MEN OF GOOD CHARACTER

'This Society shall consist of
Men of good character'

From Article 2 of
The Friendly Society of
Workers in Copper
Instituted
14th September 1846
Held at the Sign of the
Box Tree
Gravel lane, Hounsditch,
in the City of London

MEN OF GOOD CHARACTER

A History of the National Union of Sheet Metal Workers,
Coppersmiths, Heating and Domestic Engineers

TED BRAKE

LAWRENCE AND WISHART
LONDON

Lawrence and Wishart Limited
39 Museum Street
London WC1A 1LQ

First published 1985

Photoset in North Wales by
Derek Doyle & Associates, Mold, Clwyd.
Printed and bound in Great Britain at the
University Press

Contents

Acknowledgements   7

Illustrations   9

Foreword   13

1   The Guilds   17

2   The Early Trade Societies   38

3   The Early Trades in Action   61

4   From Tin Plate to Sheet Metal   103

5   Around the Country   152

6   The General Union   203

7   The National Amalgamated   222

8   The National Union   237

9   The Coppersmiths   278

10   The Heating and Domestic Engineers   319

11   The Birmingham Society   350

12   The War and After   385

Index   433

Acknowledgements

We would like to thank the following for permission to use photographs:

Worshipful Company of Tin Plate Workers, pp.26,34 and 36; National Museum of Labour History, p.42; Birmingham Public Library, p.47; London Guildhall Library, p.74; John Gorman, pp.78, 175; British Library, p.98; Trades Union Congress, pp.112, 223; Reading University Museum of Rural History, p.124; R.A. Lister Ltd., Dursley, Glos., pp.124, 125; Boulton and Paul Ltd., Norwich, p.149; Bradford Metal Works Ltd., pp.186, 187; Glasgow Museum, p.158; British Rail, Derby, p.192; Steve Litton, Swindon Branch, pp.192, 193; APV, Crawley, pp.252, 253, 311, 314, 422; Enterprise Sheet Metal, Aberdeen, p.257; Lef Bishop Ltd., Glasgow, p.257; Rolls Royce, p.260; National Motor Museum, Beaulieu, pp.263, 369; Business Press International, pp.266, 269, 270; Roy Ralph, p.274; British Aerospace, pp.276, 388, 391; Arthur Guinness Ltd., pp.279, 299; Tyne and Wear Council, Archives Dept., p.283; R.G. Abercrombie & Co., Alloa, pp.290, 291, 299; Vickers Ltd., p.316; R. and E. Frow, Labour Movement Library, p.318; Heating & Ventilating Contractors' Association, pp.340, 341, 343, 397, 414, 417; Institute of British Motor and Carriage Builders, p.365; Marston Excelsior, p.378; Pat Mantle, p.399; Doug Poole, London, p.404; Hanger's Shop Committee, p.407; J.B. Morton Ltd., Burton-on-Trent, p.408; Shipbuilding News, p.424; Vosper Thorneycroft, p.428..

List of Illustrations

Tools for eighteenth century tin plate shop 26
Sheet metal tools 27
1761 prices book 34
1805 prices book 34
Apprentices' badge, Tin Plate Workers Company 35
Eighteenth century tin plate worker 39
Eighteenth century brazier 39
1823 pewter collecting plates 42
London and Wolverhampton Societies' membership cards 44
1825 Glasgow prices book 47
1810 Birmingham prices book 47
Manchester and Preston tramping cards 55
Braziers' address to Queen Caroline 74
1821 tin plate workers' banner 78
Report of the Union, 1823 80
Wolverhampton strike poster, 1850 98
London Operative and Co-operative membership cards 110
London Co-operative Tin Plate Workers' emblem 112
Secretaries of various London societies in 1860s and 1870s 114
Dairy Utensil Makers' rule book 124
Page of a dairy utensil makers' catalogue 124
Dairy utensil workers, 1890 and 1912 124-5
Jewish tin plate workers' rule book 132
Gas meter workshop, 1936 145
First World War aircraft tin shops 149
Scottish tin plate workers' membership card 152
Scottish sheet metal workers' banner and plate 158
1873 cartoon banner 162
Liverpool tin plate workers' membership card 173
1838 Liverpool banner 175
Liverpool tin plate workers' arms 176
Drinks check 177

Liverpool tin plate workers' stamp   180
Bradford general shop   186-7
Making fairground equipment, 1938   186
Swindon and Derby railway workshops   192-3
John Wiltshire   203
1868 Manchester tramping card   207
Metal spinning, Bolton   214
Technical page of *Journal*   217
Amalgamated tin plate workers' emblem   223
Union badge   236
Coach-building shop, Nuneaton, 1950   246
Hollowing tank end   252
Shaping tank on rollers   253
Tin shops Rowntrees, York   255
Dressing coasterback bend, Aberdeen   257
Ships' galley equipment   257
Making lamp for House of Commons   257
Fitting door on Rolls Royce   260
Press shop, Vauxhall, Luton, 1920s   263
Van den Plas coach-building shop, 1925   264
Technical page in the *Journal*, 1921   265
Tinshop, aircraft works, 1914   266
R101 airship gondolas   269
Handley Page aircraft works, 1920s   270
Apprentice comes out of his time   274
Apprentices: time-served and model training   276
Union badge   277
Coppersmiths' shop, 1840   279
Jobbing coppersmiths' notebook, 1890s   283
Coppersmiths' Society emblem   288
Making whisky stills   290-91
Liverpool coppersmiths' arms   292
Shaping a bend, Guinness's shop   299
Planishing a condenser   299
Making aluminium tankers   311
Making brewery fermenting vessels   314
Marine coppersmithing   316
Art work in copper   317
Coppersmiths' badges   318
1811 Whitesmiths' rule book   319
Checking ductwork and lagging   340

Shaping copper pipe   341
Fitting fan housing   341
Heating and domestic engineering apprentices   343
HVCA apprentices' medal   343
Signing amalgamation agreement   347
H & D badges   348
J.V. Stevens   350
Page from 1912 general work catalogue   354
Coventry motor and general workshop, 1920s   359
Singer Motors' tinshop, 1926   359
Panel shop Daimler Motors, 1905   365
Radiator shop Rover Motor Co., 1919   369
Birmingham sheet metal worker   370
Constructing a heat exchanger   378
Making an aircraft pre-cooler   379
Birmingham Society badge   384
Nose cases for Skylark rockets   388
Making cowlings for Rolls Royce jet engines   388
Erecting shop, British Aerospace, Chester   391
Harry Brotherton   392
Concorde on test   397
London and Northern Ireland banners   399
Wheeling a panel for a Rolls Royce   404
Making artificial limbs   407
Finishing a body scanner   408
Working on ductwork for Barbican Arts Centre   414
Welding station, North Sea pipe-laying barge   416
Pipework, Pembrokeshire oil refinery   417
Prototype work on new British Leyland models   418
Core of nuclear reactor under construction   422
First woman member of skilled section SMW Union   424
Pipe bending under new technology   428
George Guy   431
Tom Nelson   431
Union badges   432

Foreword

This history has been written primarily for the members of the Union, but I hope it will also be of interest and perhaps of some value to the growing number of students of labour history. As the book deals with the various aspects of the trade, as well as the Union's history, I have prefaced the pages dealing with the Union with a chapter on the guilds and companies, showing the origins of the men who formed the trades clubs, the later trades societies, and so the Union. Whatever the difference between the guilds and the unions in structure and activities, the early members of the latter must have served their time within the guilds. They could not have come from anywhere else. Certainly, a corps of fully-skilled craftsmen could not have arrived from nowhere onto the industrial scene towards the end of the eighteenth century, when the guilds were in decline, while the journeymen of the guilds and companies, like old soldiers, just faded away.

I have tried to trace the history of the various streams and tributaries of craftsmen who made up the Union, the tin plate workers over some 230 years, the coppersmiths and whitesmiths for about 175 years, through the many changes in jobs and organisation, from local societies making mainly domestic wares from tinplate, iron, copper and brass, to a national organisation with members engaged in the sophisticated requirements of modern industry. In the process, I have been able to save from oblivion a number of long-forgotten trades societies: the Benevolent Institution of Whitesmiths, the Hand-in-Hand Society of Braziers, the Birmingham Carriage Lamp Makers Society, the Organ Pipe Makers Society, the Jewish Tin Plate Workers Society and the Dairy Utensil Makers Society, among others. I have also been able to record how workshop organisation played a vital part in the organisation of the tin plate workers from before 1802 when the Wolverhampton Society was governed by a committee made up of shop delegates. On a less serious note, we see the number of societies who paid their officers in ale for carrying out their various duties.

As they progressed to take advantage of changes in industry, the members confidently assumed that when one door closed, another opened. Their basis of general tin plate wares collapsed but they were already building motor cars in 1895, and were engaged in the aircraft industry from its very beginnings. Their skills are used in the aerospace industry, they took part in the construction of the Thames barrage and worked on the oil and gas rigs of the North Sea.

I have tried to give a picture of the life of the members in the Union and on the shop floor, the jobs they did, the material they worked on, the organisations they created and, where possible, something of the members themselves, touching on the annual processions and dinners, the occasional soirée and the brass band of the London tin plate workers' society in the 1880s, when another was formed by one of the gas meter 'establishments'.

For most of its varied life, the Union played a very active part in the wider trade union movement. Its representatives served on the committee to aid the Tolpuddle Martyrs, when the tin plate workers had been organised for some 60 years. Generally, it had an influence much greater than its numerical strength would seem to warrant. In my history this has had to compete with the domestic side of the Union's life. I trust that, in these circumstances, readers will forgive mistakes and deficiencies. There has been, inevitably, repetition, arising from the many streams of separate unions running alongside each other, coming together, parting, and finally amalgamating after years of negotiations. Many activities were common to a number of societies over a period of years. Where these were important, it has not been possible to omit them from the individual histories of the societies concerned, even at the expense of some repetition.

I hope that this history will give younger members, in particular, a pride in their organisation and enable them to play a more informed part in their new situation as the craft section of the Amalgamated Union of Engineering Workers – Technical and Supervisory Section.

Researching and writing this history has been a long and exacting task, but an enjoyable one. I would like to thank the last General Secretary of the independent Union, George Guy, and the NEC for giving me the opportunity of putting together our history so that it shall not be forgotten. I would like to thank, also, those many members of the Union who responded to my calls for help. In particular I would single out the large number of retired members, some in their 80s and 90s, who wrote in telling of their experiences, at the same time taking the opportunity of thanking the Union for all that it had done for them and the part it had played in their lives, expressing their pride in being members. I would like to assure them all that their contributions were most valuable and have been absorbed into the history they helped to make. I am extremely grateful for their contributions to this book.

While it is not possible to thank all by name, I must thank Dick Marsh, a former national officer, who read the manuscript on behalf of the Union and made many suggestions for its improvement. Les Buck, Harold Poole, Cyril Bransby and Bill Tooes read those sections relating to their own experience, the late Alf Cooper, Jim Boyle, Pat Carey, Sam Whittingham, Bill Warman and the late Frank Lane, recorded their experiences; a number of full-time officials around the country must also be thanked for their help, as must the head office staff, in particular, Wendy Delahoy. Ron Ralph and Bill Green did some valuable local research.

Among those outside the Union who gave assistance were Barbara and Ron Champion who read the manuscript, John Gorman who designed the dust jacket and gave help and encouragement, Bob Leeson, David Green, George Barnsby, I. Prothero, and Ruth and Edmund Frow. Thanks also to Ms A. Prochaska of the Public Record Office, Mr D.R. Webb of the Bishopsgate Institute and the librarians, archivists of the British Library of Political and Economic Science, the Aberdeen, the Avon, Bristol, Birmingham, Bolton, Edinburgh, Glasgow, Perth, London University, London Guildhall, Liverpool, Leeds, Lancaster, Lancashire and York libraries, amongst others.

To my Mum,
who refused to
curtsey when the
Countess passed by

CHAPTER ONE

The Guilds

The origins of the early societies that went to make the modern Sheet Metal Workers Union are lost in the uncharted years that saw the break up of the guild system in London and the main provincial cities of Britain, sometime in the eighteenth century.

It was the guilds that provided the first organisation of workers among the braziers, coppersmiths and tin plate workers, the ancestors of the present union. They were not, of course, workers' organisations as such, but comprised everyone in the trade concerned, masters and journeymen, employers and workers. The merchant guilds, that seem to have originated from socio-religious fraternities in the twelfth century or even earlier, and the craft guilds that succeeded them in the fourteenth century, however they may have originated, and whatever their other activities, were basically organisations of what amounted to class struggle, just as are the trade unions and employers organisations today – even though the guilds may have been the ancestors of both.[1]

They had their trappings of religion, naturally, at a time when the church had a dominating influence on all aspects of life. They had their fraternity bodies and looked after the social needs of their members, taking care of those who had fallen on hard times, in sickness and old age, a concern that extended to members' widows and orphans. And, what was considered most important, they ensured that all members, on dying, had a respectable funeral.

But basically they were fighting for a place in the sun for the guild brethren – at least in the early days, later they became rather more selective. This they sought to achieve by securing a monopoly of the particular trade and protecting the members practising it from outside competition by exercising control over all who worked in the trade within the city and keeping everyone else out, thus maintaining a closed shop over the whole trade in its area.

Their organisation enabled them to become an important social force that was transformed into a political force in the course of their economic activities.[2] This struggle for power became the main force that motivated them and gave them their very important place in English history.

During this struggle for power they came into conflict with the restrictions on trade and industry imposed by the old feudal forces. They had to fight the entrenched positions of the barons and prelates who, through their several bailiffs, controlled the courts that formed the early civic government. In this struggle they were, for a time, a progressive social force, only to become, in their turn, part of the reactionary ruling class, suppressing the struggling classes below them including the mass of ordinary members of their own guilds.

With the big increase in internal and international trade and the development of the guilds, there came a polarisation of the guild membership. The richer merchants who had become entrepreneurs, buying and selling raw materials and finished products in bulk, established themselves in the leading positions in the guilds. Both economically and socially the new-rich merchants rose above the mass of small masters and journeymen who formed the majority of the guild members with whom they had less and less in common. The guilds became, not the organisation of united struggle in the interest of all, but a vehicle to promote the interests of the leading clique of rich merchants and the means by which they challenged the old social order.[3]

These early merchant bankers and merchant adventurers had become extremely wealthy and they used their wealth and power, and that of the guilds they controlled, to strengthen their position and insinuate themselves into the structure of the city government. They became the representatives of the city in the regulation of trade while being themselves the main traders and the guilds they controlled the main organs of trade.[4] Eventually the new mercantile class succeeded in breaking the feudal monopoly of civil power and, coalescing with the old ruling class, became the main elements of civic government.

The working craftsmen and small masters having served their purpose were forced out of the old merchant guilds. So the craftsmen set about creating a new organisation to look after their interests which became the craft guilds. These gradually covered all the crafts in the city, at least as far as London was concerned, changing to meet changing circumstances. Mergers took place when perhaps one craft became out-moded, as when the armourers amalgamated with the braziers. Others split as divergent sections within a guild grew stronger and felt their individual interests would be better served by breaking away and forming their own organisation, as when the tin plate workers broke away from the Ironmongers Company. By the fourteenth century guilds had been organised in some 160 English towns.

The Coppersmiths

A list of the crafts 'exercised in London from times of old' drawn up in 1422 and preserved in the records of the Blacksmiths Company of the City of London, includes the coppersmiths and braziers.

The early organisation of the craftsmen, later to be known separately as coppersmiths and brass founders, united in the Founders Company of the City of London, is believed to have originated as a parish brotherhood in Lothebury in the City, a common form of organisation for workers in the same trade operating in the same area.

The work of the Founders included casting brass and copper to make stirrups, spurs, buckles, brass weights, candlesticks, spice mortars, as well as making from sheet copper pots and pans, chafing dishes, basins for various domestic and professional purposes, large washing vessels and ewers, the latter being depicted on the guild's coat of arms. In the eighteenth century the chief business of coppersmiths was said to be making boilers and stills for breweries and distilleries.

In fact, the work of the braziers and coppersmiths companies overlapped, bringing many demarcation difficulties. In 1617 the Founders Company petitioned the Mayor and aldermen for permission to take over all apprentices bound to workers in brass or copper within the City of London. The request was refused, probably due to opposition of the braziers.[5]

The Brotherhood helped its members in distress and provided a decent burial – the latter was considered particularly important and indeed was the main benefit provided by the coppersmiths' societies at least until 1850. The Brotherhood also gave help in food, fuel and rent to members too ill or too old to work. When they died it paid for a winding sheet, a burial pit and a toll of bells and followed their bodies to the grave. When funds allowed, it paid for a candle to be burned and a mass to be said for their souls. The friendly benefits side of trade union activity can be said to be well rooted in history.

The craft first appeared in the books of the London Guildhall in 1365 when it was recorded that 'the good men of the mystery of Founders' presented a petition to the Mayor and Aldermen complaining that

> divers members of the mystery make their work of false metal and use false solder which, when exposed to fire or great strain, break and dissolve to the great damage of those that do purchase them and to the great slander of the City and the whole mystery.[6]

They asked to be registered in the Guildhall as a Company of the City in order to control the trade. They would, they said, ensure that all work was well done and made of the finest metal and only the best solder would be used. No pieces should be soldered onto articles except 'such things as ought in reason to be soldered on'. They also had a rule that any goods going for sale at a fair or market had to be submitted to a warden for inspection before being packed up.

In addition they put forward proposals for the control and discipline of the craft. No one not a member of the mystery would be allowed to employ apprentices of the trade under pain of paying a fine of 40s, a considerable sum in those days. No outsider would be allowed to come into the City and open a shop or practise the craft without appearing before the Master and wardens and passing an examination, or becoming an apprentice. The petition was granted and the Founders Company was registered at the Guildhall with John of Lincoln as the first Master and given the monopoly of the craft in the cities of London and Westminster and for three miles around. The founders was one of the minor London companies. In 1472, the Court of the Company, recollecting their foundation, recorded 'we were then only 24 poor but honest men'. Both the braziers and founders remained minor companies, electing the minimum number of members to the Common Council of the City and providing only nine men to the watch.[7]

The Braziers

The braziers made the same approach when applying to the City for recognition, stressing their role in preserving high standards of workmanship in the interest of the consumer. No doubt the guilds did have an interest in maintaining high standards of workmanship. In 1602, for example, one Edward Collingwood was brought up before the Braziers' Court for having made two copper stills 'of old stuff' so that they were 'like an old whore new vampt'.[8] But these powers also helped them to exclude any non-member of the Company or others thought to be undesirable.

The Memorials of London record that on 20 March 1416 a group of 'presentable men, freemen of the trade of braziers of London', presented themselves with a petition declaring 'divers wares were deceiptfully made', as well in mixing of the metal as in the making, so that they 'cannot last one-third the time as they did of old'. They asked that they be allowed to elect yearly three or four persons of the trade to act as wardens or governors who should have the full powers of search 'of all manner of persons working at or following the trade of brazier in London and its suburbs. At least one of the masters to be a worker at the trade and the others traders'.[9] The right to search allowed the guild representatives to enter any premises connected with the craft and examine any article that was offered for sale in any shop, market stall or elsewhere in the City and to confiscate any they deemed to be of poor workmanship or inferior material. They also put forward a list of fines and suggested a cutback, offering that half of all fines go to the authorities at the Guildhall and the other half 'to the use and profit of the trade'. The Mayor and Aldermen thought the request 'sensible'.[10]

The braziers, from the beginning, had rules to keep the journeymen in their place. No one was allowed to take any journeyman or serving man from his master until he had finished his service. If any journeyman or serving man 'should be at enmity with or act in a rebellious manner toward his master', no other master should give him a job on pain of paying a fine of 40s. If any workman, serving man or apprentice refused to accept the rules laid down by the wardens or government of the trade, or failed to attend the Court when summoned by the beadel, he would be dealt with 'in the customary way'.[11] This attitude to journeymen was not something special to the braziers, or to London. In 1774 a master tin plate worker in Edinburgh had to swear that he would not seduce any of the guild members' journeymen or apprentices, or employ them, 'until they had been cleared by their masters'[12] – the employers' black circular has a long history.

Although a journeyman was in law largely free to come and go and to change his job, in practice no master would normally take on a journeyman unless he had made sure the man had got a clearance from his former master. The same applied to serving men who could be a journeyman from another town or a workman who had picked up the trade. A travelling craftsman, looking for work in London or another town in the middle of the sixteenth century, was legally liable to be whipped if he could not produce a certificate from his guild or former master.

Illegal Men

The companies' courts made great use of the powers of search granted them, not only to root out bad workmanship or poor materials, but also to discover 'illegal men' – those who had not served a regular apprenticeship – the exclusion of whom was one of the main means of controlling the craft. The searchers would often ask to see a man's indentures before examining his products. No outsider was allowed to keep a shop or otherwise sell goods retail in the City without permission from the guild concerned, a permission that had to be paid for, the money going into the guild's coffers. However, in excluding outsiders the guild had to be careful not to create a pool of unemployed craftsmen who would set up in opposition outside the gates.

There was a constant war against foreigners, and foreigners in this context meant not only the often strong competition coming from traders or craftsmen from the continent of Europe, but everyone from outside the City. For London, this meant men from distant parts of England, and also men of Kent, Surrey and Essex and even from the then London suburbs, from Stepney, Battersea and other separate villages that have long since been swallowed up by London.

In 1724 the Court of the Tin Plate Workers specifically warned that all unskilled Irishmen found working in the craft would be prosecuted,[13] probably referring to tinkers among the displaced Irish peasants forced by poverty to leave their homeland. But back in 1683, an exception had been made in the case of a Frenchman, Alexandre Dervayne, who was allowed into membership of the Company when he was able to prove that he had been brought up a Protestant, was skilled in the craft and had worked in the trade with his own shop in Paris.[14]

Journeymen complained that some masters imported goods to sell cheaper than the local journeymen could produce them. On taking the offending masters to court on one such occasion the case was dismissed and the journeymen lectured about interfering with the freedom of trade.

The London founders and braziers, and later the tin plate workers, carried on a sustained campaign against tinkers and others who hawked their wares around the streets, were tinning pots and vessels, or selling their goods at the many fairs and markets. In 1647 the Braziers' Court ruled that any free member of the Society 'hawking or proffering brass or copper wares' about the streets would be fined.[15] The masters' attempts to close down such outlets were not only directed against outsiders but also against independent journeymen and small masters without shops of their own, to force them to sell to the big traders always concerned to strengthen their monopoly.[16]

There was a constant stream of labourers and rural artisans flooding into the towns, and particularly London, in search of a livelihood and the guilds ensured that they were not allowed to overload the craft. The ends of the many wars also saw thousands of ex-soldiers and sailors looking for work. There were sufficient of them to warrent a special rule in the earliest trade society book of laws we have been able to locate, that of the Friendly Society of Tin Plate Workers of London, a revised edition dated January 1798. It is laid down that any returned soldier or sailor who had been a member of the Society would be admitted as a free member on return after one month's work in London and his previous membership would be taken into account.[17]

Later the masters would welcome any influx of labour as a means of weakening the position of the journeymen and keeping down wages. But when the guild system was in operation the 'illegal men' were a menace to the guilds, weakening their monopolistic position.

Apprentices

Another of the measures used for maintaining a monopoly was the control of apprentices. From 1340 London apprentices had to complete seven years' servitude. By the fifteenth century this had spread throughout the rest of the country and it became the law of the land in the sixteenth century under the Elizabethan Statute of Artificers. An apprentice to the Founders, before he was bound, had to be 'abled' or examined by the wardens 'in order to see that he is free born and whole of limb for the honour of the City.'[18]

The situation varied between one Company and another and at different periods, but the higher a man was in the hierarchy of the guild the less he was restricted. Generally a master or warden would be allowed three apprentices, a liveryman two, and an ordinary freeman one. Ordinary journeymen were to have none.

The minute books of the crafts show that a great deal of the meeting time was taken up with the admission and checking up on apprentices. Admission was by patrimony – the son of a freeman of the Company – servitude or the payment of a fee. In the middle of the eighteenth century this fee amounted to ten pounds for braziers and coppersmiths and ten pounds to twenty pounds for tin plate workers. From time to time masters were fined for taking more apprentices than their quota allowed. The Tin Plate Workers' minutes for 1706 report that a master who already had his limit of apprentices was given a dispensation 'to bind a boy' providing that he gave an undertaking that upon coming of age he be prevented, as an unqualified person, from following the trade as a tin plate worker. In 1726, another master was allowed to bind a boy on payment of a fee.

The type of work they could do was also restricted. The tin plate workers' records show that a master, one John Meering, went bond that an apprentice he had taken on to learn the trade of working in brass and copper, should not at any time be employed or set to work on tin plate or make any tin wares during his apprenticeship.

At that time apprentices lived in the houses of their masters who fed and clothed them but paid them no wages. In many cases they worked long hours and were badly treated, either by the master, or his wife, or both. Richard Carlisle, who later achieved fame – and many prison sentences – for his courageous fight against taxes on newspapers, told of his ill-treatment when he was apprentice to a tinsmith in Exeter from the age of 12 years of age, in 1802. He said he had to do 'the maximum amount of work for the minimum amount of food.' The minutes of the courts of the various trades tell of many cases of masters ill-treating their apprentices, in some cases injuring them so that they could not work. Whipping of apprentices was a regular way of maintaining discipline enshrined in the Companies' rules. The Braziers report that an apprentice accused of stealing from his master was ordered by the Court to be whipped to make him confess, 'and when whipped in front of others he did confess.'[19]

A report in the Founders Company books for 1572 records that an officer had to be called from Bridewell prison to whip an apprentice 'for being improperly dressed.'

As late as the eighteenth century the Braziers Company was told

> that ye give a special charge to all households of your Company that they keep their apprentices in all fear and obedience that they may know their duties towards their God, their magistrates, their masters and their elders, and that they shall by no means use swearing, blasphemy, haunting of evil women or schools of fence, dancing, carding, dicing, bowling, tennis play, the use of ruffs in their shirts, tavern haunting, and if any shall be found guilty, the same be forthwith punished by whipping openly in your Hall in the sight of other apprentices, and ye shall give in charge to the said masters that they shall not let, permit or suffer their apprentices to wear in their hosen any cloth of any colour that are here expressed, that is to say white, russett, blue or watchet, the said hosen to be made without stitching of silk, or any manner of cuts, and it is ordered that if the apprentice offend herein with the consent of the master, such master shall pay certain fines, but if the fault comes with the wiley apprentice, then his master is to see him punished by whipping.[20]

It was little wonder that apprentices ran away. The tin plate workers' minutes for 1693 record that John Chiswell of Wapping 'deserted his master's service before finishing his apprenticeship, secured work and received wages; contrary to the law and custom.' He was apprehended on a warrant and returned to his master and had to enter into bond that he would stay with his master until his time was completed.

Advertisements for runaway apprentices appeared in local newspapers much as advertisements for runaway slaves in the Deep South of America around the same period. *Aris's Birmingham Gazette* for 26 September 1791 carried such an advertisement:

> Whereas John Pickering, apprentice to Matthew Pickering of Nantwich in the County of Chester, Brazier, did on 8th September slope from his said master. This is to forewarn all persons from harbouring the said apprentice or they will be prosecuted as the law of the land in such cases decides. The said John Pickering is 20 years of age.

'The question of subordination among the apprentice class,' said the Founders Company ordinances, 'was at once both essential and difficult.'

Class Distinctions

The craft guilds were then controlled by a master and two wardens elected annually. They were assisted by a court which, in the sixteenth century, became known as the Court of Assistants.

Professor Unwin, historian of the London Guilds, has pointed out that the Court of

Assistants was not merely an executive committee, like those to which all large organisations are obliged in practice to entrust the management of their affairs, nor was it merely a court in name, it had actual jurisdiction over its members and even over outsiders who were engaged in the same trade. Members of the Company were forbidden to take trade disputes to any other Court until the Court of Assistants of their own Company had been appealed to in vain – a ruling which came into force in the Tin Plate Workers Company in 1679.

'By the Court's judgements unruly apprentices were whipped, journeymen on strike were imprisoned and masters offending against regulations were fined.' There seems to have been no provision for apprentices to be fined and masters whipped.

The guilds' set-up, with their courts, masters and wardens were far from democratic, the retiring master and wardens nominated their successors, either on their own or in conjunction with the Court of Assistants, which itself was a closed institution composed of former wardens whose members held the position for life. Together, they named the members who were to be chosen as freemen and those of the freemen who were to be made liverymen – the body of privileged members from whose ranks the masters and wardens were chosen.[21]

The records of the Founders Company show the changes in the guild's organisation as the wealthy traders established their position within the guild to the detriment of the mass of the membership: how an elite group had emerged from the original brotherhood of equal members. In April 1489 the guild had new ordinances which put the official stamp on the changes and divisions that had taken place.[22] The membership was now divided into three grades, at the top were the 'brothers of the clothing', that is the liverymen who wore a special livery or uniform and regalia to indicate their role in the hierarchy. It was this group that provided the master, wardens and members of the Court. Below them were the householders 'not of the clothing', the smaller masters who had their own workshops and employed apprentices and a few journeymen and hired servants. Finally there was the body of journeymen – the hired servants did not count, they were not members of the guild although they might be doing craftsmen's work.

At the time of the original ordinances when the guild was formed, there had been no such divisions between the elected Master and the rest of the members. Now a privileged minority had emerged, their privileges confirmed by the number of apprentices they were allowed – four each for the Master and upper wardens, three each for the members of the Court, two for the rest of the liverymen, one each of the small masters. The journeymen were not allowed any.

Later this authoritative trend was carried still further. In 1614 the guild was constituted a Company with a government consisting of a Master, two wardens and 15 assistants, but now it was not just the journeymen and the working masters 'not of the clothing' who were discriminated against. The liverymen, who were the middling sized masters, were also deprived almost completely of any say in the election of the officers and the management of the offices. Instead of elections, a narrow principle of co-option vested in the Court the entire constitutional and administrative authority and created an oligarchy in the persons of the few more successful and affluent members.[23] These changes in the guilds' organisation were part of the struggle that developed within the craft guilds between the manual workers – the journeymen and small working masters – and the rich traders. Disputes over prices for making articles – that is, disputes over wages – developed and the gulf between the conflicting interests widened. It was fundamentally a conflict between employers and employed, for the small masters had generally to sell to the merchants, or themselves act as subcontractors for the bigger traders and shopkeepers. The disputes became more acrimonious and violent and the government of the guilds brought in the Mayor and aldermen to help them impose discipline on the rebellious journeymen, the journeymen on their side, received help from journeymen of other crafts. The old craft loyalty of the whole craft against the rest was giving way to a new loyalty, that of man against master.

The Yeomanry

In the course of the struggle the journeymen formed their own organisation, the yeomanry, to fight for democracy within the guilds, in this they were joined by those small masters who were little more than journeymen, existing on subcontracts. The yeomanry had their own laws, their own elected leadership, their own contributions and their own box, with three locks in the traditional manner, in which to keep their books and money. During the reign of Elizabeth I the opposition to the ruling Courts of Assistants was most often voiced by the yeomanry consisting of manual workers who had served their time at the craft, whereas the members of the Court were usually merchants. The dissension between the courts and the yeomanry basically arose from the new class distinction that came from economic changes with the expansion of trade and increases in inventions, it reflected the antagonism between capital and manual labour.

The yeomanry were gradually defeated by the financial interests by now entrenched in control of the craft guilds. The yeomanry was not disbanded but taken over, allowed to continue, but as a very different kind of organisation, now part of the structure of the guild and firmly under the control of the wardens and the Court, who chose, or at least approved, the leadership of the yeomanry. Professor Unwin summed up the position: 'At the end of the fourteenth century the yeomanry were "journeymen on strike". The yeoman of the sixteenth century was often a wealthy bachelor on his way to becoming a Lord Mayor.' He was undergoing a brief period of probation doing a chore to prepare him for future high office. The yeomanry had become just another step on the ladder of promotion, another grade within the Company, a subordinate but recognised branch of the livery.

The growing predominance of liverymen who were not working craftsmen but engaged in commerce exercising control over the great majority, was resented by the yeomanry craftsmen. Friction increased and broke out into open revolt in 1651 under the revolutionary influence of Cromwellian rule. Sixteen yeomanry members of the Founders' Company presented a petition to the Cromwell government complaining that 'we have for many years been extremely trodden and kept under foot by the power and will of the Master, Warden and Assistants.' They added a political denunciation of the Court of the Company claiming that 'the major part of them are notoriously disaffected to the present Government and upon all opportunities have manifested their malignity in words and deeds.' The Upper Warden had served the late King at Oxford during the wars.[24]

During the time of the Commonwealth and the Protectorate there were two distinct moves for the reform of the companies. One was to return to a situation in which membership of the company was confined to members of the particular trade and so strengthen control over the trade. The other was to secure adequate representation on the governing body of the company for all classes included in its membership. Both these attempts to democratise the companies failed. They were, says Professor Unwin, similar to the 'alliance' proposed for many Birmingham trades in the nineteenth century with the object of securing 'better profits for manufacturers and better wages to work people.'

The journeymen of the Founders, although deprived of their organisation, continued, though perhaps sporadically, in their attempts to democratise the Company. In 1692 they appealed against 'unconstitutional and arbitrary acts' by the Court and called for a more clearly worded charter, only to have their "pretended complaints" dismissed.[25]

The yeomanry's struggle, was doomed to failure, not only were the journeymen up against the wealth and entrenched power of the members of the Court, it was also almost impossible to get continuous unity of action among the members of the yeomanry itself. As long as dissatisfied or ambitious journeymen believed that they could enter the ranks of the masters, or the small masters were allowed to think that they could rise to the position of a member of the Court, there would always be a weakness in the ranks.

The next wave of the manual workers' struggle was to be conducted by a new organisation, the independent journeymen's clubs.

Setting up in business

As the merchant and financial interests consolidated their position, there were complaints from both apprentices and journeymen at restrictions placed on their advancement.

With the sanction of the Common Council a rule was made that no London apprentice was to be admitted as a freeman and allowed to set up house or to trade until he was about 24 years of age. The companies also insisted that the aspiring applicant to full membership must prove that he had sufficient capital to start up on his own and that he should pass an examination in workmanship.[26]

In the middle of the eighteenth century, it was said that for braziers and coppersmiths to set up a business would cost a minimum of £100 and could cost up to £1,000. A tin plate worker could also set up a business for £100 'but one who stocks a shop handsomely can make use of £500 and he would have as pretty a business as any in London.[27] A handwritten list in the London Guild Hall Library, compiled by a member of the Court of the Tin Plate Workers Company, dated 1760, gives a list of equipment required for setting up a tin plate workers' shop:

1 Large Anvil, 1 Small Do, 3 Pairs of Large Shears, 2 Pairs of Small Do, 3 Large Beak Irons, 7 Smaller Do, 2 Smoothing Hammers, 2 Planishing Do, 7 Hollowing Do, 8 Flat Faced Do, 16 Creasing Do, 8 Creasing Irons, 3 Cannister Stakes, 1 Horsehead Stagg, 7 Hollow Punches, 36 Flat Punches, Chisels and Gouges, 3 Pairs Knippers, 5 Pairs of Plyers, 2 Squares and 1 Rule, 2 Pairs of Soldering Shanks and some Copper, a Vice and a Broken Hall Anvil, 2 Fire Pots, 3 Swages, 1 Pair of Large and 3 Pairs of Small Compasses, the above tools valued at 13 pounds, this 21 of July 1760.

With the increasing competition and restrictions imposed by the courts to limit the introduction of more masters, it was becoming more and more difficult for apprentices to gain the advantage that they felt the serving of seven or eight years apprenticeship entitled them – unless, of course, they managed to achieve what was supposed to be every apprentice's ambition, to marry the boss's daughter, but this was a rather restricted mode of entry.

The journeymen too, complained that the employers, acting through the courts, tried to stop them from becoming masters by charging exorbitant fees for proposing them for the City freedom, which was an essential requirement for carrying on trade in the City. The cost of becoming a freeman rose steadily, as did the payments to become a liveryman, going up tenfold during the seventeenth century. In some cases, it was equal to two years wages of a journeyman.

The conflict was sharpened as the masters feared increasing competition. One means of restricting entry was the introduction of a rule that every candidate must produce a masterpiece. Professor Unwin says that there can be little doubt that the insistence that a masterpiece be produced as part of the price of admission to the Guild was used as a barrier against a flood of journeymen becoming masters when the existing masters wanted to keep them in the position of wage earners. The cost of producing a masterpiece, he says, was too costly for the ordinary worker to afford.

The Tin Plate Workers

The London Tin Plate Workers Company came on this scene rather late. Tin plate was first imported into Britain from Bohemia around 1576 so it is to be supposed that the first tin plate workers hailed from about that time. Although attempts were made from 1670 in South Wales and elsewhere to establish a tin plate industry – encouraged by the newly formed Tin Plate Workers Company, whose members were complaining of the high import duties imposed on foreign tin plate – it was not until the 1730s and 40s that it really got established.

The Company was formed in 1670, just four years after the Great Fire of London. This may have had some bearing on the decision of the master tin plate workers to form their own company. The widespread destruction caused by the fire meant that there was a need for a massive replacement of household goods, which included tin plate wares, and these being for everyday use they had to be replaced quickly.

Tin plate had then been coming increasingly into general use over a number of years. London records tell

List of tools for setting up a tin plate workers' shop in the eighteenth century

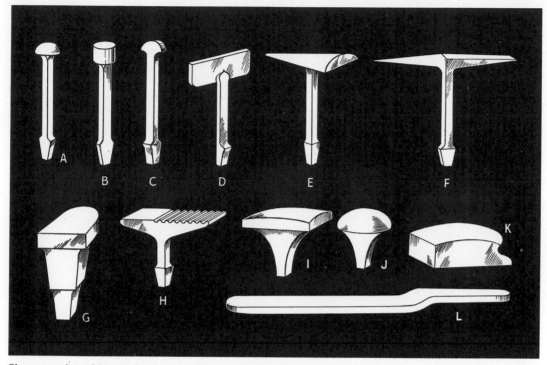

Sheet metal working tools: A: round-headed stake; B: round-bottomed stake; C: half-moon stake; D: hatchet stake; E: funnel stake; F: beck iron; G: anvil; H: crease iron; I and J: panel heads; K: block; L: spoon

of increasing conflict between the pewterers and their neighbours, the tin plate workers, who had settled in the Crooked Lane area,[28] the cause of which was that tin plate was replacing pewter for more and more goods of everyday use and putting pewterers out of work. Tin plate was so much cheaper than pewter that it sold in increasing quantities.

This was not only happening in London. The historian of the Hammermen of Dunfermline in Scotland tells that when the tin plate workers – or white iron smiths, whitesmiths or white ironmen as they were variously known in Scotland at that time – came onto the scene early in the seventeenth century, 'the pewterers' doom was sealed.' The pewterer, as a separate trade, was beginning to disappear from the Hammermen's books. Although it had taken a little time to find favour after its introduction, by the first quarter of the 18th century, 'tin plate had driven the pewterer from well nigh every town in the land.'[29]

Before forming their own company the majority of the tin plate workers had been members of the Ironmongers Company – which had been incorporated in 1463 – whose members dealt in tin plate wares in their shops. With the extension of the craft and the consequent increase in the wealth of the master tin plate workers, with the prospect of further increases in the trade to come, and possibly under the stimulation of an expected flood of sales to fire-stricken London, the master tin plate workers decided to break away from the Ironmongers and form their own company. The decision was made in 1668, the main instigator being one Thomas Aris, a liveryman of some ten years standing. But when they came to put the decision into effect they found that with fees to the City Chamberlain and other expenses it would cost some hundreds of pounds. So they joined with the wire workers who were about to break away from the Girdlers Company but were also finding the costs rather too much. When the new company was inaugurated in 1670 it was known as the Worshipful Company of Tin Plate Workers, alias Wire Workers of the City of London, a title it has retained to this day.

London seems to have been one of the few towns with separate guilds for the individual crafts of tin plate workers, braziers and coppersmiths. In other places it was apparently thought that the numbers were not sufficient to make separate guilds viable propositions, so various amalgamations and forms of organisation developed.

The Tin Plate Workers Company started when many of the older companies were breaking up or showing signs of soon doing so, but, a new broom, it vigorously applied itself to all the activities and workings of the guilds system. It operated the whole works; apprentices were expected to produce a masterpiece before being made free. Masters were fined for taking too many apprentices or employing foreigners, warrants were taken out against hawkers and 'illegal men'. Journeymen who did not take up their freedom were prosecuted, piecework lists were drawn up by the Company and as late as 1733 searches were still being carried out.

The apprenticeship system had declined in many companies but the new Company made it its business to see that within its own area of control the system was tightened up and that no irregularities were permitted. In 1676 the Court laid down that an apprentice, under penalty of a fine of 2s 6d, had to produce a masterpiece – a dripping pan, a lantherne or lantern, a pudding pan or other article in tin plate.

The Company's powers of search 'for the better discovery of bad, unskilful and deceitful goods and wares' were extended outside the cities of London and Westminster to Tottenham in the North and Norwood in the South, from Ealing in the West to Woolwich in the East.[30]

The Hammermen's Companies

In Scotland, the three crafts formed part of the Hammermen's Companies – the main qualification of entry being that the member used hammer upon metal. In the case of the Hammermen of Glasgow, who obtained their charter in 1536, the first recorded entry in the books of any one of the three crafts was of a brass smith or brazier in 1617. The coppersmith does not appear until 1665 while the first 'white-iron worker' was registered in 1652 – it was not until 1789 that the name tinsmith first appeared in the Glasgow records, translated into a tin plate worker in 1816.[31]

Apprentices aspiring to entry into the Hammermen's Company were taken by their guardian or a parent to one of the many hammermen to be found at the Cross or at their market booths. When the bargaining was completed a suitable apprenticeship fee was agreed and paid to the master. The apprentice was then 'booked in' with his name entered on the books of the craft and the occasion celebrated with a dram. Unbooked apprentices were not recognised by the craft or the guild. A booked apprentice was not only the apprentice of the individual master but also of the craft. He served five years apprenticeship during which he lived in his master's house and was fed and clothed by the master. He then did two more years of service when he was fed and lodged and received a small wage to pay for his clothes and other necessities.

The young craftsman was not allowed to carry on his trade until he had produced an assay piece. For a coppersmith this was a half-gallon measure, a 'flairbox and wand' and a copper teapot. White-ironmen had to produce a 'whytyron chamber', a block tin saucepan, a tin drainer, a block tin teapot, a block tin kettle and a jug. In 1702 a brass smith handed in as his assay 'ane broath plate and a warming pan in brass.'

Within the Hammermen's organisation the craftsmen had to restrict their activity to their individual craft. The first demarcation case recorded was in 1621 when a brass smith was told by the Court to confine himself to work in brass and 'not to interfere in the privileges of the workers in iron'[32]

The Edinburgh Hammermen's records indicate that the braziers, coppersmiths and white-ironmen were originally all minor trades, organised within one of the major divisions of the guild, but were all later admitted as full members. In 1641 a coppersmith was admitted on account of his having made a 'stoving pan and scevit' and in 1664 a white-ironman is recorded as producing as his credentials for admission 'a sugar box, a lantern, a lamp, a lantherne, and a candlestick.' Later, 'a watering pot for the gardening' was added. By 1773 the much more sophisticated requirements were 'a box with three canisters in it, a beaten work,a stuck globe lantern with 16 horns and a syphon with a brass bow curtee.[33] – whatever that may be.

The Aberdeen Hammermen also enrolled braziers, coppersmiths and white-ironmen. The records show that on 30 January 1694 the trade considered a supplication from a white-ironman, one Patrick Morgan, 'and did accept him as a journeyman on payment of eight shillings Scotch money.' He could always become a freeman 'when able to pay the trade their banquet siller.' The books further state that 'in all times hierafter,' no man would be incorporated as a white-iron worker 'until he pay the full amount that others pay'.[34] It sounds as though the tinmen were trying to get into the guild on the cheap.

The Dunfermline Hammermen's Company also included coppersmiths and white-ironmen among its members.

As with the London Guilds, those in Scotland also seized bad quality goods. The Edinburgh Hammerman's minute book records that in June 1769 a copper bucket was seized by an officer of the Company as 'insufficient'. The maker disputed the decision and the coppersmith members of the Company in the Cannongate were called together and asked to give their opinion. After some discussion the maker agreed to put new handles on the bucket 'in the sight of one of the coppersmiths,' he also agreed to pay the officer of the Company 2s 6d for his trouble.

The English Towns

The organisation of the crafts in English towns took various forms. At about 1450 in Norwich the various metal trades were drawn together in an amalgamated metal workers guild.[35] We have been unable to find anything about its subsequent history, or exactly what trades were included, but much later the Norwich freemen's rolls from 1716 to 1746 included 13 braziers, 7 tinmen and 14 whitesmiths.

Similar amalgamations took place in Chester in 1499, in Hereford around 1554 and in Bristol, Lincoln and Salisbury.[36] In Gloucester, the goldsmiths, pewterers, braziers, coppersmiths, wire drawers, cardmakers, pinmakers and plumbers combined together to form a Company of metal workers in 1607.[37] Reading and Dorchester also had mixed metal trades groups in the seventeenth century.[38] There were many parallels in other towns. In York, the ordinances of the Coppersmiths and Brassfounders Company was registered in 1681. This included braziers and tin plate workers later, if not at the time of registration, as 44 braziers and 36 tin plate workers appear on the York freemen's roll between the years 1767 and 1830.

Leeds received a charter from Charles II in 1662 in which it was ordained that all ironmongers, smiths, cutlers, pewterers, among other trades, be organised in a guild, as these were metal trades it is possible that the ' other trades' included braziers, coppersmith and tin plate workers. In some towns a rather mixed bag of trades came together in a guild. Rather like a general workers' union. In Newcastle-upon-Tyne, for instance, the tin plate workers joined up with the upholsterers and stationers.[39] The Company had only eleven members, of which only three were tin plate workers when it was founded in 1675, though the numbers built up later. The organisation provided for each of the three sections to appoint a steward. The Charter and Rules of the Incorporated Company for 1817 show the three double burner lamps of the tin plate workers among the arms of the three companies. A later report says 'the early tin plate workers made war on their nomadic competitors, the tinkers' who obviously threatened their monopoly of the craft. In 1725 one guild member, Joseph Longstaf, had a fine of five pounds remitted by the guild court on his promise to use his best endeavours to suppress the tinkers that frequented the town. In Great Grimsby in 1583 every tinker coming into the town had to pay 3s 4d if married and 5s if single.[40]

There was also a guild of tin plate workers in Preston and a flag emblazoned with the Braziers' arms was carried in the Preston guild procession in 1822, but we have not been able to find anything more of the organisation or activities of either.[41]

The Preston guilds continued to organise processions throughout the nineteenth century. In 1882 the tin plate workers led the contingent of Associated Trades. They were headed by a horseman 'in curiously ornamented tin armour, the shield being emblazoned with emblems of the trade.' This was followed by a lorry carrying men making doffin cans, wheel guards, and so on and another with men round a forge making various articles connected with the braziers' and coppersmiths' trade. The body of members, some 200 strong, carried a banner depicting the interior of a workshop. The guild no longer existed at the next procession, in 1902, although tin plate workers took part in the march.

It must be remembered that at the time when the guilds were in operation the town population was very small, in the fifteenth century even London had a population of 30,000 to 40,000, York had 11,000, Bristol 10,000 while the present industrial centres like Birmingham and Manchester were mere villages. By 1700 the population of London had grown to 674,000 and by 1801 when the guilds had virtually ceased to operate the population amounted to some 900,000. In the sixteenth and seventeenth centuries individual trades in many towns might have no more than half-a-dozen members. In Norwich in the middle of the sixteenth century, the guild officers were being elected by seven or so members, so it was natural that various trades should come together, especially among related trades, like the various metal workers.

Times of Change

Changes in customs, as well as in the economy, brought changes in the guilds and guild organisation. In 1708 the Braziers Company of London amalgamated with an even older and previously extremely important guild, the Armourers. The reason was the same as that which has brought amalgamations among trade unions in recent years, financial difficulties arising from a lack of demand for the products it was making. Changes in warfare and weaponry generally ended the wearing of armour, the Company's finances suffered and it was faced with extinction unless it diversified, so it looked around for a company with which it could relate and amalgamated with the Braziers. The new Company took the name of Armourers and Braziers. Their charter, granted by Queen Anne in 1708, covered workers in copper and brass, wrought and hammered with the hammer commonly called braziers who work or trade in wares of copper and brass in the cities of London and Westminster and five miles adjacent who have served the full seven years apprenticeship.

The new company, however, did not confine itself to this work and claimed jurisdiction over all metal work, which brought it into conflict with other companies.[42]

Decline of the Guilds

By the middle of the eighteenth century there were many signs that the guild system as a means of regulating the trades, was on its way out. In Glasgow, journeymen members of the Hammermen's Company formed their own independent club as early as 1748, electing a deacon and master separate from the guild organisation, and made rules and laws to protect their interests. The masters attacked the organisation as 'repugnant to the laws and acts of the Craft.' The journeymen maintained their organisation and entered into a bond among themselves not to work after 7 o'clock at night; they petitioned the craft government for shorter hours, saying that the work in the trade was hard and that they had no time off during the day 'except for their meat,' while other trades had one hour off for breakfast and another off for dinner. They also complained that as they did not finish work until 8 o'clock they had no time for schooling. The craft council refused to accept the request and ruled that any master who gave shorter hours and any member who joined the journeymen's society would not be allowed to vote or stand for election for seven years. The journeymen were not intimidated by threats and took the law into their own hands by going off without leave at 7 o'clock.[43]

The records continued to show masters' complaints against the journeymen. In 1773 complaints of the losses they were suffering from the spread of 'moonlighting' – journeymen jobbing on their own behalf after working hours. The Court ruled that any journeyman caught jobbing would be prosecuted 'with the utmost rigour of the law.' Earlier, the masters had complained of 'unfree' hammermen practising the craft in the outer suburbs – the surrounding villages of Gorbals, Govan, etc., which were outside the jurisdiction of the borough of Glasgow. The masters were able to control these men for a time by appointing one of their number in Gorbals as an overman who regulated the activities of his colleagues.

In London, in April 1789, the Court of the Armourers and Braziers ordered that a committee of masters and wardens be convened

to consider how far the Brasing Trade is likely to be affected by these modern inventions and what steps are necessary to be taken by the Company to support their Charter and by-laws to put a stop to or prevent their pernicious affects to the trade.[44]

From 1791 to the end of the century journeymen and apprentices were summoned before the Court to answer why they had not taken up their freedoms and in 1792 ten were fined 20s each for failing to answer the summons.[45]

Then in 1785 the Company abandoned the rights of search after some 370 years and much of the activity of the Court as reported in the minutes concerned the administration of the Company's property and investments.

It was noticeable in the Founders that the Court minutes were becoming more concerned with administration and internal discipline than with the protection of the craft. The old economic function of membership as a means of preserving the closed shop was giving way to a polarisation of the rich traders on the one hand and working mechanics and small masters on the other. The livery was refusing to mix socially with the ordinary manual workers, in 1781 the Court ruled that 'on account of their behaviour the journeymen would not be admitted to the Company's Hall for the celebrations on Lord Mayor's Day.'

During this period of economic change throughout the country, with the development of what afterwards became known as the industrial revolution, the bonds of the guild system were slackening everywhere. In the main provincial towns and cities its restrictions were more and more ignored. In London the situation was somewhat different; the city increased tremendously in size and as an industrial centre, largely through the influx of country craftsmen and labourers, the impact of this was bringing changes. Many of the rich industrialists and traders who governed the guilds were apprehensive of change and feared what would happen when controls were lifted.

Neither the majority of the working masters nor the journeymen were keen to discard voluntarily the old traditions and customs that had stood them more or less in good stead for so long. The struggle to maintain the old order can be seen in the steady stream of petitions to both the civic authorities and to Parliament. Appeals were made by journeymen to the Justices of the Peace to use the powers they possessed to fix wages, but received little response. On the other hand the many petitions from masters to Parliament to ban combinations in their trades met with a sympathetic response.

Many of the smaller masters felt that they, as well as the journeymen, would be swept aside once they had opened the floodgates of change, they made agreements not to employ foreign workers and to set up a fund to prosecute any masters who broke the agreement, but the agreement was not honoured, the offending masters saying that they could not compete with suburban masters who could draw on a big reservoir of alien and country labour at lower prices than free journeymen of London were prepared to work for.[46]

Within the trades the journeymen appealed to the masters not to end the restrictions on the number of apprentices and as late as 1811 the freemen journeymen of the Founders Company were petitioning the Court, complaining that the masters were employing many men who had not served an apprenticeship to the trade, the petitioners said they had applied to shops for work but could not get employment. The Court dismissed the petition.[47]

The journeymen of many trades who had served their time and were registered with their companies could not find work with new labour flooding into the crafts and were forced to 'wander' in search of jobs, in their wanderings they were helped by journeymen's clubs in the localities, a form of job hunting that was organised and developed later as a tramping system by the trade societies.

In 1780 the Tin Plate Workers' Court resolved that 'in view of the great dislocation the trade is labouring under from the limited number of apprentices, each freeman will be allowed to take one additional apprentice.'[48] This was later extended to a total of three apprentices, then in 1787, all restrictions on the number of apprentices were abolished.

The position of the journeymen had also changed with the economic and social changes. Originally the journeymen had lived in their master's house, fed at their master's table, and contracted to work for a year or term of years, but with the growth of a large class of journeymen and serving men who had no prospect of setting up as masters, this arrangement fell into disuse and the journeymen joined the class of wage earners.

The Journeymen's Revolt

Throughout the eighteenth century the London Tin Plate Workers Company carried on a running battle with journeymen who refused to take up their freedom of the Company. This was somewhat sporadic in the early years but grew more sustained as the years went by and the numbers involved increased.

Even while the Court of the Company was revoking all other laws that preserved the interest of the mass of the membership, it still tried to subject the journeymen to its discipline.

In 1700 the Court decreed that all tin plate workers who had not taken up their freedom should be proceeded against, but there is no record in the minutes of any action being actually taken. Again in 1719, orders were given to take proceedings against a number of journeymen. Then in 1758, its own authority obviously having little effect, the Company petitioned the Court of Common Council to grant an order that all London tin plate workers must take up their freedom of the Company or suffer a penalty of five pounds. This made no difference. Journeymen continued to neglect to take up their freedom, the Court continued to summon them to attend before it and the journeymen continued to ignore it. As late as 1822, certainly many years and probably many decades after the journeymen had broken with the company and formed their own trade society, the orders were still being issued and ignored.[49]

Another important means the Company used to control the trade was the fixing of prices to make the various articles produced. The first such price list of which we have been able to find any record was a two-sheet list giving the prices and sizes of the more general wares, put out in 1683, details of which have not survived. Originally a means of ensuring that the members of the Company did not undercut each other in pricing their wares, they were later more useful in fixing piecework prices paid to journeymen. But in none of the prices lists issued by the Company did the journeymen have any part in drawing up, negotiating or settling prices which decided what their wages should be. This was done by a committee appointed by the Court on which the journeymen were not represented.

A fuller list was produced in 1690. In regard to the latter list the minutes report a scandal concerning two members who had copies made, which they circularised contrary to the laws of the Company. For revealing trade secrets they were fined £7 10s each and warned that they would be expelled from the Company 'if their misdemeanour was repeated.' In 1721 a committee consisting of the Master, wardens and six members of the Court was set up to settle prices of all manufactured articles, and the resulting list was published the following year. Others were published in 1733, 1738 and 1761 but only the latter has been preserved.

The list published in 1761 included

apple roasters, basters, biscake frames and pans, boilers, round boxes, boxes for candles, flour, pepper, sugar, and snuff, candle safes, candle sticks, cannisters, cheese toasters, coffee pots, covers, cullenders, funnels, globes, graters, pot kettles, upright kettles, kettles for fish, fountain lamps, lamps large with two or three spouts, middle with two spouts, small lamps with one spout, standing lamps, lanthornes, outsize lanthornes, single and double ovens with grates, pans and hooks, pans for dripping, pastry pans, patty pans, pudding pans, pans for chairs, pans for sauce, pans for tobacco pipes, plates for fish, porringers, pint pots, quart pots, pudding pots, pots for watering, pots to spit in, rims for cakes, scales for flour and soap, scoops for coal, spitting basins, spring funnels, speaking trumpets, water candlesticks. Planished work: drawing boxes, boxes for matches, small candlesticks for lamps, candle sticks, extinguishers, graters for the pocket, japan mugs, lamps for spirits, ladles for eggs, pots for chocolate, slices, strainers for oranges.

WAGES

FOR MAKING THE VARIOUS SORTS OF

TIN WARES,

PROPOSED BY A GENERAL MEETING OF THE MANUFACTURERS,

AND,

After due Examination by a Committee appointed by the Court of Affiſtants of the TIN-PLATE-WORKERS COMPANY of *London*,

Agreed to and confirmed by a SPECIAL COURT, held at GUILDHALL, the 29th Day of AUGUST 1805.

JOHN RILAND MANDER, MASTER.

WILLIAM MATHEWS....} WARDENS.
WILLIAM SLARK ......}

ASSISTANTS.

Daniel Foffick,	Samuel Chamberlain,	Nicholas Robinſon,
William Hallier,	Robert Howard,	Robert Beton,
Joſeph Lucas,	Thomas Axtell,	Thomas Flather,
Joſhua Owen,	Richard Jones,	Samuel Emly,
Wilfred Reed,	James Smethurſt,	Daniel Joſhua Owen,
William Coulſery,	William Bull,	Samuel Thorpe,
Edward Collinſon,	Garnet Terry,	Daniel Maſterman,
Nathaniel Ravis,	John Smith,	Robert Hayward.
Joſeph Harris,		

London:

PRINTED BY S. COUCHMAN, THROGMORTON-STREET.
1805.

A

LIST

OF THE

PRICES for Making the feveral SORTS of TIN WARE

HEREIN MENTIONED:

ORDERED and AGREED to be paid to WORKMEN, by a COURT of ASSISTANTS of the Company of TIN PLATE WORKERS of LONDON, November 3d, 1760.

MASTER.

THOMAS KYNASTON, Efq;

ROBERT WALE,   } Wardens.
THOMAS BECK,   }

ASSISTANTS.

George Harrifon,	Naboth Tarrington,
Thomas Wilfon,	Daniel Harris,
John Howton,	George Conftable,
John Miers,	Henry Smith,
Jeremiah Garrard,	Benjamin Powles,
Thomas Willfon,	Thomas Higgins,
William Millis,	William Sumerfet,
Nicholas Bull,	William Nafh,
Henry Margerum,	Benjamin Aris,
George Knight,	James Love,
Thomas Nowell,	Thomas Lamb,
John Drinkwater,	Edward Wallby.
James Moore,	

LONDON:

Printed by SAMUEL CLARK, in Bread-Street.
MDCCLXI.

This time the journeymen did not accept the prices arbitrarily fixed for them by the Court – the employers. The Court minute books for December 1769 record that a petition was received from several journeymen, who had also put forward a petition to the trade in general, complaining 'of divers grievances and apprehensions in respect of their work and the rules of prices for the same.' The petition was rejected by the committee which claimed that although the petition had been put forward with sixty names, it had only been signed by sixteen and only one quarter of those who signed were freemen of the Company.

One year later the journeymen came back with another petition, putting forward a revised list of prices. The committee claimed that the prices were exhorbitant and recommended that they should not be paid, which was accepted by the Court who dismissed the petition.[50]

The journeymen continued to press for higher wages but apparently got nowhere and on 7 August 1786 a committee of seven assistants and seven traders was appointed 'to regulate the wages of the journeymen.' The committee was dissolved on 11 April 1787 'having been unable to affect an agreement.'

The Court minutes for 16 August 1805 report 'great disputes have arisen between the Company and the journeymen respecting prices of work and wages.' It was resolved that a committee of twelve be appointed to regulate the prices of tin wares to be made by freemen of the Company. This was hurried through at unprecedented speed and on 29 August, only thirteen days after the Court first met, it was completed and unanimously approved. Orders were given that the new book – containing the prices of making some 1,500 separate items – be printed and as a general book of wages 'be observed by all and every member of the Company for the future.'[51]

A manuscript copy of this book has been preserved in the union's archives which would suggest that Union members worked to these prices although they had no part in drawing them up, and were no longer controlled by the guild.

The records of the Company go on to report that after the book had been printed, a number of copies disposed of, and the expenses of compiling, printing and distributing settled, the remains of the sum apportioned to the project was set aside 'to reimburse the subscribers to a certain fund which has been raised by the masters in the trade to meet legal charges in proceedings against the workmen.' There is no intimation in the minutes of the nature of the charges but they could have been connected with the journeymen's petition to the magistrates to set new wage rates – the reason why the prices book had been rushed through the guild organisation – or perhaps to pay for secret action against the journeymen's society which was illegal under the Combinations Act.

This, however, was very much a rearguard action by the Company for they had by then completely lost control of the journeymen who had long had their own separate organisation.

Although the Tin Plate Workers Company continued throughout the nineteenth century as an organisation of the masters, it had no economic significance. As late as 1900 the employers' side in negotiations with the Union over a new prices book was presided over by an Upper Warden of the Company, who was also managing director of the Army and Navy Stores tin plate works and at the conclusion of the meeting the employers thanked the Company for arranging the meeting and for 'the continued help it had given to the trade.' This was something of an exception. Generally, the activities of the guilds, where they continued to exist, were the management of their investments, almshouses and education, including, of course, the London City and Guilds trades examinations.

But by 1800 the divergence of interests had already brought the break-up of the guild organisation. Both sides tried to use the guilds' customs and practices to help them in the economic struggle. At first the journeymen got a measure of support from the courts, and even from Parliament, but not for long, as Parliament and the courts were marshalled on the side of the wealthier manufacturers.

Throughout the eighteenth century there had been repeated legislation against the organisations of the journeymen and combination in a large number of trades had been made illegal, culminating in the Combinations Act.

The journeymen, needing all the support they could get in the economic struggle, came to take up a position of protecting the ideals, customs and practices of the guilds, appealing to tradition to bolster up their weak economic position. It was in their interest to maintain a position whereby the trade was regulated by traditional workshop practices, with restrictive entry to the trade through the control of apprentices. The preservation of these practices became more and more 'a battle cry in the class struggle.'[52] This tactic was maintained even when they reached a stage when the journeymen's interests could no longer be obtained through use of the guilds and companies or through the journeymen's clubs which had been increasing in number and activities. The next stage in the struggle was the development of independent trade societies.

Apprentices' badge, London Tin Plate Workers Company, front and back views

1. G. Unwin, *Guilds and Companies of London*, London 1908.
2. Ibid.
3. L. Bretano, *On the History and Development of Guilds and the Origins of Trade Unions*, London 1871.
4. Ibid.
5. G. Hadley, *Citizens and Founders*, London 1976.
6. W.M. Williams, *Annals of the Worshipful Company of Founders*, London 1867.
7. W. Cardew Hazlitt, *The Livery Companies of the City of London*, London 1892.
8. S. Hewitt Pitt, Clerk to the Company, *Notes on the History of the Worshipful Company of Armourers and Braziers*, London 1930.
9. H.T. Ridley, *Memorials of London and London Life*, London 1868.
10. Ibid.
11. Ibid.
12. J. Colston, *Incorporated Trades of Edinburgh*, Edinburgh 1891.
13. Worshipful Company of Tin Plate Workers alias Wire Workers, MS minute books, Guildhall, London.
14. Ibid.
15. Worshipful Company of Armourers and Braziers, MS minute books, Guildhall, London.
16. Unwin, op. cit.
17. Friendly Society of Tin Plate Workers, Rule Book, Public Record Office FS 1/408 B.
18. Hazlitt, op. cit.
19. Pitt, op. cit.
20. Ibid.
21. Unwin, op. cit.

22. Hadley, op. cit.
23. Worshipful Company of Founders, MS minute books, Guildhall, London.
24. W.W. Hibbert, *Worshipful Company of Founders of the City of London*, London 1925.
25. Worshipful Company of Founders, MS minute books, Guildhall, London.
26. Unwin, op. cit.
27. J. Collier, *Parents' and Guardians' Directory*, London 1761. G. Kersley, *Table of Trades*, London 1786.
28. Tin Plate Workers Company, MS minute books, loc. cit.
29. D. Thomson, *History of the Dunfermline Hammermen*, Paisley 1909.
30. G.M. Warner, *History of the Tin Plate Workers Company*, London 1964. E.A. Ebbelwhite, *A Chronological History of the Worshipful Company of Tin Plate Workers alias Wire Workers of the City of London*, London 1896. D.L. Simmons, *Worshipful Company of Tin Plate Workers alias Wire Workers of the City of London*, London 1958.
31. H. Lumsden and Henderson B. Aitkin, *History of the Hammermen of Glasgow*, Paisley 1912.
32. Ibid.
33. Colston, op. cit.
34. E. Baines, *Merchants and Craft Guilds: History of Aberdeen Incorporated Trades*, Aberdeen 1887.
35. T.C. Tingey, *Some Notes on the Craft Guilds of Norwich*, Norwich 1906.
36. G. Unwin, *Industrial Organisation in the Sixteenth and Seventeenth Centuries*, Oxford 1904.
37. W. Blazey, *Bristol and Gloucester Archaeological Transactions*, xiii, 1901.
38. Unwin, op. cit.
39. Charter and Rules of the Incorporated Company of Upholsterers, Tin Plate Workers and Stationers of Newcastle-upon-Tyne, 1817, Newcastle Public Library.
40. Unwin, op. cit.
41. W.A. Abrams, *Memorials of Preston Guilds*, Preston 1882.
42. Pitt, op. cit.
43. Lumsden and Aitkin, op. cit.
44. Armourers and Braziers Company MS minute book, loc. cit.
45. Ibid.
46. Unwin, op. cit.
47. Hadley, op. cit.
48. Tin Plate Workers Company MS minute book, loc. cit.
49. Ibid.
50. Warner, op. cit.
51. Tin Plate Workers Company MS minute book, loc. cit.
52. Unwin, op. cit.

CHAPTER TWO

The Early Trade Societies

There was no sharp break between the days of the guilds and the days of the unions. We cannot say that at a certain date the guilds ceased to function and the unions took their place. There was much overlapping, and both existed together for decades, in some cases for half a century or more, although circumstances differed between trade and trade.

The local trade clubs that were the earliest forms of trade unions can be traced back at least until the beginning of the eighteenth century when the guilds, if not still at the height of their powers and influence were still very much in evidence and actively concerned with at least some aspects of the trades with which they were associated.

As long ago as 1700, five London clubs of journeymen tailors reportedly came together to form a union, and in 1721 employers complained that there were 'unlawful combinations' of curriers, smiths, and farriers, sailmakers and coachmakers, and that bricklayers, carpenters and joiners were about to form such combinations and there were no doubt many others also.

We are told that in the eighteeth century the London Tin Plate Workers had already established their House of Call which was advertised in the press for members of the trade from the country to apply for help – perhaps the beginning of an early form of tramping system.

The Webbs, whose classic *History of Trade Unionism*, first published in 1894, is still the most comprehensive history of the British trade unions, were adamant that there was no connection between the guilds and the unions. Inasmuch as the guilds, as such, did not turn themselves into trade unions this is, of course, correct. For one thing, as we have seen, for most of their effective life the guilds represented, or at least included, all those engaged in the craft, masters and journeymen, employers and employed. At the time of their decline they were controlled by the big traders, indeed they had been for many years, and as far as they continued to have any economic activity, they represented the employers. Many of the old guilds continued in being, but they retained merely the shell of their old organisation, not the old activities.

There can, however, be no doubt about the connection between the journeymen members of the guilds and the trade societies. Many of the old trade clubs and trade societies will almost certainly have originated as journeymen's clubs that increased in numbers and independent life during the decline of the guilds in the eighteenth century, when they not only no longer represented the journeymen's interest but were antagonistic to them. From where else could the trades societies' members have come but from the journeymen who had served their apprenticeship and most of their working lives within the guilds and who had experienced the organisation of the guilds, much of which they took over into their new societies?

For many years the guilds and the journeymen's and trades' clubs existed side by side, sometimes in co-operation in the general interest of the trade, but more often in confrontation as representatives of employers and workers.

Many, probably most of the members of the new trade societies, would have been recruited from those many journeymen who, as we have seen, had not taken up their freedom of their

A tin plate worker (*left*) and brazier (*right*) at the end of the eighteenth century

particular company or who had drifted out of the company. In other cases the whole of the old journeymen's club would take on the activities of a trades club, breaking its already tenuous links with the company. Late comers, like the tin plate workers, would have been following the example of journeymen of other trades who had already made the break. After all, they both – journeymen's club and trade society – existed for the same reason and were both doing the same job, looking after the interests of the working men in the trade.

The very language and terms the trade societies used and the forms of activity they indulged in carried memories of guild life and organisation.

As late as 1870 the Manchester Tin Plate Workers Society was refusing to allow Society members to work for a certain local employer because he – the employer – had not served his apprenticeship to the trade, a clear throwback to the attitude of the guilds.

The first reference to a trade society among any of the crafts in which we are interested here comes in an advertisement in a Liverpool newspaper of 1756. In the 'wanted' columns of the issue of 20 April of that year the following appeared:

Journeymen Pewterers, Coppersmiths, Tin Plate Workers and Brass-Founders may meet with constant work and suitable encouragement by applying to Mrs H. Houghton, Pool Lane, Liverpool. They are requested to be good workers.

The issue of the following week carried another advertisement with the following reply:

Journeymen Pewterers, Coppersmiths and Tin Plate Workers. We the journeymen of the above business now residing here, do hereby give notice that the person that advertised hath not above three or four at the time working for her that are not interlopers in the above business and the scope of the said advertisement is to get men to instruct them, as we are determined not to do it. N.B. If any journeymen come here of these branches they will not be relieved as here are men able and ready to serve the town.[1]

The wording of this reply seems to indicate that there were already societies of coppersmiths and tin plate workers in Liverpool. They may have been engaged in strike action, the tone of the advertisement gives a hint of that. Moreover, the statement 'they will not be relieved' suggests that they were part of a tramping system, though whether this would be a national organisation or only on a regional level it is impossible to say.

The first edition of *Gore's Liverpool Directory,* appearing in 1766, does not mention Mrs Houghton's shop. It does, however, mention 21 businesses of braziers, tinmen and pewterers. The directory for the following year adds four more braziers and another tinman. These would be shops employing perhaps a few men each.

Advertisements for craftsmen were appearing in other papers at the time, suggesting that the old work relations were loosening as the guilds went further into decline. *Aris's Birmingham Journal* for 30 November 1761 carried such an advertisement: 'Wanted, a journeyman brazier can do black and bright work. Apply, Mr Jordan at the Dolphin in Birmingham.' In the issue for 14 March 1785 a C. Blunt of Birmingham advertised for 'Journeyman Tinman, good hand, and an out-apprentice.' The description of the apprentice required is an indication of the break-up of the old apprenticeship system in which the apprentice lived in the house of his master who fed and clothed him in return for his unpaid labour.

In Sheffield in 1780, a Braziers' Society was meeting at the Rose and Crown Inn in the High Street.[2] According to the sums disbursed, it was one of the most important of a number of local friendly societies, paying out £133 7s to members over the year. It was independent of the guilds but its officers included a Master – no doubt in imitation of or because of relations with the guilds. It could well have been the same society referred to in the *Sheffield Iris* of 17 December 1816, which then had 622 members and funds amounting to £1,768. This was one of a number of local friendly societies which were 'essentially trades unions.' said the paper. The braziers of Sheffield made trays, salvers, bowls and other articles of copper which were afterwards silver-plated, a speciality of the town. It was an extensive industry and the braziers were among the highest paid craftsmen in the city.

In London throughout the eighteenth century, as we have seen in the last chapter, some braziers and increasing numbers of journeymen tin plate workers refused, or at least failed to take up their freedoms of the company, although threatened that if they did not, proceedings would be taken against them in the courts. While some may have been unable to afford the high fees, others undoubtedly refused because they no longer considered themselves members of the company and bound by its rules. A number will have been members of an independent organisation, either a journeymen's club, friendly or benefit club, or a trade society.

The existence of such a club could well have been the explanation for a complaint of the committee to the Tin Plate Workers Company in 1769 that a petition for higher piecework prices, claimed to be in the name of 90 journeymen, had only 13 names 'and of those signing only a quarter were freemen of the Company' [3]– the 13 being possibly officers of the club. This petition was rejected and the journeymen came back with further demands, continuing their struggle against the Court of the Company for many years. This could be an indication that they already had some form of organisation of their own – even if not continually active – as without one it is unlikely that such opposition should have been maintained.

In 1805, a petition by London journeymen tin plate workers to local magistrates for an increase in wages was presented on behalf of all tin plate workers in the County of Middlesex, obviously the work of the trade society with one of the petitioners referred to by the employers as 'secretary of the workmen's club' and two others as 'delegates.' From the tone of their argument in the petition it would seem that the break with the employer-dominated Company had already taken place in 1760 when the last book of prices had been presented to the journeymen, in fact the employers referred to 'wages paid in 1760.'

The First London Society

The first real documentary evidence we have of union organisation in the trades is a handwritten book of articles of the Friendly Society of Tin Plate Workers of London, dated January 1798, whose club house was the house of John White, at the sign of the White Swan, Fleet Lane.[4]

The declared aims of the Society were sufficiently vague not to cause the members trouble in this difficult period when trade union activity was largely illegal. They were 'to raise funds for the laudable aim of benefitting such persons respectively as shall become entitled thereto in the manner directed.' In practice, they seem to have concentrated much of their effort on getting work for their members and providing relief for those out of work.

Although the articles were dated January 1798, they were not deposited with the new Registrar of Friendly Societies until November 1799. The fact that they were registered at all was probably due to the passing of the first of the Combination Acts in the intervening period, which could have made the members feel that it was better to be safe than sorry. The name adopted, the Friendly Society of Tin Plate Workers, which was also taken by the early Wolverhampton, Liverpool and Manchester societies, may have been deliberately used as a cover to make the authorities think it was just another friendly society.

The law on the registration of friendly societies had been brought in in 1793, supposedly for the protection of the members and their money. But the workmen's organisations viewed the new measures with suspicion, believing they were a device for the government to get its hands on their money and also to stop the friendly society funds being used to finance strikes. The result was that by 1800 still only about half of the known societies had registered.

The condition of the tin plate workers' rule book shows that the Society's origin dates back even earlier than the 1798 date it carries. The limp, stained exercise book containing the articles had been handled many times before being deposited with the registrar and there had been many crossings out as the rules were changed. The officers, too, had been replaced. James Mallendain had replaced John Cunningham as president and there had been a number of changes in the composition of the committee.

One of the main changes of the rules was that the government of the Society was to be in the hands of a president and two stewards instead of, as previously, a president and committee of nine. The book states that the present president and committee shall continue in their respective offices until the Society's next Quarterly Night after the allowance and confirmation of these articles and then the committee shall be dissolved.

The first rule, or 'Article ye First' as it appears in the book, says that meetings were once a month, 'each member to pay one shilling and two pence, the two pence to be spent for the good of the House whether the members were present or not.' Members paid an additional 4d each quarterly night, one penny to the servant of the House, two pence for the secretary and one penny to the box for paper, etc.

Membership was confined to 'Tin Plate Workers who have been legally bound apprentices to the said trade or sons of those who have been legally bound.' A member leaving his employment should report to the stewards 'the time and cause of his discharge (and likewise the branch of the business he was most accustomed to work at).' The steward should 'endeavour to hear of employ for him.' But stewards must not give any information about jobs to anyone not on the list of the Society, 'on pain of being fined 5s for each and every offence.' Any member informing the stewards of vacant jobs which resulted in an unemployed member getting a start, was excused two months contributions.

One notable absence from the rules is any specific reference to a tramping system. It was laid down, however, that any out-of-work member unable to get a job in London who chose to go to the country after a job would be allowed 10s.

Benefits included 8s a week to any free member out of work through no fault of his own. There was no sick pay, but at 60 years of age and after ten years' membership a fully paid-up member could claim superannuation of 3s 6d a week for the rest of his life; 6s after 15 years' membership and 6d a week for every year's membership thereafter to a maximum of 8s. A

Pewter collection plates, London Tin Plate Workers' Society, 1823

death benefit of £1 after one year's membership, £2 after two years and £3 after three years was paid 'out of the box' to widows or next of kin of paid-up members, plus a collection from every member.

Former paid-up members, 'so reduced as to being in the workhouse' were given 1s each week – an indication of the fate that many working people could expect in those 'good old days.' So, too, the many references in the rules to members undergoing imprisonment for debt – accepted, for example, as a reason for non-attendance at meetings – tell of other misfortunes likely to overtake them.

A feature that continued throughout most of the nineteenth century was the provision of a box – such as had been used by the guilds – with four different locks and keys, for holding the Society's cash and other valuables. The landlord, who was also the treasurer, kept one of the keys and the president and the two stewards the others. There was a drawer underneath, of which the secretary had the key, for the cash book. The box was kept in the club house and the president and stewards were responsible for seeing that it was 'carefully delivered to the landlord' after they had seen the books closed at 10 o'clock.

A book containing the officers' names and addresses was also kept at the bar of the club house. In fact, the public houses and their landlords played an important part in the organisation of trade societies. It is understandable that the landlord should act as one of the officers of the society as he could be contacted when the regular officers were at work – although it would appear that there was little objection to them being visited at work in these early days. Later, when factory discipline was more strict, notes appeared in the rule books or reports that the secretary should not be contacted at his place of work. Landlords were not, however, taken completely on trust. The rules stipulated that he 'shall give such security for the value deposited in the hands on trust for the Society as shall be approved by the Society.' Publicans, as a body, were generally friendly to the working-class movement. Of course, they benefitted financially from the ale consumed by the members, but many landlords lost their licences for harbouring 'illegal societies' and buying 'seditious' papers and pamphlets for the use of their customers. One Yorkshire publican, at least, was sent to prison for three months for allowng a trade union committee to meet on his premises.

Another rule states 'that the only object of this society is the relief of honest industry,' any member leaving his employment without finishing his work, unless through want of materials, would not be allowed to draw benefits 'unless he either finished his work or made proper satisfaction for same.' Whether the reasons given for this rule are the true ones or not, the fact remains that leaving one's work unfinished was punishable at law by imprisonment and was often so used in times of strike action. But the rule persisted in some form throughout the nineteenth century with successive tin plate workers' societies making themselves responsible for seeing that work was completed, often paying for the work to be done and trying to collect the cost from members later.

A rule common at the time was concerned with 'preserving decency and good order' at Society meetings.

Any member introducing Political Discourse, Seditious sentiments, or Songs, calling nick-names, or who shall curse, swear or use any obscene discourse, or shall lay wagers, promote gambling, or will not keep silent when called on by the President, shall pay a fine of six pence for each and every offence.

There were also fines for members or officials coming to meetings drunk. Later rule books also prohibited members from sleeping or reading during meetings.

Finally, the rules declared that it was 'firmly agreed to and resolved that this Society shall not be dissolved nor the cash shared out contrary to Act of Parliament' – a regular happening with mere friendly or benefit societies. All members had to agree to this on joining the society and any member 'publicly advocating the break-up of the society under any pretence whatever' would be fined £1 – the heaviest fine in the book.

The Society re-registered on 5 April 1805, having changed the club house to the George Inn, St Martin's le Grand and again on 8 January 1811 – when it appears in the register just as the Tin Plate Workers – meeting at the George Inn, West Smithfield. Unfortunately, in neither case have the rules deposited with the Registrar been preserved, so we do not know what changes may have been made in the organisation.

In 1805 there were apparently a number of organised tin plate shops in the St Pancras area. A list of workers made out by the employers mentions a Richard Steer, 'secretary of the workmen's club' and James Wilson and George Le Clere, 'delegates,' acknowledged although this was the time of the combination laws.

The Wolverhampton Society

There must already have been close contact between the various tin plate workers' societies as the 1798 London Society has a number of rules identical with some appearing in an early rule book of the Wolverhampton Society – as well as others. Unfortunately, the printed rule book of this Society bears no date. But inscribed on the blank inside cover in a childish hand in ink browned with age is 'Ann Clinton, her book June 1802' – no doubt the daughter of a member, perhaps the secretary, who would most likely have odd rule books around the house.

The preamble of this Friendly Society of Tin Plate Workers declares:

> It is the object of this institution, to dispence necessary relief to such of its members as may be out of employ and others on travel in search of the same; therefore a number of journeymen tin plate workers of the town

Membership cards

and neighbourhood of Wolverhampton have agreed, for the mutual relief and assistance of each other, under such afflications, to found and establish a society, for raising a common stock or fund, for the said purpose, under and subject to the rules, orders and regulations here-in-after mentioned.

Conditions of entry were the same as in the London Society but the rules also stipulated that any applicant 'whose character and elegibility is found agreeable' would be accepted in a ballot of not less than eleven. 'Any applicant lately out of his time bringing a card clear of the books where he worked' – perhaps the first mention of shop organisation – paid only 2s entrance fee whereas an applicant who had been a journeyman for more than 12 months when applying had to pay one guinea and the regular entrance fee of 6s.

As with other societies, the rules ensured that the maximum number of members participated in the running of the Society. Two stewards were chosen each quarterly night to manage the Society, taking the names as they appeared on the roll, and any refusing office were fined.

A standing committee of seven, all of whom must have been members for at least twelve months, was elected to decide matters that the stewards could not handle. The members served six months with half going out each quarter. Five of the committee had to attend each meeting night. On any business of importance the committee was empowered to call a deputation from each factory or shop of as many members as they thought proper. The two oldest members of the committee acted for the first month of the quarter, the two next for the second month and the two youngest for the third month. The two acting committee members received all letters from any other town and all letters that went from the Society, and one of the two members had to see them put in the post.

A president was chosen by ballot every quarter and the president, stewards and committee had to attend the meeting the night following the election one hour early to hand over to their successors all keys, books, cash and accounts 'properly examined by the committee.' A secretary was elected by ballot for a term of twelve months 'renewable at the pleasure of the Society.' The other officer was a marshal appointed every quarterly night from the next on the roll. His duty included control of the ballot box when it was wanted, 'likewise to call for ale and keep the account and distribute the same without partiality.' Any member calling for ale without leave of the marshall was fined 6d for each offence.

Disputes between members and the Society were settled by arbitration, each side nominating three people, and if these six were unable to agree another three were appointed from each side 'and what they settle and determine shall be conclusive on both sides.' General questions were settled by the majority present at an ordinary or specially summoned meeting of members, unless two or more members called for a ballot.

Contributions were 6d a fortnight until the Society's stock had risen to £200 when a general meeting would consider whether to lower contributions or increase benefits.

Unemployment benefit, the main benefit of the Society, was high, 12s a week for any member clear on the books when out of work through no fault of his own. Any unemployed member 'on the box' had to report to the steward daily. A member of two years standing sent by the committee to a job in the country was allowed 15s, but if he went on his own account he got only 7s 6d. Any young member forced to leave town for want of work was allowed 5s for the first three months, rising by 10d a month up to 10s, but any young member going to suit his own convenience only got half that amount.

The rules stated that the house where the Society was held was appointed for the reception of tramps – unfortunately any other regulations concerning tramps have been lost, as the rest of the pages are missing.

The element of conviviality, which played an important part in the early trade society meetings, was provided by an extra two pence paid by every member on top of his normal contributions each fortnightly meeting night, 'the members present to spend the money.' There was also an annual feast on 12 July for which every member paid 2s before the dinner to specially appointed officers, and a further 2s a month later. The Society also celebrated 'Mr Perry's Feast' on Shrove Tuesday, for which every member had to pay 2s for ale – those not attending had to pay their 2s the next quarter night.

The 1834 rule book of the Friendly Society of the United Operative Tin Plate Workers of Wolverhampton – the very year of the trial and transportation of the Tolpuddle Martyrs – contains a hint of ritual that surrounded these early trade unions, including the so-called secret oaths which were used as a means of convicting the six Dorset labourers. The rules lay down that 'as soon as a member enters the lodge he shall give the sign' and 'the word brother be only used during lodge hours.' The Lodge was 'conducted by a President and Vice-President, with Right and Left hand Supporters to each; a Warden, two Conductors and a Tyler; and two Stewards,' the kind of set-up used for elaborate initiations, and another rule states 'all the Officers shall attend the initiation ceremonies when summoned' or be fined three pence. It decreed that 'The President, Stewards and every member of this Society are hereby strictly enjoined not to publish or give any information respecting the affairs of this Society to any person whatsoever whose name is not on their list.' Anyone contravening this rule would be subject to a fine of 2s, later increased to 10s.

It is interesting that the Society was directly run by the men on the shop floor. 'The number of the Committee to be regulated by the number of shops in the Town in which the members are employed. The Hall Shop to choose two Committee men and the rest one.' The President, Vice-President and Stewards were selected from the committee.

Two Marshals or Ale Stewards were appointed, 'whose duty shall be to call for ale at the order of the President, pour it out and distribute it without partiality. The Officers to be allowed two cups each, and all the rest one.'

Liverpool and Manchester

The Liverpool Tin Plate Workers Society was established in 1802, according to later rule books. But the earliest documentary record we have (other than the 1765 advertisement) is the articles of the Humane Society of Tin Plate Workers of Liverpool which were filed at the Court of Sessions at Ormskirk – a small town a few miles from Liverpool[6] – on 29 April 1811. The Society met monthly at the house of Mr Eaton, at the sign of the Swan, Thomas Street, Liverpool. From the rules it would appear to have been purely a friendly society. Its benefits were a small superannuation and a burial payment. There is nothing in the rules confining membership to tin plate workers but it is probable from the title that this was the case, nor is there any other reference to the trade. But by 1819 the Society was taking part in real trade union activities. The omission may have been a precautionary measure taken because of the new combination laws which were used more frequently against trade unions in industrial areas like Lancashire than in most other parts of the country. That, too, may have been the reason for registering the Society in the small town of Ormskirk rather than in Liverpool.

The 1838 rule book of the Manchester Tin Plate Workers also claims the Society was founded in 1802. Here the earliest record we have been able to find is a tattered cash book beginning 21 March 1807, inscribed Tramp Book of the Tramp Society of Tin Plate Workers, Manchester. There is also a membership register of 1814 and a tramp card dated 1819. The Manchester Society took an early lead in opening up communications with societies in

LIST OF PRICES

ALLOWED FOR MAKING

TIN-PLATE WARES,

AS

ARRANGED BY COMMITTEES,

APPOINTED FROM THE

Manufacturers & Journeymen Tin-Plate Workers

OF

GLASGOW;

And agreed to at a Meeting of the Journeymen, held in their place of meeting, the 16th day of December, one thousand eight hundred and twenty-four years.

Journeymen's Committee.

WILLIAM STRATH, Sec
JOHN RIDDELL,
JOHN DOUGALL,
JOHN DODD,
JAMES McMILLAN,
JOHN CARMICHAEL,
JOHN McCORMICK,
GEORGE GRAHAM,

Manufacturers' Committee.

ALEXANDER KERR, Sec.
WILLIAM DREW,
GEORGE LYON, Jun.
JOHN HOGG,
JAMES JACKSON,
JOHN McALPIN,
HENRY FIELD,
JAMES GALBRAITH.

GLASGOW:

PRINTED BY JOHN GRAHAM AND CO. 136, TRONGATE.

1825.

BOOK OF PRICES,

FOR THE

MANUFACTURING

OF

TIN GOODS,

IN THE

TOWN OF BIRMINGHAM.

July 16, 1810.

Birmingham,

PRINTED AT MARTIN & CO's OFFICE, PECK LANE.

1810.

neighbouring towns on matters of mutual interest. There was an obvious need to get co-ordination on prices, rates of pay, hours and conditions of work, questions of membership and assistance in cases of dispute. This was particularly important in industrial Lancashire with the proximity of so many local societies. The first such letter we have was written on 28 February 1819 by William Nichols, then secretary of the Manchester Society, to the secretary of Liverpool Society, James Hogarth, enquiring under what circumstances the Liverpool Society had given a membership card to a Manchester man who had been refused in his own town.

The old Manchester tramping cash book shows that already in 1807 there were local tin plate workers' societies in Wigan, Ashton-under-Lyne, Warrington, Bolton, Chester, Stockport, Nantwich, Altrincham, York, Preston and Lancaster, as well as London, Liverpool, Dublin and Glasgow. We know little or nothing of these smaller societies, other than that they apparently were part of the organised tramping system.

In a side light on Lancaster,however, we do know that one, Abram Seward, set up as a master tin plate worker in Sun Street around 1780. His one claim to fame, as far as we are concerned, is that he is the only tin plate worker, as far as we know, to have been awarded the Royal Warrant. This was awarded in March 1797, appointing him

> … unto the place and quality of tin plate worker in ordinary to His Majesty, to have, hold, exercise, enjoy the said place, together with all the rights, profits, privileges and advantages thereto belonging.

The Preston Tin Plate Workers Society was already well established by June 1819 according to a list, still preserved, giving the names of the 12 men belonging to the Society and the four 'rats' in the town. The regular appearance of the names of tramps from Preston in the Manchester Society tramp book of 1807 to 1809 would seem to indicate that the Preston Society goes back at least to the beginnings of the nineteenth century and the fact that the tin plate workers were members of the Preston guilds could indicate that the organisation of the trade in the town was even much older.

Of the other industrial towns, the Birmingham Tin Plate Workers Society can 'trace its ancestry back to 1812 when a society had been founded to protest against low wages.'[7] There is also a book of prices dated 16 July 1810.[8] There is no indication who published it but the cover bears the sign of four clasped hands which would seem to indicate that it was a product of a trade society.

Similarly in Scotland, a book of 'wages for making various sorts of tin wares, proposed by a general meeting of the manufacturers in Glasgow' is dated 1811, but has nothing to show that it was the result of any negotiations or other communications with an organisation of workers.

A secretary of the Glasgow Tin Plate Workers' Society related in the 1890s how an old member, then deceased, had told him that before the formation of the 1833 society members would hold their meetings in secret and bury their books after the business was over – that would probably refer to the Society affiliated to the National Union in the 1820s.[9]

London coppersmiths also have a long history. The first records we have been able to find of any organised society is the registration on 9 April 1810, of an Amicable Society of Workers in Copper whose club house was at the Golden Lion, Fore Street, in the City of London – a favourite trade union meeting place at that time. Other entries in friendly societies' records show a coppersmiths' society met either there or at the Golden Hart Inn, Lamb Street, Spitalfields, until 1839.[10]

A Friendly Society of Braziers, meeting at the White Hart Inn, Chancery Lane, was registered on 12 January 1809. Unfortunately, the rules of none of these societies have been preserved in the records.

A Lamp Makers Union was started in Birmingham in 1824.[11] The preamble to the rules, appearing under a drawing of two clasped hands, states:

> We, the Journeymen Brass Lamp Makers, Gas Lamp Makers and Carriage Lamp Makers of Birmingham and its vicinity, after mature consideration, have thought proper to turn ourselves into a society upon laudable and benevolent principles, for the good of each other, and every other legal Professor of the calling.

No one was admitted 'who had not served five years in the business except in particular circumstances when the committee shall be empowered to investigate the matter and act as they think proper.'

It was 'the duty of every member to provide work for another out of employ (knowing of a place of work vacant) it is requested the earliest information of the same will be given to the landlord, where books will be kept for the purpose.' If an unemployed member refused to go after, or accept a position, without giving sufficient reason, the committee would be called together to consider the matter and if they found the objections frivolous or unfounded the member would be fined 2s 6d. An out-of-work member would get a ticket from the secretary bearing his name and number and he had to take it to the landlord to be entered in the book. If he did not he was fined one shilling for 'every six hours of neglect.'

The landlord did not escape fines for neglect of duty. His duties included delivering all letters to the secretary within six hours of receiving them; seeing unemployed members sign the book and accommodate the members with a suitable room or rooms if required and provide sufficient fires, candles, etc for the respective meetings of the society or committee or forfeit for such neglect three shillings.

The entrance fee was 3s 6d and subscriptions 6d a fortnight, 'two pence to be spent.' Members were free in six months and received unemployment pay according to wages at the rate of 15s in the pound. The death benefit was £5 but this had to come from a 6d donation from each member, with any deficiency to be taken from the fund.

It is difficult to believe that with such a small subscription and high benefits the society could have lasted long and it probably went down in the great depression of 1825 to 1826, if it lasted that long. We have not been able to find any further reference to it. But as members of the Birmingham Society of Tin Plate Workers made all kind of lamps from the very early days, it is possible that the lamp makers ultimately joined the Birmingham Society. It may, however, have managed to continue some form of existence, ultimately becoming the Carriage Lamp Makers Society which, with 149 members, joined the Birmingham Society in 1890.

The earliest record we have of the London Iron Plate Workers is a rule book, dated 1836, of the Friendly Society of Iron Plate Workers which had its club house, at that time, at the Sign of the Pickled Egg, Pickled Egg Walk, Clerkenwell.[12] Admission into the society was regulated by ballot, and if the applicant was approved by the majority of members present he was admitted.

According to one rule, 'any member in or out of employment, free or otherwise, refusing to make any article for less than what was paid by the shop shall receive such sum as the members deem proper.' The money to be raised by a levy of members. Another rule declared that: 'If any member takes such member's place at work at a reduced rate, he is excluded and never more allowed to enter the society.' Further rules laid down 'that if any member loses his time in consequence in endeavouring to detect a supposedly imposter member of the society; he shall have reasonable remuneration of the time he has lost, and as the committee may decide that the case shall deserve.' Where the rules are silent on any matter the issue would be settled by arbitration. Many of its other rules were identical with those of the tin plate workers society.

There was also an Iron Plate Workers Society in Birmingham already in 1824 but we have no information on its membership rules or activities.

London coppersmiths and braziers, in addition to having their separate individual societies, were also catered for by a joint society with the brassfounders, a grouping which had existed under the guilds and may easily have been formed by journeymen members of the Founders Company. We do not have any early records of any of these trades.

The Work They Did

On the work they did, according to a contemporary account, coppersmiths were mainly engaged on work for breweries and distilleries, making vats and boilers for sugar refining and soap boiling, and were also engaged on work for shipping, as well as making copper utensils and other equipment.

The work of the tin plate workers at that time, according to the 1805 prices list of the London Company,[13] included pots, pans and kettles of various shapes, sizes and uses – tea and coffee pots, fish and ham kettles – muffin covers, dish covers, cake tins, dripping pans, flour and dust pans, and a whole host of other domestic items. They made various baths – an item not included in the 1761 list – hot (5 feet 5 inches long and 1 foot 9 inches deep) and cold, foot and shower. The book lists a number of lamps of various kinds and descriptions – sedan chairmen's, footmen's, workmen's and wagon lamps, weavers' lamps, chain and hanging lamps, moon lamps, horn lamps, bull's eye lanterns and many more. For the dairy trade they made milk pails and measures, milk and cream skimmers. For shops they made tea and other cannisters, scales, measures and scoops. For the army there were barrack cans, camp sets, gunpowder magazines, powder flasks and signal lamps. Other items included cash and deed boxes, hearing and speaking trumpets, watering cans and garden squirts. In addition, of course, there would be many one-off jobs which could not be listed and would be paid day work rates. There were more than 300 different items, many of them in a whole range of different sizes and various finishes. Many of the prices were so low that it is difficult to imagine the workers could make a living wage. Sedan chairmen's lamps were priced at 4s, 12 inch dish covers 1s 3d, funnels ranged from 4d for a half-pint size to 2s 6d for the eight quart, tin kettles were 6d for the pint size going up to 3s 3d for the three and four gallon, small speaking trumpets with bell mouths were 4s, all priced in dozens. However according to the 1811 Book of Trades, tin plate workers, 'if sober, workmen' could earn 35s to 40s a week'.

A few pages remaining from an old Manchester Society prices book, published between 1810 and 1815, show how local tin plate workers contributed to industry, particularly to the needs of the local textile mills. The factory work included bobbins and doffin cans, roving cans, waste cans, cotton conductors and weavers' suckers, rollers for textile printers as well as repairing old cotton cans and skeleton cans and providing factory lanterns and tin drums.

The book also records conditions of work:

Regulations for Day Work

In Summer

From six o'clock in the Morning, until seven in the Evening, from March 10th to October 1st; during that time no candle. To be at work at eight o'clock on Monday Morning, and to work until six on Saturday Evening.

In Winter

From eight o'clock in the Morning until eight o'clock in the Evening from October 1st to March 10th. To be at work at eight o'clock on Monday Morning and to work until five o'clock on Saturday Evening.

Holidays Allowed

Christmas Day and Good Friday

An 1811 book of wages for making various sorts of tin wares proposed at a meeting of the manufacturers in Glasgow,[14] also included a number of items for cotton mills – bobbins, cop or slipping cans, pullies, skewers, drums, conductors for work lamps and fountain lamps for weavers. Also on the list were ventilators, steam pipes, conductors for electrical machines, furnace lamps, lamps for colliers, street lamp burners, coach lanterns, oil bottles for stables, coach and watchmen's horns, binnacle lamps, cabin candlesticks, sailors' tin pots, soldiers' oil bottles, gun powder magazines, cartridge boxes, and camp kettles – also whistling luggies, both small and large, whatever they were.

The prices book was 'made out' by a committee appointed by the manufacturers of Glasgow and, 'after due examination, unanimously agreed to.' There is no mention of negotiations with the journeymen, or even of consultation. The title page of the book is headed by a coat of arms identical with that of the Tin Plate Workers Company of London, though whether this means that the manufacturers formed a section of the local guild organisation, the Glasgow Hammermen, or whether they were receiving prices lists or other communications from the London Company we cannot say.

The next Glasgow prices book, date 1825, was definitely a joint effort, with initiative, apparently, coming from the journeymen. The title page indicates that it is a

List of prices allowed for making tin plate wares as arranged by committees, appointed from the Manufacturers and Journeymen Tin Plate Workers of Glasgow and agreed at the Meeting of the Journeymen, held in their place of meeting, the 16th day of December one thousand eight hundred and twenty four years.

The page is headed by the arms of the Glasgow Journeymen Tin Plate Workers showing the beehive for industry, the bundles of sticks and the clasped hands for strength and unity, the dove of peace and the Glasgow city coat of arms. Interestingly, the thistle is flanked by the shamrock and the rose, showing the Glasgow Society's adhesion to the national union.

Throughout most of the eighteenth century, if not earlier, many of the larger London craft establishments, particularly those making high class and fashionable wares, sent their products to many parts of the country. In 1825, according to a contemporary book of trades, the large manufacturers of tin plate wares in London were employing travellers to sell their wares more extensively throughout the country. They took 'in their saddlebags, drawings of all the works of taste such as moulds for puddings, jellies, etc'

But the large manufacturers were still the exception. The handicraft form of industry which had persisted throughout the eighteenth century both in London and the main provincial towns, still continued in the early decades of the nineteenth century. In 1815 London still had 30,000 separate small businesses. Birmingham was described, in 1800, as 'the greatest centre of general hardware manufacture in the world.' Quasi-independent craftsmen and their labourers produced 'an amazing range of products' from tin, brass and copper, as well as iron.

In London in 1790 there were 81 tin plate workers' businesses, 72 coppersmiths and 18 braziers.[15]

What was called the domestic system was still largely practised, with the journeymen working rather like a small sub-contractor, receiving orders and materials from a master, either renting a place in a small workshop alongside members of his own or other trades, where he might have employed an apprentice, or even another journeyman, or working at home. In the latter case he probably employed the members of his own family with even the children having a job to do. Professor Dorothy George, in *London Life in the Eighteenth Century*, mentions one such tin plate worker in 1785 who made lanterns and other tin ware articles at home which his wife lacquered. Outworkers among tin plate workers, braziers and coppersmiths would make up work for direct sale to local ironmongers or ships chandlers, particularly in the smaller towns, but also in London and other cities, perhaps getting an advance from their customer to buy small quantities of metal. The danger to the artisan in the trades societies was that these outworkers could not be controlled from selling under price, particularly when trade was bad, so bringing down prices to starvation level all round. The rules of the London Tin Plate Workers Pension Society, formed in 1828, warned that any pensioner

> in the habit of selling tin goods at less than fair trade prices, he shall immediately forfeit his annuity, as it is the opinion of the founders of this society, that the practice of making up what is commonly called 'hawkers' wares' is a serious injury to the fair trader, and also a gross fraud upon the public.

Even in London, the great centre of the craft trades, the self-employed seem to have only amounted to five or six per cent of the working people. The most usual form of industrial organisation in the metal trades was the small workshop where the master worked alongside his employees, perhaps some five or six, possibly rising to twenty or so in busy times. In these cases the division between the journeymen and the small master was a nebulous one, with the master receiving little if any more money than his journeymen. The master might sometimes revert to a journeyman or a journeyman become a small master, but this would only happen at the poorer end of the trade, the cost of setting upon one's own was too costly in the more remunerative sections of the trade. The small masters were often members of the trade society and the two would often combine against the big employers who exploited them both. In bad times the small employer with little or no capital would go under and get employment as a journeyman.

In the early nineteenth century, however, the picture had begun to change. The bigger employers, with more capital, expanded and the journeymen became wage workers, more and more divorced from the materials in which they worked.

In 1804, a petition from 160 London journeymen tin plate workers stated that several of the masters had established factories and furnishing materials for the workers, varied the work and had reduced prices. All the 160 journeymen were employed by four manufacturers. Of these Jones & Taylors Manufactury employed 50, Howard & Co. 42, Fowler 20, with Oliver employing the rest. Another manufacturer associated with this group of employers was King, of Snow Hill in the City, who in 1824 claimed to employ 80 tin plate workers (this would have been where Richard Carlisle was employed when he worked at the trade in London). An account of trades in London of 1824,[16] reports that Jones & Taylor, then of Tottenham Court Road, and Howards of Old Street were the principal tin ware manufacturers in London, seldom employing less than 100 to 150 men each, and 'those who manufacture tin ware on a smaller scale may be found in every part of the metropolis.'

The 1831 Census

To get an idea of the numbers of members of these crafts there were in Britain at that time we can only go to the 1831 census. Although it is slightly later than the period we have been dealing with, and is not completely reliable, it is the best evidence we have. Under the classification 'tinmen' there are recorded 4,399 for England (plus another ten already calling themselves tin plate workers, all of them in London), with 685 in Scotland and 161 in Wales, a grand total of 5,195. In addition, there were 6,721 classified as brass workers and tinkers: 6,155 in England, 487 in Scotland and 79 in Wales. The number listed as coppersmiths was only 486, almost entirely in the London area and in Scotland, but it is possible that some coppersmiths were included in those classified as brass workers and tinkers.

The London area, of course, had by far the greatest number of tinmen with 1,140 under Middlesex – the main areas being East London, Holborn and Finsbury – and 181 under Surrey, who were concentrated in the Southwark and Brixton areas of South London. There were also a number in Woolwich, Deptford and Greenwich, which were then included in Kent but are now part of the Greater London area.

Of the other industrial areas, Birmingham had 150 tinmen – there were, in addition, 1,785 brass workers and tinkers, 7 braziers, 6 iron plate workers, 11 tea urn makers, 6 tea pot makers and 34 coffee pot makers (a Birmingham directory for 1826 listed only 33 master braziers and tin plate workers). Wolverhampton had only 62 tin plate workers listed, with a further 356 down as brass workers and tinkers. Of the 470 tinmen in Lancashire, Ashton-under-Lyne had 12, Blackburn 12, Bolton 21, Bury 10, Lancaster 8, Liverpool 97, Manchester 165, Oldham 6, Preston 33, Warrington 11 and Wigan 14. The 281 in the West Riding of Yorkshire included Barnsley 5, Bradford 18, Doncaster 9, Halifax 33, Huddersfield 19, Leeds 54, Sheffield 22 and Wakefield 10. The city of York had 33 and Sheffield also had 55 brass workers and tinkers.

There were 114 tinmen in Cheshire, 21 of them in Chester, 30 in Stockport and 11 in Macclesfield. In the North-East coast area, there were 37 in Newcastle-upon-Tyne out of a total for Northumberland of 80; and 20 in Gateshead and 11 in Sunderland out of a Durham County total of 82. Bristol accounted for 92 of the 157 in Gloucestershire, with 15 in Cheltenham and 11 in Gloucester; Bristol also had 188 listed as brassworkers and tinkers.

The total of 209 tinmen for Devon seems rather large for a predominantly rural area although 51 of these were in Plymouth and 30 in Exeter. Norwich accounted for 27 of the 59 in Norfolk while Derby only had 11 out of the County's total of 53. But, in nearby Nottinghamshire, the City had 40 of the 54 listed for the County as a whole. Bath had 15 tinmen and Taunton only 6 out of a Somerset total of 73. In Hampshire, Portsmouth had 36 and Southampton – where an 1811 directory listed only three businesses of braziers and tinmen – still had only 8 out of a county total of 85. Sussex had a total of 66 tinmen with 16 of them in Brighton. Worcester City had 15 tinmen out of 56 for the County, most of them probably in the industrial north. Nearby Coventry gave no indication of its industrial future in the metal industry with only 8 classified as tinmen, whereas rural Kendal had 17 out of only 22 for Cumberland.

In Scotland, there were 130 tinmen in Edinburgh and district and 35 in Dundee. But the vast majority were in the western side of the country, particularly in Glasgow – 58 in Lanark, 29 in Greenock and 15 in Kilmarnock.

Wales had a sparse sprinkling of tinmen throughout the country, Glamorgan having the highest total with 29, with 11 of these in Merthyr and only 6 in Swansea.

There were a few tinmen in every English county, no matter how rural, even the smallest, Rutland, had 9. In Wales, Radnor was the only county without any but in Scotland, the concentration was in the industrial areas while the more remote counties had to make do with travelling tinkers. The tinmen seem to have lived up to the title given them later as: 'that indispensable artisan in the way of our culinary needs.'

At this time there were 7,660 whitesmiths in England, 105 in Wales and 430 in Scotland, a total of 8,195. Of these, 2,313 were in London, 1,135 in Lancashire, 644 in the Birmingham area, 504 in Staffordshire – of whom 229 were in Wolverhampton – 992 in the West Riding of Yorkshire – 250 of them in Bradford. In Scotland, the only significant number was in Gorbals, where there were 150.

We do not know the extent of trade union organisation in these crafts throughout the country, though from what records we do have it could be expected that most of the towns with sizeable numbers of such craftsmen would have some form of organisation. The records of the Union, a federation of local tin plate workers' societies, show that there were societies even in many of the smaller towns where there were only a few craftsmen.

The annual report for 1824[17] gives a list of local societies paying into the organisation and the membership on which they affiliated. London had 390 members, Manchester 90, Glasgow 70, Wolverhampton 64, Dublin 53, Liverpool 36, Birmingham 30, Edinburgh 24, Bristol 22, Preston 20, Belfast 18, Brighton 15, Nottingham 12, Cork 11, Aberdeen 10, Southampton, Sheffield, Worcester and York 9 each, Derby, Hull and Perth 7 each, Bath 6, Cheltenham, Doncaster, Maidstone and Reading 5 each, Gloucester 4 and Colchester 3 – a grand total of 945. There were other local societies mentioned. Northampton was thought to have seven members. Bilston and Norwich were included in a list for 1822 but with no membership figures. Leeds was also associated with the Union and there was some contact with Chester. There was also a society in Oxford and may have been others but our records of the Union are incomplete.

An important aid in bringing together these local societies scattered throughout the country was the tramping system, which was operated by many trades very early on in the life of the trade union movement.

We have already mentioned the important part played by the landlords of public houses in the life of the early trade unions. They often acted as treasurer of the local society, their pub provided the society with a club house and a house of call, a kind of informal labour exchange under the control of the society. Here was kept a vacancy book and the unemployed member would enter his name and, in the case of the London tin plate workers, the branches of the trade in which he had worked. The employers would either give notification of vacancies or go to the House of Call to recruit labour. This meant that many of the unemployed workers would spend a lot of their time at the pub waiting for work, at the same time consuming a lot of beer and, as they had no money, it went 'on the slate.'

The Tramping System

The landlord also played a key part in the tramping system. One of his duties, apparently, was booking tramps in and out, and as the tramping book was kept at the bar for convenience, the landlord also used it for booking in the beer of those waiting for work. The early tramping books of the Liverpool and Manchester tin plate workers societies, which were also cash books, and of the London coppersmiths, show the extent the men got into debt.

So, in choosing a club house, attention had to be paid to whether it had accommodation for tramping members – a clean bed and possibly provision for suppers and breakfasts – and conscientious trade society officials would inspect the beds to see that they were suitable.

The tramping system was devised when there was no unemployment pay for the vast majority of workers. It would take them out of the labour market in areas where work was short and get them to go in search of a job where work might be more plentiful. Even the few societies that provided unemployment pay would encourage young single men to go out on tramp to lessen the drain on their funds in times of high local unemployment.

The system was also used in times of strike action, both to lessen the call on funds and to strengthen the bargaining position of the society by removing workers and showing the employer that there was not a pool of labour he might draw on. This occurred in the 1822 Wolverhampton tin plate workers strike, when the National Union reported that they had 'ordered several of the men out on tramp.'

The members of local trade societies were usually glad to talk with tramps visiting their area, hearing about the position of work in the various towns through which they had passed as well as general talk about the trade, wages, prices, living and working conditions and probably a few tall stories of adventures on the road after being treated to a few pots of beer. This did much to strengthen the societies as national organisations, preparing the way for closer working, as well as helping to break down the isolation of the smaller societies. This was especially the case in the days when travel was difficult and people did not often move outside their own areas.

But life on the tramp was not all conviviality. It possibly had its attractions for young men when the weather was fine and the dirt roads not too dusty. But for an older man, when the weather was cold and the road hard, with boots leaking and in holes, and drenched with rain, when the road went on and on and the days went by without a job, it was not something to be enjoyed. They also suffered separation from wives and families: only two of the many tramping members recorded in the books we

Tramping cards

have of the tin plate workers had their wives with them.

A number of societies devised tramping networks with a list of towns in set order to which tramps had to keep. One of these lists that has been preserved is that of the old Brushmakers' Society. Its itinerary totalled some two thousand miles, with an extra shilling for stretches longer than 20 miles and 1s 6d for those over 60 miles. The whole circuit had to be covered before a member could return home and claim benefit. We have no information of any tramping organisation of the coppersmiths or braziers, but it would appear that there was no such system.

The tin plate worker tramps relieved by Manchester, Liverpool and Glasgow, some of whose records we have, came from and went on to a variety of different towns. At each town where there was a local society of their trade the tramp made for the club house, presenting his tramp card – or blank as it was sometimes called – to show that he was a member of the society and in good standing – and enquiring about the possibility of work. He would receive a bed for the night and perhaps supper and breakfast, and always beer. If there was a job vacant in the town he would be told of it and generally introduced to the foreman or master. If there was no work he would receive his allowance and tramp on to the next town.

Some societies paid a set allowance to their members on tramp, others, particularly in later years, paid on mileage. In the Manchester 1807 tramping book the allowance set against the name of the tramp is usually 1s 6d; a bed is charged at 6d, breakfast 4d.

The payment to be made to the individual tramp was often indicated by the colour of the card he carried or was printed on the card. The usual classes for payment were free members – those who had been in the union for at least twelve months and were fully paid up – members not free, and those on strike, the latter receiving preferential treatment.

In an 1822 report to local societies,[18] the secretary of the national union of tin plate workers writes:

> complaint has been made of societies not being sufficiently careful in issuing their cards, we hope that the laws of the union in this respect will be strictly enforced: if any alteration is necessary it will be duly attended to, and proper notice given to all interested therein: observe that no Green Card should be given without consulting the committee in London on the subject. No Blue Card can be issued until the member has been in the society twelve months, and paid all arrears and subscriptions. The Black Card is not to be given unless members have paid into the fund the amount of £1. This card only serves to identify the bearer as a member of the union, the state in which he left his former society and the provision, as stated in the Thirty-second Law, but not to claim benefit to tramp. To members not having paid £1 to the fund, a Card with one-third cut off and the money he has paid into the fund stated thereon.

The 1833 rules of the Glasgow Society state that a red card would be issued to free members on tramp; a black card to tramps not yet free, these members could draw up to half the money they had paid in. A blue card would be issued to members 'in calamitous circumstances' (on strike). The rules allowed each branch of the Society in Scotland to 'keep for issue as needed one blue card, two red and three black cards.' These variously coloured cards seem to have been standard to the different local societies throughout Britain as the Glasgow Society annual report for 1841 (the earliest we have been able to consult) refers to red and black cards, and an occasional blue one, as being carried by members from all parts of the country.

A blue tramp card of the Manchester Society for 1819[19] has on the back the signatures of the secretaries of the local societies visited and the amounts of money allowed – Wm. Nicholson (the Manchester secretary), 3s; 16th Bolton, Hammond, 1s 6d; 17 Blackburn, John

Folds, 1s. For want of employ May 24 Abm. Meaden, 1s 6d; May 27, Liverpool Jas. Hogarth 2s 6d.

The earliest rule book we have been able to find which mentions the amount of money to be paid to tramps is that of the Manchester Friendly Society of Tin Plate Workers for 1838. The rule states:

> that any travelling Member, coming toTown, and bringing with him a lawful card, from a similar Society, and is in want of employment, he shall be allowed to draw on it, according to the state and claim of the same, the sum of two shillings and upwards, together with two nights lodging and one pint of ale (not to be charged thereon) once in six months.

The rules only allowed one night in each town, except for weekends, but in a few of the large cities two nights were allowed. London was always an exception and usually a stay of three or four days was allowed. The minute book of the Operative Society of Tin Plate Workers of London for January 1847 records guidelines agreed for the general committee and secretary to follow:

> That tramps coming from towns where there is no society to be relieved with one shilling not more than once in each year. That tramps coming from a society town with no card be not relieved. That tramps with cards not free to be relieved with 2s 6d. That tramps with strike cards to be relieved four days pay and four nights lodgings. That tramps with free cards to receive four days pay and four nights lodgings. That London members going on tramp to receive a card and 10s. That London members not free, having paid six months contributions and going on tramp to receive five shillings.

There were a number of attempts to get standardised allowances. In 1858 the Glasgow Society received a letter from the London Society regarding the amount of relief they had agreed to advance tramps in future, saying that dissatisfaction had been expressed at the scale of advances laid down, but Glasgow replied they would operate according to their rules. Again in 1862 Glasgow considered proposals from London and other English societies on a new way of paying members on tramp but Glasgow again replied that they make no changes. The society went on to lay down 'that any men coming from a society of tin plate workers whose principles are the same as our own shall receive 3s gratuitously if three months a member with a blank card.'

Local societies could usually rely on the tramping members' own societies refunding monies paid out on relieving their tramping members. A Preston tramping card for 1854 has a message to that effect written on the back and signed by the secretary, William Morgan. This is also stated in the 1839 rule book of the London Operative Society –

> Members going to tramp shall be furnished with a card, stating the amount they are to receive, all monies so paid by the different societies shall be charged to London, the accounts to be paid up to Christmas in each year.

The accounts seem to have been sent in, or at least settled rather irregularly. But around 1840 there seems to have been an attempt to set up a body for adjusting or equalising the accounts. The Liverpool Society cash book for that time carries the address of the Heywood Refunding Society and an item appears in the accounts 'by balance of general tramp account for 1840 £2 9s 4d.' However, the scheme, whatever it was, did not seem to last as the 1841 tramp accounts were settled on the basis of individual societies – though not until 1845 – perhaps killed by the dilatory attitude toward book-keeping and accounts that went with spare-time secretaries more at home with the hammer than the pen. It was problems like these that would strengthen the idea that a national union was necessary, though it was many years before they were to bear fruit.

Most of the tramping members who appear in the Manchester Society's cash book from 1807 to 1809 were from Lancashire and the adjacent counties – from Altrincham, Ashton, Bolton, Chester, Glossop, Lancaster, Liverpool, Nantwich, Preston, Warrington, Wigan and York. A number also came from Dublin which was in constant communication with both Manchester and Liverpool, with members constantly coming and going throughout the whole period of the tramping system.

Generally, the tramps travelled alone, but occasionally two or three members from one town arrived together; an entry on 31 October 1807 records: 'Paid two Warrington men 3s' on rare occasions a man would be travelling with his wife, as recorded on 20 December 1807: 'Mathew Wilson and his wife, supper, bed and breakfast 5s, by cash 2s' and on 31 March 1808: 'Josh Bamford from Preston going into Derbyshire 1s 6d. Dinner himself and wife 1s 9d.'

Manchester, like some other local societies, seems to have had a rule that allowed the giving of a lump sum to members leaving the society to seek work elsewhere. There is an entry in the book: 'Aaron Meadon to London 10s.' This was too big a sum to be paying out to a man of another society passing through the town 'Robert Hares leaving the limmitts July the 22 8s' was probably a similar incident. But Wm. Nicholson (a future secretary of the Manchester Society) 'leaving town,' was only paid 1s plus 'bed, supper and breakfast 2s 2d.'

The charge on the Society for tramps at the time was not large, if an entry, probably referring to 1808/09, was correct: 'Expended on tramps 24 September to 29 October 8s. 29 October to 29 December 7s; 29 December to 25 February 2s.' Liverpool Society cash books for the 1830s and 40s show a more continuous stream of tramps passing through the town. In the three months to May 1837, 35 tramps were received. While the majority were still from the surrounding districts, they included a number from most other parts of the country. They came from Ashton-under-Lyne, Blackburn, Bolton, Bradford, Bury, Barrow, Birmingham, Brighton, Bristol, Belfast, Cheltenham, Derby, Doncaster, Dudley, Dublin, Glasgow, Lancaster, Leeds, Leamington, Manchester, Nottingham, Peterborough, Rochdale, Wigan, Warrington and Wolverhampton.

The Glasgow report for 1844 mentions a tramp from Inverness, where nine tinmen were recorded in the 1831 census, and others from Arbroath, Ayr and Montrose, as well as Aberdeen and Edinburgh, appear in the early 1840s suggesting there were already branches or sub-branches of the Scottish Society, or some kind of organisation in the smaller Scottish towns.

From the beginning of the 1840s to the early 1860s, when the original branches of tramping members were generally recorded, tramps reaching Glasgow came originally from Ashton, Accrington, Belfast, Berwick, Blackburn, Bolton, Birmingham, Bradford, Bury, Derby, Durham, Lancaster, Leeds, London, Liverpool, Manchester, Oldham, Preston, Rochdale, Wigan and Wolverhampton. As well as Scottish towns recorded above. As befits a major port, some Glasgow members took jobs aboard ships. Others, who must also be classed as travelling members rather than tramps, although they were issued with tramping cards, are recorded as bound for Gibraltar, Lima, Newfoundland, New York, Spain and Sweden.

Study of the tramp books can give some idea of what local societies were facing difficulties – strikes or layoffs due to bad trade. During the 1842 Wolverhampton strike, more Wolverhampton tramps than usual arrived in Liverpool and an entry in the cash book reported: 'To Wolverhampton tramp beds extra 15s.' There was also an influx of Birmingham members in 1844 – when there was a strike in Birmingham – and again in 1846.

The 1807 Manchester tramp book would appear to bring further evidence to the claim, made in connection with the 1756 advertisement in a Liverpool paper, that the tin plate workers' tramping system had a long history. It may well have been continuous from that date. It certainly goes back into the eighteenth century.

This seems to be the conclusion one must draw from a series of entries appearing in the early pages of the 1807 book. They record card numbers ranging from 574 to 679 – with one numbered 364 – presented by tramps from various towns. As only 38 tramps were relieved in the year from April 1807 to April 1808 it would obviously take many years to use up so many cards. It would appear that the cards were issued by some central authority covering the union, though whether on an area or national basis it is impossible to tell, and issued to local societies in batches. The evidence for this is two consecutive entries on 3 August of men from Lancaster with card numbers of 606 and 607 – the card numbered 364 could have been from a society whose members had not been on tramp. We cannot check this with other entries as no town is given for this or for a number of other entries. The system seems to have finished around the time this book was started as, while most of the entries in the earlier pages carried these high numbers, only a few did in the entries for later on in the year, and only one in 1808. When card numbers appear again in the books we have, those of the Liverpool Society for the 1830s and 1840s, they are the numbers of the membership cards of the tramps' own local society not of a special tramp card.

Further evidence of a central card issuing organisation would seem to be provided by a card bearing the modified crest of the Tin Plate Workers Company, the title Friendly Tin Plate Workers Society, with a blank space to fill in the name of the Society – in this case Manchester – a number which could be 196 and 'this 15 day of March 1819' filled in on the space provided. Another card, with a different crest, bears the title Tin Plate Workers Tramp Society, the name Preston written in ink and the year 4 added to the 185 printed on the card.

The tramping system continued as an important part of the life and activities of the early local societies. It was reorganised as far as Lancashire and Yorkshire societies were concerned and put on a more business-like footing with the formation of the General Tramping Union of Tin Plate Workers in 1861. But with the development of public transport, the increasing national character of the trade union movement and the more general provision of unemployment benefit, tramping declined in the latter decades of the nineteenth century. However, tramping or travelling as it had become known, did not completely die out until the First World War. The London tin plate workers were issuing tramping cards at least until 1905 and in 1885 a proposal by the EC of the General Union to do away with the travelling benefit was defeated by delegates.

Finally, in April 1915 the General Union of Braziers and Sheet Metal Workers, which evolved out of the General Tramping Union, decided by 38 votes to 8 to 'expunge the travelling rule' from its rules 'as no useful purpose would be served by retaining such a relic of a bygone age.'

1. *Billinge's Liverpool Advertiser.*
2. S. Pollard, *A History of Labour in Sheffield*, Liverpool 1959. Sheffield Public Library, Miscellaneous Papers 145L.
3. Tin Plate Workers Company MS minutes, loc. cit.
4. Friendly Society of Tin Plate Workers Rule Book, loc. cit.
5. The restriction of at least one year's membership before being allowed to take office would seem to indicate that the Society had been in existence for more than one year when the rule book was drawn up.
6. Liverpool Public Library.
7. Asa Briggs, *A History of Birmingham*, Vol. 2, London 1952.

8. Birmingham Public Library.
9. British Library of Political and Economic Science (BLP&ES), Webb Collection.
10. Public Record Office.
11. Place MS Collection, British Library.
12. A.T. Kidd *History of the Tin Plate Workers and Sheet Metal Workers and Braziers Societies*, London 1949.
13. MS edition contained in an old notebook is in the possession of the Union. It is dirty with much handling and was probably in regular use until the 1860 book of prices was agreed. A printed copy is in the Museum of Rural Life, Reading University. Whereas most other lists seen were designated 'Book of Prices' this printed list is entitled 'Wages for making the various sorts of Tin Wares, Proposed by a general meeting of the Manufacturers.' This would seem to indicate that the Company now looked on the journeymen as wage earners and no longer members of the Company. A list of the Glasgow manufacturers, dated 1811, is also classed as 'wages' but this could have been drawn up in association with the London Company as it carries the London Company's arms.
14. Copy at Glasgow University.
15. *Wakefield's London Directory 1790*, Guildhall, London.
16. *The Book of Trades and the Library of the Useful Arts*, London 1811 edition, Goldsmith's Library, University of London; 1821 edition, author's collection.
17. Liverpool Public Library.
18. Ibid.
19. Liverpool branch of the Union, archives.

Further information on trade union tramps is to be found in R.A. Leeson, *Travelling Brothers*, London 1979; E.J. Hobsbawm, 'The Tramping Artisan' in *Labouring Men*, London 1964 and J.W. Ronsfell, *On The Road*, Horsham 1982.

CHAPTER THREE

The Early Trades in Action

With most industry in the eighteenth century still operating on a handicrafts basis, widespread strikes were not usual. This does not mean there were none. The London tailors, who had been strongly organised, carried out a series of London-wide strikes. And the miners, the workers in the new textile industries, and in other industries where a considerable number of people were employed together, resorted to strike action to get wage increases, improve conditions or shorten hours of work.

The general pattern of strikes at this period involved just one master and a few journeymen. One historian recently listed all the strikes and disputes he could find recorded in a period covering most of the eighteenth century. Throughout the country there were only 280 between 1717 and 1780, some four and-a-half a year. And although the numbers increased later, he was only able to find 153 in the last 20 years of the century, less than eight a year.[1] While there would certainly have been a number of strikes not recorded at that time when communications were poor, and newspaper space limited and newspapers of the period have been destroyed, this sample suggests that the overall total would have been small.

At the beginning of the nineteenth century this pattern of industry continued over much of the country, although more factories in London and other big cites were increasing the number of their employees. The deteriorating economic conditions from wars and a series of bad harvests which pushed up the price of bread and other provisions also contributed to a big increase in the frequency of strikes. But many trade societies were reluctant to give up their trust in the laws that had governed their actions for so many generations, particularly in the Statute of Artificers of Queen Elzabeth I – 'Queen Betty's law' – of 1563, which gave the Justice of the Peace the right to fix wages.

As late as April 1805, at a time of mounting inflation, the result of the French wars, the tin plate workers of London made such an application to the Middlesex magistrates for an increase in piecework prices when they could get no response from an application made to the masters.

The journeymen's petition[2] declared that on 3 November 1760 the Tin Plate Workers Company had agreed to a list of prices 'for making several sorts of tin ware' and for some years the masters had paid the journeymen these prices. But afterwards several masters, 'having established factories and furnishings and material for the workers, varied the work and reduced the said prices.' There had been no material advance in the price of labour of a tin plate worker 'within these 40 years and upward' although the price of provisions and other articles of life had more than doubled and there had been alarming rises in the cost of clothing and rents. During this time the masters had frequently advanced the price of their articles to the retailers under the pretence that the workers' wages had been advanced. Unable to support their families without some advances for their labours 'and being desirous not to offend the laws by unlawful combination,' they had 'engaged to submit their sufferings to their employers and to humbly petition them for an advance in the price of labour.' They presented the petition in November 1804, pointing out that mechanics in most trades had already had similar petitions granted.

They had no doubt that the masters, sensible that there had been no advance in the price of labour for 40 years and that some prices had decreased 'while every support of nature had made a rapid increase, requiring the immediate intersession of humanity' the employers would afford them immediate redress. A total of 152 journeymen signed the petition and a further 8 illiterate made their mark, probably acting on behalf of the rest of the London journeymen.

Some masters asked for a list of the prices the journeymen wanted advanced. So 'after great labours' they finished a book of 735 prices they wanted advanced, leaving 453 for which, although not advanced for some years, they were not asking an advance, presuming that good workmen could get a living at the price. Although a few masters considered the prices fair and were paying the advance, the rest had rejected them and refused to meet the men, although on presenting the petition they were given to understand that the employers would be setting up a committee to consider the prices.

The magistrate set a date in May for the hearing but the employers asked for an adjournment for some weeks as they were not prepared. They must have continued to put off a hearing as the masters' meeting did not take place until 8 March 1806. The committee, including all or most of the big employers, consisted of Howard, Jones, Fowler, Judson, Oliver, Maggs, King, Smith and Benham, the latter making his mark.

The employers' submission claimed that several advances had been made in the years 1773, 1800 and 1805 – although the latter was made as a result of the journeymen's application – and that the 1805 advance

was a fair, reasonable and just and proper an advance and as liberal as the absolute safety of the Trade demanded and such as a workman of even moderate ability might earn as much money as is paid to the best workman in most other trades.

This list, you will remember, was the one hurried through the committee of the Court of the Company in 13 days in August 1805.

The employers accompanied their submission with a list of the wages said to have been earned by the 160 journeymen signing the petition for the previous four weeks, together with observation on the men's ability or character. These vary so much that little of value can be obtained from them: one man, listed as 'a steady man' was said to have earned £2 a week while the next one who 'loses much time' is also listed at £2, two of the 42 men at Howards were said to be 'tolerably industrious' but all the rest were idle, time-losing, slow, infirm, old, newcomers, drunken or mischievous. Only 13 earned £2 or a little over, even if helped by their sons; the lowest was 18s a week and the others varied around £1 10s. One 'steady man' at Fowlers was said to have earned over four weeks £3 2s, £2 2s 4d, £2 8s 1d and £6 9s. Another, also a 'steady man' earned £2 7s 6d, £1 19s, £5 5s 6d and £6 6s, most of his other workmen earned less than £2 and some less than £1. The secretary of the workmen's club, Richard Steer, was described as an industrious man and his earnings were said to be £2 13s. The two delegates were also said to be industrious but lost a lot of time – no doubt on Society business – nevertheless one, James Wilson, was said to have earned £7 2s and the other, George le Cere, £5 8s for the week in question.

We have no record of the magistrates making any award and it is probable that they found a reason for declining as the manuscript copy of the company's 1805 list, preserved in the archives of the Union, shows signs of being greatly used, which would seem to indicate that the men had been forced to accept these prices though a comparison with the 1760 prices book shows little if any actual increase in prices for the various articles.

The right of workers to apply to the Justices of the Peace to settle wages was by then used more as a last desperate attempt by unions in various trades to bring pressure on the employers, who strongly opposed it as interfering with their right to run their businesses as they liked. This clause of Queen Betty's Act was repealed in 1813, part of the dismantling of the laws that for centuries had provided the workers with some rights and afforded them a little protection.

Disappointed over the appeal to the magistrates, the Union apparently turned to more orthodox methods with the reported establishment of regular wage bargaining machinery among tin plate workers, as well as other trades, around 1812.[3] We have no details of how successful it was or how long it lasted.

Other kindred trades also continued to pursue wage advances. In May 1826 the London braziers presented their employers with a new prices list which had been considered at a meeting of the whole trade in the capital on 23 January, at their club house, the Golden Lion, Fore Street, Cripplegate.[4] Again this bare report is all the information we have.

The Apprentices Campaign

The bigger employers continued their offensive against the old laws which they claimed were interfering with their business. They hoped that if they could remove the restrictions on apprentices it would weaken the bargaining power of the journeymen and at the same time give themselves a new source of cheap labour. Already in 1791 a Parliamentary Committee had strongly recommended that many laws related to trade and manufacture should be repealed and singled out those relating to apprenticeships. Then as the custom of apprentices living with families of their masters declined, many employers took the opportunity to employ a large number of lads, lodging them out and employing them as cheap labour, so contributing to the growth of unemployment among skilled workers. Unemployment among artisans soared and the great distress throughout the country led to the setting up of a Parliamentary committee which reported on the widespread use of boys instead of journeymen, the situation varying with the state of workers' organisation in the trade. The committee, however, was only the means of damping down agitation and did not lead to any action.

In their campaign to get rid of restrictions on apprentices the big employers had the support of most members of the House of Commons but the journeymen were not entirely on their own having support not only of many of the small masters but also of a number of the City of London livery companies who wanted to preserve stability and prevent competitive anarchy in their trades.

Although the artisans' concern was mainly for securing the means of earning their livelihood, their action was not entirely economic. They were proud of their craft skills, of the dignity of their craft and the place it gave them in society. The art and mystery of their trade was something they had bought dearly with seven years apprenticeships. It was their only property and bargaining power in the struggle to keep up their living standards and which gave them the exclusive right of working at their trade. It restricted entry into the trade and by the exclusion of 'illegal men' prevented excessive competition for work and helped to preserve standards.

The Statute of Apprentices stated that anyone engaged in any of the various crafts must have served a seven-year apprenticeship. Although this was still the law of the land it was honoured more in the breach than in the observance.

Some employers questioned whether their trades came under the Statute, claiming that only those actually listed were covered. This would have meant that a whole range of new trades would be outside its scope. The London Tin Plate Workers Company had taken counsel's opinion back in 1735[5] and were told that if the trade had been in use at that time anyone exercising it without having served an apprenticeship would have been liable to be proceeded against.

But whatever laws or by-laws had existed, by the first decade of the nineteenth century the apprentices provisions depended upon the strength of the trade societies to enforce them. In their bid to maintain apprenticeships the trades first turned to the law, prosecuting masters who had either not themselves served a regular apprenticeship or were employing 'illegal men' – men who had not served their time at the trade.

A number of cases were brought against employers in London for violating the statute, all by the same attorney, a William Chippendale, who at a later enquiry, agreed that he worked for the trades, confirming that the cases were all part of an organised campaign.[6] This was probably the work of a body of representatives of the London trades societies calling themselves the Mechanics of the Metropolis. We do not know the names of the members but it is probable that one or more of the craft-conscious tin plate workers, braziers or coppersmiths were included. Although they do not seem to have been initiators of campaigns they were great joiners, figuring on most committees.

We do know that one of the cases brought by Chippendale – the case of Johnson v Braham, heard in the Court of the Kings Bench in 1812 – was on behalf of the Society of Whitesmiths. They complained that the employer had set to work a journeyman who had not served a seven-year apprenticeship. The judge ruled that the work he had been doing had not existed at the time of the Statute and was therefore outside the scope of the Act, giving a verdict against the Society, which had to pay £20 or £30 for the employer's costs.

This was a regular occurrence. Although the trades were only trying to get the law of the land enforced and not attempting to extend or change the law, in most cases magistrates rejected cases brought by the trade societies. When they had no alternative but to find against the employer, they generally inflicted a penalty of only 40s, the minimum fine for an offence lasting only one month, although in all cases the offences were of long duration. Moreover, the trades had to pay their own expense, even if they won, and if they lost they had to pay their own costs and those of the employer – and they lost in 12 of the 19 recorded cases, securing fines of 40s in only four of all the cases brought between 1809 and the end of 1812.[7]

It cost the trades societies £40 to bring a case and when they lost they could expect to pay around a further £30 – all to try and get the law of the land enforced, something that should have been done by the authorities. To pursue this line further would obviously be financially crippling, while not producing results and it became clear that the trades would never gain their objectives through litigation.

The Mechanics' Committee changed its tactics and about the same time changed its name to the United Artisans' Committee, sometimes known as the Artisans' General Committee. Again we do not have a list of all the trades represented but delegates from the London Braziers Society[8] certainly attended the first meeting and appeared on one of the subscriptions lists while the London tin plate workers took part in its activities and were probably on the committee.

The artisans set up a special delegate committee to devise means of preserving and extending the old Statute of Apprentices, ensuring that only a person who had served a regular apprenticeship would be allowed to work at a trade. They did not propose to interfere with those already engaged in a trade, either as employer or workman, but would restrict entry of new, unqualified people. Their aim was to guard against an unlimited number of inexperienced workmen flooding into the various trades, creating unemployment, lowering wages and standards.

The artisans' committee met each week and quickly grew in strength. Its members decided that the best way of achieving their aim was by sponsoring an Act of Parliament, having obtained counsel's opinion that it was not illegal under the combination laws to petition Parliament providing that they did not try and stop masters employing unapprenticed workmen, which would have been an offence under the combination laws as well as a conspiracy at Common Law.

The committee then set about running a very well organised campaign.[9] Advertisements were inserted in newspapers in London and provincial towns calling on the trades there to elect a local committee comprised of two representatives of every trade. These were urged to set up a fund with subscriptions of 1s 3d from every member, to agitate, collect signatures for local petitions and to maintain contact with the London Committee to whom funds should be sent to defray expenses. Meetings were to be held in every town 'as soon as convenient after receiving these resolutions' and 'masters are to be invited to give their advice and assistance in the furtherence of the objects in view.' 'Departments' were set up in many of the main towns. Contributions were received from the London trades and from 70 provincial towns. There was widespread response to a directive from London 'that every city and town throughout the United Kingdom prepare a petition to be signed by masters, journeymen, apprentices, artificers and mechanics,' praying leave to bring in a Bill to explain the Statute, amend it and to make it more effective. A total of 32,755 were reported to have signed – over 800 masters and 13,000 journeymen in the provinces and 1,154 masters and 17,517 journeymen in London.[10]

The petition was introduced into the House of Commons by George Rose MP, who had spoken on behalf of the trades in Parliament on a number of occasions. He declared that a petition signed by such a great number of tradesmen was worthy of the greatest attention, but asked that a committee be set up, instead of introducing a Bill, as urged by the Artisans' Committee, who finally accepted his suggestion that it be delayed until the next session.

The Committee proposed that every town in the land draw up new petitions of their own and that deputations of electors wait on their representatives on their return to the country after Parliament had been dissolved. It was an impressive campaign. A circular dated 18 June 1813 and signed by the Secretary, P. Cunningham, called for a subscription of 2d per month from all members of trades taking part 'so that a measure of such importance may not be lost for want of funds to support it.'[11] The money came in both to support the increased activities and to deal with expected opposition in Parliament. By August 1813, £448 had been subscribed by the London trades and £538 from 76 places in the country – £103 from Liverpool alone. Eight more London trades and many more places in the country joined the campaign.

Between the time Parliament reassembled in November and when it rose again on 20 December, 22 petitions were presented with 62,825 signatures. A further 18 petitions came in between March, when Parliament reassembled, and May. Among these was one presented on 18 April 1814 from 'the Master Manufacturers of tin ware, otherwise called tin plate workers, resident in the Metropolis and its vicinity praying that leave be given to bring in a Bill to 'explain and amend' the 1563 Act.[12] It was ordered to lie on the table, as was another from both masters and journeymen tin plate workers of London and its vicinity which was presented on 12 May.[13] Unfortunately we are unable to report what support came from our trades in various parts of the country as the petitions were all lost when the old Houses of Parliament were burned down in 1834.

The employers became alarmed at the activities of the artisans and set up their own committee, the Associated Manufacturers. The masters were not very active but their secretary, John Richter, was a friend of Francis Place, a master breeches maker and a former secretary of the journeymen's society in his trade, now a strong supporter of free trade. The two were as assiduous as the members of their committee were idle, carrying out a newspaper campaign, circularising MPs and provincial manufacturers as well as producing pamphlets attacking the Statute of Apprentices, and preparing a Parliamentary Bill to repeal the Statute.[14] The Masters' commmittee included Roger Davey, a brazier of Shoe Lane, Fleet Street, Harvey and Goldwin, zinc workers and coppersmiths of Hounsditch,[15] East London.

The artisans' committee, in turn, also stepped up its activity. They held a public meeting in London. Every Member of Parliament was canvassed, including the Prime Minister, Lord Liverpool. One MP said he was canvassed by a very large body of artisans and manufacturers who had voted for him, pressing him to oppose the employers' Bill, as well as by a London Association. The artisans secured the support of the Recorder of the City of London, the City Remembrancer and the Common Council. They also canvassed the London livery companies – it was probably as a result of this that the London master tin ware manufacturers presented their own petitions against the employers' Bill. This had its first reading on 27 April, and between 10 May and 6 June, 27 petitions were presented from many parts of the country.[16]

Even when the Bill was going through the Lords the artisans continued to steadily send in more petitions from the London trades and their supporters in the metropolis – there was no time to organise more petitions from the provinces after a request for a delay to allow this to be done was refused. The result was foregone. Although the artisans ran a remarkable campaign and received massive backing from all over the country, it was to no avail. Despite widespread apathy among manufacturers and an extremely feeble effort on the part of their committee, the employers' Bill went through. The Members of Parliament were almost all by then unquestioning supporters of *laissez-faire*. The publication of Adam Smith's *Wealth of Nations* in 1776 had given 'economic self-interest a justifying ideology and new intellectual vigour.' As one historian commented:

> The support of one or two Members of Parliament and thousands of signatures from all over the kingdom were as nothing in the scales against a few pages of Adam Smith and the growing fear that, despite the Combinations Acts, organised working men represented a growing and serious threat.

But the artisans were unlucky in that their attempt to whip up public opinion during the later stages was overshadowed by the invasion of France, the fall of Napoleon and the peace settlements.

The artisans' Bill which would have extended and strengthened the apprenticeship clauses never came before Parliament while that of the employers for the Act's repeal went through without serious opposition and was finally passed on 17 July 1814.

This defeat of the strongest and best organised campaign pursued by the trades marked an important stage in the class struggle. Following the repeal of the wage fixing clause of the old Statute the previous year,

> the last major legislative limitation on the labour market had been removed and the need of the capitalist employers for a mobile labour force whose supply and price would be determined by the 'natural law' of a free labour market would be recognised in law as it had long been allowed in practice.

Henceforth, the trades would have to rely on their own strength for the protection of their organisation, the preservation of their customs and practices and defence of living standards and conditions.

As far as apprenticeships were concerned, it was very much carry-on-as-before for the tin plate workers. In shops where union organisation was strong the Society continued to limit the number of apprentices. Where it was weak or non-existent, the employers continued to do much as they liked. Some flooded the shops with boys, others recognised the need for some control. The number of apprentices allowed in a shop was not normally stated in the rules of the Society but fixed by the committee and varied with different sections of the trade.

Although the campaign had failed in its objective, it was recognised as a high watermark in the development of co-operation among the trades and it was decided that the London Artisans Committee remain in being. The committee had already seen itself as more than an ad hoc body, limited in function to the apprentices question. Its leaders stated

it will also be the means of keeping up the spirit of Mechanics by having the opportunity of meeting monthly. For the Attainment of an Object which is entirely legal.

They saw it as a means of continuing trade union activity without being prosecuted under the combination laws. It was, in fact, the forerunner of the long line of metropolitan trades committees that continued to give more or less continuous leadership to the trades until the formation of the London Trades Council.

The employers certainly saw the London committee as being concerned with more than the apprenticeship laws and as a potential threat. The group of engineering employers, led by Maudsley, who had formed the committee to repeal the Statute of Apprentices, wrote to the Home Secretary complaining that the Committee discussed other objects at protracted meetings, consolidating their power in order to present a united front to the employers.[17]

It was probably from these meetings of the committee that the idea developed for a national general union, known as the Philanthropic Hercules, put forward by the shipwrights' secretary, John Gast, which was still-born. It seems that the London Artisans' Committee must have been responsible for the publication in 1812 of the first trade union paper, *The Beacon*, a short lived weekly.[18] No copies are known to survive but from a contemporary account of the contents it would seem to have put forward the ideas of the artisans.

All this was taking place in a period of fundamental change both in social and economic conditions. It was a period of rapid expansion of population and rising production, with new productive methods and economic and industrial organisation. It saw the end of the old order which often ruled with at least some degree of paternalism, and the rise of a new one with unbridled competition, a ruthless drive for increased production and maximum exploitation, when the workers were merely 'hands.' It was a period of violent, raw and naked class struggle.

The apprentices campaign should be seen in the context of a high level of union activity, partly as a result of these economic changes and partly in an attempt to combat spiralling prices. It followed a big increase in the number of strikes, both in London and in the country. Most of those involved were also concerned with maintaining the apprenticeship system as a means of preserving their very existence.

The next arena of the national struggle was the fight against the Combination Acts. These were by no means the first laws against the unions and union activity. Before the end of the eighteenth century there were already more than 40 Acts of Parliament to stop workers combining in trade societies, most of which covered individual trades, passed by the government of the day at the request of the employers in the trades concerned. As Adam Smith said in his *Wealth of Nations,* 'Whenever the legislature attempts to regulate the differences between masters and their workmen, the counsellors are always the masters.'

If workmen managed to escape prosecution under one or other of these many laws they were always liable to be tried for conspiracy under Common Law. Most of the magistrates were of the same social class as the big employers and actively looked after their interests, pursuing journeymen suspected of forming or belonging to combinations, employing a host of informers for the purpose as they had done for years. In the 1760s the Bow Street magistrate, John Fielding, asked the Duke of Norfolk for a knighthood on account of 'those bodies of journeymen of almost every trade whose combinations I have been industrious to break by the vigorous execution of the penal laws.' In 1755, the Bristol magistrates announced their intention to put 'in strict execution' the laws against combinations of workmen. The magistrates' drive against trade societies and trades combinations was made easier over the years by the multiplicity of laws making the organisations of working men, and their activities, illegal. While a few employers were sent to prison for short spells of correction for paying their workmen more than the official stipulated rate, we have found no record of employers imprisoned for being members of a combination, though most of them were.

The Combination Acts

The 1799 Combinations Act had its origins in a request from the master millwrights of London that Parliament bring in an Act to make combinations of journeymen millwrights illegal, as if there were not enough laws to do that already. When the Bill came before the House of Commons, William Wilberforce MP – of hallowed memory for his part in outlawing the slave trade – proposed that, since trades combinations 'are a general disease of our society,' the scope of the Bill be enlarged to make all combinations illegal.[19] As it was not possible to enlarge that specific Bill it was dropped. Instead, the Government acted on Wilberforce's proposal and a Bill was introduced by William Pitt, the Chancellor of the Exchequer himself, on 17 June 1799 and rushed through Parliament in the last four weeks before the end of the session.[20] Newspaper reports on the debate were even scantier than usual so that it became law almost unnoticed. The Liverpool journeymen, petitioning against the Bill in 1800, complained that they did not know about it until it had become law. There was only time for two hurried petitions to be served against it and no time to mobilise the trades.[21]

The Hammonds, in their *The Town Labourer,* suggest that the Combinations Acts were a result of changing economic circumstances and methods of production. Employers were using much more capital, plant and machinery so that they were that more vulnerable than the old masters in the event of strike action. This meant that for the first time combinations provided a weapon of real power in the hands of a class that had no other weapon when facing the superior forces of wealth and influence, particularly influence with the legislative authorities. This new situation had brought a new attitude among politicians. The State, which had previously regulated industry, was to abdicate in favour of the employers – the employers' law was to be the public law. Workmen were to obey their masters as they would obey the State and the State was to enforce the employers' commands as it would its own. 'The Combinations Acts remain the most unqualified surrender of the State to the discretion of a class in the history of England.'

By the end of the eighteenth century combinations assumed a new threat in the eyes of the establishment. Since the French Revolution they had been seen as a political danger to the ruling class. The Home Office papers are full of warnings of revolutionary plots with the trades combinations filling the role of the villain of the piece. So, for both political and economic considerations the State – an amalgam of the establishment and the new capitalist employers – declared war on the trades combinations.

The new combination laws met the employers' complaint that, although under the old laws legal action could be taken against artisans engaging in combination, by the time the journeymen concerned could be summoned to appear before the court they had gone on tramp and could not be found. The magistrates courts, which acted under the combination laws, went into action much more quickly.

The threats of the combination laws to the organised trades were quite an important part of the web of legislation that restricted the unions in their struggles to improve the wages and conditions of their members. They were blanket laws, covering trades left out in the mass of laws forbidding combination to many individual unions. They also restricted the rights of workers as citizens. If a worker was convicted under the combination laws he could appeal to the quarter sessions but he first had to enter into recognisences with two sufficient sureties of £20 – a large sum when wages averaged around £1 a week. As the Act forbade anyone collecting for or contributing to expenses for such an appeal, the expense put the remedy beyond the reach of workmen who earned barely sufficient to maintain themselves and their families, said one petitioner against the Acts.[22]

Anyone having charge of trade societies' funds could be questioned on oath and forced to incriminate himself and others, contrary to what had been the law of the land, said another petitioner. If they refused to answer the justices could commit them to prison without bail to remain until they gave the evidence required. Magistrates were reported to have threatened workers with imprisonment or service in the fleet as alternatives to accepting what wages employers chose to offer them.

A journeyman bootmaker told how his employer had halved their pay and when six or seven workmen had refused to work for the new wages he summoned them before the Lord Mayor for combination. The Lord Mayor said it was a hard case, and sentenced them to 14 days' hard labour but gave them a choice – they could do two months without hard labour.

'Impartially' the Combination Laws forbade combinations among masters as well as among workmen but magistrates turned a blind eye on employers combining to reduce wages – in fact there was hardly a manufacturer in the country who was not a member of a combination. An opponent of the Act pointed out that only journeymen were to be sent to prison and that the Act did not allow them the right to be tried by jury. This taking away of an Englishman's basic right was the main objection raised in Parliament to the Bill.

Although the penalty in cases tried by jury could be two years imprisonment, against three months in a magistrate's court, journeymen felt they had a better chance of getting justice from a jury than from a magistrate who was perhaps an employer himself or at least came from the same social class.

The rightness of this opinion was shown in a trial, in the Middlesex Quarter Session of 1812,[23] of 17 journeymen tin plate workers, who worked for a firm in St Pancras – then a centre of the tin plate trade. According to one account they 'threw caution to the wind' and went on strike when one of their shop mates was sacked for asking for a wage increase, in what appears to have been an organised attempt to increase piece-work prices. They first told the employer to take back the sacked man – who had been with the firm for three years – and when this was refused they demanded that not only should he be taken back but also given the increase he had asked for, which should also be paid to themselves and all tinmen employed by the firm. When the employer persisted in his refusal the men 'unlawfully' refused to work on any job normally carried out by their sacked colleague – in good trade union style – and were said to have harassed another workman and stopped him working at the old prices. The 17 were tried, not under the combination laws but at Common Law, for conspiring to raise wages and carrying out harassment and injury to their employer. They were all found not guilty by a jury which included a printer, a baker, a grocer and a butcher, and acquitted.

Tin plate workers who a few years later took part in a 'great strike' at Wolverhampton in 1819, also prosecuted at Common Law, were not so lucky as their London colleagues. The employers were said to have called in the 'Robin Redbreasts' or 'Bow Street Runners' to crush the strike. Members of the Wolverhampton Tin Plate Workers Society, 'hearing whispers that the Society's club house was to be raided,' stationed themselves in front of the entrance, delaying the police as long as possible while officials of the Society destroyed documents and records within. When the police did manage to break in by force of numbers, all evidence had been destroyed. Nevertheless, all on the premises were said to have been arrested and some, if not all, being found guilty, were transported to Van Diemen's Land.[24]

Strikes continued throughout the period of the combination laws and in many cases no charges were preferred, probably because, with no prosecuting authority, it was left to the employer to bring proceedings against the strikers, and as they would frequently have to employ the strikers after the proceedings were over they would not do so. This was particularly the case with the many small masters who worked alongside their journeymen, which would have been the case with tin plate workers. Moreover, if the strikers were sent to prison, the employer had to find replacements.

This may have been the reason we have not been able to find any record of a strike of London braziers and tin plate workers in 1810. Both societies received money from the London Gold Beaters Society – the braziers a loan of £10 10s in July of that year and the tin plate workers were paid the rather substantial sum of £30 in October.[25] Such payments from trade societies were usually made in response to requests for help during a strike, or to help meet commitments after a strike, and the fact that braziers and tin plate workers, who often worked for the same employer, were both recipients of financial aid around the same time, is significant.

The artisans called for petitions to be sent to Parliament from all over the country for the repeal of the 1799 Act. They pointed out that the new law 'erected new crimes of so indefinite a nature that no one journeyman or workman will be safe in holding any conversation with another on the subject of his trade or employment.'

Petitions were presented to Parliament in June 1800 from the trades of Bath, with 2,400 signatures, Bristol with 7,000, Derby, Lancaster, Leeds, Liverpool, Manchester, Newcastle, Nottingham and Plymouth, as well as from London. The large measure of similarity in their wording and the fact that they were all presented simultaneously suggests they were directed by a central organisation. Even the Lord Mayor of London presented to the Commons a petition from the journeymen of the cities of London and Westminster praying for the repeal of the 'injurious, unjust and oppressive law.'

They did not succeed in getting the Act repealed but they did force the government to bring in an amending Act. The main alteration was that cases would have to be heard by two magistrates instead of the one of the original Act, and that neither be engaged in the trade or industry concerned. In the 1799 Act the single magistrate hearing a case could even be the employer concerned.

The employers made a number of attempts to make the combination laws even more drastic. Wilberforce supported one such call in 1802 and masters in Lancashire, Nottingham and Glasgow sent memorials to Parliament in 1814 and 1816. All these, of course, were directed against the journeymen, but the law officer opposed any change, saying that the existing laws were sufficient.

Although the trades evaded the law wherever possible they felt its restrictions, never forgetting it was there, and during upsurges of union activity a call would be raised for repeal. It was a demand of the Lancashire cotton spinners in 1818, 1821 and 1823. In 1818 Gast wrote against the injustice of the laws and in 1819 the progressive journal, *The Gorgon,* called on the trades to get petitions signed for their repeal and a number were presented to Parliament from 'journeymen, tradesmen, and mechanics of London and Westminster.'[26] The Lancashire cotton spinners' leader, John Doherty, was outspoken in agitation against the laws which he charged had been used 'to crush the union'. The 'odious laws' had been used against the spinners during strikes. They 'forced unions to meet in secret,' a secrecy which led to violence.

The agitation for repeal gained strength as the 1820s proceeded. Francis Place, who opposed the laws as interfering with the freedom of relations between master and men, was interested and support came from some Members of Parliament. In 1822 Joseph Hume, MP, introduced the question of repeal on the floor of the Commons, using information supplied to Place obtained from several Northern trade societies. Gravener Henson, the Nottingham stocking weavers' leader, also drew up a Bill for repeal which Peter Moore, the radical MP for Coventry, introduced into Parliament on 3 March 1823. The Bill sought not only to repeal the combination laws but a number of other oppressive laws. It also proposed to set up machinery to regulate wages, hiring and firing and hours of work, for settling disputes and abolishing truck (forcing workers to buy from company-owned stores). Some of its provisions anticipated subsequent factory legislation. Criticisms that it was before its time and would not have got support of Parliament were probably correct. However it did get support among some trade societies, including the Manchester weavers, and eleven petitions in its support were secured, mainly from Nottingham, Derby and Norwich. Moore agreed to a suggestion that it be left till the next session of Parliament. This allowed Place and Hume to get in ahead and sabotage Moore's Bill which they said would antagonise Parliament and make difficulties for their own Bill. There was the inevitable horse trading and it has been suggested that Huskinson, for the Government, allowed Hume's Bill to go through to defeat Moore's; Moore eventually agreed to Huskinson's appeal to withdraw his Bill in return for a Select Committee to consider the question in the next session.

By this time, a considerable body of working-class support for action on repeal had grown up independent of promptings from Place. His strength lay in his singleness of purpose, the simple repeal of the combination laws – although he linked with it the repeal of a law forbidding the export of machinery, which he also supported, in order to get the support, or at least the neutrality of the employers. He was the architect of the 1824 Bill for the repeal of the Combination Acts and his achievement in getting it through Parliament has been described as 'a remarkable feat of intelligent wire-pulling, enormous industry and well-informed lobbying.' He took full advantage of the fact that Parliament was full of country gentlemen who were bored with trade union matters and disliked manufacture. They did not understand the issues and were largely indifferent. Moreover, most of them were devotees of *laissez-faire* and could be appealed to on anything smelling of restrictive practices. Place, with the support of Hume, played on this.

Place complained of the 'apathy' of the workers and of their distrust and antagonism to him. But distrust and antagonism were understandable when Place had been largely responsible for the campaign on behalf of the employers, some ten years earlier, which had defeated the trades' attempts to preserve apprenticeship legislation. While he believed that the combination laws were unfair as they were applied only to the workers, he was also of the opinion that they were not capable of preventing strikes or combinations. They merely caused the workers to break the law and caused bitter relations between masters and men. He was convinced that if the laws were repealed the trade societies would just wither away.

He made no attempt to work with the trade societies through consultation and common agreement but sought to manage the union delegates as he manipulated MPs, channelling their efforts in the direction he desired. The union leaders, for their part, seemed to have summed him up, saw he was in earnest, and, having some influence, stood a chance of success, and gave him qualified support. Though his Bill did not seem to be the one they wanted they accepted that half a loaf in the hand is better than no bread.

Place increased his contacts with the trades. He wrote a letter to the trade societies, explaining how to draw up a petition – though in view of the brilliant petitioning by the trades during the apprenticeship campaign this was largely a case of telling your grandmother how to suck eggs. He delivered these to the club houses of the London societies, including the tin plate workers and the Society of Brassfounders, Braziers and Coppersmiths, who elected a committee to consider the petition.[27]

Hume was made chairman of the Parliamentary Select Committee to consider the question and he circularised the towns for information. Place carefully selected the witnesses, including some manufacturers who were interested in the repeal of the law opposing the export of machinery, as well as hand-picked members of the London trades.

He did not trust the trade unionists to give the right evidence in the select committee and arranged to meet delegates coming from all over the country, carefully arranging what they were to say. Trade society members lobbied MPs, organised the collection of subscriptions and the signing of petitions, over 100 of which were sent in from the country and nearly 30 from London. The Liverpool tin plate workers seem to have been engaged in this activity as they subscribed to the purchase of a silver salver presented to General Gascoigne, a local MP, 'for his activities in the repeal of the combination laws.'

Hume's Bill had been drawn up even before the Select Committee had agreed on their resolution. It went a lot further than the Committee had decided, repealing not only the combination acts but also a number of potentially dangerous statutes. It even relieved combinations of the liability to be prosecuted at Common Law. The Bill passed through Parliament between 25 May and 5 June 1824 without serious opposition and apparently became law without a number of MP's knowing what they had voted for.

A wave of wage claims and strikes swept the country on the repeal of the Acts, despite lectures by Place that wages had nothing to do with the law but were governed by supply and demand. The Birmingham Iron Plate Workers placed an advertisement in the *Birmingham Journal* of 6 September 1824, informing their employers that they would expect an increase. This was one of a number of similar advertisements from various trades that appeared in the paper about the same time, advertisements so similar in wording that they must have been the result of concerted action, possibly by some form of trades council.

The employers were alarmed, demanding that the combination laws be restored, and Huskinson, for the Government, set up another Select Committee. The trades societies went into action to retain what they had gained. Gast, with help from Place, circulated nearly 40 trades and secured a committee with two delegates from each trade, including the London Brassfounders, braziers and coppersmiths, and the tin plate workers. They were joined by a number of provincial union leaders. The societies presented 97 petitions from various trades and towns all over the country, including the Stockport coppersmiths and the London tin plate workers, with a total of over 100,000 signatures opposing the reintroduction of the Acts. The employers could only manage to get seven petitions. Nevertheless the Select Committee ignored the trades, hearing only evidence from the shipwrights and coopers, who were then on strike, accusing the Trades Committee of 'being under the influence of agitators.' The final report of the committee and the chairman's address in favour of reimposition of the laws aroused a great deal of alarm in the trades.

The sustained activities of the trades societies, the organisation of Place and the pressures by Hume in Parliament seem to have had some effect as the Bill introduced by the Attorney General did not put into effect the demands of the most vocal of the manufacturers. In fact, the shipbuilding employers distributed leaflets outside the House of Commons opposing the new Bill and calling for greater restrictions against the trade societies. The Bill made all associations illegal *except* those who met together for consulting upon and determining the rate of wages and prices, on work and hours. This made the trade societies legal as such and free of any liability to prosecution under Common Law. But it excluded important questions like apprentices and contracts. There was also a clause against intimidation of other workmen and molesting, all rather vaguely worded so that they could be open to different interpretations. Hume had been able to get some modifications during the Bill's progress through Parliament and when it finally became law Place expressed himself generally satisfied and the trades accepted that it was not as bad as they had feared.

The campaign for the repeal of the Combination Acts was another step forward in the development of the trade unions, particularly in the extension of united action, improved organisation and general solidarity. Its influence was particularly seen in the provincial centres. In Manchester, the threat of the reintroduction of the combination laws was responsible for the calling of a meeting of the local trades. They set up an Artisans' General Committee, which co-operated with the London committee. Committees of local trades were also formed in Birmingham, Sheffield, and Sunderland. The tin plate workers, braziers and coppersmiths all played a part in this struggle.

Queen Caroline

While action against the combination laws was the most important activity, the trades societies continued with their organisational, economic and political activities during the 25 years in which the laws were in operation. One of the most bizarre actions was the campaign waged by the London artisans in support of Queen Caroline, together with artisans and radicals in the rest of the country.

Princess Caroline of Brunswick had first gained popularity among the working people of London when rejected by her husband, the highly unpopular Prince Regent – generally referred to by Londoners as 'the pig of Pall Mall.' When she returned from abroad to take up her position as Queen after her husband acceded to the throne as George IV, she was met by cheering crowds from Dover, through Kent to Greenwich and from there to London, by a solid mass of people in what was then a spontaneous demonstration. The crowd molested any who did not take off their hats and cheer and later broke the windows of unpopular ministers, and booed the King.

The trades were in the forefront in collecting some 30,000 signatures to an address of welcome and the procession that turned out to present it stretched in one continuous line from Hyde Park to the Queen's house in Hammersmith. Public agitation forced the King to abandon his attempt to get a divorce through a trial of the Queen by Parliament. The working class areas of London celebrated for three days with bonfires and fireworks. Crowds attacked the offices of newspapers supporting the Government, shattering their windows with a hail of stones. Police who tried to disperse them were put to flight.

ADDRESS OF THE BRASS-FOUNDERS & BRAZIERS.

TO HER MOST GRACIOUS MAJESTY QUEEN CAROLINE.

MAY IT PLEASE YOUR MOST GRACIOUS MAJESTY,

We, the Brass-Founders and Braziers of the City of London and its vicinity, anciently denominated the Workers in Brass, feel infinite pleasure in being permitted the high honour of again humbly and dutifully approaching your Most Gracious Majesty, to express our sincere acknowledgments for the honours already received at your Majesty's Royal Pleasure, and to offer our heartfelt Congratulations on the triumphant conclusion of the base proceedings instituted, matured, and conducted with such unexampled severity against your Gracious Majesty's person and honour, under the fictious title of a "Bill of Pains and Penalties,"—proceedings which will ever be considered as derogatory to the laws, and be deprecated by all true Englishmen, as an invasion of their rights, however high or humble the station

The radicals, supported by the leaders of the trade societies, saw this as an important political opportunity to attack the reactionary government and kept up the agitation. The individual trades collected 20,000 signatures to an address of support from the 'Artisans and Industrious Classes' and almost every trade in London turned out to deliver it. Prominent were 10,000 sailors and 3,000 shipwrights, with bands and banners.

The tin plate workers were there, riding in four barouches![29]

But one of the most splendid contingents was said to be the braziers, brass and copper workers. their union took up the cause of Queen Caroline in a big way. On 30 October 1820 they presented a loyal address, welcoming her return, expressing disgust and abhorrance at her treatment and pledging their support. This was signed by the chairman of the Union, Thomas Cheney, the secretary, Robert Dowding, the treasurer, David Bickham Irwin, and 800 members of the union taking part in a meeting. It was presented in a brass case carried by a member in brass armour on horseback, attended by four pages in brass and copper helmets, accompanied by the officials bearing brass wands surmounted by stars and members 'bearing brazen devices' with other members clad in armour, complete with bands and banners.

A second address was presented on 22 January 1831. It was printed on satin and signed by the officials, the 45 members of the committee and 1,200 members of the Union. It was even more fulsome in her praise and condemnatory of her traducers. It was accompanied by an ever bigger procession, yet more elaborate. It was preceeded by three trumpeters, a number of 'knights' mounted on 'chargers' clad in full brass or steel coats of armour with others in half armour and 'cuirassiers' mounted and on foot, all attended by 'esquires'. The address was carried in an even more elaborate brass casket, embellished with a dove and laurel wreath, together with mitres tied with white ribbons, crowns and coronets carried on cushions, with music from three bands.

The slogans on the specially made banners were of a kind surely never seen before or since on trade union banners: 'Hail! Queen of England, Peace be unto thee', 'Hail! Star of Brunswick, the Muses bend to thee', 'Disloyal? No! She's punished for her Truth, and undergoes more Godess-like than Wife-like', 'The Queen and her Rights', 'It is better to trust in the Lord than put confidence in Princes'. Another showed the Eye of Providence looking benignly on the initials C R with a crown between and the motto 'As it should be'. A flag proclaimed: 'The queen's Guard are Men of Metal', and there were a variety of trade flags, banners with the arms of the Union and one showing a workshop scene.

The Queen replied to both addresses, thanking them for their loyal sentiments, pledging support for the freedom of the press and praising the brass devices made and carried by members.[29]

Then in the middle of it all the Queen died. But this did not end the agitation, the most dramatic was yet to come. Fearing further demonstrations, the Government and Court decided to rush her body abroad bypassing the then radical City of London, where they feared her body might be held to lie in state. But they reckoned without the people of London, led by the trades societies, who were determined that the funeral procession should pass through the City where it would be received by the Lord Mayor. A call went out for the people to assemble at six in the morning outside the Queen's house. The brassfounders, braziers and coppersmiths society was one of those that decided to attend as a trade body.[30] Despite pouring rain a solid mass of people took part, accompanying the procession. When the cortège tried to turn off the road to the City, at Kensington, they found the road blocked by vehicles, with another added as soon as one was removed. The next road had been dug up, and this continued all the way. The first lot of gates into Hyde Park were padlocked and there was a race between the cortège and its accompanying Life Guards and the crowds to get to another gate. Here the Life Guards attacked the crowd, first with the flats of their swords and then opening fire, killing two workers and wounding others. But the demonstration continued. All turnings off Oxford Street were blocked and at Tottenham Court Road lines of carts and coaches padlocked together, and trenches dug across the road, stopped all progress to the north. Eventually the authorities gave up and the cortège arrived at the boundaries of the City to be met by the Lord Mayor and other City officers who accompanied the procession through the City, the running battle having taken all day, criss-crossing the streets of London's West End.

Even this was not the end. The trades decided on a public funeral of the two artisans who had been killed, a bricklayer and a carpenter. There was a huge procession in trades groupings, with the braziers reported as one of the first groups to arrive.[31]

Although there was genuine sympathy among the people for the Queen, who was said to have made some radical statements in the past, the agitation was political. The radicals and working class leaders saw the affair as being cruicially important in re-establishing political campaigning, involving the mass of the artisans in political activity while discrediting the reactionary government and the political system, laying the basis for the later reform agitation.

The period of the combination laws also saw the wave of machine breaking known as Luddism, which lasted from 1811 to 1816. It mainly affected the hosiery and lace making machines of the East Midlands, the woollen industry of the West Riding of Yorkshire and the cotton industry of South Lancashire and North Cheshire. It was born in the fears of handicraft workers that the new machines would completely take away their livelihood and add to the mass unemployment that had already reduced the majority of these workers to near starvation. The frustrations of the combination laws which in some areas prevented or severely restricted normal forms of action and weakened the trades societies, also played a part. For unorganised or poorly organised workers, particularly those working in groups in close association, it took the place of organised union activity and has been called 'collective bargaining by riot.' It was sometimes used to intimidate wage-cutting employers or those employing blacklegs during a strike. It was not a method used by the mass of the urban artisans to any extent, although at this time they too were concerned at the spread of machinery which undermined their skilled status and the strength of their position in wage bargaining.

This concern was expressed in a letter sent on 25 August 1820 by F. Cook, secretary of the Wolverhampton Tin Plate Workers, to other local societies in the trade.[32] He said that they had been told by their employers that there was a man in Sheffield 'now stamping all manner of articles that can be stamped, such as Tea Kettle Tops, and Coffee Pot Tops, etc, etc.' They had been shown these articles which were 'ready for making up in such style that has not been equalled before.' They were being offered at low rates to induce employers to buy. Both the employers and the union in Wolverhampton were 'determined to set their faces against it knowing in the end that it will terminate in the ruin of employer and employed' and, if allowed to continue, 'we shall not one half of us be in employ long.' He went on to say it is the wish of our employers that we should as promptly as possible communicate our joint resolution to you which is 'that we shall not buy or make one article up, likewise wishing you to call the trade together to make known our determination around your neighbourhood and where you may think proper. We've no doubt but you and the trade in general will see the utility of this prompt communication. Unity in our trade is necessary and desirable with us when things are going smoothly, but when either our trade or our rights are invaded it becomes us to form in one general body to act as *ONE MAN, FIRM, INDEPENDENT AND JUST*; not giving way in a righteous cause nor acting unjust to others. We've not forgot what sacrifices our parents made on our behalf to gain a knowledge of the Trade and we, therefore, should strenuously endeavour to transmit it to our sons and future posterity in as good or better condition that we found it. Believing these to be your sentiments.' Soon after this – partly as a result of this letter – proposals were received from London about the setting up of a national union.

The National Union

This move by the London tin plate workers was part of a desire for national unity stimulated by the need for stronger organisation to meet the greater strength of the capitalist employers.

A covering letter, dated 24 April 1821, which introduced the printed circular calling for the setting up of 'the union' stated: 'It is very desirable and essentially necessary to our existence as a trade that a union should be immediately formed throughout England, Scotland and Ireland for the purpose of making a stand against the encroachments of the masters.' The secretary, W. Smith, asked for the sentiments of the trade in the area to be forwarded to London, if possible by 30 April, when there would be a general meeting of the trade there.

The circular stated that, due to 'the great depression in prices and a threatened continuance of the same,' the trades in the principal manufacturing towns had appealed to the London Society 'as a parent society' to consider uniting the trade throughout the country 'to stop, if possible, the ruin thereof.' A general meeting of the London Society had unanimously agreed on the necessity for an immediate union and had drawn up 'a code of Salutary Laws' on the principle of equality, 'both in expense and advantage, for protection from penury and distress.' It warned that 'the smaller branches of the trade will find themselves unpleasantly situated in consequence of the measures adopted by the union; but if united, will participate in equal advantage and be respected as members of union.'[32]

Another letter from London, dated 26 July 1821, showed that the Union had been established and that the secretary was F. Stokes. He said the Union 'met with approbation and wherever we can obtain an address of a society it gradually extends itself to all quarters.' The laws had been approved and were at the press.

A letter from London to the Liverpool Society showed the difficulties these early societies worked under when post masters were liable to open letters and packages and report their contents to the Home Office. In the letter dated 17 September 1821, the secretary stated: 'in making up the parcels I thought it would go more safely by way of Scotland, as I was sending there through Belfast, one parcel inside another.'

The first quarterly report of the Union, up to 25 June 1821, claimed support from all the principal manufacturing towns,

> convinced by reason and necessity, that it is only strength united with ability, brought into action by such liberal principles, that can be calculated on with confidence to unite the trade and check the growing danger of oppression, or effectively deliver those who have fallen victims to the rapacity of their employers.
>
> To unite the trade, the Audit Committee judged it expedient, in order to remove false prejudices, and explain the principles of the union, to appoint and send a proper person on a mission through the trade, in England, Ireland and Scotland, which by extraordinary exertions was accomplished in one month.

The 'missionary expenses' amounted to £43 9s 8d.

The report mentioned the unorganised state of several societies that had joined the union 'but in general societies begin to wear an organised form and are very active in extending the union all around.'

The Audit Committee in London decided to call a national delegate trade conference on 2 July 1822 to be held in London 'for the welfare of the union and the trade.' A letter from the secretary dated 20 June, informing local societies of the arrangements, called on them to send 'a competent and confidential representative, with full powers to assist at the conference, and invested with such questions, propositions and resolutions as your society might think proper to lay before the deputation.' Societies too small to send a representative were invited to send, in due time, any questions, propositions or resolutions which would be 'duly attended to and fairly discussed.' All societies were asked to 'furnish the names of all men working at the trade both the society members and the rats, the number of each, and description of card in hand,' for the information of the conference. The local societies were asked to pay the fares of the delegates to and from London, the London Society undertaking to accommodate and provide for the deputies while in London during the conference. Small societies were asked to make a financial contribution if they did not send delegates.

The next communication we have, dated December 1822, lists local societies from 24 towns – Bath, Birmingham, Brighton, Bristol, Belfast, Bilston, Cheltenham, Derby, Doncaster, Dublin, Edinburgh, Glasgow, Hull, Liverpool, Manchester, Maidstone, Norwich, Preston, Reading, Sheffield, Southampton, Wolverhampton, Worcester and London. It says 'there are prospects of additional strength from the application of two or three respectable societies, who on hearing of the union, have offered their financial and material support,' and is signed 'By order of the Committee.' Subsequent communications are signed 'the Trade Committee.' This is probably something to do with a comment in the report that

> Some remarks have been made by our friends of the Union respecting the late alterations which have taken place in the London Society and likewise of the managing committee of the union. We take this opportunity of explaining and removing any unpleasant sensation our friends may have entertained, by informing them, that we revere the Laws of the Union generally; and consider that no alteration or addition can be made, without the consent of the Union, or a Deputation from them. The measures alluded to, were only experiments, to ascertain and determine how far a saving could be effected in doing the business of the Union. If a saving could be effected, and the business transacted in a manner equally satisfactory, we feel it a duty incumbent on us to recommend this system of economy to the consideration of the Union; if, on the contrary, it is deemed impracticable, to relinquish the design.

The Third Annual Report, dated 28 January 1825, returns to this question:

Banner based on the Tin Plate Company's coat of arms, with supporters depicted as eighteenth century craftsmen, the spherical ships' lantern of the arms shown as a globe and the seventeenth century lamps greatly simplified. This design seems to have been used by a number of societies who were a member of the 1821-25 Union; this one was bought by the Liverpool Society in 1821, at a cost of 5s

> To remedy some errors that have crept into our system through negligence in doing the business of the Union, we are induced to adopt measures y way of experiment to remedy this evil and to have the affairs of the union more strictly investigated.

Explaining delays in preparing the annual report, it says

> in consequence of making up the books and accounts of the ex-secretary, whose mode of transacting the business of the union, and whose manner of making up the accounts and giving up the books has been by no means satisfactory.

The Committee also announced an increase in subscriptions to 1s a week per member, 'to meet the present and future demands on our funds.'

It reported on the 'validity and stability' of the Union in London with a doubling of the membership since the formation of the Union. In February 1822 it had credited the London Society with 250 members. By the time of the 1824 general report London membership was up to 390. By that time the total membership of the Union was 945 with societies in Aberdeen, Cork, Gloucester, Perth and York joining as well as Northampton, which had not by then returned figures of membership. It reported that Leeds had been lost to the Union for some time through the improper conduct of their Secretary, Robert Phayre, who disappeared carrying with him their little funds amounting to almost £4. It is but justice, however to add that he has repaid part of it and solemnly pledged himself to repay it all in a short time. We are informed from the best authority that this Society is on the eve of again re-entering.

The September 1823 report was not so good, however concerning Oxford.

For the past few years we have spared no pains (by letter) to convince the men at the above place of the utility of their strict adherence to the Union, but all our efforts proved in vain.
THEY ARE A SET OF INCORRIGIBLE RATS!

The Committee requested the names of masters who employed an undue proportion of apprentices.

As every mechanic has a little circle in which he moves, he can influence parents who have boys to put out that avaritous masters had one bad reason for taking so many apprentices, which is to inundate the business, reduce mankind to a state of pauperism, fill their own coffers, and then turn them out into the world without any prospects of employment either as master or journeyman.

The January 1825 annual report, declares

on taking a retrospective view of the transactions connected with the trade and the Union since our last report, we have much cause to rejoice. We cannot help congratulating our friends with the animating prospect of a flourishing trade, which brings to our recollection the happiness enjoyed in former times, the Union is increasing in every quarter both in numbers and moral strength.

Earlier, however, the report declared that 'the various attempts to lower wages has called every power into action to counteract their designs.' In fact a great deal of the energies, time and money of the Union, in the five years of existence which we have documentation on, was connected with strikes, all under the combination laws. First there was the big strike in Wolverhampton which started in January 1821 and lasted over seven months. It arose in opposition to price-cutting by the employers. After a reduction of ten per cent in prices two years previously, the Wolverhampton employers decided to cut prices by a further ten per cent at Christmas. The men took immediate strike action. After remaining solid for nine weeks it was discovered that five men had returned and were secretly working. The Society condemned them as 'rats' and printed their names and addresses on posters which were posted up in pubs, shops and around the streets. The Union took over the running of the strike, quickly providing financial assistance, and sending as many strikers out of the town as possible. London, at a special meeting, agreed to levy themselves 1s 6d a week, in addition to their subscriptions and made loans 'to be repaid when circumstances permit.' Some men were said to be paying as much as 5s a week to the strike fund.

London provided £200 from their own funds – the amount of their stock in hand – and circularised the Union. Many of the local societies found difficulty in raising the money asked of them – a shilling a week from each member. But the secretary praised the societies which 'have certainly performed wonders providing the infant state the Union' and he congratulated some societies on the help they got from other trades. The final total of subscriptions for 29 weeks was £944 4s 8d of which £592 5s 11d came from London.

In order to reduce expenses the Union ordered several men out on tramp – 'three to the North Road, two to the West Road, four or five we now have in work in London.' The committee told the local societies to see by the list of correspondents where to send tramps

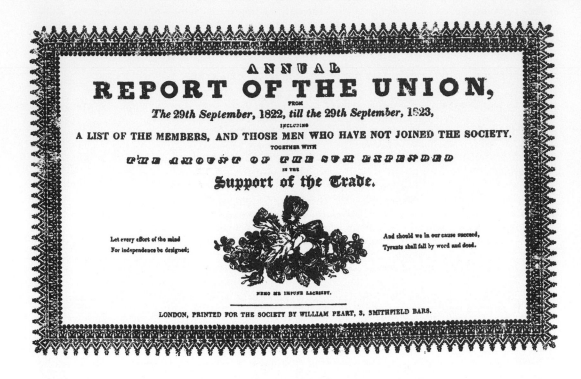

without cards – 'those who will not support the trade let them support the tramps.'

The final report we have on the strike declared 'we trust that with a little more of your assistance we shall be able to terminate the contest with honour to ourselves and credit to the trade.' The employers' combination was broken 'for of the eight who started out, only three stood out.' When the strike started there were nearly 60 men working and paying to the Society. At the time of the report there were only 20, all of them getting full wages 'and they have formed themselves into a society expressly for the purpose of helping their fellow warriors in the struggle.' Twenty had left the town and nearly all had employment, most of them in London. About 16 were left, a few of them with large families, to be provided for at a cost of about £15 a week. They were prepared to leave Wolverhampton and it was proposed that all local societies with more than 30 members take one of these men and provide for him out of local funds until a job was available. London would take a proportion based on its membership.

In 1824 there was a strike at King's factory in Snow Hill, London where all the 52 men withdrew their labour because they had 'been assailed by unexampled acts of oppression and deprived of rights and privileges enjoyed at every respectable manufactory in London.' Everywhere else

small beer or Beer money is allowed to the workmen, but at 66 Snow Hill no such privilege has been enjoyed for several years!! Tyranny is carried to such a height there that men are not even allowed to drink what they pay for out of their own pockets, and have frequently had the mortification to see their beer upset in their presence by their Employer and his Sons!!![33]

Beer played an important part in the lives of working men then, as it had done for centuries. As these tin plate workers declared it was the custom to drink while at work. In the eighteenth century a potman from the nearest inn would come to the workshop two or three times a day to fill up the pot, collecting payment at the end of the week. Many London printshops had an alehouse boy in constant attendance to supply the workers who customarily drank a pint before breakfast, a pint with breakfast, a pint between breakfast and dinner, a pint with dinner, a pint in the afternoon and another pint when they finished work. Shop fines were usually spent in drink, and beer was the main way of celebrating any special occasion such as a lad coming out of his time; a new man coming into the shop was also expected to pay his footing, treating the rest of the shop. So the reaction of the tin men at the stopping of this age-old custom was not as outrageous as might seem today.

King carried on a campaign against the men in *The Times* and they, unable to break into *The Times,* put their case through posters and placards posted up around the town. They used the same means to ridicule his advertisements in the *Morning Advertiser* and provincial papers like the *Birmingham Journal* for 70 to 80 workers, saying he would not find such workers who were not members of the Union.

During the dispute 33 tin plate workers employed at the Royal Laboratory at Woolwich were given a week's notice.[34] None of them were members of the Society and the Union was worried that they might be recruited by King. They therefore approached the men and got them all to join the Society. After about a week half of them were called back to Woolwich and most of the others got work elsewhere in London. The 52 strikers from Snow Hill also got work quickly and there seems to have been no appeal to other societies in the Union for help.

In the end King was said to be left with only two workers, one of them his brother-in-law, and several of his former 'best hands' said they would never work for him again, although 'several are making great sacrifices,' said the report. The cost of this 'contest,' including support for the men from Woolwich who were out of work, came to £233.

The Union then took up the case of the men in the Glasgow area. The low wages being paid and the 'multitude of apprentices' employed had long been the concern of the Union and it had been one of the items of discussion at the nation delegate conference, the 'oppression on the one hand, the generous stimulation held out by the Union on the other, at last aroused the men of Glasgow from their slumbers.' They paid off their debt to the Union and began to raise a fund to finance a campaign for better pay and conditions. They petitioned the Glasgow employers on 'the grievances which for a long period we have borne and submitted to.' The wages allowed by the piecework prices were

> altogether an inadequate remuneration for our service and the work performed, but is even in many instances insufficient for our subsistence; and when again a family has to be supported and educated the trifling mite of wages entirely vanishes. A good and experienced workman cannot earn more than ten shillings a week; and that though we work eleven hours in the day: while other Mechanics work only ten hours.

It went on to say 'The present Table of Prices, too is in many respects inapplicable: in as much as it contains articles not made in this Town – and others are omitted which are daily made in it.' They had therefore 'presumed to frame a new Table which we respectfully submit to your consideration.' They proposed that the two sides should get together 'to alter the rate of Prices so as, on an average, to allow a good working Journeyman Eighteen shillings per week,' which was not unreasonable. They also asked the employers to seriously consider limiting the number of apprentices to 'one Apprentice to two Journeymen, and in a shop where no

Journeymen are kept the first apprentice to be in his sixth year before another taken on.' It proposed that hours of work to be considered from 6 o'clock in the morning to the same hour in the evening.

While the changes proposed may have been revolutionary, the wording of the petition certainly was not. It concluded: 'We accordingly respectfully crave your humane interference in the premises and to grant us redress and relief from the grievances above set forth and as in duty bound Your Petitioners will ever pray.'[35]

There were a number of meetings between the society and the employers 'to discuss these and other regulation,' but the employers could not agree among themselves and the meetings broke down. As trade in Glasgow was then good the Society asked the Union in London for permission to strike. This was granted and on 26 October 1824 77 men, most of them single, 'turned out.' On the following day the principal employer called in the ten men he employed and 'complied with their wishes.' Two others followed his example. A report, dated 28 January 1825, declared 'The Cause is gained and it has cost the Union £223.'

During this time it was reported that 'several of the masters at Cork have taken upon themselves to dictate to the men in an improper manner.' Local societies, particularly Bristol, 'being the nearest place in England,' were asked not to send tramps there. This dispute was also settled with the employers 'complying to the wishes of the men.' The cost to the Union – £20.

A 'contest at Preston is next in succession which proved equally propititious and attended with little expense to the Union but infinite satisfaction to themselves. It only cost £20.'

During the 'encounters' in London and Glasgow the Bristol Society 'solicited the aid of the Union on their behalf, being, as they stated, on the eve of a calamity, and requiring the assistance of the laws which the union provide in such cases.' As the Union already had nearly 150 members on strike (or calamity as they called it) and being unwilling to take on more than they could accomplish, they felt they were unable to comply with this request. The report expressed the belief that 'to our friends in Bristol and the Union at large, this must seem reasonable.'

Throughout its known life the Union was concerned with the organisation of the trade throughout the country calling for lists of members of local societies and of the non-Society men, and exposing the rats. There was a widespread and bitter feeling against 'rats' – men who persistently refused to join the society and worked under rate. They are the subject of the preamble of the 1839 rule book of the Operative Tin Plate Workers of London.

> A Rat is to his Trade what a Traitor is to his Country: and though both may be useful to one party in troublesome times, when peace returns they are detested alike by all; so when help is wanted, a Rat is the last to contribute assistance and the first to grasp a benefit he never laboured to procure, he cares only for himself, but he sees not beyond the extent of a day, and for a momentary and worthless approbation would destroy friends, family and country; in short he is a traitor on a small scale; he first sells the journeyman and is himself afterwards sold in his turn to his Master, until at last he is despised by both, and deserted by all; he is an enemy to himself – to the present age – and to posterity!

The corresponding secretary made great use of ridicule combined with personal abuse in his war against the 'rats' using the most fanciful and convoluted language to undermine their position and to get members not to work with them, repeatedly publishing their names, nicknames and addresses, workplaces and activities.

The last communication we have of the Union is a report dated January 1825 but that does not mean it ceased to exist after that date as our records of the union are by no means complete and it spent all its known life in illegality during the period of the Combination Acts. The most likely answer is that it went down sometime during the great depression during the latter half of 1825 and through most of 1826 when possibly a number of the local societies faded out and others were unable to pay affiliation fees. All that is left behind are a few letters, circulars and brief reports and a banner dating from July 1821, soon after the Union was formed, with a popularised version of the arms of the London Company and bits of another which would seem to indicate that it was the general banner of the Union.

But in the minds of many tin plate workers of that time it must have kindled and developed the idea of unity throughout the trade and so made a contribution to the eventual formation of the National Union.

The Trades Newspaper

The end of the combination laws saw a big upsurge in trade union activity. One of the first acts of the London artisans was the publication of a weekly newspaper, *The Trades Newspaper and Mechanics Weekly Journal*. The trades had long complained that they did not get a fair hearing, their views were either ignored or misrepresented, a charge that was to be made many times down the years. In the words of the first editorial

> A new and important era has commenced in the history of our class of society ... the day is close at hand when by reason alone, we shall assert, successfully, our rights and interests at the bar of Public Opinion ... what the British Mechanics still want, is ... a newspaper of their own ... a common organ which may give better effect to their common appeal to the hearts and understanding of men, and which may, under all changes of circumstances, through good and evil, report, advocate and uphold the interest of the working classes, as before all others entitled to consideration and protection.

They called for £1,000 capital to be raised by £5 shares to be owned only by trades societies of more than 25 members. The paper would be run by a committee of management of 11 representatives of shareholding societies, plus a secretary. Half of the committee would retire on rotation every six months, their replacements elected by a general meeting of shareholders. The first chairman was the shipwrights' leader John Gast who almost certainly had been the driving force in getting the newspaper started. The editor was a journalist appointed by the committee at a salary of £6 a week – the usual payment to London reporters of morning newspapers. The first number appeared on 17 July 1825.

Not enough preliminary work was done to get the paper established, so it was too much of a London creation with few shareholders or sellers in the provinces. In a hurry to get it out before a projected rival, the *Artisan's Chronicle,* its target of £1,000 working capital was not attained. As a result it only managed a top sale of 700 copies a week and was soon in financial difficulties. Among others the London Society of Brassfounders, Coppersmiths and Braziers responded and at a meeting at the Duke's Head, Bloomsbury, agreed 'to advance £2 per share held in the *Trades Newspaper* to encourage circulation.' But financial difficulties continued and in June 1827 the paper amalgated with the *London Free Press* to become *Trades Free Press.*[36] It still continued to carry both general and trade union views and to be managed by a committee of trades representatives. But its financial difficulties continued and in December the paper was sold. Its name was changed to the *Weekly Free Press* and trades societies' news was gradually dropped in a bid to woo more non-working class readers.

During its lifetime the *Trades Newspaper* carried not only news of the economic and political activities of the trades, it carried trade society notices from, among others, the braziers and tin plate workers and also recorded such activities as the annual procession and dinner of the

Society of Brassfounders, Braziers and Coppersmiths, held on the first Monday in July – 'St Monday' holiday was still honoured by many of the London trades in the 1820s, and most had an annual 'anniversary day' for which a committee was elected annually together with other officials, to make the arrangements.

According to the report the colourfull procession was led by a 'Peace Officer' on horseback and three trumpeters followed by the president on horseback wearing a complete suit of copper scale armour with other members dressed in armour on horseback, groups of members with banners and bands and some of the products of the trade following behind.[37] It started from Lincoln's Inn Fields and 'presented a grand and imposing spectacle.' In 1826 they marched to the Mermaid Tavern, Hackney. In 1827 the procession was not held because of the apathy of members. But in 1828 the secretary, J. Callahan, Junior, called on all members to provide themselves with a blue favour with ornament to be attached to the left breast and to carry some device 'displaying to the public the very peculiar advantage of our body (second to none) in forming a public procession.' They marched some six miles to the Eyre Arms Hotel, St Johns Wood, where the bill of fare included: roast fowls, ducks, geese, quarters of lamb, sirloins of beef, fillets of veal, boiled leg of lamb, ham and pigeon pies, savoury pies, giblet pies, jellies, plump puddings, tarts, marrow puddings, custards, vegetables in season, cheese salads, etc, etc, porter with dinner and a glass of brandy afterwards, at a cost of 7s. This was followed by songs and other entertainment and a ball.

The paper also provided a service to the unions with its subscription lists to strike funds. The publicity thus given undoubtedly helped many workers in local struggles which would otherwise largely have remaind unknown outside their own localities. Support for a fund set up by the London trades for the strike of the Bradford Woolcombers and Weavers and the Leicester Framework Knitters came from societies all over the country, including the tin plate workers then meeting at the Flying Horse, Charterhouse Street, and the Braziers whose club house was the Pewter Platter, Hatton Garden, as well as the Liverpool tin plate workers and a number of braziers shops, some of them making weekly contributions. The coppersmiths and braziers are also recorded as contributing to the long and bitterly fought strike of the Kidderminster carpet weavers. During the 21 weeks struggle the paper reported meetings and demonstrations all over the country protesting at the use of troops, and strike-breakers, blacklists and the arrest of strikers for 'begging.'

These were only the better known of a number of strikes and conflicts which came with the end of the short-lived boom in the latter part of 1825. A deepening depression followed throughout 1826 to make the year one of falling wages and widespread distress. Despite short recoveries, the next six years was a period of high unemployment and want, made worse by bad harvests and consequent high food prices in 1829 and 1831.

Among the host of unpublicised strikes one in February 1826 brought ten braziers before the Liverpool magistrates charged with having left their employ at Sutherland's 'without finishing the different sorts of work upon which they were severally engaged and refusing to complete the same without an advance in wages from 24s to 28s a week.[38] Mr Sutherland said he considered their conduct the more reprehensible because they had taken advantage of a temporary pressure of business to enforce their demands, notwithstanding that he had on previous occasions kept some of them at work when he could have done without them and they could now, by extra work, earn from 30s to 40s a week. He did not want to press the case against them if they would return and finish the jobs they had in hand. The Mayor addressed each of them in an impressive manner, and recommended them to comply with the reasonable request of their master which they severally refused to do, upon which they were all committed to Kirkdale House of Correction for one month's hard labour – a harsh sentence for just not finishing their work, work moreover for which they would not have been paid.

As Adam Smith rightly said

> A master was at liberty at any time to turn off the whole of his workers – all at once – if they would not accept the wages he chose to offer them. But it was made an offence for the whole of the workmen to leave their master if he refused to give the wages they chose to request.

Despite the growing depression the strike wave continued, with the London tin plate workers taking action in 1828. The strikes became fiercer and a growing bitterness developed among the workers toward their employers. Instead of looking for the real cause of militancy, the press and employers blamed 'Owenism' – the socialist bogey of the period – and the repeal of the combination laws. As the economic position worsened more and more strikes ended in failure. As a consequence many of the more politically conscious workers turned again to political forms of action.

Others turned to education, taking part in the activities of the Mechanics Institutes in which Johnson, secretary of the London whitesmiths, had long played a leading part. It was probably his enthusiasm for education which was responsible for the whitesmiths' own library.

This seems to have been a period of great intellectual and organisational ferment. New papers and periodicals were brought out almost every week, some of them legal, others illegal. Many radical publishers refused to pay the stamp duty, which they dubbed 'taxes on knowledge,' instituted by the government to stop the circulation of papers among the working class. A number of these radical publishers and sellers of papers went to prison for their activities, including former tin plate worker, Richard Carlisle, who spent many years in prison for his part in the campaign for a free press. It was also a period of mass meetings, debates, lectures and discussions on all manner of subjects, political, economic, scientific, and religious. Nothing was barred, however crackpot.

Many artisans supported action to force the repeal of the Corn Laws. Adopted in 1816, the laws put a tax on the importing of foreign cereals. The main opposition to these laws was the new manufacturing class who complained that the laws restricted their competitiveness in overseas markets and only helped the already lightly-taxed landowning interests. The artisans supported the repeal as a means of reducing food prices. They also supported protectionism and opposed reductions in tariffs. This working-class opposition to the Corn Laws continued until their repeal and many years later the London Tin Plate Workers Society decided unanimously to send a subscription book round the trade in support of the Anti-Corn Law League.

A report in January 1842[39] quoted a worker in a Birmingham lamp manufactory as saying that in 1815, before the Corn Laws, they were earning good money, 'now wages were reduced by two-thirds.' Formerly 78 workers were fully employed, 'now there were only 36 and those on a $4\frac{1}{2}$ day week.' Trade had fallen off very much since 1829. A journeyman tin plate worker is quoted as saying that there had been a reduction of one third in the number of men employed in their manufactory and those that remained were only partially employed.

Reform Act

The industrialists saw that the landowning interests controlling Parliament would not make the legislative changes they required and so began to advocate parliamentary reform, for which the artisans had long campaigned. By 1830 the economic crisis had reached its height. Factories were closing down and unemployment increased rapidly, while the wages of those who still had jobs fell. As in the past, economic distress strengthened the demands for parliamentary reform. The industrialists and their allies who now added their voice to the demand did not support the granting of the franchise to the artisans, let alone manhood suffrage, although they were prepared to use working-class discontent as a weapon for securing their own political ends.

The main object of attack were the 'Rotten Boroughs', places where the vote had dwindled to a mere handful in the control of the local landowner but still returned Members of Parliament, whose seats were bought and sold. The greatest scandal was Old Sarum, categorised as a 'ditch in Wiltshire,' where no one lived but which returned two Members of Parliament while industrial centres like Birmingham, Manchester, Leeds, Bradford, Sheffield and Swansea returned none. The electorate was then a mere 220,000 for a population of 14 million.

The industrialists were quite prepared to let the aristocrats continue to govern the country while they got on with their own business, providing Parliament looked after the interests of industry – which meant themselves – and they wanted the vote for the towns to ensure that their interests were looked after.

The politically-aware artisans who controlled the trade societies wanted real reform and the main organisation campaigning for their demands was the National Union of Working Classes, formed in April 1831. It demanded manhood suffrage, a secret ballot and no property qualification for Members of Parliament. The demands gave it the support of radical politicians. But the main body of the working class gave their support to the less millitant National Political Union formed in November by Francis Place to counter the NUWC. The mainly middle-class leadership of the NUWC put their support behind a Bill sponsored by the Whig reformers giving the industrialists much of what they were demanding while leaving the working class out in the cold.

The two years of struggle for reform saw many clashes throughout the country, especially when it seemed that reform was to be defeated yet again. Working class discontent mounted. In October 1831 the authorities in Bristol lost control of the city for three days as the mass of the people demonstrated. Twelve people were killed and the Mansion House, the Bishop's Palace, the Customs House and the Excise House were burned down.

Nottingham Castle was set on fire, Derby gaol sacked and prisoners released, a detachment of soldiers was ambushed at Merthyr Tydfil. Mass meetings and demonstrations were held all over the country. More than 50,000 congregated on Town Moor, Newcastle-upon-Tyne, demanding the enactment of the Bill. In Glasgow on 8 September 1831, 150,000 marched in a demonstration organised by the Glasgow United Trades with the tin plate workers marching in the Hammermen's contingent, 'which included representations of three tinmen and a blacksmith at work.' Flags were carried by the trade representatives calling for reform and justice. Some 200,000 from all the surrounding towns took part in a demonstration in Birmingham. This was said to be one of the most class-conscious and serious disturbances in the nineteenth century and Britain was believed to be closer to revolution than at any time since the seventeenth century. Parliament hastily pushed the Reform Bill through but although it did away with the worst of the Rotten Boroughs and gave representation to the new industrial towns, it confined the suffrage to the middle class.

The mass of the trade societies' members gave a tumultuous welcome to the news of the passing of the Reform Act before they realised that once again they had been taken for a ride by the middle class. On 10 August 1832 the Edinburgh Trades staged a great demonstration said to be the most spectacular. It was led by a Champion encased in Black Tin Armour, mounted on a fine horse decorated with a beautiful cover. The Champion carried a Shield and Battle-axe made of Tin. His armour covered every part of his body even over the finger points, and his helmet bore a profusion of black Ostrich feathers. His appearance was very much admired. He was supported on either side by three men in Highland costume. Then followed a Block-Tin Grecian Flower Vase, filled with Thistles, Roses and Shamrock. A yellow silk flag with the Tin Plate workers' arms above which were the words in gold letters 'United Tin Plate Workers' motto below 'Amore sitis uniti,' ornamented with Thistle, Rose and Shamrock. On top of the staff was an elegant tin thistle.

Another of the six banners carried showed 'hands united' encircled by laurel with a motto above 'We have achieved a Victory over the Enemies of the People, with a 'Scottish Star' and a Lion Rampant in the centre while another with a golden hammer and crown bore the motto 'We hail with pleasure the prospect of a brighter future.' Demonstrators carried a block-tin triumphal arch and poles with tin spears, a tin pineapple and a kettle and stand on top. The banner bearers wore tin hats and the whole body carried tin batons and wore medals.

The brassfounders, which apparently included braziers and coppersmiths as in London, carried a model of a gas meter and various lamps, as well as banners.[40]

A similar but separate demonstration took place in neighbouring Leith when the tin plate workers marched jointly with the coppersmiths. They carried a yellow flag with a shield depicting a coffee filter and lamps. Another banner was carried by the apprentices and the contingent was led by a man in armour on horseback.[41]

It was soon seen that the warnings of the NUWC were correct and that the Reform Bill would only deliver the working class into the hands of the employers. Dropped by their erstwhile allies of the Reform campaigns the workers turned once more to the normal day to day activities of their own trade societies.

This included participation in the rising co-operative movement. A large number of co-operative retail shops had come into existence during 1829 and 1830 to provide the working people with cheap and unadulterated food. From and around these developed other co-operative organisations and activities and a complete co-operative philosophy. The years 1831 and 1832 saw the beginnings of co-operative production and in 1832 the first co-operative labour exchanges were formed to exchange and sell goods made by co-operative members. They sought to develop a new system of currency based on labour value in which the cost of labour and raw materials in the article were in hours of labour instead of pounds, shillings and pence. They were accepted by members of the co-operative and even some private tradesmen for a time. Several of the stores employed trade union members including some tinmen to make goods for sale. By 1830 some artisan leaders had become interested in co-operative production for the employment of their out-of-work members. Soon a number of single-trade co-operative societies developed – one, the Hand-in-Hand Society,[42] was composed exclusively of braziers and brassfounders – largely as a form of unemployed relief. In April 1833, the braziers were included in a number of societies that came together to form the United Trades Association which provided loans to member societies to buy raw materials.

All trades were now seriously hit by unemployment and although the co-operatives were some help, the practical artisans leading the trade societies turned again to the formation of a general union to fight the unemployment and wage cutting resulting from the deepening economic crisis.

In 1829 and again in 1830 the Lancashire cotton spinners' leader, John Doherty, raised the old question of a general union of trades. A meeting in Manchester supported by the local whitesmiths and other metal trades, as well as the main body of the textile workers, launched the Union of Trades, later to change its name to the National Association for the Protection of

Labour with Doherty as secretary and editor of the organisation's paper, the *United Trades Co-operative Journal*.

The Union obtained some strong support in Lancashire and the Midlands, mainly among textile workers but also from miners and some sections of the metal trades. Among the latter we again find the Manchester Whitesmiths who are recorded as having paid their £1 entrance fee and taken part in meetings. At its peak, the Union is believed to have had about 150 affiliated societies with between 10,000 and 20,000 members. But due to internal dissensions, apparently arising from discontent at the lack of help given to strikes, it faded out in 1832.

All was not lost, however, for some of the achievements of the NAPL stuck. In the Midlands, a number of unions of trades on a town or county basis remained in being, loosely uniting the local organisations of the various trades. These provided the basis for maintaining and extending trade union organisation, provided a forum for ideas and gave local leadership.

When the economic revival began in 1833 there came a new burst of trade union activity. Grand lodges of the tailors and cordwainers were established and the General Union of Carpenters joined with the Builders Union. Trades and occupations never before organised formed unions. A wave of strikes swept across the country as many trades tried to make good the economic losses of the previous years. In the forefront of the demands were shorter hours of work and a minimum wage. More and more trades were reporting that they had gained the shorter day, finishing work at six instead of eight in the evenings and that the employers had granted a time work wage of 5s a day. The copper, brass and steel workers lodge at the Welsh Harp in Holborn, publicly thanked their employer in a letter to the press 'for his shining and manly example' in reducing their hours of work to 6 am to 6 pm instead of the former 6 am to 8 pm.[43]

This situation did not last, however. Soon, with the encouragement of the Government, the employers combined to wage war on the trade unions, sacking all who refused to give up their union membership. Employers in many places, including Derby, Leicester, Glasgow, Worcester and Yeovil, presented their employees with a document stating that they would have nothing more to do with the trade unions, locking out those who would not sign it. With the spirit of elation surrounding the recent wave of union activity the workers were in no mood to be bullied. So the two sides went into action with masses of workers fully believing that they were about to enter a new era, that the struggle would open the gates to the co-operative commonwealth.

For some reason the lockout of the workers in Derby struck a sympathetic chord in the working people throughout the country. It started with a lockout of the workers in the silk mills but soon spread to other trades in the town. Over 1,000 were involved. Financial support poured in from all parts of the country, from the old trade societies and the new factory workers, from individuals, from collections on the shop floor, in pubs and even collections taken door-to-door. They included the London societies of braziers and coppersmiths, brass and copper shops, tin shops, the Oxford tinmen and the London whitesmiths, with many of them sending regular donations.[44] There were, no doubt, many more contributors of whom we have no record, as the whole working class seemed to be involved. Some of the contributions went to set up co-operative workshops for the Derby silk workers, the Worcester and Yeovil glovers, the Leicester hosiery workers and the Glasgow weavers. Despite this great popular support the lockouts placed a great strain on the unions, especially as more and more workers were either locked out or came out on strike.

The Grand National

This was the situation on 13 February 1834, when the union delegates met in conference in London with the object of consolidating all the unions throughout the country in a single united body – the Grand National Consolidated Trade Union. In a short time the new organisation caught the imagination of the working people and despite an extremely short life became the best known episode in the history of the British trade unions. The movement embraced 'Owenism,' the co-operative ideas of Robert Owen – co-operative workshops, the settling of the unemployed on smallholdings in communities, retail co-ops, labour exchanges in which goods changed hands on the basis of the amount of labour taken in their production, all based on education. Although Owenite ideas governed the GNCTU, in actual fact he did not join it until April, when he was made grand master.

Following the conference there was an immediate inrush of trade societies wishing to affiliate and unorganised trades clamouring for organisation and recognition. Lodges of 'industrial females,' female gardeners and tailors, were set up and general unions – called 'miscellaneous lodges.'

The working people do not seem to have been intimidated by the lockouts, or the continued widespread attacks on the union by the employers with the backing of the Government and the Press.

The mass of the working people throughout the country, both the members of established unions and those who had not been previously touched by union organisation, seem to have believed that the New Jerusalem was just around the corner. The state of enthusiasm, of euphoria even, that surrounded the GNCTU may be judged by the description of the meeeting at which the tin plate workers of London decided to become members of the organisation. They were normally a hard headed body of men, always ready to play their part in all union activities, but cautious in their approach. Yet at the 'numerous meeting of the tin plate workers of London and its vicinity,' held on 24 February 1834, at the Mechanics Institute, they carried with acclamation a resolution that,

> viewing as this meeting does, with pleasure, the rapid motion made by trade unions toward effecting a great and beneficial change in the condition of the working classes, we are of the opinion that the Tin Plate Workers of London ought to become a branch of the same and contribute to the sacred cause of man's regeneration.

They hoped that this example 'would stimulate all others working in the same trade throughout the kingdom to do likewise.' And the report concluded 'when man an' man o'er all the earth shall brothers be an' all that.' They did join the organisation in March remaining a branch of the GNCTU throughout its existence.[45] The brassfounders, braziers and coppersmiths also joined. In a meeting held in March in the Institute of the Working Classes in Theobalds Road, they decided to become a branch of the GNCTU, demanding a Union of the whole of the working men of the trades, giving to each member a perfect equity of rights and privileges. That such a Union be called the first Lodge of the United Branches of the Metal Trade.[46]

Similar meetings were being held of most trades throughout the country. Among other activities, the various trades also organised giant funeral processions for Union members who died during this period. The London Tin Plate Workers inserted an advertisement in the trade union paper. *The Pioneer:* 'Funeral of Bro. Alexander Napier, Tin Plate Worker. All Brothers respectfully invited to attend at Clerkenwell.' Those taking part were not only showing respect to their dead colleague but were also getting round the laws which forbade political demonstrations on Sundays.

In March, within weeks of the formation of the GNCTU, the local magistrates in Dorset ordered the arrest of six agricultural labourers and sparked off something that was to make them the best known group of men in British trade union history – the Tolpuddle Martyrs, a legend in their own lifetime. The men, active locally as Methodists, formed a trade union – the first lodge of the agricultural workers of the GNCTU – to try to stop reductions in their miserable 9s a week wages. For this they were sentenced by the Dorchester court to seven years' transportation – they were actually charged and convicted on administering unlawful oaths, similar to ceremonies used in lodges of the Masonic order.

The GNCTU quickly went into action. Petitions and protests against the sentences began to pour into the Home Office from the beginning of April. Protest meetings were held all over the country. Bradford led with a big demonstration on 4 April, followed by Leeds, Huddersfield, Newcastle-upon-Tyne and Manchester, where between 20,000 and 30,000 were said to have taken part in the demonstration. A conference in London brought delegates from all over the country who planned a monster petition to be presented to the government by a massive procession demanding the release of the prisoners.

The agitation continued and by 21 April, the date fixed to present the petition, 260,000 had already signed, calling for the men's release. The trades escorted the petition when it was presented to the Home Secretary, lining up in Copenhagen Fields in North London behind their individual union banners – with the tin plate workers going 8th – each man wearing a red ribbon in his lapel. *The Gentlemen's Magazine* said that 30,000 lined up at the start and many more thousands joined in; the *Poor Man's Guardian* reported that altogether 125,000 took part. The trade unionists marched in silence and in perfect order, five and six abreast, and the procession took more than two hours to pass at ordinary walking pace. The petition, mounted on a big roll, was carried by six men at the head of the march. Even though the Home Secretary, Lord Melbourne, refused to accept the petition with its huge escort, the day passed off without violence and the hundreds of special constables, enrolled by a government fearful of an uprising, were not used.

It was obvious that the government was backing the employers and had decided to make an example of the six men. The trial had been rushed through and the Dorchester Victims, as they were called, were already in the hulks awaiting transportation when the demonstration was held. Lord Melbourne ultimately rejected the petition and protests and the victims of the employers and government were taken in chains in the terrible conditions of the convict ships to serve their sentences in Australia.

The trades societies did not accept this defeat and a Central London Dorchester Committee was formed in February 1835 to press for the return of the victims and to provide money for the upkeep of their families in Tolpuddle. The committee included James Gray as representative of the London Tin Plate Workers, J. Burkingyoung of the coppersmiths and representatives of the braziers and whitesmiths. The committee kept up a continuous campaign both inside and outside Parliament and finally secured the men's release, though due to official bungling it was two years before they arrived home. The committees raised enough money to pay the families a total of £7 a week and to pay for the campaign with regular donations from the trades societies – the London Tin Plate Workers Society contributed directly and through shop collections, including Crossley's Gas Meter Manufactury. When the released men did finally arrive back in London a massive demonstration of welcome was staged on Kennington

Common in April 1838. It was reported that many of the trades marched to the ground preceded by their colours and bands of music, and the tin plate workers and whitesmiths were among those singled out as the most colourful.

Despite the uncompromising attitude of both government and employers in their attempts to destroy the unions, the workers remained on the offensive. When the brewers Coombe, Delafield and Co. discharged all trade unionists working for them, the unions boycotted their beer and then went on strike. More and more groups of workers came out and the GNCTU tried to damp down this action as they were unable to meet the demands for financial support. The dissatisfied trades left the organisation when they did not get the support they wanted. First the cordwainers broke away, others followed and support melted away as quickly as it had arisen, so that by August 1834 the GNCTU, to all intents and purposes, had ceased to exist.

It had a short life but even so it contributed to the feeling of national solidarity among a variety of trades and brought into organisation groups of workers who had hitherto been thought to be outside the trade union movement. It also left behind an acting national leadership in the Central Dorchester Committee which remained in operation until 1839.

With the GNCTU now only a memory and Robert Owen moved to fresh fields, the established unions returned to their normal activities of day-to-day protection of their members' interests.

The Dorchester Committee – with its tin plate workers and coppersmith delegates – was the first to organise support for the Associated Cotton Spinners of Glasgow, who, in the middle of 1837,

> were ruthlessly seized, in the lawful execution of their duty, by a band of police, dragged to prison as felons, and treated in a manner unparalleled in the annals of the history of the worst days of Sidmouth or Castlereagh.

They were charged with conspiracy, unlawful oaths and secret transactions which were said at the trial to include arson, molesting and attacks on persons and property. Their cause was later handed over to the Glasgow Committee of Trades who briefed attorneys and organised the defence. Despite a vigorous campaign by the Glasgow Committee and financial support from towns in many parts of Britain, including the Glasgow tin plate workers, the men were convicted on a majority verdict of eight to seven. Despite this almost even split of the jury they were sentenced to seven years transportation.

A vicious anti-trade union agitation was carried out by the press during the cotton spinners' trial as a result of which the government set up yet another special committee in 1838 to enquire into combinations. A provisional committee of the trades was set up by O'Connell to keep an eye on the proceedings. Another committee, called the London Trades Combinations Committee was set up by Lovett, helped by Place. The London tin plate workers' was one of the 16 societies that was a member of both, while the Bristol tin plate workers gave support to Lovett's committee.[48]

The London tin plate workers was also prominent in the Metropolitan Trades Hall Movement. A delegate from the Society attended meetings of a company formed for the purpose of building a centre for the London trade union movement with a place for meetings, committee rooms, library and other facilities. The Society delegate moved a motion of support for the project in order to get away from 'the bad influence of the public house.'[49] A meeting to support a similar project in Birmingham was attended by Walter Thorne of the Birmingham tin plate workers. Like similar projects put forward in the days of the Grand National

Consolidated Trades Union, on which these proposals were probably based, neither materialised.

In October 1841, a delegate from the London tin plate workers attended a meeting called by the Metropolitan Trades Committee to discuss ways of helping the strike of masons engaged on rebuilding the Houses of Parliament. At a similar meeting in Birmingham a delegate from the local braziers' society said he was instructed to tell the masons that they had the braziers' support. 'Theirs was a strike of principle. The strikers showed that they had moral feeling and were not to be trampled on.' Walter Thorne, for the Birmingham tin plate workers, was more cautious. He wanted to know if they were going to form a committee of the trades. The tin plate workers were prepared to assist but wanted to understand the real grievance.

According to one historian, the London tin plate workers was one of the chief group of strong societies giving help to those engaged in a wave of strikes. At the end of the decade, October 1839, we find them contributing to a fund for the Newcastle shoemakers who had been out for 14 weeks 'to defend the working class.' Support for strikes came from workers all over the country with the setting up in 1838 of a new independent working class newspaper, *The Operative*. This stemmed directly from the widespread anti-trade union campaign conducted in the press throughout the country which convinced trade union leaders of the need for the movement to have its own paper.

The capital of *The Operative* was divided into 4,000 shares of 5s each so that ordinary working men could become shareholders but the organisers were impatient to get started and launched the paper as soon as 500 shares were taken up. It was run by a committee of management consisting of 12 London trade unionists including R. Fowler, of the whitesmiths, and was said to have been 'established for the working classes, for the defence of labour.' Its aims were defined as

> reform of the Reform Act, universal suffrage, a fair day's wage for a fair day's work, abolition of the corn laws, an improved system of taxation, cheap and honest government, equal administration of the laws, justice for the employee as well as the employer.

Its campaigning strength can be seen from the support for the bookbinders' strike that came after the paper had taken up their cause. Among others, donations flowed in from tin plate workers' societies in Birmingham, Bolton-le-Moor, Bristol, Bury, Glasgow, Huddersfield, Liverpool, Wolverhampton and York. Meetings were held up and down the country – one called by Bury General Trades Committee was supported by the local tin plate workers' society who sent a delegate.

Among letters from tin plate workers appearing in the paper was one supporting universal suffrage and another condemning the apathy among the mass of workers to a strike of London boot makers. The London tin plate workers had received a delegate from 'their suffering brethren,' lent them £25 and formed a boot and shoe club. As the general press did not report such happenings it was necessary for all workers to read *The Operative*.

Unfortunately, the paper had a rival in *The Charter*, the organ of the London Working Men's Association, which did not like the militant attitude of *The Operative*. Both were supporters of the Chartist Movement, of which the editor of *The Operative*, Bronterre O'Brien was a leading member. Instead of sinking their differences and amalgamating, they continued in rivalry and *The Operative* ceased to appear in May 1839 while *The Charter* was incorporated into another paper in March the following year.

Chartism

The Chartist Movement was brought into being by the Working Men's Association, formed by Lovett, composed of moderate and respectable artisans, among them many of the Dorchester Committee, including Burkinshaw of the coppersmiths, as well as Simpson, Tome and Jones of the whitesmiths. The chairman of its Northampton branch at one time was Walter Thorne, who later became secretary of the Birmingham tin plate workers.

Britain at this time was going through one of its cyclical periods of trade recession. The years 1838 to 1842 were years of distress and unemployment. Frustrated in their attempts to improve their position by economic means the working class movement turned once again to political action, Chartism, which with its ups and downs, was to last for well over ten years.

Chartism started with a meeting at the well-known trade union pub, the Crown and Anchor, in February 1837, organised by the WMA. The Association put forward five points, drafted by Lovett, for a petition to Parliament, which afterwards became the points of the Charter. These were universal suffrage – for women as well as men – annual Parliaments, secret ballot, equal electoral constituencies and no property qualifications. To this was added payment for MPs. A further demand for the reform of the House of Lords was apparently dropped.

The six points were adopted as the People's Charter in May 1837 and so began the British workers' greatest and most class-conscious protest movement of the nineteenth century. It was deliberately working-class in character, and largely in leadership, but from the first there was a deep split in the movement.

This was between the 'moral force' Chartists with their roots back in the artisans of the London Working Men's Association and the 'physical force' Chartists whose source was the unemployed, casual and unskilled labourers led by George Julian Harney, editor of the *Red Republican,* who constantly called on the workers to arm.

But the divisions were not purely a matter of principle they often reflected conditions existing in various parts of the country or an assessment of the situation. William Lovett was a respectable artisan and a typical 'moral force' man but at a public meeting in Birmingham he seconded a resolution calling on the people to take up arms in their own defence when he saw the authorities planning to put down Chartism by force. He was arrested and incarcerated in Warwick Gaol. And the London tin plate workers, who were also inclined to the 'moral force' side, came out in his defence expressing 'at a very large meeting,' deep sympathy for all those imprisoned for political offences, especially for Mr Lovett. The Society declared that it was not only determined to 'memorialise the Queen, but to open subscription lists for the families of the victims.'[50]

It was the artisans who provided the demands of Chartism, but hunger and hatred were the drivng force that made Chartism the great mass movement it remained for some years. The hatred was that of the workers for the new machines being installed in the factories and for the masters who used them to grind down the poor.

> The new machines set a pace of output which reduced to dire penury those who were forced to compete with them by the older methods of handicraft. They flung men out of work by thousands and sent them to struggle wildly for jobs at any wage the employer would offer and under any conditions of work. Hours of labour in the factories were stretched out to almost unbelievable lengths throwing more workers out of jobs and making the scramble worse.

The employers fought fiercely against the trades unions which demanded a standard rate of wages and limits to the working day. They 'were an affront to freedom,' to the freedom of the manufacturer to govern as he wanted and the freedom of the individual workman to agree his own rate of wages with his master – a master who held all the cards. The employers also objected just as strongly to attempts to regulate hours of work by law for children as well as adults. This was the general attitude of a large section of employers in the textile areas and in the mining areas where miners were still working on a yearly bond.

It was these workers who formed the mass movement of Chartism, together with the poor of East London, the workers around the docks, the navvies and unskilled workers and the mass of unskilled labourers in Birmingham and the Black Country, another centre of militant Chartism.

In its early days, when trade was bad and there was much distress among the skilled trades, as well as the poorer sections of the people, Chartism had the support of the trades societies.

The London coppersmiths formed themselves into a branch or 'locality' of the Chartist Movement. The London tin plate workers supported the non-militant paper *The Charter*, advertising their meetings in its pages, an indication that the officials expected it to be read by their members.[51]

The trade in Birmingham also supported the Charter. Among the donations toward the expenses of holding the Chartist convention in that city was one of 17s from workers at a lamp manufactory in Newell Street.

In 1839, when John Frost, Henry Vincent and others were sentenced to transportation for their part in the uprising in Newport, Monmouthshire, Walter Thorne, secretary of the Birmingham tin plate workers, in a letter to the *Birmingham Journal*[52] appealed for financial support for the families of those transported, and for support for George Thompson, then in Chester gaol, 'for selling the labour of his own hand,' apparently pamphlets regarded as seditious.

The majority of those elected to the national council of the National Chartist Association were trade unionists, though normally in their individual capacities rather than as representatives of their trades. Nominations in 1841 included two tinmen, William Henderson, for Gateshead, and William Morgan, for Bristol, a brazier, William Tipper, for Marylebone, London, a tin plate worker, Edmund Powell, for Cardiff, and another, George Dudley, for Bilston and 'a tinner,' James Webster, for York. A whitesmith, A. Cummings, was nominated sub-secretary for Devonport and another, William Scott, as sub-treasurer for Woodhouse. The nominations for 1842 included a tinman, William Dallibar, for Chelsea; a tin plate worker, S. Taylor, for Salford and a coppersmith, George Goddatt, for Shoreditch, where the club house of the London coppersmiths was situated. The tin plate worker, George Dudley, was again nominated for Bilston and the 'tinner,' James Webster, again had the York nomination.

There is no record of any of these trades being represented at the delegate meetings of trade unionists who met in Manchester to organise the 1842 General Strike which supported the demands of the Charter, although it is quite possible that whitesmiths, who were strong in the area, were among the many bodies of smiths that took part in the strike, which was largely confined to Lancashire, parts of Yorkshire and some areas of the Midlands. Although it had its main strength in the textile areas, mechanics, engineers, millwrights, moulders and smiths played a prominent part.

Some 500,000 workers were said to have answered the strike call with an active discipline that brought into being decisive expressions of working class power. Strike committees that organised and ran communities, outfaced local magistrates and army commanders, issued permits to work, ensured policing, collected and distributed food and brought together mass meetings by which entire populations were involved in determining the course of the strike.

After some three weeks the army crushed the strike, firing on unarmed crowds at Preston, Blackburn and Bolton. Some 1,500 were arrested and charged, most of them getting long terms of imprisonment, and in some cases, transportation.

In May of that year the National Petition calling for the six points of the Charter was presented in Parliament. It was signed by 3,317,702 people and was six miles long. There was hardly a town in Britain that was not represented, but Parliament rejected it by 287 votes to 49.

After the rejection by Parliament of the National Petition and the widespread strikes in the Northern and Midlands counties, put down by military force, the Chartist Association again turned its attention to the trade societies. *The Northern Star* changed its name to *Northern Star and National Trades Journal* in 1844 and a convention of trades was held in London in March 1845. This was supported by the Operative Tin Plate workers who sent Allen as its delegate,[53] representing 300 members. but although Chartism continued as an important organisation of the people until 1848 and maintained some form of organisation until the 1850s, with the improvement of trade and employment the leaders of the trades were looking for new industrial organisation to carry the struggle forward.

The London tin plate workers was one of the 17 societies who attended a meeting in the Bell Inn, Old bailey, in 1839 which set up the Central Organisation of London Trades. This led the activities of the trades societies in the capital until 1844 or 1845 when it apparently merged with the newly formed National Association of United Trades for the Protection of Labour to give a lead to the Movement nationally.

National Association of Trades

The National Association of United Trades was another attempt to build unity and give direction to the whole of the trade union movement. According to its rules

> it was based on two great facts: first, that the industrious classes do not receive a fair day's wages for a fair day's labour; and, secondly, that for some years past their endeavours to obtain this have, with a few exceptions, been unsuccessful. The main reason for this state of things was to be found in the isolation of the different sections of working men and the absence of a generally recognised and admitted authority of the trades themselves.

The Association was the result of a proposal by John Drury, the able secretary of the United Trades of Sheffield. He persuaded T.S. Dunscome, an aristocrat and dandy who nevertheless supported the trade unionists and Chartists in the House of Commons, to give it his support. Dunscome became the patron of the Association and was later elected its president, and turned out to be very valuable, playing an active part and conscientiously attending its committee meetings over the next three or four years.

The proposal to set up the organisation was considered by the London Committee of Trades at the Bell Inn, Old Bailey. Allen attended on behalf of the tin plate workers and was elected a member of the seven man committee which organised a national delegate meeting in London at Easter 1845, with 110 delegates representing the London trades, the Lancashire miners and textile workers, the Yorkshire woollen workers and Midlands' hosiery workers, as well as the United Trades of Sheffield, Manchester, Norwich, Hull, Bristol, Rochdale and Yarmouth. But few of the bigger unions actually joined and it became largely the organisation of the smaller or less well organised trades. Allen was elected both to the Central Committee and the Central Metropolitan Committee.

In contrast to the Grand National Consolidated Trades Union of some ten years earlier, which was all excitement and wordy resolutions of ushering in a co-operative commonwealth, the NATUPL 'was distinguished by the moderation of its aims and the prudence of its administration' and provided help and advice for a number of struggling unions.

However, Owenite views were still held by many of the union leaders and a sister organisation was formed, the National Association of United Trades for the Employment of Labour, specifically to form co-operative production organisations.

No attempt was made to supersede existing trades societies or to bring them into any form of general trade union. The rules insisted that

> the peculiar local internal and technical circumstances of each trade render it necessary that for all purposes of internal government its affairs should be administered by persons possessing a practical knowledge of them.

Its purpose and duty was

> to protect the interests and promote the well-being of the associated trades by mediation, arbitration and legal proceedings (by promoting) all measures, political, social and educational which are intended to improve the condition of the labouring classes.

Altogether, it seems to have been a body tailor-made to appeal to such old craft organisations as the tin plate workers.

But, although its delegate to the conference had been elected to the committee and reported back to the Society, the London tin plate workers seemed very lukewarm in their relations with it. They refused to participate in a questionnaire from the Association and appeared to be rather reluctant in their decision to affiliate after a delegate had attended and answered all their questions.[54] This would seem to be due to internal differences within the Society itself.

At the September 1846 conference of the Association, Williamson, who joined Allen as representative of the London tin plate workers, pursued a cautious line. He warned that many of the most powerful unions stood aloof from the Association for fear that they would continually be called on to pay for support for trades with low wages who were not only the most in need of improvement but also the most numerous. A sliding scale of payments was the only way of meeting these prejudices. This view apparently agreed with the attitude of many of those present as both Williamson and Allen were elected to the Central Committee and were also appointed full time paid organisers. They travelled as 'missionaries' to all parts of the country, visiting the various trades, helping them with organising and other problems, interviewing employers in cases of dispute, arbitrating, as well as holding public meetings and meetings of individual trades, putting the views and policies of the Association and calling for affiliations.

Support for the Association seems to have been one of the bones of contention in a split that occurred in the London Operative Tin Plate Workers' Society just then. Under the influence of the new secretary, S. Ching, the Society immediately broke off relations with the Association and when representatives tried to meet the committee of the Operative Society to arbitrate and try and heal the split they were told to go away and mind their own business. Allen, who remained a member of the Operative Society, then left the Association but Williamson, who had joined the breakaway Co-operative Society, continued as a full time official.

In March 1846 the Association held a national delegate conference on unemployment, which was attended by representatives from both the Wolverhampton and Birmingham societies. The Association seems to have been a businesslike organisation with annual national meetings lasting several days to decide policy and with regular weekly meetings of the Metropolitan Central Committee, presided over by Dunscome, at their Tottenham Court Road headquarters.

Although the Association did not favour strikes and had no intention of getting swamped by them as the GNCTU had done, it invariably received many requests for support for strikers and the claims were gone into by the travelling officials, including Williamson. Most were refused but it did support the Holytown miners in Scotland and the calico printers of Crayford in Kent, to which both the London Co-operative and Wolverhampton societies contributed.

In March 1847 the London Co-operative tin plate workers sought the help of the central committee of the Association in a dispute with an employer near Leicester Square who had demanded big reductions in the price of railway lamps. Negotiations were entered into by a member of the committee but when the employer would not move the Association asked its sister organisation to employ the men in a co-operative.[54]

The Wolverhampton Society had joined the Association in March 1845, followed soon afterwards by the Birmingham Society, while the Glasgow Society attended meetings of the local branch of the Association.[55]

The 1848 rule book of the Wolverhampton Co-operative Tin Plate Workers Association indicates its strong adherence to the Association. The preamble declares that 'we have agreed, for the mutual support of each other, to maintain (in conjunction with the National Association of United Trades) by all legal means our rights and interests in the trade.' Rule No 1 states that members are excused local payments when sick or out of work 'but all contributions to the National Association must be regularly paid.' Another rule laid down that any member suffering from an imposition or oppression by an employer will, if necessary, have his case laid before the Central Committee of the National Association for the Protection of Labour. These references to the National Association are also included in the 1856 rule book. And, a letter, dated January 1847, from William Brodie, the Wolverhampton secretary to the secretary of the newly-formed London Co-operative tin plate workers, says they are 'bound together' in the National Association and regrets that the other London society had withdrawn. He declares 'nothing but a grand national association can ever relieve us from the state we are in.'

Although the Association advocated arbitration rather than strike action, they were still met with hostility from the employers. Williamson, on a visit to Wolverhampton, was requested by the tin plate workers to 'wait upon' an employer named Fearcombe who had declared a reduction of 70 per cent in the price of a job without consultation, or notice. After being insulted by Fearcombe and ordered off the premises, Williamson took the case to court and obtained judgement against the employer.[56]

The Wolverhampton Strike

It was a strike by the Wolverhampton tin plate workers that dealt an almost mortal blow to the Association and one from which it never fully recovered. It arose from a long-standing campaign to get all the manufacturers in the town paying on a standard book of prices.

The Society drew up a new prices book which was unanimously agreed at a special meeting

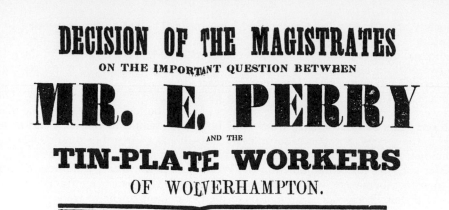

DECISION OF THE MAGISTRATES

ON THE IMPORTANT QUESTION BETWEEN

MR. E. PERRY

AND THE

TIN-PLATE WORKERS

OF WOLVERHAMPTON.

THE Worshipful the Mayor, *agreeably to the request of Mr. E. Perry*, convened a Meeting of the Magistrates at the Town Hall this day, to which Meeting his Worship invited Messrs GREEN and WINTERS, the delegates of the United Trades' Association, likewise four Tin-plate Workers from Mr. E. PERRY'S Manufactory, one from the OLD HALL, and one from Messrs. SHOOLBRED'S; R. H. BARTLET, Esq., Solicitor, was also in attendance, on behalf of the Working Men, and their differences were submitted to the Bench, the Mayor being in the Chair. A lengthened statement was made on both sides, and listened to by the Bench, we are happy to say, with the usual attention and interest. The gist of the complaints of the men was, *first*, that Mr. E. PERRY had inveigled his men into unfair and one-sided agreements; and, *secondly*, that Mr. PERRY objected to pay the same price (for the labour of his workmen) as had been and is being paid by Messrs WALTON and SHOOLBRED (*the two largest manufacturers in the town*) to their workmen. It should be understood, that the Mayor and other Magistrates assembled and acted as mediators in this unpleasant affair, *with the consent of both parties*. The *Magistrates* having retired for a considerable time, *returned into Court, and the Mayor delivered the unanimous opinion of the Magistrates in the following words :---*

The Mayor said, "It is a great satisfaction to me, that on this occasion other magistrates, unconnected with manufacturers, "have kindly given me their assistance, and being unanimous in the opinion we have formed, we have determined to give it "without binding any other party to it; we think such a course the most likely one to terminate these dissensions.

"Mr. PERRY has addressed us at great length, and requires from us protection in the carrying on of his business; he "represents that workmen willing to work for him are insulted and intimidated, and that he is subject to great annoyances, "because he does not subscribe to a certain Book of Prices settled by the TIN-PLATE WORKERS of the town. Since the Com- "bination Acts have been repealed, the working classes have the fullest right to meet and discuss their interests, and to be "advised by whoever they please, but they have no right to interfere with others by coercion or insult, and if there be any one "duty more incumbent than another upon magistrates, it is that of restraining the power of physical force against individual "liberty, and Mr. PERRY may rest assured, that he will not appeal in vain to the Magistrates of Wolverhampton on that point; "we will sit at midnight, if necessary, to enforce law and peace. With reference to the Book of Prices, we have nothing to "do with it unless assented to by all parties; nor is it by any meeting or printed book that the price of labour can ultimately "be adjusted; it must depend upon the varying state of trade and other circumstances, too numerous to mention. The "workmen may be emphatically assured, that it is not by their meeting and writing down any list of prices that will in the "end determine the price of labour. In the absence of exact terms, the magistrates can know nothing but the market price "of work for the time being. And this brings us to the question whether Mr. PERRY is now bound to pay that price? It "seems that all the workmen usually employed by him have left his manufactory, except those who are under written con- "tracts. By those contracts, judging from the one before us, he engages to pay each workman such wages as he pays other "workmen in his manufactory; but if they are all hired, to what standard are we to refer? Others can remain or not, as they "like, and a manufacturer can employ them or not, as he can afford, and it is one of the objections to long agreements for "service, that if wages rise, and those hire I are bound to work for less than their fellow labourers, discontent is sure to arise. "The magistrates, therefore, do always regret to see agreements for long periods, and they have an objection to commit upon "them, unless absolutely necessary; but Mr. PERRY must not conclude that this implies any objection to give him every pro- "tection in our power. The question, however, now resolves itself into this—What rate of wages is Mr. PERRY bound to "give under existing circumstances? To whom are we to refer for the market price of the day? To Mr. PERRY'S own list "and the list of three other houses acting avowedly in concert with him, or to the other houses of the town? In our opinion "we should be obliged to refer to the latter as the standard of value, for this amongst other reasons, that if a workman were "not bound by contract, he might go to those houses and obtain their wages. This, we think, would be the rule adopted in "Courts of Law, and we hope this expression of our opinion will terminate these unfortunate differences."

Magistrates present: The Mayor,---G. ROBINSON, Esq.; W. F. FRYER, Esq.; H. G. B. WHITGREAVE, Esq.; Aldermen J. WALKER and ANDREWS.

Dr. MANNIX, one of the County Magistrates, having been informed of the decision of the Bench on this important subject, although not present on the occasion, has given permission to publish his name as coinciding most cordially with the above decision of his brother Magistrates.

Dated this 24th day of October, 1850.

W. S. WHITE, Printer, 38, King-street, Two doors from Holborn.

of the Society at its meeting place, the Red Cow Inn in Dudley Street, in August 1850, and then submitted to the employers. It was thought that the main manufacturers had agreed but Perry, who had been concerned in a strike over prices in 1842, refused to accept the prices and another two or three employers with him. The Society then withdrew its members from those shops, except members bound by long term contracts.

The practice of some employers of binding men was also a source of conflict. The trade societies were strongly opposed to their members being bound by contract to one master for two or three years or even longer, which was both detrimental to the men and a source of weakness in the society. Some local societies had a rule that no member should engage himself to an employer so that he could not leave after giving the customary notice. The Liverpool and Manchester societies had complained to the Wolverhampton Society a number of times that some of their members were working in Wolverhampton on long-term contracts.

It was said that Perry offered premiums to men in distant towns to work in his factory in Wolverhampton on such contracts and when he had sufficient of these contract men he felt himself to be in a position to defy the Society. The following statement that was printed and widely circulated in the town during the strike, although no doubt an extreme case, supports the unions' strong feelings against the practice:

> James Totterdale, greatly reduced from want of employment, caused by sickness, left Liverpool, leaving his family behind him and engaged himself to Mr E. Perry under one of these agreements. Having been a short time in Wolverhampton, he received a letter from his wife, informing him of the dangerous illness of one of their children, and that if he desired to see it again (alive) he must instantly set off for Liverpool. He left Wolverhampton without stopping for Perry's permission and reached his wretched home in time to witness his child in its last agonies of death, and another stricken down with the same grim enemy. An officer from Wolverhampton was in Liverpool armed by the authority to search for those who had absconded from Mr Perry's service. This officer found Todderdale with a few boards he had been begging to make a coffin for his dead child. The officer had but one duty. Totterdale was brought a prisoner to Wolverhampton, leaving his child uncoffined and unburied and another child and his wife on a bed of sickness. He was taken before the magistrate when the above facts were pleaded in his defence, and corroborated by the officer. The magistrates were disposed to view the case somewhat leniently, but Mr Perry's solicitor was instructed to press for a committal. The magistrates refused compliance with so harsh a request and ordered the man to return to his employment, and to pay the expenses of his capture and removal (between £3 and £4). It was urged by the solicitor that the man was not in a state of health to be of much service to Mr Perry, but that the object was to make an example for the others.[57]

After the Society had called their members out, Perry had applied to the courts for protection in carrying out his business, saying that his men were willing to work for him at the old prices but had been intimidated. He was assured of protection and the magistrates acting as arbitrators, observed that no manufacturer could be bound by book prices as prices were determined by the state of trade.

They then turned to the position of the men on long contracts who were employed on the basis that they would be paid the same rates as Perry paid to his other workmen. But, argued the magistrates, if all the other workmen had left, what governed the rate of wages? Should they be paid by Perry's book or that of the other manufacturers in the town? They decided that it should be the latter because if the contracted workmen were free to leave they would go to these other firms and get the rate of wages that they paid. There was much rejoicing among the Society men but Perry refused to accept the verdict, and the strike continued.[58]

Deprived of his English workers he 'seduced from their homes 19 French tinsmiths with false promises of how much they could earn.'[59] Interviewed by representatives of the Society they said the money they had been earning at Perry's was not enough to provide them with a livelihood and they agreed to return home. Perry, however, refused to give them their books and passports that he was holding. The Frenchmen, after applying to the magistrate who said he could not interfere, appealed to the French chargé d'affaires who arranged with the customs that the men could be let in without documents. Perry then sent for some German workers who also returned home when they found they were blacking on a strike.

The strikers were attacked in a *Times* editorial but the NAUTEL came to their support and the trade union movement, both local and national, rallied to their cause. The strike became a national issue. Then Perry attacked the leaders of the Association as 'Chartists' and prosecuted the three members engaged in running the strike – William Peel, Frederick Green and Thomas Winters – as well as the secretary of the Wolverhampton Society, Henry Rolands, and five other members of the Society, George Duffield, Thomas Woodnorth, John Gaunt, Thomas Pitt and Charles Platt. An indictment of 20 counts was drawn up charging the men with conspiracy, harassment and intimidation, to be heard at the Staffordshire Assizes.

A benefit performance in aid of the men was held at the Wolverhampton Theatre and a public meeting attracted 1,500 people. A national defence committee was set up at the Bell Inn under the chairmanship of the general secretary of the engineers, William Allan, and supporting committees were set up in Liverpool and Manchester. Societies in towns throughout the country were visited and told of this threat to peaceful combination. More than £2,800 was raised with donations coming from tin plate workers' societies in Accrington, Belfast, Birmingham, Bolton, Bradford, Bristol, Bury, Dublin, Leeds, Liverpool, London, Manchester, Nottingham and Oldham, as well as from members in Wolverhampton, and also from the English gas meter makers in Paris. The ASE gave £202, the stonemasons £163 and the compositors £150. Other donations came from such diverse groups of workers as the bobbin makers of Ambleside, the carpet weavers of Kidderminster, the tapestry weavers of Bridgenorth, the silk ribbon weavers of Congleton, the shoemakers of Cirencester, the rock salt miners of Northwich and the coopers and brushmakers of London.[60]

The old London Operative Society of Tin Plate Workers under Ching was very antagonistic, accusing the Wolverhampton men of ingratitude over the 1842 strike on which the London members still had to pay for money borrowed. They refused to take part in the Defence Committee accusing its members of 'wanting to lead the London trades astray.'[61] It was not until March 1952 that they made a grant of £20 and sent a representative to the committee and the London tin plate workers' support for the strike came almost entirely from the Co-operative Society.

Due to 'official bungling' the trial had to be held three times and finished up at the Queen's Bench. Five of the accused were sentenced to three months imprisonment and one to one month; the others were acquitted.

During the struggle, Ernest Perry's seat on the town council came up for re-election.[62] The tin plate workers put up their own candidate and with support of local trade unionists canvassed the town, winning the seat. His brother then resigned his own seat and Perry stood again. Again the tin plate workers put up an opposition candidate, and again Perry was defeated. Two more seats fell vacant but the Perrys, afraid to face another defeat, put up two of their cronies. Once more the Society nominated opposition candidates and again they were successful. Unfortunately the verdict of the court was not that of the people.

The National Association continued, and as the rule book shows, the Wolverhampton Society continued to support it. But although it lingered on for many years, helping and advising a number of minor trades societies, as well as promoting Bills in Parliament in support of conciliation, it no longer played a major role in the movement. During the period of its existence it had occupied a place somewhere between the rather loose, politically inspired general union bodies and the new type of trade unionism which a few years later led to the formation of the Trades Union Congress.

1. C.R. Dobson, *Masters and Journeymen*, London 1980.
2. Greater London Council archives MA/W/26.
3. I.J. Prothero, *Artisans and Politics in Nineteenth Century London*, London 1979.
4. *Trades Newspaper*, London 6 October 1825.
5. Tin Plate Workers Company MS minute books, loc. cit.
6. *Journals of the House of Commons*, i xv iii 426.
7. *House of Commons Parliamentary Papers*, 1812-13, iv 50.
8. Broadsides Collection, 20 31 and 20 32, Guildhall, London.
9. Ibid.
10. *House of Commons Debates*, 3 May 1813.
11. Broadsides Collection, loc. cit.
12. *House of Commons Journal*, 18 April 1814.
13. *House of Commons Journal*, 12 May 1814.
14. E.P. Thompson, *Making of the English Working Class*, London 1965.
15. *Meeting of the Committee of Master Manufacture ... to consider the best means of Supporting Mr Sergeant Onslow's intended motion for the repeal of the Statute of 5th Elizabeth.* Pamphlet in the Senate House collection of the University of London, Ms755 fol 211.
16. *Journal of the House of Commons*, i xv iii 426.
17. PRO, Home Office Papers 42 133.
18. *Trades Newspaper*, 9 November 1826. *Gorgom*, 17 October 1818.
19. *House of Commons Journal*, 5 April 1799.
20. *Parliamentary Reports*, 10 June 1799.
21. *Parliamentary Reports*, lviii 110-112 218/224.
22. *House of Commons Journal*, iv 645.
23. KB Michaelmas 53 George III Mid. II KB 28 443 PRO.
24. Kidd, op. cit.
25. BLP & ES Webb Collection.
26. *Parliamentary Debates*, 16 and 30 January 1800.
27. Place Add MS 2760 p222.
28. *Artisans London and Provincial Chronicle*, 17 June 1825.
29. Prothero, op. cit.; Broadsides Collection, 2 9 and 2 17, loc. cit.
30. Prothero, op. cit.
31. Ibid.
32. Kidd, op. cit.
33. Place Add MS 27799 pp 174-5.
34. Liverpool Public Library.
35. National Union of Sheet Metal Workers' archives.
36. *Trades Free Press*, 17 August 1826.
37. *Trades Newspaper*, 3 July 1826.
38. *Billinge's Liverpool Advertiser*, 7 February 1836.
39. *Birmingham Journal*, 20 January 1842.
40. Edinburgh Public Library, Edinburgh Room, YJN 1213.832.
41. Ibid.
42. Prothero, op. cit.; *Weekly Free Press*, 24 July 1830.
43. I.J. Prothero, *London Working Class Movements 1825-48*, unpublished Ph.D. Thesis 1966, Guildhall, London.
44. *Pioneer*, February-March 1834.
45. *Pioneer*, 15 March 1834; *Crisis*, 8 March 1834.
46. *Pioneer*, 29 March 1834.
47. Ibid.

48.   *The Charter*, 15 and 18 August 1838.
49.   *Northern Star*, 16 May and 14 November 1840.
50.   *The Charter*, 25 August 1839.
51.   *The Charter*, 21 April 1839.
52.   *Birmingham Journal*, 7 March 1840.
53.   *Northern Star*, 5 October 1839.
54.   *Northern Star*, 13 March 1847.
55.   *Northern Star*, 7 March 1845.
56.   National Association of United Trades for the Protection of Labour, Monthly Report, October 1847.
57.   Place Collection, Set 59, Vol.2.
58.   *Northern Star*, 11 January 1851.
59.   *Northern Star*, 4 January 1851.
60.   Balance Sheet of the Central London Defence Committee, 28 February 1853.
61.   London Operative Tin Plate Workers, MS minutes, loc. cit.
62.   *Notes to the People*, Ernest Jones, London 1851.

CHAPTER FOUR

From Tin Plate To Sheet Metal

When Britain began manufacturing tin plate after it was introduced from the continent in about 1665 the first centres for the fabrication of tin plate wares were Pontypool where tin plate was made, and London. By the middle of the eighteenth century, however, South Staffordshire had taken over from South Wales with Wolverhampton the headquarters of the trade, outside London. Neighbouring Bilston, then a hamlet, appears to have been the seat of manufacture of the lighter and cheaper kinds of small tin wares. A century later tin plate ware was still one of the stable trades of the area, Wolverhampton mainly making the most expensive kinds and Dudley turning out the commonest articles at the cheapest prices. By then Birmingham had begun to challenge its older, more established neighbour with the bulk of its trade in the middling class of goods while Wolverhampton had been developing a great variety of novelties for household purposes, a field Birmingham was to follow.

Generally the Midlands tin plate workers made toilet wares, jugs, cups, bottles, kettles, coffee pots as well as baths of all kinds, many of them for the colonial trade.

The workers were said to be descendants of the old travelling tinkers who had made common wares for the villagers and country fairs. They were not too skilled and many of their early products were pieces just soldered together instead of shaped. At the beginning of the nineteenth century, most of these wares were hand made in small factories. Some fifty years later, 24 factories – 14 in Wolverhampton and 10 in Bilston – were employing 2,000 workers, 400 of them skilled tinmen. But stampings were increasing – 'the aid of machinery being introduced to the old indespensibles, the mallet, the hammer and the stake', to quote a contemporary chronicler.[1]

In the smoke blackened country of broken down buildings, and the ravages of early industrialisation that made up the Black Country, the skilled tin plate workers were among the higher paid, earning 30s. and more a week, with hardly any overtime in the larger factories, except on special occasions. In Bilston, however, where the wages were lower in line with the lower quality of the work, both men and women toiled until nine at night, and on occasion until 11.00 pm. An 1866 historian, describing the area, allowed that the social conditions of the hardware workers 'was up to the average of the mechanic class' but deplored that 'there is a high amount of intemperance among them and they are very improvident. Homes are sadly wanting in order and general domestic comforts. But there has been some improvement of late.'[2]

The leading tin plate workers' societies at that time were London, Wolverhampton and Birmingham, with Manchester in the North and Glasgow, the main society, in Scotland.

There was more or less close working between these main societies and they each had an influence on the smaller societies in their immediate areas. London, both because it was by far the biggest society and because of its special position as the capital, played the most important part and was called on to give special aid to other societies in times of crisis.

In the 1840s and 1850s the London Society was closely involved in a series of strikes in the Midlands. We have seen in the previous chapter the national ramification of the long drawn out and bitter 1850-1851 strike of the Wolverhampton society and the division in the attitudes of the London tin plate workers toward it.

This division had its origins in another bitter conflict between the Wolverhampton Society and a section of the employers in 1842, due to competition between various employers 'and the trade in general'. Early in the year, the Wolverhampton employers called for a review of the prices so that all should pay the same. The Society agreed and its committee produced a new prices book. Seven of the ten main employers accepted the new prices but the other three refused, including Perry and Farncombe, the most ruthless exploiters of the men.

The Society retaliated with a strike at the three firms on 10 August 1842 and turned to London for support. An initial grant of £50 was sent within a few days with a request for information on what further help would be required. London members were levied $\frac{1}{2}$d in the shilling earned, declaring that they would give of their utmost as by supporting the Wolverhampton men they were supporting themselves. On 10 October, two delegates were sent to Wolverhampton to try to 'bring the business to a termination.' This failed and the financial support continued, but on 31 January the London committee reported difficulty in raising money to continue the strike. The levy was raised to 1d in the shilling and a general meeting of Society members and nons was held to see what else could be done. A deputation was sent to the London masters to get signatures for an appeal, visits were made to the small shops and subscription books were sent round the trade. An appeal to other trade societies brought in £1,752. The Liverpool Tin Plate Workers Society levied their members 6d a week and pledged £3 every other week 'throughout their calamity'. In May 1843, they increased their levy to 1s a week. Manchester sent at least two monthly donations and the Glasgow Society made a loan of £41 7s 6d.

The strike having dragged on for seven months, and showing no sign of ending, the London Society took a hand in negotiations to bring it to a close. A deputation met Perry and Farncome in London and obtained proposals for a settlement which, the London Society thought, could be accepted by the Wolverhampton members. A meeting of London members, attended by Rowlands, the Wolverhampton Society secretary, called by a large majority for the terms to be accepted. This the strikers refused to do and London accused the Wolverhampton committee of not doing their duty in forcing the men to return. However, the London officials asked their members to go out and get what money they could so that as good a donation as possible could be sent to Wolverhampton, and a meeting agreed that those earning £1 a week should pay 1s with an additional $\frac{1}{2}$d in the shilling for those earning more than £1.

However, for some reason things began to go sour and at a meeting on 4 June the secretary read a letter from Wolverhampton said to be 'most insulting', and a reply was sent giving the London view. Wolverhampton was asked to send a report on the strike which would be printed together with a London report. The reply brought condemnation of Wolverhampton at a general meeting which decided 'that in the present state of our funds we cannot remit more money to Wolverhampton.' Eventually, the strike was called off.

The Midlands struggle then moved to Birmingham. The Society sent out letters and circulars at the beginning of April 1846 telling of a strike against one of their employers, a Mr Griffiths, who was demanding a 20 per cent cut on book prices. London sent £10 immediately and the Liverpool Society records 'lent Birmingham £5 to help them in their calamity' and later sent an enquiry 'to know their circumstances. If they need assistance the Secretary to send them £5.' A deputation from the London Committee saw Mr Griffiths in London, who apparently convinced them that he was prepared to pay the book prices if other manufacturers would do the same but complained of undercutting, employers farming out work privately to their employees, and of having to pay more than the Wolverhampton employers. The London Society sent a deputation to urge the strikers to return and proposed to print and circularise a report of what had happened, promising that if the Birmingham men then had to strike to maintain the book prices London would bear their share of the expenses. The deputation, with one representative of each shop on strike, met the employers and were 'very favourably treated'. So the strike ended in May and the Birmingham Society was told of the necessity 'of establishing and maintaining a better organisation than they had done hitherto.'

In 1855, Birmingham was again in trouble, Liverpool Society recording on 6 May that year an instruction to the secretary to write to the Birmingham Society concerning their strike, adding on 5 June 'sent £5 to Birmingham and another £5 in a fortnight if required.' The London Co-operative Tin Plate Workers' Society seems to have taken over something of the organisation as the London Operative Society had done some ten years earlier. They held a special meeting of members on the strike, sent two delegates to Birmingham for 12 days, provided £40 in cash and cards to the value of £7 15s, which suggests that the Birmingham Society was being reorganised.

The final word on that strike echoed the sour notes on which previous strikes ended, with a minute in the Liverpool Society's books for 18 January 1856 'That this Society records its indignation in the manner in which the Birmingham Society has acted in reference to the late strike in not giving intimation of its closure and no particulars of its progress.' The London Operative Society's minutes reported a similar message to Birmingham.

The industrial Midlands was a rough and tough area and this was reflected in their industrial struggles. The activities of other local tin plate workers' societies for the most part followed very different lines.

Now let us look at the pattern of the trade, especially in London.

The Operative Society

Early in the 1842 minute book of the London Operative Tin Plate Workers' Society, meeting in the Ben Johnson, Clerkenwell, we come across the important question of pricing new jobs in a trade society which was then almost entirely piece-work.

At the July meeting, it was reported that a new job of soap cases required pricing, and in August a new horn lantern was introduced to the meeting. This was the usual practice when a new job had to be priced or a new price put on an altered job. There were committees for the different items manufactured – baths, lamps, gas meters and so on. The pricing committee would get together with an example of the job to be priced and after deliberations on the work entailed would put forward a recommended price. If the job had already been sent round the shops the committee would have the benefit of the reactions of the men who would have to do the work. And it was usual to have examples of the new job at the meeting of the lodge which had to endorse or reject the recommended price.

This was a time of poor trade and the employers were on the offensive. In April, two members asked the Society for guidance. Their employer had issued each of them with a notebook and told them to enter the times taken for every job, both special and jobbing work. It was the opinion of the men working in the shop concerned – as with many since when confronted with time and motion and similar studies – that 'this would be an evil.' It was a new development and they were suspicious of it. The meeting does not seem to have appreciated the possible significance of the move and decided that the Society should not interfere, recommending that the members try it out and assured them that they were at liberty to apply to the trade again if necessary.

However, the meeting did decide that there should be closer working between the different shops and that a sub-committee of six members from different factories go into the best means of improving communications between shops to provide a better basis for arriving at prices for new jobs or jobs that had been altered.

This was the 'Hungry Forties', a time of high unemployment and reduced wages. The tin plate workers suffered like the rest of the trades and the various pricing committees were frequently called upon to deal with demands for reductions in established prices. A survey of wages in the East end of London at that time found tin plate workers averaging 21s 2d a week.[3]   The work position worsened through 1843 and by 1844 the London Society was in a very bad way. A sub-committee reported that unless something was done to raise money the Society 'would not be able to carry out demands.' A proposal to raise subscriptions was rejected on the grounds that it would not help the situation and would lead to more men leaving the Society. It was also decided that there could be no reduction of benefits to men out of work or on strike.

It was finally decided to compromise. Those who could afford to should pay an increased contribution of 1s a week but members who could not afford to pay more than the existing dues of 9d should still be considered 'a payable member'. All were asked to pay what they could for the ensuing months and £20 was borrowed from the Manchester Society. A sub-committee was appointed to enquire into the state of the Society and report on measures that might be adopted to put it on its feet.

Still the difficulties mounted. Three employers asked for price reductions and the sub-committees, having enquired into the prices of the articles all over London, decided that slight reductions could be made. It was reported that all the best work was gradually leaving the factories and being given to private workmen to be made more cheaply. The situation was so serious, said the report, that strong action would have to be taken soon if the Society were to continue.

The committee decided on a policy of recruitment. A meeting of 'non-payable members' was held at the Bell Inn. The meeting was told of the urgent necessity for all those present to support the Society, otherwise prices would be reduced. But with the support of all men working in the trade further reductions could be avoided.

Speakers also declared that the Society had a claim on all tin plate workers in London because of the great sum it was paying out annually to assist men arriving in London on tramp. Great destitution frequently occurred and was relieved, not by the tin plate workers of London but by the fraction who belonged to the Society. All present were called on, 'in the name of humanity', to come forward and help the Society. Those present agreed to inform their shop mates of what had been said and to attend the next lodge meeting. At the June meeting, 58 new members joined up.

Suggestions put forward at later meetings included dissolving the Society and reducing subs to 6d, but it was pointed out that the Society had debts amounting to £500 and that a 6d sub would not pay outgoing expenses. So it was decided to set up a committee to consider changes in the laws of the Society.

The spokesman of the committee, Thomas Lavender, gave his report to the lodge meeting of 20 September 1846. He was followed by another member of the committee, Samuel Ching, who put forward his own proposals in direct opposition to those of the committee, whom he had not consulted and who expressed complete astonishment.

The minute book reports 'Here a scene of great confusion took place which baffles description. There was uproar, with many members wanting to speak at once.' The rest of the minutes of that meeting are written in a completely different hand – the Society had effectively split in two.

Ching's report proposed the election of a treasurer, tougher measures on the relief of tramps, a quarterly audit and changes in book-keeping, an account made of the money owed to the pension society. It also proposed an immediate withdrawal from the NAUTPL.

The five other members of the committee condemned Ching's action and the clamour and confusion was so great that the business could not be heard. After the chairman had restored order he put the two proposals to the vote – the committee report received 120 votes and Ching 110. The Committee proposal that a committee of six be elected to run the Society was then put and carried by 80 votes to 70.

Despite this double defeat, the Ching faction continued to hold sway. An ad hoc committee, obviously the result of some behind the scenes activities, made a 'protest' at the next lodge meeting, part of a successful coup. They

> introduced the necessary elections, which were carried, as the best means to oppose alterations proposed by the committee of enquiry, and were to continue to act until such time as the contemplated alterations be carried out.

The members of the group who took over the society announced that any who wanted to remain members should make payments before the end of November and the shops were to be acquainted 'with the decisions of the lodge.'

The Secretary, James Johnson, being unable to produce the books, resigned, and Samuel Ching was elected pro tem.

At the January Lodge meeting, Ching's proposals, that had originally been defeated, became 'regulations for guidance of General Committee and Secretary.' It was decided that the Western branch be continued for another six months on trial and Ching, who had been confirmed as secretary at a salary of £20 a year, was also to be secretary of the Western branch at no extra salary. A new club house, the Pewter Platter, was chosen from five pubs recommended by various members.

The reason for the split, which seems to have been cleverly engineered, was apparently based on political differences, as well as differences of opinion in the way the branch should be run, and the difficult financial position brought things to a head. The old society under Ching, which retained the name of the Operative Society, played a less active role in the wider trade union and labour movement in the succeeding years. They retained something more than half of the old membership, together with the title, assets and liabilities, books, goodwill and whatever of the old Society.

After the split in 1846, the slimmed down Society tightened up its organisation. This included putting the pension fund on a sounder footing, paying into the pension society amounts owing and instituting a more formal separation of the funds, as well as the election of new officers.

The tin plate workers' pension society had been established on 11 August 1828 'for the relief of aged, infirm and distressed Tin Plate Workers and their dependants.' It was run by a committee of members with ten leading employers acting as patrons and two trustees each from the employers and Union. The administration later included three representatives of the pensioners. The committee met four times a year in the Welsh Harp, Holborn, to collect subscriptions, receive the name of applicants for membership and other business. A book was kept at the bar for the entry of subscriptions.

There were three classes of subscriptions, the 1st class received a pension of £10 a year, 2nd class £6 and 3rd class (widows of subscribers who paid 10s a year) received £5 a year, all paid quarterly.

The committee had the right to refuse admission or stop the pension of 'any person who shall have been proved to have been guilty of any flagrant act of vice or immorality', against which the accused could appeal to the next general meeting.

Election of pensioners was by ballot. Members were first elected to second class membership, succeeding to first class by seniority as vacancies occurred. Subscription was 5s a year but members could take out a number of subscriptions, each one entitling them to an extra vote. A life subscription of 10 guineas in a single donation brought five votes at elections.

One of the first acts in tightening up the organisation was a more rigid attitude in the application of rules governing the relief of tramps, London always having been something of a Mecca for those seeking work, a tightening up on payments could no doubt save a considerable amount of money.

Immediately after the split the Operative Society withdrew from the NATUPL which was strongly attacked by the new leadership. In 1848 a delegate was sent to a London trades meeting at the Bell 'to consider the present alarming state of trade' but he reported back that 'the political views expressed were so extreme' that he could not conscientiously attend any longer and therefore tendered his resignation. This was accepted and no replacement was sent.

But a different attitude was adopted to an appeal to help John Drury, a Sheffield union leader who, with others, had been imprisoned on 'questionable evidence' and sentenced to transportation. After a report from a delegate to the defence committee, that the issue 'had been the means of rousing the London trades and effecting a better understanding than had existed for some years, and would undoubtedly be of advantage to our trade should we require assistance from other trades', £5 was taken from the box as a grant plus a £5 loan and the promise of a subscription list if necessary. The Society also sent a delegate to a committee proposed by the engineers to set up a metropolitan association of trades.

By this time the Society had paid off more than half the money owing and had set about calling in the money lent to others. About this time they received an invitation from the London bookbinders for delegates to attend a reception to celebrate the liquidation of debts entered into during their struggles in 1839 – seven years before.

The general depression of trade worsened with large numbers out of work 'and no possibility of getting any'. Extra contributions had made it possible to assist men who had run out of benefit and £40 was voted for a trial emigration plan. Contributions were increased to 8d a week, including 3d for out-of-work pay, and members were encouraged to lend the Society small sums weekly to help maintain funds.

Meanwhile, employers took advantage of the wide-spread unemployment to get prices reduced. One employer demanded reductions in bath prices to bring his prices down to those other firms were paying. He was told he would have to provide the same facilities and operate the same conditions – groups of men making separate parts instead of one man making the whole bath, not using iron heavier than 24 gauge and not less than six baths at a time. The committee regretted that

the competition that existed and the desire for cheap and inferior articles was producing a system alike injurious to the customer, the workman and the employer agreed that strike benefit be paid to men discountenancing the system of cheap work and cheap workmen.

At one meeting a member complained that his employer was refusing to pay for patterns – either to have them made or for patterns the men had to go out to get. This was said to be contrary to general usage 'and not be submitted to without trying to alter same.'

The most extensive activity of the Society at this period was the compilation of a complete new book of prices, the first new prices book since the one produced by the London Tin Plate Workers Company in 1805, the first in which the workmen had been engaged and to be mutually agreed between employers and the unions. It was a joint work of the three societies: the Operative, the Co-operative and the Gas Meter Makers, signed by the three secretaries, J. Doggett, I. Merryweather and W. Flood.

It had 96 printed pages including eight pages of different kinds and sizes of baths, five pages of lanterns, more than five of kettles of various kinds and four of saucepans. The only bow to the industrial revolution included were railway carriage warmers, and refrigerators. It was a colossal task for men working at the bench, most of the work being done in their spare time, with each item subject to discussions and agreement by members followed by negotiations with the employers' committee. It came into operation in 1868.

The London Co-operative Tin Plate Workers Society

After the split, the other five members of the committee and their supporters, numbering something less than those who stayed with the old society, formed a new organisation called the London Co-operative Tin Plate Workers Society.

They first held their meetings at the Literary and Scientific Institute in Tottenham Court Road, the headquarters of the NAUTPL, but soon moved to the Craven Head in Drury Lane, the club house of a number of trades societies. They later transferred to the Black Jack in Portugal Street, Lincoln's Inn Fields, and for most of their existence were known as the Black Jack Tin Plate Workers.

Their rules were largely based on those of the old society, with some minor changes in wording and the benefits were the same. They included members from all sections of the trade, including meter makers.

But the rules were prefaced by a political address drawing attention to the great increase in the country's wealth and the inequalities in the division of these newly created riches, and went on to stress the need for working-class unity. It concluded

> Among the several objects of this Society the most important is to obtain a just return in exchange for our labour and to defend those who sacrifice their employment in maintaining same. To assist each other in obtaining employment. To allow a sufficient sum to admit of the respectable interment of a member or a member's wife.

It was signed by Thomas Lavender, William Williamson, Edward Pritchard, Richard Leeming and George Swainton (Secretary). Thomas Lavender later took over as secretary.

But the best known secretary the Society had in the 28 years of its life was Tom Jones, who served from 1860 to 1865. He was born in the small market town of Ledbury, in Herefordshire, on 1 September 1822 and learned his trade from his father who had a small tin plate business in the town. He went up to London to work where he joined the Operative Tin Plate Workers Society on 13 February 1839 and became active in the Society and the general trade union movement. In 1859 he was elected to a committee of the London trades formed to get support for the London building trade workers, locked out by their employers who were demanding they should sign a 'document' renouncing the unions before they could be taken back. This long and bitter dispute brought home to the London trades the necessity of a permanent organisation. Tom Jones, who had become a leading member of the lock-out committee, was one of the nine leaders of trade societies who drew up a circular calling a meeting which formed the Council and was its first secretary, seeing it through its formative period. In the first circular he sent out as London Trades Council secretary to the London trades he asked

> Are we not grievously deficient in respect of our own duties – our own self help? Because so isolated, keeping aloof from co-operating with each other, as in all cases we should, and thus forgetting the great principle – that Unity is Strength.

He was responsible for the publication of the first national trade union directory in 1861, and took a leading part in the creation in the same year of a new trade union newspaper, the *Beehive*, of which he was a director. His friend and colleague, the carpenter Randall Cremer, later wrote

> he was as popular as the Tin Plate Workers Society due to his genial nature and steady unionism. But more than that, Tom was a character, a study, particularly in hats, where he bought them, who made them nobody knew. But he was never seen out of doors without a tall silk hat of the most peculiar build and tilted upon his head at the most delicately poised angle so that the wearer and his hat, once seen, were not easily forgotten.[4]

When he retired as secretary, representatives of both the Operative Society and the Gas Meter Makers Association were present at the farewell ceremony and tribute was paid to his success in helping to bring the three societies closer together.

He later became foreman at one of the biggest shops in the trade at that time, R.W. Wilson. But he retained his union membership and was elected to the pension in 1892, retiring to his native Ledbury where he died in 1919 – 81 years a member of the Society.

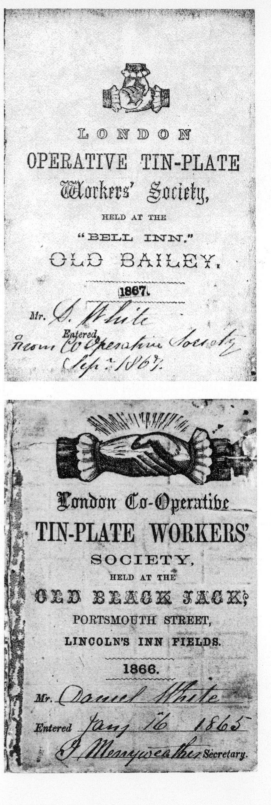

In 1864 the Society was active in the London Trades Hall movement, to provide the trades societies with a place of their own, Tom Jones playing a prominent part in the movement.

In December 1846 the Society had accepted into membership English tinmen working in Paris who had formed their own Mutual Benefit Trade and Sick Society, giving them the full benefits and rights of regular London Society members when they returned home. The Operative Society had refused to take them in as free members, saying that they could not change the rules to make this possible. There were a number of these groups of English tin plate workers in Europe – in Dordrecht, Rotterdam, The Hague, Marseilles, Milan, Barcelona, Brussels, Berlin – and at least one man in Montevideo. Most, if not all, were gas meter makers and it was said that they could earn as much as in any London shop. They were later accepted as 'country shops' or 'country members' of the London Society, going abroad on their own responsibility, though they expected advice or intervention when they were in difficulties, which happened from time to time. In the later 1880s they were beginning to experience real difficulties with what they called 'the natives' moving into their jobs and were told by the local managements to go, unless they wanted to work for the same rates as the local men, which they said were up to 41 per cent below what they had been receiving. Most, therefore, made their way home, looking to the London Society for help.

The Co-operative Society's delegates continued to play an active role in the London Trades Council. One of them, Bawden, was a leader of the London trades campaign for electoral reform in the mid-sixties and was one of the speakers in meetings on the franchise organised by the London Working Men's Association. Another delegate, Butler, was a member of the Trades Garibaldi Demonstration Committee, together with Fast of the Zinc Workers. The Society was a shareholder in the *Beehive* newspaper, a working class paper started in October 1861 by the building workers' leader, George Potter – the Society bought 26 5s shares in 1862 and its trade council delegate followed Tom Jones as a director of the paper. The Society also provided financial help for the paper when it was in difficulties, a position also taken by the Gas Meter Makers' Society.

The year 1866 saw the development of the second reform movement in which the three tin workers' societies were active. At the meeting of the London Trades, organised by the London Working Men's Association to plan the Reform demonstration, Bawden was elected to the campaign committee and was one of the speakers at the Hyde Park rally, in October, in which 150,000 workers were said to have taken part. Each trade was headed by a band, carried a banner and exhibited specimens of their particular craft.

In December the 'Black Jack', and the 'Bell' societies, the gas meter makers, coppersmiths, iron plate workers and zinc workers marched in the 35,000 strong demonstration of the London trades. The tin plate workers' contingent was said to have given 'some relief to the procession. They carried with them on a cart drawn by two good horses, various articles of their manufacture, such as gas meters, measures, etc., surmounted by the legend 'measure for measure'. They carried also various devices in tin and a bannerette bordered with chippings of the same metal.' One of the two marshals of the demonstration was a tin plate worker named Scanes, a former army drill sergeant.

At the February 1867 meeting of the trades delegates Bawden urged all working class organisations to do everything possible to extend the franchise having earlier pledged his Society 'to render every assistance, pecuniary and otherwise'. At the LWMA Trafalgar Square meeting he declared the government was incompetent to deal with Reform, and at a St Martin's Hall meeting he urged the House of Commons not to allow the government to trifle with Reform any longer. In August 1867, both the 'Black Jack' and the 'Bell' societies attended a Reform fête at the Crystal Palace.

Emblem of the London Co-operative Tin Plate Workers' Society, copied from that of the Central Union;
it is signed by Thomas Jones

Tin plate workers' societies in other parts of the country also took part in Reform demonstrations. Members of the local trade society took part in the Birmingham demonstrations together with other trades. In November the tin plate workers and coppersmiths were prominent both in the Edinburgh and Glasgow demonstrations.

The tin plate workers of North and South Shields and Newcastle took part in the Great Reform Demonstration of the workers of Tyne and Wear on Newcastle Moor on 29 January 1867, with their marshal Thomas Hunter. The newspaper report says

> Great amusement was created by the device which this body of men carried, representing Mr Lowe placed under a shower bath in full operation. Underneath were inscribed the words, 'A cooler for Lowe' and the cry of the League 'Manhood Suffrage and Vote by Ballot'. Devices of St Nicholas Tower and Earl Grey's Monument were also carried.

Lowe under a shower bath was also depicted on a banner carried by the Edinburgh Tin Plate Workers.[5]

This activity of the trades did much to ensure the passing of the Liberal Party's Reform Bill which enfranchised the urban artisans.

Then in 1867, as the result of a deputation from the International asking for support for the Paris metal workers on strike, the Society agreed to join the International Working Men's Association – the first International, founded by Karl Marx – and 'voted a sum of money'.[6]

The Society, together with the Operative Society and the Gas Meter Makers' Association formed a committee to collect funds for the destitute Lancashire tin plate workers during the 'cotton famine' in 1862. Representatives of the three societies sat together at the Bell on Saturday evenings to receive collections from the shops. Fast, the secretary of the zinc workers' did the same at his union's club house.[7]

But this was one of the brighter spots in relations between the two rival societies. After the split relations varied from strained to hostile. Within a few months of the break the Co-operative Society accused the Operative of trying to poach its members, by passing a resolution that any free member of 'another tin plate workers' society in London' could join them and come into benefit in three months. In September 1847 the Co-operative Society sent a deputation to its rival complaining that their members were not being allowed to work in factories employing Operative Society members but were told that rules or working conditions could not be altered and that the committee could not interfere with decisions made in the factories.

But by December 1848 relations had improved to the extent that the Operative Society agreed that all petitions signed by the Co-operative Society could be received in their shops providing there were reciprocal arrangements (petitions were collecting sheets sent round the shops to get financial aid for members in difficulties. Applications had to be approved by a general meeting of members and vetted by the special petition committee to see if they were worthy of support and that there were not too many going around at the same time). In these early days individual feelings were still rather raw so that co-operation gave way to discord or squabbles. In March 1883, Co-operative Society members were participating in the Operative Society's annual dinner and providing stewards. By December the same year they were again accusing their recent hosts of trying to poach members, this time by issuing a statement that any member who came over would be credited with the same financial position 'as they were in the society they had left.'

Joseph Doggett.

Thomas Jones.

John Deans.

Ebenezer Brown.

Alfred J. Harris.

William Hood.

Secretaries of the various London societies in the 1860s and 1870s

After 1853, however, the two societies began to work together with regular meetings to iron out differences arising in the shops relating to piece work prices and working conditions. It was agreed that a deputation should be convened by either society for discussions of whatever was in dispute. They also took part in joint negotiations with the employers – bringing in the meter makers' association when appropriate – and sharing expenses.

In 1856 the Co-operative Society formed a pension society of their own, modelled on that of the society they had left. And in 1872 they appointed a committee to consider the question of setting up a sick and funeral fund for the members of the two societies and the Gas Meter Makers Association. There were already such funds in some of the bigger factories, Wilson's had had one since 1866, but members had to sacrifice benefits when they moved from one firm to another.

With all this joint working it was not surprising that there had been an increasing number of proposals for amalgamation between the three societies.

In October 1873, the Co-operative Society recorded that at two previous meetings of the three societies, pledges had been given that they would all support attempts to return to a united society, 'believing that the time was now opportune'. Now that the protagonists of the original split were no longer around the joint sub-committee formed to work out details reported in April 1874 that the main difficulty encountered concerned the form the amalgamation should take.

Then on 5 January 1875, the Operative and Co-operative societies united to form the Amalgamated Tin Plate Workers Society of London. The 144 members of the Meter Makers Association voted to stay out, maintaining their independence for another 13 years.

The Gas Meter Makers Association

For very many years the gas meter makers formed one of the strongest, and certainly the best organised and most influential, section of the trade – at least in London, and their influence spread over much of the country.

Gas meters were invented around 1815 and, according to a pamphlet published in 1840,[8] the domestic meter was already in use, to some extent, by 1820, or thereabouts. These would be wet meters in a cast iron case, with the rotating float and certain internal divisions made in tin plate. Some of the best known names in the gas meter industry of later years were in the business from the start, or very soon after. Parkinsons was established in 1816, Cowans in 1822. Both Thomas and George Glover's were also early on the scene, the latter's 'improved dry meter' contained in a tin plate case was first brought out in 1844 and was regarded as something of a landmark. In the 1820s and 1830s it became usual for consumers to have a choice of being supplied through a meter or by the declared hour.[9]

The first regular repairs of which we have any record was the claim by George Glover to have had the first contract for repairing meters from the Gas Light & Coke Company of London in 1871. This involved all work for the western part of the city and Thomas Glover got the contract for the eastern area soon after.

We cannot say exactly when meters first became established as part of the trade of the tin plate workers' societies but it seems probable that the London Society members got in, either at the start, or very early on. The first reference to organised trade unionism in the meter industry, however, comes from Edinburgh, where a model of a gas meter was carried by the tin plate workers' contingent at the 1832 Reform demonstration in that city.[10] Soon after, in 1834, we find union members at Crossley's Gas Meter Manufactury in London contributing to the fund for the Dorchester victims (the Tolpuddle martyrs), the first recording of many such contributions by gas meter makers down the years to strike appeals and other acts of solidarity.

What is certain is that by 1842 the meter section was well established among London Society members. The minutes record that the December 1842 lodge meeting was shown a meter made at Edge's factory over which there was a dispute concerning the price to be paid for extra work involved. The Meter Association – the men's pricing committee – had already met and supported the claim of Edge's men. The lodge endorsed this action and decided that a deputation from the shop should act in conjunction with the committee of the Society in the event of any action being necessary, but there is no record of any further development.

Then in 1843, there was trouble when the same firm introduced a new meter 'smaller than a regulation three light'. A special lodge meeting heard that the firm had offered 30 hours for making a dozen cases and 32 hours for the wheels. The men said they required 36 and 38 hours respectively 'and they could not make them for less.' The lodge endorsed the Meter Association's price and all was set for a strike. Both the men and the firm gave notice and the lodge agreed there be a levy of 1s 3d a week for two weeks. The dispute dragged on and after some weeks the men were allowed to drift back to work, it would seem on the employers' terms.

The strong position of the meter makers and their attitude, real or fancied, to the rest of the trade was not universally welcomed by the non-meter maker. The following incident may have been the first recorded friction between the meter makers and the rest, but it certainly was not the last.

Tensions over incidents now long forgotten must have built up during 1843 for at the end of the year things came to a head with charges that the meter makers were operating a society within a society.

On 16 January 1844 a special lodge meeting was called on the requisition of 48 members 'to consider the laws and objects of the Meter Makers' Association.' A motion was moved that the Association was 'incompatible, injurious and illegal' and that it was

> destructive to the general interest for one section to set themselves up as a body, have a reserve fund to protect one particular branch, no matter under what pretences. It was incompatible inasmuch as it destroyed the confidence between man and man and would always be looked on with jealousy. It was illegal and fractious to set up such a body without first consulting the parent body. Undue interference by the meter association caused great expense and dissatisfaction and occasioned serious injury to the men themselves employed in that branch of the trade and ought to be abolished.

Feelings ran very high but an amendment was finally carried that meter makers had the same rights as any other body of men to subscribe any sum they may think proper for any purpose not opposed to the trade society. But it considered that the present Meter Association 'had discussed and given opinions on the conduct of the trade committees, which was highly wrong and hurtful to our general interest.' It proposed that the Meter Association should continue but on no account discuss or question any general trade matters'.

This seems to have papered over the cracks for the time being. But bad feeling must have remained as meter makers split away from the general London body of tin plate workers in 1861 and formed their own London Operative Gas Meter Makers Association with an initial membership of about 144. Their club house was the Bull's Head, Lever Street, St Luke's.

The Society consisted of

Journeymen Tin Plate Workers who are, or who have been, employed in the manufacture of Gas Meters, or of such persons who have served their time in the manufacture of the same, who shall be proposed and seconded by members of the Society on a regular Committee night.

Its declared aims were

To obtain a just return in exchange for our labour, and to defend those who may sacrifice their employment in maintaining the same. To assist each other in obtaining employment. To grant a pension to our aged and infirm members. To allow a sufficient sum to admit of the respectable interment of a member or member's wife.

Prospective members had to attend the committee of management for approval and became members on the payment of 2s entrance fee and a free member after paying twelve months' subscription at 6d a week. Country members with a free card from another local society were admitted free and became entitled to all benefits except funeral and petition allowance after three months. Any applicant 'who had held himself aloof from, or done anything to the injury of the Trade' could be fined before being admitted.

In an attempt to attract members of other London societies into the Association, it was decided that 'a free member of a duly recognised Tin Plate Workers' Society, working in the Meter trade' would be 'placed upon the books of the Society the same as he stood upon the books of the Society he left: and be free of all benefits at the end of the three months.'

Meter makers, as a body, were perhaps the most stable section of the trade but, as with other skilled craftsmen, there were always some taking advantage of their skilled status to move around looking for something better, or perhaps just a change of scene. So very soon the Association was joining with the other two London tin plate workers societies in negotiating on behalf of its members working in other branches of the trade, such as general work, refrigerators and the cannister industry. There were also a number of meter makers in the other two tin plate workers' societies – with the three co-operating in negotiations – as well as quite a few unorganised workers.

The meter makers' society joined with the Operative and Co-operative societies in the talks leading up to amalgamation in 1875 but finally decided to stay out on their own, and it was not until the 16 April 1888 that they finally linked up with the Amalgamated Society.

The London Amalgamated Society

The meter makers were probably persuaded to return to the fold by the employers' attempt at a wholesale revision of the 1868 book of prices. The first intimation that the employers were planning such an attack came in a letter dated 5 February 1886 from six employers who between them employed some 200 members on general work, styling themselves 'the whole of the Tin Plate Manufacturers paying the full price'. They enclosed a new price list they had drawn up between themselves, unilaterally, comprising about 1,000 items with reductions on the 1868 prices of between 5 and 50 per cent, to take effect from 27 March. They graciously intimated that they would be prepared to discuss any suggestions received by 8 March 'as we do not apprehend (having regard to the studious moderation that has governed us in making these reductions) that the suggestions would amount to more than a few matters of detail.' The reductions were 'necessary and expedient' arising chiefly from the considerable growth of factories not paying the full price for work. They also claimed that the labour saving appliances introduced having immensely facilitated the work in comparison with the conditions prevailing when the prices were fixed in 1805 as have also the increased size and improved quality of the tin plate ... [Moreover] ... The reasons urged for the 1868 advances – the continued high price of provisions and house rents – does not now exist.

When the employers refused to meet the Society a ballot of the members decided on strike action 'to defend the 1868 prices', which were not an advance on 1805 but 'an assimilation of the prices rendered necessary in consequence of changes made in different factories during the long period of 60 years, some being reduced and others advanced.' The Society prepared for a long strike. A statement was drawn up and, with the backing of the London Trades Council, was issued 'to the trades unions of the United Kingdom'. Delegates attended meetings of the other London trades and tin plate workers' societies throughout the country. Circulars were also sent to the latter asking them to dissuade tinmen from going to London for jobs. It was pointed out that many non-unionists who had come out had to be supported as well as Society members, and soon the donations began to roll in; £120 from the gas meter makers and £100 from the East London Society with smaller amounts from the National Amalgamated and from Birmingham, Bury, Hull, Glasgow, Edinburgh, Liverpool, Wolverhampton and Worcester societies, from the London zinc workers and from other trades in many parts of the country. However, within a few days the employers gave in and, with one exception, arranged for their men to return at the old prices.

The firm continuing the dispute, Groom's, was one of the oldest in the business and many of their workers had been with the firm for 50 years and more. But they refused to take any man back unless he severed his links with the Society.

Groom then tried intimidation, prosecuting two of the Society pickets under the 1875 Conspiracy and Protection of Property Act, on a charge of 'illegally watching and besetting the said factory', in other words picketing a shop on strike. One of the few blacklegs had complained that a picket had threatened him as he tried to enter the factory to go to work, saying 'Bloody shame on you. What bloody man do you call yourself?' and told him that if he continued to work he would 'never finish the job.' As this was considered an important case affecting the right of peaceful picketing, the two pickets elected for trial by jury and the Society briefed counsel. The court was crowded with trade unionists anxious on its bearings on trade union rights. However, they need not have worried, after a number of witnesses had been heard, the foreman of the jury intervened saying 'My Lord, we do not think there is any necessity to examine further witnesses as we are of the opinion that the case for the prosecution has broken down.' 'Well, gentlemen, I have been of the opinion for some time past', replied the judge and dismissed the case.[11]

Earlier, in 1872, the three societies protested 'against the injustices of the laws relating to trade unions as expounded by Judge Brett in the case of the gas stokers.' For years, one of the main targets of the trade union movement was the Criminal Law Amendment Act which admitted the legality of strikes but anything done in pursuance of a strike was a criminal conspiracy. Despite protests and deputations from the unions the Gladstone Cabinet refused to amend the Act. But the movement exploded into action when the gas stokers were sentenced to 12 months' imprisonment on a charge of conspiracy to coerce or molest their employer by merely preparing for a simultaneous withdrawal of their labour. The TUC, which by then had 1,100,000 affiliated members, now led opposition to the Act, first getting the gas stokers released after a few months. Then, in the 1874 General Election the newly enfranchised artisans used their vote to effect, opposing the Liberals and putting up 13 trade unionists, two of whom were successful, the miners' leaders Burt and MacDonald, the first Labour Members of Parliament. The Liberal Party was defeated, the hated Criminal Law Amendment Act was repealed and the Conspiracy and Protection of Property Act and a new Master and Servants Act were introduced. The results of the prosecution of the pickets was therefore of vital interest to the movement. Their participation in this led to a broadening of outlook in the London tin plate workers and to their decision to send a delegate to the 1875 Trades Union Congress.

Fair Prices

The question of prices was of paramount importance to the big piece work section of the trade and in 1891 the three main piece working societies, London, Birmingham and Wolverhampton, met to consider a prices book for Government work, as a number of unfair manufacturers were putting in 'ridiculous prices'. As a result of pressure from friendly members of Parliament, the government agreed to pay the prices operating in the town where the work was done, so it was the responsibility of the local societies in the various towns to maintain fair prices. In addition to drawing up a new list, the London Society asked Sidney Buxton MP to get the War Minister to pledge the Government to give contracts only to firms paying fair wages. This was an important step in the Unions' fight against sweat-shop employers and it remained in force until the 1980s, but its application was never automatic, and had to be fought for.

Another long-running source of conflict was the societies' attempts to stop the employers using female labour on tin plate work. In 1893, when Suggs proposed using women to produce some parts of a job, the Society called a general meeting of members which resolved that 'under no circumstances can any member be allowed to finish any work or use any portion of work for the making of any article which has been wholly or partly prepared by female labour.' When the gas meter manufacturers put women on assembling parts for automatic meters at Wrights, Cowans and Milnes, the employers were warned that if the women were not taken off the job the men would all leave, which they did and a prolonged strike, supported by the whole trade, was fought before the men won their case. The women were paid 6s a week, working from 8.00 am to 6.00 pm and 1 o'clock on Saturdays. But it was not the low wages, as such, that the Society objected to. They were against the employment of women at all and in many cases men refused to go into a shop where women were working. In 1898 the committee called for 'resolute action to be taken against female labour as the employment of females or unskilled labour was detrimental to the best interests of the trade and should be prohibited at once.'

A related question was the employment of boys as cheap labour, which had concerned the trade from the beginning and was one of the issues behind the apprentices campaign in 1813 and 1814. A shop at Newington Causeway was found to be employing young men at 3d to 5d an hour making lantern parts and Wilsons, one of the biggest trade shops on general work followed in 1896, opening a shop for boys with a man to teach them, but after the Society had warned that they would not accept this method of working, Wilsons abandoned the idea.

There was a continuing fight on the number of boys allowed in a shop. In 1896 the committee laid down that gas meter shops be allowed one boy at the bench for every 10 tinmen or gas meter makers employed. In general or lamp shops not more than one boy was allowed for every five tinmen employed, the average to be calculated on tinmen employed for 12 months.

At a joint meeting after the conclusion of negotiations on the new prices book in 1900 the employers proposed apprentices and boys doing general work should not exceed one boy for every four men. This was accepted by the book committee although there was some objection within the Union, who would have liked to get something in return, London organiser Gordon said London shops showed an average of one boy for every seven men. It was agreed that the ratio of one in five remain in the shops in other branches of the trade and that there be also no interference with the numbers in meter shops.

The meeting also agreed that boys be bound as apprentices for not less than five years and that those in the last year of their apprenticeship be not included in the average when counting the percentage of apprentices to men. For the first six months apprentices should be paid a minimum of 3s a week; after that they should be on piece work; paid half of their earnings for the next year and for the remainder of their apprenticeship two thirds of their earnings calculated at book prices. One employer thought it would be in the best interest of both the firms and the boys that the payments be more liberal and it was left to the employers to do as they thought best for payment in the concluding years.

The perpetual question of 'unruly apprentices' was also discussed but, like many before and since, they had no answers to the problem and the minutes say no conclusion was arrived at.[11]

The meeting does not seem to have considered the training of apprentices and the subject is almost completely missing from the minutes of the Society as are also the questions of apprentices' hours and conditions of work. In 1843 it was reported that there was 'discussion and opposition to the system of training apprentices at Mr Warner's.' Then there is silence until 1894 when a delegate was sent to a conference of the technical education board, but that does not seem to have led to any discussion or even report back at Society meetings.

Not until the First World War were boys allowed to be members of the union. It was decided unanimously, on a recommendation of the EC in December 1917, that apprentices or boys learning the trade should be admitted as junior members from the age of 15 with one third of the benefits per rule for a contribution of 2d a week until they qualified for adult membership.

Most of the general work, dairy utensil making and gas meter making, was piece work and prices for these were negotiated between the Union and the employers. Books of prices for general tin plate ware contained the result of these negotiations for all the range of general wares in current use. The 1805 prices, produced by the guilds without reference to the journeymen, continued, with minor adjustments until 1868, when the trade societies produced another list more in keeping with the period.

It was not until the 1890s that work began on a new all-embracing book of prices for general work, to add to the list of new articles introduced, eliminate the old fashioned or discontinued articles and to provide prices in line with modern conditions. This was the work of a 'book committee' elected at a meeting of Society members, all of whom, including the secretaries of the two unions, were working at the bench so that most of the work, which occupied some six or seven years, had to be done in the men's spare time with a minimum of days off from work for which they were only paid the actual loss of earnings. Nevertheless, the Union had to call for higher contributions to meet expenses of compiling the book.

This resulted, eventually, in a book of 285 pages, without the extensive index, with 1,259 separate articles, most of them in various sizes, so that there could be 30 or more different prices for each basic article.

This went further than earlier books as in many cases it gave details of making; particulars of measurement, materials, the gauge of sheets and wire used and other information for the guidance of all concerned, such as the number in each job given out and the sorts provided. All the work was done by the members of the Union which paid all the costs.

It was only then submitted to the employers and the first joint meeting of the two sides was held on 10 May 1899 under the auspices of the London Labour Conciliation Board. The committee of the employers' association met separately once or twice a week to consider the prices in the list. Their first meeting was held in the Guildhall under the chairmanship of the

Upper Warden (Master Elect) of the Worshipful Company of Tin Plate Workers.

Then in August direct negotiations between the two committees began in earnest. Every item was gone into in detail with one or other of the employers questioning each one. Progress was slow and the secretary of the London Amalgamated Society, James Dean, regretted the way in which the employers were cutting the proposed prices, pointing out that no increase in wages had taken place for 30 years.

After a series of meetings the Union issued a printed report of 80 pages giving a list of the prices agreed, with changes from the original price and items still outstanding as a preliminary report, which was put to a general meeting for endorsement and guidance on the attitude to be taken on those still outstanding. Joint meetings continued sometimes twice a week until finally completed and agreed that it should come into operation on 1st October 1900. The employers then stated they would only pay $8\frac{1}{2}$d an hour day-rate on general work – lower than any other section of the trade, which had minimum rates of 9d and 10d, but despite protests the employers would not be moved.

Club Houses

As we have seen, the unions relied a great deal on pubs and the landlords who provided them with a club house, gave them fires, beds for tramps, looked after the vacant books and often acted as treasurer and bankers, their only, or almost only, return, being the cost of the beer consumed by members. Yet many of the Unions seemed to change their club house merely for a change of scene. Most landlords were a friendly lot but 'mine host' of the White Swan in Tudor Street, which the London Society used in 1887/88 did not take kindly to the Society or the use of his house. He was too busy to act as treasurer and complained at out of work members monopolising the tap room all day and using 'very rough language'. Finally he asked them to move.

London seems to have been very late in using shop secretaries for collecting contributions and to attend to certain other aspects of Union business. This made the club house a particularly important part of the Union organisation.

Most of the London Society's club houses over the years, until the First World War, were in the Fleet Street/Holborn area of the city, central to the area where most tin plate workshops were located, an important consideration when workers generally made their daily journeys on foot. But with the spread of London and the scattering of work places, a single location was no longer convenient and members living in other areas with a number of tin plate shops began pressing for their own club houses.

In 1888, a petition from 19 members living in East London and working in the local ship repair yards along the Thames asked for a club house to be opened in that area where the secretary could attend once a week to collect contributions and where an out of work book could be kept. On ship repair they were frequently changing their jobs, working around the Millwall, Victoria and Albert docks, and could not journey to the club house each time to sign the book. With the agreement of the committee they settled their club house at the Oriental Tavern whose host offered them a room for £1 a year. Later the same year a tinman working at Woolwich Arsenal asked if he and his workmates could join without having to travel to central London to pay their contributions and see to other Union business. The secretary and president visited the Arsenal and enrolled seven members, agreeing for one working in the laboratory to act as dues collector. In February 1889 they formed a sub-branch, appointed a secretary and set up a club house at the Sussex Arms, arranging for an out-of-work book to be kept there. Then in 1898 a recruiting meeting brought in 40 new members.

Members at Tilbury docks then asked if they could appoint one of their number as local secretary and sign the out-of-work book locally, complaining that attending the central club house took so much time that they could lose the chance of any job that might be going in their area.

Meetings of the East London sub-branch continued at the Oriental Tavern and in June 1892 they called on the committee to take up the question of a minimum rate for day work, saying that members at one shop had left the Society because they felt there was no protection for men on day work. The committee fixed a 9d minimum and decided to put in for overtime rates after the normal nine hour day. A survey showed that 33 shops would be affected. A joint committee of the London and East London societies began an organising campaign but the going was slow as they could only manage one shop a night with most tinmen in the shipping shops working overtime. In five months only 16 had joined and a few pay increases had been obtained.

The Oriental Tavern also acted as strike headquarters during a long and bitter struggle over a 3s a week claim by members at the P & O Steamship Co. at Albert Dock. The men declared they would stay out until their claim, which would have brought their wages to £2 2s a week, was conceded. But they were not only up against non-union labour, members of other trades helped the company by doing work usually done by the tinmen – coppersmiths were making lifeboat tanks, plumbers making ice boxes, boilermakers making brass funnelling and ventilators and joiners were lining washrooms with tin or zinc. The P & O shop was blacked but in January the following year the organising committee announced that the firm was paying the minimum rate and non-union workers there wanted to join, so the shop was reopened. In 1902 a meeting was held at the Oriental to 'rekindle interest in the Society', but only four new members were made. It was said that most shipping work had left London, so after a time the organising sub-committee was disbanded.

The East London Society

Around the early 1840s the London Operative Tin Plate Workers Society, which was largely centred in and around the City of London, formed a West End sub-branch and the London secretary visited the club house once a week to collect contributions. Even after the sub-branch was dissolved and the club house discontinued, the high class work continued to be known as West End-work in the trade.[13]

Similarly, the cheaper, lighter gauge wares with an inferior finish, produced largely, but not exclusively, by manufacturers in London's East End, were known as East End-work. From around the middle of the nineteenth century this cheaper class of work increased and in February 1874 the tinmen working in these shops formed their own, independent organisation the East London Society of Tin and Iron Plate Workers.

As time went on there was a great deal of overlapping in the type of work made by members of the two societies and with workers changing jobs there was an increased intermingling of members of the two societies in the shops. There were even 'East End men' working in meter shops which had been the preserve of the Operative Society. Amicable relations continued between the two organisations but in 1882 the committee of the London Amalgamated considered what could be done to defeat 'the evil' of the spread of factories making the cheap class of work 'which would not provide a living however long one worked.' Workers in the higher class workshops foresaw the increasing competition leading to lower prices and wages in their shops. A proposal was made in 1888 for the amalgamation of the two societies as a means of strengthening the fight against lowered standards but this was turned down by the Amalgamated. A proposal for a prices book for the cheaper class of work for which no list existed was agreed but does not seem to have materialised. However, the East London Society did co-operate with the 1900 prices book committee on general work. In 1892 the two committees worked together to get out a list of prices for work for the London County Council schools, asylums boards and other municipal bodies. They also co-operated in organisation drives, particularly in ship repair, with an amicable allocation of the members made. There was even closer working when the two London Societies helped to form the National Amalgamated Tin Plate Workers of Great Britain, and in 1894 a joint general meeting decided to fix an 8d an hour minimum rate for London. There was some friction on East London shops being closed to members of the Amalgamated while there was no restriction on East London members working in Amalgamated shops. But this was not serious and there was no surprise when the long-mooted idea of amalgamation actually came to fruition in July 1901, largely the result of the work of the East End President, Charles Gordon, with the East London Society bringing in some 300 members to the new London Society of Tin and Iron Plate, General Sheet Metal Workers and Gas Meter Makers.

The Dairy Utensil Makers

The London Society of Dairy Utensil Makers was formed in 1890 with its meeting place the White Hart, Windmill Street, Tottenham Court Road. It took only men who had served five years in the trade or apprentices in the last year of their time. Benefits were confined to unemployment and funeral. They made the milk measures, $\frac{1}{2}$d, half pint, pint and quart and milk cans that the pre-war milkman brought to the doors and the milk churns with their dished and raised lids and polished brass-banded decoration that was the main feature of the horse-drawn milk floats, as well as the more substantial railway milk churns, the milking pails, milk strainers, milk coolers and other equipment for dairies.

General tin plate workers were employed in dairy shops and relations seemed to be generally amicable. Then in July 1901, Gordon reported to the London Committee that the Dairy Utensil Makers' Society had collapsed. In an attempt to salvage something from the wreckage, he called a meeting of dairy representatives at their club house which was attended by 16 representatives of dairy shops as well as the chairman, Batsman, and the secretary, Green. They asked the terms for admission into the London Society and in particular wanted to know whether they would be allowed representatives on the management committee. There was some fear that they would have to work for 8d an hour. Gordon suggested that a minimum rate for dairy work should be 9d and as most dairy workers were on piecework that a new prices book be got out. He told the dairy men that if they came in *en bloc* and brought in the funds in hand, said to be £70, in a given time, they would be free members within three months, but men over 40 would have to wait one year before becoming eligible for funeral benefit.

On 16 September the dairy officials reported their members had accepted the terms and cards were made out for 81 members immediately, the following week the number was increased to 105 and finally 113 ex-dairy society members joined. The funds were transferred and several shop representatives elected.

But the dairy members proved something of a mixed blessing. In June 1903, it was reported that of the 113 who had joined, 29 ran out in 1902 and six more the following year. Of the remaining 72, only 36 remained in benefit. The persisting high amount of arrears provided a

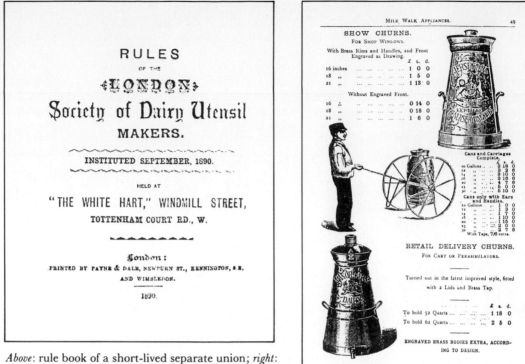

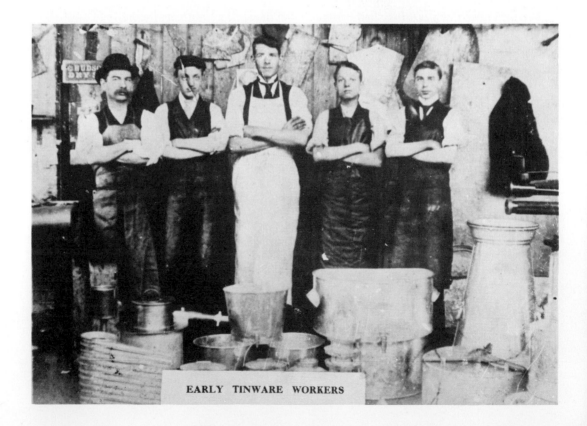

Above: rule book of a short-lived separate union; *right*: page from price list of H.S. Pond, dairy utensil makers, Blandford, Dorset

EARLY TINWARE WORKERS

The making of dairy utensils was an important part of the tin plate trade in many parts of the country until the 1930s. *Left* (*bottom*): dairy utensil workers of around 1890; *Above*: tin plate workers in the cream separator works of R.A. Lister, Dursely, Glos., and (*below*) the tin shop in the same works about 1912

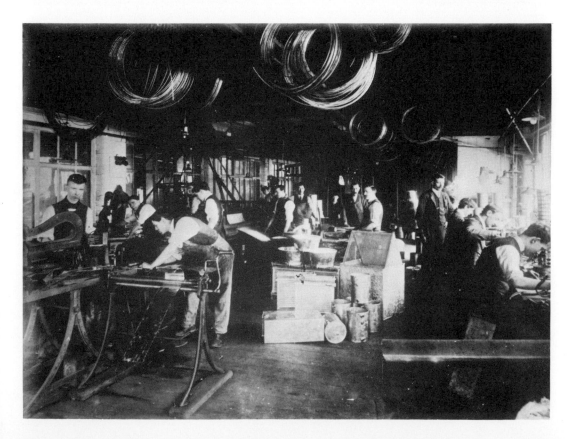

long-running headache for the London officials. A member of one of the bigger shops blamed the fact that soon after taking up membership they were faced with a six months levy in support of the Jewish workers' strike.

A committee had been set up with representatives from the main dairy shops to get a new prices list but officials said it would be foolish to press for new prices based on 9d an hour when few members of the section were interested enough to pay their dues. It was decided to first form an organising committee of eight with three each from Higginbotham's and Gilling's and two from Dairy Supply, the main shops in the trade. Organisation remained bad, with only four or five out of 14 at Dairy Supply union members in 1911, said to be typical of the trade. A visit from the organising committee gained 10 applications for membership.

But the dairy section remained a black spot with low wages and bad organisation. Boys were making and soldering small cans. When war broke out the highest rate at Dairy Outfit Co. of Hemel Hempstead was $8\frac{1}{2}$d an hour plus 5 per cent. One man was earning as little as $4\frac{1}{2}$d an hour, others $5\frac{1}{2}$, 6d, $6\frac{1}{2}$d and 7d. Men were working $64\frac{1}{2}$ hours a week and overtime was paid at piece-work rates. Apathy was rife. When reactions were asked for concerning a general application for a wage increase not a single dairy shop bothered to reply. In 1918 men at Hemel Hempstead were working from 7.30 am to 8.00 pm for £2 5s a week. A man was paid 4s 6d piece work for making a supply churn, planishing his own brass work, compared with a London book price of 18s 6d.

Later, as the Society put in applications for wage increases and obtained some successes during the war years, more dairy members took an active interest in the affairs of their section of the Society and 35 to 40 took part in a meeting following which they obtained a 15 per cent increase, early in 1918, and at the end of the war 90 members took strike action to force an acceptable advance in wages. But the dairy section never became one of the most militant sections of the Union.

The Iron Plate Workers

The iron plate workers seem to have been particularly prone to the periodic failure and breaking up of their organisation, probably because most of the trade was low paid.

The trade was mainly centred in the Midlands and the first London organisation of which we have any record is the Friendly Society of Iron Plate Workers formed in 1838 and meeting at the Sign of the Pickled Egg in Clerkenwell.[14] Then in 1842 an iron plate workers' society contributed to the London strike fund on behalf of the Wolverhampton tinmen.[15]

In November 1866 a new society was formed, the London Iron Plate Trade and Protection Society with its club house at the St John of Jerusalem in Clerkenwell and having Thomas Doherty as secretary and William Craig as chairman.[16] The inaugural meeting decided to adopt the Birmingham society's rules for the first six months and then review the position. The same year they took part in the London demonstration for electoral reform, the only record we have of its activities.

Then in 1892 the Deptford branch of the iron plate workers' society announced a strike at Gardeners had been settled and from then on there was more or less continuous organisation in South and East London. A couple of years later King, secretary of the London Tin Plate Workers, received a letter from a man who said he had been acting as secretary of an iron plate workers' strike in Birmingham and had had to change his name. They had formed the South London branch of the National Iron Plate Workers and Braziers Society with 16 men joining in one shop and were trying to extend their organisation. They were asking to join the National

Amalgamated 'to give them some standing'. King reported on the resulting meeting saying that the price they were receiving for Waterloo scoops was low but dustbin prices 'were not too far removed from ours'. They had decided to form a committee of one representative from each of their seven shops and call a meeting of the committees of the two societies. At that meeting it was recommended that the iron plate workers form a society with the assistance of the joint committee of the London and East London tin plate workers and to come under their control. At a meeting in the Princess of Wales in Deptford it was decided that they ask to join the tin plate workers, but the committee doubted whether they would be able to get their prices increased to those of the London prices book and decided that they would assist the iron plate workers to form a society by granting financial aid and nominating members from their society to take part in its management. This was put into operation in March 1900 and continued throughout the life of the organisation.

The TPW nominated from their own society the secretary, treasurer and one committee man and paid part of their salaries. H. Turk was appointed secretary and was accepted by the members of the new organisation. By August he was able to report a membership of 54 creeping up to 112 by the end of the year. Wages were low, members in some shops receiving only £1 1s a week which was a threat to the tin plate workers, many of whose jobs overlapped. Prolonged strikes took place to try and stop the attempts of two employers to reduce prices even further but seem to have petered out and in 1904 one of the main shops was said to be paying only $8\frac{1}{2}$d an hour, 'which was not enough for men capable of working from drawings', but the firm wanted even lower prices. A shortage of tools in some shops with only 12 pairs of shears and two jennies for 80 to 90 men was said to be reducing earnings and the Society managed to get this improved but was unable to stop the excessive use of boys and improvers as cheap labour. Piece-mastering was continuing at Braby's, one of the biggest shops, which remained unorganised 'due to family influence'.

Turk had resigned as secretary in July 1903 and the tin plate workers replaced him with James Ford but in January 1904 the iron plate workers decided to elect and pay their own secretary, although they re-elected Ford, who later in the year was replaced by McAllister.

In 1905 the iron plate workers again asked to join the tin plate workers and again were turned down as they were said to be working considerably below prices. But after this had again been pressed by a crowded meeting, with only five out of 55 voting against, the Committee agreed to recommend that they be accepted. But they would not take in any more mounting forgers – the blacksmiths who made and fixed the iron fittings used on the jobs and who had always been organised in the iron plate workers' societies. The iron plate workers took strong exception to this and were backed by Charles Gordon of the National Amalgamated, but a ballot of the tin plate workers opposed fusion.

MacAllister retired in 1911 and a deputation from the society met the TPW committee to urge fusion, asking why they could not be treated in the same way as the cannister makers. Again they were turned down because of low prices. Instead, W. Rae, a leading member of the Committee, was given responsibility for the organisation, whose members were still pressing for a merger. By 1911 he was able to report a membership of 166 with funds totalling £172, some prices had been increased and there was a growing interest among members with bigger attendance at meetings.

In 1913 when applications for a merger had again been turned down, Rae asked what the iron plate workers had to do to be accepted. They now had recognition in many shops, some with 100 per cent organisation, the general rate was now 10d an hour and the members were prepared to increase their contributions from 6d to the London rate of 9d. While keeping up the pressure for fusion Rae continued to build up the Union pushing up the membership to 181 by

November and 228 by April 1914. Braby's were now well organised and had three rises in the past 21 months. Eventually the tin plate workers had to give way and fusion took place on 4th July 1914, with the iron plate workers contributing 230 members and £300 in funds. They retained their club house, the Kings Arms at Deptford, with the London secretary and president attending fortnightly to take part in meetings and collect contributions. So ended 12 years as second class citizens; the London iron plate workers were received into the kingdom.

London Cannister Makers

The London Canister Makers and Tinmen's Society was formed in 1881, with its club house the York Minster, off the Commercial Road.[17] It provided out-of-work, strike and funeral benefits. Membership was around 100 but the trade was not well organised and even in the organised shops there were non-Society men, as well as members of the tin plate workers' society and the Gas Meter Makers Association.

The best work was the manufacture of provision tins, mainly for the export market. The larger provision merchants made their own tins and maintained a fair sized permanent staff. In busy times a good man at around the turn of the century could earn 50s a week. The main London shops were in the East End, particularly around Millwall. But a number of members from London and elsewhere worked in the fishing ports in the season travelling as far north as Stornoway, Aberdeen and Fraserburgh, continuing by way of Grimsby and Lowestoft, and finishing up at Mevagissey, but they were mainly younger, single men. Working long hours on piecework they were able to make it pay.

An old price list of canning work in Aberdeen includes the following 'impossible' prices:

> Making: 1 1b square or oval 2s 6d a gross; 1 1b tall open tops 1s 2d a gross; Red herring, hand cut and flanged 4s per $\frac{1}{2}$ gross; Red herring swaged $\frac{1}{2}$, 1 and 2 dozs. 5s per gross; Floating by machine: 1 1b open tops 5d per gross; Soldering up: 1 lb square or oval 1s 8d per 100; 1 lb tall round 1s per 100; Cupping by machine: $1\frac{1}{2}$ and 2 oz 2d per 100; 1 and 2 lb herring 4d per 100. Closing: Herring 1d per 100.

These were the prices London members (and others) worked to on the fishing trail and from which they made a living, earning on average £3 to £3 10s a week of indefinite hours. They are unlikely to have been much different in the London shops.

In addition to the Canister Makers' Society and some members of the London tin plate workers' society, a high proportion of the Aberdeen and Lowestoft Societies were canners around this time.

Much canning work was very seasonal. December and January were usually dull months but in February the preserving trade picked up, making tins for potted meats, tongues and brawn. Sausages were tinned in March and on until the weather got too hot. Fruit and fish followed in the autumn. Then a little of everything for the Christmas trade, with the general trade filling in.

A lot of the work was casual, with the men turned off immediately in slack times, so there was a lot of moving from shop to shop, to sections of the trade that might be busy.

Most jobs were piecework, with only the better, usually permanent men on day work. There was also a form of 'task day work' with payment by the hour on the understanding that output would be up to a given amount. Only quick workers were kept on and for top men rates compared to the general tin plate trade, ranging from $6\frac{1}{2}$d to 9d an hour in the early years of this century.

By 1907 the Society had changed its name to the London Society of Tin Canister Makers, Preserved Provision Case Makers and General Sheet Metal Workers, meeting at the Bell, Houndsditch. The Union had been able to cut out most overtime, the members were against it, other than in exceptional cases.

More and more machinery was now being introduced, simplifying the work, so that the Society was faced with a decreasing number of jobs as more women and boys were taken on at low rates of pay. Machines also meant that an increasing amount of Society time was spent in looking into accidents, the result, said the Union, of the machines not being properly guarded.

A number of firms which are still household names today were already trade shops around 100 years ago. The first record we have of members working in canning shops was at Cross and Blackwell's where a man named Hooper was dismissed in March 1843 for pilfering. He pleaded 'custom and practice'. A general meeting of the London Operative Society decided that

> while we strongly discountenance any member taking anything of the smallest value from his employer, yet in consideration of the practice of men working in soup places to helping themselves to a small portion of vials, we allow Hooper his out-of-work pay, this time,

but he was warned not to let it happen again.

In January 1900, there was correspondence between the secretaries of the canister makers and the tin plate workers on prices, when it was stated that Bovril was paying 9d an hour. Concern was expressed over one man making biscuit tins, priced as 30s a gross, who was earning £3 a week. It was feared that if men earned so much money the price would be cut. The men at Morton's, one of the biggest names in the canning industry, earned a maximum of 45s in their main factory.

Another big employer was Moir's, provision merchants of Aberdeen, said to be paying the lowest wages in the town. In March 1870 the London Gas Meter Makers Association, which also organised canister makers, called a meeting at their club house, the City of London Tavern in City Road, to consider a proposal by Moir's to cut their already low prices. The men had called meetings in the shop and had waited on the employers but the only result was that they had all been given a week's notice.

They had been given a stamped contract to sign before they could start work again. This laid down that a tinman would have to work from 6 am to 6 pm every weekday. In addition, for every day except Saturday he would have to work such times after 6 pm as consigned to him by the employer 'to which he would be bound to adhere'. For this he would get a certain, unspecified weekly wage. A sum of 2s a week would be stopped out of his wages and kept in the hands of the employer until the complete fulfilment of the worker's obligations under the agreement, after which the money would be handed back to the worker. However, in the event of a breach of the agreement or obligations, or of conducting himself disrespectfully to his master, or if unsteady or intemperate in his conduct or behaviour he would forfeit all the money in the hands of his master, plus a fine of £2. Moreover, should he prove to be an inefficient workman – that is, if he turned out more than 1 per cent of defectively soldered tins – he would be immediately dismissed, fined £2 and would forfeit the money stopped from his wages and held by the employer, as well as make good the defective tins at his own cost. The employers would be 'constituted the sole judges of what tins be held improperly soldered'.

The meeting strongly supported the Aberdeen men 'in resisting such a tyranical document' and voted £5 to the strike fund. They also asked for copies of the document to be sent to Thomas Hughes, MP (the author of *Tom Brown's School Days*) and barrister Frederick Harrison, both of whom were good friends of the trade unions. As with many strikes, we do not know how not ended.

Morton's, whose main factory was at Millwall, and had other factories in all the main fishing ports, were engaged in a succession of disputes with their men. In 1903 a dispute continued over several months concerning the rates to be paid to London workers going to Mevagissey during the season. The tinmen, who worked a 12½ hour day there, were guaranteed 30s a week plus a 5s lodging allowance. They wanted at least 45s, pointing out that many of them would be keeping two homes going.

Then in 1909, one of the biggest struggles in the canning industry dragged over many months. Starting in Morton's Milwall factory, it gave the death blow to the London Canister Makers Society, 30 per cent of whose members were involved. Reporting before the conclusion of the strike the secretary, C. Abel, said that if the London Society had not taken on the responsibility of paying the canister members the dispute pay of 20s allowed by their rule 'we should have been forced to succumb'.

Pickets were out as far distant as Aberdeen, where about 170 were still in at Morton's Rosemount factory and 24 at Fraserburgh. With the fishing fleet moving down the east coast of England, the London Society proposed that the struggle be mounted at Lowestoft during the first two or three weeks of the season there.

A conference of the societies concerned could see little likelihood of a successful conclusion and recommended an ending of the dispute, which was agreed by the National Amalgamated management committee unless some arrangement could be made with the firm, and this dispute seems to have petered out as did so many others.

The total cost of the dispute was £1,097 14s 11½d without the cost of out-of-work pay for those still out and unable to get work at the end of the strike. The main contributors were the canister makers and London tin plate workers' societies with lesser amounts from the National Amalgamated and the Case Makers.

The canister makers' society was in a very bad way. From its inception membership had hovered round the 100 mark. It had not responded to invitations to join the National Amalgamated in 1896 but had gone into the organisation toward the end of 1900. It had been generous in its help to London tin plate workers in dispute. Now its application to them for amalgamation was turned down as being too much of a liability at that time, but it was said that the National Amalgamated had a duty to see that the Society was saved from extinction.

The secretary, Abel, then wrote for assistance, spelling out their desperate financial position. They only had £1 8s in their funds and an income of £1 5s a week; with five members out of work who were in benefit and entitled to £3 a week, on top of all this the society had received a death claim for £10. He appealed for a loan to help them over their difficulties until some scheme could be adopted. The preserving trade itself was in a very bad way, and he said they had been badly hit by female and boy labour.

Gordon said that the management committee of the National Amalgamated had helped them to the extent of 6d per man during the last year, apart from dispute benefit. The Society had 45 names on their books, who were paying 1s a week, but 12 were out of work, including some not entitled to benefit. The London Society agreed to lend them £2 immediately and at their meeting, in November 1909, the proposals for amalgamation were discussed. The committee pointed out the difficulties – the low minimum wage of 8d an hour; the fact that the Society's members worked with female labour; the age of the members; the fact that canning was a dying industry; the Society's lack of funds; the increased contributions the canister makers' members would have to pay on joining the London Society. Those pressing for the amalgamation said that the canister makers were good trade unionists, and although their contributions were only 6d a week they had regular collections for those in distress, paying a levy of 2s during the Morton dispute, out of a minimum rate of only 8d an hour. It was decided by 42 votes to six to recommend the acceptance of amalgamation.

The takeover took place in February 1911. There were only 30 members left in the Society when it was finally taken over and funds totalled only £25. It was said that the numbers and the way the Society was constituted could not offer success as a separate branch or enable the members to maintain their position. There was every possibility, if left to itself, that the Society would become extinct and be a menace to the trade. Moreover, their 29 years of trade union organisation must have some appeal to the London sheet metal workers' consideration. The aim would be to establish a 9d an hour minimum wage within a year.

The takeover was finally endorsed at a general meeting of the sheet metal workers where assurance was given that most of the canister makers could take on work in various branches of the trade, 'many would make meter makers'.

Jewish Branch

The 1900 annual report of the East London Society drew attention to 'the increasing number of Jews engaged in the manufacture of light tin work in the East End of London'. The committee had 'deemed it necessary, in conjunction with the London Amalgamated Society, to organise them' and in spite of difficulties, had set up a special branch. The difficulties included opposition from members of the London Society and a deputation from various shops waited on the committee to protest against Jewish workers being taken into the Society 'although paid at low rates'. They put forward a motion, already drawn up, that before any such step be taken it be put to a specially called meeting of members. This was rejected by the committee which, nevertheless, decided to call a joint meeting of the London and East London societies. The real opposition would appear to have been racial as, when the question came up before a general meeting, the chairman expressed the hope that members 'would not use language leading to dissent'.

The leaders of the London societies were not, of course, being completely altruistic in organising the Jewish tinmen. The men were working in sweat shops at low prices which were a threat to the established societies. The chairman of the general meeting said they must 'calmly consider what was best for themselves and the trade'. It was decided to set up a separate branch which, although only a branch of the London Society, had its own rule book. There was also some suspicion on the part of the Jewish workers about the Society's motives, one of them telling their newly formed branch that they would be dropped as soon as they had served their purpose. The hard-headed leaders of the London Society expressed themselves satisfied on the returns on the money they had spent in setting up the branch – £15 6s 10d, including £10 for the secretary's salary, saying 'the new branch sets fair to become a useful adjunct to the trade', and in the near future 'we shall be making an effort to obtain for them the same rate of wages as we have ourselves'.

This was a time when refugees from Eastern Europe were flooding into London's East End, many of them skilled craftsmen in various trades. It was pointed out that another difficulty in organising them was that of language, '80 per cent of them having no knowledge of English'. Branch business was carried out in Yiddish with a translator provided when the London officers attended. The 1901 rule book of the branch had its front cover and front half of the book printed in English and the back cover and back half, reading from back to front, in Yiddish with Hebrew characters.

'The Jewish Tin Plate Workers, a branch of the London Tin and Iron Plate Workers', to give it its correct title, was formed in 1901 and had its meeting place at the Duke of Hesse, in

Whitechapel. The London Society kept a firm control over its new branch. The secretary, president, three of the committee and one of the trustees were all nominated by the London Society and chosen at a meeting of the branch. The committee comprised six members, the branch being allowed to nominate the other three. Three were to retire every six months and were eligible for re-election. The assistant secretary was chosen by the committee. The treasurer had to be a member of the London Society and was chosen at a general meeting remaining in office at the pleasure of the branch. One of the trustees, in whom were 'vested all the monies and other properties of the branch', also had to be a member of the London Society.

The object of the branch was 'to secure to the Jewish tin plate workers the standard wages and conditions as contained in the London price list of 1900'. Contributions were necessarily low, 6d a week, and members were free after 12 months. Out-of-work pay was 1s a day after six months membership and 2s a day after twelve months for 36 days, renewable after six months. Dispute pay was 14s a week for a single man and 16s if married, continued for eight weeks then transferred to out-of-work benefit. Out-of-work members were exempted from signing the book on feast or fast days.

At the end of August, Gordon reported that 110 members had been enrolled in the branch since its inception but about 20 of these had emigrated and 40 had not been heard of again.

Some 50 were now paying regularly. There had been no improvement in wages and a general meeting of members agreed to put in for an advance to be made in two stages, the first application to be for a 50 per cent increase on average prices paid – a copy of the new prices list to be sent to all the Jewish employers. It was further recommended that working hours should not exceed 60 a week and that no member should teach a 'greener'.

When, on the 1 November deadline, the employers had not paid the increase, all members of the branch were called out and with the exception of one or two, all had responded. On the first day, 78 signed the book and on the second day 74. One employer called on the special police service but no action was taken as the picketing was conducted 'in a very quiet and satisfactory manner'.

Meetings were held with a number of employers and the men were allowed to return to those who agreed to pay the increase. The rest stood firm and had it not been for the return of the workers – all Englishmen – at one shop, it was said that the leading opposition among the employers would have given in. At the beginning of the strike the London Society agreed by 104 votes to 3 to a 6d a week levy. Then, as the strike dragged on, an appeal was sent out to the trade.

The National Amalgamated, urging affiliated societies to give financial assistance, declared 'if they are victorious it must have a beneficial effect on the general trade throughout the country besides emancipating these poor, helpless creatures from a state little removed from slavery'. The London Canister Makers was the first to respond with a donation of £50 and a letter indicating that all members in work were being levied 6d. Donations followed from Wolverhampton, Edinburgh, Aberdeen, Bristol, Exeter and Halesowen.

Calls for meetings were ignored with only those employers paying the increased prices turning up, then some put forward offers of 15 per cent to 20 per cent increases and one put out his own list, which turned out to be the old prices with pennies added here and there. There was no sign of a break through and to make matters worse, orders dried up and the men who had returned to those shops agreeing to pay the increase were stood off and had to be paid unemployment benefit.

Some employers told their men that if they would give up the Union they would give them money to celebrate the Passover. On being told of this the Society countered with £30 for loans of £1 for married men and 10s for single.

The Society called a special meeting on 9 April to put forward a new compromise price list which would give 35 per cent above the old prices. Four of the employers accepted this, leaving 30 men still out plus a similar number of 'greeners'. Gordon thought they should lower their sights to a 20 per cent increase as 'more realistic' and holding out the possibility of a settlement. Although the Jewish members seemed prepared to hold out, the Society wanted the strike brought to an end and gave the officers powers to negotiate 'an honourable settlement'. On the 9 May the officers were told to get the best settlement they could and wind up the strike. They gave up the strike room at the Beehive. A general meeting of the Society agreed that it would be futile to continue the strike although ending it in defeat would be detrimental to the Jewish branch whose members 'had acted with determination and loyalty throughout'. No further payments would be made to 'greeners' who had come out in support and members still out would be put on out-of-work pay. It was left to the committee to bring the strike to an official end 'when expeditious'. On 13 June at a meeting at the Prince of Hesse Gordon brought the strike to an effective end 'after a good fight' lasting seven months. Although they had not been successful, 'they had shown they could fight for their rights.' They were urged to stand by the Society and so be able to improve their position 'in the near future'. The levy ended on 28 June.

All 35 members present at that meeting decided unanimously to continue the branch but on 21 July the London committee decided to wind it up and destroy all rule books that were left. All monies standing to the credit of the branch were transferred to the London Society funds. So, after some 12 months, the first Jewish organisation was brought to an end.

Three members were transferred to the London Society, some emigrated, a few went back at the old prices and the 14 who were left continued to receive unemployment pay. It was decided that those members who had taken a more prominent part in the affairs of the branch and the strike, should not suffer from possible victimisation. Some active members who could not get a job were paid 23s each a week victimisation pay.

Some members of the old branch formed a new independent Jewish Tin Plate Workers Society on 24 January 1903. The secretary, Lively, and the president, Cohen, invited the committee of the London Society to attend meetings of the Jewish Society to give 'encouragement and assistance', but a general meeting decided by 58 votes to 8 'not to entertain the question.' A request for the ledger and other books used in the strike was also refused and the new Society seems to have sunk into oblivion.

But the Jewish tinmen persisted and formed another independent society in May 1906. There seems to have been a certain continuity as a statement of the assets of the new society included '£7 handed over from the previous Society'. In a letter to the London Society it was said they had 60 members in East London whom it was thought, 'would stick together'. The EC of the London Society met a deputation from the new society when the secretary, Yankebvitch, asked for moral and financial support. They had had 73 members but eight had gone to America. There were about 20 Jewish shops in the East End of London, the biggest having only six or seven workers. Working conditions were very bad indeed. Some of their members, who had six or seven children to support, were not earning more than 7s 6d a week and they felt powerless to improve their position without help from the London Society.

The deputation reported that Epstein's were supplying Perkins, one of the big London general shops, with cut priced toilet cans, jugs, dustpans and other wares. Jackson's and Nathan's were also cutting prices. The secretary presented a financial statement, 'in Yiddish', that the total receipts for the six months the Society had been in operation amounted to about £20. Expenditure was about £11 and the balance in the hands of the treasurer was £9. Members were about £6 in arrears. Members of the committee were invited to attend branch meetings. They 'listened with sympathy' to the appeal but said they had no powers to sanction an official deputation and decided 'no further action be taken.' They did, however, send them a rule book and a prices book, with a warning that the latter must not be shown to the employers.

The Society held a recruiting meeting at Kings Hall, Commercial Road, in October 1908 with a speaker from the London Society and an attendance of 35, and another meeting the following month.

Nevertheless, this society, too, must have folded up as we next read that Jewish members had begun to join the London Society. It was reported that Asserton's, where all the workers were Jewish, and had been completely unorganised 12 months before, now had 14 out of the 15 men there in the London Society, 'thanks to the untiring work of Sam Clugman', who had got the employer to recognise the Society and had obtained increases of 2d and 3d to bring the rate up to 10d and 1s 1d an hour, and the employer had also agreed to pay a ½d an hour war bonus.

However, the desire of a number of workers to have a society of their own persisted and the London Jewish Tin Plate Workers and Sheet Metal Workers was formed on 8 November 1913.[18]

The new Union had the usual officers and all were eligible for election after only three months membership if not more than eight weeks in arrears. Only the treasurer and delegates were paid for their services. General members' meetings were held when the management committee considered it necessary. But any member could attend meetings of the committee, though not allowed to vote. Any member, too, had the right to inspect the books, funds, and list of members. During the slack season 'a fair and equitable division of trade' was compulsory in all workshops.

The committee was not allowed to declare a strike in cases of important dispute involving ten or more members without the sanction of a special general members' meeting and they should first do all in their power to settle a dispute amicably. The committee, however, had power to end such a dispute, although neither the committee nor the officers could settle any dispute without the concurrence of the member or members concerned.

The poverty of prospective members was indicated by a ruling that workers wanting to join could pay the entrance fee by instalments if they were not in a position to afford the entire sum at once – the fee was 1s. Anyone who had been a member of a union 'in England or abroad' was accepted as a full member and exempted from paying an entrance fee.

Any member acting contrary to the interest of the Union or working in a shop where there was a strike or lockout could be fined up to £3, which must have seemed a small fortune to members who had to pay 1s by instalments.

L. Lesser was elected secretary, a position he held throughout the life time of the Union. But in May 1914, a deputation consisting of Lichinsky and Octovich asked the London Society not to insist that Lesser sever his connection with the Jewish Union, of which he was secretary, in order to join the London Society, as if he gave up the secretaryship the Union would fail. The committee refused to reconsider their ruling and Lesser chose to remain with the new Union. The initial membership was only 16, but by 1914 they had between 50 and 60 and had a peak of 86 members in 1916. In March 1916 they complained that the London Society was making their members leave the Union and join the London Society and said they would call on all unions to help them fight for their existence. The London Society replied that they were not compelling anyone to join their Society but no man could be a member of two unions.

In the early days of the Society, the general rate was around 6d an hour, although some men were earning £2 a week; contributions were 4d a week. Their funds were hit by a strike lasting six months in one shop in support of a member whose workmates considered to have been victimised. The strike was not closed but the men ran out of money and with no strike pay they began to wander back.

On 13 August 1917 a deputation attended a committee meeting of the London Society to discuss the possibility of a merger. Lesser explained that the majority of members were of military age and five had already enlisted but were keeping up their membership. The remaining 36 were all receiving 1s an hour and were paying 6d a week in contributions, but were prepared to pay the London contributions. All members were allowed to join the Society and credited with 12 months membership in calculating benefits. A couple of weeks later the Union asked about the position of self-determination after the merger, pointing out they would like to continue their own meetings to discuss problems in their own language, Lesser giving an assurance that no action would be taken without the approval of the EC, but it would seem that they got little satisfaction on that score. However, the Union members agreed to fusion and paid their full funds of £70 into the Society. The secretary and president of the Society, on request, addressed the Jewish union before it was officially broken up and the Union, the last organisation specifically for Jewish sheet metal workers, was officially dissolved on 24 November 1917. Reporting the fact, the London EC declared: 'the Jewish Society is now part of the Society, another step to better organisation and solidifying forces in the London area.' This episode of the Union's history ended with the presentation of a silver watch to the last secretary, Lesser, 'for his splendid services', and he went on to play a leading part in the London Society, serving on the committee.

The Zinc Workers

Commenting on three entries in the Liverpool cash book for June 1833 'committee expenses on zinc business', Frances Turner, the historian of the Liverpool Society, says that this was about the time that sheet zinc was first put onto the market and was recognised as a metal that could be worked up into shapes though the method was held to be something of a secret.

The workers in zinc tended to be members of the tin plate workers' societies, or perhaps more correctly, tin plate workers took over the working of zinc. But special zinc workers' societies were formed in London and Birmingham.

The Birmingham and District Operative Zinc Workers' Society, consisting of 'foremen and journeymen zinc workers' had its club house at the Nottingham Arms Inn in Bristol Street at the time of the 1898 rule book.

The London Operative Zinc and Galvanised Iron Workers' Society was founded in 1853 with only 37 members but dropped the latter from its title in 1873.[19] Membership increased to 95 in 1886 but the Society never organised more than one-fifth of the workers in the trade. Nevertheless, income always exceeded expenditure and at one time in the 1890s the value reached the high figure of £11 3s 1½d per member. Strike benefit was then £1 per week and unemployment 2s 6d a day for 36 days and 1s 3d for a further 36 days in any six months.

The secretary, Fast, was very active in the general trade union movement in London in the 1860s. He was an active member of the London Trades Council[20], the Garibaldi demonstration committee, a keen supporter of the *Beehive* newspaper both inside his own Society and outside, and took part in trade union activities to get working men's clubs opened in various parts of London. As the Society's delegate he took part in the London Trades Council activities and his Society gave financial support to many strikes.

The 1901 census recorded 935 zinc workers in London of whom only a little over 100 were members of the Society. By 1913 the Society had changed its name to the Zinc and Copper Roofers and General Sheet Metal Workers' Society, reflecting changes in the work of members. But the change did not bring any increase in membership.

The work consisted of laying zinc and copper 'flats' on roofs and, in the workshops, making cowls, flues, dormers, ventilating work and similar jobs. The centre of the trade was the Euston Road – known to the trade as 'the road'. There were five or six large shops employing up to 90 men regularly throughout the year, as well as a number of small masters who one week would be employing one man and the next a dozen. Besides the permanent staff in the large shops there was always a drifting section of casuals.

About half the men were on day work which was the general rule in the small shops. The employer would price the job in piece-work shops and if no one would accept or there could be no compromise agreement, it would be given out as day-work. Many of the big jobs would last weeks, even months, and were done on a gang system with the men drawing weekly on the job and then settling up at the end, with the employer giving the leader of the gang what was left, for him to divide between the men. If it was a 'dead horse' job they would have to make it up on the next job.

Wage rates at this period, before the First World War, were 8d, 9d or in some cases 10d an hour, giving an average of 36s to £2 a week throughout the year. On the outskirts of London rates were 1d less. Men were paid 'walking time' at normal day work rates for the time it took to get to a job, with 1s 6d a night lodging money if they worked outside London.

A few lads were apprenticed until 21, usually in the smaller shops where they were able to learn every branch of the trade, working under the master. Full members of the Society were allowed to have their sons working with them at rates below the minimum. But generally a lad worked with a man, carrying the tools, holding up and gradually picking up the trade until able to do the work on his own and claim the full rate. Toward the end of the nineteenth century, however, the Society started technical classes in zinc work, open both to Society and non-Society men.

All applicants for membership of the Society had to be earning the minimum rate – in the 1900 rule book this was 8d an hour up to the age of 23 and 9½d at 26 years of age. Those earning less were given four months to comply. No one was admitted under 21 years of age or over 45 and all applicants had to be sponsored by two men 'who can speak of their ability as a workman'. Those joining after the age of 40 had to pay one quarter more contributions, they were entitled to only one-half of the funeral benefit and did not receive sick or superannuation benefits. There was a 3d fine for non-attendance at meetings without a valid reason. Hours were then 54 a week 'and in order to give all men a fair chance of employment, overtime shall be discouraged as far as possible.' Included among the objects of the Society was 'to aid other trade societies having for their object, or one of them, the promotion of the interests of workmen.'

Tentative discussions on possible fusion were held with the London Society which was told that although they wanted to be affiliated to the National Amalgamated, they wanted to remain a zinc workers' society. The membership was generally conservative in outlook but some of the younger members were eager for a change. They had got the impression that the London Society had blocked their bid to join the National Amalgamated. While denying this the London Society indicated they thought it would be better if the zinc workers joined up with the London Society rather than have several similar societies in one town.

The zinc workers secretary, R. Warren, pointed out that they were in a good position with 116 members and funds of over £1,000. They paid lower contributions and had similar benefits to the Tin Plate Workers except that they paid sick benefit, which the London Society did not. A sub-committee of the two societies met to work out proposals, reporting that the London Society had 3,000 members with funds to the value of £5 per member; the zinc workers had 100 members valued at £9 each. Just over half the membership was over 40 years of age. The four members of the zinc workers on superannuation would be taken over and the tin plate workers agreed to accept the two members then in waiting for super with an agreement that there would never be more than four of the zinc workers on super at any one time. The zinc workers were to retain £300 to fund the sick scheme, the other £600 to be paid to the London Society. A ballot of the zinc workers resulted in 60 in favour of fusion and 33 against. It was thought that the big minority against reflected dissatisfaction over the sick scheme agreement. The London Sheet Metal Workers voted in favour of fusion by 1,993 to 48. The amalgamation took place on 31 December 1913, but this was not the end of the story. There was a lot of dissatisfaction and eventually 30 former members of the zinc workers' society resigned – all of them working in Braby's shop – and rejoined the Zinc and Copper Roofers' Society which had been reformed in January 1922. Part of the grievances was the handling of a funeral claim by the EC of the London Society. There can be no doubt these who reformed the old society were those who had voted against fusion in the 1917 ballot.

The Braziers

The London Braziers was an old established society with a guild background.[21] A Friendly Society of Braziers was founded in January 1809, meeting at the White Hart, Chancery Lane. Whether this was the origin of the London Hand in Hand Society, founded in 1827, is not known; nor do we know the position occupied among London braziers by the Operative Braziers' Society, which in 1834 was meeting at the Rockingham Arms.[22] There were also braziers associated with the coppersmiths and brassfounders and, as we have seen, a 'Hand-in-Hand' braziers co-operative was operating in 1834.

A braziers' society was meeting at the Pewter Platter, Charles St, Hatton Garden, in 1825 when it gave financial support to the Bradford wool combers' strike[25] – with other donations and weekly contributions coming from various braziers' shops – and in 1861 the Hand in Hand Society was still meeting there. In 1841 a brazier, William Tipper, of Marylebone was elected to the General Council of the National Chartist Association.[26] The same year the Society was engaged in a strike at Pontifex London shop on the number of apprentices.

A Birmingham Braziers' Society was active in 1843 when its members went on strike over prices. The employers thought the prices being paid were too high and asked the men to draw up a new price list but when they did so the employers would not accept it and offered a new list of their own, 25 per cent lower. The men rejected it and went on strike.[23]

In 1861, a Liverpool Braziers' Society was meeting at the Barlow Mow, Cheapside, another local society, in Bristol, had its club house at the Sportsman Inn, Temple Gate and probably others existed we have not been able to locate. There seems to have been no attempt to form a national society and they probably faded away, their members joining the coppersmiths or sheet metal workers.

The 'braziers' in the titles of some sheet metal workers' societies refers to that method of joining metal and while the members of the braziers' societies did practise this, they were actually copper and brass smiths, working in light gauge metal, and their work and that of the coppersmiths often overlapped. They made such things as tea kettles, kitchen ware, copper bowls for preserving and sugar melting, and long chaldrons for feather dyeing. The rule book of the Hand in Hand Society[24] said they organised men on copper goods and other copper work, either on bright or brown work – the former apparently the light gauge, polished wares for retail sale and the brown work the more commercial and industrial jobs that did not require a highly polished finish. A 1903 report said they were busy before and after Christmas but slack in the summer until the fruit season when jam makers wanted new coppers and sent their old ones in for repair. They were almost entirely on piece-work and at that time were earning 9d to 9½d an hour.

In 1889 the Society had moved along the street to the Sir Ralph Abercrombie Tavern. Its membership was then 76 and apprentices could join the Society after seven years at the trade. Contributions were 1s 3d every monthly meeting night of which they got back a 3d drinks ticket. Members leaving their work unfinished would not be allowed 'benefits from the box', the rule book also stated:

> On all occasions when any free member is under necessity of complaining of undue restriction in the price of his labour, either by day or by the piece, the same shall be forwarded to the committee to consider and if they find he has a just grievance they shall afford the complainant temporary assistance, if required, not to exceed 15s, and shall call a committee as speedily as possible and if the complaint be just make a grant of £1 4s until the grievance can be adjusted or he be found employment.

In 1905 the Society moved to the Coach and Horses, St.John's Square, Clerkenwell, Thomas Whiting was elected secretary and the name was changed to the London Braziers and Sheet Metal Workers Society, organising men 'who had been at their business five years'. In 1911 they were engaged with the London Sheet Metal Workers in a strike and as a result moves were proposed for amalgamation but it was put off because of talks with the coppersmiths who, it was thought, might object as the braziers were more allied to their trade. The following year the braziers asked if the two societies could be federated for the purposes of the Insurance Act. It was not until 1918 that amalgamation moves were again made. Membership had then dropped to 27 with an average age of $58\frac{1}{2}$ years, the oldest being 83 and the youngest 43. Their value per member was £13 and funds totalled £322 15s 1d. The Sheet Metal Workers offered them a calculation of 20 years membership for all benefits, including superannuation. Their benefits were eight weeks at 12s in any one year and dispute 24s, contributions were 2s a week. However, the braziers decided to stay on their own. Their subsequent history was one of decline and death. Their club house had been bombed and they met at the secretary's home. Every year registered more members over 65, more dying, a few of the younger ones resigning to join the sheet metal workers or coppersmiths. Finally in June 1928, when they only had 11 members, it was decided to dissolve the Society 'owing to so many having died', and the monies divided equally among members on the books.

The Organ Pipe Makers

In June 1917, the Society received a letter from R. Nichols, secretary of the Organ Pipe Makers Society, asking for a meeting to discuss the fusion of the two societies. At that meeting it was said they had only 20 members in London, with four or five in the army. But they produced a list of 60 unorganised men working in various non-union shops in London. There were also others in different parts of the country. Their rates of pay were 8d to 9d an hour and Union contributions 6d a week. Although they were highly skilled they had no form of apprenticeship.

It was explained that members not only made the pipes, they also made the metal from which the pipes were made and part of their skill lay in getting the right mixture, as this was essential for getting the right tone. Tin, lead and zinc were used in various mixtures with the tin content varying from 20 to 90 per cent; increasing the tin content brightened the tone to 'string quality'. Broad tones were produced by an alloy rich in lead. Most modern organ pipes contained a number of 'spotted metal' pipes of 50 to 55 per cent tin. Tin alloys in this range produced large crystals or 'spots' and provided a particularly rich tone. The metal was cast on a 12ft long table of York stone, covered by a thick layer of fustian overlaid with glazed linen. The stirred molten metal was poured into a wooden trough on runners stretching the width of the table and trundled along its whole length, the metal escaping from the trough to leave a thin, semi-liquid sheet of shimmering 'spotted metal'. The edges were then cleaned, the metal rolled into a pipe, a V scraped along the seam which was then soldered. The men then cut and shaped the pipe and fitted the conical sections and ends, making bends and slots. A big organ could have 'hundreds' of pipes, the pitch depending on the length.

The London Society committee considered their skill merited a higher rate of pay and that this could be achieved with the backing of the London Society and the unorganised men brought in. Merger terms were agreed, London taking over the pipe makers' funds and crediting their members with two years' membership for benefit purposes.

Tin Case Makers

Around this immediate pre-war period the EC considered proposals that the tin case makers be brought into the Union. This was a small specialised section of the tin plate trade making packing cases for the export market, organised in their own section of the London Wood and Tin Packing Case Trade Society. There was some overlapping with Society members in packing case shops while case makers worked in the canning industry and a few in meter shops. An unsuccessful strike in 1912 for a recognised rate left them worse off than before, some shops closed and although a few members were getting 8d an hour most were on 5d and 6d. In this situation the EC rejected merger proposals although Gordon, the National secretary, told a London meeting that tin case makers were already members of the Manchester, Bradford and Bolton Societies, that Glasgow and Birmingham also organised them and the situation was working well.

After a strike over boy-labour, Hammond, the case makers' secretary, applied to the Society for a working agreement and recognition of each other's cards in a bid to fight dilution – they had 60 to 70 members on tin work in London and all their cards were stamped 'tin section'. An increasing number worked in Society shops as the war progressed and many of them stayed on after the war. A further merger proposal in 1917 brought a report from the committee 'their tinmen do not think themselves as good as ours and would not be able to do some of our work, but they were all handy men and no doubt, with practice, they would be able to pick up some lines.' The EC again turned down the suggestion for taking them in en bloc but ruled they could be accepted individually.

Other Societies

During the war applications came from a number of small craft societies, whose members were not on war work, to allow their members to work in tin plate workshops for the duration. The general attitude of the London Society was that if they could do the job and the men would work with them, they would be accepted, but they would have to join the Society. The majority of these were silversmiths, said to be good craftsmen and expecting to return to their trade after the war, although some remained in the Society. It was reported that already at the end of 1914, 11 members of the Gold, Silver and Allied Trades Society were at Short's Rochester, all of them working to sheet metal workers' rules, although the shop was unorganised. In 1917 members of the scientific instrument makers were working in gas meter shops and proposed joint moves to get a wage increase but the EC was affronted and their proposal was brushed aside. The following year the Musical Instrument Makers were told that their members could work in Society shops, only if they joined the London Society. Then in 1919 Thorpe, the secretary of the wire workers, suggested amalgamation with the London Society. They were formed in 1871 and had 140 members working both day and piece work but thought it best to join up with a stronger organisation. In view of the coming formation of the National Union, they were asked to delay the proposal for three months.

Craft to Industry

Throughout this period the Society was trying to grapple with the problems arising from fundamental changes in its whole basis with the beginnings of its own industrial revolution from a local craft based trade society towards a national union based on industry. In the early years of the new century the dislocation caused by the decline of the old domestic tin ware trade which had been the early basis for its existence, coupled with ever increasing periods of economic depression, elevated unemployment and under employment to a major problem.

In 1908, trade was so bad that the Society lost £1,100 in unemployment pay and arrears of contributions. A special committee reported that unemployment must now be regarded as a permanent feature of the trade, both in times of boom and depression, and was bound to increase with the introduction of more and more labour saving machinery. It was the inevitable development of the present system of production for profit. The number of members working in the general trade had greatly diminished. Machinery, speeding up and sectionalisation had displaced many men in the gas meter section. Ship repair work had largely left London. On the other side of the coin, a number of motor shops had sprung up. However, their existence was not known to the office until they had been largely manned by non-union labour.

One suggested line of action was to opt out of the system through co-operative production. It was rejected by the majority because of lack of capital, difficulty of getting work, and doubts that it would solve the unemployment problem anyway – the movement had a long history of failed co-operative schemes that could not be forgotten.

Eventually, two proposals were accepted, the complete organisation of the trade and the institution of a limit or 'maximum target' on piecework earnings. This was said to be already in operation in some shops. It stopped some men earning 'excessively high wages' and so menacing prices, and also helped to spread work. It was agreed by 243 votes to 29 to circularise the shops asking them to fix their own limits, so starting a practice that became a feature of the trade, strictly controlled in the strongly organised shops with fines imposed on any who 'broke the shop limit'.

The Society took part in the 'Right to Work' Movement and its banner was out to lead a contingent of members on an unemployment demonstration through the West End. It also sent a delegate to a more respectable two-day conference on unemployment at the Guildhall. There was strong feeling among the long-term unemployed that they were not getting a fair deal. They took part in more rowdy, 'unofficial' demonstrations to the annoyance of officials, invaded Parkinson and Cowan's meter shop complaining of the shop working overtime when men were out of work, and threatened to break up the clique they said were keeping unemployment benefits down. They were admonished by the committee which then went on to decide that members who had been out of work for two years should get the Christmas grant and members in the workhouse should receive 2s.

Almost as soon as the new London prices book was issued in 1900 there was grave concern in the Society at the decline of general work. A special meeting in September 1906 discussed the problem of the big London general shops which were no longer making the mass of wares they sold but bought in from cut price makers.

Hardings, who at one time employed 100 men, now only had 50; Wilson, Parkins and Lewis who had a total of 150 were down to 90; Spokes only had seven or eight men on special work and Keeves were in the process of getting rid of their last eight or ten men, saying that they could buy in at about half the cost of making in the shop.

Most of the ware was supplied by the Midlands, but some of the commoner kind was made in the Jewish and other shops in East and South London.

The London Society called a meeting of representatives from the Midlands to discuss the whole unsatisfactory position. Six London shops were represented as well as three shops from Birmingham and the secretaries of the Birmingham and Wolverhampton societies. Smith, the Wolverhampton secretary said they were in a similar position to London; one shop which had employed 90 men now only had five and for ten years general work had been seen as a dying trade. Birmingham, on the other hand, said they were busier than they had been for 10 or 12 years with about 150 men on general work. When asked about producing a prices book as they had promised they said they had no intention of adjusting their prices to suit London when they had not been consulted about the London book.

The EC later agreed that Birmingham competition and machinery were the main causes of the trouble, together with the uncontrolled employment of female and boy labour, the mixing of piecework and day work, low minimum rates, the failure to bring out a prices book, sectionalisation coupled with machine made parts produced in factories where Union members were not allowed. The Society should try and control machinery – the knife, rollers, angle benders and folders were all claimed as tinmen's tools in general shops but in meter shops they were used by labourers, this should be altered. Sectionalisation was already a danger and would be more so in the future in meter and motor shops. Although men working in shops with sectionalisation and machinery were actually earning more than men in traditional shops, the EC warned that indiscriminate sectionalisation would mean the ruin of the trade. It was decided that where large quantities were involved sectionalisation could be accepted but the extent must be decided by the EC as cases arose. Although it was pointed out that female labour was in the trade to stay, and the Union should recognise this and try and control it, it was decided that a protest be sent to Birmingham that the prevalance of female and uncontrolled boy labour in the Midlands was detrimental to all branches of the trade, at the same time advising them to increase their minimum rate to somewhere near the standard achieved in London.

This brought an angry riposte from Stevens who accused London of dictating to them as well as encouraging sweating, the premium bonus system, piecemastering and the prevalence of female and Jewish labour, and refused to apologise. The bickering, arising from the attempts of the local societies to get for their own members as big a slice as possible of the decreasing amount of work, showed the increasing need for a national union to replace the many local societies.

Most of the displaced general workers got jobs as motor work increased and other doors opened to new avenues of work.

One of these was the ventilating trade. In 1897 the organising committee called a meeting of men working in ventilating shops. About 50 turned up from four shops. They complained that work was being made up in the shops at 8d an hour but was being fitted on the sites by joiners and bricklayers at 11d and 1s an hour. They were ashamed to mention their wages when working on building sites. It was decided to go in for 9d an hour but there was little enthusiasm for action to back up the claim. These years before the war saw a great development in heating and ventilating work with the great number of large buildings going up, changing the whole face of London, but there were only sporadic attempts to organise the shops where the trunking and equipment was being made.

Organising

Already in 1897 concern was being expressed at the poor organisation of the trade and the rigidity of the rules which interfered with recruitment especially the ruling that applicants for membership must be in receipt of the recognised rate. This was a major consideration of the whole pre-war period. A suggestion was made to get round this by allowing a six month probationary period. It was reported that there were men in many shops who would like to join but who were stopped by the earnings rule. In 1906 the secretary was asked to get out a list of shops to be organised so that they could be visited in a systematic way and the following year two members of the EC were made responsible for organising. There were said to be tinmen not in the Union at Chelmsford, Slough and other places in outer London, as well as in Woolwich, Fulham and Hammersmith. Proposals were made for a full-time organiser to be appointed as there were many shops to be visited, meter shops as well as motor and lampmaking shops, many had lapsed and municipal work was being done in 'hole and corner shops'. The proposal was turned down on account of cost and there not being enough work for a man full time. In 1910 a six-member committee was elected to work with the EC and officers on the question of systematically organising the whole of London district, covering all sections of the trade. The state of organisation in the motor shops was particularly poor and low wages and piecemastering persisted in coachbuilding.

The following year the committee issued a printed report. Special efforts should be made to organise shops springing up in and around London and other towns in the area. Known shops should be visited to extend the Society's sphere of influence. J.C. Gordon reported that he had visited motor shops in a number of places; there were groups of men working in Reading, Bedford, Peterborough, Huntingdon, and Luton. He had found 12 men working at the latter but the PB system was rife and he could not see his way clear to forming a branch. It was proposed that when a shop was organised it should be visited periodically. There was a lot of arrears among all sections and effective control should be maintained to ensure that Union rates and conditions were observed. It was reported in October 1912 that as a result of all this activity, 300 had been added to the roll and the total membership was 1,833.

The Meter Shops

The gas meter shops, a continuing and relatively stable section of the trade, were not exempt from the problems arising from changing patterns of industry, despite the meter makers' own strong organisational set up.

In the 1890s a considerable amount of non-unionism was reported in meters, as in the trade generally. It was not until 1897 that the old established firm of G. Glover's became a trade shop, yet Mr Glover had no objection, merely hoping that his older employees would not be forced to join. In the event, one man aged 77 and a number over 60 put in applications to join. Cowan's London shop organisation had also been allowed to slip as a number of members had accumulated arrears of contributions and been allowed to lapse.

In some shops women and boys had been recruited as cheap labour. In 1892, as 50 years before, Wright's was a main source of trouble, first over prices and a charge of victimisation then, in 1895, on the employment of women and boys. The two London societies jointly warned that they could not allow female labour on gas meters and when the management ignored this, Union members were withdrawn and the shop picketed.

A couple of months later, it was reported that Wright's were getting parts stamped and employing boys on rows of benches, on a kind of simple line production, each boy doing a section of the work, passing the job along the line from one to another until it was completed. They were paid 16s a week and no skilled men were employed in the shop. This attempt to do without skilled meter makers did not succeed – perhaps the work of unskilled women and boys would not pass the stringent tests to which each meter is subjected at the public testing stations. Whatever the reason, Wright's came under new management the following year and reverted to the employment of Society members only.

Another bitter and long drawn out dispute over the employment of women took place in Cowan's Edinburgh shop in 1897, which soon affected all the main gas meter making centres with shops in Manchester, Wolverhampton and Cowan's 90 strong London shop giving the Edinburgh men their solid backing. Faced with this united opposition, the firm pledged that no more women would be recruited, those recently started would be withdrawn and women would all gradually be eliminated on meter work.

Cowan's London shop was a source of trouble of a different sort when it was first established. The works were in Smith Square on the site now occupied by Transport House, not far from the House of Commons, and Members of Parliament and other VIPs complained of the noise of hammering early in the mornings, so the men were not allowed to start work until 8.30 am instead of the usual 6.30 am.

In the 1890s the gas meter trade received a boost with the introduction of the pre-paid or slot meter. Not only was there much more work in these than in the old 'ordinary' meter but there was also a great increase in demand as many more people could afford a penny in the slot than could meet a quarterly bill. Gas had come to the people. About the same time the incandescent gas mantle was introduced, giving a much brighter light, and so helping to stimulate the demand for gas. Most of these new meters were hand made and of intricate shape (at least one well known manufacturer was producing completely hand-made meters until the end of the First World War). All this meant the recruitment of a lot more meter makers, many of them coming from the old declining general shops.

A survey on the eve of the war showed that meter makers were getting an average of 1s an hour, with a maximum of 1s 3d, against an average general trade rate of 10d.

With the end of the war the trade experienced another boom. Four and a half years with few meters being made, plus a backlog of repairs, was a bonus in itself. But that was not all: gas was now being put to new uses. Instead of its sole domestic function being lighting, gas was now increasingly being used for cookers, fires and heaters. This made obsolete the old '3 light' and '5 light' meters, which with their 18 feet and 30 feet an hour, did not have the capacity to pass sufficient gas to operate these new facilities. So new meters were designed, able to pass 150 and 200 feet an hour, bringing a lot more work in the shape of replacements.

But the section got a shock at the end of 1911 with the threat of a foreign invasion when a German firm opened a warehouse in Birmingham, offering cut price meters. The Leicester Corporation was the first to be tempted, ordering an initial 3,000 but Union and employers co-operated to fight this and after a visit to the Leicester Corporation the order was withdrawn and ended that particular attempt at foreign invasion. Another aspect of joint working occurred about the same time with the request from the employers for collaboration in getting together a strong skilled labour force to staff new meter shops being opened in Nottingham. Together with the Wolverhampton Society the London Meter Stewards' Association helped recruit men from London, the Midlands, Manchester, Bury and Exeter and also helped to ensure that the men received the meter rate.

Typical London gas meter shop between the wars; this photograph was taken in 1936

One of the last actions of the meter stewards association before the outbreak of the war was to call a meeting of shop delegates to consider recommendations of the meter pricing committee on new prices for industrial meters. These were referred to as 'big meters' although, as with domestic meters, new designs had replaced the old panel meters for industrial use that could be the size of a double door. The new industrial meters were anything up to five feet high and were a completely hand made job made up out of the flat from sheets of Manchester plate. The war put the recommendations into cold storage and closed the discussion for the duration.

Since the beginning of the century the meter section had been improving its organisation and quietly raising their rates through delegate meetings and conferences with the employers, reinforced with small strikes here and there. This was continued on into the war. In 1916 a conference with the employers procured a war bonus but a claim for overtime rates for pieceworkers was put off for 12 months or the end of the war. A few months later the Society's officials met the employers at a Leeds conference to press a claim for a 25 per cent increase, 'but they were out-generalled and got nothing.'

A number of meter shops made a limited amount of meters during the war and some repairs were also carried out. But most of the younger members went into aircraft shops and most of the floor space in the meter shops themselves was given over to war work with mess tins and ammunition boxes turned out by the million, together with sub-contract aircraft work, Parkinson's, for example made 12 gallon and later 15 gallon petrol tanks for Sopwith Camel fighter planes.

Lamp Makers

The 1901 census recorded 532 lantern, lamp and candlestick makers in London, and that did not count those registered as tin plate workers or sheet metal workers who were employed on lamp making. The London 1901 prices book lists 21 different lamps, all of a number of sizes or other variations with special lamps for police, customs houses, lamplighters, pawnbrokers, butchers, contractors and servants. Also, not listed, were shops making railway, ships and carriage lamps. A report a few years later claimed that except for the output of a few carriage lamp makers and art metal workers, few lamps were being made in London and wrote off lampmaking as a dying trade. The Society seemed to concur in this as in 1903 it merged the lamp and general work committee. But within a few years there was a great resurgence due to the rise of the cycle and motor industries.

Motors

The first references we find to the motor industry in the books of the Union was, appropriately, from the Midlands with a report from the Birmingham secretary, J.V. Stevens, that they already had five members working in motor shops and 'earning good money'.

That was in 1897, and the same year he was writing to the London Society enquiring about 'motor car lanterns' being made at Braby's and requesting information about other firms that were engaged on that work. He also enquired about the price being paid for 'heaters for motor cars' – possibly referring to ignition tubes.

It was this accessory type of work that seemed to engage London motor shops in those very early days. A meeting was held to price acetylene lamps for buses. The following year the men at Randall's were making dust caps for motor cars – reportedly earning $11\frac{3}{4}$d an hour with the employer wanting a cut because of 'the fierce competition, especially from a French house'.

At both the Incandescent Co. and Salisbury's there were bitter and protracted disputes in 1903 and 1904 about the price of making motor car tail lamps, which turned into a battle about female labour.

Salisbury's advertised in *Vorwarts*, the German Social Democratic Party's paper, for lampmakers and three or four Germans turned up for work, but when the pickets told them there was a dispute on they returned home, their fares and expenses paid by the Union, as did a Frenchman and men from other parts of Britain. The Society contacted the German trade union, which circularised a report to all German papers with information about the strike.

The committee tried to take the case to arbitration but Salisbury refused. The Society was more concerned with getting the women taken off the job but Salisbury would not discuss it, insisting that he must have cheap female labour to compete with the Midlands and the Continent, although Stevens denied there were any women on motor lamps in Birmingham. The Society intimated that if extra facilities were provided they would be prepared to consider reducing the price but in no circumstances would they allow women to be introduced onto motor work, although by that time the infant motor industry was staffed by largely unorganised labour. Salisbury then took his machines and work to Germany but soon returned. The dispute cost the Union well over £1,000 but this, the first real struggle for the Union in the motor industry, seems to have ended inconclusively.

But London was also beginning to develop a reputation as a top class coachbuilding centre.

In 1901, H.J. Mulliner, of Mayfair, started making bodies for Di Dion and Benz using a large amount of aluminium. They also built bodies on Daimler, Rolls Royce and Napier chassis. Already in 1898 the first petrol buses, built on Daimler chassis, were running on the streets of London. By 1904 Talbot, Vauxhall and Napier cars were being built in London. Around 1905 many of the best known names in the coach building trade were becoming established, Mulliners being followed by Barker's, Hooper's, Thrupp and Mabberley, Windover's and Cunard, with, in the Home Counties, Salmond's of Newport Pagnell, Vincent's of Reading and Maythorne of Biggleswade.

New doors were opening in this rapidly expanding industry and the old tin plate workers were pushing their way through, developing new skills as sheet metal workers, especially the new line of panel beaters who became something of an élite grouping in the trade, in such demand that they could command their own rate. In one South London shop, the panel beaters turned up for work wearing 'Churchill' type hard hats and carrying their dinner in Gladstone bags. The woodwork of the old coach builders had given way to steel and aluminium, leather wings had been replaced by metal, usually soldered or rivetted, to be followed by the domed wing, beaten out by hand – shaping a pair of 3 inch domed wings was considered a hard day's work. The whole back of the bodies with their double curvature sweep, was made in one piece, as was the dash, finished all over with the planishing hammer. All jobs were hand hammered, doors being shaped on the anvil head with a four pound hammer and planished. On some jobs valences and shields were hand seamed. The wheel was now being more widely used but many still preferred the power hammer.

The Society had a running battle against the premium bonus system in which the time was fixed for a job by the management and if the man did it quicker than the time allowed he got a bonus of only half the time saved, the other half going to the management, and without any safeguard that times would not be reduced. The main protagonist in the operation of PB was the Daimler Co. in Coventry and although the London Society took part in national meetings and had a number of men working in Daimler's, the main burden of the struggle was in the Midlands. However, PB was operated quite widely in the motor trade, in London as well as elsewhere, and caused some hesitation over organising shops where it was in use.

It was not until 1904 that London got around to fixing a minimum rate for motor work, deciding on 9d at a meeting of the general work pricing committee who did not even feel the need to invite any motor shop to attend. By then a number of firms were paying more than that, Rothchild et Fils, a trade shop, was paying 11d. No real attempt had been made to organise the motor shops when in 1906 the committee was told of a works at Willesden Junction, the Albany Silent Safety Car Co., employing some 30 tinmen at 50s a week. Although men there had asked for a visit of the officials it was not until ten months later that they went and called a meeting at which 32 men turned up, 13 of them non-unionist. All handed in application forms and a secretary and shop committee was elected, two each from the radiator and bonnet shops, to make Albany the first trade shop among the London motor manufacturers.

The secretary reported that about 35 sheet metal workers at Napier's wanted to join the Society. They were of many different nationalities but had an interpreter. The committee called a meeting and although only ten men turned up, one, acting as pro-tem secretary brought 14 filled in forms from men who were working. Three were for men from Riga, two from Vilna, two from Divinsk, and one each from Libau, Warsaw, Berlin and Cologne. Nearly all were working under a bonus system and were earning between 34s and 38s a week. The committee seems to have recognised that if they were to organise the motor trade they must be prepared to countenance some unorthodox methods of payment. At another meeting four months later the Napier men reported that they had started a shop fund and were getting out a book of shop rules.

The Society organised the string of garages of the Taxi Cab Co. and also the garages of the Vanguard bus service where all the 18 men on bus and radiator work had come out on a 16 week strike in support of the Union at a cost of £300.

After repeated calls to the committee to do something about organising the motor shops they asked for a list of names. Most of those quoted were small sub-contract shops employing a few panel beaters, or making radiators, wings, bonnets, tanks and exhaust silencers. But they also included the coach builders who now included Van den Plas of Acton, Park Ward and Mulliners of Chiswick. Rates varied, anything from 8d to 1s. A number of shops were operating the premium bonus system or were paying below the rate, employed piecemasters or an excessive amount of boy labour, which meant that the Union would not touch them. Most of the actual organising seems to have been done by Union members moving into unorganised shops and signing-up the men they worked beside. By this means Panhard and a number of other firms became Union shops. Often conditions could also be improved providing there was the will to do something about it. Members at Van den Plas came out when the firm put boys on panel jobs and the firm promptly withdrew them. A lightning strike at Napier's persuaded the management to substitute straight piece work for the premium bonus they had intended. But the old protest of leaving the job lost the Union the Motor Appliances shop when the firm insisted on keeping 23 boys to 11 men and the EC just withdrew members.

In a move to raise rates of pay in the motor shops it was only with great reluctance that the officials were given full powers to negotiate piece-work prices when suitable day-work rates could not be obtained and a motor work pricing committee was elected to maintain rank-and-file control. A survey on the eve of the war in connection with the claim for a 10d an hour minimum found that 150 to 160 men in 54 shops were already on or above that rate while a similar number were still lagging behind.

At the end of 1913 the first works' committee was formed at Darracq with a member of the London Society elected as its chairman but in line with its old policy of keeping aloof from entanglements with other unions in negotiations, the EC decided by four to one that 'Society members should steer clear of works committees.'

Aircraft

The newest of all industries to attract the labour and skills of the sheet metal workers at this period was aircraft, though until 1914 only a handful of members worked in the industry. With their wood and linen wings and fuselage there was not a lot of work for metal workers – mainly fuel and oil tanks, engine cowlings and wheel spats – and production was small.

Most aircraft work was more or less experimental. Harold Blackburn, who later became London district secretary, said:

> The craftsmen were called on to give a far greater degree of technical knowledge coupled with practical efficiency than was generally expected in other branches of the trade. Sheet metal workers had, to all intents and purposes, to train managements, along with draughtsmen and designers, the fundamentals of the trade.

These were the pioneers, engaged on such legendary planes as the Sopwith Camel.

Little or nothing was done by the Union to see that members working on aircraft received wages commensurate with the very high degree of skill that was called for. Providing members

Sheet metal and metal spinning shops, Boulton & Paul, Norwich, during the First World War

received the prevailing minimum district rate, that seemed to be sufficient. The officials gave little or no leadership on wage rates, according to Blackburn. 'In the years from 1915 to 1918 the earning capacity of the Union's members was increased according to the strength of the shop organisation, without any set policy by the national executive.' From documents available, this would seem to be a valid criticism. Officials were quite prepared to negotiate and press for the demands made by the members working on aircraft, but they were only responding to rank and file action, not formulating policy. When a promise by the authorities to give civilian workers at RAF Farnborough a rise to bring their money up to £2 5s for a 48-hour week was not honoured, no action was taken by the Union. But as members from all branches of the trade were drafted into the industry rank and file wages movements were set up and by 1916 they were operating in RAF Farnborough, Sopwith's of Kingston and the Aircraft Co., Hendon.

It was also action by members in the shops that maintained Union conditions. A proposal by the Farnborough authorities to put women on cutting out was quietly shelved when the shop organised a protest meeting. Sopwith's proposed introducing the premium bonus system and expressed surprise that the tin shop should oppose the system when others accepted it but when the Union's position was explained to the management they dropped the idea as they would 'do nothing to upset the sheet metal department.' Action by the shop was also responsible for bringing the nine nons into the Union. In 1917 the military director at Farnborough announced a decision to introduce piecework and open a rate-fixing department and was told that if such a scheme were brought in the men would down tools.

It was not until May 1917, when firms doing aircraft work were springing up everywhere, that it was decided to fix a standard rate for aircraft work. A meeting of shop delegates was held and a claim was put in for a 1s 1d an hour minimum. Although some firms agreed that this was fair, when it went to a meeting of the aircraft employers' association it was rejected out of hand by the chairman, the only one to speak, and he refused to put forward any alternative proposal. The aircraft sheet metal workers' answer was to set up an association of secretaries and chairmen of aircraft shops, with monthly meetings and special sub-committee meetings as required. Within three months it was reported that Fairey, Brown and Melhuish, Regent, Handley Page, Nieuport and Thrupp and Mabberley were paying the increase. A mass meeting at 'the Ring' stadium, Blackfriars, called by the stewards' association and addressed by H.J. Crucefix and R.B. Pattison, secretary and chairman of the association, put in for a 1s 3d minimum. After a two-week strike the men were persuaded by the Union to go to arbitration, where they lost, blaming the officials.

Gordon, the general secretary of the Amalgamated, warned that the then methods of working was not producing results and unless members on aircraft work agreed to some form of payment by results they would be faced with dilution. The stewards' association spokesmen strongly opposed piecework and insisted that it would only be accepted after the employers had acceded to the claim for 1s 1d plus 25 per cent. This was only granted after what they called 'a cessation of work' which lasted two weeks. Surveying the action in March 1918 the association complained that owing to the structure of the Union only the one district had been called out and that while they were on strike their work had been sent to other parts of the country where it had been done by members of other local societies. They had been blacklegging on the London aircraft workers and a demand was made for solid amalgamation so that this could not happen again. With the advent of piece-work the association formed an aircraft pricing committee of seven members whose task was to enquire into the prices of jobs in various shops and advise shops in the section on the position. As a result of this action Pattison was elected to the EC. He resigned so that he could help in the build-up of the campaign, preferring to work with the Association as secretary, and was re-elected to the EC when the campaign was concluded, J.E. Adams succeeding him as secretary of the Association.

The motor and aircraft industries, developed under wartime pressures, brought new problems of organisation for the Society. It was decided that the large influx of semi-skilled workers connected with the trade must be organised by the Society if it were to have any control over them. A special auxilliary section was organised with its own rule book setting out rates and benefits but the Society chose to ignore the problem of whether trainee wounded soldiers and women dilutees should also be organised.

1. S. Timmins, *Resources, Production and Industrial History of Birmingham*, London 1866.
2. Ibid.
3. *Journal of the Statistical Society*, Vol. 11, 1848.
4. *London Trades Council, A History*, London 1950.
5. *Newcastle Courant*, January 1867.
6. International Working Men's Association MS minute book, Bishopsgate Institute.
7. *Beehive*, 15 November 1862.

8. J.O.N. Butter, *The Advantage of Gas Light in Private Houses*, London 1840.
9. Institute of Gas Engineers' Journals.
10. Edinburgh Public Library, Edinburgh Room, JYN 1213.832.
11. *Important Trade Union Case*. Report of Proceedings at Middlesex Sessions, 21 June 1886 before Mr P.H. Edlin, Assistant Judge, R V Lowe and Jordan, Amalgamated Society of Tin Plate Workers, London 1886.
12. BLP&ES Webb Collection.
13. *Ironmonger*, 22 September 1900.
14. Kidd, op. cit.
15. BLP&ES Webb Collection.
16. *Beehive*, 3 November 1866.
17. Charles Booth, *Life and Labours of the People of London*, London 1903.
18. PRO FS11/197.
19. Booth, op. cit.
20. *Beehive*, various.
21. PRO FS3.
22. *Pioneer*, 29 March 1834.
23. BLP&ES, Webb Collection.
24. Braziers Hand in Hand Society, Rule Book, Trades Union Congress.
25. *Trades Newspaper*, January 1826.
26. *Northern Star*, 8 February 1841.

Other material used in this chapter has been taken from the books of the various tin plate workers' societies still in the possession of the Union.

CHAPTER FIVE

Around the Country

It might be interesting and useful at this stage to take a look at the local tin plate workers in various parts of the country, their activities, organisation and changing work patterns. This period was one of changes, from a trade based on many small local societies, mainly engaged on hand-made domestic ware, toward a single national union with a more industrial outlook.

The Scottish Societies

The Glasgow Society was reorganised in 1833, the second attempt to get the Society into running order, with 34 tinmen taking part in the inaugural meeting. The previous effort had lasted six months but the members taking part had agreed not to take out the money they had contributed but to leave it as a basis for another go. This reorganised Society differed from its predecessors in that it included in its territory the whole of Scotland, proclaimed in its title: The United Tin Plate Workers Protective Society of Scotland – Western Division. We do not know what happened to the Society which existed in 1825 or how long Glasgow tinmen were without an organisation but it cannot have been very long as the new society retained the records of the old.

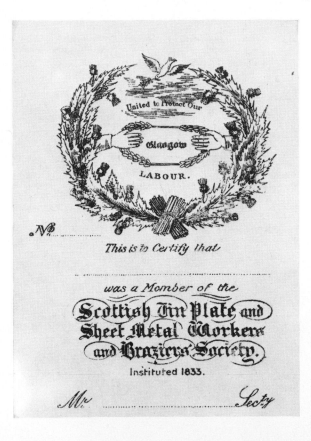

Among these records was the Glasgow Journeymen Tin Plate Workers' list of prices agreed with the manufacturers' committee in December 1825 after their long and bitter strike. The prices book also included working regulations agreed by the journeymen's committee headed by the secretary, William Strath. They laid down that

> a man going into the country to work to be allowed bed and board. A piece workman, taken off his regular work for any length of time less than five hours, to be paid one-sixth in addition to the average of his regular wages. A man's labour to be ten working hours daily.

The refurbished, new-look Society came into

being in April 1833. The need for strong organisation was urgent with local wages only 14s for a week of 66 hours. The preamble to the 1833 rules puts the situation that then existed: 'There can be few arguments wanting to convince us of the fact that we, as operatives, are descending rapidly in the scale. The trade is rapidly being encroached upon.

Their first annual report, issued on 14 April 1834, mentioned recent strikes from which the men failed to get what they considered their due. As the report otherwise records the success and prosperity of the Society the strikes could have been the cause of a disintegration of the old Society and the need for a reorganisation. It goes on to say

> This attempt to form a union has been laughed at by some in the trade, they have taunted us with our failure more than once already, and allege that we are again doomed to disappointment ... [but] ... if all the journeymen tinmen in Scotland were united, could they not force, where resistance is encountered, a reasonable demand? Is it possible, or at all likely that we would permit one half of the employers of Glasgow to compel their workmen to work one hour longer each day than the other half is doing, and in almost every case, with wages considerably less?

But the report declared that the Society would not use force, except the force of argument to get the nons to join. It went on to reply to insinuations by the press that union members were misguided men, keeping the office-bearers in idleness. It pointed out that only one official was paid, directly or indirectly, their rewards were more often to be marked out as victims of employers' resentment.

The constitution indicated that the organisation was designed to unite existing clubs or societies throughout Scotland on a purely trade basis. The country was divided into three districts: Glasgow was to act as head of the western division as well as the parent body of the whole organisation, Edinburgh was the governing society in the east and Aberdeen in the north. Within a few months Dundee, at its own request, was given responsibility for the central division with the task of organising neighbouring towns. The four societies seem to have been autonomous bodies as each was to act for the others in collecting contributions and paying out benefits for members of the other societies working in their area. That there were local societies is indicated in the 1844 report which mentions a tramp from Inverness where nine tinmen were recorded in 1831 census. Others from Arbroath, Ayr and Montrose appear in other records of the early 1840s.

The subscriptions were realistically set at only 2d per week and the proposal was to make wide use of levies on members to pay for specific needs. Out-of-work benefit was 4s a week for four weeks and dispute benefit 6s a week for a single man and 10s for marrieds. In the case of 'calamity', application had to be made to the branch secretary who would consult all other branches on what amount of help could be expected.

In contrast to the usual procedure of the time, the rules stated:

> 'As the compulsory recourse to fines to force the acceptance of office or attendance at meetings has a tendancy to generate disquietude, we leave to those who may be chosen to give consciencious attendance to the trust imposed on them.

Among the officers was a Corresponding Secretary as well as a separate Glasgow secretary. The branch was run by a committee of six, three elected from Glasgow and three taken from the roll. Very soon there were small but active sub-branches in Paisley and Greenock, each with its own secretary.

Despite their protestations of conciliation and pacific intentions, members were soon having to fight for the right to belong to a union. There were strikes with two separate employers in

Glasgow and another in Greenock. The first two ended in quick victory, the Greenock business taking rather longer. The Society then set about reducing the hours of work. First they dealt with the shops, about one-half the total, who were working one hour longer than the rest. This done, in 1837 they succeeded, within one month, in reducing the general hours of work from eleven hours a day to ten, without loss of earnings. They then went on to get a 2s advance in wages throughout the city.

In 1841 new laws were drafted for a more up-to-date administration, with friendly society benefits – giving sick, idle (unemployment), funeral and dispute benefits. The Society changed its name to the United Tin Plate Workers Sick and Protecting Society for Scotland, Western Division. The report proudly stated that the Society 'had upwards of £172 at our command.' If used with caution, together with the activity of the members it 'must be a great object in stopping avaritious [*sic*] employers from taking advantage of us – of our lawful rights.' In this year they succeeded in getting agreement on 'dropping out' at 4 o'clock on Saturdays.

The year 1841/2, the beginning of the 'Hungry Forties', was one of

> unprecedented melancholy throughout the Empire. Operatives of every class have and still are feeling its scourge ... Nothing but the strong bonds of that Union which has so firmly cemented us could have prevented our utter subjugation, but for it we must have been in the hands of many of our employers as clay in the hands of the potter, acted upon as their lust for greed directed, ... [though] ... avarice did indeed put forth her unrelenting hand to prey on some of our Members.

Even so, the membership was down to 65 for Glasgow, seven for Paisley and seventeen for Greenock. Rebuilding the membership was a long and patient business but by 1847 the numbers had grown to 126. By that time both the Paisley and Greenock sub-branches had disappeared from the annual reports.

In 1847 the designation 'Western District' was dropped from the title, in 1850 the separate secretary from Glasgow was discontinued and in 1854 the name was changed to the United Tin Plate Sick and Providing Society of Glasgow.

But Glasgow seems to have continued as the parent Society for the rest of Scotland. In 1855 Aberdeen was complaining to Glasgow of trouble with a number of employers who were installing machinery to make herring cases, using men engaged for tinning to cut, square and prepare cases, and using labourers for rivetting plates. Supported by Glasgow, the branch warned the employers not to interfere with tinmen's work. The same year, Aberdeen was asking Glasgow's permission to elect a committee with John Eade as secretary. This was approved after a lot of discussion. But the following month the Glasgow committee decided that all Aberdeen business, except for collecting money, examining claims for sick and 'idle aliment', and funerals, would be subjected to revision by Glasgow. Later, Aberdeen was given permission to have employers apply to their committee for men, and the branch was allowed to keep £10 in hand. In March 1857, when 47 Aberdeen members were excluded for non-payment, the Glasgow committee discussed the reasons for a falling off in membership in the Northern city. But they still decided that there could be no office in Aberdeen, the men there should correspond with Glasgow. Their present laws would not allow the Glasgow Society to be part of a federal union.

However, by 1864 Aberdeen had again become independent. In August of that year a meeting of the Aberdeen Operative Society of Tin Plate Workers urged that a connection be opened between the two societies, that Glasgow recognise the Aberdeen Society, and that each should recognise one another's tramps. This was agreed to and Glasgow decided that men going to Aberdeen 'be given tramp cards as in the case with members going to England and

Ireland.' Men staying there should remain members of the Glasgow Society.

With the demise of the Paisley and Greenock branches, organised tin plate workers in both towns were treated as country members of the Glasgow branch. The falling membership in Paisley in 1858 was put down to the cost of sending subscriptions by post and it was decided to send a deputation to discuss with the Paisley men what could be done. The trouble continued and in January 1861 it was decided that the secretary maintain correspondence with Paisley and then in March that the secretary attend both Paisley and Greenock meetings to give the men better facilities for joining the Society.

The 1852 accounts record 'expenses incurred on account of calamitous circumstances £144 14s 5d,' a considerable sum which would seem to indicate a big strike. But we have no record of it.

But the report does refer to preparations for a recruiting drive and a campaign for a general advance in wages. 'Large numbers of shops are still under-paid. How can we expect better paid shops to rise when so many are under-paid? A uniformity of wages throughout the city is desirable,' declared the secretary. The Society purchased some 9,000 circulars, 250 membership books and 700 copies of the Society's laws, and spent £5 19s 11d on deputations to non-Society men. As a result membership went up in the year from 250 to 378.

In October 1855 a vote was taken at a general meeting on whether to go for a reduction in the working week to 57 hours or for more money; eleven voted for a reduction in hours, seven for an increase in wages, one would take either and one was content with what he had. The following month's lodge meeting took a straight vote calling for an advance in wages, which was carried unanimously. A survey of wages throughout the trade in the City showed a variation from only 16s 6d to 24s. The meeting decided that no man would work for less than 20s and that men already earning from 20s to 24s a week should receive 1s rise. A circular to this effect was sent to the employers. An indication of the low wages prevailing, even after this, is to be seen in an entry in the minutes that two men had been ordered by their employer to go to work at Loch Shields at 4d an hour or not to go to work on Monday. The meeting decided that the men could work at 4d an hour because of the state of trade.

The depressed state of trade continued, some employers reduced wages by 10 per cent, unemployment mounted and membership dropped until by 1859 it was down to 220, even below what it was before the recruiting drive. The worst year was 1857 when fifty men dropped out of the Society.

With the improvement in trade in the early 60s another drive to bring in non-Society men was attempted. After some little success in early 1863 other nons were told they must join within a fortnight 'or other measures would be taken.' As a result membership began to climb again. It was 264 in April 1863, 354 the following year and 415 in 1865. By 1864 the committee felt strong enough to put in for a 2s a week general advance 'for both town and country.' This was generally conceded in Glasgow after some strike action. In Greenock and Paisley strike action had to be taken in some shops to get the rise. The 'corresponding member' in Johnstone reported that all employers had paid the 2s except one who would only pay 1s. Port Glasgow was also successful. Glasgow seems to have been steadily improving membership in the countryside. There had already been reference to a group of members in Kilmarnock in 1857 and members were enrolled in Bonny Bridge and Largs in 1865, followed later by Barrhead and Camsie.

By this time the Society had given up all claim to being a national organisation, confining its activities to Glasgow and the surrounding area.

In the 1860s concern began to be felt about the training of apprentices, which had been a problem forty years earlier. Then, at a lodge meeting in March 1826, it was agreed that we apply all the moral means in our power to induce an employer to bind or engage their apprentice for a proper term of years so that they may be the more likely to become efficient workmen before they undertake the responsibilities as such.

In October 1863 a circular was sent to all employers in the City –

That boys three months in your employ, or, at all events when they begin to work at the trade, should be Bound or Engaged for six or seven years; but should there be sufficient reason for the said binding or engaging being broken, they should produce a certificate from their late employer, so that they may work out their time in accordance to their first Agreement. It is now expected that from this date, the conditions of the Agreement will be carried out and also in future strictly adhered to.

Sixty employers signed the agreement and received a letter giving 'best thanks for your co-operation, from your humble servants, the Journeymen Tinsmiths.'

The Society, as a body, was strongly opposed to piece-work and in April 1859 a lodge meeting decided that it was 'against the rules and principles of the Society' to work by the piece except for work given out by the gross or 100. But in August there was a demand for piece-work on gunpowder boxes 'as was operating in other shops' whose earnings were 24s to 30s. And in 1865 men were being paid 30s a gross for making passage lamps. At the May 1865 lodge meeting it was decided unanimously

That, as piece-work in our trade has been virtually abolished in Glasgow for upward of 20 years, and as when it was in practice it occasioned misunderstanding and disputes between employers and employed to a.disagreeable extent … we cannot agree to return to it, and in those isolated cases where it exists at present we shall do our best endeavours to get it abolished there also.

But in April 1870 it was decided to agree to let men make dyers' poles by the piece on a short-time basis – and in September it was unanimously agreed to allow the introduction of piecework at the Townhead Gas Works. But in 1872, after talks with the Edinburgh secretary, a general meeting in November decided that no member working in the corporation gas works 'can remain a member of the Society who continues or resumes piece-work on tin plate or iron gas meters.' It was decided that dispute benefit be paid to both members and non-members. As so often happens there is no record of the result but as the dispute benefit paid out for the whole year amounted to only £21 it would appear that any dispute there may have been was not a long one.

The Society's rules forbade members from engaging themselves to an employer so that they could not leave after two weeks notice and in February 1860 the Society wrote to Birmingham asking for information on three Glasgow members who had engaged themselves to a Birmingham employer named Griffiths for one year without first checking on his relations with operatives there. The secretary had first to send a telegram to Manchester to get the address of the Birmingham secretary, an indication of how isolated from each other were some of the trade societies in different parts of the country, even at that comparatively late date.

In the same year they took a stand on seasonal work, ruling that

Any member of the Society leaving his employment to go to work at the salmon case making, or any such job or place which he knows to be for a short or limited period, without first obtaining the permission of the office bearers or committee to do so, shall not be enabled to receive his idle aliment on his return, although failing to obtain employment.

Members rebelled against the committee's lack of enthusiasm to claim work on galvanised iron during a clash with the plumbers and agreed to accept into membership a young man who had served his time in the galvanised trade. They also rejected the plumbers claim for work on zinc.

In 1866 the Society joined a committee of the iron trades campaigning for a shorter working week and voted 1d per member for the funds. It issued a circular to the trade for a 55-hour standard working week but agreed to accept an employers' offer of 57 hours at the same rate of wages as previously, with all hours above 57 to be paid for at time-and-a-quarter. A survey of the trade showed that there were 64 tin plate workers at the Caledonian railway works who were not in the Society, that some of the smaller shops were still working 60 hours and men at Johnstone were having difficulty in getting the 57 hours. Average wages were found to be £1 2s 9¼d. This was in 1868, a time of high unemployment and it was decided to put off activity until trade was better.

With the improvement in trade it was decided the following September to make a wage application through the shops and got the 2s a week they asked for. They followed this up with an application for a 51-hour week with no loss in pay.

The Society also played its part in the wider trade union and Labour movement, reaffirmed its confidence and support of the Glasgow trades council then being attacked in the press. (Later, one of the Society's delegates to the trades council, George Carson, was its secretary for fifteen years, from 1901 to 1916.)

It was active in the trade union agitation in support of the 1865 Reform Act to give adult urban male suffrage, buying a new banner at a cost of £13 which, incidentally was oversubscribed by £4 12s 3d when subscription lists went round the shops, the extra money being used to give a bigger banner by adding a border to it. Members in Dumbarton were also out with the banner in the town's own demonstration. A levy was put on members to pay the expenses of the Reform demonstrations.

In September 1867 delegates were sent to a meeting to protest at unjust criticisms of the unions following the Sheffield 'outrages' and to demand legislation to give trade union funds the same protection as that afforded to friendly societies. The banner got another outing at an even bigger demonstration demanding the repeal of the Criminal Law Amendment Act in November 1873. A general meeting of the Society recognised 'The oppression and important strictures placed upon trade unionists' by this Act and resolved to join the demonstration of working men of Glasgow and the West of Scotland to demand the repeal of the measure. The committee bought 300 rosettes out of the funds and sent postcards to all shops instructing them to appoint delegates to attend the office and collect rosettes for all members of the shop.

In 1881 it was recorded that 'the dark clouds hovering over industry during the last few years' had passed away. But in the trade there were large numbers of men not connected with the Society and still a large number were being excluded for non-payment of dues – 92 new members had been made but 67 were excluded. In 1883, the jubilee year of the Society, 175 joined and 63 were excluded but this influx seems to have been the result of the festivities around the jubilee, in which 1,400 people took part, as the following year 108 were excluded. By 1885 depression was again hitting the trade with large numbers out of work and idle benefit was extended from four to eight weeks.

In 1883 there had been activity over the payment of a minimum wage which was conceded with very little strike action and a later survey of eighty shops employing members recorded 376 Society members earning an average of £1 8s 11½d and 185 non-Society men at £1 8s 2d plus 74 apprentices. One shop had 34 apprentices to eleven members and fifteen non-Society men. Wages varied from one man on 17s to four at £1 16s. Membership in 1893 was 649 out of

Scottish banner dating from 1891 based on emblem of the National
Amalgamated Society, *left*: identification plate carried in demonstrations.

about 1,000 tinmen in the city. Despite instituting a system of shop
delegates it had not been possible to reduce the number of non-Society
men or to stop the large number of lapsings each year. The names of
members excluded for non-payment of dues was printed in the annual
report in the hope of shaming them into paying up. In 1896, too, a black
list of members expelled was included. A strike on the Clyde in 1896
pushed up payments of strike benefits and expenses but the Society
claimed a victory 'in maintaining our position and principles,' gaining $\frac{1}{2}$d
an hour on the standard rate. Success was also obtained in Barrhead and
at Ayr, where fourteen members and six nons were out for over three

months. Before that wages after serving an apprenticeship of six years were 'the handsome amount of 12s to 14s a week,' the highest paid man getting 26s.

A dispute arose with the Manchester and Liverpool societies in 1900 in connection with an official strike of case makers in the Vale of Leven when the two English societies replying to a request from Glasgow said that while they would ask their members not to reply to advertisements from the firms concerned they could not stop them doing work for the firms where Union members were on strike. The Society took the unusual step of circularising all tin plate workers' societies in the country to bring pressure on Manchester and Liverpool.

In 1899 the membership topped the 1,000 mark for the first time and the secretary's job was divided into two, a corresponding and a financial secretary, to deal with the increased amount of work. They were both part-time although it was said that a levy of $\frac{1}{2}$d per member a week would have paid for a full-time official. A technical committee was also appointed after the education authorities had agreed to open a sheet metal class.

The year 1902 saw a depression of trade and increased unemployment so that 'idle benefit' was increased to 16 weeks and a levy of 6d a week was put on all at work to pay for it. A by-product of the unemployment was an increase in the number of members lapsed through non-payment of dues.

Then in 1907 the local employers formed their own organisation and immediately gave notice of $\frac{1}{4}$d reduction in wages. The Society decided to fight the cut and members were levied ls a week. The number on strike gradually increased until 300 were out and after three months the levy was raised to 5s a week. The cost of strike benefit amounted to £3,759 the first year and £3,209 the second, including payment to some nons who also came out. The strike came during a slump in trade and after it was called off a number of members could not get work but the Society prided itself on paying strike benefit until the last man was back at work and in some cases that meant close on two-and-a-half years.

Just before the strike started the Society had joined the National Amalgamated which immediately came to their aid with a grant of £200 and also put a 3d levy on all affiliated members which meant a payment of £1,400 the first year and £1,115 the following year. A loan of £200 came from London, £150 from Birmingham and £50 from Wolverhampton, Aberdeen Society made a loan of £50 and a grant of £10, the engineers made a loan of £500 and a grant of £40. Eventually the men had to go back and accept the reduction. The Committee reported the members could have gone back earlier,without the loss of the $\frac{1}{4}$d if they had been prepared to accept the employers' terms 'which were too obnoxious for us to agree to.'

By 1910, due partly to the loss of members in the strike, partly the poor state of trade, and partly by a purge of those in arrears, membership had dropped to 651. Recruiting meetings were held in Dumbarton and Greenock and members were made in Falkirk, Alexandria, Camelon and Kilmarnock until, on the eve of the war, membership had climbed again to 900. By 1913 the Society was able to afford a full-time secretary and Thomas Sanders was elected to fill the post at a salary of £116 5s a year. As elsewhere, there was some serious unemployment at the beginning of the war but by April 1915 114 members were in the forces and most of the rest were on some kind of munitions work.

As the war dragged on the Society was concerned 'at the invasion of the craft by unskilled and female labour with no visible sacrifice by the employers' side.' They supported the Clyde Engineers Vigilent Committee, the Munitions Act Enquiry Committee, the Glasgow Workers' War Emergency Committee, the Falkirk Munitions Committee and other such defence organisations while they continued to take part in the annual May Day demonstrations with banner and bands throughout the war.

The end of the war saw a return to unemployment and strikes to enforce the 54-hour week without loss of pay. The Society also supported the great 40-hour week strike. The Committee's recommendation for support had been turned down by a general meeting in favour of a ballot of members but when the strike started a large number of members came out and a special meeting declared in favour of a general strike to enforce the demand. After the end of the strike the Committee disciplined members who had remained at work. One, Garroway, refused to pay the fine and took the Union to court to prevent his expulsion or suspension from the Union for refusal to pay. He lost his case but together with others who had been disciplined he set up the West of Scotland Sheet Metal Workers Society which lingered on through the 1920s before winding up and its remaining members returned to the fold.

The Society formed an apprentices section for 'workers in the following metals, sheet tin, iron, copper, brass, zinc, aluminium and other alloys.' The newly-elected general secretary, W.J. Clark, said that there should not be too many restrictions on apprentices. They should be directed into sections of the trade that would be most beneficial to them and to the trade and where the demand was greater than the supply, so helping to stop encroachments of other societies on the trade.

After a number of meetings with 'kindred trades' in the previous few years the general secretary, greeting the proposed National Union of Sheet Metal Workers, said undoubtedly its formation would be 'the first step towards fusion of kindred trades, coppersmiths, sheet iron workers, plumbers, etc.'

Edinburgh Society

A meeting to revive the Edinburgh Society, attended by 94 local tinmen, was held in the Mason's Hall in April 1866. No mention was made of any previous society – although we know that a society existed in the 1820s, if not earlier and in 1842 and 43 tramps from Edinburgh, with cards, passed through Glasgow – or why the 1866 revival was necessary. It is difficult to believe that organisations would have been allowed to collapse and disappear, and the local tinmen left with no organisation, without Glasgow moving in, but there is no reference to Edinburgh in the annual reports around that date. The meeting elected acting officers and a committee of sixteen to draw up rules for the government of the society. The laws were drawn up, printed and sent to one hundred local tinmen before the Society was formally established at a meeting on 16 July 1866 as the United Tin Plate Workers of Edinburgh and Leith Protecting and Friendly Society with a membership of 44, which had been pushed up to 60 by October. Edward Forbes was installed as secretary at a salary of £8 a year.

Apprentices were admitted one year before ending their time. It would appear that some difficulty was experienced in recruitment as in 1872 it was decided that any tin plate worker could join the Society at a lower rate of contributions for trade protection alone – which included 'idle aliment' – but could not join for only the friendly benefits.

The new society affiliated to the trades council but in 1869 the secretary was instructed to write to the council protesting at their 'interfering in politics'. The Society continued its membership on receipt of a 'satisfactory reply' but members were not entirely happy with the relationship and in 1875 decided to have no representative on the council. In 1869, however, they joined other trades in agitation for a 51-hour week and in 1872 participated in the meeting to set up the local 51-hour League. Then in 1875 the secretary represented the Society at a meeting to form a 'protecting association' to protect the 51 hours 'and such trade union privileges as we are in possession of.'

In 1873 protests were received at the low rate of wages and at the secretary for 'not taking up the matter', but a special committee decided 'not to proceed any further' and there seems to have been no general movement for an advance in wages.

Although earlier Edinburgh societies had been party to tramping agreements, it was not until April 1874 that 'a movement to get tramping cards' was started after several members had asked for them. A sub-committee to draw up a card asked the lithographers 'what can be got in the way of arms or clasped hands?'

A motion 'that we agitate for an eight-hour day through Parliament' put forward at a general meeting in 1888 was defeated by an amendment that the eight-hour day be secured by the Union without the aid of Parliament. Another motion calling for support for three working men candidates for the school board was defeated.

In 1890 the Society moved to the Labour Hall and the secretary was accused of misleading the members as they 'Didn't know it belonged to the Socialists' and the demand was made that they vacate the premises immediately. A compromise was reached that they remain for a year – they stayed five.

In January 1874 the new Society was involved in the first of what was to be a continuing series of disputes in the meter industry, which employed the biggest section of its membership. It arose through a decision of Cowan's to end special overtime rates. Both members and non-Society men came out, with the Society paying the same aliment to both and the brass finishers agreed that the two societies should 'work heartily together.' Collections were taken in local tinshops, particularly in the other meter shops in the town. And during the strike the men went on the offensive, putting in a demand for a wage increase as Cowan's paid the lowest rate in town. After three months some of the members returned and a general meeting decided they could remain members of the Society, whereupon the secretary resigned, and soon the rest went back. In August Cowan reduced the price of 'soft metal work' without notice, saying if the men did not like it he could get women to do the work more cheaply.

Then in 1878 both Cowan's and Donaldson's reduced prices by 10 per cent and day work rates by 5 per cent. The men at both firms were called out and a 2s levy put on the shop. Cowan's called a meeting of their employees and said they would take any worker back on the old terms if they would leave the Society, offering to start a new one for the men. They also proposed a 10 per cent general reduction in prices with a 20 per cent increase on bad jobs. They later offered to maintain old prices until September 1878 and the Society called off the strike, only to put it on again when Cowan's only offered short time working. The Society then called on London for help which brought Deans, the London secretary, to Edinburgh, and after meetings with both the Society and the management he got an agreement to operate both in Edinburgh and London, bringing to an end a dispute that had lasted on and off for fifteen months.

Cowan's was the scene of another big dispute in 1898 when the management put in to operation a long-cherished aim of using women labour on meters. The men countered with an overtime ban but action had to be taken by workers in Cowan's shops in London and other towns before the management climbed down. In 1906 the men at Grant's came out in resisting a price reduction and in 1907 members at Milnes struck to stop sectionalisation.

With the meter shops forming the core of union organisation in the town, employing some 400 tinmen, of whom Cowan's, Alder and Mackay and Laidlaw's accounted for about 100 each, the Society decided to tighten up organisation. In 1888 a joint committee was formed of representatives of the six meter shops in the town, each shop supplying a complete list of prices. In 1899 chapels were formed at Cowan's and Laidlaw's and others followed later. The Society was now better equipped to take part in the struggles in the meter shops, whose tale of strikes, lockouts and victimisation continued throughout the life of the Society.

Banner carried by the Edinburgh Society in a local demonstration on 23 August 1873, to protest against anti-trade union legislation

There was continued suspicion of political activities in the Society and for some years it was luke-warm in its attitude toward the trades council. Despite this, a member of the Society, George Holburn, was elected president of the council in 1873. Speaking at a peace conference in Glasgow that year he told how, as a youth, he had been on board a transport vessel in the Crimean War and 'saw the bloodshed of that strife.' He was town councillor for Leith as a Gladstonian Liberal from 1890 to 1895 and was then elected Liberal and Labour Member of Parliament for North-West Lanarkshire, holding the seat until he died in 1899 at 56 years of age.

The Society also took part in a demonstration on 23 August 1873 to protest against the Criminal Law Amendment Act, and other anti-trade union legislation.

In 1895 it was agreed to send two delegates to a trades council conference on support for working-men candidates for the parish council but a request from the Independent Labour Party in 1899 that their working-men candidates be allowed to address the Society meeting was refused. There was still resistance to 'political activities,' the Society did not participate in the trades council May Day demonstration the following year 'through lack of interest in the shops,' and decided to take 'no action' in a call for support for school board elections. But in 1897 agreed to send a delegate to the Scottish TUC and to a conference on building a Labour Hall. In 1905 it was agreed the Society take part in the local Trades Dispute Bill demonstration, 100 tin batons were ordered and the Society was to pay its share in hiring a brass band. But despite high unemployment in the trade the Society refused to take part in a trades council unemployed demonstration in 1912 or a Budget Protest demonstration.

The aspirations for unity of the trade for the whole of Scotland that had inspired the Glasgow members when they re-formed their Society in 1833, still persisted, coming to the surface from time to time.

In 1869 the Aberdeen Society proposed that they, Edinburgh and Glasgow, should work closer together for their mutual advantage, but although Glasgow was in agreement and wrote to Edinburgh proposing action, nothing came of it. Then in January 1872 the Edinburgh Society took action, sending a deputation to Glasgow to urge closer working on wages, idle members, labour requirements and other relevant matters, as well as discussing methods of work in the gas meter shops. In December 1875 the Edinburgh Society made another attempt, suggesting a meeting to consider the formation of a confederation of tin plate workers in the whole of Scotland with the object of forming a National Tin Plate Workers Union. The following June saw the Edinburgh Society again pushing its proposals for unity with a suggestion that a conference be held in Glasgow and putting forward a 'scheme for confederation the basis of which was mutual support in disputes.' Glasgow's reaction was to offer the other tin plate workers' societies in Scotland 'amalgamation by joining us individually.'

Edinburgh refused to accept this brush-off as final and its persistence bore fruit with a conference in August at which delegates agreed 'that the tin plate workers of Scotland unite in a simple federation to relieve each other of their idle members and to intimate monthly the state of trade and any vacancies that may arise and to aid each other in cases of dispute.' The following February a delegation from the Edinburgh Society spent a week in Glasgow discussing joint problems. However, whatever the outcome, there is no record in the minutes of further joint action other than a request from Aberdeen for help in a big strike in which a number of their members were engaged. Edinburgh responded with an immediate donation of £15 and a guarantee of £1 10s a week, following this with another £10 grant. Donations totalling £39 were sent to Aberdeen in 1886 in response to another strike appeal.

Attempts by the Edinburgh Society to form branches in Kirkaldy and Perth do not seem to have materialised but more basic co-operation came in 1892 when Aberdeen proposed joint action to revive the Dundee Society. The Dundee trades council was appealed to and organised a meeting of tinmen in the town with representatives of the two societies attending. After the Dundee Society was reformed the other two societies continued to send delegates to its meetings and gave general help until the Society was able to stand on its own feet. Edinburgh then took over the Society as a subsidiary. It had to get permission from Edinburgh to affiliate to the trades council and to send a circular to employers for an advance in the minimum rate to 7d. In 1905 it was stressed that although the Dundee accounts were treated separately in the annual report, it remained a branch of the Edinburgh Society. Pressures from Dundee branch for independence were resisted for a time and it was not until 1912 that a separate independent Dundee Society was established – twenty years after it was reformed.

Membership of the Edinburgh Society stagnated with only some seventy members in 1890 out of a total of around 300 tinsmiths in Edinburgh and Leith. An organising drive, taken with the help of the trades council, brought in only twenty new members but ten years later the Society could boast a membership of over 300.

The Society then felt strong enough to put forward rules for apprentices. Not more than one apprentice would be allowed for each five journeymen. No apprentice was to be allowed to work piecework until he had been four years in the trade. No employer should take an apprentice who had broken his time with another employer. Overtime and lost time were to be included when reckoning an apprentice's six years' service.

The Edinburgh Society joined the National Amalgamated Tin Plate Workers in 1889, immediately after the accession of the London societies to the Birmingham and Wolverhampton organisation had allowed the affiliation of other societies. Edinburgh was the first to join and was soon followed by Aberdeen, then with 99 members, which it pushed up to 170 by 1900. Glasgow was invited to join but declined and Dundee was told to affiliate through Edinburgh.

The Wolverhampton Society

As we have seen, the Wolverhampton was one of the earliest tin plate workers' societies in the country and it seems to have had an unbroken existence from its beginnings sometime before 1802. It had an active and colourful life, something of which we have chronicled elsewhere.

Like London at around the same time, Wolverhampton also had two societies in the 1870s. But this was not due to any split or breakaway, rather it arose from the aristocratic attitude of the members of what was called the No. 1 Society, which only took in members working in the 'better class' of shop, turning out best quality work and where rates and conditions met with the approval of the Committee. There was no attempt to get all shops up to this standard; no directing of members into these non-Society shops to fight for better rates and conditions for all. These were decreed non-Society shops and remained outside the pale, the workers there regarded as rather unfortunate. Any member going to work in a non-Society shop was liable to be fined or even expelled from the Society.

There were not always two societies. Before 1873 there were just the organised and unorganised shops and only one is recorded as having made the change from one to the other – Tower Street Works was accepted as a Society shop as this is 'the general wish of the men working there and in view of the straightforward manner in which the men conducted themselves with their employers on his consenting to pay book prices.'

In 1873 the Wolverhampton and Birmingham Societies put in a joint claim for an increase in prices only to have the Wolverhampton employers say they could not accede to the claim as they would not be able to compete with the cheaper non-union firms. The Society then invited the 'nons' to their meeting, and to take part in the strike. They did not invite them to join the Society, instead they suggested that they form their own Society. So the No. 2 Society, the Wolverhampton Co-operative Tin Plate Workers Society, came into being.

There had already been a Wolverhampton Co-operative Tin Plate Workers Society in 1848, but that seems to have been only a change of name, possibly something to do with the strike of 1842. There is certainly no reference to two societies previously in such contemporary records as we have. The rules of the Co-operative Society were similar in nature to those of the Operative Society and it was also based on representatives of the organised shops with shops of up to twenty members providing one committeeman, from twenty to forty members providing two, those with sixty members three and so on in multiples of twenty.

The books show the old Society was extremely generous to other societies and other sections of the trade on strike or in other difficulties – '£10 to the strikers and another £10 in a month if still out' appears frequently in the minutes. A resolution strongly condemning the policy that led to the Franco-Prussian War of 1870 and expressing sympathy for the 'poor, brave and unfortunate soldiers on both sides prostrate' was backed up with a vote of £10 for the wounded. The same sum was offered in 1871, if required, for action on the Trade Union Bill then before Parliament, coupled with a pledge to co-operate with the London trades and a proposal that two delegates be elected by each shop to help the officials if necessary. The Society also gave material support to the working-class newspaper, the *Beehive*, taking one copy 'for each manufactury.' It was an early member of the trades council and a strong supporter of the co-operative formed by Willenhall lockmakers during a strike.

The Society itself had to ask for support from the trade union movement in times of need, as we have seen; but during the 1868 depression it applied to its own members for loans of money so that it could pay out-of-work benefit.

In 1872, while considering it 'inexpedient' to apply for a 10 per cent increase because of anomalies between prices in the various shops, the men in the non-Society shops were told to put in for book prices and support was pledged for those doing so. For the next six months the Committee held talks with the Birmingham Society on joint action for a rise of 15 per cent. It was agreed the prices of the 1850 book were not fair for 1872 conditions with provisions, rents, fuel and other things increased in price. Wolverhampton favoured a 10 per cent claim and insisted on choosing the right time but offered the Birmingham Society financial support if they wanted to go out on their own. As part of the preparations the No. 2 Society men were invited to a meeting where they reported that the men they represented backed a call for a rise. They were told to pay attention to regular dues payments for 'though unity is indispensible, money is the sinews of war.' On general working it was agreed that members of the two societies could work in each other's shops while maintaining membership of their own societies.

A mass meeting preceded by shop meetings agreed that the three societies make a joint application for an advance at the beginning of November but no reply was received from the employers and in the following January the men at one shop refused to work at the old prices and gave notice – the following day the advance was agreed. The success of this joint action led to calls for closer working and a proposal from the No. 1 Society committee for an amalgamation of all tin plate workers throughout Britain. The Birmingham Society proposed that a start be made with the amalgamation of the three societies to be called the Amalgamated Tin Plate Workers of the Midlands District with funds equal to 5s a member and contributions of 1d a week. The new organisation came into being on a January 1876 and was soon directing the joint affairs of the three societies.

There followed one of the periodic depressions of trade and the Operative Society was forced to levy members 6d a month 'because of the large numbers out of work and on strike and other heavy expenses through the depressed state of trade.' In 1881 it was decided that any member who had been 'on the funds' for twelve months, drawing out-of-work pay, must take his card within two weeks and go and look for work in other towns or forego his pay.

With the old established society in such straits it was not to be wondered at that the No. 2 Society, so recently formed, should be asking for assistance, having expended all their funds with the heavy expenses of the past two years. The No. 1 Society granted them £25 and proposed discussions on the amalgamation of the two societies as soon as possible. However, the situation was brought to a head by the collapse of the No. 2 Society and proposals were made for the take-over of its members. There was opposition in the shops and a deputation asked if it were in the interest of members of the No. 1 Society to admit members of the No. 2. After discussion with the Committee it was agreed to admit the majority

> as a means of preventing any further reduction in prices and as a means of inculcating the principles of true trade unionism into the present and rising generation for the protection of rights of Labour and of our craft.

The committee declared that, while it was willing to open the No. 1 Society as wide as possible to the members of the late No. 2 Society, they felt justified in arranging the conditions of admission 'according to antecedents of members making application.'

The names of applicants were to be taken by shop secretaries two weeks before the meeting to discuss their admittance. Men over sixty would have to go before a general meeting of members. The minutes go on to record the admission of members from the various shops over the next two months or so, with 21 from one shop, 52 from another. But acceptance was by no means automatic. In October 1881 it was recorded that

> we do not recognise Messrs Williams or Brandens as Society shops because of the low prices paid, and leave it to the general meeting to decide if members be admitted as soon as they get work in shops paying the rate, as they have previously been good paying members of the Society now broken up … any members of the late No. 2 Society delaying their application to later than one month from today will not be dealt with so leniently as those admitted previously.

It was also laid down that general meetings be confined to members of the old No. 1 Society as the meeting room did not have room for all to be accommodated.

Much of the subsequent history of the Society is covered by that of the National Amalgamated but we can record that in 1896 a resolution was sent to all local employers that all gear case work in the town would be done day work at 7d an hour. Shop secretaries were asked to discuss with their members the advisability of the day work system applying to all work. Reports from the shops turned down the idea of giving up piecework entirely in favour of day work but to establish a minimum day work rate, 7d an hour was agreed and established early in 1897. It was not until 1911 that there was an increase to 8d with a further ½d an hour for motor and gear case work to 9d. The same rates applied to Birmingham but while Birmingham continued to work piecework Wolverhampton put in for a 9d day work minimum on both gear case and motor work.

National Iron Plate Workers

As we have seen there was an iron plate workers' society in Birmingham in 1824[1] when it greeted the repeal of the Combination Acts with a demand for a wage increase and in London a Friendly Society of Iron Plate Workers existed at least as far back as 1838[2]. It, or its successor, was still in existence in 1842 when it made a donation to a tin plate workers' strike. There may have been others in different parts of the country but we have not been able to find a record of any at this period.

Their work generally was heavier and rougher than the general work of the tin plate workers, although there was a certain amount of overlap and members of the two societies sometimes worked in each others' shops; in Birmingham this was particularly the case in the metal trunk making section of the trade.

The Birmingham Iron Plate Workers Trade Protection Society was formed in 1864[3] and was still in existence in March 1866 when it gave £2 to the patternmakers then on strike and in November that year a newly formed London Society was using the rule book of the Birmingham Society as a guide, In December 1866 the Iron Braziers and Iron Plate Workers Societies were attending meetings of the Wolverhampton Trades Council.[4] Then in October 1867 an accumulation of grievances led to the Birmingham Society taking strike action. There was dissatisfaction over the apprenticeship system at some firms: some of the largest had promised to employ only union men and then broke their word, putting non-unionists on the job and at the same time issuing a list of reduced piecework prices. The strike continued on into 1868 but finally collapsed and the Union with it.

Although it was a separate organisation the Wolverhampton Society seems also to have declined because we hear of a new organisation being formed in 1872. This seems to have inspired the Birmingham men to have another go and a new Birmingham Society was formed in 1874, but the two remained separate organisations.

This was a period of good trade with rapidly developing trade unions and the new Birmingham Society was an instant success. In 1875 it won a bonus of 10 per cent on piece-work prices and the following year could boast of almost 350 members, practically the whole of the men in the trade in Birmingham. It continued to organise most of the trade members until 1881 when the employers gave notice of the withdrawal of the 10 per cent bonus. The Society replied with a general strike of the Birmingham trade. But this was a time of deteriorating trade and although more than 350 men stayed out for some months they were eventually beaten by the employers bringing in outside blacklegs. The Union had to call off the strike and those that could returned to work without the 10 per cent. The defeat and with it the 10 per cent reduction in piecework prices brought a decline in Union strength and from 1881 to 1888 its membership did not exceed eighty to 100 men. As a consequence piece-work prices fell rapidly as employers were able to take as much as 20 per cent to 30 per cent off the prices of many jobs with the Union not strong enough to deny them.

The year 1888 saw a revival of trade and new unions springing up in all Birmingham trades. The Society determined to rebuild their organisation and shop meetings were held all over the town. Membership, which numbered only eighty at the beginning of 1889, shot up to about 450 by the end of the year with the trade almost completely organised once more. The Society still remained a purely Birmingham organisation.

In December 1889, trade being very good and confident of their newly-acquired strength, the Society put in for a return of the 10 per cent they had lost some ten years before, with the local iron plate workers' societies in Wolverhampton and Bilston making a similar claim. The employers refused but after a strike lasting five weeks in which all the men in Birmingham and a large number of those in Wolverhampton and Bilston took part, the men were successful. The employers conceded the 10 per cent on condition that the Society produced a new minimum price list and did their best to enforce it in all shops where the trade was carried on within a radius of fourteen miles of Birmingham. These terms were agreed at a joint meeting of the Society and a newly-formed employers' organisation presided over by an independent chairman, W.J. Davies, the highly respected general secretary of the brass workers' union.

At the cost of £120 the Birmingham Society, with the help of the local Wolverhampton and Bilston societies, quickly produced a new complete list of prices and presented it to the employers who declined to accept it unless 10 per cent was taken off, asserting that the bonus was included in the new list. No agreement could be reached and it was referred to Judge Chalmers as arbitrator. He awarded in favour of the men but then largely nullified his decision by suggesting a new and revised list be drawn up. A joint committee of employers and men was formed to draw up the proposed new list but could not reach an agreement and finally adjourned indefinitely.

In April 1890 the employees distributed a new list throughout the trade in the whole of the Midlands and gave notice that these would be the prices they paid in future. This gave price reductions of from 10 per cent to 40 per cent on many jobs and was rejected by the men, and as the employers were adamant another great strike took place with more than 500 men out in Birmingham, Wolverhampton and Bilston and another 130 in Lye. After six or seven weeks the employers agreed to withdraw their price list and the men everywhere returned victorious at the old prices and bonuses.

The Birmingham Society then sent out delegates all over the country to try and organise a national union. New societies were formed and old ones revived and the National Amalgamated Iron Plate Workers Society was set up with Birmingham as its headquarters and branches in London, Liverpool, Manchester, Bristol and Walsall, as well as Wolverhampton and Bilston.

Only Lye remained aloof from the new organisation. But Lye was important to the trade and was rapidly becoming the centre of the industry, the number employed having doubled in the previous few years to some 450 men, all belonging to the Knights of Labour[5], a general political and industrial organisation that had originated in the USA, and had helped the Lye iron plate workers obtain a unified list of prices. They were understandably loath to desert those who had helped them in their hour of need but they too came in within a few months. Each of the towns still had its own local price list on which they received the 10 per cent bonus, except Lye, which already had the 10 per cent incorporated in the prices.

Early in 1892 trouble began again with some employers giving notice they were withdrawing the 10 per cent bonus, and trade being very bad, they succeeded in getting the better of the men in the strike that ensued. Other employers, clamouring against unfair competition, also wanted the bonus taken off and toward the end of the year all Birmingham employers withdrew the bonuses. Trade was still very bad and the Society was practically without funds, strikes and unemployed pay having absorbed all but £250, and the committee was prepared to let the 10 per cent go, but the men would not hear of it so in December 1892 another general strike took place with more than 500 men out in Birmingham, Wolverhampton and Bilston. After the first week strike pay dropped to 5s a week and that was only possible because of levies of 5s a week for those still in work. The Society made desperate efforts to get a meeting with the employers who refused until forced by public pressure through the local press. A joint meeting was held in January 1893 and when no agreement was arrived at, the employers suggested the Editor of the *Birmingham Gazette* act as arbitrator. When the men turned this down they proposed setting up an arbitration and conciliation board to which all matters could be submitted. But the employers wanted the men to return without the 10 per cent until the arbitration award and the men were determined not to return without it. The deadlock continued until at a joint meeting on 28 February 1893 the strike was closed on much better terms than the strikers could have expected, with the 10 per cent retained for three months to allow the Society to force all outside employers to pay Birmingham prices and the bonus, failing which the bonus would be taken off. The employers agreed to take back all men who had gone on strike.

But the long and rather inconclusive strike took its toll and members drifted out of the Society. Moreover, trade remained bad and men who had fought a long and bitter fight to retain the 10 per cent traded it for the chance of a job. Men who would not give up the 10 per cent were discharged and eventually, in order to stop the victimisation of its best members, the Society had to agree to drop the bonus. In the next few months Union membership in Birmingham dropped from 450 to 300.

Despite this setback, the National Union continued and in 1894 claimed a membership of 1,225. Lye had become the biggest branch with 350 members and was said to be strong and well-organised although there were 70 non-unionists in the town. Birmingham still had 320 members and some 130 nons who had dropped out during the strike. Wolverhampton had 300 members and there were another 70 non-union men in the town since the strike. Bilston had 80 members and another 20 ex-members. London had some 70 members and it was estimated a further 100 non-unionists were also working in the trade but shops were scattered over such a wide area it was difficult to tell what was the real position. Manchester, which had only been set up in 1890 claimed 50 members and reported some 20 unorganised men. Bristol had 30 members and indicated that a further 20 men, not in the Society, were generally making specialities. Walsall had only 20 members but these were said to be all the men working in the trade in the town. The trade was also very small in Liverpool where the branch, set up in 1890 still had only 15 members.

The trade continued to decline in Birmingham and Lye established itself as the centre of the industry. Branches were opened in Dudley and Darleston and by 1898 the hollowware industry, as it was becoming to be known, had shifted to the Black Country with the headquarters of the union established at Dudley.

The trade was engaged in making such things as baths, buckets, boxes, bins, boilers, bowls, braziers, mangers and troughs, stoves, kettles, scoops, scuttles and tubs. The metal worked was generally of heavier gauge than that normally used by the tin plate workers and generally a cheaper class of work. There was singularly little demarcation and although there was some graduation from the iron plate workers' society to the tin plate workers this was by arrangement. The work was heavy and laborious and low paid, the average wage at the time of the struggle to retain the 10 per cent was about 25s a week, without the bonus, for a week of 56 to 60 hours, and the trade was subject to periods of short-time working. Work was mainly piece-work with many of the shops having their own individual lists to suit the different patterns of work and facilities available. There was a certain amount of piecemastering when the Union was weak although it was against Union rules.

There were never many women employed in the trade in Birmingham, but in Lye – and particularly in the Brierley Hill district – there were very many until the Lye Society, with the help of the Knights of Labour, spent a lot of money and had a number of strikes in the late 1880s 'against these women and succeeded in abolishing them in nine cases out of ten.' The women were generally employed on machines with one or two men to do the heavier or more skilled sections of the work, which was sectionalised, using machine-made parts, and a job would pass through twenty or thirty hands before it was finished.

Boy labour was also a problem. Apprentices were not registered or limited and men were allowed to take their sons into the shops. Employers would take on more and more lads until the men complained and the Union took steps to try and get them removed. A bigger problem was sub-contracting with a couple of men renting a small shop, filling it with lads on sectionalised work, threatening the men's jobs, while the lads never learned the trade. Where possible the Union limited the number of boys to one to every five men and insisted on a five or sometimes seven year apprenticeship. Machinery was then being introduced to a greater extent, reducing the amount of work and cutting the price of jobs.

The Union also had a section for blacksmiths working in the iron plate trade and took in galvanisers, especially after the Good Intent Society of Galvanisers, formed in Wolverhampton in October 1893 under the secretaryship of Isaac Grafton, was dissolved in February 1899. The iron braziers, too, had their own section and own list of prices.

The dominant figure for the rest of the Union's life was Simeon Webb, who became chairman after the removal to Dudley. He resigned in April 1900 and was elected General Secretary in April 1901, at a salary of £2 5s a week. Simeon Webb was the Union and he raised it from a weak organisation catering for a low-paid sweated industry 'to a respected society of workers whose wages and conditions compared favourably with the rest of the sheet metal trade', part of the established trade union movement. Webb seems to have been the very pattern of a respectable Edwardian trade union leader. He was a member of the Tipton Urban District Council and chairman of its education committee, chairman of the Dudley Board of Guardians, a Staffordshire county Justice of the Peace, a leader of the Netherton Noah's Ark Primitive Methodist Church and active in the Sunday School Movement – when he became General Secretary the Union's meeting place was immediately changed from a pub to the Temperance Institute. It was only fitting that he should end his career being awarded an OBE.

But the problems of the industry were well-established and, despite Webb's dynamism, progress was slow. The continued arrears, lapsings and members running out of the union kept it weak. In 1898 an organiser was appointed and after only two weeks 160 new members were made at Wolverhampton and Lye so two assistants were appointed 'with reasonable expenses paid.' In 1900, after Dudley had drawn attention to the bad state of the shops and falling off in contributions, all branches were asked to appoint two organisers at 8d an hour with expenses of not exceeding 5s a week. New membership drives included 'Sunday parades' in Lye, visits to factories and the offer of 6d for each member made. This was rewarded with an increase of some 400 over five years to 550 at the end of 1906.

Another problem was the old custom of employers charging workmen for the use of gas, heat and blast used during their work. It came to a head in September 1901 when a blacksmith member was dismissed for refusing to pay for the blast used in the forge he operated. Webb intervened and the man was reinstated on the understanding he used bellows instead of the firm's blast. The following months two branches called for an end to the custom of charging for gas lighting 'during the short days' which was still widespread. A circular was sent out to 26 firms in Birmingham, Bilston, Lye and Wolverhampton asking them to discontinue the practice which was illegal under the Truck Act of 1883. Eleven refused, some did not reply and members at one Birmingham firm told the Society not to interfere, while the Birmingham branch thought it was not worth fighting for. Members working in offending firms were told to work only during day light and they would be paid 2s 6d a week for lost time. Complaints by the Union brought a visit by a factory inspector to one firm but no action was taken so in May 1902 the Union itself prosecuted one firm under the Truck Act, only to have the magistrates at Stourbridge court throw out the case when the defending solicitor claimed that only a factory inspector could prosecute. An appeal to the Home Office ruled that anyone could prosecute under the Factory Act or Truck Act but still the inspector took no action. The Union pursued some cases but finally it was allowed to drop.

But most disputes were about piecework prices and there always seemed to be a dispute on the go. We read in the minutes of members on strike asking permission to go hop-picking if they took only two-thirds of strike pay and left their address with the Society. A major activity was preparing price lists. In 1898 the blacksmiths' section called a meeting of one delegate from each district to get out a new list – it was not completed until September 1904.

In September 1901 the List Committee presented a new list of prices for government work for which London was asked if they wanted to include any items. Before presenting it to the employers a meeting of all branches was called to prepare the members for the struggle that lay ahead. The response was hardly enthusiastic; it was accepted but only the regulars attended the meetings. The Society tried to pressurise the employers by getting men to sign forms giving in their notice, many signed and the forms were presented and later withdrawn to consider employers' objections. The employers were invited to a meeting to discuss the list but only a few of the more sympathetic ones turned up. It was then thought necessary to strengthen the non-Society shops before making a move. By this time it was reported that trade in some shops was very bad and was not very good anywhere, so the list was held in abeyance until more favourable times.

A list of prices for municipal work was then produced and a circular sent to all trades councils asking for their support in getting it accepted, 'with entirely satisfactory results.'

The day workers numbering around 200 were a neglected section. In June 1904 a survey found that 130 of them were receiving less than 6d an hour against a minimum rate of 7d but no action was taken. The only general claim in the ten years covered by the minutes was in 1899 when Dudley reported obtaining the 10 per cent without difficulty and most other branches reported the reception 'favourable'.

The Society was concerned at the number of 'contractors' who not only did cut-price jobs but also took over the jobs of men on strike. In 1903 the TUC Parliamentary Committee was asked to get questions raised in the House of Commons about 'sub-letting' of jobs and sweating on government contracts, and a protest was sent to the War Office on price-cutting on a job of 19,000 mangers and 2,000 horse buckets. The position of the Society was often undermined by members accepting cuts or new prices without notifying head office, unmindful of the effect this would have on other shops. A joint committee was set up with the tin plate workers to decide on prices of work they had in common to try and avoid price-cutting through competition.

The years 1906/7 saw a return to bad times with large-scale unemployment, some men had been 'at play', as unemployment was euphemistically called, for twenty weeks and more. The regular meeting of branch delegates was told that there was a reluctance among members to pay higher contributions to provide out-of-work pay but a willingness to make voluntary shop collection.

In 1906 the Wolverhampton tin plate workers complained that the Union's members at Sankey's were accepting sweated rates for day work that would jeopardise the established motor trade minimum day work rate of 8½d an hour. The TPW called out all their members at Sankey's and urged the iron plate workers to do the same. The Union felt all they could do was to call out the few men on motor work and expel two members who refused to give up piece-work.

As with the sheet metal workers there is no record in the minutes of any attempt to get better apprenticeship training in the shops but Webb was successful in getting a technical class opened in Lye in 1904, and he persuaded the Society to put up an annual prize of one guinea for the best student. Earlier, in response from a request from the National Union of Teachers, the Society wrote to the Minister of Education calling for the age limit to be raised for boys working part time.

There followed a spate of political activity. In 1904 the committee sent a protest to the Foreign Secretary, Lord Lansdown, at the massacres in Macedonia and urged the great powers to carry out the Treaty of Berlin. The same month they expressed their support for an international anti-military conference, protesting at the huge burden of military and naval expenditure. In 1906 the secretary reported on a 'very successful' national peace conference in Birmingham. He also attended a conference of the International Metal Workers in Holland. From 1905 to 1922 he was also active in the General Federation of Trade Unions, a body set up by the TUC to help smaller unions by spreading the financial load during disputes and other times of crisis. In 1904 the Society took out £20 in shares in an abortive Birmingham Trades Hall project. Its response to the usual strike appeals was conditioned by its own poor financial position with a 10s or occasional £1 donation the most they could afford, with local appeals sent round the shops.

The National organisation was building up close relations with the sheet metal workers in the Midlands and 'after a long wooing a quiet wedding' took place with the organisation joining the National Amalgamated in January 1910. By this time the Iron Plate Workers were in a bad way, membership had dropped to 558 and funds were down to £612 18s 5d; its branches confined to the Midlands – Lye, Wolverhampton, Birmingham, Bilston and Dudley – except for a few members in Belfast and the small Bristol branch in the process of joining the local tin plate workers. The National body gave itself a new image with a change of name to the Galvanised Hollowware and Sheet Metal Workers Union, and Simeon Webb was given a bigger stage on which to demonstrate his undoubted capacity.

But the National Amalgamated did not count the affiliation as all gain, stressing the 'handicap' of women workers engaged on the manufacture of common house buckets and pails, although Webb said they desired to resist any further increase in the number of women. The Women's Trade Union League was interesting itself in the women but the National Amalgamated made Webb fully aware

of our refusal to recognise women labour in the trade and had been advised that the Society should not identify itself with the movement in such manner as would give colour to the idea that we, as a trade, were willing to depart from the policy of strenuously opposing the introduction of women labour into the trade.

Trade was good in 1911 and the Society doubled its membership to 1,186 – which Webb said was 95 per cent of the workers in the industry – and record funds. The position enabled the Society to get wage increases for 75 per cent of the lowest paid men in the trade, something that had not been done for twenty years, but it had only been achieved with a number of disputes. The struggle was maintained during 1912 resulting in a uniform minimum standard piecework list and uniform rates for day work in the various grades with a general rate of 7½d and 8½d for government work on a 54-hour week. Their target was now the five or six firms still clinging to the pernicious system of sub-contracting or sweating. Membership had gone up to a record 1,324, including youths of 16 who were now admitted to the Society.

With the formation of the National Union, the Midlands' Hollowware Society became a district of its own, 3B, for some years before being incorporated in the general Midlands district; Simeon Webb became district secretary, served on the national executive of the new Union until his retirement and was national President for five years.

The Liverpool Society

The books of the Liverpool Society tell of the continuing relationships between the various local tin plate workers' societies. The cash books from 1830 to 1832 record regular parcels from London, probably containing literature, despite the demise of the National Union some five years or so earlier. There were also parcels from Wolverhampton and Bristol. Many of the other entries deal with the relief of tramps and payments for ale. These give the only reference we have of the existence of some societies. The minutes for May 1840, for example, record that 'the secretary shall send two copies of the laws of the Society to Wrexham and a letter of introduction and to congratulate them on coming forward.' Similarly, an entry in 1848 'Jas Marton's card from Shrewsbury' gives an unexpected early record of a society in that town. An entry in the cash book for July 1830 'Parcel from Oswestry 2s' could also indicate a society there. But why Liverpool should be sending three dozen cards and a book of rules to an old-established society like Nottingham in December 1855 is another matter, unless perhaps it was being revived or reorganised for some reason. An entry recording the receipt of 36 cards from Manchester in June 1837, at the high cost of 6s, is possibly an indication that tramp cards were already supplied by the Manchester Society.

The 1842 minute book gives a list of local societies with which the Society was in contact, with the name of the secretary, the landlord and the club-house. They include Belfast, Dublin, Glasgow, London, Birmingham, Wolverhampton, Nottingham, Stourbridge, Bristol, Doncaster, Bradford, Manchester, Ashton-under-Lyne, Bolton, Preston, Blackburn, Wigan, Rochdale, Heywood and Stockport.

The books also record the financial assistance given to other trades in difficulties. They include such nationally famous disputes as the 1825 Bradford Wool Combers and Stuff Weavers strike (for which the Union still has a receipt for a donation of £4) and the London Building Trades lockout of 1859, as well as such obscure and forgotten disputes as that of the London Umbrella Silk Weavers' Association of 1861 and many more too numerous to mention.

The Society, generally, played its part in the wider trade union movement, both locally for the improvement of conditions, and in national causes – at least up to the 1870s.

In August 1845 a committee of five was elected 'to meet the trades working with us to petition for a reduction of hours on Saturdays, with full powers to act' – hours of work were said to be commonly 69 a week. This was obviously a long-running campaign as we read that

in January 1849 it was agreed 'that John Cook have his quarter's contributions returned to him in consequence of the sacrifices he has been at defending the hours of labour.'

The next reference to hours of work is July 1860 when a deputation of three was appointed to meet with a deputation of brass finishers and coppersmiths on the question of obtaining a half-holiday on Saturday. A special meeting decided that all legitimate means be used to ensure that 'labour cease at 12 o'clock on Saturdays.' Many seemingly took French leave as it was agreed that two members be allowed benefit 'having been locked out at Bennett's for leaving work at midday on Saturday.' In March 1866, having won the day in Liverpool, the Society resolved to help the men at St Helen's to get Saturday afternoons off.

The slow steady campaign to get hours reduced continued. In November a delegate represented the Society at meetings of the Nine Hours League and at the end of December the Society decided to step up its activities. It called for a report on how the Nine Hours League was being received in the various shops, held a meeting to consider the position of the trade in the Nine Hours Movement and set up a committee to supervise activities.

The only reference to action on wages in this period was a resolution in January 1856

that the wages recognised by this society be 24s a week and members are generally recommended not to work for less, and that no person be allowed into the Society who works for less than 22s a week.

Then in 1863 Ashton-under-Lyne employers, during the widespread unemployment and distress among tinmen in Lancashire due to the cotton famine, circularised a new prices book. The Manchester, Blackburn and Preston societies apparently accepted the lower prices, but Liverpool replied that their system of working was so materially different from other towns in Lancashire that the prices could not be entertained. They went on to submit, 'most respectfully, that it is ill-timed and unwise to attempt on the part of employers or employed to make any alteration in the price paid for labour in the present crisis.' While the Society members 'rejoice at the peace and order prevailing in Lancashire' they sympathised with their fellow labourers in their suffering and distress caused by the American War. They were

convinced that any attempt at the reduction in the price of labour at the present time may lead to serious consequences, the responsibility for which would rest with the Ashton masters. ... [and they] respectfully recommend the desirability of avoiding such a conflict with their men at the present time.

The Society was one of fourteen which got together in February 1847 to form the local Trades Guardian Association, sending two delegates and affiliating on the basis of 80 members at 1d per member. The records show a continuous active support of the Association and its activities. It channelled much of its financial support for other societies in distress, as well as for activity of the wider trade union movement through the Association and the history of the Trades Council singles out the tin plate workers as one of seven societies giving a wider measure of support.

The Society rallied round when, at the end of the 1840s, the engineering employers tried to smash the trade unions. In 1847 Selsby, the general secretary of the Mechanics Protective Association (known as the Old Mechanics) and 26 strikers were arrested during a strike and in an indictment said to be forty yards long, charged with 'unlawfully conspiring, confederating and agreeing to oppress' an employer – though Selsby's only action was to issue calls for voluntary collections for the strikers and transmit to them the money donated. The Association's offices were ransacked and Selsby and the others dragged off to prison without any legal authority. The case aroused great concern among the unions, the Liverpool Society gave £5 toward expenses for attending the trial and made up to £3 available toward the defence. Selsby and seven others were found guilty and although the convictions were quashed on appeal, the unions were alarmed and began to consider action to strengthen the unions' legal position.

Their concern increased when 21 London stonemasons were indicted for conspiracy and when the secretary of the Sheffield razor grinders and three members of the society were tried and sentenced to ten years' transportation at the instance of the local employers' association, on the uncorroborated evidence of two convicts that they had incited them to destroy machinery. The National Association of United Trades organised protest meetings and indignation at this perversion of justice was so great that the indictment was quashed on a technical point. A new indictment was immediately preferred against the men and it was only after widespread protest that they were finally released after one year. The Liverpool Society contributed £4 to each of the defence funds, and also took a collection for the Sheffield men. (Financial support also came from the London societies, from the tin plate workers societies of Birmingham, Wolverhampton, Blackburn, Bradford, Rochdale, Oldham and from the London Zinc Workers.)

After this the Trades Guardian Association became more involved in parliamentary action and the Society with it. Records show a payment of 10s to the secretary for loss of time in 1853 in forwarding a petition to Parliament – this would have been in connection with the Combination of Workmen Bill. A local paper reports that a Liverpool MP introduced into Parliament petitions in favour of this Bill from a number of local trade societies, including the tin plate workers.

Then in 1854, the Society put a 1d levy on members to defray expenses in connection with the Friendly Societies Bill then going through Parliament. The unions lobbied members of the House of Commons, getting a clause added to the Act to include the trade unions in its scope, believing that this would give them legal status, allowing them to take legal action on their own account in cases such as proceedings against absconding officials. A number of unions, including the Liverpool tin plate workers, deposited their rules with the Registrar, after making the necessary alterations required by the Act but a later Queen's Bench ruling of four judges headed by the Lord Chief Justice, declared that the unions were outside the scope of the Act and moreover, while they were not now actually criminal, they were so far in restraint of trade as to make them illegal associations.

The unions responded to this setback by increasing their Parliamentary activity and in

Liverpool Society banner believed to have been purchased in 1838 for the procession to mark Queen Victoria's coronation

January 1857 the Society voted £3 for delegates taking part, in conjunction with the Guardian Association, 'in the proceedings of watching the Bill in Parliament relative to workmen.' In July 1859 10s was paid through the Association to support 'the Combination Bill in Parliament,' a short Bill designed to expressly legalise peaceful persuasion to join a trade union and peaceful picketing to obtain higher wages or shorter hours of work, the legality of which was in some doubt. It apparently originated with the executive of the NAUT and Thomas Duncombe was involved in bringing it before Parliament successfully.

About this time the Society was involved in a number of activities concerned with arbitration, mostly originating from the NAUT. In April 1858 it decided that action on a circular received from the National Association in relation to 'McKinnon's Bill in Parliament on arbitration' be left to the Society's delegates to the Guardian Association and a 2d levy was put on all members for expenses in 'watching the Bill in Parliament.' Then in January 1860 it petitioned Parliament in favour of the Conciliation and Arbitration Bill then going through the House which called for the setting up of 'equitable councils' between masters and workmen 'invested with power to decide all questions relating to existing contracts.' And in January 1861 a delegate was appointed to attend a London meeting organised by the National Association.

In November 1871 the Society sent a delegate to the United Trades Association meeting concerning the repeal of the obnoxious clauses of the Trade Union Act, part of the struggle against the Criminal Law Amendment Act.

From then on activities to obtain legislation favourable to the unions was channelled through the TUC Parliamentary Committee to whom the Society sent a £1 donation in April 1878 but in its national activities the Society tended more and more to act collectively through the General Union.

In April 1864 the Society was a member of the local Trades Garibaldi Demonstration

Committee and with other sections of the working-class movement took part in the tumultuous reception he received on account of his progressive role in the unification and liberation of Italy.

But all this was only a small part of the activities of the Society, most of which were concerned with domestic affairs. Not all these were connected with work. An entry in the cash book for June 1838 records 'Sundry Bills for the Colour 13s 6d' and '1s 6d to officers, allowance for looking after colour.' This would be a new Society banner for the city's celebrations of Queen Victoria's coronation when all the trades took part in a procession including 'tin plate workers in tin helmets with tin battle axes and braziers displaying sundry kettles, urns, etc.'

Already in 1811 the Society had a superannuation benefit; any fully paid up member of ten years' standing was entitled to 2s 6d a week for life on reaching the age of sixty, if fifteen years a member 3s a week and after twenty years 3s 6d. We do not know when this was discontinued, it certainly does not appear in the 1853 rule book and was reintroduced in 1859. The preface to the 1853 rule book states the Society was founded 'for the good of the class to which we belong' and looking after the welfare of members and their families played an important part in that work. A special widows' and orphans' fund was set up in 1888 to give help to needy widows of members and payed a golden sovereign to every widow on the books at Christmas. When a member died his widow received a funeral benefit and the Society was well represented at the funeral provided for by a twelve-member funeral committee consisting of the president, secretary and ten members off the roll who served for six months. They were paid 2s 6d for attending each weekday funeral but were fined if they did not attend every funeral or send a substitute.

Polished tin-plate shield used at all Liverpool Society trade demonstrations and 'walkings'

This, I suppose, brings us to drink, which became a bone of contention in the latter half of the nineteenth century. Drink played an important part in the life of the society. The society met in a public house, with the landlord usually acting as treasurer. The rules laid down that 3d of the contributions should be spent on ale, whether the member was there or not, and one of the members acted as ale steward at meetings. The Society had drink checks, round brass tokens stamped with the initials of the Society, issued to each member when paying his dues and exchanged for ale, the secretary redeeming them later. The minute book for April 1860 records 'that 100

3d drink checks stamped from 20 gauge brass were given to members on payment of their subscriptions at the Liverpool Society clubhouse where they could be exchanged for ale, to be redeemed later by the secretary

drink checks be made and that Wm Tower make them' for which, no doubt, he was paid in ale. This was the usual form of payment for all jobs done on behalf of the Society, for going to the bank or post office, or relieving tramps. It was not until July 1860 that it was resolved 'that the secretary be paid in money instead of in drink on paying members and tramps.' About this time, probably as a result of the rising strength of the temperance movement among responsible artisans, arguments began to be heard against meeting in a pub. The following March it was moved .'that we pay rent for the room and do away with drink entirely' but it took another seven years before it was put into operation.

The Society was extremely generous in its financial support over the years both to other tin plate workers' societies and to other trades. In 1841 it sent £4 to the Dublin Society to help them in a law suit; in 1842 a 6d levy was put on the branch to help the Wolverhampton Society, sending £3 a fortnight during their calamity, reducing the levy to 6d a quarter the following year, in 1846 £4 was sent to Birmingham and in 1847 £3 to Wigan. Liverpool provided £15 during the 1850/51 Wolverhampton strike; in 1852 they sent £2 to Bolton and in 1853 £8 to Preston. In 1862 a 6d a week levy was put on members to help the distressed Lancashire tinmen.

The books show a similar record in help for other trades: 1839, £3 to the London bookbinders; 1840, 10s to the cork cutters; 1841 another £2 to the cork cutters and £4 to the London masons; 1847, £2 to the basketmakers, £4 to the glassmakers and £3 to the engineers, 1851 £2 10s to the glass bottle makers, 1853, £2 to the upholsterers, £4 to the shoemakers, £5 to the Manchester dyers and £7 to the Wigan factory operatives; 1856 £1 to the London ships' carpenters; 1857, £20 over a period of three months to the cabinet makers; 1859, £1 to the window blind makers and £3 to the glass blowers. Also paid in 1859 was a total of £35 over three months to the locked-out London building workers, £2 10s to the Nottingham lace makers, £10 to the Welsh miners, £2 to the Warwickshire miners and £2 10s to the London cabinet makers whose members had been prosecuted for picketing, and so on until the 1913 Dublin strike when they made a grant of £10 and put on a levy of 2s per man.

A less happy relationship with other trades was the constant disputes over demarcation, a particular problem in shipbuilding and repair where the majority of Liverpool members were employed. The EC was given powers to take action against infringement on tinmen's work, especially by boilermakers, plumbers, brass finishers and joiners, as well as by whitesmiths and sheet iron workers. When the plumbers complained that covering pantry tables and dressers with block tin and zinc on White Star ships was their work, the Society wrote to 40 local employers for evidence that it was traditional tinmen's work. The boilermakers demanded that all workers on sheet iron be members of their union. On the other side the Society objected to brassfinishers doing lagging and whitesmiths making templates. When sheet metal classes were started at the technical school in 1905 the Society objected to other trades being allowed to take part in classes on practical work and sent a deputation to try and stop whitesmiths' apprentices being taught alongside sheet metal workers.

In the mid-1880s a new meter shop opened in Liverpool with production on a piece-work basis. The Society ordered its members there to go on day work and if the management would not accept to withdraw from the shop. Most of the men ignored these instructions, were ultimately expelled from the Society and the shop blacked. The expelled members started their own organisation, the Independent Liverpool Sheet Metal Workers' Union which spread into other shops as some of the original members moved and pieceworkers, rejected by the Liverpool Society, joined. But after a few years members of the Independent Union accepted that they could not build up a viable union and disbanded, dividing up the funds. They still continued working as piece-workers, the Society still refused to accept them, so the shop remained non-union. This caused concern to meter makers in other parts of the country and Gordon paid a number of visits to Liverpool urging the Society to organise the shop which was undercutting the established firms. He warned that with forty or fifty men earning only 33s the shop was a menace to the gas meter trade; they were also doing the work of shops on strike. The Society remained unmoved and refused to have anything to do with the shop while it remained on piece-work. It was not until 1915 that the men working at the Parr Gas Meter Co were accepted into membership, piece-work having given way to day-work.

In reponse to a notice from the employers that they were cutting wages, the committee resolved to maintain a rate of 30s a week and, anticipating a long battle with the employers put a 1s levy on all members while getting powers from a general meeting to raise it to 2s if necessary. Arrangements were made for all shop stewards to pay in contributions with the minimum of delay so that the struggle would not languish for lack of money. It was not until eighteen months later, in July 1881, that the levy was discontinued. A wages check the following May found only thirteen on the minimum rate and the vast majority earning 32s or more. The committee then raised the minimum rate to 32s and there was a continuous run of strikes until 1884 when the employers threatened to reduce wages to 28s and a couple of years later demanded still more cuts. The strike list was still in operation in 1888, but the following year the Society went on the offensive, demanding special overtime rates and holiday payments. By 1893 the employers were again posting notices for cuts both in wages and overtime payments so the committee put a levy on all overtime worked, 1s for each half-day's overtime and 2s 6d for all night work and in April 1893 levied all members 6d a week to provide for out-of-work members who had run out of benefit. The levies were not taken off completely until March 1895. This continuous battle to maintain standards of its members was the longest in the Society's history and was waged in the final days of Victorian prosperity when Britain was still the workshop of the world, and Liverpool one of its major ports.

Back in 1879, at the beginning of this struggle, entry into the Society was tightened up. No more new members were to be admitted by vote on ordinary club nights but each case would be considered by the Committee of Management and all those it passed would have to be approved at the next general meeting before becoming members. This rigid attitude to membership continued and we read of a refusal in 1905 to admit an apprentice in his final three months as being 'too young' and a 61-year-old man as 'too old'.

Their experiences in these long years of struggle brought realisation that the economic struggle was not enough with the employers occupying all the seats of political power and in 1894 a special meeting was held with a speaker from the local trades council who urged members to 'put away all consideration of Liberalism and Toryism' and make sure they were represented on all public bodies by people of their own class. The Society responded to his call and affiliated to the Labour Representation Committee and elected delegates.

In 1909, confronted with high unemployment, the Society considered the position of shops closed to members because they were not paying the rate or otherwise not conforming with Society standards. The Committee ruled that in the then condition of the trade, members already working in shops not paying the rate should be allowed to continue in the shop but under no circumstances should other members be allowed to start.

Men working in ironmongers' shops, where no shipping work was done, should be allowed to work for 36s for a week of 53 hours, but not for less than 8d an hour: men on ventilation work for the building trade should get 38s, they would be allowed to work piece-work but must report to the officers the conditions under which they worked; the rate for sheet iron work at mills and sugar houses was fixed at a minimum of 36s for 53 hours but any man taking such work should report to the officers. In November 1914 the minimum rate for motor work was fixed at 44s.

Charge hands should not be allowed to handle tools when in charge of five men or more. They should be paid an extra 1s a day above the rate when in charge of up to 20 men and 2s a day extra when in charge of more than 20. The wartime demand for labour allowed a claim of time-and-a-quarter for working in bilge spaces and on oil ships, time-and-a-half for work on oil tanks on oil ships and 64s a week for men on welding and burning, to be paid for the whole day at that rate after five minutes of this work. Men working 15 feet above deck or above ground were to be paid 1s extra per day and men sent to work aboard ship should have the assistance of at least one labourer.

The Society used a system of levies on members for a large number of objects. In 1909 the levy was 3s a fortnight, bringing contributions up to 5s a fortnight. In April 1910 this was reduced to 4s a fortnight, and in April 1912 a special 6d a week levy was put on to help fund the Joint Wages Committee that the Society had joined. The Society gave its full support to this movement which in May 1914 gave notice to the employers for a 6s a week advance. It also joined the Short Hours Movement, calling for a 40 hour week. The employers responded in July that year with an offer of 40s for a 47 hour week which was accepted.

Although it agreed in June 1915 to suspend rules to allow greater production of munitions the Society still opposed demands from both employers and government officials for dilution. The Committee obtained a list from the General Union of the various classes of work to which members could be drafted to ensure the retention of the maximum amount of work. In November 1916 the Society called a Town Hall meeting of shop stewards to hear an outline of the government's 'Organisation of Labour' scheme. After the officials had declared it was useless to resist the meeting agreed that the Society sign the agreement only five voting against. Then in January 1917 it was decided there was no alternative but to accept the Government's dilution scheme for private and commercial firms, carrying with it the provision of cards for exemption from military service. In 1915 a number of Canadian tradesmen arrived to work in union shops and were welcomed by the Society which admitted them into membership at reduced fees, conscious that they would help in the fight against dilution.

There had long been Society representatives in the various shops and yards and in 1911 they were reinforced with the election of members into an all-trades vigilance committee to ensure 'trade union bonafides' of workers at Cammel Laird's yard. In July 1916 the Secretary wrote to all shops urging them to elect shop stewards in the interest of the trade. In a number of shops it was difficult to get anyone to accept the position. This was the position at the Aintree munitions factory where over 100 Union members were employed, many of them from various other local societies. Despite repeated attempts by the Society to get a steward elected, it was not until they were told they would have to appear before the EC, charged with violating the rules, that the members conformed.

The war, with its introduction of new industries and new outlets for sheet metal workers, stimulated the Society into a drive to improve organisation. In the course of this it was reported that officials 'had come across a section of workmen known as tank makers' and asked the General Union for guidance on how to get them into the Union. They were told that tank makers could be organised into an auxiliary section then awaiting approval by branches. Then in 1919, on the very eve of the end of the Liverpool Society as an autonomous body and its incorporation into a National Union, it was finally agreed to admit welders into the branch, a controversy that had been going on almost from the first days of welders working in the industry, and even at this late hour sixteen voted against.

Oldham and Ashton

The first reference to the Oldham Friendly Society of Tin Plate Workers we have been able to find is a report in the Liverpool books for October 1837 of a tramp from Oldham with a card No. 10, followed by many others throughout the whole of the 1840s. In 1847 the Society's club house was the George and Dragon in the Market Place and the secretary was J. Johnson. By 1861 it had moved to the Woolpack, Greenacre Moor. The Oldham Society was a founder member of the General Union and attended the preliminary meeting in October 1861. In the 1872 report it was credited with 79 members. It left the General Union and joined the National Amalgamated in 1899, when it had a membership of 150.

In 1906 the Tin Roller Makers employed in one of the largest shops in Oldham joined the Society after it had neglected this branch of the trade for years. It was a small group of tradesmen and seems to have increased the membership of the Society by only fourteen.

The Society refused invitations in 1898 and 1899 to join the local trades council but changed its mind in 1903 when it affiliated to both the trades council and the Labour Representation Committee, although resigning from the Metal Trades Federation. It gave strong support to the Trades Union Congress policy on the Taff Vale Judgement, calling for mass meetings and pressure on local MPs. They made grants of £5 to the Bristol Society whose members were on dispute and lent £150 to the neighbouring Ashton Society, as well as £5 grants to the metal dressers and the Penrhyn quarrymen. The secretary also wrote to the Members of Parliament on evasion of the fair wages clause by local employers on government contracts in the making of field kitchens.

A large proportion of the Society's members were employed on gas meters and a depression in the trade put 132 members out of work in 1908 and 138 in 1909, out of a total membership of 208. Members on piece-work earning more than the standard rate were required to put 1s into the box each month to help maintain the local out-of-work fund. The Society began to look beyond the town's boundaries to increase its membership, giving attention to organising the trade in Middleton and elsewhere in the district. On the eve of the war another slump hit the meter trade, and a number of men were put off but the outbreak of war, after an almost complete stoppage of work for a while, brought work on munitions, pushing up membership to 250.

The Ashton-under-Lyne and District Braziers and Sheet Metal Workers Society claimed in its rule books that it was established in 1825. In fact the pages of the Manchester Society tramp book for May 1807 record an Ashton man given relief, there may have been more but most of the entries do not record the tramp's society. But others appear in the Liverpool cash book during the 1840s. In 1847 the Ashton Society was meeting at the White Lion, Booth Street, with Jos. Anderson as secretary. By 1861 it had moved its club house to the Crown Inn, Old Street. Ashton was also a founder member of the GU and in 1872 had a reported membership of 31. At the end of 1909 it severed all connections with the GU, complaining that the dues were too high for the benefits received. It continued on its own for a year or two and then in 1912, after opposition by the General Union, it affiliated to the Amalgamated with a membership of 133. That year it achieved a general advance of wages, increased overtime and working-out rates and an agreement on apprentices. By the start of the war membership had been pushed up to 164.

The 1919 minute book shows the Society as highly politcal, starting with a speaker on the 'Hands off Russia' movement and later another from the trades and labour council after which a resolution was passed

that the Allied Governments cease at once all armed intervention in Russia; recall all Allied troops at present in Russia; raise the starvation blockade of the Russian people; stop aiding by finance or otherwise the old reactionary gangs and by so doing guarantee to the Russian people that right of self-determination which is the right of every nation.

The Society affiliated to the Manchester Labour College and to the Labour Research Department, sent delegates to Ashton Labour Party and invested £100 in the *Daily Herald*. They also sent £20 to the Cheltenham branch to support members in dispute at Gloster Aircraft, £5 to a Wolverhampton dispute and £20 plus the result of collections to the moulders' dispute.

Support was registered for the joint committee demand for all overtime to be paid at double-time and calculated on the basis of a seven-hour day and for the demand for a 40 hour week.

It was decided that all time men spent in the forces should be counted as Union membership so that they remained on full benefit and in the case of apprentices it was to be counted in their time. Apprentices should not be allowed to do piece-work and their numbers limited in the shops. Each shop should elect one committee member who would also act as shop steward and collect contributions. A call was made for the abolition of piece-work to be taken up nationally and opposition was expressed to the signing of an agreement on procedure for the avoidance of disputes.

Wigan

Although Wigan did not feature in the societies affiliated to the Union in 1821 to 1825 there was, apparently, a society in the town before that time as the Manchester tramp book records '3 April 1807 Thos. Jackson from Wigan.' A Liverpool cash book for 1842 lists a society meeting at the Coach and Horses, Market Street, Wigan; the secretary was then J.Bolton, having replaced J. Udale. Two tramps from the Wigan branch with cards numbered three and four appear in the Liverpool books in April and July 1846 and the following year the Liverpool Society lent £3 to Wigan 'to assist them in their present calamity.' The Society also had support from Manchester during strikes in 1870 and 1875.

Wigan registered its support for the formation of the General Union in 1861 but did not send a delegate until the following meeting and in 1872 it is recorded as having only 11 members, and needed support from time to time to remain in business.

The only account we have of the Wigan Society's own records are contained in a minute book covering the period from 1913 to the end of its life as an independent Society and its absorption into the National Union. Its secretary in 1913 and for a few years afterwards was H.C.Veal. Most of the business of general interest is concerned with money in one form or another. In January 1913 membership application forms were issued to all non-union tinmen in the town and the committee decided to levy members 3d a fortnight for 12 months in preparation for the coming struggle. In April it was again agreed to make a drive to get all men working in recognised shops into the Union before putting in for an advance and we read in the September minutes that an application had been made for an advance of 2s a week, making a minimum rate of 38s for a 53 hours week. The employers said they could only pay 1s and this was unanimously accepted by branch members, who extended thanks to the employers. In March 1915 the branch put in another application for 3s a week, to bring their money up to 40s, complaining that Wigan rates were the lowest of all towns in a 20 mile radius, nearby Bolton receiving 42s for the same class of work. This time their application was granted in full.

A shortage of money continued to dog the branch. In April 1913 it was decided that after all expenses had been paid the surplus should be handed to the secretary as his fee until there were enough members to pay his salary. The society wrote to the National Amalgamated for a greater administration allowance to pay the salary but were told not to use Society money. This was still a problem in 1916 when the September minutes recorded a 1d levy to pay the secretary's salary. Neither was there enough money to pay unemployment benefit and so the remains of the fund was divided between the two members out of work. However, despite its own difficulties, the branch made a grant of £1 10s to the 1913 Dublin lockout. And in 1916, it was decided to put on a levy in answer to an appeal to defray the expenses of Labour councillors who lost time from work on council business.

The drive for members brought applications from corporation workers including one man who had spent practically the whole of his working life repairing night soil cans. His eligibility as a sheet metal worker was questioned but it was pointed out that this was a craftsman's job and he was accepted. It was then revealed that the corporation was paying less than the district rate and an application was made for an advance. A proposal was also put to the corporation that the gas department open a shop to repair meters.

Bradford

The Bradford Tin Plate Workers' Society first appears in the existing records in 1842 in a list of societies in contact with the Liverpool Society. Its secretary was then Thomas Smith and its club house the Bawton Arms in New Street, later moving to the Royal Oak, West Gate, where it still was in 1861. Tramping members of the Bradford Society in search of work appear in the Liverpool books for 1844 and 1845 and the Society itself must have been an important link in the general tramping network with the entries in its cash book mainly dealing with the relief of a large number of tramps.

Every month without exception up to 1882 the relief of tramps is the most important item, including those without cards who were receiving 2s 6d relief in 1862 but reduced to 'casual tramps' in receipt of 6d in the final days. Very few names are recorded but in 1871 a man arrived from Kendal, the only record of tin plate worker connections in the town. According to an 1897 entry one tramping-round took in Bradford, Halifax, Ashton, Manchester, Wigan, Bury, Rochdale, Burnley, Warrington and Bolton. But otherwise, over all these years the visiting tramps, sometimes referred to as tinners, tinmen or tin-smiths, remained an anonymous bunch, coming from and going to one knows not where, leaving only a record in the cash book of so many beds, sometimes so much ale and a few pence or shillings of relief and untold stories of hardship, separation from families and fading hope.

We know nothing more, either, of the activities of the Bradford Society until 1861 when it affiliated to the General Tramping Union in whose books it was credited with 57 members in 1867. Its secretary at that time was John Blackman and president Matt Ashley. Its recorded activities are very sparse, no doubt because the activities were too. In 1868 it was decided unanimously to affiliate to the Bradford Trades Council and also to bear its share of the expenses of sending a trades council delegate to a meeting in Manchester that decided to set up the Trades Union Congress. It also convened a meeting of the employers 'to discuss matters belonging to the trade'. The first wage claim appears in 1872 when an application was made for a 2s increase. In 1869 the management committee saw a local employer, Rowbotham, about limiting the number of apprentices with a repeat visit in 1871 and the August branch meeting decided that 'any clubman shall report any excess of apprentices or improvers, any neglecting to do so to be fined.' Then in 1878 it was resolved 'that by-laws respecting apprentices be abolished.' The August 1871 meeting ruled

that if any man thinks he does not get a fair wage he shall call a shop meeting to consider the same. If they think it is advisable they, along with the committee of management, shall do what they think best and, if the man or men have to come out they shall be supported on the same rate as strike pay'.

The September meeting decided 'that the Nine Hour Movement be adopted in the trade and committee of management be empowered to adopt means to bring it about.'

In June 1868 the committee met to consider the Preston strike and in September a grant of £5 was made to the locked-out Accrington Society. In 1871 interest free loans were made to Halifax and Blackburn. The minute books indicate that Bradford was always prepared to pay its whack of expenses, recording in April 1872 that the Society agreed to take part in the trade union demonstration 'and pay a share of expenses according to numbers.' It also offered to make an advance of £10 toward the expenses of the emblem if required; we later read of framed emblems being presented to Widow Smith and Widow Garnet 'at the expenses of the Society'.

The end of the 1870s was a period of depression and bad trade, and in 1879 the Society levied all members 6d a week 'to meet the present heavy expenditure' to apply to all except out-of-work members who were to be excused unless receiving the full out-of-work donation. This was originally for three months but continued for a year. In April 1884 superannuation benefit was suspended for two years and in 1887 it was decided to abandon it altogether. In 1886 all members were levied 2d a week for two years and the following year it was decided that any member who was out of benefit, who had reduced his arrears to six shillings, should be allowed a blank card in order to travel in search of work. In this period many members left the town. Membership continued to decline from 32 in 1886 to 25, 19 and finally in 1895 to only 13. However, the situation then eased and membership climbed up to 40 and the Society felt able to make each member a grant of £1 out of trade funds, first stopping all arrears, because of the bad times they had suffered during the great depression.

With the improvement of trade the Society went onto the offensive against cut-price low-wage employers. It drew up a list of fair shops which was sent to all secretaries and chairmen of public bodies in the town. The secretary also wrote to the Board of Guardians for dealing with unfair shops and with the help of the trades council's Fair Contract Committee, was able to get the Corporation to transfer its dustbins order to a fair shop. This 'fair trading' attitude was maintained by the Society in its own dealings. It employed the Co-operative Society's bakery department for its annual anniversary dinner and vetoed the booking by its entertainment committee of a pianist who was not a member of the Bradford Chairmen's and Pianists' Society.

Committees were a regular feature, part of the organisation of the Society. When something had to be done the first move seems to have been to elect a committee to consider it. The entertainment committee was only one of a number. There were different committees to deal with various aspects of the trade, meter committee, lamp committee and so on. There was an anniversary committee and when a cricket match was proposed a committee was appointed 'to carry same forward.' Another committee was formed in 1903 to get technical courses on metal plate work started. There does not seem to have been a political committee although the members generally supported Labour and the Society's delegates on the trades council voted for the canditure of ILP member F W Jowett for the West Bradford constituency. Nor have we been able to find any reference to an organising committee.

In 1901 the Society joined the national Amalgamated and the following year J.C. Gordon paid an organising and recruiting visit to the town as part of a tour to deal with the 'general disorganised' state of the trade in Yorkshire. The result was a general 1d increase in wages to a 7d minimum rate – including the packing case makers – a 54 hour week, a six year apprenticeship and limit of apprentices to one for every four men, all obtained with a minimum of strike action. It brought an anguished cry from the employers who demanded the organisation of the surrounding towns, Shipley, Dewsbury and Cleckheaton, to remove unfair competition.

The next general wage claim came ten years later with an application for another 1d to make the rate 8d. The employers offered $\frac{1}{2}$d after a one week strike which the Society was prepared to accept when the employers made it conditional on a guarantee that Leeds, Halifax and Huddersfield would get the same, which the Society refused to accept and members were locked out. But, supported by the Amalgamated and with additional financial aid from other societies, particularly London, Leeds and Bristol, the men stood firm and finally got the full claim without any conditions attached, although at a cost of £52 for the strike and £666 for the lockout. In 1914 the tin and zinc packing case makers called a strike over pay. The Society took over the running of the strike and got them a rate of 32s for a 51 hour week, taking the members into the Society.

Bradford entered the Amalgamated with 41 members. After Gordon's organising visit membership amounted to 62 and after the 1910 conflict they claimed 80 members and entered the war with 105 and had 125 at the end of the year.

According to a report of an old member, a typical Bradford general work shop in 1910 employed eight tinsmiths with two indentured apprentices and seven labourers, mostly employed in crating and despatching products. These were tin pans and cook ware, copper wash boilers, pans and possers, galvanised iron slipper baths and portable gas ovens, brass ash pans, fenders, lamps, fire-extinguishers, etc. The machines consisted of one screw press plus the usual assorted folders, guillotines and rollers; there was only one power driven machine, a polisher with emery wheel. Wages were 8d an hour; apprentices received 5s a week for the first year and a 1s increase each year until they reached the age of 21, when they came out of their time. Jobs were all day-work for which there was a set time. Each man had a slate as a time sheet on which he entered jobs done and time taken. Amenities were a can of hot water to make tea in the dinner hour plus a bucket of water for washing – no soap or towel supplied. There was no ventilation or dust extraction, and consequently many of the men had sore eyes and skin rash from packing slag wool into the gas stoves, a black face and cough from the polishing machine and yellow teeth and stained hands from acid fumes. Although most of the tinmen in the shop were Union members, none 'confessed' to it. A number of the unorganised men in the town worked for ironmongers making things for the shop or for the cotton mills. One, two or three men worked with the employer in a cellar, working all day by gas light. In these places it was generally 'how cheap can you do it,' never using 24 gauge metal when the job could be done with 26 gauge. Some of the bigger mills employed from four to six sheet metal workers, with an apprentice, on maintenance work. Before 1914 the trade in Bradford was only about one-third organised.and the same proportion probably held for other towns during this period.

While Bradford remained a general-work town, the year 1905 saw the advent of Jowett cars, producing popular two-cylinder cheap utility models, giving way to aluminium-bodied sports cars after the Second World War. The firm provided work for up to 50 members over the years until it folded in 1954, when the works and work-force were taken over by International Harvester.

Leeds

The 1901 Rule book of the Leeds and District Trade and Friendly Society of Sheet Metal Workers claims that it was instituted in 1857. That was probably one of the many reorganisations of the Society. We know there was some form of organisation in 1824 and a union tramp with a Leeds Society card No. 10 was relieved by Liverpool in 1846. A Leeds Tin Plate Workers' Society was in existence in 1847, one of a group of societies in the main towns which kept in touch with each other. Its secretary was J. B. Hurst and its club house the Boy and Barrel in Bridgate Street.

There seems to have been a breakaway society formed around 1900 as the General Union received a letter from an organisation calling itself the Leeds Independent Tin Plate Workers Society, asking for a mutual agreement for relieving each others' tramps. The General Union replied that it would cause confusion to have two relieving stations in the town. The Society had joined the General Union in 1861 but had left and affiliated to the National Amalgamated in 1903 when it had 64 members and funds totalling £570. The following year membership increased to 82. The year 1908 was the worst in the history of the Society with bad trade persisting throughout the year, but, as the economic situation improved they were able to push membership up to 106 in 1912 and the last quarter of 1913 saw a rapid rise to a record figure of 150. The secretary reported that they had established the rate at 7d but that 90 per cent of the members were getting more. With the help of the Labour members on the Council they had persuaded the Corporation to make and repair its own street lamps, providing additional work for members; some one-fifth of the branch membership was already employed at the Corporation's stove and meter department.

Entries in the Society's minute book of 1905 to 1914 – the only one we have – show the Society was concerned with organising tin plate workers not only in Leeds but also in the surrounding area. In 1907 the committee decided that a deputation 'go to Barnsley to get the

Bradford Street Metal Works, a typical general shop, turning out a wide variety of work. *Above*: making equipment in stainless steel for a national confectionary company; *right*: making machinery guards for a local engineering company; *left, top*: ducting system of tinned iron for a local paper manufacturer; *left, bottom*: fairground dodgem cars in the making at Willis panels, Coventry, 1938

few men there to join the Leeds Society'. A recruiting meeting was held at the FitzWilliam Inn and 13 of the 17 local tinmen attending joined the Society, and a few months later the Leeds officers helped them to form a society of their own. A recruiting meeting was later held in Wakefield and 12 members signed up as members of the Leeds Society. Then in 1913 the secretary wrote to the Bradford, Halifax and Huddersfield societies asking if they would co-operate in organising the West Riding but nothing further was heard of the proposal; it was probably killed off by the war. The committee did not neglect its own home pitch. In January 1910 it appointed an organising secretary supported by a committee of four with powers to add to their number and £10 was voted to pay organisation expenses. A list was drawn up of shops to be visited. Branch building suffered a temporary set-back with the outbreak of war in 1914 when a large number of members were stood off but by 1915 membership had been advanced to an all-time high of 187.

A meeting of Society and non-Society men working at Wilson Matheson, one of the largest general shops in the town, sent a joint deputation to 'wait on the masters' in an attempt to get the town rate. Later Society and non-Society men again combined, taking strike action when the employer tried to reduce prices and the minimum rate.

Gas meter makers accounted for a goodly proportion of the branch membership, with branches of many of the main manufacturers in the town, and it was a meter shop that provided the longest-running strike in the Society's history, when 12 men in the local shop of Milne's Meters came out in solidarity with their colleagues in the main shop in Edinburgh. Pickets were put on the shop and some Glasgow members were persuaded to take an expenses paid return visit home. The Leeds men were out for six months, the terms of settlement providing that the men went back exactly as they came out, without any prejudice shown on either side and with all blacklegs removed before the strikers returned to work.

The EC drew up a list of fair shops in the town and about half-a-dozen doubtfuls were written to asking if they would be prepared to pay the minimum rate and recognise standard hours. The Society's officials met the local Fair Contracts Committee, members of which accompanied them to put their case to the Corporation.

The Society also played its part in political activities. In 1905 it invited representatives of the Labour Representation Committee to address the lodge, which led to the affiliation of the Society and support of Labour activities, but a proposal to nominate a Leeds Society member as a Parliamentary candidate at the cost of 4d extra on the contributions was 'not entertained'. In March 1906 the Society sent a letter to local Members of Parliament asking them to support the Trades Dispute Bill then going through Parliament and later it was represented at a local Labour Party meeting to consider political and trade union activity in support of the Bill. It also sent representatives to a conference in Wakefield on old age pensions. The Society took up 20 ten-shilling shares in the Labour Publishing Society which produced the local Labour paper, the *Leeds and District Local Citizen*, and invested £50 in the Leeds Trades Council Club.

Nor did the Society ignore the plight of fellow tradesmen in difficulties. When Bradford Society men were locked out over a pay claim Leeds made an immediate grant of £2 and levied members 3d a week for three weeks. It also made a grant to the Hollowware Workers on strike in the Black Country. The Society sent £2 to the food fund in support of locked out Dublin workers, but a letter from the Women's Suffrage Societies, West Riding Federation, was allowed to 'lie on the table.'

Hull

There was a Hull Society already in existence in 1824, and probably earlier. Although it was listed as only having seven members it was able to meet all its commitments to the National Union of the day. It was also part of the tramping system, although we have been unable to find any reference to organisation in the town until 1862 when Hull joined the newly formed General Union. This society collapsed the following year but was resurrected in August 1866.

Several previous attempts to form a Society had met with defeat 'due to the distrust and apathy of the men', but the 1866 Society survived, even if it did not exactly flourish. According to a report by the secretary, Proctor, in 1893 there were 120 'eligible men' working in the town of whom only half were in the union – even this was a gain of 34 over five years. However, the employers still refused to recognise the Society. As a result, although the minimum was officially 30s for a 53 hour week, 26s was 'the common figure' of wages in the town. The Society had turned down an invitation to join the Federation of Ship Building and Engineering Trades 'as they could not take the responsibility of a strike with so few in the Union and so many non-unionists in the town.'

Members were primarily engaged in shipyard work and iron cask making. In the yards they often came into conflict with the boilermakers although last minute concessions had up to then avoided open conflict between the two unions. The sheet metal workers had resisted proposals to form a joint committee and draw up lines of demarcation because they felt they would not get fair play, the boilermakers being so much stronger and more numerous. In 1903 they were still having difficulties with the boilermakers but reached a compromise that the boilermakers did the sheet iron work in the boiler room and the sheet metal workers in the engine room.

The 1893 report said they had joined the local trades council but had withdrawn 'believing it to be nothing but a clique of radical proletarians.' They had recently rejoined but were still dissatisfied and were thinking of withdrawing again over the fact that radicals were supported in recent elections, quite regardless of their conduct as employers of labour.

In the years immediately before the First World War, the Hull sheet metal workers took part in many attempts to get a stable branch organised in Yarmouth, where a sub-branch of the Hull Society was finally set up in 1915. Like that of sheet metal workers in many of the east coast fishing ports, much of the work in Hull consisted in supplying ships chandlers or ships' stores as well as a certain amount of boat building and repair. Grimsby reported a claim for extra money 'for specially laborious work' in stokeholds and engine rooms. They were also engaged in fitting up acetylene gas lighting then extensively used on fishing vessels. The rate paid for this work was said to be considerably below that paid in Hull and this threat of undercutting gave Hull the incentive to get the other east coast ports organised.

Derby

The Derby and District Friendly Society of Braziers and Tin Plate Workers was formed in February 1872 by a group of some twenty tinsmiths from the local railway workshops, with E. Elliot as its first secretary.[6] There is said to have been a guild or fellowship of tin plate workers in 1822 and certainly there was a union branch with seven members in 1825. Union organisation existed at least for part of the interim period as the Glasgow tramp records for 1841/2 show, while the Liverpool tramp book records relieving a tramp from Derby bearing card No. 6 in 1843 and another with card No. 11 in 1845. The new society joined the General Union on a basis of 24 members within months and like the General Union, was concerned with friendly benefits; new members were required to provide a doctor's certificate of good health.

The new union met at the Market Tavern, its club house until 1920 and where, after the lodge meeting, members' wives could call for them at around ten o'clock on a Saturday night to complete their weekend's marketing – valuable pennies could be saved by late-night shopping among the leftovers in those pre-refrigeration days.

Derby was then a quiet country town set in good dairy farming country famous for its cheeses, brought into the old open market by the waggon-load on Saturday market days. The farmers provided work for some of the small tinkers' workshops making milk churns, pails, milk skimmers and other dairy equipment. Other small shops made vats and coppers for the breweries and drip pans and zinc counter coverings for the beer houses. Yet others of these one and two-man tinkers' shops scattered round the town made goods for ironmongers, baths, buckets, ladles, saucepans, breakfast cans and a range of tinware domestic utensils. One small firm specialised in making highly polished copper coffee grinders which were sent all over the country.

Some of the local engineering and other works employed a tinman or two, mostly on maintenance work. But most of the branch membership for the first thirty years of its life came from the shops of the old Midland Railway which came to the town in 1836. The railway shopmen were by way of being little aristocrats among local working men, envied for their regular jobs, relatively well paid and with a few shillings pension on retirement.

After 1900 the cycle gear trade developed and the local gas company employed some tinmen on meter work, but the big day for Derby sheet metal workers was when Rolls Royce moved into the town in 1908 followed by British Celanese in 1910.

From 1911 onwards a number of members of Northern and Midlands branches came to the town to work and considerably strengthened branch organisation and activity. Then, with the govenment take-over of the Rolls Royce factory for war-time aircraft engines, some 60 outside tinmen were drafted in. There was some conflict at the pre-war Rolls Royce Motors, first over the Company's insistence on operating the controversial premium bonus system, and then a big strike over the victimisation of a shop steward. The newcomers helped to establish a town rate for motor work – previously the tinkers' wages had been decided at the employer's pleasure. The new rate for a 54 hour week was 1s a week above the fitters' and turners' rate and the railway shopmen's rate was 2s under the district or town rate, and was for 54 hours, the difference was supposedly to offset the free tickets, quarter fares, free firewood and other 'concessions' that were railwaymen's perks.

The branch, along with the Allied Trades Movement, resisted an attempt by the Company to have three grades, makers, repairers and other. British Celanese works at Spendon recognised the Union which, after many meetings, was able to negotiate a wage a little above the town rate. The branch was also successful in negotiating a lieu rate with the Gas Company 33 per cent above the engineers rate. After the war a number of new shops opened, including one by the Derby Co-operative Society. Membership topped 100 mark after members of other branches were allowed to transfer to the local branch. In 1920,the Derby Society ended its separate existence with 144 members and £500 to become part of the National Union, soon pushing up its membership to 200.

Swindon and other Railway Branches

The Swindon branch started off as a one-works branch formed as a result of a visit by J Corbett, secretary of the Crewe branch of the National Amalgamated on 22 May 1915 when he had a meeting with nine tinsmiths of the local rail shops in the Great Western Railway Coffee Tavern.

Although this was in effect a company town it is still remarkable that it was not until 1915 that trade union organisation had penetrated to the tinshop. Gordon reported that 30 or 40 tinmen were employed in the railway shops, averaging 33s for a week of 54 hours. Many were over fifty and having been brought up in the shop regarded their situations as permanent, so saw no reason for a union; the younger men held aloof for fear of victimisation. But after a talk by Corbett the nine tinmen agreed that it would be in their interest to form a branch, and promised they would get some of their shop mates to another meeting to formally set one up. This took place on 1 June at the same coffee tavern when nineteen tinmen turned up, but the formal opening was delayed until 5 June when J. Corbett, J.C. Gordon, for the National Amalgamated, and Hall, secretary of the neighbouring Eastleigh branch, also based on railway shops, all spoke and 22 men signed membership forms. The branch strength was pushed up to 25 on the first paying-in night, when W. Golby was confirmed as secretary and A. R. Cooke as president.

The local trades and labour council was written to for a book of rules and guidance on how to run a union branch, an emblem was obtained, framed, hung up on the club house wall, and the branch was away. The officers and members of the branch were very raw, holding long discussions on how to proceed when anything new came up and were continually applying to the trades council and union head office to ask what they should do, Hickin commenting that the branch secretary was 'very persistent in his writing.'

Membership built up by ones and twos and then in October, on the recommendation of the general secretary the branch took in eight tradesmen working in the GWR shops in West London; the London Society, was unable to take them in as they were not earning the district rate. In 1917 eight lads were accepted into membership.

The district rate was fixed at 40s, and a pricing committee was formed. In 1920 the members decided to divide up the funds after paying all head office dues, copying the share-out policy of the old friendly societies. However, the branch continued and even formed a second sub-branch at Oxford. A joint meeting rejected proposed cuts of 6s 6d a week and pressed for the National Union to be represented by a member working in a railway shop at negotiating conferences.

Swindon was the last of a number of rail shops visited during organising tours of the general secretary. The first was Crewe – which was also the first branch of the National Amalgamated as distinct from affiliated societies. It came as the result of a meeting organised, at Gordon's request, by the local trades council, aided by a number of Labour councillors, attended by a number of young and enthusiastic tinsmiths employed in the locomotive department of the London and North Western Railway. A branch with 27 members was formed at the beginning of 1906 which had grown, six months later, to 34 with an average age of 29. The works followed the usual railway pattern of poor piece-work prices and low earnings which largely contributed to the branch's boast that by the end of 1907 they had 48 members out of a total of around 60 tinsmiths at the works. Although this was followed by three years of continuous short time, membership kept up between 40 and 45 and at the beginning of the war totalled 66.

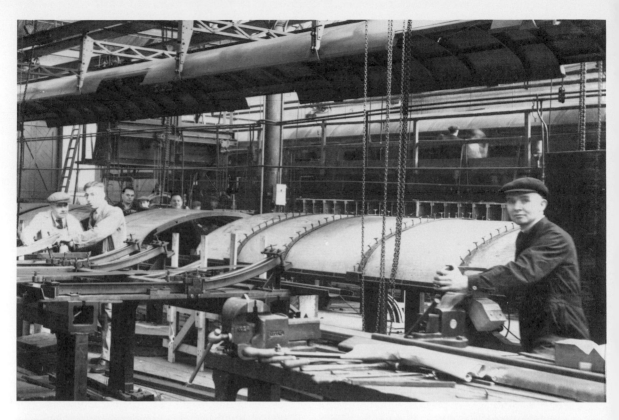

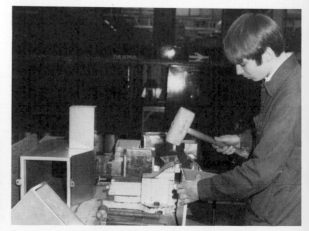

Railway shops. *Right*: welding repairs on a diesel locomotive at Swindon; *Opposite page, top*: fitting coach roof and side panels, Derby; *bottom, left*: making tail lamps and *right, top*: making diesel tanks at Swindon; *bottom*: making air conditioning systems for diesel railcars, Derby

The Crewe secretary, J.Corbett, continued to press for the other railway shops to be brought in but it was not until 1913 that any advance was registered. First Gordon set up a branch of the tinmen working at the London and North Eastern Railway works at Wolverton, largely engaged on making various kinds of lamps. This was in January 1913 and by October the same year the number had grown to forty, the full complement of tinsmiths in the shop. (Some fifty years previously the works had been organised by the old London Co-operative Tin Plate Workers Society.)

Then in November that year he got a branch going in Eastleigh for 17 workers in the London and South Western Railway works but here they were only able to get the membership up to 25 by the end of 1914. That same year tinsmiths working at the North Staffordshire Railway works joined the Hanley branch of the Union. Further organisation of railway tinsmiths had to wait until after the war.

Bristol

The Bristol Society was another that dated its formation to the end of the nineteenth century when in fact a society existed long before that time. Bristol is credited with 22 members in the 1824 membership list of the National Union and in that year was said to be 'on the eve of a calamity' – of strike action – its contributions and strike payments to that Union are both under two separate accounts A and C: there is no explanation for this and it is the only society in which it occurs. The Liverpool Society provides the next reference to the Society with an entry in its cash book for August 1837 'Postage from Bristol 11d.' In October that year a tramp from Bristol with card No. 28 was relieved and another with card No. 3 a couple of days later. Bristol tramps were also relieved in Liverpool in 1843, 46 and 48. Liverpool records for 1842 also list a Bristol Society, meeting at the Cock and Bottle, Castle Green, whose secretary was Geo. Tomkins. The same club house is given in the London trades directory for 1861. In the mid-nineteenth century Bristol appears on contribution lists to various strikes and on committees.

Then in 1898 the National Amalgamated decided to set up a branch in the City. There is no mention of any other society that might have collapsed and none of the tinmen that joined seem to have had any experience of a union. The Amalgamated called a meeting of local tin and iron plate workers at Sheppards Hall, Old Market Street, with a local trade unionist, Councillor J. Sharland in the chair. J.C. Gordon of the Amalgamated, J.V. Stevens of Birmingham and M. Preston of the General Union spoke and the men present unanimously agreed to form a union, Councillor Sharland agreed to be chairman for the first year, a secretary, Wilkins, was elected and it was decided that the club house be at the Jolly Meter Coffee Tavern in Queen Street. The Union joined the National Amalgamated and the trades council. They later started a political fund of 1s per member a year and affiliated to the Labour Electoral Association.

The following year the Union was responsible for getting a class in sheet metal work started at the technical college. The officials made their first wages application, on behalf of members working at Fry's the chocolate firm and then wrote thanking them 'for the kindness in the liberal advance to their employees.' A six-man organising committee was elected and the London and Midlands societies helped with the drawing up of a prices list. One of the main employers refused to pay the new prices and a strike developed. The employer first tried offering the men ½d an hour increase if they would leave the Union, when this failed he imported men from Lye but the Union was able to persuade them to return home. The London societies sent £35 to the strike fund and the General Union sent a further £5. More assistance came from other societies in the trade in the shape of a gift of £5 to help the Society to start a superannuation fund.

The new society was also generous in its aid. In 1902 it made a grant of £10 to the strike of London Jewish tin plate workers. In July 1901 it granted £2 to the Penrhyn quarry workers strike and the following month levied members 3d per week to help the locked-out Bristol tramwaymen. In the depression of 1905 stewards were asked to get a minimum of 1d per week per man for the trades council's unemployed fund. The members gave the secretary the power of discretion in relieving members of other societies 'on the road' with a maximum of 2s 6d each.

In 1900, at the request of the National Amalgamated, Bristol took in Society members at Llanelly until they were able to form a Society of their own. The following year three of the Llanelly members refused to work under rate and were discharged. They were paid strike pay by Bristol but told that in future any member must inform the Society of any grievance before taking strike action.

Thereafter the Society seems to have led an even more placid existence. It started the 1900s with a membership tottering around the seventy mark and slowly rose until in 1913 it registered a total of 104, reporting that motor work was 'very good', general work 'very fair' and the one lamp shop 'fair'. There was a general absence of disputes. The end of the first year of the war was celebrated with a membership of 135.

Smaller Societies

There must have been many small societies dotted around the country of which we have little or no record. We do not know how many of the small societies associated with the Union went down when it apparently collapsed around 1825: Maidstone with five members, Bath with six, Colchester with only three or Gloucester with four are likely candidates for collapse. Gloucester's neighbour, Cheltenham, which had five members in 1824, appears again in the 1837 Liverpool books with the relief of a tramp bearing a Cheltenham card No. 4 and the Society contributed to a strike fund in 1843. But nothing more about the Society appears in our records until a Cheltenham branch became part of the National Union in 1921.

In the same area was the Worcester Society with nine members in 1824. The next we read of the Society is a record in the Liverpool cash book of three tramps from Worcester relieved in 1847 and 48. One, arriving in Liverpool in February 1848, had been on the road since October 1847. Another had arrived in Liverpool via London. Then in 1877 the Society was re-formed during a missionary visit by officials of the newly-formed National Amalgamated. It appears on the Amalgamated's records in 1907 as a sub-branch of Wolverhampton so we know very little about it. When it was re-formed in 1877 it had 23 members: at the outbreak of war in 1914 it still had only 25 members, rising modestly to 38 by the end of 1917. The secretary, Jackson, wrote to London in 1893 asking for prices of signal lamps for the South Western Railway as they were having trouble with a firm who would not pay the rate. But the Society's main shop was Williamson's, a general shop which turned out a number of good craftsmen.

One of these was J. Sambrook who in 1911 was taken on as the first foreman of the tinshop at the Morgan three-wheeled cycle-car works at nearby semi-rural Malvern. As a strong trade unionist he only took on Union members and the tinshop remained a closed shop, continuing through the aftermath of the General Strike when the few local trade union branches were going under, employing up to 34 members at its peak. It remained an oasis of union organisation in a desert of anti-trade unionism, part of the Worcester branch, until the National Radar Establishment moved there during the Second World War and employed a number of sheet metal workers. It was by such means that the Union grew and spread.

The Manchester Society

From the records available, the Manchester Tin Plate Workers' Society would seem to have led a very parochial existence during most of the nineteenth century, considering the key position it occupied in the trade in the North of England. Although it was affiliated to the local trades council it did not seem to have made its mark in the wider activities of the trade union and labour movement.

The Manchester Society was one of the older tin plate workers' societies; the earliest rule book we have, that of the Manchester Friendly Society of Tin-Plate Workers, the second revision dated 1838, states that the Society was established in 1802. The earliest record we have is a cash book bearing the title *Tramp Book of the Tramp Society of Tin Plate Workers, Manchester* for 1807 and 1808. It records the amount of money expended in the relief of tramps, with varying but regular amounts for beer consumed by members 'on the slate', some postage and sundries. One different entry, for March 1808 records: 'To the four members for drawing up a memorial 4s 0d' – probably beer money for writing a wage application to be sent to employers. Another mysterious entry notes: 'Gave John Gledhill his travelling Card, allowed him 7s out of which he paid his arrears up to 24 April, gave him 12 years Bounty Money and 8s tramp money which in all amounted to £3 2s.'

Then on 28 February, 1819 the Manchester secretary wrote to his fellow secretary in Liverpool, James Hogarth:

Gentlemen:
I am desired by the Society of Tin Plate Workers to inform you that they desire to hold a correspondence with you once in six months or oftener if necessary, in order to know the good men from the bad as we often get imposed upon. There is a man in the name of John Dixon, that served his time in this town and through his bad conduct we did not think him worthy of being a member here, he came to Liverpool and has now returned with a card. We wished to know on what terms you

entered him, and likewise to know as to the reason he gave you that he was not entered here. Be so kind as to answer this as soon as possible.

Yours respectfully for the Society
Wm Nicholson

Direct from me at the York Inn, Shude Hill, Manchester.

On the back was a rough pen and ink sketch of a dog chasing rats.

The Manchester Society also had a membership register dated 1814 and a tramp card for 1819. The 1838 rule book is largely unexceptional, its preface stating that

> the Journeymen Tin Plate Workers of Manchester have agreed for the mutual support of each other and to maintain, by all just and lawful means in our power our rights and interests in the trade ... [their objects including] to lend assistance to Members of similar Societies who are travelling in search of employment, etc.

It consisted of 'Journeymen Tin Plate Workers only, who have served a regular apprenticeship to the trade, or the eldest sons of such who may have been working with their fathers or others in the trade.' Any free member wanting to go elsewhere in search of work would be entitled to receive the full 1s 2d a day unemployment pay from any Society he may call at which would be repaid by the Society at the end of the year; Members not free would be entitled to half the contributions they had paid into the Society. A Children's Funeral Society, formed in August 1819, was to become an integral part of the Society, paying parents from £1 to £4 at the death of a son or daughter 'plus 4s worth of liquer from the club house.' Drink figured largely in the affairs of the Society, the subscriptions of from 5d to 1s a week was specified in the rules as to include drink. The old cash book for the 1830s and 1840s has a regular entry each quarter 'secretary's ale' the amounts varying from 12s to 18s and the stewards had a regular monthly 1s 8d ale allowance. It was not until October 1870 that it was decided 'that no drink be supplied by the Society and we ask the landlord what rent he wants for accommodation' – previously the landlord received no rent for the rooms, his money coming from the drink consumed by members at the club house.

The old cash book dating from 1838 to 1847 underlines the lack of outside interest during that period. Apart from the contributions, benefit payments, salaries and tramp accounts, they only record a £3 repayment of a loan to Rochdale and two £10 grants to the Wolverhampton strike in 1842.

Although there is no record of the Manchester Society taking part in political or even trade union demonstrations, it did have an annual anniversary procession and participated in appropriate civic functions, such as the Town's celebrations for Queen Victoria's coronation. This was probably the reason it purchased a Society banner and regalia in 1876. The banner had 'the Society's emblem painted on one side.' The regalia consisted of a suit of tin armour and a large crown. The following year it added tin battle axes and a sceptre. These were 'got up' by a member of the Society.

All were the responsibility of the contingency committee which had the power to lend it out to other local societies providing they paid all expenses, including those of the banner carrier who accompanied it, and the cost of repairing any damage. The member appointed to wear the armour in the procession was paid 7s 6d, as were the four members deputed to carry the banner. The four members who attended to the guy ropes of the banner each received a free ticket for the anniversary dinner, as did the eight marshals and eight apprentices who carried the crown. A horse was borrowed for the occasion to carry the man in armour. Later, unemployed members were appointed to wear the armour and carry the banner and other regalia. These were all proud possessions of the Society and when Bolton split off to go its own way it was decided, in the division of the assets, that Manchester should retain the banner and regalia but that Bolton should have the use of it whenever it wished.

The Manchester Society was always very orientated toward welfare benefits and a lot of the committee's time was taken up with approving grants for sickness, unemployment, superannuation, funeral and other cases of need. The 1847 rule book allows a widow of a free member, 'so long as she retains her husband's name and maintains a good moral character' to have the privilege of having her name on the Society's books on the payment of a 1s entrance fee and contributions of 1s a quarter, allowing her next of kin to receive a funeral grant of £6. The 1846 rules provided for two sick stewards whose job was to examine all claims for sick pay and to visit every sick member at least once a week or be fined 1s 'for each neglect'. Some years later the Society divided the city into four districts with one doctor appointed to each to provide members with sick certificates as required. A lot of other time was taken up with the consideration of applications for membership. From a perusal of the minute books it would seem that the question of wages, hours and conditions of work came a bad second to these welfare and social questions.

In July 1862 it is recorded 'that the business regarding the new prices book issued by the masters' association be left to the secretary', then in April 1872 a committee was appointed, consisting of the president, treasurer, secretary and seven members to draw up a new piece-work prices book and the employers were given three months notice of the intention. In January 1873, the book being completed, the secretary asked the employers for a meeting, warning them that they would 'not be granted the privilege of objecting to any member of the deputation.' In April it was resolved that if a certain employer refused to pay the new prices the men should ask for the case to be referred to arbitration by an equal number of journeymen and employers and if the employer should refuse then the men in the shop should decide on their own line of action, which seems to indicate that the majority of the employers had accepted the prices, or at least reached agreement on them. In January 1875 the Society accepted an increase in day work rates of 1s in the first week in January and another in the first week in March.

There was a gradual reduction in the standard hours of work during this period. In 1871 a notice was sent to the three Manchester papers, the *Guardian, Examiner* and *Courier,* with copies printed and sent to all employers:

> That we, the journeymen tin plate workers of Manchester, Salford and the surrounding district, beg most respectfully to tender our sincere thanks to our employers for the generous manner in which they have conceded the 54-hours per week and at the same time we beg most respectfully to intimate that it is desirable that from 1st January 1872 we may be allowed to cease work at half past 5 o'clock in the evenings and 12 o'clock on Saturdays so that by this arrangement we may be enabled to feel the benefit of the concession you have so kindly conferred upon us.

It was signed by the president, Jas.Lomas, and secretary, Thos. Unsworth. No reply was received and it was assumed there was no opposition to the proposal so the committee prepared to put it into operation but in April 1872 the masters summoned Society representatives to a meeting after which the committee declared 'it was considered advisable not to alter the present system of working the 54-hour week.'

That same year the Society negotiated payment to men sent a distance of three miles from the shop, for staying out overnight and for anyone sent out suddenly without food. If the distance of the job was over twenty miles the men would be allowed to return home once a week and if over twenty miles, by special arrangements. 'Ironmongers to make their own arrangements with their men.'

Speaking at a meeting in London in 1862 the Manchester secretary, James Dunn, told of the suffering among tin plate workers in Lancashire due to the cotton 'famine' resulting from the American Civil War. Many Lancashire tin plate workers were dependent on the cotton mills for work and these had long been closed through lack of cotton. A total of 116 members of the various local societies were out of work, some had been out for from nine to fourteen months, most had families who were suffering 'the greatest privation and misery too heartrending to describe.' Another 200 were working only three to four days a week; only about 100 were working full time but their numbers were decreasing daily, adding to those out of work. He undertook to distribute monies collected by the London societies and in August 1863 reported that he had paid £55 to members out in Manchester, £33 15s to Ashton, £34 15s to Preston, £33 15s to Oldham, £14 4s 7d to Rochdale, £12 16s to Bacup, £12 5s to Blackburn and £2 10s to Bury, a total of £200 6s 7d received from London. He also distributed money sent by Liverpool, Wolverhampton and other societies.

In March 1863 it was decided that, 'as the funds of the Society are as low as it is possible for them to be, any expenses arising from decisions taken at meetings be raised by levies on members both in and out of work. A contingency fund was set up in January 1873 to help other societies both within the trade and in other trades who were in distress and 'other cases thought to be satisfactory.' It was funded by a levy of 3d a quarter on every member and a like sum taken from the general fund when there was a clear gain of that amount at the end of a quarter. The fund was kept separate from other accounts and was administered by a committee of the president, vice-president, treasurer, secretary and three sick visitors who could make grants of not more than £3 for any contingency or emergency if satisfied it was a case worthy of support. A second grant could only be made by bringing the case before a general meeting of members. The levy was stopped when the fund reached £30 and restarted when funds were reduced to £15. Grants had, of course, been made to other societies before the fund was set up.

In 1865 the result of a 1s levy was sent to men on strike at Platt Brothers, Oldham; in 1866 £5, raised by a levy was sent to striking bakers; in 1867 the results of a 2d levy was sent to the Derbyshire miners and £5 to the London basketweavers; in 1868 a 2d levy was put on members for the smallware weavers. In July 1868 £3 to £4 a week was taken from the funds for locked out members of the Accrington Society with a final sum sent in December with the recommendation 'that they do the best for themselves after this date.' In July 1871 members were levied 6d per week to support the Blackburn Society 'on strike for a reduction in the hours of labour.' Two grants of £5 were made to miners locked out in South Wales. After the fund was set up the grants continued: in 1873 10s a week for six weeks for the smiths' strikers and a similar amount to the umbrella frame makers, £1 to the Nottingham lace makers, £2 10s for the boot rivetters, £2 to the file smiths; 1875 £7 to the Wigan Society, 1876 £5 to the fine spinners, 1877 £1 10s to the silk hat band weavers, £8 to the carpenters, £5 to the Bolton hand mule spinners, £3 to the spindle and flyer makers and a levy of 1s for the relief of famine in India. In 1878 a promise of support of up to £15 was made to the Edinburgh Society 'forced to take strike action.' And so it went on with a levy of 6d a week in 1897 to provide a guaranteed £5 a week for engineers locked out over the claim for an eight-hour day 'to continue while the dispute lasts', a grant of £3 a week for four weeks in 1899 for 20,000 textile workers in Bohemia on strike for a reduction in hours from eleven to ten a day, a similar amount to 40,000 locked out members of the United Trades Unions of Denmark and a grant to striking carpenters in Brussels.

The support the Society gave to the engineers in 1897 struggling for an eight-hour day was rather different from its attitude to the Nine Hours League in 1871. Then, although the secretary attended a meeting of the League it was decided to take no part in its activities. This was in keeping with its attitude to other sections of the trade union and Labour movement. Invitations from the trades council to be associated with May Day demonstrations, it was decided, should lay on the table and the same fate befell early appeals and invitations from the Labour Representation Committee and the Social Democratic Federation. Then in 1891 the Society agreed to be associated with the Manchester and Salford Trades Council Labour Electoral Association and around the turn of the century it was responding to appeals to help defray expenses of Labour and trade union candidates in elections to municipal bodies.

The Society remained small and select while the majority of the trade remained unorganised and a strict and rigid interpretation of the rules on membership, and a reluctance to go out and get members kept it so. In 1874 the committee refused to entertain a request for labour from a tin can shop, Horrocks and Sons, because Mr George Horrocks had not served his time at that branch of the trade. Only allowing two apprentices to a shop, irrespective of the number of journeymen, further restricted the size of the Society, as did restricting membership to those working in Society-approved shops and earning the standard rate of pay. In 1870 the Society insisted that two men working below the rate in one shop be discharged before members would be allowed to work there. Members were continually being told that they must leave their place of work if they could not obtain the minimum rate and members were excluded from the Society for working in non-Society shops or below the rate. The result of all the restrictions and the attitude of mind that insisted on their retention could be seen in a shrinking Society at a time of rapidly growing industry. In 1873 there was a slight relaxation with a decision that 'aged' tin plate workers, over fifty years old, working at the trade as ordinary journeymen, would be allowed to become members of the Society. Then in 1893, in order to reduce the superannuation claims, members who had reached the normal retiring age would be allowed to work below the standard rate on a part-time basis.

It was not until the end of the 1860s that we find any record of moves concerning organisation of the trade and that was only a proposal that did not get off the ground. In 1883 a proposal was made that any shop where a man could earn the minimum rate should be opened to members but it was heavily defeated. But some concern appears to have arisen over the state of the Society during the 1886 depression when funds were so depleted that a 3d levy had to be put on all members and benefits reduced. The committee was urged to 'devise some means to induce non-Society men to join and so strengthen our interest and their's also'. But it took until 1890 before a circular was sent to non-Society shops inviting qualified tinmen to join. Men at a ventilating works and the Manchester Carriage works were invited to meet the committee to discuss joining the Society and improving wages. An inducement of membership at one-half the normal entrance fee was made to non-unionists at Cowan's meter shop.

Manchester had, however, shown a responsibility in salvaging remains of broken Societies in its vicinity. In August 1861, together with the Blackburn Society, it had successfully resuscitated the Wigan Society. Then Accrington tinmen were approached to form a branch of the Manchester Society in January 1864. The same year the Society took in Bolton members after their own society collapsed. It was run as a sub-branch of Manchester with its own club house where the secretary attended once a week to collect contributions. This continued until January 1895 when the Bolton membership had reached 96 and re-formed their own branch. Stockport was also run as a sub-branch of Manchester which controlled its activities (although in the 1840s it was a separate society) countering a proposal to apply for a wage increase with a request that it be left in abeyance pending a meeting of Society and non-Society men with the secretary to discuss improving organisation. When the Stockport secretary resigned in 1897 Manchester appointed his successor and when he too resigned his successor, elected by Stockport members, was 'subject to endorsement by Manchester.' Stockport also had to get permission to affiliate to the local trades council.

In November 1865 it was resolved that the lowest rate for general work should be 28s a week with 32s for cylinder workers. Bolton members were to be allowed a standard rate of 26s. It was also decided to fix a rate of 32s for casemakers, 'except for the aged and infirm.' Then in 1885 it was decided to take into membership the body of tin packing case makers whose members had 'lately commenced making tin cases.' In an attempt to organise the trade non-Society men were invited to meet the committee to discuss entry and told that they would be admitted at one-half of the normal entrance fee. They were also assured that if they lost their employment in resisting employers' demands for wage reductions they would have the support of the Society. A special casemakers' meeting was called to consider the continuing serious state of the trade and a joint committee was set up with the wooden packing-case makers which produced a registered trade stamp to mark all cases made with union labour and organised dockers, sailors and lorry drivers were asked not to handle non-union cases. Employers were asked to use their influence among shippers and merchants to honour the trade mark.

In an attempt to give employment to members another committee was set up to consider costs and working of a Union-owned casemakers' shop but after being talked around for some five years it quietly faded away. Following a report in June 1899 that there were still thirteen non-Union shops employing 33 men and 28 lads, compared with thirteen union shops employing 75 journeymen and 24 apprentices it was decided that another attempt to organise the trade be made before any other action could be taken. Three case-makers were co-opted onto the committee to work out a plan of action. They reported that a number of men in the 'outside shops' would be prepared to join but they were working under the rate so it was decided that the earnings condition be waived and all men admitted who had served a seven year apprenticeship. A new organising drive was then made on the 'outside shops' and a number of recruits made. But it was not until 1917 that all the case makers were enrolled in the Union which was then able to bring the rate up to that of the rest of the trade.

Manchester was an important centre of the gas meter industry and in 1894 the Society called a national conference on the wide difference in prices paid in Manchester, Edinburgh and London, which had a measure of success in obtaining a uniformity of prices. But generally Manchester followed the much stronger London meter makers' section.

It was also a centre for a number of railway workshops and in the 1870s took steps to maintain rates on various lines. In 1893 a meeting was organised of all men working in railway shops 'to devise any legitimate means by which the standard rate could be obtained.' After the men at Horwich, who were receiving £2 a week, piece-work, expressed fears that any interference might bring difficulties, it was decided to leave things in abeyance. There it remained until 1896 when a deputation from the Gorton works complained that their wages had been reduced to bring them 2s below the rate. Joint efforts to improve the position seem to have had little result. A meeting was called in 1899 to monitor the conditions under which the men were employed, their piece-work or day work earnings, and the position regarding apprentices.

Horwich works of the Lancashire and Yorkshire Railway reported thirty men employed, including one non-Society man. There were also seven apprentices. The standard rate was 32s for a week of 53 hours. The men had waived their claim for a wage advance, made in a circular to the management, as they considered the time was not opportune. At the L & Y Railway coach department there were 25 men employed and seven apprentices. Wages were noted in the Company's books as being 32s for a 53-hour week but practically no day work was done as each job stood by itself and was rated by the men at time and a quarter, to give them an average wage of £2 a week. The two shops of the Great Central Railway employed thirty men with three apprentices in each. At the locomotive depot there was no piecework operating and the average wage was £2. Eighteen months before a deputation went to the management for an advance in wages which was refused and then were told that if they chose to strike all work would be sent out. At the Great Central Loco Department there were eight men wholly engaged in engine lagging who wanted to work by the piece and in the other shop the five men on general work were on day work.

The committee called a meeting to discuss this mixed bag of conditions and asked all those present it they were in favour of a circular being sent to the companies seeking an advance of wages at the same time as one was sent to other employers but there was no enthusiasm for it.

The Society engaged in many demarcation disputes, putting up a strong resistance to any other workers doing work which they claimed belonged to the tin plate workers In 1889 they issued a printed statement opposing the growing practice among some employers of putting labourers on an increasing number of tin plate working machines. The Society declared that straight cutting machines, circular cutters, swaging rollers, jennies, folding machines, bending machines, wire bending and cutting machines, wiring machines, gassing machines, slipping tin punching machines, card can binder cutting and punching as being the ordinary tools of the tin plate worker. Labourers would be allowed to use all presses operated by steam power, hand presses that they were already allowed to use and steam power guillotines for rough cutting that had to be recut to a mark or gauge.

Firms were told that on no account could members of the Society use sheets cut, squared and folded by labourers. All work done on the guillotine for use by Society members must be done by members. But the Society had never regarded the screw press used for notching corners as one of their tools.

Demarcation disputes with the coppersmiths were 'regular', and in 1901 it was decided to try and reach agreement. The Society set out their members' rights to work all sheet metals including copper, brass, zinc, lead, block tin or white metal-coated iron or steel and any other sheet metals in commercial use. They maintained the right to such operations as making cramped or other seams or joints in the working of any of these metals which necessitated brazing, rivetting, grooving, soft soldering and chemical burning. Any qualified workers on these sheet metals – sectionally or collectively – were eligible to become members of the Society After making an article they claimed the right to fix it if required. The Society was prepared to meet with the coppersmiths' representatives and agree on reasonable demarcation but could not give way on any of the points mentioned which constituted the trades of the members of the Society.

After five members had been appointed by the two societies to work out demarcation lines, the sheet metal workers agreed that none of their members would go on out-work except for fixing hoppers, repairing refrigerators, lining rounds, squares or other class of lining. They also claimed, in brewery work, to do anything in sheet copper that could be made and fixed at the brewery. They would not do copper pipe fitting except so far as work directly connected with jobs already mentioned and required to be done when at the brewery. Sheet metal workers would under no circumstances do any copper pipe fitting if there was a coppersmith working at the brewery at the time. They would not use the forge or blowpipe to soften or braize copper for anything that was not already their work. No sheet metal worker would use or work any copper above fourteen BWG except when working with a coppersmith and they would expect coppersmiths to work hand in hand with sheet metal workers.

For years the Society had been concerned at mounting arrears of contributions. Lists of members in default were read out at branch meetings, money had been stopped out of benefit payments, but it was not until 1900 that collectors – called stewards – were appointed in shops where a majority of the members 'thought it desirable.' Collectors were paid 2 per cent commission and fined for failing to pay-in on time.

So, rather late in the day, this important development in the trade union movement came to Manchester. The shop stewards became the voice of the workers on the shop floor, a great step forward for industrial democracy, strengthening the unions where it was most necessary, at the point of production, giving strength and representation to the workers in their day-to-day dealing with the once all-powerful management. They became the foundation on which the democratic organisation and fighting strength of the National Union was based.

For some 120 years the Manchester Society had played an important part as an individual Society, protecting the interests of the sheet metal workers it represented. But of all its activities, the greatest contribution the Society made to the craft was to take the initiative in the setting up of the General Union which was born on 1 January 1862. This was the first regional or national organisation of the trade since the Union disappeared around 1825. It made the National Union possible.

1. *Aris's Birmingham Journal*, 6 September 1824.
2. Kidd, op. cit.
3. BLP&ES, Webb Collection.
4. G. Barnsby, *Origins of the Wolverhampton Trades Council*, Wolverhampton, 1965. The Society was one of the founders of the Council in 1865 and one of its two delegates, E. Davis, was elected Vice President, becoming President the following year. He was very active in support of the locksmiths during their long strike and in the formation of a production co-operative. In April 1866 he moved a successful resolution that the Council discuss the International Working Men's Association, but nothing seems to have come of it. Barnsby suggests that Davis was interested in the functions and activities of the International 'in preventing the import of foreign blacklegs during strikes as the tin plate workers had had experince of these blacklegging activities.'
5. BLP&ES, Webb Collection.
6. This section is largely based on research and a report by H. Dennis, a former Derby branch secretary.
Most of the rest of the material on which this chapter is based was drawn from such books of the former societies as still remain is national, district or branch offices.

CHAPTER SIX

The General Union

The formation of the General Union in 1861 was the first of two decisive steps that led to the eventual formation of the National Union of Sheet Metal Workers – a goal to which the craftsmen in the trade had been struggling for 100 years.

The other was the setting up, in 1876, of the Amalgamated Tin Plate Workers of Birmingham and Wolverhampton, which developed into the National Amalgamated Union of Tin Plate Workers – later Sheet Metal Workers – to which the General Union later affiliated.

The General Union started off with a much more modest aim, as the General Tramping Union of Tin Plate Workers, but as the years went by the 'tramping' part declined and the 'general' aspect

John Wiltshire, General Union Secretary 1882-93, part-time and full-time General Secretary 1893-1913

took over. It came into being as the result of a call by the Manchester Society to other Lancashire tin plate workers' societies to a meeting 'on the present unsatisfactory tramping system' and on the adjustment of contributions paid by members of one society working in an area covered by another. (What was considered 'unsatisfactory' about the existing tramping system does not appear in any of the relative minutes.) The meeting took place on 19 October 1861 when the Liverpool, Blackburn, Oldham, Bury, Preston, Ashton, Rochdale and Bacup societies accepted Manchester's invitation

It was agreed to set up a co-ordinated tramping system governed by a secretary, president and committee of five, the committee appointed by the Manchester Society – known as the No. 1 Society – with all member societies providing the same benefits for members on tramp in search of work.

After agreement by the several societies, the proposals were endorsed at a meeting at the Manchester Society's club house on 19 December when the founder members were joined by the Bradford and Leeds societies with Wigan and Lancaster approving but not represented. William Dunn of Manchester was elected part-time secretary on a salary of £5 a year, and John Brown of Liverpool president and the new union went into operation on 1 January 1862.

The governing body was the annual meeting of delegates from affiliated societies, each playing host in turn. The decisions of the annual delegate meeting were binding on all branches and the General Union rules were binding on all members: but if branches or local societies wanted they could have their own individual rules so long as they did not conflict with those of the General Union.

Prior to the formation of the Union many of the local societies were little more than old-fashioned trade clubs, with a mere handful of members and little or no power. Their operations were restricted by their small membership and limited finances. Each stolidly maintained its own independence, with its own rules, contribution rates and benefits, negotiating individually with local employers and largely unaware of what was happening outside its own immediate area. A society might disappear from time to time when trade was bad or when no one could be found to take on the job of secretary, to be resurrected during a dispute or at other times when the local tinmen felt the need of a society.

Very soon the modest declared aims of the Union were seen to be insufficient. Industry was growing rapidly and big factories were taking over from the small workshops run by individual masters, with trade union organisation changing to cope with industrial change. The tin plate workers could not remain completely aloof, although many of the old craftsmen resisted change. Delegates to annual conferences voiced the growing need for closer working on general policy, on wages and hours, working conditions, the formulation and timing of claims to be made to the employers, support for societies in dispute. Slowly the Union began to consider these matters.

More than that was needed, however. If the Union was to deal with these successfully it would have to take up the organisation of the many non-unionists in the trade. But it was in no way a dynamic campaigning body. Its method of expansion was to take in existing societies rather than go out and organise in fresh fields.

It did, however, save some local societies from foundering and helped resurrect others that fell by the wayside. When, in 1863, the Hull Society broke up, the former secretary was told to join the Leeds or Bradford branch taking as many of the late Hull members as he could persuade to follow him; meanwhile he was to continue to relieve tramps that came to the town until the branch could be re-formed. Keighley was advised to join the Bradford Society and Dewsbury went into Leeds, acting as a relieving station for tramps. Already in 1867 the Union's management committee asked the secretary and a representative of the Rochdale Society to visit Bacup and try to avert the break-up of this, the smallest of the affiliated local societies. They succeeded at the time but soon Bacup was in difficulties again, too small to be viable and, recognising the inevitable, the management committee decided that the Bacup members be given clearance to join another society.

The report for 1872 credited the Manchester Society with 315 members, Liverpool 133, Oldham 79, Bury 76, Ashton 31, Bradford 57, Leeds 64, Preston 38, Blackburn 40, Rochdale 28, Halifax 24, Bacup 8, Hull 21 (having been re-formed), Huddersfield 13, Lancaster 16, Belfast 37, Wigan 11, Burnley 16, Derby 24, Nottingham 36. Later Newcastle-upon-Tyne was admitted with 53 members, Sheffield readmitted after seceding in 1870 had 28, Sunderland 16, Uttoxeter 6. So that by July 1877 there was a total of 28 branches with a membership of 1,404. Voting in the deliberations of the Union was based on membership with one vote for the smallest society with six members to 11 for Manchester.

Cork and Limerick, with nine members, wrote enquiring about affiliation. Grimsby Society joined, as did the Potteries (or Staffordshire) for a time. The secretary was empowered to open a branch in Barrow-in-Furness – which eventually joined with an original complement of ten members. A visit was paid to the North East coast to look into the position of Sunderland, Stockton and Middlesborough, and the possibility of forming a branch in Shields. Liverpool was also allowed to open a relieving house for tramps in St Helens.

Structure of the Union

The financing of the Union was based on an equalising system, an old-fashioned method which it was introducing at a time when other unions were discarding it. The system was based on branch quarterly returns which gave the names of members who had received benifit payments during the quarter from branch funds or by means of advances from the General

Union. These expenses, together with the general cost of management, were totalled up under various heads of expenditure, and then the whole cost was levied equally upon the total membership. The secretary then issued a statement setting out these levies and charges in due proportion upon each branch to recoup the year's expenses. Consequently, these levies formed the main income of the Union, and the payments of benefits to members the expenditure.

The local societies fixed the contributions of their individual members, the General Union not interfering with the amounts subscribed unless the society failed to meet such payments as might become due after the regular quarterly balancing.

This rather antiquated method of funding was generally popular with the local societies because it gave them a large measure of local autonomy; but it also kept the General Union short of money, so restricting its activities.

Some attempt to give the Union greater funds was later made by putting the equalisation figure higher than the actual amount required, so that a small fund could be built up to assist any society that did not have enough funds of its own to meet the claims of its members.

It was later seen that the levy system severely handicapped efforts at organisation, especially in areas where wages were low. The need to make provision for such cases had been considered on many occasions and eventually a draft rule covering contributions and scales of benefits was drawn up by the EC and put to the societies for endorsement. It eventually came into effect, but not until January 1898.

This covered new branches opened in areas where wages were so low that the contributions the new members could afford would not provide sufficient funds to meet the full liabilities to the Union and benefits to branch members. In such cases the EC was empowered to allow new branch members to pay not less than 6d a week, entitling them to one-half benefits with the branch charged one-half the levies. Payment of a 9d contribution would allow three-quarters benefits and levies. This would only apply to new members and new branches in low-paid areas. In all other cases the full amount under the old system was retained.

All the activities of the Union erred on the side of caution, which was built into its constitution. Proposals were put forward at one delegate meeting to be decided at the next, normally held one year later, to allow local societies to consider the proposals. While this was very democratic it did tend to strangle initiative and quick action.

At the 1862 conference the Blackburn Society put forward proposals for funeral benefit and a superannuation fund, extended to those incapacitated by accident or disease 'not incurred by improper conduct.' This was agreed at the 1864 meeting. A sick benefit was added later. By 1884 all branches also subscribed to out-of-work, dispute, benevolent and travelling benefits.

An attempt to give the General Union greater control over the constituent societies was made at the 1868 meeting when it was laid down that before any society on strike could appeal to other societies for aid it must notify the Union so that it could be decided whether it was worthy of support. But the Union could only recommend and not order individual societies in cases of strike action.

The General Union slowly changed from a loose federation of like-minded societies into one in which the management committee took over the administration of a whole range of benefits. It also assumed greater control over strikes, with a ruling that the Union could not recognise any strike to uphold a standard of wages, only those resisting a general reduction. It also decided that no strike pay could be made to any member society from the Union funds without the consent of the majority of the societies making up the Union – a further restriction on quick action.

In the mid-1870s a great trade depression hit the area, lasting six years and greatly testing the union. There was great distress among members and at one time one third of the membership was unemployed.

The depression played havoc with the organisation. Two branches foundered and there is no doubt that more would have disappeared had they still remained small individual societies relying on their own resources. As it was, all branches were allowed loans from the Union's contingency fund.

Wigan was typical of the smaller branches. It appealed to the General Union for relief as all its own funds were exhausted, members having only had a few days work in six months. They were all in benefit 'having paid contributions with money that should have been spent on bread.'

The secretary reported that a number of societies had not been able to relieve tramps as all their funds were exhausted. He recommended that societies should not issue travelling cards and should advise members not to travel during the trade depression – though that was precisely when members were forced to go on tramp in search of work. If they were compelled to travel, they should avoid Blackburn, Halifax, Huddersfield, Nottingham, Lancaster, Wigan, Newcastle and Sunderland, as these societies had all used up their funds.

Any society with money not being used was asked to make loans to the union. The decision to suspend societies with excessive arrears was put into abeyance for the duration of the depression for fear of losing more affiliated societies. As it was, the General Union was left with a mere fifteen societies and an affiliated membership of only 892. The important Oldham and Leeds societies seceded. It was decided that the Wigan Society, 'because of its reduced state', be joined to the Bolton section of the Manchester Society for twelve months.

The practical difficulties brought into being or shown up by the depression strengthened the movement for changes in the General Union. The Manchester Society proposed a tightening up; overtime, piece-work and apprentices should be regulated. No employer should be allowed more than two apprentices. Systematic overtime should be discountenanced and where overtime was unavoidable, it should be paid at time-and-a-quarter for the first two hours, time-and-a-half for the next two hours and then double-time till the next day's work, and societies should fix allowances for working outside the shop.

The General Union started off and remained an organisation largely concerned with the North of England, most strongly based in Lancashire. But in 1877 the management committee invited the London, Birmingham and Wolverhampton societies to join. There seems to have been no response and when the matter was raised again some years later the societies, immersed in their own organisation, decided to take no action. The next move came from the National Amalgamated in 1890 which sent a top level delegation to Manchester to urge a fraternal friendship closer than then existed. They wanted to come to a business arrangement with the General Union on purely trade union matters.

But the two organisations operated from different standpoints. While the National Amalgamated was only concerned with purely trade union matters, such as the conduct and settlement of trade disputes, day work wages and piece-work prices, and their only benefit was dispute pay, the General Union covered the whole range of welfare benefits. The General Union was not constituted, in organisation or in the outlook of its leadership, to operate as a fighting organisation, while the National Amalgamated brushed aside welfare benefits as the concern of friendly societies that existed for the purpose.

Wiltshire, then secretary of the General Union, who was on record as being 'against the amalgamation idea',was contemptuous of the Amalgamated, telling the deputation that their *ONE* benefit had been one of many benefits of the General Union for many years, 'only we call it contingency and you call it strike benefit.' The constitution of the Amalgamated was 'too narrow.' It was not enough merely to profess sympathy for fellow tradesmen in need. But perhaps his greatest opposition stemmed from the fact that most Amalgamated members were on piece-work and closer working could lead to General Union members getting drawn into 'this most obnoxious system of working.' He agreed on the need for unity – he could hardly have objected to the principle – but opposed the practice advocated by the deputation.

The question came up at the 1891 General Union biennial delegate meeting and was rejected. Then in 1897 delegates unanimously demanded that the question be put to the branches but the EC turned it down as leading to possible friction. In 1899 a motion from Manchester calling on the General Union to affiliate to the Amalgamation was defeated by 278 to 96 in a vote of the delegates' present. But when Manchester put a similar motion in 1900 it was carried and the General Union was accepted into the Amalgamated as a body, continuing with its own organisation, funds, officials and delegate meetings – a union within a union, its control over its constituent members maintained.

In 1893 it was decided to create a position of full-time General Secretary and John Wiltshire, who had been doing the job on a part-time bais for eleven years, was the natural choice and was elected unopposed. This, of course, strengthened his influence, and his rather narrow traditionalist viewpont was to largely dominate the General Union for another twenty years.

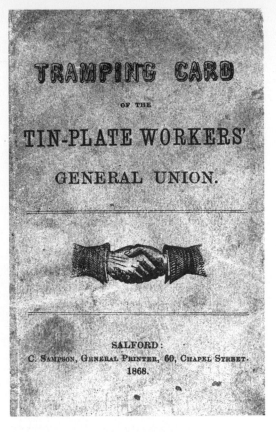

The previous year the General Union's name was changed from 'Tin Plate Workers' to Braziers and Sheet Metal Workers' in recognition of the changing work of the members. The inclusion of 'braziers' in the title did not indicate an amalgamation with any local braziers' society. It was adopted by many local societies that were changing their name to sheet metal workers at that time and was probably just a means of laying claim to braziers' work more specifically than was indicated in the general title of sheet metal workers.

But it was not until 1899 that the rules were changed to give legality to the extension of the trade in conformity with the title. The new rule specified that in future branches and affiliated societies could admit into membership men in receipt of the recognised rate of wages working in the following metals: copper, brass, zinc, block tin (white metal), tinned sheets, iron, steel or any other sheet metal in commercial use.

Previously the Union was officially confined to tin plate workers and this was strictly adhered to. A request from Bury in 1880 for permission to take some coppersmiths into membership was turned down by the EC on the grounds that the rules specified tin plate workers only. But even the change in rule did not let workers in any metal join; as late as 1918 an attempt by the Sheffield Society to enrol three silversmiths was vetoed by the EC.

Although a number of the affiliated societies changed their titles at the same time, it was not until 1916 that the EC ruled that all societies must adopt a common title, 'obliterating' the term 'tin plate workers' and replacing it with 'sheet metal workers.' Already in 1892 contribution cards and books had been standardised throughout the General Union.

At the same time the rule changes allowed apprentices to be admitted in their final year; in which case they would become free members in fifteen months. It laid down that on average there should be two apprentices to every five men.

Another new rule gave the EC powers to start new branches in any town in the UK where there was no other branch of the trade, distinct from the affiliated societies, coming directly under the control of the EC. These rule changes did not alter an EC ruling that no society was allowed to take in new members over the age of forty.

Modernisation Attempts

The old trade club attitude toward membership persisted and was a great handicap in organising the many non-unionised tin plate workers. This attitude must take the blame for the fact that in a period of rapidly expanding industry, especially in the metal trades, the organisation of the General Union remained largely static showing little gain in membership until the war. One of the main stumbling blocks, common throughout the trade, was the absolute refusal to take in men working below the district rate, or to even allow members to work below the rate. But this was only one factor hindering organisation. There was strong opposition to opening new branches in areas where there had previously been no members 'as this would not give anything to build on.' Wiltshire ruled that there must be people in the area with knowledge of the Union to act as officers, otherwise organisation would be unstable. Taken together this meant that membership could only be expanded through the adhesion of apprentices from organised shops.

Although the committee was empowered to visit any town where there was a likelihood of a branch being formed or other towns, 'in or out of the union', for the purpose of enlarging or strengthening the Union, in practice visits were rarely made except at the request of an existing branch in the area. The formation of new branches or the resuscitation of defunct societies depended largely on the enthusiasm of active members of neighbouring societies. For example, in 1890 the General Secretary was invited by Blackburn members to Accrington to meet tinmen not in the Union. As a result, thirty nons joined the Blackburn Society, eventually forming their own Society.

So actual results were small compared with the size of the problem. Hull was reportedly taking steps to develop the Union in Grimsby. Bury arranged a meeting to form a branch in Warrington – although tramping Warrington tinmen were recorded as far back as 1807. Halifax members arranged a meeting in Huddersfield addressed by the secretary which brought in 18 local tinmen and the formation of a Society. Sheffield held a meeting in Chesterfield but only recorded hopes plus some intimidation and victimisation of intending members.

In 1900 the EC appointed an organising committee 'to strengthen the Union' but this did not bring any real change. Some attempts at organisation were made in the North East, largely the work of James Campbell of Newcastle, but there is no record of other action. Campbell later complained that restrictions on making new members made it almost impossible to do the job properly. A branch was formed at Hartlepool in 1902 from members he had made earlier and who had been held by the Newcastle branch.

A lot of dissatisfaction was expressed at the high cost of benefits, some members complaining that the high-benefit, high-cost society restricted organisation, citing a survey which found that members did not want a regular out-of-work benefit. Societies began to vote with their feet. Nottingham seceded because of the sick scheme. Ashton broke away because dues were too high for benefits received, objecting to paying more than 7s a month. Warrington, giving notice of seceding, said members would not pay more than 1s a month and benefits should be optional. By dropping dues to 1s they had recruited twenty members.

However, when Sheffield branch said it would only be possible to organise men working on a sheet iron dust extractor plant for a local granary if a trade-only membership was allowed, they were told they could enrol the men at half rates under a rule for organising men on low wages.

But that was not the usual pattern. When Newcastle complained that it was difficult to compete with the sheet iron workers for members because of high fees to pay for all the welfare benefits, their plea for a 6d a week trade-only section was rejected after the General Secretary declared the Union was not going to emulate the sheet iron workers.

Despite the dissatisfaction with high-cost benefits and their undoubted interference with recruitment, the national delegate meeting decided there could be no opting out. Societies had to subscribe to all fixed benefits if they were to remain in the GU. These were: donation, management, funeral, superannuation, benevolent, travelling, sick and contingency.

These benefits may have helped strengthen the loyalty of members to their local society but they not only hindered organisation, they made it difficult to transfer a member to a new society when he moved to another town. Before a member could be transferred from one society to another both had to agree on the value to be placed on the member, based on his length of membership and the amount of dues paid which varied from one society to another. A transfer fee then had to be paid to allow the member to keep in benefit.

Later, when he was President, Campbell complained that sheet metal workers were being organised by other unions such as the engineers, tool makers, coppersmiths and even by non-craft unions like the railwaymen's and labourers' organisations. The sheet iron workers had a branch of 100 in North Shields and yet there was no branch of the General Union. The same position prevailed in other towns in the Northeast – in Darlington, Middlesborough and Stockton – as well as in Wales and even in some parts of the Midlands, Yorkshire and Lancashire. 'Our work is being poached simply because there is no branch of the Union there or because the local branch lacks the energy.' He also complained that some societies, such as Barrow, did not have a single apprentice while the sheet iron workers and other unions had many. This would ultimately mean the phasing out of sheet metal workers in those areas. He attacked the old constitution which, designed to preserve the old structure, rendered the EC helpless, unable to do anything if the branches would not take action. The EC must have the right to interfere, to exert supervision and control over Union activities at all levels in the interest of the trade. That meant a centralised form of organisation.

A number of attempts were made over the years to reform the constitution to give the Union a more centralised character in line with modern ideas. All were defeated by the conservatism of the local societies who saw the moves as attacks on local autonomy.

In all these attempts at change the traditionalists in the local branches had always had the support of the GU leadership. But here changes were on the way. In 1907 it was felt that the burden of work on the General Secretary was too much for him, and Archibald Kidd of the Liverpool branch was elected Assistant Secretary – at a salary of £2 a year. John Wiltshire's health began to deteriorate and Kidd more and more took over the reins of power until in July 1913, after a total of 31 years in office, Wiltshire retired. Kidd was elected to the top post – at a salary of £130 a year – with a four-year term of office, elegible for re-election. At the same time it was decided the President should be changed every two years.

Kidd was a man of very different outlook to his predecessor and at a special meeting in April 1918 called to consider alteration in the rules to do away with the levy system, the EC came out in support of those demanding change, undoubtedly due to Kidd's influence. The critics declared the system was holding back the Union from organising the non unionised mass of tin plate workers, urging a centralised organisation to take in all sheet metal workers. They argued there should be no embargo on men over 40 years of age. For years there had been but slight change in the methods of running the Union; no initiative was taken in dealing with the problems of the day. The Union was becoming a mere benefit society and appeared to have forgotten that its primary reason for existence was to carry on a ceaseless war against capitalism. To the leadership of the Union 'friendly benefits were more important than the class struggle'. In the 40 years since the formation of the GU there had been an unparalleled expansion of industry while scientific methods of production had increased the productivity of the workers. But the Union had not taken part in that expansion.

Walter Hulme, the leading spokesman for the modernisers and editor of the Union journal whose pages he had used to press the claims of centralisation, said that the antiquated structure of the GU could not face the possibility of a big strike. When 120 Liverpool members were locked out, the GU came within four weeks of bankruptcy. A lock-out or strike of the much larger Manchester Society would break the GU and the militant employers, determined to break the power of the organised workers, could bring that about. The levy system made it almost impossible to organise as it threw the branches back on their own resources. There were 18,000 to 20,000 unorganised sheet metal workers and in 22 years the GU had created only three new branches. How long were they prepared to allow this to continue?

The President stated the EC were proposing the centralisation of the Union to increase efficiency, broaden the basis or organisation and provide facilities for organising. The constitution must be altered to create a fighting unit to meet the organisation of the employers. Kidd, in his first major conference as General Secretary, backed the EC's scheme attacking the fear of change that paralysed some members. A centralised Union was a step to one national union for the whole industry and a stride to a strong organisation of all unions that would mean the downfall of the wages system and the abolition of capitalism.

The supporters of the old system and local autonomy were not impressed. They were joined by those who said they could not support centralisation of the General Union on its own, for 2,800 members in 30 branches, leaving the other 9,600 of the National Amalgamated – of which the GU was then a member – in 36 other branches, outside. 'If we are to have a National Union of Sheet Metal Workers, let us aim at the solidification of coppersmiths, sheet iron workers, etc.', said Fred Mason, secretary of the Manchester Society, which sounds rather like an attempt to put off the 'evil day' of amalgamation until some distant future. Together, the opposition defeated the EC proposal by 57 votes to 32.

The centralisers kept chipping away but it was not until March 1919 that their attempts bore fruit and centralisation was accepted by the overwhelming majority of 932 – 1,326 votes to 344. By then it did not really matter as the General Union was on the eve of disappearing into the National Union.

So much for the history of the struggle to reform the Union structure. Now we must return to chronicle some other aspects of the life and activities of the GU and its members.

In the Shipyards

Shipbuilding and ship repair work constituted an important though numerically minor section of the work area covered by the GU. It was concentrated on Merseyside, Barrow and the North East coast, although organisation in the latter area was patchy. There was also a certain amount of shipping work at Hull and Grimsby.

For much of the time, from at least 1900, the activities of members of the Union in the shipping industry were concerned with demarcation, trying to hang on to sheet metal work claimed by the the more aggressive plumbers, boilermakers and sheet iron workers.

Earlier, in 1891, the Newcastle Society complained that the plumbers were claiming 'all kinds of work that had been done by our members.' This included the making and fixing of sheet iron ventilators as well as trunking, tubes and boxes; lining metal lockers, bins, mail and store rooms using tin, iron or zinc; machinery guards and pipe casings in sheet iron, tin, copper brass or munz metal; storm boxes and gratings in iron, tin, brass or copper; galley and donkey funnels, stove funnels and casings in iron; urinals and latrines in sheet iron; wash basins, stands and troughs; ships' lamps, light boxes of every description in copper, brass, tin or sheet iron; mouth-pieces and sound bells for voice tubes in copper, brass, tin or zinc; boxes for side or mast head lamps in sheet iron; drip trays of every description in copper, brass, zinc, tin or sheet iron; making iron flanges, flanging and rivetting and all pipes where such work is attached.

The Society members decided to put up a fight for their work and with the approval of the EC asked the engineers to join with them against the plumbers' trespassing on the work of other trades in the shipyards of the Tyne and Wear.

Around the late 1890s the Barrow Society wrote to the EC saying that the boilermarkers in the local shipyard of Vicker's and Maxim's were all working on 'comparatively light sheet iron', with the suspicion that they wanted to take over all sheet iron work. The EC suggested a meeting be called of all local societies concerned – Barrow, Manchester, Hull, Liverpool and Newcastle – and they should draw up demarcation lines, limiting their claims to working on sheet iron not more than $\frac{1}{8}$ inch thick or Birmingham wire gauge No. 10. The EC should approach all firms concerned to establish the Union's claim to the work and also affiliate to the Shipbuilding and Engineering Federation.

Barrow also proposed that a committee be formed in societies faced with this problem to determine a course of action. At a meeting with the boilermakers in Barrow, the GU claimed all sheet metal work in the engine room – casings, steam pipes, lagging cylinders, guards – and all kinds of sheet iron work that sheet metal workers had done for 25 years. The boilermakers categorically rejected the claim and counter-claimed for all work on sheet iron from 3/16 inch down to 18 gauge. Members of the boilermakers' sheet iron section went further and demanded that all workers on sheet iron must join the boilermakers' society ' or steps would be taken to make their position in the yards untenable.'

After 1900 an even more aggressive organisation came on the scene – the Light Plate, Sheet Iron and Range Makers Society formed in Glasgow in 1900. It soon began to penetrate the Northern English ports. Having nothing to build on it had to somehow carve out a territory for itself. In the rough conditions of dockyard life it maintained a tough, aggressive image as it moved into new areas, not only organising the large number of non-union sheet iron workers but also poaching members of other unions in the face of increasing competition. This it did by a combination of threats of physical violence and offering a much lower rate of contributions than the established unions. On a trades-benefit-only basis, it was able to offer membership for only 6d a week which was very attractive to workers in the low-paid shipbuilding and repair industry.

Unable to deal with the sheet iron workers in the yards, the Newcastle branch proposed that efforts be made to control them, either by their affiliation to the National Amalgamated or through the Shipbuilding and Engineering Federation and when in 1908 the sheet iron workers applied for membership of the Federation, the GU, under pressure from the Newcastle Society, opposed the application, charging the sheet iron workers with getting men to fill the places of sheet metal workers during a recent dispute. The boilermakers and smiths made similar accusations and the Federation turned down the application.

The harassment of sheet metal workers in the yards continued. At Palmers', Hebburn, sheet iron workers refused to work with members of the GU and the foreman ordered all GU members to leave the ship. Wiltshire protested to Richmond, the sheet iron workers' secretary, who backed his members' action. The GU took the case to the Federation whose Tyne and Wear Committee instituted an enquiry in 1913. After a lengthy hearing the GU claim was substantiated and it was said the sheet iron workers' methods were 'to be deprecated in wanting in the spirit of fair play and recognised trade union principles.' The enquiry suggested there was plenty of work for all as neither union could fulfill the then demands for sheet iron workers in the shipping industry.

This brought no real change and the struggle for work continued. At Barrow, only strong action enabled sheet metal workers to retain work long done by union members against sheet iron workers' claims, and a similar stance was taken at Camel Laird's, Liverpool. One result of this attitude was that the Birkenhead sheet iron workers sent a deputation to the Liverpool sheet metal workers to suggest a working ageement. No satisfactory arrangement was reached, however, and guerrilla warfare continued.

Rail Shops

Another specialised section of tin plate workers covered railway workshops, although the degree of organisation was sketchy. There were no branches in such important railway towns as York, Doncaster and Middlesborough, and one was formed in Darlington only toward the end of the life of the GU – although there was a branch of nine members at York in 1824 and one at Doncaster with five members. A Doncaster branch had its club house at the Blue Bell, Baxters Gate in 1842 and Liverpool Society relieved tramps from Doncaster in 1846 and 1847 bearing the local society cards Nos.5 and 6 and another in 1850. It was tinsmiths at the old Midland Railway depot who re-formed the Derby branch in 1872 and who formed the basis of the branch for the rest of the century. In Newcastle, the branch complained that sheet metal workers were being organised by the general railwaymen's union.

From the books it would appear that the main activity in the railway workshops was in the Lancashire depots at Horwich and Newton Heath. One of the difficulties of organisation was due to the union set-up. Union members came from a variety of individual local societies based in the surrounding Lancashire towns; so in 1899, the Bolton Society reported that several of the 30 or so members in the Horwich workshops had run out of the union.

Bolton's difficulty was that only 12 of the workers there were members of the Bolton branch. Five came from Wigan, four from Liverpool, two from Preston and one from the Bury branch and four men were not in any union. However, the branch arranged for one of their members to visit the Horwich loco works once a month for the next three months for a card check.

Railway wages were notoriously low and men at the loco works at both Horwich and Newton Heath were said to be paid 4s below the district minimum rate. It was doubted whether wages in the tinsmiths' shop at Newton Heath reached £2 a week.

Practically everything there was done piece-work, including repairs, and a special shop committee supervised and arranged prices. Horwich had no such organisation. It was left to the foreman and the individual workman to fix prices between them and they were often altered without any consultation with the men in the shop as a whole. The General Union asked Bolton to get this individual bargaining stopped.

The war brought a break-through in railway shop organisation in the Northeast with all sheet metal workers in the Darlington works of the old North Eastern Railway joining the Union and becoming members of the Newcastle branch, forming their own Darlington branch in 1919.

In 1915 Derby Society took part in a move under the auspices of the engineering allied trades committee to improve rates and conditions in the Midland Railway Depot and again in 1917 to bring rates up to what was paid in other districts. In 1918 members at the Great Central Railway Gorton Tank depot in Manchester went on strike with other trades to force a 12½ per cent bonus on earnings. Workers at the Warrington depot of the Cheshire Lines got a 2s increase to bring up their wages to 40s and a rise of 7½ per cent on piece-work prices. But even in wartime, and with the help of the allied trades movement, railway workers still occupied the lower ranks of the earnings table. Even the appointment of a member of the EC as railways organiser could not greatly improve the position.

Meters and General

Gas meter making and repair provided employment for a number of members and was particularly important in Manchester and Oldham. They had very close relationships with London and Edinburgh branches where the main shops of the various firms with Lancashire branches were situated.

General work seems to have continued as a sizeable section of the trade in the area from which the General Union drew its main strength later than it did in the South. A number of the smaller Lancashire societies had long been dependent to a high degree on supplying tin plate wares for the textile mills, and guards, etc., for the engineering factories. But new sources of work were challenging the old, even in this heartland of the old tin plate workers' trade, bringing new problems.

Motors and Aircraft

When the first GU members started work on motor cars is not known,but the first reference to the industry in the Union's books did not come until the end of 1908, and then only the report of the admission into the Halifax Society of a metal spinner, engaged on spinning sheet metal for motor car lamps.

However, Crossley's were making motor cars in Manchester from 1903 and employed some sheet metal workers. Union members or not, the coachwork of the early Crossleys was said to be 'particularly pleasing' and the 1910 models were 'good solid workmanship throughout.' In August 1914 members were certainly working at the firm on War Office contracts for staff cars, lorries and tenders which were a prominent feature of the Western Front. The Belsize car was also being built in Manchester from before 1904. At the same time the Eagle was being produced in Altrincham and the Horbick in Pendleton from 1900 to 1909. Though not employing large numbers of men, they must have been giving work to an increasing number of members.

Soon after 1908 there was a report that members from Manchester, Liverpool, Bolton and Blackburn had gone to Derby 'to work in the new motor car works' – Rolls Royce – which had originally been made in Manchester. The reports indicated that there were six members working there for 36s for a 54-hour week, which was less than the 8½d an hour minimum laid down by the National Amalgamated for the motor industry. It was then found that the men

Traditional metal spinning; making main baffles for a Jaguar aircraft at a Bolton general shop

were increasing their earnings by working the Premium Bonus (PB) system, although they assured the Union that they had a say in fixing fair times for the jobs. The GU was in something of a dilemma. Although it subscribed to the general opposition in the trade to the system, it did not want to lose the foothold obtained in the factory. The men had 'regained some ground from the unscrupulous coppersmiths' trade who had assisted employers elsewhere to defeat our trade union efforts to keep clear of PB', said the General Secretary. However, he did not want to get officially contaminated and turned down a request from the Derby branch to visit the Rolls Royce works 'because coppersmiths were taking tinmen's work', saying that he could not visit the works while PB was in operation.

From then on motor work became a regular and increasing outlet for GU members, though compared with the Midlands area the numbers employed was very small. But it was not all plain sailing. The new motor car employers were a different class of men to the masters of the old general work whose lives had been spent in the general trade. The newcomers were impatient to make their mark, insisting on doing things their own way and objecting to any questioning of their methods by the Union.

It was reported that in 1908 14 men at the Pendleton Radiator Co. in Manchester went on strike because after the employer had used their knowledge to build up the firm, he was gradually replacing Society men with nons.

Organisation of the industry increased. In 1912 a member working at the Vulcan Car Co., which had been building cars at Southport since 1904, called on the secretary to organise the tinmen there. As a result the men joined the Bolton Society, accepting the Society's rates and conditions. They were working piece-work but were pushing for 38s a week day work. The tinshop also joined the joint trades committee at the works. Leyland motors was apparently already organised as it was reported that the firm's proposal to operate PB had been called off after a warning of action by all trades. The members were pressing for a minimum rate of 40s for 53 hours.

Ford's, then at Trafford Park, Manchester, were also in conflict with the Union in 1912, over the victimisation of a member for his trade union activities. Members objected to the firm putting a labourer on a folding machine and were told by the management that they would do as they wanted and would brook no interference from any trade society. When one member objected and was sacked the rest of the shop came out. The Manchester Trades Council and the joint trades movement in the factory gave them support but after a deputation from the Union members were withdrawn and the shop blacked.

The 1914-18 war saw the closure of some of the smaller motor companies but the bigger factories were all busy on war work. The war brought aircraft factories into the GU area but apparently it was not until quite late that it had any impact on Union organisation.

In March 1918 the EC arranged a meeting between representatives of the Manchester, Bolton, Blackburn and Bury societies to discuss aircraft work. The conference discussed prices and agreed that attempts would have to be made to level them up. They would also have to get an agreement on prices for petrol tanks.

The EC reported in August that the GU had '13 districts more or less on aircraft work' and urged all of them to send delegates to a national meeting of members working on aircraft to be held in Derby, organised by the National Amalgamated. The delegates agreed to an aircraft rate of 1s 4d an hour, plus all war allowances, plus $12\frac{1}{2}$ per cent. The EC circularised branches calling on them to set up pricing committees, to tabulate lists of times and prices for day-work rates and piece work earnings operating in the shops under their control, facilities provided and working conditions in the shops, to be sent to the General Secretary. As a result the Manchester Society appointed an aircraft secretary and shop organisations were developed at A.V. Roe and other aircraft factories.

Wider Activities

The General Union, as such, does not seem to have played a very active part in the wider trade union and labour movement. As far back as 1890 complaint was made of the GU's lack of contact with other sections of the movement and a survey showed only five societies out of 16 connected with their trades council; a request went out to the others to affiliate. In 1893 the President represented the GU at a London protest against the contracting-out provisions in the Employers' Liability Bill then going through the House of Lords. But this was not repeated and for many years there appears to have been a general reluctance to take part in anything that might be labelled political, and the verdict on a letter from the TUC Parliamentary Committee urging support for Independent Labour Party candidates was that 'it cannot be entertained.' As late as 1911 the EC's response to an appeal to the Union to take up shares in the Labour papers the *Daily Herald* and the *Daily Citizen* was that they 'ought to refrain.'

This lack of participation in labour movement activities makes the purchase of a banner for 25 guineas in 1899 rather surprising. It was kept in the Manchester Society club house and two members were appointed caretakers to look after it with instructions to take it out of its box carefully from time to time for an airing; the wooden box was lined with zinc to protect it from damp. Branches were allowed to borrow it if they paid the expenses of the two caretakers who must accompany it and provide and paid for any extra help needed. Already in 1872 the EC had ordered emblems for sale to members and later bought a supply of badges for members to purchase.

Surprising, too, was the Union's early support for independent working-class education. This may have been the work of Kidd as the first contacts coincided with his election as Assistant Secretary and he retained close connections with the movement for many years. The Union made a £5 grant to Ruskin College, Oxford, and accepted a half-scholarship which would enable it to send a full-time student for a year's study at a cost of £25, covering board, lodging and tuition. There were two applicants, both from the Liverpool branch. They submitted essays and the successful one, Henry Slack, took up the scholarship although the Union would not pay the maintenance grant of 15s a week he had requested. Requests for further support were turned down in 1911 because the college governors had dismissed the Principal Denis Herd for his support for the working-class movement, and for teaching Marx's labour theory of value.

Support was given to the Central Labour College (providing independent working-class education based on the unions, without charity support) which had come out of a strike of the students in defence of the Principal. An offer by Ruskin of a second scholarship was turned down by 295 votes to 81 and it was decided that the result of an annual 2d levy be sent to the Central Labour College. This later became the National Council of Labour Colleges to which the Union affiliated and strongly supported for the rest of its existence.

Around the same period pressure mounted for a Union journal and despite some opposition four journal pages were added to the 1908 quarterly reports, giving way to a quarterly journal the following year, which became a monthly a year later, continuing under the editorship of Walter Hume, Blackburn branch secretary, until it was taken over as part of the duties of the assistant secretary of the new National Union. Technical articles and drawings, a popular and regular feature of the Journal, were started in 1911, (in more than 70 years there were only three technical editors. Francis Turner of Liverpool, followed by F.W. Mann of London from January 1934 and from February 1973 by Fred Rooum of Bradford, who had been contributing technical 'short cuts' items since 1967.) When they were first introduced, the EC, in giving the Editor permission to obtain blocks for illustrating pattern development, warned him that he must not see this as a precedent and not order any more without permission.

Shorter Hours

The General Union was not an active participant in the 1897 movement of the engineers for an eight-hour day. However, they became involved, willy-nilly, when members were locked out with the rest of the workers in the engineering employers' reply to the claim. In response to appeals for financial support the GU gave the maximum grant allowed by the rules, £10 to each of the main unions involved, the Amalgamated Society of Engineers and the United Machine Workers Association and later contributed £106 to the Manchester and London lock-out funds. Members levied themselves 3d a week. In all, 128 GU members were involved, receiving about £455 in strike pay. Despite wide support from the movement during the whole of the protracted dispute the engineers had to go back without having achieved their objective.

Another attempt to gain the eight-hour day was made in 1913 at a number of meetings between the engineering employers and the 32 unions with members in the industry. There were complaints by delegates to the Union's conference at the position taken by the EC and the apathy of the members, said to be due to lack of leadership and the withholding of information from them. Some objected that branch agreements with the employers precluding them from

A typical technical page from the *Journal*

Technical Matters

Cones or triangles?

by
Fred
Rooum

OUR main item is a transformer, round top and an oblong base with semi circular ends; developed here by the oblique cone method, then by triangulation. I think triangulation is the best method but I may be wrong. However, the second item, a cone-headed ventilator, is certainly best developed as part of a cone.

Item (1) The oblique cone method. Set out the half-elevation and quarter-plan as shown. Divide the larger quarter-circle into three equal parts as at A,B', C', D'. Draw a line from D' through the lowest point of the small quarter-circle to meet the base line at V'. Erect a vertical line on V' and cut this by a line from A, through a, to obtain point V. From centre V' swing arcs from B', C', D', up to the base line, as at B, C, D. From them draw lines to the apex V.

Pattern. Erect the centre line VA, equal to VA in the elevation. Using V as centre scribe arcs of indefinite length with radii equal to VB, VC, VD in the elevation. Starting from A, step off from one arc to the next a distance equal to the curve AB' in the plan, obtaining points B,C,D. Join ABCD by a smooth curve. Draw lines from B,C,D, to V. Cut these lines from V with distances equal to Va, Vb, Vc, Vd in the elevation. Mark the new points a,b,c,d, and join them by an even curve. With d as centre, radius dD, scribe an arc down from D. Cut this arc by a line from d, equal to twice the length of D'm in the plan, to obtain the point D". The rest of the pattern is copied from the part already drawn, as follows: From D" draw a line through d and make it same length as VD. Mark its end with a small v. Then from v the pattern lines VC, VB, VA, are repeated as shown.

The above construction is adapted from an 80-year-old drawing. The symmetrical pattern is artistic and attractive. But if we care to ignore these qualities the work can be shortened. One quarter only — the portion between Md and Aa — really needs developing. It can then serve as a template for the other quarters.

The same transformer by triangulation. Draw part-plan and elevation as before. Divide the quarter-circles each into three equal parts, lettered ABCD and abcd. Join these points by the usual false length lines. Obtain their true lengths by erecting a height-line same height as the elevation. Along its base set out the false lengths taken from the plan. Join these points on the base to the top of the height-line to get their true lengths.

Quarter-pattern. Erect the true length line Aa. From centre a, with compasses set to true length aB, scribe an arc to the right of A. Cut this arc from A with a distance equal to the curves AB in the plan. From centre B, compasses set to true length Bb, scribe an arc to the right of a. Cut this arc from a, by a distance equal to the curve ab in the plan. Continue this process as shown, noting that DM in the plan is already true length. The true length dM completes the quarter-pattern.

Item (2). The sketch shows a simple ventilator, made in two pieces. It illustrates the joining of a cone to a round pipe. The joint between the two pieces will be elliptical, and obviously the two ellipses must be the same size and shape. To ensure this, set up an elevation (plan not needed).

First draw the outline of the pipe, and inside it, near the top, scribe a circle same diameter as the pipe. Next, draw the full cone and place it so that its sides touch the circle. Now from the points where the outside line of the cone meet those of the pipe, draw the joint-line. Draw on the base of the cone a semicircle, divided into the customary six equal parts. From the points on the semicircle draw lines, parallel to the cone's axis, to the base of the cone, thence to its apex V. From the points where these radial lines cross the joint-line, draw lines square to the cone's axis, to the side of the cone. Number them 0 to 6, as shown.

Pattern, for the conical head. Draw the pattern of the full cone. Divide its perimeter into 12 equal parts and from the points thus found draw lines by distances V6, V5, V4 etc. taken from the elevation. Join the ten points by a smooth curve to complete the pattern.

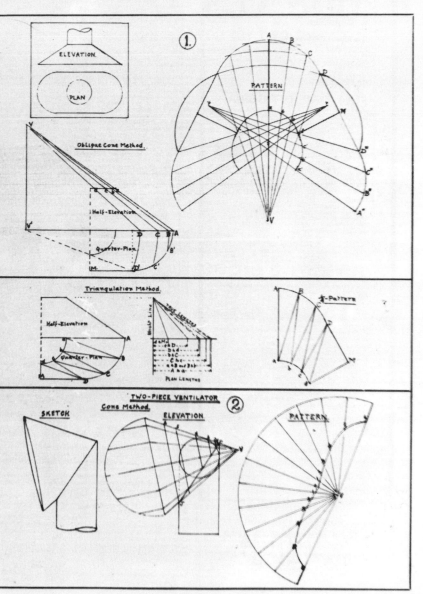

taking action and were told by the militants that 'flimsy agreements should not be allowed to get in the way of an eight-hour day.'

During the talks members taking part in a rank-and-file 'short-time movement' were able to get some local successes with a general 48-hour week for workers at the Cunard Steamship Co., and a 44-hour week for all outside trades, as well as for all workers during the winter months.

Continuing discussions between the employers and the unions were eventually caught up in the war and shelved for the duration. They were immediately resumed at the end of hostilities and after a ballot vote of the members a 47-hour week was accepted in December 1918.

Shop Stewards

In the years immediately before the war there was widespread militancy among many unions on a wide range of issues, with close working between members on the shop floor and the evolvement of the shop stewards movement. There was wide support for the allied trades movement. In 1913 Warrington members asked for support of the GU in their activities to get all sheet metal tradesmen into the Union, part of the allied trades movement in the stove and grate industry.

In August 1914 the Manchester Society reported that shop stewards had been appointed to every shop in the City. Their duty was to collect contributions and examine members' cards, their expenses were paid out of a 6d levy on the membership. Soon afterwards the GU ruled that stewards be appointed in 'every manufactury where members are employed.' They should collect not only the contributions from GU members, but from all sheet metal societies, examine the cards of any new members starting in the shop and report any arrears to the branch secretary.

Although the shop stewards as constituted had only limited functions, they did lead to a strengthening of the members on the shop floor and factory level. Soon they evolved as the leaders of the Union in the workplace.

In 1913 members at Vickers shipyard at Barrow had taken part with other trades in the Allied Trades Vigilante Committee for the limitation of overtime and the restriction of Sunday and holiday working. The branch also helped to develop the Allied Trades Movement – also known as the Joint Trades Movement – as did other sections of the GU. On the eve of the war this movement had helped bring pay increases in the Warrington loco works and wage advances for 40 GU members at Leyland Motors. In 1916 the Barrow members had joined with the movement in ending the Premium Bonus system.

In the localities, branches of unions in the engineering industry got together to form local Allied, or Joint Trades Movement committees. The Hull and Derby branch secretaries – and perhaps others – took part in local meetings of the movement with the employers to negotiate rates, conditions and other relevant subjects. Barrow and Sheffield had strong joint shop stewards committees and there was also organisation at Manchester and maybe other towns within the GU area. We do not know how far GU members participated but there must have been a considerable activity in the light of an NEC ruling in 1918 that the position of members who went on strike at the instance of the shop stewards or the Allied Trades Movement would be considered by the branch committees as early as possible. Claims should be forwarded to the EC who were empowered to grant strike pay if they considered it justified. This speeding up of strike recognition and payment was said to be due to the fact that the shop stewards movement had brought about a new set of circumstances and the rules must be changed to suit. A couple of years earlier, the president had drawn attention to the fact that the Allied Trades Movement was able to bring out the whole of the members in a branch or area.

These joint activities, plus the change in the leadership, brought a distinct change in the GU's attitude – it became more political and more militant. During the 1913 Dublin general strike, on the initiative of the Derby branch, the GU pressed the TUC to send food ships every day until the strike ended. The EC also congratulated the Irish union leader, James Larkin, on his release from Mountjoy prison and called on all organised workers to 'emphatically protest against the unjust imprisonment of Irish workers, demanding that all those imprisoned for peaceful picketing be released' and called for the immediate withdrawal of police and soldiers protecting employers and blacklegs in Dublin.

This rather revolutionary attitude continued after the war with, in 1920, the EC passing a resolution 'approving and appreciating' the action of 'forming a Council of Action and issuing such a courageous and leading manifesto to the whole of the labour movement bearing upon the Russo-Polish war.' They recommended to members that 'a prompt and loyal response be given to any instructions emanating from the Council of Action which has for its object the prevention of any declaration of war against Soviet Russia.'

The war brought some change in attitude towards organisation, especially in new areas, though this was probably mainly influenced by members going to work in different parts of the country on war work, particularly in aircraft factories often located in non-industrial areas.

A central branch was set up to take new members when there were less than ten in an area, not enough to form a branch. The members of this branch sent their contributions directly to head office or through someone chosen to act as shop steward. Announcing the innovation in 1917 the President, Fred Mason, said 'in this way the Union can stretch out the hand of friendship to the loneliest sheet metal worker in the most out-of-the-way place in the kingdom and lay the foundation for new branches in the future.'

But the General Union had to be pressurised by branches to take in welders, even as second-class members. Newcastle, Barrow and Derby all raised the question but Bolton opposed. The rules must be obeyed and they stated that members must be time-served men, whereas welders had not served an apprenticeship. There was a demand for welders at the moment but after the war the demand would be reduced. A motion that welders be admitted into the branches and affiliated societies, as welders, paying the same contributions as other members, on the understanding that they do not do sheet metal work, was defeated. Finally it was agreed to take in welders but in a separate branch. They would be enrolled by branches but their contributions would be sent en block to head office. They would not be allowed to do sheet metal work. It was not until the last days of the GU, in August 1919, that the EC agreed that it was essential to organise an auxiliary section. It would be in the best interest of the Union that workers, other than skilled men, in the sheet metal industry, be taken into the Union. Branches and local societies should organise these workers into an auxiliary section, they would include keg and drum makers, canister makers, tank makers, etc. They further agreed, surprisingly in view of their past attitude, that 'females in these trades be eligible to become members.'

Wartime

The first few months of the 1914-18 war brought widespread unemployment in the GU area. Unions and employers held a joint meeting to discuss ways and means of reducing unemployment and the Director of War Office Contracts issued a memorandum on maintaining employment during the war, suggesting doing away with overtime as a means of spreading the work available.

In Barrow, on the other hand, there was a shortage of sheet metal workers for the shipyards. The secretary was told to provide 50 men or other tradesmen would be put on sheet metal work. However, 30 or 40 Belgian refugee tradesmen arrived and were put on the work. The management gave an assurance that they were all time-served men who belonged to the Belgian sheet metal workers' union. They were receiving the rate and there was no intention of keeping them on after the war. After checking the EC agreed, and the Belgians were later taken into the Union.

The General Secretary attended a government meeting with the secretaries of other unions and afterwards the EC agreed that they must acquiesce in providing increased production, but if attempts were made to put unskilled labour on skilled tradesmen's work there would be common resistance.

At the 1915 delegate meeting the President, James Campbell, reported a government request to relax custom and practice but so far, with the help of the branches, they 'had been able to maintain their principles.'

In 1917 a schedule of reserved occupations exempted from call-up to the forces sheet metal workers, irrespective of age, engaged in shipbuilding or on marine engineering. There were age limits for tradesmen in other sections. Members were advised to see that they had scheduled occupation certificates. Those under 24 not on war work were advised to enroll as War Munitions Volunteers and members generally were asked to put themselves at the disposal of their branch officials so that any surplus labour could be placed on war work and used in the best interest of the trade.

In December, Halifax branch protested that four members had been taken to the colours and demanded that all sheet metal workers under the age of 24 on aircraft work be protected.

For branch and shop officials the whole period of the war was one long battle against dilution. At one point the Union called on Ministry of Munitions officials to hold an enquiry, rejecting the findings because the official involved had first held a meeting with the employers who provided him with false information; it was able to force another hearing which was favourable to the Union.

There would seem to have been greater militancy during the war and the minutes record a number of strikes. Men at Lowestoft and Yarmouth were out for three days protesting against a non-unionist being started and opposing the introduction of piece-work, and were successful on both issues. Later the same year members at Vulcan's of Southport stopped work 'as the only way to enforce payment of a wage increase awarded by the Committee on Production.' This was in May 1917 and in April 1918 they came out again against the victimisation of an active union member.

In 1918 there was a strike of members at Crossley Aircraft and at A.V. Roe Aviation, Manchester, 45 members were out for a month protesting at the victimisation of shop stewards. Action at Kerr's Aircraft, Preston, stopped the management's proposal to introduce the Premium Bonus system.

In May 1917, members at Manchester and Derby joined engineering union stoppages against the Munitions of War Bill, then going through the House of Commons, which could give the employers power to bring in dilution on private and commercial work. Their application for contingency pay was refused by the EC 'as these were unauthorised strikes, strictly prohibited by the rules.'

In June 1918 members joined a meeting of Bedfordshire aircraft workers protesting against the government's withdrawal of free rail vouchers for war volunteer munition workers. They called on the organised workers throughout the country to take action, saying if the government was honest it would withdraw all first class dining and sleeping compartments as they were not used by soldiers, sailors or munition workers, and so were not necessary.

This was the way General Union members went through the war individually and as part of the National Amalgamated. There were no big, spectacular strikes but members were generally ready to take action when they felt their craft status, union organisation or customs were threatened, with an eye on the post-war situation and warnings that they would need even stronger organisation to meet employers' attacks.

With the formation of the National Union the GU, unlike the branch and district organisations throughout the country, had no function. While it could be said that the organisation of the National Amalgamated was translated into the National Union, whatever separate functions the GU had disappeared, ending its life as a union. The 3,000 or so members it covered at the time were absorbed into the new union and, on 31 December 1920, after an existence of just on 60 years, it was dissolved.

Chapter 6
This chapter is wholly based on the minutes of the General Union which are still in the possession of the Union, complete from the first meeting in October 1861 until it was wound up in 1921 and became part of the National Union.

CHAPTER SEVEN

The National Amalgamated

The National Amalgamated Tin Plate Workers, as we have seen, also started off very modestly as a federal organisation of three societies, two Wolverhampton and one Birmingham to provide closer working of the tin plate workers' organisation in the Midlands, particularly in disputes with the rather tough employers in their area.

The initiative came from the Birmingham Co-operative Tin Plate Workers' Society following a dispute, and was discussed by the committee of the Wolverhampton No. 1 Society in conjunction with an invitation just then received to join the General Union, and suggestions from some members of their own committee to establish an amalgamation of all tin plate workers of the United Kingdom.

The committee decided it preferred an organisation concerned with just strengthening the unions for dealing with strikes and lockouts and that 'no other project will advance the interest of the trade'. A committee was formed and a fund established to promote the idea and the Wolverhampton No. 2 Society was brought into the discussions.

So the Amalgamated Tin Plate Workers of Birmingham, Wolverhampton and District duly came into being on 3 January 1876 at a meeting of the joint committees at the Pack Horse Inn, Dudley Street, Wolverhampton, bringing together some 800 members. The first Secretary was Edward Davis of Wolverhampton and the President William Evans, the Birmingham secretary. This system continued, with the Secretary from one organisation and the President from the other. The contributions were 1s per member per quarter.

The first annual meeting discussed inequalities in prices paid by various employers and a proposal to establish a system to prevent anomalies. The meeting also elected a delegate to attend the next Trades Union Congress and voted £2 to the TUC Parliamentary Committee. One of its first actions was to approve a strike over a Birmingham employer trying to force men to finish at an unagreed piece-work price army mess tins on which women had done the preliminary work.

The committee soon got down to organising the trade – then called 'mission work' – deciding there and then to visit Worcester and Bilston and form local organisations as branches of the Amalgamated. Both had previously had their own local societies in the 1820s, and Worcester had a society in 1848 and 1849.

The President, Vice-president and Secretary all visited Worcester and spoke at a meeting of 23 local tinmen who agreed to form a Society. This was accomplished at a second meeting on 2 June 1877. The members promised to consider joining the Amalgamated but did not do so until 1907 and then only as a sub-branch of the Wolverhampton Society.

A delegation visited Bilston in September and had a discussion with 'a representative committee' of the local tin plate workers who were said to total not more than 20 to 25. But

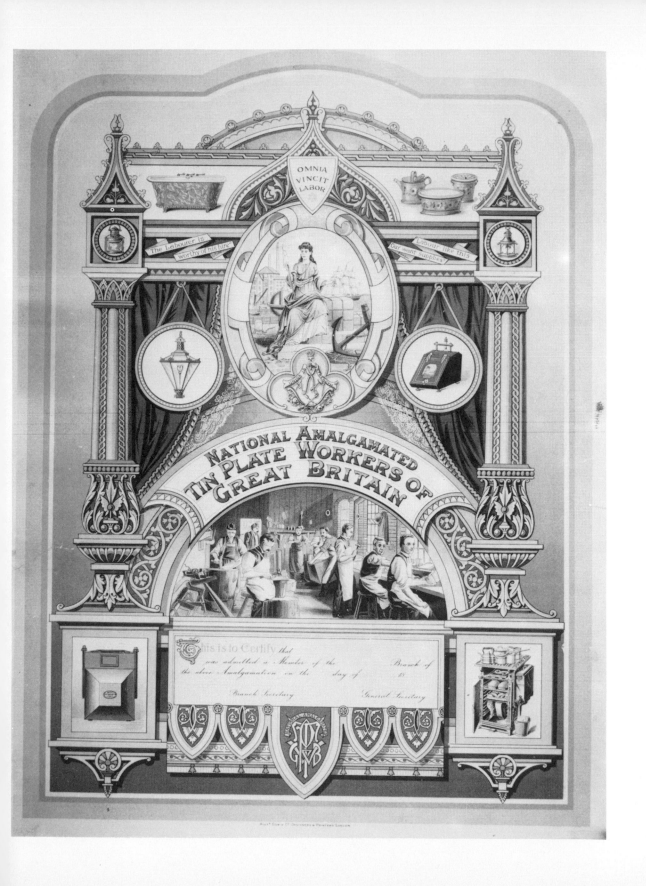

assurances were given that those present would arrange a meeting and try to either start a society in Bilston or get the local tinmen to join one of the Wolverhampton societies. The latter option was probably taken up as we have been unable to find any mention of Bilston in the organisation until they too came in as a sub-branch of Wolverhampton.

The following years were taken up by a succession of strikes, mostly resisting employers' attempts to cut prices. So, early in 1878 it decided that the system of pricing work by committees, as set forth in the rules of the societies, should be strictly adhered to. Any infringement would be 'visited with the utmost fine specified therein'. No article new to any shop should be priced until an attempt had been made to find out if it had been priced elsewhere. Any price fixed by a shop committee should be sent by the shop secretary or shop steward to the secretary of his society, together with a description of the mode of making. The information should then be sent to the other secretaries as early as possible.

The 1878 meeting set up a Victim Fund with £5 a quarter drawn from the funds of the Amalgamated, for the benefit of any member victimised for carrying out trade union practices, for advancing, defending or protecting the rights and interests of the trade and as a defence measure against any tyranny by employers.

A big strike and lockout, in line with the bitter Wolverhampton strikes of the past, took place in 1880 at Jones Bros, one of the important Wolverhampton factories. Over a four year period of trade depression, Jones repeatedly attempted to reduce prices and in resisting these attempts the Wolverhampton societies, particularly the No. 2 Society, were financially weakened. Taking advantage of this, Jones Bros tried to smash the union in their factory, insisting that the men sign a document that they would leave the Society. If they refused they would have to give up their job.

A deputation from the three societies was rejected by the firm who ignored a call from a mass meeting that they should do so, and they declared that in future they intended to be non-union. The Amalgamated wrote to the firm warning that if they did not receive a deputation they would be denounced from the platform of a public meeting and this was duly done, without effect.

There were 24 Society men out of the 27 tinmen working in the shop and seven of them were discharged for standing by the Union. The rest of the men were called out and a meeting held to put their case before the public. A levy was put on the rest of the trade and married men were given £1 a week strike pay and single men 15s. However, a number of men went into the struck firm and eventually the strikers were told to get work elsewhere and the shop was given up.

This strike, on top of the already shaky finances of the Wolverhampton No. 2 Society, brought about its collapse. Unable to pay expenses or to resist attacks on book prices, the Society decided to close.

The drain of funds resulting from a large number of small strikes, and especially the long depression of trade, shook the foundations of the other two societies, despite increases in contributions and a limit put on strike pay.

In 1885, with the depression still continuing, the Amalgamated broke a long tradition of tinmen's societies and allowed their out of work members to take jobs in non-trade shops until they could get something better. Both societies had suffered through the long drain of high out-of-work pay. Birmingham lost members but the Wolverhampton Society succeeded in maintaining its position.

The perilous state of the Amalgamated and the continued depression of trade, forced the management committee to the conclusion that they must get more societies to join them. It was resolved to first approach London. Talks began with the three London Societies early in 1887 and finally the London Amalgamated Society and the East London decided to join – the third, the Gas Meter Makers, had by then gone back into the London Amalgamated Society. But it was not until 1 January 1889 that the affiliation was effected and the National Amalgamated Tin Plate Workers of Great Britain came into existence, with H. Ricket of Wolverhampton as Secretary, E. Fooks of Birmingham, President and F.B. Monk of London Vice-President, all part-time. The London Amalgamated brought in 692 much-needed members and the East London 112.

The business of the early years of the expanded organisation was mainly concerned with consolidating their position and providing financial assistance to members on strike, particularly those resisting employers' attempts to cut prices.

The new organisation was seen as a step toward forming a united federation of the trade over the whole country.

The leaders of the Amalgamated saw the adhesion of the General Union as the most obvious way of strengthening their organisation and the trade as a whole. They made many overtures, sent invitations and tried to get meetings to bring this about. However, in 1892 it was reported that

the Lancashire Union still continues to shuffle, willing to talk on trade matters but refusing to meet a deputation, from the Amalgamated, to discuss the amalgamation of the two bodies.

One of the major stumbling blocks was piece-work, considered an evil by most of the General Union members but the way of life for the bulk of the Amalgamated.

However, the Amalgamated received a number of requests for information and for rule books from societies affiliated to the General Union, which the National Amalgamated felt, indicated that there was some opposition in the General Union to the position of its leadership.

The 1890s saw a big development in trade unionism throughout the country. The great London dock strike of 1889 had helped with a boost to the new unions of general labourers and the unorganised generally.

But the National Amalgamated had not fulfilled the promise of its foundation. Edinburgh had been the first to join, bringing in 300 members. Aberdeen had come in with 99 members, Dundee had expressed a wish to join but had been told they should come to an arrangement with Edinburgh to save expense. But Glasgow turned down an invitation, adding to an earlier opposition to the piece-working activities of most of the Amalgamated's members, a complaint that the management committee provided strike pay only for members whereas in Glasgow it was necessary to support non-members during disputes.

Fair Wages

Early in 1891, a meeting was held to discuss what could be done about the low rates of pay on government contracts and the evils of sub-contracting which was rife in this work. One London firm was said to be in receipt of large government contracts but had no workshops of its own and contracted out the whole orders to another firm which employed lads and a few non-union men, turning out cheap work of poor quality. It was decided to bring out a price list of all government contract work, applicable to the whole country, which would be sent to employers and government offices concerned. But again there was no mention of getting the sub-contract shops organised. The all-pervading attitude of craft purity seems to have blinded the unions to the value of 100 per cent organisation. It is true that on this occasion members were asked to get jobs in 'unfair' shops, but only to get evidence for the House of Commons

Fair Wages Committee which a friendly Member of Parliament, Sidney Buxton, had been able to set up. The National Amalgamated also asked the TUC Parliamentary Committee to help and persuaded trade union members of Parliament John Burns and Henry Broadhurst, as well as Joseph Chamberlain, a Birmingham Liberal MP who said he would take the matter up in the House if he could be given specific cases.

The Fair Wages Committee got an undertaking that firms would be told that unless they paid the agreed rate of wages they would not be given further contracts. But this depended on the Union complaining to the committee and so tabs had to be kept on all government contracts to see that the recipients did not evade the conditions laid down. The Union price list was completed in 1894 after nine days of deliberations on prices put forward by joint pricing committees with representatives from all sections, including the preserving trade, and men from Birmingham lamp shops, as well as members of a Midlands' wheeling committee, each brought in when their own speciality was being discussed. It was further agreed that most lamp work and general work would normally be done day work. The price lists were later accepted by the county councils and municipal authorities.

In 1902, probably as a result of the big increase in government orders from the Boer War, a committee was set up to renew the 1894 price list which covered both War Office and Admiralty work, and to establish a new minimum rate.

The committee was to consist of three from London and three from the Midlands so that it could remain a national list. It was agreed that the Midlands list be used as a basis, with specialists co-opted onto the committee for discussions on the various items – lamps, general work, baths, biscuit tins, zinc linings, canisters, hospital dressing wagons, workers on copper and brass, wheeling etc. A minimum rate of 8d an hour was imposed and conditions laid down on the amount of machinery used and on what jobs, day-work and piece-working, special rates, sectionalising, tinning, the labour of boys and youths. The list was to be the minimum charged for the whole of the United Kingdom except London, which was allowed to charge extra.

Societies on government contracts must appoint a special committee to price all new work and work that differed from that specified on the list. All new prices must be forwarded to the secretary who would forward them to other societies and branches. Attempts to get the conditions imposed were made more difficult in that the period was one of acute trade depression in the four years following the end of the Boer War. In some areas of the North, 30 per cent of trade members were out of work and virtually all areas were affected. A London report said they had paid out more out-of-work benefit than ever before, blaming the increase in machinery, new lines in enamel ware and 'the effect of the waste of public money over the late unnecessary and inglorious war in South Africa.' Dispute pay also increased as men resisted employers' attempts to cut prices.

Building the Union

In 1891, the Liverpool Sheet Metal Workers Society – a breakaway from the day-working General Union Liverpool-affiliate by men who wanted to work piece work – joined, to acclamation from the members of the Management Committee but indignant complaints from the General Union. It did not last long, breaking up in 1894. In an attempt to overcome this stagnation an organising committee was set up in May 1894, but still it concentrated on trying to get existing societies to affiliate.

Then a few years later it was agreed that societies be allowed to start branches outside their own area, the Amalgamation paying initial expenses, a licence that was to be later taken up by the Wolverhampton Society. J.V. Stevens, who was something of a driving force inside the Amalgamation, moved that the committee be instructed to draft rules and establish branches of the Amalgamation wherever the opportunity presented itself, with a view to strengthening its organisation and power and make it in reality a national amalgamation.

On this basis, attempts were made to form branches where none had existed. A satisfactory start was made with Exeter, largely due to the efforts of Wolverhampton backed up by Birmingham. This was based on Willey's gas meter shop but also took in some general workers, and it was hoped it would soon bring in members from all over Devon. The Bristol Society was also revived in 1898, but visits to Norwich and Crewe proved abortive, the latter town having, it was said, few tinmen except those in the railway works and it was thought that they would have to join the Railway Servants Union. The biggest success was the accession of the old established Oldham Society with 150 members in 1899, which had broken with the General Union, but this was the result of Oldham's own initiative.

The management committee seem to have been aware of the inadequacy of their efforts as in 1900 it was decided to appoint a national organiser, choosing J.Charles Gordon, President of the East London Society, who had been active in organisational work. The following year he was elected as the first full time secretary with a vote of 2,632 to 1,704 for A. Harvey of Birmingham, and he took office on 1 January 1902.

The position was for an initial period of three years and he would be eligible for re-election. It could be terminated by three months' notice on either side, at annual conference, or by a two-thirds vote of the affiliated societies on the recommendation of the management committee. In addition to secretarial duties, he should also act as an organiser and his services would be available to local societies in cases of special problems or difficulties in organisation. He was paid £2.10s a week plus 2s.6d a day expenses when away from home and 2s. for a bed with third class railway fares when required.

The management committee, which consisted of the President, Vice-President and four delegates elected by annual conference, were to direct the secretary in all matters of organisation and were vested with the power to establish branches wherever opportunities offered.

The appointment of Gordon was of great importance to the future of the organisation. He not only had great energy and drive, he was also a great believer in getting the unorganised into the Union and was not restricted in these efforts by any concern for an examination of the craft purity of every potential member when organising new branches. He put his trust rather in the strength of unity. He appears to have had a national, rather than a local, outlook and his activities in setting up branches in new areas largely provided the pattern for the spread of the later Union.

Gordon's first visit was to the Black Country where a branch was set up covering Halesowen, Stourbridge and Lye, joining the Amalgamated in November 1902. This success was possible because of the assistance provided by Wolverhampton and Birmingham, taking the new Society under their wing for the first year. Wolverhampton provided one of their members, W. Huyton, to act as secretary, paying his expenses, while Birmingham provided and paid for the president, W. Barnet. They also provided £50 jointly to pay for printing rule books, contribution cards and other requirements and made a contribution to local funds.

In 1901, Gordon also paid the first of a number of visits to South Wales. A small Cardiff society had briefly affiliated, joining the Amalgamated on a membership of 15 in October 1891, but had broken up at the end of 1892, the Secretary, Samson Hill, who had apparently been the driving force, reporting that they had been unable to get a viable membership although they had offered increased benefits.

Gordon visited Cardiff with a view to restarting the branch, and was told that there were between 50 and 60 sheet metal workers in the district, half of them in shipping shops and others in general shops in the town or in mills in the district. However, his meeting was so sparsely attended that it was decided to abandon the attempt for the time being.

He then visited Llanelly, where he settled a dispute over a foreman's attempts to cut prices, and Swansea where workers in the general trade said they were willing to join if a society were formed; here the trades council offered assistance.

He reported on the difficulty of organising South Wales as no town had enough tinmen to form a viable branch. Cardiff, where there was perhaps a possibility of 25 members, might form the centre for a branch for the whole area, with secretaries in the other towns sending the contributions in to the centre weekly. There was a possibility of 30 members in the Swansea district, 20 in Newport, 12 at Llanelly and a few in such places as Neath and Aberdare. But this organisation would be both expensive and unsatisfactory. Meanwhile the members he had made at Llanelly were included in the Bristol branch. He made other visits, notably in 1906 and 1907 but without any recorded success. Even the Llanelly members seem to have dropped out, as in 1916 an enquiry was made about forming a branch in the town.

Gordon next turned his attentions to the Eastern counties, forming a branch of 24 at Lowestoft, all of them in the preserving trade, in October 1901. This was extended to cover Yarmouth and the membership was pushed up to 39 by December but with the end of the fishing season members left for other ports and were never heard of again. Nevertheless, the branch remained in existence until sometime before the war and was re-formed in 1918.

Difficult as it undoubtedly was to form new branches, it seems to have been even more difficult to keep them, particularly in the more isolated areas. Norwich was a case in point. A branch was formed there in 1902, after some support had been given by the local trade council, but it had disappeared by 1904, and was then back again by 1916, reportedly with 100 members. The same situation applied at Lincoln where a branch was set up in 1907, with 14 members, but does not appear in the 1909 report, reappearing in 1916.

This was generally an outpost of low wages and poor conditions and it was not until the coming of 'numerous' aircraft works during the First World War that organisation came there to stay. One of these was Ipswich – where soon afterwards the men active in getting the branch formed were sacked. During the organising drive in East Anglia in 1917 a branch was even formed in Huntingdon with 24 members 'with good prospects of building up a good branch' and there was some activity in Chelmsford and Loughborough, and toward the end of the war a branch was started in Downham Market. No doubt many of the members from established branches who went into the area to work in the new aircraft factories helped with the formation of the new branches, and in some cases provided the officers.

One man who played an important part in organising the railway shops was J. Corbett, the secretary of the Crewe branch, which was formed in 1907 with 45 members, concentrated in the railway shops.

In 1907 a call was made to organise all rail shops and the secretary visited Doncaster, Wolverton and Howden, 'but was unable to induce the men to combine.' He had paid a visit to Doncaster, Eastleigh and Ashford, as well as Gloucester, Cheltenham and Chelmsford in 1907 with a similar lack of results: the tinmen in the rail shops apparently felt they had a secure job and did not want to jeopardise it – this was the time when the railwaymen were classed as railway servants.

Then in 1913, Corbett visited Wolverton and succeeded in getting the men together and formed a branch with 20 members. In 1915 he paid a visit to Swindon and talked to the tinmen there, one of whom became interested enough to organise a meeting.

After an earlier visit to Portsmouth by Gordon had not yielded much in recruitment as 'most tinmen in the town worked in the Government service and saw no need for organisation', a branch of 13 was set up in 1907. Another was formed in neighbouring Southampton with 16 members.

The year 1907 seems to have been a bumper one as far as new branches was concerned. One was started at Leicester. Around the same time there was a joint effort by Wolverhampton and London to organise the meter shops in nearby Nottingham, where the branch seems to have fallen on difficult times. Wolverhampton reorganised it, provided funds, and took it in as a sub-branch. Then in 1908 Gordon formed, or revived, the branch in Huddersfield with 18 members, 'most of the tinmen in the town', which seems to have been neglected by the General Union in whose area it was. The former Potteries branch, now called North Staffordshire, also joined.

Other branches came into being as a result of the spread of aircraft or munitions factories. A branch was formed at Weybridge in 1916 with 24 members. A number of members of other societies were working in the many aircraft shops in the area and one of them, A.J. Smith of Wolverhampton, acted as secretary. The same conditions applied to Yeovil where a London member, J. Sage, took over as secretary of the newly formed branch with 12 local members. A Derby member took on the secretaryship of Rochester, which was started with 20 members during the same period.

As the General Union had at last affiliated at the turn of the century, when Bradford branch had also joined, and other associates or former affiliates of the General Union had come in over the years, the National Amalgamated had become really national as J.V. Stevens had hoped for in the 1890s – although by then his Birmingham Society was outside the organisation. Nevertheless, at the end of 1916 the affiliated membership was over 11,000.

The organisation drives brought many problems to the old craft unions. It was no longer a question of deciding whether an applicant had served his time, was obtaining Union rate, had not offended against the union in any way. After the start of the war the committee had to decide what should be done about men who had learned their sheet metal work at a government training centre, or the semi-skilled working on jobs that had previously been done by Union members. Their instinct was to refuse to have anything to do with them, but in a general organising drive this was not so easy and in many cases if a man could and was doing the job he was accepted, at least in areas without strong Union traditions.

There was also the position of the auxiliary workers and the new oxy-acetylene welders: Should they be taken into the organisation and if so what was to be their relation with the tinmen?

Early in the war a new branch had been formed at Hadley, Salop, centred on a vehicle factory and the welders there applied to be members of the branch. The Hadley branch members opposed and a special welders' branch was formed after it was pointed out that the Amalgamated had claimed welding as the work of their members.

In April 1915, due to slackness of work in Hadley, the welders were scattered round the country and there was great difficulty in maintaining the special branch. So the branch was transferred to Wolverhampton where a lot of welders had joined. The following year it was reported the branch had doubled in size and had members in Birmingham, Sheffield, Farnborough and Earlstown as well as other districts. From then on the Union claimed all welders working on sheet metal work. Barrow, where members had previously only tacked the job in position, leaving welders to do the actual welding, then claimed the whole of the welding work, although this was made more difficult by having previously rejected it. Other branches had the same difficulty where they had let other unions claim the work.

Premium Bonus Problems

The relief given by the rise of the motor industry in providing jobs to offset losses by the decreasing general trade, was compromised in the minds of the leaders of the National Amalgamated by the spread of the premium bonus system through the industry. The Amalgamated refused to recognise the 'obnoxious system', condemning the fact that neither the Union nor the workers in the shop were consulted about a fair price, just given the job and the price with it, to make the best they could of it. The tendency of the management to cut times they themselves had fixed when they considered the workers were earning too much money was another objection, and the fact that the workers only received one half of the money saved by their increased efforts.

The Amalgamated first publicly condemned the system at the 1904 National Delegate Conference when it recommended that no society should enter into any agreement that would allow their members to work under the system. The sheet metal workers were apparently the only trade to object strongly when the system was introduced by the Daimler Motor Company in Coventry, members were told not to operate it but to continue on day work. In co-operation with the Birmingham Society, the EC called a conference of all societies with members working at the plant, which included the coppersmiths. By 26 votes to 3 the meeting resolved that none of the societies present would allow their members to work under the system after 1 September. When the London and Provincial Society of Coppersmiths continued to allow their members to defy the agreement to which they were party, the EC condemned their action as a betrayal of the unions and took the case to the TUC whose inter-union sub-committee found that the coppersmiths had not infringed any trade union rule.

Encouraged by the coppersmiths' action, a number of sheet metal workers defied their Unions' instructions and continued working the system for which they were expelled on the decision of a general meeting. All other members of unions affiliated to the Amalgamated were withdrawn and the shop blacked, although production continued.

The Amalgamated continued its opposition to the system, although General Union members worked under it at Rolls Royce, Derby, in Barrow shipyards and elsewhere. The Union's refusal to organise shops where the system was in operation weakened the position of the Union in this important and rapidly expanding new industry for very many years.

The dispute over the bonus system was also responsible for the rise of a rival, breakaway union, the Progressive Sheet Metal Workers' Society, formed in Coventry on 14 September 1907 by the expelled members working at Daimlers.[1] Its first Secretary was A. Osborne and the President W. Stokes, said to be former London Society members. Their first meeting place was the Canal Tavern and they later moved to the Lamp Tavern in Coventry. They only took in men 'skilled in the trade' and their objects included 'to defend our principles and to assist those who sacrifice their employment in defence of same.' It was also laid down that shop stewards be appointed in any manufactury where members were employed. The organisation spread to other factories in Coventry and its membership rose to a peak of 150 on the eve of the war, only 45 of them working at Daimlers. Its members moved around and got jobs in London, Lancashire and other places. In some cases there was bad feeling between them and members of the old unions who refused to work with them; in other places no one bothered. It was a time when sheet metal workers were on the move.

When the Amalgamated saw this was to be no fly-by-night organisation, but could cause trouble, the General Secretary arranged a meeting with the Secretary of the Progressives, A.

Ross and the President Easton, suggesting that the new union be disbanded and the members rejoin the old societies. Ross was doubtful about the response without any inducement but they agreed to call a general meeting to be addressed by officials of both the Progressive and Amalgamated societies. The meeting turned down the proposal and a suggestion that they should amalgamate with the London Society was rejected by the London officials. The Amalgamated tried again, calling a meeting of all societies concerned, which was attended by representatives of the London, Birmingham, Manchester, Glasgow, Coventry, Crewe, Wolverhampton, Bristol and Hadley societies, the General Union and the Iron Plate Workers. It decided that any member of the Progressive Society who wanted to join any other society should be admitted on terms decided by the local society concerned, on the distinct understanding that the member give an undertaking not to work the PB system and to conform to prevailing conditions. But it was stressed that in future no member of the Progressive would be allowed to work in shops of any other society. This does not seem to have been very vigorously applied and it was not until 1918 that it was agreed to disband the Society – about a year after Daimlers abandoned the bonus system. To facilitate this, a new rule was introduced by the leadership of the Progressive Society to allow any member leaving the Society to receive his full valuation in the Society, which then had 102 members and £1,499 in the funds. The last five members left in 1920 and the Society was wound up.

One of the features that made it easier for the Progressive Society to continue to exist as a breakaway society in Coventry was the large number of metal workers from all over the country working there at that time. The havoc this caused in the organisation of its affiliated societies, and the large number of men falling into arrears was causing concern to the Amalgamated, as well as their almost complete isolation from branch life.

In 1913, some of the more active trade unionists wrote to the Amalgamated complaining that they had no say in affairs affecting them, particularly as Coventry was under the jurisdiction of the Birmingham Society. Again in 1916 the officials received complaints that the members had no voice in determining their conditions of work and were virtually disenfranchised. There were now more than 200 members of societies affiliated to the Amalgamated working in Coventry's various munitions factories.

With the Amalgamated's agreement a meeting was called and a committee set up with the responsibility of collecting dues and forwarding the money to the various local societies. The Coventry activists were then able to check who were union members and who were in benefit. The Committee also paid out benefits on behalf of the local societies and co-operated in a joint committee with the Birmingham Society for trade purposes.

From this developed the Coventry Sheet Metal Workers' Committee which campaigned for one national union of sheet metal workers all over the country, and sent out proposed rules for this national union, to be discussed at a national meeting in Coventry to be held in March 1918.[2] The introduction by James Moody, the pro-tem Honorary Secretary urged all societies to elect a delegate, declaring that 'the organisation as it exists at present is altogether inadequate, out of date, and not strong enough to meet the aggression of the already organised employers, which we shall have to meet no doubt in the near future.' It suggested the following rules. 1. That there be one society for the sheet metal trade, one card, one contribution, one benefit, all for trade purposes. 2. That there be one national minimum rate, one national price list for repetition work. 3. That every branch in a district shall have complete local autonomy and have complete local power in disputes. 4. That the action of any local body shall be supported by the whole of the country to the extent of a down tool policy. 5. That a national conference be called, elected from each branch, to decide a national policy in the case of an aggressive dispute. 6. That the country be split up into districts, each district to appoint its own administrative council.

In 1914, faced with the mass movement of workers all over the country, the Amalgamated management committee discussed the transfer of members from one affiliated society to another. All they could suggest was the fixing of a transfer value of a member based on the society's funds and the member's length of membership. This would allow him to go on drawing benefit when he transferred to another society. It does not seem to have been of much use in enabling members to transfer readily and it was very slow.

The war showed up the weakness of getting quick decisions so necessary in dealing with a succession of new problems, something almost impossible when it was necessary to convince a number of local societies with different interests and experiences. The question of dealing with the problems of the aircraft industry was a case in point. Although members in aircraft factories had been crying out for a national policy for much of the war, it was not until March 1918 that the Secretary was able to get in touch with the affiliated societies concerned to consider a conference of members from the industry, and the conference was not in fact held until 7 December 1918, after the end of the war. The meeting, in Derby, fixed a basic national time rate for all aircraft work of 1s.4d. an hour, plus all war awards and $12\frac{1}{2}$ per cent. Each district was urged to elect a pricing committee who would compile a complete return of prices of jobs, day and piece-work facilities, conditions and other relevant information. By the time this proposal could be acted on, the effect would be severely limited with the big cutback of work on military aircraft and only a slow change over to the production of civil planes.

The Birmingham Split

The year 1909 brought the biggest blow the Amalgamated had suffered since its formation, and a catastrophic rupture of the unity of the sheet metal workers that was to weaken the organised trade for the next 60 years. This was the secession of the Birmingham Society, one of the main founders of the organisation and second only to London in size and importance.

The ostensible cause of the rupture was the action of the management committee in increasing contributions and putting a levy on branches and societies to provide help for the Glasgow Society then engaged in a strike involving almost the whole of its members. Birmingham refused to pay either the levy or the increased contributions saying that they were against the rules and were not necessary. But many were of the opinion that the Birmingham secretary, J.V. Stevens, irked at the restrictions the Amalgamated placed on his freedom of action, had made use of the occasion.

The Birmingham Society asked for a special delegate conference to discuss two motions:

1. That no increased contributions above 3s be recommended as no greater increase was needed if the rules were adhered to and strict economy practised.

2. That no grant be given to assist societies in distress without sanction of a conference of one delegate from each society in order that it be considered and best advice given. Help to societies must be of a purely voluntary character.

The Birmingham delegates came to the meeting supplied with a sufficient number of their motions to provide each delegate with a copy, and both the mover, the Birmingham president, G. Challenor, and the seconder, the secretary, J.V. Stevens, read their remarks. When the meeting turned down both of their motions, the Birmingham delegates read out a prepared statement and left the meeting and the Amalgamated.

Despite regular assertions that they wanted unity and were in favour of a 'solid amalgamation', many members of the Amalgamated expressed the opinion that the

Birmingham leaders did not want to return to the fold. Many invitations were presented to them but there were always 'good reasons' why they should not accept.

In January 1913 a joint meeting was held with Birmingham to try and get an agreement. The Amalgamated delegates agreed with a number of the points brought forward. But when asked would Birmingham join up again with the Amalgamated if their proposals were accepted, they were not able to answer.

But the Amalgamated persisted and in response to another invitation to return Birmingham spelled out what it meant by a 'solid amalgamation'. This called for one united society for the whole trade with equal contributions and equal benefits and a common fund to administer benefits common to all members – dispute, out-of-work and funeral benefits and any other trade benefits agreed on from time to time. Local societies could provide from their own local funds any other benefits to suit local requirements. General fundamental laws should be binding on all sections and all members without exception and decisions of a national conference with votes based on the size of the branches, should also be binding on all. A small central executive would supervise the carrying out of laws and all national affairs and no general strike could be called without its permission. There would be a system of district committees covering the whole country with their own laws and full powers of local government under the central committee, while branches in the towns would also have their own local laws subordinate to those of their district. The other rules covered the long standing opposition to working with women, piece-mastering, contract work and the premium bonus system.

In August a deputation was received from the Birmingham Society to discuss the proposals. J.V. Stevens complained that as at present constituted, the Amalgamated had no powers to enforce resolutions. Each society pleased itself. He was a great believer in local autonomy and in keeping as much local power as possible, but believed that, if carried to excess, it resulted in anarchy. While the central committee would have to be consulted in cases of general dispute, wage rises and attempts to improve conditions should be dealt with by district committees.

There was considerable support for many of the proposals and the management committee said nothing must be allowed to stand in the way of getting Birmingham to return. A sub-committee was set up to draft a scheme of contributions, benefits, etc.

But the Birmingham leaders turned their proposal down, saying that they did not create a solid and united amalgamation, there were no provisions for fundamental laws governing the amalgamation, no central fund and no provision for district committees. So the rift continued.

The management committee's proposals were put to the delegate meeting and approved, but the majority was so small that nothing was done to implement it at either the 1916 or 1917 delegate meetings.

According to reports 1918 saw mounting support for the idea of a national union, with wide local discussions on the plans, the main opposition coming from Wolverhampton and Edinburgh. The management committee drew up new plans and submitted them to the 1919 delegate conference at which representatives of the Birmingham Society were present, including Challoner and Stevens.

The proposals laid down specific contributions and benefits, including the taking over of superannuation funds and the payment of benefits. The country was to be divided into six districts each managed by a committee elected by ballot vote of branches. Each district would be represented on a national executive by one delegate for districts of up to 2,000 members and an extra delegate for bigger districts. A sum of 10s a member was to be paid into a central fund to put the new union on a sound financial basis.

The Birmingham Society's first objection was on the superannuation proposals. Under no circumstances would they pool their superannuation funds. They also demanded that if branches withdrew from the amalgamation, they should be able to take with them their share of funds. They further wanted the proportion of the contributions left after paying out benefits to go to the local societies to pay for their administration expenses, pointing out that these, in some of the larger societies, were extremely heavy because of frequent meetings which were held daily and to cut these down would injure the effectiveness of the organisation.

The management committee pointed out that if the Birmingham proposals were put into effect they would have a number of local societies, not a national organisation and if they were not prepared to compromise there was no point in continuing discussion. The Birmingham amendment to retain superannuation funds locally was put to the vote and defeated, after which the Birmingham delegation walked out. The proposals were then accepted by the rest of the meeting.

Joint Action

The need for closer relations and joint action with other unions became more and more apparent as firms became bigger and improved their joint industrial organisation. The Amalgamated affiliated to the Trade Union Congress and also to the Engineering and Shipbuilding Federation.

It also became aware of the need to have access to Members of Parliament on such questions as fair wages for government contracts. Finally came the Taff Vale Judgement of 1901 in which the Union of Railway Servants were successfully sued for damages resulting from a strike on a small railway in South Wales, destroying at a stroke the generally held belief that the 1871 and 1876 Acts conferred immunity on a union from being sued as a corporate body.

For the Amalgamated, the judgement had the opposite effect than was intended. The 1902 conference decided to affiliate to the Labour Representation Committee to help defend members 'from the dangers which undoubtedly menaced them from trusts and combines.' It urged every effort be made to get Labour representation in national and local bodies.

The management committee then asked all societies for their approval to affiliate on the basis of a membership of 6,000 with an affiliation fee of £25, which was generally agreed.

From this basis, the 1907 delegate meeting went on to decide unanimously that members should be eligible to stand as Labour Parliamentary candidates and that an extra 4d be called for on top of the 2d already agreed for affiliation, to set up the necessary fund.

However, what has become known as the Osborn Judgement intervened. In 1908, W.V. Osborne, a member of the Society of Railway Servants, liberally backed by employers who feared the support being given to the Labour Party, succeeded in a legal action to restrain the union from spending any of its funds on political purposes, which was not rectified until the Trades Dispute Act of 1913.

Nevertheless, in 1909 the Union called on all local societies to get members elected to various local bodies and to work with other Labour men in such councils. It also agreed to increase subscriptions if necessary to meet LRC demands. All this persuaded the management committee that the time had come for the trade to be represented in Parliament and in 1913 the EC was asked to prepare a scheme.

It was suggested that a political levy be instituted on a voluntary basis, with members able to claim exemption as provided by law. It was estimated that 7,000 would pay the 6d annual levy required to provide necessary electoral expenses estimated at £850. All members and officials would be eligible for nomination by local societies or branches and those elected by the Union, using the second ballot system, would go forward for consideration by local Labour Parties.

Any member elected to Parliament would be under the control of, and would have to report to, the management committee. They would be expected to engage in organisation work for the Amalgamated during the recess for which they would be paid at the rate of 5s 6d a day expenses, exclusive of bed.

This, like so many other activities, got caught up in the war and was never put into effect. While the National Union did affiliate to the Labour Party and while many members, with the blessing of the Union, became local councillors, and even mayors in many parts of the country, it was not until the 1970s that the first members were nominated to be official Union Parliamentary candidates. And it was not until 1982 that a Union member, sitting in Parliament for Glasgow, Springburn, Michael John Martin, was officially sponsored by the Union.

The Amalgamated also invested £25 each in the Labour papers, the *Daily Herald* and the *Daily Citizen*, in token of the papers' support for the trade union movement and particularly for the support they had given to the strike of the Galvanised Hollowware workers.

As the trade unions became a more accepted part of the industrial scene – something of a necessary evil – even the smaller craft unions were drawn into the government's industrial orbit.

With the introduction of National Insurance in 1911 the National Amalgamated registered as an approved society and campaigned for all members to register with them. This meant that a large amount of the time of the few full time officials, was taken up with this work.

Then with the war came a whole host of official regulations, of meetings with government officials, conferences on production, manpower and all the other aspects of labour and the war, pepped up with occasional lectures from government leaders, which took more of their time.

The Amalgamated leaders were quietly opposed to the relaxation of union rules which was a constant theme of these meetings and of printed documents that flowed into the union offices. 'This was not necessary for a Society that could supply the labour required by Government'. In any case it only applied to controlled establishments and the Amalgamated were only involved in a few of those – Wolverhampton reported 20 and London 100 – the only one giving a little trouble at that time was Darracq.

Several attempts had been made to introduce dilution. Government officials visited the Union head office and called conferences but the Amalgamated had always been able to put off the evil day by supplying the workers required. Some employers had tried to introduce dilutee labour into their shops on their own account, as they had done long before the war. Where and when the Union became aware of this they opposed it, either directly or with the help of the Ministry in cases when the correct procedure had not been pursued, but it meant that the Secretary had to be dashing off all over the country.

At various times and places, wounded and disabled soldiers were being introduced into the shops after a short training on sheet metal work. The employers used them as cheap labour and when the Union insisted that they be paid the minimum rate, most employers lost interest in them and they were discharged.

In June 1916, a representative of the Ministry of Munitions declared there was a great shortage of sheet metal workers and no more should be taken for the army. The Amalgamated circularised the trade recommending that all members who were not already on war work should register as war munitions volunteers – although there were already hundreds of such registered volunteers waiting to be placed on war work – so that employers could not say that no sheet metal workers were available. 'There was no need for dilution.'

In fact, in April that year a number of members had been brought back from the forces and the Ministry of Munitions asked for another 200 sheet metal workers which the Amalgamated was able to supply.

Not all the Amalgamated's activities at this time took a purely defensive form. It recorded the opposition of its membership to the 1916 Compulsory Services Bill and asked that this should be taken up by the Labour Party conference. And, of course, it was continually on the offensive on the wages front, supporting the interests of its members both against the employers and government representatives.

The war over, the National Amalgamated pushed forward with proposals for amalgamation and the creation of a real national union, the dream of 100 years. Financial proposals were finalised, the proposed rules were printed and submitted to the affiliated societies and branches.

A national ballot of the whole membership of the Amalgamated was held and resulted in 10,045 votes in favour of a National Union and 965 against. It was regretted that the Birmingham Society had decided to remain outside but it was pointed out that otherwise all the societies and branches connected with the National Amalgamated, with the exception of Dublin, decided in favour of the proposals and a National Union.

The National Union of Sheet Metal Workers and Braziers came into existence on 1st July 1920 with benefits to commence from 1 January 1921, completing the task for which the National Amalgamated Society had been formed.

1. PRO FS11/112. Union registration number 1426 T.
2. Circular setting out the demands of the Coventry Sheet Metal Workers' Committee, a rank and file and file organisation, urging the setting up of one union for all sheet metal workers.

The chapter is otherwise based on the MS minutes and printed reports of the National Amalgamated and of local societies.

CHAPTER EIGHT

The National Union

The National Union came into being at a particularly difficult time for the trade union movement. While immersed in the task of welding together a collection of local societies with a great variety of different rules and customs into one efficient national organisation, the leaders of the new Union were faced with an economic crisis of unprecedented magnitude. The lack of cohesion among the old local societies making up the former National Amalgamated and the General Union made the task even harder.

The situation surrounding the change-over from a war-time economy to peace-time production and all its attendant problems, was something completely new. Every problem had to be dealt with individually and very often there were many clamouring for attention at the same time.

The 'land fit for heroes' that the government had promised when demanding sacrifices from the workers quickly faded away once the war was over. Working people were back to the old pre-war scramble for jobs and the struggle to earn a living. Employers, hit by the loss of lucrative war-time contracts slashed wages and piece-work prices in the no-holds-barred struggle for new contracts. To get the cheap labour necessary to undercut their rivals, many employers hung on to the war-time dilutees, pushing skilled men out of work, and the London district shop stewards' association were soon knocking at the doors of the Union, wanting to know what was being done about it.

A number of employers tried to go back to pre-war job prices, ignoring the great changes that had taken place, including a 50 per cent increase in living costs since the last national increase in wages. As for the inflation since the beginning of the war, the Labour Party cost of living committee recorded a rise of 176 per cent in food prices between July 1914 and September 1920, a 313 per cent rise in the cost of clothing, 43 per cent rent rises, a 193 per cent increase in heating and lighting charges and a 207 per cent rise in the price of other necessities.

In an attempt to protect the members' living standards in this bear garden, the unions tried to get the various war bonuses consolidated into an enhanced base rate; but all the engineering employers would offer after protracted negotiations was a stabilisation of wages for six months, a 'concession', it became apparent later, to give them time to plan their line of attack on wages in this new post-war situation.

The shipbuilding employers refused even that. They wanted a reduction in wages and they wanted it immediately. After a number of meetings of a joint sub-committee had achieved nothing, the Shipbuilding Employers Federation issued a statement announcing a unilateral decision to discontinue from the last week in April 1921 the last 6s award for day workers and 15 per cent for piece-workers.

Union resistance brought a slight modification. The cut would come in two stages; the day workers' wages would be reduced by 3s a week and piece-workers' prices by $7\frac{1}{2}$ per cent at the beginning of May and the rest, a similar amount, a month later.

A National Union ballot of the shipbuilding districts recorded 926 in favour of acceding to the employers' demand and 2,933 for strike action to fight the cuts. In separate ballots the shipbuilding unions as a whole turned down the demand by 39,959 to 22,479 but the union leadership ruled it did not give the two-thirds majority for strike action. A meeting of National Union members at the London docks later voted to accept the cuts pointing out that there were only thirty to fifty sheet metal workers among some 17,000 other trades working there, so they had to go along with the majority. A similar situation existed in the bigger shipbuilding and repair areas.

The general secretary Charles Gordon complained in the Journal that there was an unremitting, inspired campaign to pin on the workers and their supposedly high wages the blame for the economic crisis, the depression, high unemployment and most of the manifold ills the country and the economy were suffering from. The government, the employers 'and their servile press' kept up a chorus of demands for wage reductions to meet foreign competition.

The focus of the campaign was the engineering workers and, in preparation for the end of the period of wage stabilisation, an attack was launched on 9 March 1921 at a meeting convened by the Engineering and Allied Employers National Federation to which the unions had been invited to hear their fate. They were told that the wage stabilisation could not be maintained. The employers had hoped that it would attract export orders, they said, but it had not paid off. Germany and the US were quoting from 50 per cent to 75 per cent less than Britain and it was impossible for British firms to compete. Drastic cuts in the cost of production would have to be made to keep the wheels of industry turning. There must be sacrifices and this meant wage cuts.

The actual demand was released on the 200 leaders of the engineering unions at a recall conference on 12 May 1921. The stunned union representatives protested vigorously at the severity of the cuts that were even worse than those inflicted by the shipbuilding employers. But the employers would not budge so the meeting broke up and the Federation and AEU leaders recommended that the executives of all societies represented should immediately issue instructions to their members to stop work when the notices went up announcing the cuts. These instructions should remain in force until further notice.

This made the employers hesitate and after a series of meetings, with the Minister of Labour playing his part, they retreated a little, proposing to spread the reductions over a period. A ballot of union members turned this down by a majority of two to one. The National Union ballot showed an even greater opposition of three to one.

The strength of rank and file opposition brought a further modification in the employers' demands. The cuts would now be spread over three stages: 3s a week would come off time workers' wages and $7\frac{1}{2}$ per cent off piece-work prices from 31 July 1921, plus a similar reduction from 15 August. The decision on the $12\frac{1}{2}$ per cent and $7\frac{1}{2}$ per cent Ministry of Munitions war bonuses would be announced at a joint meeting in September when it would be established whether the economic situation had changed sufficiently to allow any modification.

At that meeting there was no surprise when the employers declared that the situation demanded the full reduction and that the 16s 6d cut would be spread over three months, July, August and September.

National Union members voted against acceptance by nearly eight to one and ballots of all trades also rejected the cuts. But the Federation executive decided not to order the withdrawal of members. They felt that the workers had taken a battering from both unemployment and wage cuts and the financial situation of the unions would not allow them to put up a fight.

The sheet metal workers took strong objection to the Federation executive agreeing to a settlement, and a ballot of members voted 4,306 to 1,837 for the Union to secede from the Federation. The NEC decided to leave the question until the next national conference when they judged, correctly, that tempers would have cooled sufficiently for a reconsideration.

The shipyard workers had already been deprived of their 16s 6d war bonuses but the shipyard employers decided they must have more and announced the withdrawal of the remaining 10s war bonus. A strike was called and then the Federation ordered a return but at the London docks, and perhaps elsewhere, a rank and file committee was set up to continue the strike and obtain better terms. The National Union held a ballot in which only 95 voted for acceptance, 2,778 voted to continue resistance by strike action if necessary and 2,431 for the union to make the best possible terms, which should be put to another ballot. Eventually the dispute was concluded with an agreement that the 10s be withdrawn over four equal stages with no more cuts to be made until the following March.

Meanwhile unemployment continued to mount. In 1920 the Union paid out a total of £48,575 in unemployment benefit, more than the whole income from contributions and levies. The total expenditure for the year was a crippling £123,000. A large proportion of the new National Union membership was reportedly signing on the dole and many more were working short time. There was widespread distress throughout the Union, many members having had to sell off much of their household possessions until there was nothing left to pawn. Men had to go on the poor law to get food.

Nationally, the jobless total was 1,500,000 in April 1921, with a further million on short time, rising to an official two million in the following February.

By March 1922, about 75 per cent of National Union members signing on the dole in London had used up all benefits due to them under rule. Many were destitute. The district committee set up a central unemployed committee, responsible for getting collections taken in the shops from members still in work and distributing the proceeds in small weekly donations to those out of benefit. It also set up a 'stop evictions fund' to help out-of-work members who had fallen behind with their rent.

A deputation from the district's central shop stewards' association urged the committee to increase out-of-work pay to prevent increased distress among unemployed members. This depression was not going to go away and there was no prospect of putting members on in the foreseeable future. It was agreed to augment unemployment pay for the 440 out of work in the district by 2s 6d a day, to be financed by a compulsory levy of 2s 6d a week from those in work. This caused an outcry with shops protesting that with the low wages being earned the levy was causing hardship for those members in work. Farwig's, one of the bigger general shops, complained that $7\frac{1}{2}$ per cent had been taken off their prices and the shop was only working $21\frac{1}{2}$ hours one week and $17\frac{1}{2}$ hours the next, so that members could not afford to pay the levy. The NEC then stepped in and told the London district committee that they had no right to put on a levy, it was against the rules and moreover was illegal. The London committee then made the levy voluntary. When this did not bring in the required amount it was proposed that a delegate be elected in each shop to the central unemployment committee and that the Union organise general meetings with unemployed members as speakers. The shop stewards, 'exploring all avenues', suggested that the Russian Bank in London be approached to discuss the possibility of obtaining direct contract work from Russia to employ out-of-work members.

Action of one kind or another was being taken in other districts of the Union. Wolverhampton branch set up a distress committee which supervised collections and made fortnightly grants to those out of benefit. Edinburgh branch had paid out £2,550 in 1921 to alleviate distress among members, using surplus funds accruing after the amalgamation. Others gave what help they could.

Lost Work

A certain amount of demoralisation seems to have set in during the post-war depression. Shop organisation deteriorated and in some cases ceased to exist. With no one in these shops collecting contributions, members got into arrears and lapsed.

One member of the district committee estimated there were 1,000 sheet metal workers unorganised in London. If the National Union did not get them in they would join other unions. The chairman, MacWilliam, criticised the meter section for their complacency, concerned only with their own shops. The motor shops were not 50 per cent organised. In London, the trade as a whole was only 60 per cent unionised. During 1924, 181 new members had been made and 276 had lapsed.

The London secretary reported on visits he had made to various shops. At de Havilland there were now only ten men in the shop and they 'were not good quality craftsmen.' He made one member and persuaded another to become shop secretary, who had since changed his mind. At Leyland's, Kingston, some forty men were handling sheet metal but only eleven were eligible for membership as the Society was constituted. Boy labour was a big problem. One shop was comprised only of boys, aged between 14 and 17, working from seven in the morning till seven at night, with one hour for dinner the only break, and also working Saturday afternoons and Sunday mornings. Considering the problem, the NEC said that 8,390 men on sheet metal work in London could be organised into the auxiliary section. But the London district committee decided not to take any further steps to organise auxilary workers.

Proposals that a national organiser be appointed came up from time to time from various branches, were regularly opposed by the NEC and regularly defeated.

This reflected a growing difference of attitude toward the Union, between those who thought that the best interests of the members and the trade would be served by retaining the craft purity of the Union with membership restricted to skilled craftsmen and those, usually younger members, was thought that the changes in the trade, the deskilling, the breaking down of jobs and new methods and materials could only be met by taking in all workers in the sheet metal and related industries, with the development of the ancilliary section.

Concern at the amount of work being lost to Union members by the employment of semi-skilled workers on increasingly-sectionalised sheet metal work was raised regularly during the inter-war years but inevitably came up against the sterile attitude that all sheet metal work belonged to members of the National Union by right, an attitude unaccompanied by any action to try and retain it. Nor was there any serious attempt to organise these people into the Union. The Ashton-under-Lyne branch tried unsuccessfully at the 1927 National Conference to get the implementation of a sub-committee report on organising auxiliary workers. Other voices were raised in similar calls from time to time but were unheeded.

Membership of the Union was for skilled male sheet metal workers who had served their time at the trade and all applicants for membership had to convince the branch committee that they were indeed eligible on that basis and had not transgressed Union principles in any way.

As late as 1937 National Conference turned down a Bristol motion drawing attention to the large amount of sheet metal being sectionalised and given to semi-skilled workers, and urging that they be organised into the Union to give some control over them. Only eight voted in favour out of 53 voting delegates. Most still insisted that all the work was craftsmen's work and should be done by members of the Union. Another motion that steps be taken to organise the workers in the mass-production motor and other sheet metal factories was lost by 27 votes to 17.

Critics blamed the rules as being too inflexible to deal with the problems arising from the development of the industry. There was, in fact, provision for auxiliary workers to be enrolled in a special section of the Union but it did not find great favour with those running the Union, who declined to use it for the purpose for which it was supposedly created, using it largely to segregate welders. An attempt by the NEC to stipulate those workers eligible to join the auxiliary section, instead of leaving this to the branch committee – and therefore often ignored – was defeated right on the eve of the war, at the 1939 National Conference. It was only accepted at a special conference after the start of the war, in 1940, smuggled in with war-time provisions for relaxation of customs. This belated acceptance of the facts of life enabled the Union to survive and grow in the wartime and post-war years but it was almost too late and the delay did have an effect on limiting the Union's place in industry.

Shop Stewards' Associations

In the early days of the National Union the London district played a special part, working closely with the national office, both because the head office was in London and because the district, in effect the old London Society, was by far the biggest section of the Union, with about a quarter of the whole membership.

The very size of the London district allowed it to do things that were not possible in the numerically smaller districts, including an extension of the democratic process of consulting members and bringing them into greater participation in Union affairs, giving a voice to members on the shop floor extra to the ballots conducted during periods of national negotiations.

This was achieved by the creation of a number of shop stewards' organisations catering for the various sections of the trade. They were formed from the shop organisation on which the Union itself was based. Each organised shop was expected to have its own elected secretary, chairman and committee, holding regular quarterly meetings, as well as special meetings to deal with anything that might arise, and fining members who did not attend without reason. They acted rather like branches of the Union within the machinery of the district – they were well able to do this as many of the shops had more members than a number of provincial branches – distributing ballot forms and other communications from the district office.

The more active shops sent their secretaries and chairmen to regular meetings of the shop stewards' associations for their particular section of the trade. These were rank and file organisations, with their own secretaries, chairmen and committee and delegates running their own affairs. At the same time they were a recognised part of the organisation of the London district encouraged, and even, if necessary, set up by the district committee, as they had been by the old London Society before it. We have just seen how, when confronted with a large body of unemployed members, the reaction of the district committee was to set up a central unemployed committee, acting rather like a shop stewards' organisation with its own officers and even delegates from shops, with regular meetings, having access to the district committee and consulted by them.

The inspiration of them all was the Gas Meter Stewards' Association which had its origins in the pricing committees that had existed for all the main commodities made as far back as there are records and were then still in operation. At this time the Meter Stewards Association was still very much a power in its own section of the trade and was maintaining an influence on the district committee that came from strong organisation. When, during the war, gas meter makers went to work in the aircraft shops, they helped to create an aircraft sheet metal shop stewards' association.

Although the inflated aircraft industry of the war years had collapsed, providing work for only a small number of members, the aircraft shop stewards association still lingered on, rather moribund and only a shadow of the body that was so active in defence of members' interests a few years before. Its place was taken by the burgeoning Motor Shop Stewards Association, embracing many former aircraft shops now engaged on work for the motor trade, with Harry Brotherton, a former meter maker, then aircraft worker and later General Secretary, as its first secretary.

A co-ordinating shop stewards' organisation had been set up at the end of the war, known as the Central Committee and later as the United Shop Stewards' Association, with R.B. Pattison as one of its leading lights. Its stated objects were to 'build up a strong and co-ordinated rank and file movement in the workshops for the purpose of increasing the efficiency of our trade union.' Each branch of the craft should have its shop stewards' association sending representatives to the Central Committee or United Association, funded by a contribution of one-halfpenny a month for each member in the affiliated body. It declared

> that in the event of any branch of our Society considering the time opportune to down tools they should, before ceasing work, approach the Central Shop Stewards Committee who will immediately consider, with the executive committee of our Society, their grievances.

It was this body that first called together the motor shops to form a stewards' association.

The first circulars of the new Motor Shop Stewards' Association set out its position in the Union. It emphasised its 'friendly and cordial relations with the district committee during the critical period of the Union's history', giving assistance to men on dispute at Handley Page, the Aircraft Manufacturing Co. and Brown and Melhuish 'when the breakdown of the ordinary machinery of the Union necessitated the calling together of all available stewards.' It also had long discussions with the district committee on dilution and on the advisability of signing the Agreement on the Procedure for the Avoidance of Disputes, the outcome of which was the calling together by the district committee of all shop stewards 'to discuss the position and outline a policy' – it decided against signing.

The Association also set up a sub-committee which tabulated the shifting conditions and policies of the shops in its section, giving the rates paid, systems worked and the general conditions obtaining. This information was available to the district committee as well as to stewards negotiating with managements.

London also developed other organisations to deal with special problems. In 1921, when it seemed that the railwaymen and transport workers would come out on strike in support of their 'Triple Alliance' partners, the coal miners, the London district committee of the Union discussed action to be taken in the case of a national stoppage. It was decided to divide London into eight areas, with two centres in each, with their own sub-committees to arrange ways of keeping in contact with members, providing information on what was happening, delivering messages to shop stewards and arranging to call stewards together if necessary.

Out-of-work members with bicycles were asked to volunteer to act as couriers. A circular was drawn up reporting what had been arranged, to be delivered by the cyclist couriers.

There is no doubt that a general strike was expected. As it happened, the railwaymen's leaders fought shy of taking part in a sympathetic strike although a ballot vote, made public later, showed that their members were in favour of action. So the machinery was put in cold storage for use in the future and was actually brought out during the 1922 'Managerial Functions' lockout.

The 'Managerial Functions' Lockout

The lockout was part of the continuing post-war offensive of the engineering employers. There is no doubt that it was deliberately contrived to weaken the unions. They picked on the AEU, the biggest union in the industry, as the target for their first attack, accusing them of interfering in matters that were managerial functions and of no concern to the unions. Sir Alan Smith, secretary of the engineering employers' federation, said the question at issue was 'whether the industry was to be conducted under the Soviet system or on the basis of private enterprise.'

After declaring that the unions had no business to interfere with the manning of machines, the employers seized on overtime as a better field of attack, insisting that all decisions on the working of overtime would be made by the employers. When the AEU suggested that it should continue to be the subject of mutual consent, as it had been in the past, Sir Alan Smith jumped in with a notice that unless the union made a declaration not to interfere in managerial functions – and that was apparently anything the employers liked to include in that category -'the services of their members would not be required in federated establishments after 11 March 1922.'

From the intransigent attitude of the employers it is difficult not to believe they were spoiling for a fight. If it had not been on the issue of overtime – which in that period of mass unemployment and short time working was hardly a burning issue – something else would have been used to foment a dispute. The employers obviously felt they had the unions where they wanted them, weak after a long period of unemployment and wage cuts, and now was the time to end their powers for good and all. They gave the union an ultimatum not to interfere with the right of employers to exercise managerial functions and the employers 'would not interfere in the proper functions of the unions.' The Procedure for the Avoidance of Disputes must be adhered to during which time the employers' instructions would be observed. Firms would refuse to employ members of any union that did not comply with these terms. This was to be only the beginning; when the terms were accepted the unions would be summoned to a meeting at which future working conditions would be 'set up on an economic basis.'

The unions of the Engineering and Shipbuilding Trades Federation were told that they must also accept the terms within eight days, although they protested they had no quarrel with the employers. They were later allowed 14 days to ballot their members when the employers realised that this was a constitutional necessity for many unions, but they were told that if they had not indicated their agreement by first post on 25 March 'the services of their members would be dispensed with.' The National Union voted against any further negotiations, pointing out that the employers would be able to put dilutees on any skilled man's job. Eventually, when no agreement could be reached, the union members were locked out at the end of April.

In London, 3,613 members were locked out immediately, with 910 in Wolverhampton, 800 to 900 in the North of England, 600 on Merseyside, 300 in Glasgow. Other members were told to come out as soon as notices laying down the employers' ultimatum as a condition of employment were posted up.

The general attitude of members was that they had to stand up and fight. The men at the Gothic Works of T. Glover, gas meter and lamp makers, in North London jumped the gun, voting to come out as soon as the AEU was locked out and marching round to other works to get the men out. London put its courier scheme into operation and arranged for a member of the committee to be at each centre to give guidance and information. Joint lockout committees were set up in many towns.

Nationally the Union took steps to prepare for a long struggle. A protracted period of unemployment had depleted Union funds which then totalled only £11,444.10s 6d. Of this the trustees recommended that £2,000 be set aside for superannuation payments and a further £2,000 for administration. The CWS bank was approached for the biggest overdraft possible on securities held and the districts were asked to help. The London district handed over the deeds of its office property as collateral, Glasgow sent Clyde Navigation bonds with a face value of £1,000, Ashton-under-Lyne offered £200 invested in Ashton Corporation stock and £100 in the *Daily Herald*, Wolverhampton and Manchester each made loans of £2,000 and other districts lent what they had. But still money was short with so much to be paid out in dispute benefit. Of the £12,000 overdraft allowed by the bank, £5,000 had already been paid out early in May. The salaries of full-time officers was cut by £30 a year and cuts were made in branch secretaries' and shop stewards' commissions.

Still the situation continued to deteriorate and finally the NEC had to suspend dispute and unemployment benefits as the Union just had no money to pay them.

The other unions were in a similar position, but all managed to hold out until the end of May and then, financially crippled, they asked for talks at which the employers' federation offered essentially the same terms as before the lockout, but slightly modified its terminology. A ballot of all unions recorded a majority in favour of acceptance but with 52,423 still voting for continuing resistance as against 99,313 for a settlement.

Work was resumed on 2 June 1922 but it was some time before the majority restarted. Some shops stayed out against discrimination and demanding that as all came out together all should return together. But the London district secretary reported later that about 100 of their members would never be taken back.

During the lockout a national ballot was held on a proposal to levy all members in work 2s 6d a week for four weeks. This was carried by 3,840 to 2,770 but there was so much vocal opposition that it was decided to leave it in abeyance until the next national conference.

The No. 3B district – the old iron plate and hollowware workers in the Black Country, who had separate employers and were not affected by the lockout – carried their opposition to a levy to the point of holding a ballot on seceding from the Union when five branches voted in favour and two to 'wait and see'. The NEC expressed surprise and concern at the 'demagogic attitude' taken by the district secretary, Simeon Webb. At the national conference the district's delegate called for the National Union to be dissolved and for a return to the old looser amalgamation, but found no support elsewhere. But the conference did decide not to put the 2s 6d levy into effect, the 3B district decided to take no more action for another twelve months so the matter was allowed to fade away. The whole incident was a warning that the National Union had not been consolidated and that the minority in various parts of the country who had voted against the formation of the Union were still not convinced.

On the other hand, a number of members wanted still further amalgamation to strengthen the fight against employers' attacks. The wage cuts followed by the lockout had brought new amalgamation motions on the conference agenda. Glasgow, supported by London, called for amalgamation with kindred trades. Wolverhampton asked for talks with the Birmingham Society, the Sheet Iron Workers and the Coppersmith's Society and urged the TUC to form the unions into one body to meet the power of capital as represented by the employers' federations.

Wage Cuts

In addition to the national wage cuts, local employers' associations took advantage of the situation to enforce their own reductions. Sheet metal workers were under special attack in a number of selected districts to bring their wage rates down to those of other skilled workers. The London Engineering Employers' Association issued instructions to member firms to lock out sheet metal workers if they refused to accept the fitters' and turners' rate. They announced a new London day work rate of 1s 1d plus £1 6s 6d plus 12½ per cent, which was rejected by a mass meeting of members. A compromise was reached with the Union accepting the 1s 1d and plussages and the employers agreeing to ability rates.

Birmingham and Wolverhampton had both accepted local rates that meant cuts of 2d an hour. In Coventry the new rate meant a drop of 31s 6d a week. Edinburgh employers reduced the local rate and the Dundee rate was cut to 1s 8d all-in. The RAE at Farnborough and other government establishments followed the line of private industry and cut rates to conform with those outside. With the London settlement, members in most districts had been forced into conformity. The various trade groupings and individual firms also took their slice.

The gas meter employers called for a 5 per cent reduction in piece-work prices which they said would be deducted from selling prices 'to save the trade.' The men opposed but Hickin, the then General Secretary, said the Union had no money to fight and the cut would have to be accepted. 'If it was left for a fortnight, the men would be running after the employers and the shops would be full of blacklegs.' The men gave in and soon the employers were demanding an end to 'dirty money' on meter repairs.

An all-round cut in prices demanded by the dairy utensil employers was bitterly resisted by the dairy workers, one of the weakest sections of the trade, who put up a good fight, lasting many months, before being forced to return.

The London general work employers followed with a demand for book price percentages to be cut from 120 to 100 per cent and a penny to be knocked off the day work rate. General workers in Birmingham suffered a reduction of 5s 6d a week, but an attempt by Austin Motors to cut prices was successfully resisted.

Among individual employers taking up the attack was Vulcan Motors of Southport. They demanded a reduction of 30s a week and gave the men the alternative of accepting the demand in full or be locked out. The district committee supported the men in resisting but after three months accepted a settlement and closed the dispute, though not without objections.

One after another the London motor firms made their demands for cuts in piece-work prices. Hooper's, one of the top high-class coach-builders, specialising in hand built Rolls Royce bodies, wanted the price of limousines with beaten head panels reduced from £18 to £13 10s but eventually accepted the men's offer of £16; the landaulette price was cut from £13 to £9 5s; the phaeton from £15 to £12. A set of four wings with beaten spare wheel wells was cut from £12 10s to £11 10s.

De Dion demanded that the price of panelling a body be reduced from £10 to £7, claiming that they could get the job done for that money outside, which was probably true as the multiplicity of shops that had mushroomed during the war on aircraft sub-contract work were fighting now for motor work. A number of the aircraft firms were also on motor work as there were few orders in their own industry. Fairey was buildings bodies for Singer at £8 each but then sub-contracted the job to Scott and Sadden at £3 15s. They cut the price of Hillman two seaters from £4 4s to £3 14s and then sub-contracted them at £3 10s. General Aircraft was

Building coachwork bodies and wings from the flat at Car Panels, Nuneaton, on Daimler and Lea Francis cars, made up from the flat, early 1950s

building Buick five-seater bodies at £15 which they wanted cut to £6 11s, raised the price to £8 and then sub-contracted the job at £6 5s. They also made Morris Cowley bodies in the 'dilution department'. The Union men were told they could have the job at the same price, 22s 6d each, raising the price to 28s when the men could not make them pay, no doubt saving money by not having to pay for putting right bad work.

The Union was very worried by the undercutting of the main shops by sub-contractors, using non-union and dilutee labour, putting members out of work. The number of men employed in 16 shops on motor work dropped from 553 to 191 in twelve months: General Aircraft from 70 members to 12, Auto Rad from 30 to 10, Adam Grimaldi from 15 to 2, Graham White from 70 to 8, Brown and Melhuish from 40 to 20, Darracq from 60 to 5, BMC from 30 to 12, Camden Sheet Metal from 80 to 40. In some motor body shops there were more dilutees than skilled metal workers.

At a joint meeting of the district committee, the Motor Shop Stewards Association and the motor pricing committee, it was decided that as far as possible the pricing committee, composed of members elected from the section, should price all new jobs and jobs on which there had been alterations or had been in dispute. The London assistant secretary visited a number of shops and 'read the riot act', reporting that many had no shop organisation and non-unionists were working on sheet metal work. At least 32 motor shops were in a bad state of organisation, including a number of well-known shops, 30 were without secretaries, many of the workers were non-union or lapsed members and long hours were worked at ordinary rates.

The employers followed up their success in cutting wages with pressure on the Union to accept the Procedure for the Avoidance of Disputes. The Union was one of the few in the engineering industry that had not signed the agreement. Now the employers were insisting that there would be no settlement of disputes accept through procedure. There was strong opposition to this from Union members all over the country and widespread resistance to any agreement.

In particular, they objected to management making temporary decisions which would remain in force throughout procedure, saying that temporary decisions had a habit of becoming established customs. But there was also general opposition to the whole concept, complaining that it took too long and by the time a dispute had gone through the machinery the situation which gave rise to it no longer existed. They wanted settlements by mutual agreement to continue.

However, the NEC decided by six votes to three to sign the agreement to bring the National Union into line with other unions. The decision was widely condemned, with Manchester and Oldham branches refusing to recognise it or to attend any meeting at York where national arbitration decisions were made.

General Strike

The all-out confrontation with the employers that the London district committee, at least, had expected in 1921, came in May 1926 with the nine days of the General Strike. Again the issue was one of solidarity with the miners threatened with punitive cuts in wages combined with an increase in the working day, imposed as an ultimatum by the most rapacious set of employers in the country, backed by a government representative of big business. The confrontation of miners and mine owners had come in 1925 and the TUC General Council had been forced into a position of having to inform the government that the whole of the labour movement was prepared to back the miners. All active trade unionists were well aware that if the coal owners were allowed to get away with their demands, their own employers would be making similar calls soon after. At that stage the government was not prepared to take on the trade unions and agreed to continue the coal subsidy for a further nine months, using the time to prepare for a showdown with the unions. The TUC General Council, on the other hand, did nothing to prepare the workers to meet the challenge. Burying their heads in the sand they refused to see what was obvious, vainly hoping that the threat would go away if they ignored it.

When it did not, the General Council wriggled, trying to find a way out of their dilemma, holding meeting after meeting with government ministers. But life had caught up with them and soon they had no room to manoeuvre. On the one hand was the government who had taken over from the coal owners, refusing to move from what they saw as an impregnable position. On the other was the mass of trade unionists resolved not to let down the miners yet again.

On 30 April 1926 the lock-out notices to the miners became operative. On 1 May a conference of trade union executives gave the General Council a mandate to call a general strike with a vote of 3,653,529 to 49,911 with 319,00 awaiting instructions from their members. With the strike notice not taking effect until 3 May the General Council held further meetings with ministers and thought they had found a formula to get them off the hook but the government was not prepared to let them escape. Coal stocks were built up, a strike-breaking organisation all prepared, the government would not accept anything but complete surrender. This the Movement was not prepared to tolerate. So the TUC leadership stumbled into a strike they did not want and called out certain key sections of workers from the evening of 3 May.

The National Union, with the rest of the unions, sent out telegrams to all district and branch officials to bring their members out as instructed. Not only did all the members working in key industries come out, others not scheduled for immediate action came out as well. Members of district committees were sitting continuously to deal with problems and the London secretary reported that the phone was ringing all day with members seeking instructions.

The first to be called out were members working in transport – road, rail, shipping and aircraft. The London General Omnibus Co shops had not been included in the first line of attack, but members of all trades walked out and the National Union members were told to do the same. The steward at Woolwich Arsenal wanted to know why the members had not been called when other trades were walking out. The steward at the Daimler depot at Hendon rang in to say the firm had been requisitioned and 'everything that could be put on wheels was being prepared for the government.' He was told to bring the men out immediately. Members at RAF Kidbrook, ringing in for instructions were told to stop, as were members at the LNER depot. Members working in gas and electricity were told to await instructions, but the meter stewards decided that all meter makers still working should be called out.

The district committee decided that when some workers were unable to get to work because of transport stoppages, the whole of the shop should stop, rather than have some in and some out. Members at Baker's, Willesden refused an offer from the management for free transport for men living some distance away, preferring to strike.

The courier service designed for the 'Triple Alliance' emergency was put into service with motorcycles supplementing the bicycles of 1921. They delivered leaflets giving members information and instructions and were commended by the district secretary at the end of the strike. Meetings were held at the various centres, attendances varying from 14 to 98 but the assistant secretary reported that 'officious police' at Camberwell would not allow him to consult members.

The district committee was told that non-unionists were not only coming out on strike but were asking to join the Union. Up to 100 had signed forms in the first four days. It was decided that they should be allowed strike pay and also that arrears would be ignored in paying those members who were out on strike.

Writing in the Union Journal later, the Ashton branch secretary, Booth Wimpenny, told of his experience on the local Council of Action:

> We found ourselves in an entirely new situation. The first thing to be tackled was the improvisation of an organisation. As the situation developed we had to make changes to meet rising needs. To this committee each affiliated union appointed its representatives and as the area was extended the numbers grew and it became somewhat unwieldy. We then split up into a general committee and three sub-committees and by so doing were in continual session to deal with any questions that came along. We were called upon to deal with all manner of questions, the area was extended daily. Numbers of men were being brought into contact with a set of conditions the like of which they had never experienced before. For a moment power had passed into the hands of the workers. Here was a body of men fresh from the factory or workshop dealing with questions as to who should remain and who should cease to carry on in the usual way. At each session that I attended we were discussing the question of permits for this purpose or that necessity; employers of labour coming, cap in hand, begging for permission to do certain things or, to be more correct, to allow their workers to return to perform

certain customary operations 'Please can I move a quantity of coal from such and such a place?' or 'Please can my transport worker move certain foodstuffs to this or that direction?' What an experience! So-called captains of industry in the hands of the common or garden worker. Most of them turned empty away after a most humiliating experience, for one and all were put through a stern questioning. Some of them tried bullying, but that was no use. Some of them tried persuasion, referring to us as Mr Chairman and gentlemen, but only a rigid examination of the stern facts moved our activities ... There is another matter that stands to the credit of the workers and that is the excellent manner in which they conducted themselves. Many attempts to provoke them were made, but there they stood, perfectly orderly, as firm as a rock ... One lesson is that there should be a link between the local trades councils and the Trades Union Congress so that we do not have to improvise machinery ... Another point clearly demonstrated is the need for our closing ranks on the political field.

When, on 12 May, the strike was unexpectedly called off, the London district told members to return 'where the terms of employment were no worse than before the dispute and providing always that all sections of organised labour returns without victimisation.' But there was victimisation. The management at Dougal's gas meters gave the men their cards and money and told them they would call any men they wanted. LGOC told half of the members that they could start, all of them single men; no married men were to be started until later. Fairey also said half their employees could start but the men said 'all or none'and the management increased the proportion to 70 per cent with a promise that the rest would be back within a fortnight. At Metal Propellors, Croydon, 15 were victimised. At Edinburgh most meter shops 'were inclined to be selective' in taking men back but management was told that the men all came out together and would all return together, and solidarity won the day. Members at Strachan and Brown's on motor sub-contract work, were told they could have their jobs back if they tore up their union cards – they stayed out and received victimisation pay.

A total of 1,967 were on strike in London and £2,480 was paid out in benefit. Nationally the Union paid out £11,000.

Collections were taken in the shops for the victimised members and grants were made out of local funds to supplement the Union benefit payments. Soon they were paid wholly from union funds and the collections were switched to providing help for the miners. Collections for the miners' relief fund totalled £4,157 7s 1d with probably as much again from independent shop collections sent separately.

The General Secretary, writing in the Journal, congratulated the members on their 'splendid response' confronted 'with all the forces of the State, armed and otherwise' and mis-representation of the media.

There was a lot of criticism from active members of the Union on the handling of the General Strike and particularly on the way it was called off. At the 1927 meeting of union executives to hear the TUC report on the strike the National Union delegation voted to accept the report made by Pugh. This was finally endorsed by the Union but not without a lot of criticism by members who wanted to know why the strike was so hurriedly called off, why it had been called off without any demand to end the lockout of miners or any guarantee against victimisation.

Political Action

The Union took part in the TUC Hyde Park demonstration against the Tory Government's vindictive attack on the movement with the Trade Union Reform Act following the General

Strike. This included an attempt to cripple the Labour Party finances with changes in the rules for paying the political levy, so that those wanting to pay had to sign a paper indicating they wanted to contribute instead of signing a contracting-out form if they did not want to pay the levy, as in the past. The Union had set up a political fund in 1923 after previous pre-war moves had been overtaken by the Osborne judgement on the legality of any payments, followed by the outbreak of the First World War and the formation of the National Union. Now in 1927 the whole question of the political fund was being challenged again in the attempt to hobble the Labour Party. How right the movement was to question this new legislation can be seen from the fact that in 1938 only 38 per cent of members of the National Union were paying the levy – 78 per cent of the London district, 34 per cent in the 3B district – the old hollowware area – 30 per cent in Yorkshire and the Midlands, 27 per cent in Lancashire and 26 per cent in the East Midlands and the South West. Appeals were made from time to time for more members to pay the levy, but apparently with little success.

In 1932, a call was made in the *Journal* for branches to link up with local Labour parties in campaigns for a million more members of the Labour Party and for an increase in the circulation of the *Daily Herald*.

But a letter from the *Sunday Worker* asking that a speaker be allowed at one of the meetings of the Union was rejected because 'he would be speaking for one particular paper rather than for the national workers' press.' Calls from the Ashton-under-Lyne and Coventry branches for the Union to affiliate to the National Minority Movement – rank-and-file Communist and left-Labour organisation to 'ginger-up the unions' – was rejected and a number of letters to the London district from the NMM were ordered to 'lie on the table.' Even letters from the National Unemployed Workers' Movement, asking for support for the Hunger Marchers, suffered the same fate in 1927 and again in 1930.

But right from 1936 there was strong and widespread support for the Spanish people against Franco fascism and for the International Brigades, with collecting sheets sent round the shops from time to time, with motions criticising the National Council of Labour for its lack of action in support of the Spanish people. In the 1930s, there was growing support, particularly in the aircraft shops, for joint political action by all left wing parties in opposition to fascism.

The Aircraft Shop Stewards Association had its own library, mainly of Left Book Club books, which members could borrow, in an attempt to provide political education, particularly for young members.

Eventually the left wing members, Left Labour, Communist and left wing members of no party, began to get elected to positions in the Union, particularly in London.

Recession

The inter-war years was a period dominated by recession, with a few minor booms, as far as the Union was concerned. There had been an improvement in trade in 1924, but the improvements gained suffered a setback with the employers' attacks on the unions following the General Strike of 1926. The gains made in 1928 and 1929 then disappeared in the slump of 1930. This was the time of record unemployment when some three million were on the dole, the period of depressed areas, closed factories and yards, and Hunger Marches.

In the National Union 10.5 per cent of members were out of work in 1930, going up to 16.4 per cent in 1931, 18.7 per cent in 1932 then dropping slightly to 15.5 per cent in 1933 as the economy began to improve. The Union paid out £20,000 out-of-work benefit payments in 1931 peaking at £25,896 the following year: more than half the money received in contributions.

Payments then began to decline as unemployed members ran out of benefit and benefit was reduced.

At the end of 1932 the NEC called a special conference to consider the precarious financial position of the Union. The bank balance had fallen from £20,170 to £7,863 between the previous January and December and was continuing to fall by more than £1,000 a month. In 1931 the NEC had asked for an increase in contributions but had dropped their request in view of opposition from members faced with threats of wage cuts by both engineering and shipbuilding employers. The 3d a week increase that had been put on later had not been sufficient. There must be further increases in contributions or a cut in benefits. It was decided by 30 votes to 13 to cut out-of-work pay by half and sick pay by a quarter, to consider cuts in officers' salaries and to make a charge for the *Journal*. It was not until 1936 that it was possible to restore the cuts and reduce contributions.

In Wolverhampton in 1931 out of 825 members on the books, 270 were unemployed. Liverpool paid out £2,199 in unemployment benefit with only £1,728 coming in from contributions. Glasgow paid out £2,287 to unemployed members and received £3,029 in contributions. In most branches collections were taken in the shops but with many men on short time this did not bring in enough, a football competition was added to raise money. Members whose unemployment benefit was cut off under the means test were dependent on the grants from these sources. Already in 1931, 150 London members had run of out benefit and were dependent on the Union grants of 10s a week to buy food. In 1932 it was reported that a number of the men unemployed had been out for years and could not expect to ever get another job.

The London unemployed committee charged the Union with not doing enough to get men jobs. It appealed to the shop stewards to get the benches filled in the shops before allowing men to work overtime. It called on members to take part in marches against the means test and in support of the hunger marchers, and in 1933 the district committee, with the Union banner, led the Union contingent in the TUC march and demonstration in support of the unemployed.

It is not easy to convey a real understanding of the sufferings of the mass of long-term unemployed. After running out of benefit on the dole there was no automatic national assistance payments, the unemployed had to go through a means test under which earnings of children and other members of the household were assessed and their possessions sold before assistance would be given. One London district secretary tells how the meaning of the stark poverty of those times was brought home to him with the finding of a box in the district office filled with slips of paper. They were IOUs dating from that period, each one for a shilling – how desperate members must have been to borrow one shilling from the Union.

These years of mass unemployment, of course, weakened the unions and the engineering employers took advantage of this weakness to announce a worsening of conditions. Hours of work would go up from 47 to 48 a week; overtime rates would only be paid after a full week's work instead of on a daily basis, and payment for the first four hours would be cut to time-and-a-quarter; piece-work rates would be cut to 25 per cent above day-work rates, instead of $33\frac{1}{3}$ per cent. Despite agitation, the Union had not been able to get the pre-1931 situation restored by the outbreak of war.

In October 1932 the War Office joined in, taking off the war bonuses of their engineering employees, on instruction from the Treasury, to bring them in line with rates of outside workers.

However, the men stuck to the Union and membership remained remarkably constant through the years of the slump, new entrants compensating for those lost through deaths and lapsings. The Union entered the slump with a membership of 14,758 at the end of 1929 and still had 14,250 at the end of 1933 and 14,645 at the end of 1934.

Organisation

London still accounted for about one quarter of the membership and so the position of London decided the position of the Union. The London district was actually one big branch 3,250 or so strong with members working in nearly 500 shops, employing from six to 300 members. Around 120 of them were organised at least to the extent of having a shop steward.

There was a general dissatisfaction among active members at the state of organisation in the trade and the London district committee came under strong criticism for the large number of non-members working at the trade in the capital and surrounding areas. Members of the United Shop Stewards' Association felt that London was too big and should be split up into branches; members would then be able to attend branch meetings and from greater member involvement would come greater organisation of the trade. After some hesitation the district committee agreed to give it a try with a West London branch for members living in the area. However attendance was little better and as support dwindled still further the experiment was abandoned. A special organising meeting was then held, based on the Southall area, but despite a great deal of publicity including advertisements and circulars to the shops, only a handful turned up. A proposal for general meetings on a delegate basis with votes based on the

Hollowing a dished end for a tank by power hammer at APV, Wandsworth

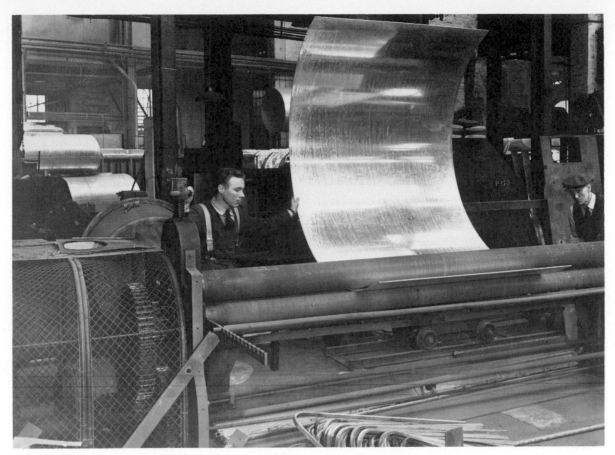

Shaping a tank on the rollers at APV, Wandsworth

membership was considered but apparently did not reach fruition. It did, however, bring out the facts of membership for 1937: 598 working in aircraft shops, 728 on general work, 979 on gas meters, 865 in motor shops and 352 on ventilation, with around 1,000 private members – that is members who worked in places with no organisation and paid their contributions individually. The term probably dates from those early tin plate workers who worked privately – at home. It was pointed out that one reason for lack of attendance at meetings was that all the livelier shops were already organised and operating very much as a branch with their own regular meetings taking place after work in the shop or elsewhere locally, so that members were only delayed for about an hour or so before making their journey home.

At this stage it might be useful to give some indication of the various sections of the trade at that time, the changing work of the members and its impact on the activities and organisation of the Union in the inter-war period that was laying the basis for greater technical changes to come.

The General Trade

In the 1920s the general shops still provided jobs for some hundreds of Union members. Although some quite big shops – by Union standards – remained, the general trade was only a remnant of even twenty or thirty years before, when it provided a sizeable portion of the nation's domestic ware, plus equipment for the armed forces. The main areas had been the Midlands and London. Now, in their decline, the London shops were complaining of undercutting by the Midlands. Vanloads of utensils were said to be going into the Army and Navy stores, which used to be made in the stores' own workshops. Most of these were said to be coming from the Midlands, some would be machine-made, the others had machine-made parts of items otherwise said to have been made up by National Union members at prices with which London could not compete. There seems to have been no attempt at this period to get a meeting of the two and sort things out. Other firms were buying from Belgium and Germany, at a price cheaper than the cost in Britain for materials alone. A meeting was called in 1924 to try and sort out the position and provide a better basis for this section of the trade. Charges of undercutting on the galvanised iron section brought a retort by a representative of one shop accused that their prices 'allowed a man of 70 to earn £5 a week on coal bunkers in a 38-hour week', while apprentices and men just out of their time could earn £4 a week on scoops and waterloos. Differences seem to have been the result of facilities provided and methods of work.

The London district committee thought something should be done to obtain an advance for the general shops but it was not easy as those in the most need were the least militant. The Assistant Secretary eventually managed to see the men from Keeves shop in the East End but they were not too keen to meet him and, fearing they might be seen by the management, eventually met him in a nearby churchyard at dinner time. They were reluctant to 'stick their necks out' by putting in for an increase and agreed that one man should do so for the lot of them – no doubt they were older men who had spent most of their lives in the shop and were afraid of the unknown outside world.

The general employers still worked by the book prices agreed between the employers and Union in 1900 and revised in 1917, but by the 1920s plussed by up to 100 per cent. This book had over 1,200 sets of prices for the various articles manufactured, each with an average of five sizes. By the 1920s one employer said he only made 100 book items and another 24. Like the rest of the employers, the manufacturers of general work wanted reductions in prices, generally proposing that the 100 per cent increase on book prices be reduced to 75 per cent for such things as uniform cases and deed boxes. The men at one shop agreed they could accept the new prices because of 'modern facilities' that other shops did not have, another thought the new prices would still allow them to earn 2s 6d an hour if given out in bigger quantities. The 1900 prices book stipulated that 'a wheel, treadle guillotine and a large angle bender shall be found.' If smaller quantities than a dozen were given out 'extra is to be charged' and where a larger quantity of any free-selling article than is stated is the custom 'shall still obtain.'

General trade workers were also employed at many factories on maintenance and equipment. There might be one man or, as in the case of Rowntree of York, over 150 sheet metal workers, in the mid-1930s. One section of men was kept busy all the time making and fitting ducting, fans and other equipment for the air-conditioning which was essential for all workrooms to maintain a constant temperature, for the chocolates, not the work-people. Another section shaped, flanged, fitted and sometimes made up the 'miles' of copper pipes and the vats and boiling pans with dovetailed brazed joints, all the work done on the

Tinshops at Rowntree's, York, which at one time employed over 150 members on maintenance, ventilation equipment and chocolate moulds

blacksmith's-type coke-fired forge in the centre of the shop. About 30 men were employed in a special shop making moulds for the various chocolates, Easter eggs and chocolate bars, some hundreds of which were fitted to each endless belt, taking the liquid chocolate which was then passed through a freezing chamber before being delivered to the packers. A lot of moulds, all made by hand, were required before a new line could be started. Others were engaged in making and hand soldering the tin linings of packing cases for the export trade. Rowntree at that time was still run by the family and all employees had to join their appropriate trade union before they could start. The management had a weekly meeting with the shop stewards and the stewards' chairman had his own office for dealing with complaints. All apprentices had to attend evening classes at the local technical institute.

Members were also employed in a similar capacity at the other chocolate firms, Cadbury at Bournville, Birmingham and Fry at Bristol. Flour mills, too, employed a number of members, mainly on trunking and other equipment.

Another big shop employing general workers was Joseph Lyons, of tea shop and Corner House fame. They made ducting and ventilating equipment out of galvanised iron, hand-made buckets, galvanised tables for stripping meat, poultry, vegetables, etc., as well as bakery equipment including large capacity mixing bowls and dough mixers, and copper pipes and copper vats. Later much of the work was done in Firth Staybrite, the original stainless steel.

Among those on the edge of the general trade were a number of firms specialising in various classes of sheet metal work. One of these was the group engaged on laboratory and hospital work. A group of stewards representing members working in London shops on this work met for the first time in November 1937 with a view to discussing prices and setting up a shop stewards' association. A number of members had been working on artificial limbs for some years by then, but they had no stewards' association until after the war. Another section was the expanding sign trade.

The Rail Shops

Members working in the railway shops were another section of the Union that did not do so well in these inter-war years. The pay was comparatively low, the railway companies' traditionally stressing job security in order to retain their workforce, and seem to have been remarkably successful in doing so.

Members were employed in the depots, doing repairs on locomotives and rolling stock, making and repairing the various lamps used in the railway service, station equipment and so on. In the shops they worked on locomotive construction and in the carriage works they carried out the metal panelling, made ventilators and other sheet metal parts. A number of carriage works, like the works in Gloucester, made carriages for countries all over the world. These were shipped in zinc-lined containers 30 feet long by 12 feet deep with the joins soldered up by hand and a zinc lid soldered on to keep out the sea water – all done with a two pound copper iron heated in a coke-fired stove.

The National Union, with a comparatively small membership in the industry, generally went in with the trades with bigger memberships in negotiations for wages advances or better conditions. An attempt was made in 1922 to get a wage increase that would bring railway shopmen more in line with craftsmen doing similar work in outside industries. This failed when the Industrial Court ruled that the railways were a separate industry and not bound by the results of agreements in other industries. The following year the members at the GWR shops in Swindon urged the National Union to resist attempts by the companies to reduce

Top: dressing a coasterback bend at Enterprise Sheet Metal Works, Aberdeen; *left*: checking stainless steel dough mixers for ships' galleys at Thos. Bishop, Glasgow; *below*: making a special lamp for the Houses of Parliament at an East London general shop

wages by 6s 6d a week. They also called for the Union's representative at the negotiating conference to be a working railway shopman. They succeeded in neither. However, in October 1929 continued pressure obtained the restoration of $2\frac{1}{2}$ per cent deducted from shopmen's wages in 1928. But the deteriorating economic situation allowed the companies to get it back very soon, with an announcement in 1931 that wages would be reduced by 4s 6d a week for day workers and by 6s 6d for those on payment by results.

In the General Strike, the members in the railway shops had been among those most deeply involved. The members at Swindon, and no doubt elsewhere, were already out when they received the Union telegram calling them out, and they remained out for eleven days. The union was represented on the strike committee that was in daily session throughout the strike. The branch also took an active part in the setting up of the Federation of Trades Committee in Swindon which carried out joint action in the shops.

Shipbuilding and Repair

The worst-hit in this period were the members working on shipbuilding and repair. Not only was their industry devastated, yards closed as a matter of policy by the employers' organisation – they were also dismantled so that they would never reopen – but the branches were mainly in areas where there was little alternative work. Already in 1928 unemployment among members in this section of the Union amounted to 24.6 per cent.

In the 1920s, the members played their part in resisting employers' demands for wage cuts and pressing for wage advances. In 1928 the Union, through the joint trades movement, put in for a rise of 8s for men on shipbuilding and 5s a week for those on ship repair. This was rejected by the employers and the NEC expressed its disgust with the joint trades movement which, it said, did nothing but talk, with no results, and it was decided to attend no further meetings of the movement.

The position of members in the minor ports was much better. London, which was confined to ship repair, remained fairly busy. Southampton branch, with a number of its members at Harland and Wolff and Thorneycroft among others, kept up a constant fight to improve the position of members and to retain work, on the one hand in conflict with the employers, and on the other with the boilermakers who tried to use their size and strength to take over whatever jobs were around. In 1924 branch members took part in a long local strike for a 3s a week advance, but had to return with only half their claim. In the fight for work they got an agreement that Union members would do the shaping and fitting of panels for insulating holds on Union Castle ships. In 1936 they successfully fought off a boilermakers' claim that only eight sheet metal workers would be employed. And in 1938, in reply to a boilermakers' edict that sheet metal workers would not be allowed to fit trunking on ships, Union members in the shops stopped work on making the trunking until it was agreed they should fit it also.

Among the more forgotten members of the trade were those on fishing vessel building, outfitting and repair. Their period of apprenticeship in the port of Hull, in the early 1920s was seven years, and that meant seven full years and at the end of their time they had to serve extra days to make up time lost on days off or hours lost in lateness for work before being able to claim the man's rate, then £2 3s. As boys they had been paid 4s a week for the first year, rising by 1s a week per year. Their work was skilled and varied. They made the forecastle and the galley stoves – originally coal fired, then oil and later electric – frying pans, kettles, steamers and all the tin plate wares used for cooking; they made and fitted the shaped ventilators for the engine room and all cabin ventilator shafts, oil and water tanks, made the side, stern and mast lamps – these were originally for paraffin, and paraffin lamps were still carried as stand-bys when they changed over to electric. Until the end of the Second World War trawlers were lit by gas and Union members made the acetylene tanks and generators, and made and fitted the brass piping. They made ash chutes and lagged the engines and boilers, first with 18g galvanised iron and later with blue steel. Other sheet metal equipment included fish washers and tanks and boilers for making cod liver oil while the trawlers were at sea. Grimsby, Fleetwood and other ports also had members in this forgotten section of the trade.

But for members in the main shipbuilding ports it took the advent of the war to return them to any kind of relative prosperity.

The Ventilation Trade

The ventilating trade, on the other hand, was one of opening doors. At a meeting of ventilating shops at the beginning of 1933 it was established that there were 14 shops in London engaged on ventilating work and two more were in the process of opening. With the continuing increase in the size of buildings – domestic, commercial and industrial – there was obviously going to be a developing demand for heating, ventilating and air-conditioning, with a consequent increase in work prospects.

It was decided to go in for a ls 10d an hour minimum and an improvement in overtime rates and outworking allowances. Applications had to be on an individual basis as, it was said, there was then no employers' organisation for the trade.

Gas Meter Shops

The gas meter shops maintained their traditional militancy in looking after their sectional interests. Already in 1922, after a national conference of meter shops, a national ballot voted for a wage claim. Even during the heart of the slump, in mid-1930 the meter makers stopped work when the employers put up notices announcing reductions in rates, and refused to take them down. In London 380 were out on dispute, going back after a week. The meter makers' determination to get the cuts restored had to wait until 1936, when 924 members, the whole of the gas meter makers in London, took strike action. Throughout the period the meter makers continued their well-tried method of continually putting in for small increases in pay for changes made in a variety of jobs on different meters. They built up their shop organisation so that, with the exception of the gas companies, there was no chance of getting a job in a London meter shop if not a member of the Union. In the provinces the situation varied but on average the meter shops throughout the country were then the best organised section of the trade.

Coachbuilding

Although some top-class coachbuilders were scattered throughout the country, London in the late 1920s and the 1930s had become the centre for first class motor body work, carrying on the coachbuilding traditions of the days of the horse-drawn carriages, sometimes with the same firms. They gave the impression that quality of workmanship was all and that no expense was spared. Indeed, bodies built by Barkers on Rolls Royce chassis were said to be 'built almost without regard to cost', but that was not how it appeared to the men responsible for

Fitting a door on a coach-built Rolls Royce at Mulliners, London

fashioning these beautiful creations.

The Union, after a meeting with the stewards of the motor shops, put in for a rate of 2s 3d an hour for panel beaters – their rate was then 1s 10½d – and 2s 1d for first class wing makers. The manufacturers meeting in 1936, who included Barkers, would not go beyond a 2s 1d minimum for panel beaters; wing makers on the top private coachbuilding work would get 1s 11d and when on public service work 1s 9½d; flat workers, who did all the other sheet metal work on the job, would get 1s 8d and 1s 7d. These were the rates paid by the manufacturers of international repute – Hooper's, Barker's, Park Ward, Thrupp and Maberley, Freestone and Webb, Gurney Nutting, Arthur and H. J. Mulliner, Connaught, Windover's, James Young.

Standards were high if wages were low. After the panel beater had finished panelling a Rolls body the foreman would examine and check it all meticulously. He would take a penny and put it between the doors; if it was tight he would mark it, if it had too much clearance he would mark it. It might take a day or a day-and-a-half to get it passed. 'You thought you had done the perfect job, the foreman was trying to prove that you hadn't. But when you saw it going out of the works after it was painted you were very proud of yourself, because it was wonderful job', said one panel beater working at James Young of Bromley. Before the Union got the shop organised, Young was paying a panel beater only 1s 6d an hour and refused to pay more, only compromising when the men walked out – but even then he did not offer a better rate, only agreeing to accept piece-work.

For the more run-of-the-mill jobs prices were equally tight. A set of four wings for a Wolseley Hornet Special, made in 20 gauge steel, semi-cycle type with a swage down the middle, brought the wing maker in 22s. For that he had to draw the metal from the stores, get the patterns and mark out, cut the shape out, mark the centre line for the swage, shape them on the wheel, put in the special shaped swage working by eye, wire the edges and finish off. It was possible to earn £4 a week by going all out with a long run on one job. But to do a one-off replacement for 5s 6d was a dead loss.

At the 1929 London motor show there were 59 specialised coachbuilding firms exhibiting the skill of the panel builder. But toward the end of the 1930s coachbuilding shops were disappearing. Barker's had closed in 1938, their goodwill taken over by Hooper's; their workers,taken over by nobody, were looking for jobs. Park Ward had been taken over by Rolls Royce. Others were going over to aircraft subcontract work and another era, another example of the sheet metal workers' craft was on the way out.

Mass Production Cars

In the early 1930s, it became obvious that the all-steel motor bodies and mass production in the car field had come to stay. The unions realised that the workers in these factories must be organised if the unions were to have any relevance in the modern economy. But the going was tough. While the unions were not exactly welcomed in any car factory, they were forbidden in these new mass production giants.

A shop steward at Briggs Bodies, part of the Ford empire, H.A. Coward, said that when any form of organisation showed itself, the Company would think nothing of sacking up to 500 workers without notice, replacing them within 48 hours. It was common to see union meetings on waste ground outside the plants broken up by mounted police with trade unionists arrested in the mêlée that followed and given prison sentences. Lord Nuffield said he would not allow any union in his factories and he would sack anyone who joined one, but he encouraged membership of a company union, the League of Industry, formed after the General Strike. It had people in each shop to represent the workers, Lord Nuffield chose the 'representatives'.

Any union that managed to exist in these factories had to operate like a secret society. At the Austin works at Birmingham, the Union dues collectors would operate in the lavatories with a member posted outside to warn of approaching foremen.

Working conditions in these plants were said to be deplorable; accidents were common, the work was dirty and there were no proper washing facilities. At the old Morris plant at Cowley, Oxford, it was not until the mid-1960s that the unions managed to get toilet paper provided, 'before that the men had to take their own *Daily Mirror* with them.' Even then the maintenance workers were ordered to screw the paper holders on the outside of the doors and it took the unions a further six months to get them transferred to the inside. At Ford men had to wear badges with numbers so that they could be easily identified for reporting, which took place for the smallest offence. In some plants men were timed when going to the lavatory.

When there was a breakdown of any kind – which was not infrequent in these early days – the men were stood off without pay and they had to get out of the works when any repairs were being done. If the job took half-an-hour they would be stopped three-quarter of an hour's pay. Men were allocated to a shift, there might be two hours' work, there might be nothing and they would be told to go home for the day, without pay. Sometimes they might be told to stay on, perhaps till 8 o'clock at night, without notice, with no special overtime rates paid or food provided. A similar position operated at Morris Motors and elsewhere. This was the heart of the depression and some men were only working two days a week. The position of the men was undercut by the large number of women employed at starvation rates. At Pressed Steel, Oxford, one girl was quoted as working all week for 3s 10d, and one man received 1s 9d for $3\frac{1}{2}$ hours work.

The big Ford plant at Dagenham, Essex, employed men from all over the country, many of them from the depressed areas. It was a swamp of non-unionism when the Dagenham trades council called a meeting to try and get them organised. The assistant London secretary was one of the five union officials and 12 Ford workers who turned up. Little impression was made but meetings were held outside the gates and he managed to make a few members and a few others went in to work there, but progress was slow. Then the breakthrough came during a strike in March 1933 when he spoke outside the gates and managed to contact some of the Union members. After four days the management retreated, offering to meet the men but not the officials. The men rejected this and the top management finally agreed to meet the union officers, offering 2s 3d an hour for skilled workers, 1s 9d for semi-skilled and 1s 6d for unskilled, with an agreement that there would be no victimisation, which was accepted at a mass meeting.

The following morning all the workers at the neighbouring Briggs body plant were out, demanding the same rates as Ford. Mass meetings of 500 and 600 were held outside the plant while officials met some 50 members in the local Labour Institute to set up a strike committee. They got increases but not their full demands, which included union recognition – that came later. Another strike succeeded in getting special overtime rates paid.

The General Secretary made one attempt to organise Morris Motors, holding a meeting outside the gates of the Cowley plant, but registered no response, although there were some 50 to 60 skilled sheet metal workers employed in the experimental department. Some other members would work there occasionally for a time, earning 2s an hour rectifying work from the presses. There was also a big radiator shop, but all the workers there were non-union. It was said that in 1939 400 sheet metal workers at Morris Motors had wanted to join the Union but the General Secretary would not take them and they all joined the Brassworkers Union.

There were a few members at Pressed Steel Oxford, where conditions were said to be even worse than at Morris and where a spontaneous strike against intolerable conditions in 1934 gave some stimulous to trade union organisation.

Better results were obtained at the other giant, Austin Motors of Birmingham, where there were strikes from time to time and where the National Union worked in conjunction with the Birmingham Society. The strikes, with 700 members of the Birmingham branch of the Union taking part in one, eventually meant the Union was tolerated, if not recognised until the war.

The skilled sheet metal workers at Vauxhall, Luton, which had been taken over by the U.S. giant, General Motors, were already largely organised.

Towards the end of the 1930s the Union organised British Light Steel Pressings, London, the Rootes answer to Pressed Steel, producing all-steel bodies for their range of Humber, Hillman, Sunbeam and Talbot cars, as well as bodies for other manufacturers. The majority of workers there were metal finishers, straightening out dents and buckles in wings and panels as they came off the presses. After a lot of soul-searching it was finally decided to organise them into the skilled section of the Union 'in the interest of the trade', and 120 joined the Union. The torch solderers who had to fill in and smooth out the final job, and the welders were taken into the auxiliary section.

In this way the Union came to terms with the mass production factories, except for Morris Motors which, being outside the main industrial areas, remained outside the organisation, but could have been drawn in if there had been the will, if there had been a policy to take them into the Union that would not have been satisfied with one meeting with the potential members under the eye of the management.

Coventry Branch

Coventry was the motor town of Britain. It was a growth area, cosmopolitan; one place where a skilled man could get a job during the depression, and they came from all over the country, from Scotland, Wales, Lancashire, East Anglia. One man, 'Manchester Jack', came down every year by canal boat, arriving without a bean in his pocket. But work was only seasonal, for a few months. After the Motor Show orders in the autumn the firms would begin recruiting workers, filling the shops. Humber would have 50 or 60 in the panel shop, perhaps 200 in the 'flat' shop. Singer's would have some 200 tinsmiths, plus panel beaters. 'Then about Easter, you would see the foreman coming round, tapping men on the shoulder, "pick up your cards tonight" and you would wonder if he would come to you,' said Frank Lane, who later became branch secretary. His wife would dread to see him come down the garden path at this time of the year in case he was carrying his tool box on his shoulder, when she would say 'Got it again?' There was no off-season work in Coventry. In the summer only a handful of workers were left in the motor shops, the élite, mostly on experimental work, and the maintenance men busy with guards, trunking, dust extraction hoppers and the like, a coveted job. They did not earn as much as production workers but they were not stood off.

In the early 1920s there was still some cycle gearcase work as well as handmade petrol tanks and mudguards for motorcycles before machines were invented to make them.

Frank Lane tells of the hard work involved in making by hand the front wings for an Armstrong Siddeley out of 20 gauge steel. It was a young man's job, and even then it 'took it out of you.' At the end of the day his ears would ring from blocking up the domed wing with a bossing mallet on a sandbag and then planishing it with a hammer. He was glad to sit down on a Saturday afternoon and took all Sunday to recover for another round.

The motor shops were already organised in the 1920s and the sheet metal workers held up after the General Strike when many other unions fell to pieces. Even at the depths of the slump, in 1930, a metal worker could not get a job in Coventry unless he was a member of the Union. All the sub-contractors were Union shops. The main shops were all strongly organised and they would not have stood for work from their firm to be sub-contracted to a non-union firm. However, the men in the sub-contracting shops were a law unto themselves; they had no shop rate and earned what they liked, worked all hours without any special overtime rate and stayed out when they wanted. 'But they were very skilled men, artists on the wheel, and fast, they would wheel up a panel in no time.'

Early press work needed a lot of hand-finishing, here being given at Vauxhall Motors, Luton, in the early 1920s

In the late 1920s mechanisation began to come in. They got a machine to take some of the work out of wing making, and halving the price, stamping out radiator shells at Singer and cutting the price from 1s 11d each to 7s 6d a dozen. That was when the rate was 1s 11½d and Singer with an output of 200 a week was the third biggest motor firm in the country.

There was still a lot of work for members after the track system took over – the cars at first pushed along – and with it the all-steel body. The early pressings needed a lot of rectifying. They did not fit, members had to fill up one-inch gaps to make the doors close, sometimes extra tinplate would have to be soldered on or the tonneau and cantrail heavily leaded to make them fit. Even so, if the finished job was 'the thickness of a cigarette paper' out when the inspector laid his rule on it, he would not pass it.

With National Union members in Coventry coming from so many different branches, to whom members' contributions had to be sent, administration was very difficult. So in January 1921 a Coventry branch was formed – after consultation with the local EC of the Birmingham Society. The first secretary, J. Moody, held the position for the next 20 years. Within months a joint committee had been set up with the Birmingham Society branch and they continued to work closely together. They jointly resisted employers' demands for wage reductions and together with the local coppersmiths organised opposition to the 1922 lockout, instructing all members to bring out their tools. The two societies set up a joint committee with the coppersmiths to eliminate the remnants of non-unionism. The AEU was later brought in to a committee of four from each union 'to promote the interests of the trade in wages, conditions and terms of piece-work.' In 1925 the Coventry National Union branch decided that all panel shops in Coventry would be open to coppersmiths. And, extending their organisation, they took part in a meeting in Birmingham in an endeavour to get a Midlands motor work pricing committee.

The branch also tried to get an organisation created in anticipation of the General Strike, with a call to the local trades council early in April 1926 to set up a Council of Action for the miners. Members had not been loath to 'put their money where their mouth was', levying themselves to reimburse the branch secretary if he were unable to get work owing to his official duties and followed this with a bigger regular weekly levy to guarantee the wages of a full-time secretary, a decision endorsed by a branch ballot of members. The branch had applied for

Van den Plas coach-building works, London 1925

ANSWERS TO CORRESPONDENCE.

All queries or replies to be written on one side of the paper only. If an answer is expected to be forwarded to the querist an addressed and stamped envelope must be included.

A FURTHER ANSWER TO DOME WINGS FOR MOTOR CARS.

Query. Can you tell me the method to use to make a set of Dome Wings for a motor car, with and without valances.

Answer. Having had a wide experience in sheet-metal work for motor cars in all its branches, I venture to contribute my experience in the best method employed in the making of Dome Wings, at the same time admitting Mr. F. TURNER's methods to be practical and correct. As to gauges and metal employed I think that TERNE STEEL would be better left out owing to the sulphur in the metal having a blistering effect, more especially at joints on the coach painting; Lead Coated Steel is very good and can be welded equally as well as Black Iron—20 and 22 are the gauges usually employed.

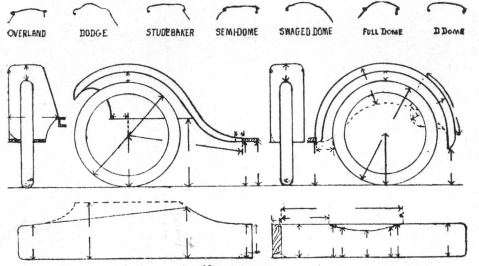

OVERLAND   DODGE   STUDEBAKER   SEMI-DOME   SWAGED DOME   FULL DOME   D DOME

MEASUREMENTS.

I enclose measurement form which I drew out for our firm. Readers will notice that not only is the diameter of the wheel required but also measurement from *ground to centre of wheel. This* is important, as the particular wheel from which the measurements may be taken may be deflated a $\frac{1}{2}$in. or more, thus altering all other ground measurements. Difficulty may be experienced in deciding the width of the wing. Firstly, one must study the type of body fitted or ascertain the type with a view to making or keeping his wings in proportion. It is the usual practice for Body Builders to fit the platforms flush with the hub caps, and, when possible, do likewise with the wings; in many cases this is not possible owing to the camber on the front wheels, but with the aid of a straight edge, an evenly balanced wing can be easily arrived at.

REAR WINGS.

In the case of Rear Wings difficulty is only experienced where the wing requires to be cut to fit close to the panel. In *this case both sides* ought to be measured and geometrical principles employed when fitting is not possible.

THE MAKING.

Very little is left to be said on the making. Mr. F. TURNER's paragraphs explained the method of contracting or crimping the edges of the wings. In this method I am a great believer. Firstly, one retains the gauge of the metal at the highest point of the dome, and secondly, when this method is mastered one can obtain the required sweeps and shapes with more speed and accuracy. This method is invaluable in panel work.—J. McK.

Tinshop, Aircraft Manufacturing Co., Hendon, 1914

permission to affiliate to the left-wing National Minority Movement, supported the 'Hands Off China' committee as far back as 1927, and was active in support of the Spanish Republic and the International Brigade during the war against Franco.

Coventry sheet metal shops gave support to the Aircraft Shop Stewards' National Council, campaigning for 100 per cent trade unionism, and helped set up joint shop stewards' committees despite discouragement from the NEC, and on the eve of the war set up a Coventry Sheet Metal Joint Shop Stewards' Committee with Bill Warman as Chairman and J. Baggott as secretary, both members of the National Union.

Aircraft

Aircraft manufacture, which had been responsible for a 'gold rush' of members from all sections of the trade during the First World War, just as quickly collapsed as a source of work for members with the end of hostilities. There were already enough machines for the peace-time Air Force and the development of commercial air lines had not got under way.

While many of the sub-contract factories went out of existence or reverted to their pre-war activities, the established aircraft companies looked around for other work to keep them going until the aircraft industry picked up. Many of them went on to motor car work, A.V.Roe of Manchester – later to be amalgamated with Crossley Motors – Blackburn's works near Hull and Shorts at Rochester got orders for motor coach bodies, Bristol did work for Armstrong Siddeley and made tramcars for the Corporation, Sopwith, in the Brooklands sheds, made ABC motorcycles.

The retreat of members from the aircraft shops continued, speeding up as the employers cut wage rates. The employers in their dilemma turned to their federation, complaining that they were unable to retain men skilled in aircraft work at the rates established by the federation, the men leaving to go to better-paid jobs in non-federated shops and in other sections of the trade. After a meeting the federation reported to their member firms in September 1923, insisting that 'as the skill on aircraft work was no greater than in general shops' aircraft workers should not be paid at higher rates. If it were necessary to pay ability-rates they should not be given without good reason and only to men 'thoroughly deserving' of extra and should not be extended to become the majority rate of the shop. The federation did not recognise a higher panel beaters' rate, and where a differential rate already existed it was to be given only to tinmen actually on recognised panel beating. Payment by results systems should be instituted wherever possible at not more than a third above daywork rates and guaranteed rates should only be paid on a day-work basis. The federation cautioned member firms to only give out sub-contract work to federated firms.

The employers fell back on their pre-war practice of employing semi-skilled non-union labour leavened with a few skilled workers for the more intricate jobs. District officers in London, visiting shops like De Havilland and Handley Page on organising trips, found very few men that the constitution of the Union allowed them to enroll.

De Havilland had broken away from the war-time Airco combination which included A.V. Roe, Sopwith and the Integrated Propellor Co., of Colindale, starting up on their own at Stag Lane, Edgware. At that time, 1921/22, they had only 14 sheet metal workers and only one or two of them were in the Union.

The shop was rather spartan. Jobs were made up from the flat and included engine cowlings and fairings from aluminium, black iron exhaust manifolds, tinplate fuel tanks and copper fuel pipes, the latter job consisting of loading the pipes with lead or resin and shaping them in a radiused bending block held in a bench vice. It was all handwork. The equipment consisted of a 3 foot treadle-operated guillotine, a 2 foot bench folder, a 4 foot standing folder, a 4 foot set of rollers, a bench knife-cutter, a fly press, swaging and joggling machines and a jenny, all hand operated, together with the usual collection of stakes, heads and anvils, and a small forge for brazing, silver-soldering and annealing. Plus, of course, the ubiquitous leather-covered sand bag, essential as all shaped work was done with a bossing mallet, finished and smoothed with a planishing hammer.

The jobs included the shaped nose and tail sections of streamlined fuel tanks of beaten copper, fitted under the top wing on either side of the fuselage on the 8-seater DH34 biplanes built for airlines operating the Paris run from Croydon, forerunner of British Airways. Here they later developed the very popular series of DH Moths.

In the early 1920s the work of members on the Gloster Gamecock fighting plane, at Cheltenham, consisted of making engine cowlings, fairings, some panels for the fuselage, shaped aluminium fittings around the cockpit – all planished by hand – fuel and oil tanks, 'putting bulbous noses on bits that stuck out and making other odd sheet metal bits.' These were the usual kind of jobs on planes mainly made up of wood and canvas.

Later, the members at Gloster worked on the Schneider trophy planes. By then all-metal planes were taking over but the legacy of the era of the 'wood and canvas jobs' was demarcation disputes with joiners, as when duralumin replaced mahogany for the floats and hulls of seaplanes. But some wooden parts lingered on until the end of the 1920s.

By the early 1920s Short's of Rochester were already developing all-metal construction with stressed skin monocoque fuselage of wrapped duralumin sheet, butted and rivetted on L section transverse frames and longitudinal intercostal stiffeners.[1] Its Silver Streak freight carrying biplanes of steel, aluminium and duralumin were perhaps the first to use methods of construction designed to suit metal. The big, for their day, all-metal, three-engined Calcutta flying boats of 1927/28 with their luxurious Pulman-type lounges, used by Imperial Airways on their long-distance routes 'to the very outposts of Empire', made extensive use of duralumin. Blackburn, which was building the luxury Nile civil transport flying boats, with 14 pairs of seats facing each other across the gangway, had also gone over to duralumin. Boulton and Paul's, was already doing away with its woodworking shop and installing folders and other metal-working tools, with sheet metal workers moving in against protests from the joiners.

In 1929, members at Saunders Roe on the Isle of Wight were working on the twin-engined Cutty Sark flying boat with a metal-framed hull covered in dural. At about the same time, in Southampton, other Union members were employed on the series of Supermarine sea planes and the big Southampton Mark X flying boats with their stainless steel hull, skins stiffened with longitudinal corregations. They also helped construct the successful, beautifully-streamlined Schneider trophy racing machines and, from the eve of the last war, the Spitfire, after the factory had been taken over by Vickers.

Then in the 1930s, members working on the DH Comet had to learn the intricacies of working magnesium which was very tricky, especially on double-curvature shaping, but they soon mastered its peculiarities.[2]

Experiments with airships provided work for some members during the 1920s, and earlier members at Brown and Melhuish had made airship gondolas during the war. The R100 was built by Boulton and Paul at Brough, near Hull where Blackburn aircraft were made during the war.

The ill-fated R101 was made at Cardington, Bedford, under Air Ministry control, using a war-time factory of Short Bros. The shop was organised in 1928 during a visit by Charles Hickin, who called a recruitment and organising meeting of the 20 or so men from all over the country at the nearby Bedford Labour Club.

The hull of the ship was built by Boulton and Paul of Norwich, a shop which had been organised during the war. It was housed in a hangar about half a mile from the other shop and the two had little to do with each other. The metal skeleton was made of 25 miles of steel or duralumin tubes in struts, rings joined together with intercostals, with a metal skin rivetted on. The airscrews of shaped metal, hollow and welded along the edges, were made at a trade shop, Metal Propellors of Croydon.

The work included the power cars and control gondolas, various tanks, air intakes for the engines, gas valves for the skins, support for the walkways, mouldings for the cabins. The gondola outer skins and some other parts were of aluminium, but much of the other work was of duralumin, a metal then only just coming into use. It was very tricky to work. It could not be beaten out with a mallet and had to be shaped exclusively on the wheel, gradually working the structure of the metal into the desired shape, often a double curvature. It first had to be treated in the heat bath and Cardington did not have a bath long enough for some of the bigger sections which were basted, 'rather like basting a joint', as one man who worked there described the process. This, of course, would not give the necessary uniformity of treatment and must have led to some structural weakness, although the parts concerned were auxiliary

Members working on R101 airship built these power gondolas with their streamlined aluminium skins

and not vital to the structure. The job itself was subject to the closest scrutiny and examination so that structurally and for finish it was as good as it was possible to get it – much better than the Graf Zepplin which, by comparison, was 'a string bag' he said. This was despite the fact that the shop was very poorly equipped.

This, he said, was a criticism of most of the aircraft factories at that time. Handley Page, who were making the big passenger-carrying planes used to pioneer Imperial Airways routes across the world, had no machinery to build these great air liners. No means of shaping metal, except by the hand. They did not even have rollers, nothing to break the metal. There was not a single wheeling machine and a man would have to beat out the whole front of a Hannibal, 'the height of a ceiling', with a bossing mallet on a sandbag and then planish the lot with a hammer. Whole lengths of metal for the fuselage would have to be cut out with snips, there was not even a bench cutter.

It was the same with other aircraft shops whose names were famous worldwide. Hawker's had one power hammer and, like de Havilland and Bristol, just one wheeling machine, Fairey was better equipped but even there 50 men could be waiting to use one jig, causing tension in the shop. There was no real modern equipment until the war when American machines were brought in at government expense.

The number of sheet metal workers employed at that time was small. At the beginning of the 1930s Gloster, Fairey and Hawker had about 50 each, but de Havilland employed only 20 and

Handley Page only six or seven. Wage rates were low in all main shops but the opportunities for overtime were high as the years went by.

In 1929 the United Shop Stewards Association sent a deputation to the London district committee complaining that the aircraft shops 'had been in a rotten condition for years.' Fairey was only paying ls 4d an hour and de Havilland 1s 6d. In most shops, 'fitters, silversmiths and general workers were doing our work.' All-metal seaplane floats had been given to boatbuilders and although members stopped work they only got partial satisfaction. Hawkers had a strike over fitters and brassworkers cutting out and shaping bulkheads and instrument panels. Men of all trades used snips and mallets, the tools of the sheet metal workers, who were increasingly kept on experimental work with production work given to other labour. At Vicker's, Weybridge, there was no Union organisation and a lot of the work was jigged up for boys.

The stewards' association offered their help, which was accepted although the district committee was doubtful if much could be done. This initiative was defeated by the slump of 1931/32 when many active members were victimised and whole shops were closed down. Before that the problem had been taken to a general meeting of the district which set up an Aircraft Shop Stewards' Association and the district had taken some steps to organise the unorganised and arrange for shop stewards in shops that were without them, but criticism of lack of drive and confidence on the part of the officials remained among the younger activists.

With the Union reeling under the burden of unemployment and members lapsing after getting into arrears, the employers announced cuts in wages that were already low, and other demands for worsening conditions.

Boulton and Paul tried to introduce the Bedaux system but had to withdraw the proposal after a sharp, unofficial strike. Fairey members hit on the idea of countering management's attacks with lightning sit-down strikes that never failed to bring prompt and satisfactory settlement. Others were not so lucky. Hawker management demanded cuts in prices including five hours off a 55-hour job although only one third of the workers there were getting the shop rate. The men were told that if they rejected the demand they would be discharged and boys

Handley Page aircraft factory, Hendon, in the mid-1920s

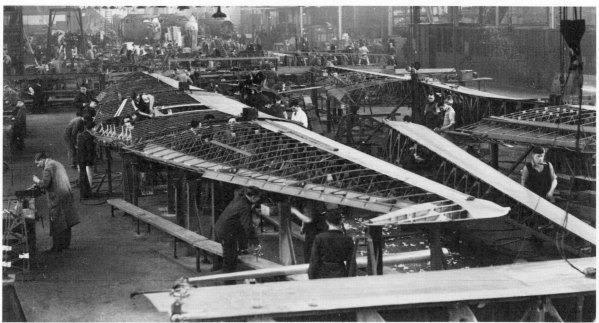

would be put on jigged-up jobs. Although prices were cut more boys were gradually introduced, working on jigs, and kept on one job until they were proficient at it. Then came a strike that was to have far-reaching effects on the Union and the engineering unions generally.

The Gloster Aircraft management, at Cheltenham, demanded that the day-work rate be cut from 1s 6d to 1s 3d an hour. The men refused to accept it and a compromise of 1s 4½d was agreed – it was not until 1935 that the shop could begin to take action to get the cut restored and then by only ½d an hour in two bites of ¼d over a three-month interval, to 1s 5d. Meanwhile the shop resolved not to accept any more wage cuts or worsening of conditions. They rejected a management proposal to introduce the premium bonus system, resisted pressures over a long period to allow more apprentices and refused to allow cuts in wages of indentured apprentices. At the same time they maintained contact with the Hawker shop and later with Armstrong Whitworth of Coventry to discuss piece-work prices – after they had become part of the Hawker-Siddeley set-up.

Inside the factory, the sheet metal stewards held meetings of the labourers to persuade them to join a union. Then, when the management put a non-union man in the fitters' shop, the whole works came out, followed by Hawkers, at Kingston-on-Thames. The 145 sheet metal workers at the Gloster and the 75 at Hawker's played a key role in the strike, but they got no help from the Union which afterwards refused to pay dispute benefit. But support came from shops all over the country, from trade unionists who saw the strike as an indication that the tide had turned. After two weeks, the men returned and although they had not obtained all their demands they achieved some success. The main achievement was in bringing 100 per cent trade unionism to the fore in the industry. It focussed attention on the question of organisation as nothing else had done.

The Gloster dispute brought about the formation of the Aircraft Shop Stewards' National Council which, during the war, was extended to cover all engineering. Branded as a Communist 'front', it was strongly opposed by most of the official trade union leaders in the engineering unions. Writing later in the Union journal, R.B. Pattison, who was active in the early days of the organisation, said that all its founders were actual workers in the aircraft industry, many of them holding responsible positions in their respective unions. 'The endeavour of the Council and its paper, the *New Propellor* was to strengthen the unions in the industry.' The paper was eagerly read by workers on the shop floor who ignored their own union journals. It played a leading role in the struggle for 100 per cent trade unionism, first in the aircraft factories and then throughout the engineering industry. It gave voice to the demands of the workers in the industry, breaking down the isolation of individual shops with reports of what was happening in the industry throughout the country, it helped workers organise shop stewards committees, gave workers confidence by letting them see that they were part of a big and successful organisation, organised support for strikes and reported successes in wage claims, trade union organisation and particularly the drive for 100 per cent trade unionism that swept the country. Not least, it forced the official trade union leadership into action.

The Council was successful because it came at the right time, when the workers were wanting to take the offensive after years of economic and political defeats and setbacks and, by appealing to all unions in the industry, was able to give the necessary leadership.

Sheet metal workers played an important part in the movement and organisation from the start. Jim Boyle, a Scot who served his time at Rosyth dockyard and was steward at Hawker's, played a leading role in its formation and was its first chairman. He was followed by Tom Schofield, originally a member of the Rochdale branch, who was then steward at de Havilland, Hatfield and, like Jim Boyle, later a member of the London district committee. He remained chairman until his untimely death in May 1939. H. Gerrard, shop steward at Gloster, and long-time chairman of the Cheltenham branch of the Union, was also a member of the council. Pat Carey, then at Handley Page, and Harold Blackburn of Fairey, Hayes, also took a part in the activities of the organisation and were later elected to district and national positions in the Union.

The success of the unofficial body stimulated the national leadership of the engineering unions into taking some notice of the workers in the aircraft industry. A National Council of Aircraft Workers was formed by all unions in the industry other than the AEU and the sheet metal workers, both of which, by then, had their own national organisations.

Having ignored demands going back to 1926, when Cheltenham branch had called for the formation within the Union of a National Aircraft Vigilance Committee with one delegate from each aircraft factory, and 1927 when the Fairey, Hayes, shop called for a national aircraft committee, the NEC accepted in 1935 a motion from Cheltenham to set up such a body. First they sent a questionnaire out to all aircraft shops which reported that 822 members were working in the industry – but they were only able to find 54 non-union sheet metal workers in the industry nationwide. So, with delegates appointed by Bristol, Cheltenham, Hull, Leeds, London, Manchester and Southampton branches, the National Aircraft Committee on which much hopes were set, came into being in November 1935.

It was welcomed by Blackburn but he urged the NEC to give more powers to the committee they had sanctioned after years of opposition. The committee, however, was already a dead duck. It had been formed, apparently, to take the heat out of the support for the aircraft stewards' movement. It held two meetings with a year between them, before the delegates were called together to have the committee's obituary read to them.

At those two meetings with the NEC the delegates discussed wage rates, facilities in the shops, the position of rate fixers, whether to press for their withdrawal or to get them replaced with union members; the ratio of apprentices; the premium bonus system; the position of sub-contractors; and the fixing of piece-work prices by the parent shop. It was agreed that before piece-work prices were fixed other related shops and the branch secretary should be informed, no price should be agreed until sanctioned by head office. An attempt by the delegates to get aircraft committees – answerable to the national committee – set up in each district, was turned down as 'not provided for in the rules.' With the other aircraft bodies pressing for wage increases, the NEC agreed to table a claim for a 2d an hour advance for all skilled members working in the aircraft industry, only to be told by the employers federation after presenting the claim, that no sectional claim could be heard as a national claim had been put in for the whole of the engineering industry. Despite its promise, the Committee seems to have achieved nothing other than a brief forum where aircraft shop stewards from the various districts could get together.

The rise of the aircraft shop stewards' movement, then, was not universally welcomed within the National Union. The Union leadership strongly opposed stewards' involvement with the unofficial 'communist' aircraft stewards' national council, claiming that it would bring Union policy under the control of other trades, going so far as to forbid members at Hawker's being associated with a works' council wages claim. Most of the stewards were seen as 'young men in a hurry', impatient with the doubts and hesitations of the older established leadership. Many were militant not only in the economic but also in the political field, taking a rather left-wing stance in this period of rising fascism and not too choosey with whom they worked so long as it advanced the struggle. While the Union was certainly not right-wing, the old 'labour aristocrat' attitude prevailed. Jealous of their status, they were afraid of losing control to the 'lesser breeds', the rising tide of semi-skilled and unskilled. The aircraft men were seen as 'upstarts'. This was particularly the position of the gas meter makers who were still dominant in the Union and afraid of losing their position of power.

Blackburn warned that the workers in the aircraft shops would not much longer stand the policy of drift and delay in bettering their conditions. The NEC was following a policy of 'wait and see' in a 'period of lost opportunity.' But with the government's expansionist policy toward aircraft, 'sub-contracting would be rampant' to the detriment of the union.

Official obstruction could not hold back the momentum of the movement. A number of strikes took place, mostly on questions of demarcation, but coming together in action helped forward organisation. One of the biggest was at Fairey, Stockport, where the management had been chipping away at the sheet metal shop organisation for some time and was suspect of planning to replace Union members with semi-skilled. The shop came out when the wheeling machine was taken away and the work given to shipwrights. The strike got widespread support after a call for donations was made in the *New Propellor*. Union members at the Hayes shop came out in support, the NEC was prevailed to take up the fight 'which was vital to the aircraft shops' and the management withdrew. Similar action took place in the Blackburn Aircraft shop in Dumbarton and 350 men came out at Marston's, Wolverhampton, when tanks were given to fitters to make. After a struggle, 100 per cent Union membership was recorded at Lucas Aircraft, Birmingham and Fairey, Hamble.[3]

The old London Aircraft Shop Stewards Association was revived on an unofficial basis with Tom Schofield as chairman and Jim Boyle as secretary. While mainly covering the London shops it also held a few national meetings with stewards from Bristol, Cheltenham, Leeds and Southampton. (Official blessing was bestowed in 1939 with R. Daley as secretary and George Varney as chairman, the former officials looking on as they were district committee members and not allowed to serve on a stewards' committee.)

In the mid-1930s the London district called a meeting of aircraft shops where it was reported that de Havilland had 200 members at Hatfield and 20 at Stag Lane. They had obtained 100 per cent membership after a strike over ratefixers, when they also obtained recognition of the shop stewards and the pricing committee as well as an increase in the bonus rate. Handley Page, on the other hand, where the management was very anti-union, was still unorganised with only nine members out of 50 to 60 sheet metal workers. When Pat Carey and other active members went there in 1938 they helped make it 100 per cent. Fairey was then 95 per cent organised, with about 100 members, but there was another 500 unorganised potential auxiliaries.

With the activities of the stewards' association, the rest of the aircraft shops achieved 100 per cent organisation. Even Vickers of Weybridge, long a bastion of anti-trade unionism and boy labour, where at one time some 900 were said to have been engaged on sheet metal work of some kind, was eventually organised. Then the sub-contractors came on the scene and the whole process of organisation had to start again, never stopping as every week saw a new shop opening or going over to aircraft work. This continued up to and during the war.

Apprentices

The successful way in which members from all sections of the trade were able to take in their stride the continuing changes in industry, the most complicated and varied jobs in the two world wars and the increasing high technology of the post-war world – so different from the jobs specifically provided for in their apprenticeship training – pays tribute to the form and quality of the trade apprenticeship training over the years. This is particularly evident in the

An apprentice comes out of his time at G. Glover's gas meter shop, Chelsea, around 1950. He was carried round the shops on the shoulders of the youngest journeyman while the others beat on their iron bench plates to hammer him out. He afterwards invited the foreman, steward and the rest of the shop to a drink at his bench, fitted up as a bar

way members are facing up to the new challenges to the craft in the rapidly developing aircraft and aero-space industry.

One member, who served his time as a trade apprentice at de Havilland in the early 1920s, tells of that time-honoured trade apprenticeship training, the 'holding-up method'. His early training consisted of assisting the men on the job, by holding up the job while the man shaped, wired the edges, soldered, or whatever process was required, and holding the dolly while rivetting. During these different operations the man he was working with would explain the reasons for the methods used and how to go about it, letting the apprentice have a go at it under supervision. He was shown how to develop patterns for various jobs and how to beat out a piece of metal to get the shape required. The same methods of training were followed when he was shown copper work, pipe bending, brazing and silver-soldering. Later he had to attend instruction classes. With this training he was later able to go to a position in the 'Engineering Methods and Planning Department' of the Company.

Other members, relating their apprenticeship and work in later life, show that the above illustration was not just 'a one-off job' but quite general for those who had received a good trade apprenticeship.

One retired member, after an ordinary trade apprenticeship at Rowntree, mainly on maintenance work, was a sheet metal work instructor for seven years – many workers from the bench became full or part-time instructors and teachers at technical schools over the years. He then spent the last twenty years of his working life on Rolls Royce jet engines and other high technology aircraft work, including the experimental work on Concorde and jump jets.

Another, apprenticed at the old Singer tinsmiths' shop in the days of coachbuilt bodies, got his training by being shown by the men but was also on piece-work while learning, at two-thirds the price of the job and receiving two-thirds of the men's rate. He and other apprentices persuaded the Coventry branch to start evening classes in sheet metal work where he got his City and Guilds. He also went on to high-class aero work. H.Brotherton – who became General Secretary of the Union – in his apprenticeship in a London gas meter shop was also on piece-work while learning, and receiving a proportion of the price the men received for the job. He worked later in the early aircraft and then in the early motor shops.

Yet another retired member made the same journey after serving his time in the 1920s at a general shop in Derby, where they made baths and dustbins as well as such things as one-off car wings, equipment for local factories and all the other kinds of sheet metal fabrication that comes the way of a small general shop, as well as making their own acetylene gas plant for welding.

He later went to work in the Rolls Royce sheet metal shop, being transferred in 1930 to the experimental department and a couple of years later was sent with a supervisor to form a sheet metal shop at the flight development establishment at Hucknall aerodrome, with a free hand to recruit as many sheet metal workers as possible. With the help of the Nottingham and Derby branches they got some 200 members including a number from the Metropolitan gas meter company of Nottingham. The management were very keen on apprenticed labour and preferred Union members. They allotted one apprentice to every six skilled men to learn the trade in the traditional way. The sheet metal workers worked on practically all the power plant prototypes, on converting many planes into 'flying testbeds', on the first steam-cooled engines and the cooling jackets of the Condor and Peregrine engines. He and another Derby branch member were sent to work on the first Miles Master trainers and in addition to the technical work they got the shop organised. So the Union and technical development worked together and were doing so elsewhere.

One tinsmith, starting at Short's in the early days of aircraft, went higher; transferred to the experimental department, studied in his spare time and obtained a degree, was moved to the design department, made a director and finished up as general manager.

A report on training by the Board of Trade a few years earlier,[4] shows that, of the number of learners and apprentices in the sheet metal industry sampled in the review, one-quarter were indentured still. Most apprentices started in the workshops as holders-up to journeymen, graduating to apprentices after a time if they showed an aptitude. They learned their trade by first doing light and simple manufacturing processes under the supervision of the foreman or, in small workshops, by the 'master', gradually working up to more exacting jobs. The employers interviewed accepted this as 'a natural and recognised means of securing a succession of thoroughly efficient workmen.' Many said they would only employ sheet metal workers who had had such a training. The report accepted such apprenticeships as 'excellent' as a means of training and commented that the great variety of articles made in general sheet metal shops made endless calls upon the skill and ingenuity of the workman. With this variety of work in the trade 'tinmen were always learning.'

The age of starting apprenticeships varied from 14 to 16 years and they lasted five, six or seven years. Apprentices' wages ranged from 1s 6d to 7s a week for the first year, rising to 5s 6d to 20s for the final year; the general rate was from 4s to 5s 6d for the first to 10s to 15s for the final year. Only a few apprentices paid a premium. Boys were said to be generally encouraged to attend evening technical classes where these existed – a number of employers were reported as paying fees and even paying for text books. But the cost of equipment meant that sheet metal classes were largely restricted to the bigger industrial centres. Already some employers were advocating apprentices being given time off work to attend classes.

But not all employers were satisfied with trade apprenticeships. As early as 1924 the

Left: time-served apprentice at Marston's, Wolverhampton, winner of the 1977 Craftex award, with examples of his work; *above*: Model training at the British Aircraft Corporation Works, Weybridge

shipbuilding employers were calling for apprenticeships not confined to one trade but cutting across all trades to give a general skill. This was turned down by the unions at that time as it would mean a weakening of the individual unions and a free-for-all with the strongest grabbing the work and the members.

Expansion

The economy, which had begun to show a limited improvement in 1934, continued to make progress and the five to six year period until the beginning of the war became the longest period of expansion and progress that the workers had experienced during the whole of the inter-war years, a situation which was helped by the drive for rearmament. This, coupled with the pressure on the Union to organise the still large non-union element in the trade, was reflected in the increase in membership. Total membership, which had changed little during the previous period, now began to take off. From a total of 15,401 at the end of December 1935 it went up to 17,338 the following year when a record number of 2,505 new members joined the Union. And the momentum was maintained with a total of 19,168 at the end of 1937, 21,523 in 1938 and 24,642 by the end of 1939. However there were still pockets of high unemployment in the many distressed areas and in certain sections of the trade, in shipbuilding – although this had been improved with the building of warships as the government moved toward rearmament – and in gas meters, which was partly allieviated as some meter manufacturers tendered for government contracts.

The improved economic climate helped the engineering unions to better the wages and conditions of the workers in the industry. In 1938 the employers conceded a week's holiday with pay. The unions also gained the right to negotiate on behalf of youths and apprentices.

The situation was also used by the unions to try and rectify conditions imposed on them when trade was bad. At the 1937 National Conference, Manchester succeeded in getting a motion carried calling for the termination of the 'York memo', which had been signed under duress when the Union was weak. When Hickin put this forward to the employers Ramsey, the EEF secretary, warned him that he would not only have the employers against him but the 44 unions that were operating the agreement. Hickin, who did not take a lot of convincing, persuaded the NEC to call a special conference and got the decision reversed after declaring that if they broke with the agreement they would have a lot of union recognition fights in the shops. He did not see a lot of harm in the procedure agreement. In ten years only four disputes had been taken to works conferences and only one to York, all of them dealing with meter shops.

Manchester and others were still not convinced and at the 1939 conference got agreement that the offending clause be modified so that 'any innovations introduced on either side to which the other objects shall be removed pending negotiations.' The employers, of course, objected and the war stopped any further attempts to do away with the offensive agreement 'for the duration.'

Attempts by the engineering unions in this period to get some satisfaction on their claim for the restoration of pre-1931 piece-work rates and conditions were also successfully resisted by the employers and lost in the clouds of the coming war, as were so many issues.

1. H. Penrose, *British Aviation, Vol. 3, The Adventurous years 1919-29*, London 1973.
2. Interview with P. Carey, aircraft shop steward and later NEC member.
3. *New Propellor*, various numbers.
4. Printed but unpublished Board of Trade Report of an enquiry into the apprenticeship and industrial training in the various trades and occupations in the UK, 1915.
The chapter is otherwise mainly baased on the minutes, reports and journals of the National Union.

CHAPTER 9

The Coppersmiths

The information we have been able to gather on the early history of the coppersmiths is rather fragmentary. In eighteenth-century London much of the coppersmiths' work lay along the banks of the Thames, where the main centres of sugar refining, soap boiling, brewing and distilling were located, as well as ships' chandlers and other forms of shipping work: later these activities were to spread to other parts of the city. As we have seen, the London Amicable Society of Workers in Copper was first registered on 9 April 1810 and continued registration until 1839. So it would seem that the Society formed on 14 September 1846, later celebrated as the origins of the Coppersmiths' trade organisation, was only a re-forming or reorganisation of the Society, decided on for reasons unknown.

In the first decades of the nineteenth century, London coppersmiths were also organised in at least one other local society, the London Society of Brassfounders, Braziers and Coppersmiths, an organisation probably formed by journeymen of the Founders' Guild which earlier organised these trades.

There were probably some early organisations of coppersmiths in other parts of the country but we have no precise information about them. A later Glasgow branch secretary spoke of a society in that city in 1820, some of the members working at R. Napier's on shipbuilding, others at shops making pans and equipment for sugar refiners and some at the Glasgow Copper Works.

The two London societies were active in the Metropolitan trades movement in the 1820s and 1830s. We find them and individual coppersmiths' shops contributing to such well-known strikes as the Kidderminster Carpet Weavers in 1828 and the London Bookbinders of 1839, among others. They formed a branch of Robert Owen's Grand National Consolidated Trades Union in 1834 and a coppersmiths' delegate served for some years on the committee to help the Tolpuddle Martyrs – J. Burkingyoung, who was prominent in the trade society movement of the period. As a result of support given to a coppersmiths' strike by the Chartist paper, the *Northern Star*, the London Society formed themselves into a 'locality' or branch of the National Chartist Association. A Chartist paper reported:

The coppersmiths held their weekly meeting on Friday, September 3rd at the Golden Lion, Fore Street, Cripplegate, when a most excellent spirit was evinced, powerful speeches were delivered by several of their members, and all appear convinced that nothing short of the Charter can remove the poverty and misery which has overspread the land.[1]

In 1842 a coppersmith, George Goddatt, was nominated to the General Council of the Chartist National Association for Shoreditch,[2] as we have seen.

Pontifex coppersmiths' shop, City of London, about 1840

In the 1830s a Brass-Founders, Braziers and Coppersmiths Armour Association met quarterly at the Black Jack, Portsmouth Street.[3] It consisted of men of the associated trades 'for the purpose of preserving the armour and attendant property belonging thereto and to divide any pecuniary sums that may be derived from lending same.' It owned a number of suits of armour made from 7,000 scales of brass, each fastened by two copper rivets. The Association had its own rule book, like a trade society, the members paying 6d a quarter. It was said to have started with the procession in 1820 in support of Queen Caroline. It held an annual procession on the first Monday in July, led by a 'Peace officer', followed by a conductor on horseback, four stewards, president on horseback, band of music, a banner reading 'Society of Brass Founders, Braziers and Coppersmiths', body of members with brass devices, knight in full armour on horseback, body of members with brass devices, another banner reading 'Brass Founders, Braziers and Coppersmiths, Men of Metal' continuing with five bodies of members, interspersed with three more knights in full armour on horseback, two more bands with big drums and flags and banners – a crimson flag on staff, large banner with trade arms on each side, Union flag on brass shaft and a banner at the rear with the slogan 'As it should be'; stewards and attendants walked on each side. The Association endeavoured to provide 'some additional splendour each year, such as a new flag or some curious device related to the trade introduced by a member.' The book lists 26 braziers' and 30 coppersmiths' establishments in London where their members were employed.

On a more ordinary level of activity, we have a report of a long strike in 1841 of coppersmiths and braziers at the important factory of Pontifex in Shoe Lane in the City of London. They were out for more than 14 weeks protesting that the employer had 23 apprentices to 30 journeymen and was employing labourers who had not served a legal apprenticeship to the trade on coppersmiths' work. In their statement to the trades they complained that boys and young men were bound from 15 to 19 years and during that time were sent to work 'to different factories of the art', such as breweries, distilleries, sugar refineries and other places connected with the copper trade, and the employer only paid them an average of 7s to 12s a week for the whole of their apprenticeship.

> Their parents were compelled, having signed an agreement, to supply their offspring with all the necessities of life and if any accident or illness befel them during their apprenticeship they received no remuneration for maintenance when they could not work.

The strike report thanked coppersmiths in London, Birmingham, Bristol, Manchester, Southampton, Salisbury, Liverpool, Glasgow and elsewhere and called on 'all mechanics, whatever their trade, to open their hearts to allow the fight for justice to be carried on.' All contributions would be thankfully received at their club house, the Golden Lion, Cripplegate. They pledged to carry on the fight until the employer agreed to terms presented in a manifesto so far rejected. This laid down that there must be only one apprentice for every four journeymen coppersmiths and two apprentices in the braziers' shop.

The reorganised 1846 Friendly Society of Workers in Copper had its club house 'at the house of Mr Viles, known by the sign of the Box Tree', Gravel Lane, Houndsditch.

Except for the name of the Society, nowhere in the articles is there any indication that the Society should consist of coppersmiths or that members should have served an apprenticeship at the trade. The articles state that 'it is designed solely for the decent interment of the dead.' A clause that it should also 'administer relief to those who may be in want of employment' is crossed out, as is the article that members out of employment 'if not by his own neglect' should receive 10s a week for the first month and 5s per week for the next six weeks in any one year.

Two stewards were appointed from the roll each quarterly night and it was the senior steward's duty to take the contributions. The stewards also had the power to call a meeting of all members 'on an extraordinary occasion', on the written request that the whole Society be summoned together, signed by three free members, presented to the secretary. A president was elected each meeting night from among those present, his duties being confined to keeping order. A secretary was chosen and re-elected every quarterly night 'to keep an account of the Society's affairs'; for which he was paid 15s a quarter. A later addition provided for three trustees to be elected on a quarterly night and remain in office during the pleasure of the society. When it was necessary to invest any part of the Society's stock the Society had to be summoned and two-thirds had to be present when the sum was agreed.

The only other condition of membership, in addition to being of good character and free from bodily infirmities, was to declare oneself sincerely, truly and solemnly attached to Her Majesty Queen Victoria:

> and will to the best of my power support the constitution of Great Britain both in church and state as by law established and also will be no means endeavour, either by words or actions, to diminish that respect due to the illustrious House of Hanover as finally settled by our ancestry at the Revolution.

Despite the exclusively friendly society, or rather burial society character of the articles of the Society, its activities were those of a trade society, as is evident from the minute book.

Very soon the day-to-day running of the Society showed that changes had to be made. Increasing the benefits to include unemployment pay was apparently soon decided on, as in September 1847 it was agreed 'that no relief be allowed from the funds accumulating for a member out of employ until the stock amounts to £100 and all benefits to cease when the stock is less than £50.' The area of membership must have soon widened, as the following year a country steward was appointed to look after the subscriptions of members outside London. A committee was provided for at some early stage and in December 1849 each members received 6d for attending committee meetings, stewards received 9d for attending monthly meetings and 'those attending to put money away in the bank' received 1s. In 1850 it was decided that every member was to have 'vote and voice' as soon as he had paid his entrance money and one month's subscription.

The first mention in the minutes of specific trade activities occurred in July 1848 when it was agreed that any member in full employ who lent himself to any other master be fined £1. Then the following year the whole committee agreed:

> that any member of the Society being lent by his foreman unbeknown to his master, and refusing to go, thereby throwing himself out of work, should receive from the Society the same amount of wages he was then receiving. The amount of wages not to exceed six days in one week.

In 1852 there was a big strike or 'turn-out' and £50 was drawn out of the bank on 12 January to pay benefit for those who were out of work due to the strike. Free members were to receive 10s per week 'while this unfortunate turn-out shall last.' The same benefit was paid to non-free members and to non-unionists who had come out with the Society men. No one was to be paid more than 10s a week during the turn-out and those in work were to be levied 6d a day to pay the benefits of those out of work. The employers introduced a 'document', renouncing the Society, that the men had to sign before being allowed to start work. The minutes recorded a decision that no member of the Society should sign the document and any that did would be erased from the books. Circulars were printed setting out the Society's case and distributed to the public to collect subscriptions. In February a committee of seven was elected from those out of work to deal with the business of collecting subscriptions. On 25 March the 6d levy paid by working members was reduced to 4d a day and the following month it was ruled that non-members should have no money from the Society. The weekly subscription was discontinued from 15 May and the relief committee was disbanded. A vote of thanks was given to members for 'standing out during the unfortunate dispute between the masters and the Amalgamated Society.' In March the following year a benefit was held at the Surrey Tavern to help build up the funds. Finally in September the following year it was stated that any coppersmith who had signed the document before 13 September would never be admitted into the Society, which seems to hint that the Society lost the strike and that it had been agreed that after 13 September members would be allowed to sign in order to get a job.

In 1855 coppersmiths in Swindon wrote asking to be accepted as a branch of the London Society but a general meeting decided that no branch be formed at that time.

The minutes of 1854 record the mounting concern of the officials about the Society's money held by the landlord, Mr Vile, who acted as a kind of unofficial treasurer. The rules said that the landlord should provide a bond or some form of security for the monies in his possession, but it would seem that this had been ignored.

The January general meeting asked for £70 to be taken out of his hands and put in the bank.

On 10 March it was decided he be asked if he proposed to pay over the money and on the 15th the secretary and two stewards were told to wait on Mr Vile and receive the money. They seem to have received some sort of satisfaction, but not all the money. On 5 September the matter comes up again in the minutes when it was decided that £40 be withdrawn from the landlord and paid into the bank. The next item on the money question does not appear until the following 18 June instructing the secretary to apply for the Society's box following Mr Vile's bankruptcy. Then the two stewards were told to attend the bankruptcy court and watch the proceedings of Mr Vile's bankruptcy on behalf of the Society.

In April the Society moved its club house to the Bell, Church Row, Houndsditch and the secretary was instructed to get the necessary bond from the new landlord as surety of money belonging to the Society passing through his hands. The secretary, accompanied by the two stewards, visited the two bondsmen who had agreed to act as surety for Mr Caley, the landlord of the Bell, to get the bonds signed and enquire into the respectability of the bondsmen.

Their expenses sheet read:

5th June 1858 expenses in going to Peckham and getting the bond signed by Mr. Shut. Money Spent: Society House 1s, Omnibus 1s 6d, The Queen 8d, Surrey View 8d, Omnibus 1s 6d, total 7s. Time: The two stewards and the secretary 6 hours each 9s plus 7s, total 16s. 12th June 1858. Getting the bond signed by Mr. Rush: Money spent: The Red Lion 6d, The Sir John Falstaff 6d, Society House 1s 6d, total 2s 6d. Time: The two stewards and secretary 4 hours each 6s plus 2s 6p, total 8s 6d.

The loss of whatever amount of money held by Mr Vile seems to have brought a lack of confidence among the members about their funds and it was moved that the whole of the money be shared out among the members. An amendment watered down this drastic proposal suggesting that the burial fund be left untouched and £100 of the £153 7s 6d should be taken out of the bank and distributed on the basis of the amount each member had paid in, which was agreed at a summoned meeting and a committee of seven was elected to deal with the share out.

The Society weathered the storm and continued its activities, voting £15 to locked-out building workers and £5 to the metal trades who were also locked-out by their employers, with a further £10 to the London building workers some nine months later. And in 1866 27 coppersmiths at Shears, Bankside, South-East London, were locked out for refusing to work overtime at plain time when they had an agreement with the employer for time and a quarter for the first two hours. A change in the set up of the Society came in the 1860 with a regular chairman, elected on a six months basis. He doubled up as corresponding secretary for an annual remuneration of £2.

In 1861, and for a long time afterwards, according to a member who came out of his time in that year, the trade in London was made up of tea urn makers, 'who were very jealous of their knowledge of the art of bronzing'; tea kettle makers; washing copper makers (who did little else all the year round but make large or small washing coppers for laundries or private houses). Other shops made all the articles for large country houses, hotels and ships – stock pots, stew pans, frying pans, omelette and beau marie pans, fish kettles, saucepans, colanders, preserving pans, warming pans, 'and many other articles in copper or brass too numerous to mention.' There were brewing copper makers and makers of stills of various kinds, dyers' coppers, sugar house pans and equipment, confectioners' pans and equipment and utensils for wholesale chemists, saccharine works and the like. Some shops specialised in diving apparatus or fire engines. There was railway work in all its branches, steamboat work and other new work coming along 'one class of work after another.'

Working notebook of a jobbing coppersmith in Newcastle-upon-Tyne at the end of the nineteenth century

He started work with a City of London firm at 13½ years of age, as a boy, and at 16 began a seven year bound apprenticeship as a coppersmith and brazier. Men and boys did a ten hour day or more, and until 4 o'clock on Saturdays. Most work was by the piece and low paid. A young man coming out of his time got £1 to 24s a week while men of 30 were earning only 25s. In some cases the foreman acted as piece-master, sometimes sharing with the men the over plus when the job was finished, sometimes not.

A boy starting his apprenticeship had to pay a footing to a representative of the men. This was spent on beer, spirits, etc., and usually lasted three days. An apprentice on piece-work got half the man's rate and in his last year was paid 13s 6d a week on a day-work basis. In his last six months an apprentice was allowed to join the men in their Saturday afternoon drinking, after they had been paid. Nearly everyone dressed in fustian or corduroy, including the foreman and most mechanics wore talls hats, changing to brown paper hats to work in. Beer was brought into the shop each morning at 11 o'clock and sold to anyone who wanted it, with time allowed to drink it up.

In the 1860s there was no compulsory education; working-class children were lucky if they went for a year or two to a charity school, one controlled by a religious society or dame's school where for a few pence a week they learned the rudiments of reading and writing until they left to start work at the age of 10. Much later, Keir Hardie, illiterate at 17, taught himself to write using chalk on the coal face, and the gas workers' leader, Will Thorne, signed his marriage certificate with this thumb print. So, with few of the men in the shop able to read, they contributed a few pence a week to buy communal newspapers and one of the literate members would read aloud to their mates during breakfast.

Coppersmiths in those days made up their own pipes from the sheet: pipe bending was very elementary, the only equipment where he worked was posts and cyder presses. Many jobs had to be done over and over again according to the whim or temper of the foreman before he would pass it, sometimes rejecting the job altogether and relegating it to the scrapheap.

With the last six months of apprenticeship to serve, he attended the quarterly meeting at the Bell, Houndsditch at 8 o'clock on a Saturday night to join the society. His workmates presented him for membership and he was voted in. He was then introduced to the Chairman, Mr Webb, the Secretary, Mr Mayo, and the father of the Society and its first chairman, W. Jones. There were not many members present but some came from nearby shops still wearing leather aprons and brown paper caps. The Society did not pay rent for the room but there was a lot of drinking and that covered the rent. The meeting broke up at 11.30 pm. Six months later he got his indentures and started life as a fully-fledged mechanic at $22\frac{1}{2}$ years of age after nine years in the shop. At that time, around 1877, the London Society employed a solicitor's clerk to do their book-keeping.

Another member told how when he started his apprenticeship before the First World War he had to pay his 'footing' by buying each 'smith in the shop a pint of beer.' When he came out of his time everyone assembled in the shop to 'hammer him out.' The 'smiths beat with their hammers on anvils or anything else handy 'while his fellow apprentices pelted him with bags of red ochre, black lead, fireclay and whiting. The ceremony over he once again had to pay his 'footing' to celebrate the occasion.[5]

The Society Spreads

Organisation gradually spread from London as members went to work in the country. Many went to jobs at ports – Chatham, Portsmouth, Devonport – working on contracts obtained by London firms. Some stayed on after the contracts had finished. They retained their membership of the London Society, eventually helping to form local branches.

A somewhat later description of the coppersmiths' trade in London records that according to the census around the turn of the century there were 933 coppersmiths in London. The majority of them were said to have been engaged on marine repair work. In this section of the trade 'men would flit from job to job, leaving one job which they thought might only last a fortnight to go to another that might last a month.' No notice was usually given or required, the man would ask for his money at the end of the day and go. Such was the nature of shipping jobs that when one firm was slack another could be busy.

Brewery and distillery work employed a number of members; the work 'came in bursts' and was usually done in winter. Railway shop work, although perhaps not so well paid, was said to be very regular, as also were some of the general engineering shops that employed coppersmiths.

In the railway and general engineering shops and on marine work, all men were on time-work but some of the work in breweries and distilleries – on coppers, stills and hop-backs – was customarily done as piece-work. The average wage for a coppersmith was then 6s a day of $9\frac{1}{2}$ hours with $6\frac{1}{2}$ hours on Saturdays, making a 54 hour week. Short time was more general than overtime and it was said to be unusual for a man to work for one firm for a whole year. The union was able to enforce a minimum wage and deputations were said to be the usual means of settling disputes. A five year apprenticeship was already taking the place of the old seven year indentured apprenticeship.

According to the 1861 census there were then 1,800 coppersmiths in Britain, 657 of them in London. In 1864 – the earliest year for which we have figures – the London Society had 189 members, going up to 204 in 1865 and 225 in 1866, staying at around that figure for the next few years.

The three years from 1867 to 1869 saw a big rise in unemployment with out-of-work pay shooting up to £286, £162 and £184 compared with only £13 and £19 for 1863 and 1864.

By 1873 membership had dropped to only 127 and the 1878 report said that the 'widespread and desolating character' of the depression then prevailing in almost every branch of industry was:

plainly evidenced in the extreme poverty which it is carrying into the homes of the working classes, causing the social conditions of their existence to become more stringent and difficult to bear.

The terrible dearth of trade throughout the country had continued so that the Society's expenditure in relief had been greater than at any time in its history and at £230 was more than double the money coming into the fund during the year. Toward the end of the following year the situation improved and the relief fund was only a few pounds in the red over the year's working. It was in this 'razor-edge existence' that these small societies collapsed. However, for the coppersmiths this improvement continued and 'assumed a permanence that entitled the past year [1881/82] to be ranked as one of the most prosperous that we have experienced for a long time.'

A big lock-out of members in 1866 in defence of wages – during which the Society paid out £20 to non-unionists who came out in support of Society members – brought financial support from Portsmouth, Southampton, Burton-on-Trent, Romford and Woolwich Dockyard as well as from a number of London shops not affected by the dispute, including Truman and Hanbury's brewery, GWR locomotive depot and Pontifex. This demonstration of solidarity helped to strengthen the ties already existing among the coppersmiths' fraternity.

Occasionally in the accounts about this time there appeared references to allowance to members for travelling. But, although there was a lot of moving around the country in search of jobs, the Society did not operate a tramping system for out-of-work members. Probably in these years, when the tramping system in so many unions was at its height, there were not enough coppersmiths' organisations throughout the country to provide a route to aid 'smiths seeking work.

Writing in 1878 the new secretary, Charles H. Quinton – who had taken over from James Mayo in 1869 – said that despite the difficulties the Society was then encountering, he had no regrets that they had started a sick fund, despite some opposition. He felt that it would become a source of strength to the Society.

In the year 1881/2 the Society changed its club house to the Duke of Wellington, then in 1889 moved again to the One Swan in Bishopsgate and yet again in 1891 to the Black Horse, Leman Street.

Toward National Organisation

But the most significant happening of 1891 was the formation of a sub-branch at Portsmouth dockyard – the first small step towards the goal of a national union. It was probably on the strength of this, together with the spread of individual members in other parts of the country, that the name of the Society was changed to the London and Provincial Friendly Society of Coppersmiths in 1892, with a membership of 364. In 1909 it added Metalworkers to its title.

In his 1897 report, the Secretary told how the Society had had to join in what he called 'one of the greatest struggles ever to take place in the history of labour.' After months of struggle in which members suffered severely, 'many losing their jobs', they had to return on the same terms on which they came out. But, he said, there had been a splendid stand by both union members and non-unionists. Support had come from the Glasgow and Liverpool Societies, and from coppersmiths in Chatham, Portsmouth, Hull, the Isle of Wight, Weymouth and the Derby railway shops, from men at the Battersea sugar house, the Wandsworth distillery, from Truman's and Whitbread's breweries and various other shops, as well as from the Joiners' Union and the TUC.

As a result of the struggle for work, a number of demarcation disputes took place with other trades in Portsmouth and other dockyards, particularly with the plumbers and brass-finishers – the first record of such clashes that continued throughout the whole life of the Society. On this occasion the coppersmiths were successful in getting plumbers taken off jobs claimed as coppersmiths' work, but the secretary warned that if they wanted to retain their work the men in the yards must be vigilant and pursue the claims locally.

New branches were formed in Hull and Bristol in 1897. The Bristol organisation allowed the establishment of Society shops in a number of Bristol Channel ports, mainly in ship repair – in Avonmouth, Barry, Cardiff, Newport, Port Talbot and Swansea.

Before that, a branch had been started in Devonport with 20 members, joining Portsmouth which had become a full branch 34 strong, and was followed by Chatham in 1902 with 23 members and Sheerness in 1905 with just 11. These naval dockyard branches had their own special problems with the peculiar position of the establishment men and the differences between them and the rest, to say nothing of the fact that all negotiations and disputes had to go through the Admiralty. But they became a strong bulwark of the Society over the years.

In 1905, the Southampton branch joined up with 51 members, mostly in shipbuilding and repair but with a few employed at the South Western Railway Works. The following year saw the entrance of the Cowes, Isle of Wight branch with a membership of 18, then mainly on marine and general work. Then in 1907 24 members were recruited in Leeds and a branch was formed in the town, where most shops were engaged on general or locomotive work.

A proposal to form a nation-wide federation of coppersmiths met with some delay because of the difficulties encountered by the Glasgow Society in the aftermath of a long, unsuccessful strike involving a large body of the membership in defence of wage rates – which had the backing of the London Society to the extent of a grant for £50 – coupled with the effect on the Society of a severe trade depression.

By July 1909, however, the position of the Glasgow Society had improved sufficiently to allow their attendance at a meeting in Manchester to finalise the arrangements of the new organisation. It was known as the Federation of Coppersmiths, Braziers and Metalworkers of Great Britain and Ireland and had an initial affiliated membership of 775.

Its declared aims were to promote the general interests of the trade; to prevent strikes and lockouts and to aid the societies in the Federation when a dispute was anticipated or in progress; to increase their influence by organising and establishing new branches where possible; to issue a quarterly magazine on the condition of trade and information of interest to the trade and the cause of trade unionism, and to raise a fund for these objectives.

In 1904 George Rick had taken over as Secretary on the death of Quinton and the club house was moved to the Goat Tavern, Tower Bridge. Rick was elected full-time General Secretary at a salary of £130 a year and in 1909 the Society moved again. But this was not just a change of club house, it was a move out of the old club house style of organisation into that of the registered office – at the Victoria Hotel, Holborn Circus – that went with a full-time General Secretary.

About this time the Society began to take a more active part in the wider organisation of the trade union movement. In 1906 it sent its first delegate to the Trades Union Congress and the following year it affiliated to Congress. At the 1909 Congress, the coppersmiths' delegate asked for TUC support to get the Trade included in the Workshops Act of 1901, which included the provision of washing facilities in workshops. A delegate was also sent to a TUC conference in support of the introduction of labour exchanges and another TUC conference on the premium bonus system of payment.

Rick died in office in 1910 but his short time as General Secretary saw a complete change of lifestyle of the Society. He was succeeded by Henry Stansfield, a man who was to have an even greater impact. Building on the new base left to him, he played a big part in forming the Society into a national union and at the same time restricting it by jealously preserving its old-fashioned craft character. He represented a day when son followed father in the trade, when an apprentice in one London shop could boast of being a tenth generation coppersmith.

In his 1911 report the new secretary claimed that in the previous 17 months the Society had made 230 new members 'and obtained better conditions and absolute recognition of the Society and its rules in the provinces where branches were established and had beaten the employers' organisations at all points.'

Branches were opened in a number of towns. Belfast was well established with 29 members but Bradford had only 10 and Halifax 9. A branch was restarted at Coventry with 22 members, most of them on motor work. These small branches were very vulnerable to take-over by bigger and long established unions, and this remained a constant danger. The new Leeds branch reported such a bid by the local engineering union. But the Leeds coppersmiths rejected 'the invitation to be swallowed up by the ASE, and thereby losing the standing of a responsible organisation.' This urge to retain the identity of their craft kept the coppersmiths, or a hard core of them, as a separate society long after it would perhaps have been in their own interest to have worked out a form of amalgamation with unions of kindred trades as a means of forming a strong autonomous section of a viable united union.

The need was there and very soon the Federation was seen to be only a prologue to a much closer form of organisation, more able to build up the Trade into a true national organisation and defend it from encroachments by other unions. The London and Provincial, and the separate Scottish, Manchester and Burton-on-Trent societies, amalgamated in 1912 to form the National Society of Coppersmiths, Braziers and Metalworkers with a membership of 1,760 to be joined the following year by Liverpool, bringing in a further 138 members.

The Scottish contribution to the amalgamation was the United Coppersmiths, Braziers and Metal Workers Association, second only in size to the London and Provincial Society, dating

from 1866. A number of societies had been formed before 'but none had endured.' The 'great curse' of the trade in Glasgow was said to be boy labour, which the Association could not control. They were also plagued by demarcation disputes and encroachments on their work by 'plumbers, brass-finisher, sheet metal workers, whitesmiths and tinkers.' A report in 1892 by the then secretary, Thomas Williams, said the general earnings were $6\frac{3}{4}$d to 7d an hour, but a few were getting 8d and others as little as 5d an hour. All were on day-work. In 1888/89 the Association had had a series of meetings to consider putting in for an advance and had formed a 'provisional committee' to organise meetings and other activities. Members of what he called the 'Old Society' joined and for a time the two organisations – the 'Old Society' and the 'Trade Society' – existed side by side, with the trade society claiming 500 members.

At the beginning of 1910 the Association had a purge of members in arrears 'to provide a realistic level for Federation levies' and was left with a total of 299 members, but by the end of the year they were back to 351. The financial secretary, Alex Turnbull, said that he expected 'at a very early date' to have their fellow trademen in the East of Scotland once more within their ranks and would be getting in touch with Dundee and Aberdeen in the immediate future. In addition to the main bulk of the membership in Glasgow, the Scottish Association also had branches in Greenock with 92 members and Paisley with 12.

Also forming part of the Scottish district of the new National Society was the Edinburgh and Leith Society with 47 members. After its formation in 1889 the branch had a rough time from members of the engineering union who tried to stop the local coppersmiths forming their own society, refusing to work with them, and sending men from Glasgow to take the place of coppersmiths on strike, in the tough free-for-all struggle to grab what work was available.

Much of the work of Scottish coppersmiths was on shipbuilding and repair, with some railway shop work. But an important, if smaller section worked on the building of stills for the whisky trade.[6] These stills, 'three times as high as a man', were all hand made from the flat, each one an individual job, differing shape and size to suit the ideas of the distillers. The 'smiths would winter in the shops building the stills and with the arrival of better weather many would be off to the glens to fit them up. At one time there were also some travelling 'smiths who went from distillery to distillery on repairs and maintenance work.

The independent Burton-on-Trent Society had a membership of only 31 when it joined the amalgamation, hardly enough to be a viable society. Most of them worked in the brewing industry. Manchester brought 59 members into the society, working in general, locomotive, marine and motor shops.

The Liverpool United Society of Coppersmiths, although one of the prime advocates of amalgamation, did not join the National Society until October 1913. It then totalled 137 members, including nine apprentices. Its records claimed that it was established in 1860 and reorganised in 1879. The members worked mainly on shipbuilding and repair.

In addition to the branches and membership coming together in the amalgamation, 1912 saw the establishment of a number of new branches. Membership of these was small. Peterborough had 15 members, working in the Great Northern and Great Eastern railway shops, at Peter Brotherhoods, the marine enginers newly moved from London, and at Merryweathers, the fire engine makers. Swindon, with an initial 15 members, was exclusively a Great Western Railway branch. Derby had 24 members working mainly in the Midland Railway workshops and Rolls Royce, with some on general work. A branch was formed at Birkenhead from Liverpool members. It was active for a while but did not last.

Early in 1914 a branch was formed in Barrow, initially with 18 members of the Glasgow branch but soon enrolled local members. It was based on the Vicker's and Maxim's shipyard, but also had some members in the shops of the small Barrow-in-Furness Railway.

Construction of stills for the whisky industry from the flat copper sheet at Abercrombie's, Alloa, Scotland

A branch was formed at Wallsend. Attempts had been made to get a union established on Tyneside three or four years after the engineers' nine hour strike of 1871, when the ASE refused to accept coppersmiths. But it only lasted a few years. Another attempt was made soon after. This time the ASE tried to take them over but the members refused, afraid that they would be swamped by the engineers and that they would be forced to accept the engineering rate which was 3s to 5s below the coppersmiths' rate. Furthermore, they did not fancy being represented in negotiations by an engineer who knew nothing about coppersmiths' work. But although they remained independent the organisation did not last long. Now, for the first time since then, coppersmiths on Tyne and Wear, mostly working on ship building, were being organised by the new Wallsend branch.

Brighton branch was established in October 1913 with members working at the depot of the old London, Brighton and South Coast Railway. The branch owed its origins to a Portsmouth member who had gone to work there three years previously and had made nine new members. They had been enrolled in the Portsmouth branch, forming a separate section until the time was right to send them out into the world with their own branch. The Southampton branch also organised a group of members working in the Eastleigh railway works.

Accounts of these new branches appearing in the monthly reports stimulated further organisation. The following year new branches were formed in Grimsby with nine members from workers engaged in the building and repair of fishing vessels, at Weymouth with 25 members working at Whitehead's torpedo works and Portland dockyard and at Acton in West London based on Napier's motor works. The Scottish district formed a branch at Aberdeen, enrolling 10 of the 16 coppersmiths in the town, and at Kilmarnock, with 11 members mainly on back boilers. As a result of this spate of activity by the members, the Coppersmiths' Society was able to claim, with some justification, that it was a real national union, even though it was still very much of a minnow compared with the many big fish in the TUC pool.

This immediate pre-war period was one of ferment in the trade union movement with strike activity spreading all over the country and demands for better pay and conditions coming from

LIVERPOOL UNITED SOCIETY OF COPPERSMITHS.

ESTABLISHED 1860.   RE-ORGANISED 1879.

HELD AT THE
NEW MARKET INN,   1, GREAT HOMER STREET,

trade after trade. The coppersmiths, working as they did in the main industrial centres, could not be unaffected by what was going on all around them. With the strength of their new national organisation behind them, they too began to make a move for wage advances.

Stirrings were reported in the naval dockyards. Chatham complained that the minimum rate in the yard was 30s a week, well below what was being paid outside. Portsmouth branch reported that wages were at the same level they had been 30 years before and there was a growing feeling of unrest in the yard. Even the older men, who were considered to be part of the very fabric of the dockyard, were begining to think that something must be done.

The branch also complained of the attitude of the Admiralty toward the workforce. All men were dismissed to the scrap heap at 60 years of age to get along as best they could, despite a lifetime of service. If and when they reached the age of 70 they were given a 5s a week pension, but nothing for the years in between, the Admiralty thinking, if they thought at all, that the men could survive on what they had put away out of their thirty-odd shillings a week.

A proposal was put forward for an overtime ban at all naval dockyards in order to bring pressure on the Admiralty to agree to a wage increase. The Portsmouth branch opposed. It would be unwise, said the branch; there was little overtime done in the yard, the 20 established non-Society men and the seven hired men would continue to work, as would the members of the ASE and Steam Engine Makers Society. There was no chance of getting a solid action. Moreover, jobs that had been reclaimed from the boilermakers, plumbers and shipwrights would be lost again. The EC agreed that the branches in the various yards should decide in the light of their own position whether to impose a ban.

Members of the Southampton branch working on commercial shipbuilding and repair came out with other trades for a 3s a week advance, but after four months they had to go back with an increase of only 1s 6d. The branch then faced the task of getting all its members reinstated which, in some cases, took considerable time.

This was a period of industrial change. Old industries, materials and ways of doing things were being jettisoned and replaced with new and the coppersmiths, like other tradesmen, had to find themselves a place in this new scheme of things. They came to the new motor industry initially on copper-pipe work and then put in a claim for the work of shaping body panels, both in the case of steel and aluminium. Some of them soon became adept at the intricate double curvature work and wheeling but in this, and in wing making, they came up against the sheet metal workers, especially the Birmingham and Midlands Society which had set out to control the industry. In the early days, members of the two unions would often be working alongside each other in the same shop. But after the sheet metal workers blacked Daimler in Coventry in their opposition to the premium bonus method of payment, and the coppersmiths continued to work, increasing their complement in the firm, the antagonism between the two increased. However, although the coppersmiths had members working at Deasey, Humber, Maudsley, Rover, Standard and Swift motor shops, they had to be content with second fiddle to the sheet metal workers in the industry. Despite regular appeals in the Monthly Report from the Coventry secretary for coppersmiths to 'take their rightful place' in the motor industry, he admitted that their apathy and indifference had meant that in the Midlands, the stronghold of the motor trade, there were only three or four shops where coppersmiths were engaged on panel work. The General Secretary confirmed that in London over 90% of motor work was in the hands of the sheet metal workers. The Scottish district secretary also appealed for members to apply for jobs in the panel shops of the Argyle and Arrol Johnstone motor works. Manchester reported some success in claiming wing making, as well as pipe work, in the local motor shops.

But by this time the coppersmiths seem to have become largely a pipe bending and fitting trade, claiming work on any copper pipes from 3/8 inch petrol pipes to large pipes of six to nine inches diameter for ship work – bending, flanging, brazing and fitting. Not that they had pipe work all their own away. The brass-finishers took all the small pipe work they could get and the plumbers, in particular, claimed all the rest, particularly when copper pipes gave way to steel. The coppersmiths had to claim usage and previous materials used, much as the shipwrights had done when wooden ships gave way to steel.

On the eve of the war the Manchester branch took the initiative in organising the back boiler and cylinder makers, who had long been the Cinderellas of the trade. Back boilers were small tanks, sometimes fitted with internal flues, made from 3/16 inch copper plate, fitted at the back of kitchen fire-places with the hot water circulating to a copper storage cylinder. These were originally made at traditional coppersmiths' shops but with the big increase in demand when vast housing estates came to be built providing bathrooms for the mass of people, specialist non-union firms began to take over, particularly in the North and Midlands, putting labourers on the work and cutting the rates so that men could earn only £2 to £2 10s a week. Boys, also engaged on the work, started at 5s a week, rising by an annual 2s until they were 21.

Although the skilled back boiler and cylinder makers had served a seven year indentured apprenticeship the branch decided to take them in as a separate section until such time as their rates and conditions could be brought up to the standard of other coppersmiths. A successful wage claim gave the men an advance of from 2s to 14s a week and improved conditions so they were transferred from the probationary section to full membership.

Manchester's action was followed after the war by other branches. Bradford decided to take them into the trade protection section but was against any discrimination or having them treated as second-class citizens in any way. With the return to normal peace-time conditions the branches with back boiler and cylinder makers in their area began an organising drive. In 1922 Manchester, Rotherham, Leeds, Bradford, Halifax, and Lytham branches got together and set up a permanent organising committee which built up opposition to wage cuts demanded by the employers although Union organisation was pitifully weak. Of the 27 firms in the employers' organisation, only four or five were unionised. Nevertheless a strike was called in these shops, involving as many of the nons as possible. The committee demanded a minimum rate of 1s 8d an hour but after nine weeks out, they settled for a payment by results agreement which guaranteed a yield of 1s 8d asked for. Later back boiler and cylinder makers in Leicester and Kirkaldy were organised and brought into the Society.

Wartime

The war brought increased membership to the coppersmiths, as to other unions in engineering. A 1914 increase of 322 took the membership total to 2,500; there was a further increase of 330 in 1915, 300 in 1916, 430 in 1917 and 309 in 1918, bringing the total by the end of that year to 3,370, an increase of some 50 per cent since the outbreak of war.

Organisation, too, was strengthened with new branches opened in Wolverhampton in 1914 and nearby Birmingham the following year. The year 1915 saw the formation of branches at the naval dockyards of Rosyth and Pembroke – the first Welsh branch. Branches at Newcastle and Norwich were added in 1916, at Invergordon, North Shields and Jarrow and also in Dublin and Derry in 1917 and at Darlington in 1918.

The war brought new openings for coppersmiths in the rapidly expanded aircraft industry as well as an overflowing of work in the ship yards. But although the Society had increased in size and strengthened its organisation, it was still a prey to bigger and much stronger unions; perhaps it was even more vulnerable than in peace time as it could not provide the greater amount of labour which the war industries were demanding.

Despite the war time restrictions there were a number of strikes by coppersmiths. Two took place in 1915, one was short and sharp, the response to Cammel Laird's Liverpool management giving 'coppersmiths' work' to other trades. The management promised not to do it again and the men went back. The second, at Fairfields on the Clyde, became of national interest when 30 coppersmiths appeared before the Munitions Tribunal, the first time the tribunal was used in Scotland. It created something of a sensation in trade union circles up and down the country, prominent union leaders attended the 'trial' and Lloyd George referred to it in Parliament. The men were charged with leaving off work without permission, which was a crime, although the men pleaded provocation in that their work had been given to plumbers. The management's excuse was that coppersmiths were some 80 short of requirements but the Union district secretary told the court that coppersmiths were often sitting around with nothing to do. He also charged Fairfield's with violation of the Munitions Act by changing conditions of work without consultation. The management agreed to keep plumbers out of the coppersmiths' shop – instead they sent the work to the plumbers' shop. Confronted with this, they agreed to put one plumber off coppersmiths' work for every coppersmith sent to the yard by the Union. The men were fined a nominal 2s 6d. When, months later, members in Cowes put a ban on all overtime when the management gave a job to other pipe benders no action was taken, although this was illegal. However, 30 coppersmiths who joined in an overtime ban with other trades at Cammel Laird's were fined. But management agreed that the men would be given notice when overtime was required and the rest of the accused were discharged. In March 1916, 64 coppersmiths who came out when a tinsmith was employed in the coppersmiths' shop were summoned before the Tribunal and fined 12s 6d for every day they were out.

Coppersmiths at Eastleigh railway works struck in November 1917 against the very low wages being paid; they were supported by the Southampton branch and the local trades council which circularised contribution sheets. And in 1918 Farnborough members came out with sheet metal workers at the aircraft works in support of a pay claim, although told not to by the EC, and achieved their demands. This seems to have been a general pattern of activity under wartime restrictions and regulations.

The coppersmiths do not seem to have been unduely worried by dilution by unskilled labour which was a problem for sheet metal workers and other craft union. Demarcation in war, as in peace, was the coppersmiths' main concern. Like the sheet metal workers, they seem to have accepted that silversmiths should be employed – 26 silversmiths were reportedly working with coppersmiths at Derby and others at Coventry, Wolverhampton and elsewhere. Belgian coppersmiths were also more-or-less welcomed and taken into the Society. Nor apparently was there much concern about the call-up of coppersmiths to the forces. There was, however, some support among Society members in May 1917 for activities by ASE members against the abolition of the Trade Card scheme which had exempted skilled workers from call-up to the forces, coupled with a protest at dilution on commercial work. Derby and Coventry expressed their support but Newcastle branch refused to join in any activities led by the ASE. Society members in Peterborough came out in a week-long strike called by the local joint trades movement and some Manchester members also joined in strike action, which was opposed by the Manchester branch secretary, who insinuated the strikes were led by 'supporters of Russia' and the shop stewards' movement that was behind it was now shown up in its true light. After a while the strike movement began to crumble and when the Government agreed to consider amendments to their new proposals the men went back.

This period saw the increase in influence and activity of the engineering shops stewards movement. Bradford branch reported that the rank and file movement was getting very popular and had 'a good few members'. But Stansfield was very dismissive of the movement and declared there was no need for it within the Society, which seemed to confirm that it did have some support among coppersmiths.

In the first months of the war Stansfield's letters to members in the monthly journal were very anti-war, uncompromisingly opposed to 'a capitalist war fought on behalf of the rich.' In October 1915 he refused an invitation to visit the Western Front, saying that the EC was well aware of its duties to the country and did not need any advisory committee and trips to France to remind them of their responsibilities. However, the President and some other members did take part in a delegation to France later. Stansfield's attacks on the war declined as he became more enmeshed in the day-to-day affairs of the Society and the increased activities occasioned by the war, but his views also seem to have changed.

There was a lot of grumbling and strong words reported in the monthly journal, about the small wage increases awarded by the authorities. Coventry, a relatively high wage town, had received 25 per cent by August 1916, Birmingham 11s and Farnborough 10s, but the average of branches through the country was only 4s 6d. In the same period, it was said, food prices had shot up – the price of six loaves had gone up from 1s 1½d at the beginning of the war to 1s 10½d; 2lbs of sugar from 4d to 1s; three eggs from 3d to 6d; ¼lb tea from 4d to 8d; ½lb cheese from 4d to 8d; 1lb of bacon from 8d to 1s 4d; 1½lb of jam from 6d to 10d; 2lbs of beef or mutton from 1s 2½d to 2s 6d; ¼ stone of potatoes from 2d to 6d.

As the war progressed concern began to be expressed in some areas at the changes in materials and methods of work and how the coppersmiths would be affected when the war was over. Weymouth regretted that steel pipes were taking the place of copper and welding superceding brazing. Coventry expressed concern about the future with castings, machine bending and welding taking the place of the old coppersmiths' work. Both were looking toward the sheet metal workers as a possible haven. The Birmingham secretary welcomed a movement to get understanding between the Society and the metal workers, pledging himself to do anything to make the movement effective. However, there was a lot of opposition in many areas to any closer working with the metal workers who were looked on as filchers of coppersmiths' work.

At the 1917 annual meeting the Coventry secretary, H. Salsbury, moved that all branches be urged to use every endeavour to get all coppersmiths working at the trade into membership, providing they were eligible according to rule. He included those 'known today as sheet metal workers, braziers and silversmiths.'

Attempts to improve day-to-day relations continued. A meeting was held in Manchester with representatives of the National Amalgamated Sheet Metal Workers and the Birmingham Society to iron out differences between the two trades. H. Stansfield expressed the hope that the meeting would be a preliminary to amalgamation of all the sheet metal workers throughout the country. The terms 'tinsmith' and 'coppersmith' were an obstruction to joint action, local difficulties should be settled through the executives of the two unions. Later he said amalgamation between the sheet metal workers' societies should precede any amalgamation discussions with the coppersmiths.

A national joint committee was then elected with two each from the coppersmiths and the Birmingham Society and four from the National Amalgamated, plus all full-time officers. All disputes would be referred to the committee as they arose if they could not be settled by local joint committees to be set up in all districts. Demarcation problems should be dealt with from the stand-point of the ability of the workers concerned. Stansfield and the president, Strugnell, hoped that the conference was a step to national unity. In fact is made no apparent contribution to that end.

Internal domestic issues were not neglected despite the urgent pressures of war-time working. The position of apprentices was of vital concern for a craft union. The National Council agreed that craft apprentices be allowed in the motor and aircraft industries. Apparently, the Society had followed the practice of the sheet metal workers which had ruled that the methods of production in these two industries did not allow the variety of work necessary to give a proper training. It was now felt that the position had changed and the methods of work gave adequate craft training.

It was further decided that steps be taken to ensure apprentices attended technical schools during working hours – probably the first time this had been raised anywhere. Branches were also requested to make local enquiries about the possibility of adult members attending technical schools to learn welding, etc.

The Council also considered the accumulating criticism of how the Society was run. The main charge, coming from a number of branches, that the Society was run by London was largely ignored. The only concession was that all branches were allowed to nominate candidates for the seven-member EC; members still had to be resident in London and were elected at the London branch by ballot or show of hands. They would meet as required, to be summoned by the General Secretary or President or by a majority of themselves.

The National Council was to consist of seven members elected at the annual conference for a three year period: one from Ireland, two from Scotland, and one each from grouped branches in the South of England, the Midlands, the Lancashire district and the North East coast.

All candidates for office had to be full, free members with not less than five years' consecutive membership, to have served as an officer for not less than 12 months and to have nominated the Society as his approved society for the National Insurance. He must be working at the trade and receiving the minimum rate and conditions of the district.

Branches were to be grouped in districts to facilitate the work of the Society, with London as a separate district branch with its own secretary, who would also be the assistant secretary of the Society.

It was decided to create the position of general treasurer and book examiner, the job of the latter being to visit branches and districts on the instruction of the National Council or EC and examine the books.

Industrial Unrest

The coppersmiths did not a take a leading part in the ferment in the labour movement at the end of the war, but were not unaffected by the upsurge of industrial militancy.

The major demand of the engineering workers with the end of hostilities was for a 40 hour week. The unions put in an application for 44 hours, the employers countered with an offer of 47 hours which the union leadership was prepared to accept, only to be met by a rising opposition on the shop floor.

The unofficial shop stewards' movement, which had increased its strength and influence in that last, desperate year of the war, led the struggle for the 40 hours, with the stewards in the Clyde shipyards and engineering shops in the van.

The leaders of the unions decided on a national ballot of the membership on the acceptance of the 47 hours. The vote in the Society's own ballot was 1,330 in favour of the 47 hours and 504 against; the main branches against being Barrow, Belfast, Glasgow, Southampton, Hull and Wolverhampton.

A similar vote was recorded among the engineering unions generally and the 47 hour agreement was signed and went into operation. But the rules and regulations with which the employers surrounded the working of the 47 hours irritated many members of the Society and other unions, and there was a great deal of agitation.

Grimsby branch members were out for three weeks at the call of the local allied trades committee and the branch secretary wrote glowingly in the journal about how the strike committee had ensured that no strikers or their dependants would go hungry, having made arrangements with a firm in the town to provide food which would be paid for later. The Coventry branch was reprimanded for sending a circular round the branches calling for action.

Rosyth branch sponsored a call in the dockyard for a 40 hour week and came out on strike in support of other trades in the yard who had taken industrial action. Many yards on the Tyne were also on strike over the 47 hour agreement, including members of the North Shields branch. Aberdeen made a call for the 40 hours and Edinburgh urged that the 40 hour claim be pursued, although only by constitutional means. The West of Scotland district agreed by 85 votes to 62 to accept the 47 hours but in the meantime to endeavour to get a new ballot. A complaint was made that the previous ballot gave no alternative but to vote for or against 47 hours. Although the Glasgow branch held two mass meetings on the question, one of them the biggest ever held, with 350 members present, no decision was reached. The district secretary declared that 'the great majority was convinced that the upheaval served no purpose' and claimed that many members on the Clyde did not go to work because of 'threats and tyranny by the pickets.' The Coventry branch secretary, on the other hand, thought that industrial unrest was 'healthy'.

In May 1919 another ballot was held, this time on whether to apply for a 44 hour week, the coppersmiths voted 1,800 for and 62 against, but no action was taken.

The 40 hour week demand, and the later rejection of the 47 hour agreement, were led by the shop stewards movement and once again there was a division in the trade unions between those supporting the rank and file movement, as being more in touch with the demands and aspirations of the workers, and those who continued to back the official union leadership which by and large had no time for the unofficial movement.

Stansfield made a number of strong, even vicious attacks on the rank and file movement in his reports in the journal, declaring they were 'anti-trade unionists' and worked through what he called 'mob meetings'. The movement was against organised labour, claiming 'might against right'. He claimed that 'few coppersmiths practise this anti-trade unionism otherwise known as the shop stewards' movement.'

He further claimed that a strike by the London ship repair workers for a 15s a week advance was the work of the shop steward's movement as were the strikes on the Clyde, in Belfast and on the North-East coast, and the fact that in all cases the men had to return without achieving their demands showed up the movement for the ineffectual body that it was. It appeared that the union officials preferred the strikes should fail and so weaken the rank and file movement, rather than give them official support and provide the base for a general advance of the whole membership.

A nine-day strike of the whole of the 6,000 workers at Rolls Royce, Derby, in support of a shop steward summarily dismissed by the management, who refused to reinstate him until there had been a local conference, was attacked by Stansfield as 'another antic of the shop stewards' movement that did not lend credit or dignity to the unions.' The unions' officials ordered their members to return without the steward.

The argument and debate for and against the shop stewards movement continued in the pages of the monthly journal. The secretary of the Portsmouth dockyard branch opposed the movement as 'unsound'. But the secretary of another dockyard branch, Invergordon, supported the shop stewards saying that troubles arose in the workshop and the place to settle them was in the workshop and not to wait weeks for a branch meeting.

But rising unemployment, attacks by the management, particularly the 'managerial functions' dispute of 1922, weakened the whole of the trade union movement, official and unofficial alike.

In the immediate post-war years, when the trade unions were still maintaining some momentum, the Society continued to strengthen its organisation with the formation of more local branches, spreading its influence into new areas. One of these was Cork, its members working at the Ford motor works. Others were at Kilmarnock where eight members and four apprentices working on back boilers and cylinders formed the basis; Lytham and Fyld, which also covered Preston and Fleetwood, where the 30 members worked mainly in general shops and on fishing boats; Alloa had 21 members mainly engaged on distillery work while Rotherham with 17 members and Halifax were on general work and back boilers and cylinders.

This strengthening and widening of the organisation not only helped the Society in its negotiations with employers, it also gave it a better bargaining position in relation with other unions.

Back in 1913 a joint meeting of the Coventry branch and the local sheet metal workers attempted to overcome once and for all the continual quarrels over demarcation. They agreed that in the local motor shops members of both trades could work together on any sheet metal work, on panels and also on pipe-bending – the very core of the coppersmiths' trade. They also decided on procedures for phasing out the premium bonus system, particularly at Daimlers, which was a bone of contention of long standing between the two societies. Stansfield backed this attitude and said the curse of demarcation should not be allowed in this new industry and all work should be available to both trades. This, of course, would have been of decided advantage to the coppersmiths, which only had a foothold in the motor shops.

Then came the war, and although various branches spoke during these years of the need of amalgamation no move seems to have been taken to translate the declarations into practice.

But early in 1919 attempts were made to end the continual pre-occupation of all sections of the trade with demarcation and losing work to other trades.

Shaping the backpiece of a bend at the Guinness brewery maintenace shop, London; *right*: planishing a condenser at Abercrombie's, Alloa

The EC protested its support, in principle, of ultimate amalgamation with both the sheet metal workers and plumbers, but said that federation was a necessary preliminary. They accepted an invitation from the plumbers for a meeting at executive level. But instead of a discussion on the setting up of a joint board to settle matters in dispute they found that the plumbers were all set to discuss amalgamation.

Eventually it was proposed to set up a joint board to establish common ground between the two trades, to devise ways of settling local disputes and allocation of work – to include an equal distribution where both trades were employed. They also agreed to examine the ground together with the sheet metal workers on the possibility of federation and amalgamation. They finally agreed to consider the situation again three months later and meanwhile to set up a joint board to establish common ground and settle disputes arising out of allocation of work. The proposals were circulated to branches for consideration and of those that replied nine were definitely against amalgamation and seven supported the EC's action.

Within the Society itself all was not sweetness and light. At the time of the amalgamation not enough thought had been given to the way the different parts of the amalgamation would work. It would seem to have been assumed that the Society would operate as before but on a larger scale.

Although there was a nine-strong elected National Executive Council together with the full time officers, this was normally only called together quarterly. The day-to-day government of the Society between NEC meetings was carried on by the General Secretary in co-operation with the committee of management comprised of members resident in London only and elected at a London branch meeting by ballot or a show of hands – much as the early national trade unions of 50 years before operated.

This 'government by London' caused a great deal of resentment and came up for regular criticism by branches in different parts of the country. The General Secretary claimed there was no other way in which they could operate. He had to have a body to whom he could apply at any time and it was not possible, and too expensive, to call the NEC together.

At the other end of the country the Scottish district committee acted somewhat like an autonomous fiefdom. It was the committe of the former Scottish Association which had undergone a change of name but little else. Moreover, it continued to double up as the Glasgow branch committee with the district secretary and president acting in the same capacity for the branch. In other words, it had taken over the territory it controlled before the amalgamation and continued to operate in much the same way. This was rather resented by other Scottish branches which at an enlarged district committee meeting were brusquely told that they could speak but not vote, only the elected Glasgow members had the right to vote and if they did not like it they could lump it.

When the district committee was called to account for their action in setting up new branches in Darlington, which was not even in Scotland, they indignantly replied that Darlington was part of the old Scottish Association and resented what they did in their own territory being questioned by London, which, it was said, wanted to retain its old power undiminished.

The Scottish President said they were prepared to take a ballot of their members whether they should stay in the amalgamation if they were to be controlled by a London based committee that they did not recognise. They demanded that the government of the Society should rest with the National Council on which they were represented. They denied the claim that the Council could not be easily called together when required. At the delegate conference that discussed the Scottish district action the Glasgow members were isolated, the East of Scotland members voting against them, although other members declared that it was undemocratic that the committee controlling the affairs of the Society be based only on one branch.

On this occasion the disagreement was papered over with all accepting a semantic solution of changing the name of the London-based Executive Council to Committee of Management and the National Council to National Executive Committee.

This allowed an agreement to be reached without too much loss of face, but it did nothing substantial to overcome the opposition of the provincial members to the dominant position London held in the Society by its complete monopoly of the Committee of Management which, despite the change of name, continued to control the Society as it had done of yore.

In many parts of the country unemployment began to rise in 1921. The Scottish district committee tried to ease the position in its area by limiting overtime but found the proposal very difficult to implement.

The national engineering employers took advantage of the increased unemployment and demanded a 5s cut in weekly wages. Branches were asked if they would favour a policy of resisting the employers' demands and 27 replied supporting resistance while others accepted the reduction with various provisos.

A series of ballots of members was taken in conjunction with the other unions in engineering. In June 1921, 1,531 voted against accepting the proposed cut and 629 in favour. A second ballot reversed the position with 1,264 voting in favour and 577 against. Then in October another ballot was held on the employers' further proposal to withdraw the $12\frac{1}{2}$ and $7\frac{1}{2}$ per cent wartime awards. This found the Society fairly evenly divided with 892 voting in favour and 768 against.

Mass unemployment increased month by month through 1921 with cuts in wages keeping pace with equal regularity. Starting from a minimum rate of £4 4s $11\frac{1}{2}$d at the beginning of the year the employers cut 3s a week in August, another 3s in November, 3s 6d in December and another 3s 6d in January 1922, then 3s 6d in July and 5s 6d in both August and September.

Shipyards closed and ships were built abroad while shipping members walked the streets.

The following year the employers made another attack, demanding limitations to the organisation and activities of the unions in the industry, in what has become known as the managerial functions dispute. The Engineering Employers' Federation laid down terms under which the unions would operate in future and demanded that all trades sign an agreement to abide by the order. The metal trades federation tried to negotiate with the employers, with Stansfield a member of the negotiating committee, but they refused to blackleg on the engineers. A ballot was held, the coppersmiths voting by 1,710 to 281 to back the Society's stand, and members in general engineering were locked out with the rest of the industry. Not a large number of Society members were hit by the lockout as many worked in small non-federated shops and a large proportion were employed in shipyards, which were not affected. After some three months the workers were forced to accept the employers' terms, the coppersmiths voting 1,174 to 559 to accept.

The shipbuilding employers also went on the offensive, demanding a reduction of 26s 6d a week. This was resisted, the coppersmiths voting 1,212 to 189 to oppose the demand. Eventually, together with the other unions they accepted a two stage reduction.

Early in these disputes the London shop stewards met and recommended that there be a levy of 5 per cent of earnings on all members remaining in work, to provide aid for those locked out. This was accepted by the branch and the NEC later asked all branches to follow suit.

The engineering employers, having weakened the position of the unions, put in a demand in July for a reduction of 16s 6d a week by the end of August, the coppersmiths opposing acceptance by only 39 votes with 594 against and 555 for acceptance. The Engineering and

Shipbuilding Trades Federation as a whole was two to one against but as this was not enough for strike action the reduction was accepted.

The Admiralty followed the example of the private employers and cut war bonuses in the naval dockyards. The secretary of the dockyards committee attacked the Whitley Councils which allowed minor concessions but ignored proposals on such major issues as hours and conditions. They were conceived as a means of containing industrial unrest, he said, arguing that the workers would never emancipate themselves by sitting round a table with employers, but must be class conscious.

The situation continued to deteriorate. Many yards were empty and the employers said they would have to go back to 1908 rates of pay to be competitive. On the 1 September 1922 the last coppersmith was paid off at Barrow and for months every member of the branch was idle. In Greenock and North Shields half the members were out of work.

In Glasgow, although half the branch had emigrated, half of those left were out of work and many of the others on short time. Over the next six months unemployment among coppersmiths in the city varied between 160 and 190. Other branches reported more or less similar situation, particularly the shipping branches.

The NEC proposed a number of financial provisions to help the Society to weather the economic storm. Unemployment pay was cut to a maximum of 20 weeks; contributions were increased by 3d to 2s a week: £1,000 was borrowed from the superannuation reserve fund; the General Secretary and Scottish Secretary took cuts in salary.

With the prolonged battering the Society had sustained from unemployment and employers' attacks, members began to look around for ways of giving the Society greater strength to defend members' interests.

The NEC agreed to have talks with the Heating and Domestic Engineers for joint action, and Manchester and Coventry branches pressed for closer working with the sheet metal workers such as had been successful in their areas. The General Secretary opposed this latter suggestion and the motion was withdrawn.

There was also some support inside the Society for the National Minority Movement, started by Communists and left-wing Labour people to 'ginger-up' the official machinery within the various unions, to strengthen members' participation and influence, co-ordinate activity and get the unions on the offensive. A discussion inside the Devonport branch was said to have aroused a great deal of support and a proposal was made to form a local branch and for the Society to affiliate. The secretary said there was no need for such a body in the Coppersmiths' Society.

With the spread of economic improvement and union recovery the Society once more began extending its organisation. A new branch was formed at Cheltenham for coppersmiths at the Gloster Aircraft Co.; Devonport organised a sub-branch in Falmouth and Peterborough extended its membership to Huntingdon.

The election in 1924 of the first Labour government heartened the industrial working class and brought increasing militancy and a new wave of strikes. The London branch decided the time had come to win back some of the wage cuts made in the last few years. The whole of the London membership took the day off and 300 attended a mass meeting which decided to put in a claim for a £4 a week minimum. A couple of months later a branch meeting decided that members should leave firms that did not pay the £4. After a month the employers proposed that agreements be entered into with individual firms for payment by results schemes that would give the £4 minimum and also concessions on overtime and working conditions. Only 13 firms agreed to the £4 and members in the rest of the Trade were out solid. They claimed that they were not on strike, only taking a holiday until the employers decided to pay to coppersmith craftsmen the minimum rate for their services just as doctors, lawyers and other professional men charged a minimum rate.

As more firms agreed to work out schemes to provide the minimum, members returned to allow them to put their proposals into practice and eventually some advances were made.

Rotherham members staged a six week strike over the employment of too many boys, insisting that no more boys be taken on until numbers had been reduced to one boy for every three men. Liverpool branch, too, was active, joining with other local trades in shipping to put in for a 10s a week increase.

Towards the end of 1925, however, unemployment began to rise again: 140 were out of work in Glasgow, 35 in Liverpool and only 11 members were working in Barrow.

The General Strike

Then came the General Strike to which the Society gave its full backing. The committee of management remained in continuous session during the conferences prior to the calling of the strike and signified their support for the TUC memorandum calling the strike. The NEC was called together, and decided on a 5 per cent levy on all those in work. Although only a minority of members were initially affected by this 'grave attack on wages and hours' all members on maintenance work at places where men were on strike were called out. Later, men obeyed the call of the TUC to all workers in engineering and shipyards (except naval dockyards), and workers in breweries, distilleries and chemical works.

Stansfield report that the leadership of the Society was amazed to receive the news that the strike had been called off. They had been doing their bit in what amounted to 'a great rehearsal' and felt that the calling out of the second line – the engineering and shipbuilding trades – had had the desired effect and the Government had succumbed. Phone calls and telegrams were received from members all over the country wanting to join in before the strike was called and then refusing to return because of the employers' humiliating conditions. They were told to 'act in accordance with the trades of the locality.'

A resolution from the NEC was sent to the TUC General Council, praising the 'splendid and loyal manner in which all trade union members had responded to the strike call.'' It went on to express 'keen disappointment at the contempt displayed' in calling off the strike without first obtaining assurances that no victimisation or humiliating conditions would be imposed on strikers on their return. It regretted 'that such a vital injury should have been done to the trade union movement by those responsible for the indifference displayed.''

The NEC expressed a belief that, despite the injury done to the movement by calling off the strike, the way in which the whole of the unions responded would revivify and strengthen the movement. Those few who did not meet the call would live to be ashamed of themselves. It was decided that no 'Judas money' would be accepted from blacklegs in the shape of the 5 per cent levy on members who were not called out. Members were asked to give the names and places of work of any known blacklegs to their branch secretary.

After the strike no member was allowed to start in the place of a discharged member and members working for contractors were told not to work in breweries, distilleries, etc., where blacklegs were employed.

From all over the country branches reported on local activities and condemned the ending of the strike. Barrow expressed great dissatisfaction at the way the strike was called off. Cowes praised the splendid way in which members downed tools. Six shipwrights were victimised and were being supported by a local levy of all trades. Doncaster proudly reported 'every man responded well'; Derby '100 per cent response'. At Farnborough Royal Aircraft Establishment, all coppersmiths came out with other trades and took part in strike committees to deal with finances, transport, entertainment etc. Mass picketing was in full force. Mass meetings held every day and reports from other areas read out. After the first few days the *British Worker* was sold daily thanks to two men going to London every day at 4 am to collect copies. These men ceased to be coppersmiths or of separate trades, just workers resenting injustice to fellow workers, the miners.

Greenock condemned the surrender and the way the workers had been let down by the Labour leaders. Leeds reported all coppersmiths and apprentices out. London had 259 members and 15 apprentices out for a total of 2,107 days. Manchester members ceased work immediately and nons came out with them, 76 members affected. Some 200 attended a mass rally, despite transport difficulties, happy to have been called out but shocked when news of the surrender became known. Portsmouth answered the call with a determination not to give in until victory was won. Rotherham reported industry practically at a standstill with most firms closed down.

Glasgow reported 90 members in loco shops and transport depots out from the first day and these were added to every day as calls came to other transport workers to come out. The second line of attack brought out 200 more and finally only some three dozen, mainly in one-man shops, were not out. The way in which so many responded enthusiastically when they had nothing personally to gain and perhaps much to lose was a victory in itself. Sheerness reported 'wonderful response and great determination shown.' Swindon: not a coppersmith turned up and all stayed out until the end. Dundee came out the first day and when they found out that they had jumped the gun decided to stay out. They could not go back en bloc as some had been given their books. Collections continued for miners at Cheltenham, Coventry, London, Liverpool and Sheerness plus £167 by branches sent to head office.

The aftermath of the strike brought prolonged short-time working on a wide scale as well as some unemployment and victimisation.

The Tory government's attempts to use the General Strike setback to cut the links between the trade unions and the Labour Party by restrictions on the political levy occasioned the Society to take the opportunity of holding another ballot to set up a political fund. A ballot had been held soon after the war and the move had been defeated with a small majority voting against. This time, early in 1928, the members voted in favour by 354 votes to 214. The Secretary appealed to members to contract in and the branches with the more politically-minded secretaries made an effort to get their members to do so, but even those who did contract in were often very lax in paying up. Although it was only 1s, paid once a year, collection was always a problem and many were in arrears.

The NEC had always been concerned at the large number of members who were in arrears with their trade contributions and about this time they proposed weekly collections of dues as a means of overcoming this. This was followed by a proposal to draw in the shop delegates to collect the dues of members in the shop. They were provided with collecting cards and were paid a commission on the amounts collected. Other steps were soon taken to make them more general representatives of the trade in the workshop. They were issued with membership application forms and distributed the monthly journal. The NEC made this more official with a ruling that all shops where two or more members were employed should annually elect a shop delegate to look after the interests of the trade. He should examine members' cards once a month to see that they were fully paid up, notify the branch secretary of any dispute, the names of the members affected or likely to be affected and provide full particulars as soon as possible. At the same time it was laid down that any member obtaining a job in a place where a branch existed must report to the secretary within 48 hours.

Other changes in the organisation included a decision that the London district secretary become a full time official paid by the Society, with a salary of £250 a year. He had previously been full time but only a London official, paid from a voluntary levy on the London members. The Scottish district secretary was already a full time paid official and the president also acted as National Insurance secretary with his salary paid by the Ministry and could generally be called on when required on Union business.

By the late 1920s trade had improved, and coppersmiths were back in demand. The Society had even made a breakthrough in the anti-union giant of the motor industry, the Pressed Steel Co. in Oxford, where members were engaged on panel work and wing making. In their first week newcomers went on day work at 1s 2d an hour but afterwards transferred to piecework, based on a rate of 1s 8d an hour. Arrol Johnstone of Paisley lifted the ban on trade union members which it had imposed in 1922. But the Society itself blacked Crossley Motors of Manchester when they would not pay the Society rate. Two members who refused to leave the firm were expelled from the Society.

The Depression

But prosperity did not last long; 1930 ushered in the great depression. The railway shops began the process and members were put off from all the main rail shops. The motor industry, never renowned for giving security of work, followed. Sunbeam Motors provided a few jobs for members on Kay Donn's world record challenger but when that was finished the works virtually closed. All workers at Beardmore Motors, Paisley, were sacked and the works closed down. The company's shipyard was bought by Shipbuilding Securities Limited – an organisation set up by the industry to reduce competition by buying up selected yards, closing and dismantling them so that they could not be used, paying the employers to leave the industry and putting men on the scrap heap. In November 1930 Beardmore's locomotive works also closed.

By 1932, unemployment affected much of the country and nowhere more than in the shipyards. Sunderland reported that of the branch's membership of 27 only three were working and two of those were out of the trade. The situation in Barrow was no better with only a dozen working out of a branch of 90, and most had been out for six months, or more. The majority of members of the Liverpool branch were said to have been unemployed for two-and-a-half years. Manchester, which had 170 members a few years previously, was down to 60. Glasgow reported at least three quarters of the branch out of work, including 22 put off when work on the liner, the *Queen Mary*, was stopped. The only men at work in Greenock were four in the torpedo works. In Alloa only the apprentices were at work, and they were on short time. Then all the shops in the town closed and the branch folded. In the Midlands, the Wolverhampton branch closed with no members left. All members of the Cheltenham branch were out of work when the Gloucester Aircraft Works went into mothballs. It was not only shipbuilding and general engineering that suffered. The distilleries throughout Scotland were caught up in the blizzard with no fewer than 30 closed on Speyside alone.

The income from branches was severely cut. Birmingham branch reported that in 1932 they had received only 15 per cent of contributions due. With a drastic cut in the money coming in and increased benefits being paid out as a result of the mass unemployment, the Society's funds were in a perilous state.

The NEC cut employment benefit from 12s to 6s for a period of 10 weeks followed by 20 weeks at 3s a week in any one year. The concession that members would not be liable for contributions while unemployed was stopped, although members could delay paying until they returned to work. Cuts were also made in sickness, superannuation and burial benefits. Part-time officials' payments were reduced and the Journal was issued quarterly instead of monthly. Even so, expenditure continued to exceed income.

In an attempt to recruit members and particularly to attract those who because of the depression could not afford to pay full contributions, a new 'trade only' membership section was started in 1933 with no entrance fee and contributions fixed at 1s a week.

The employers, of course, took advantage of the vulnerability of the unions with so many out of work to cut wages and worsen conditions. In June 1931 the Society took part, along with the other trades, in negotiations with the engineering employers. The unions were forced to accept a general worsening of wages and conditions as the depression worsened.

There was no upturn in trade until 1934, and then only in some areas. But during the year 300 new members were enrolled. A new branch was started in Leicester, largely from members of branches in the distressed areas who had gone there in search of work. The initial membership was around 30 and the work was mainly general and back boilers, with some hospital work. Members were taken on again at Weybridge as orders were received for military aircraft. But the situation in the shipyards was still very depressed. Glasgow still had 120 signing the books and it was not until 1937 that distilleries began to re-open again.

The depression and the consequent competition for jobs brought home to members the need for improving qualifications. Glasgow branch started a weekly class of 40 members at the Society's rooms on 'practical and workaday methods on drawings, pattern cutting and development, the lack of which had told against members in the competition for jobs.' Glasgow urged all shops to get the foremen to give apprentices regular practical experience in electric and oxy-acetylene welding, and apprentices were urged to enroll for copper welding classes provided by the Educational Authority. London set up a training group in the crypt of a Poplar church for practical and theoretical training in welding. The Cowes branch opened a welding class and Leicester branch persuaded a local firm to let members practise welding on their premises in their spare time.

The year 1937 saw a wave of strikes by engineering apprentices sweeping through one industrial centre after another. The strike wave started on the Clyde and a number of young coppersmiths were members of the group sponsoring the initial turn-out. Soon some 130 coppersmith apprentices were among the thousands of shipbuilding and engineering apprentices out in Glasgow, Paisley and Greenock.

Their main demand was for a 50 per cent increase in rates which had remained unchanged for nearly 50 years at 10s a week for the first year, rising to £1 in the final year. In future apprentices' wages should be negotiated by the unions, 'so freeing them from their long-standing bondage.' The rate of apprentices to journeymen should also be mutually agreed between the Engineering Employer's Association and the various unions. After five weeks they returned on the understanding that the employers would be prepared to give an increase, but once the boys were back in the shops the employers pared down the claim to rates ranging from 12s 6d to 26s.

The branch officials took up the case of apprentices in the non-Federated shops – the amount of repetition work they were given, excessive number in relation to journeymen, and low wages. They got the boys the new rates and an agreement that the Society would have to be consulted before apprentices were taken on.

An agreement was also reached with the local Employers' Association on a twelve months probationary period after a lad had finished his time. At the beginning of this period the young journeyman would be paid 10s less than the journeymen's rate, increasing by 2s 6d a quarter until he received the full rate at the end of the year.

During the strike collections were taken in the coppersmiths' shops to help the apprentices, supplementing payments from the branch funds and grants from head office. Fifty apprentices later joined the Society.

The ripples of the Clyde strike spread far and wide. Agreement was reached with the Edinburgh employers to pay the new rates. A group of apprentices in Stirlingshire approached the district committee about their wages and terms of apprenticeship and were able to get both adjusted to the new terms.

In Coventry, young coppersmiths actively participated in the strikes of 1,500 apprentices for increases in pay and trade union recognition. The Manchester branch secretary wrote glowingly of the organisation developed by the 14,000 engineering apprentices on strike in Lancashire – in which his lads participated. They only returned when the employers agreed to consider their demand for a 3s a week rise and union recognition.

Coppersmith apprentices at Rolls Royce, Derby, were affected by the militancy of other areas, complaining they were kept working for too long periods of time on the same type of jobs so that they did not get enough experience. They managed to get an improvement in the position with help of the shop steward.

In the 1930s the demarcation issue became even sharper with bitter fights throughout the slump for what little work was available. When trade improved the various trades tried to establish their right to as wide a range of jobs as possible.

Burton-on-Trent had an eight day strike in a dispute concerning the sheet metal workers, over who was to do work on aluminium in the brewery industry – which they claimed as it had superceded copper – and small utensils for the dairy trade. In the Swindon railway works there was another dispute with the sheet metal workers on welding light steel panels on coaches and with boilermakers and shipwrights on pipe work. In Manchester there was trouble over the Heating and Domestic Engineers doing coppersmithing. Early in 1938 all the coppersmiths on the Clyde came out in protest at the 'brassies' working on copper pipes. But the real villain and enemy of all coppersmiths remained the plumber who was referred to as something almost sub-human, completely without scruples, grabbing any work he could lay his hands on.

Coppersmiths who were members of the engineering union seemed to be exempt from the abuse heaped on members of other kindred trades who were caught doing work that was coppersmiths' by right, and indeed could not be done properly by anyone except a coppersmith. Whereas members of these other trades were untrained villains masquerading as coppersmiths, the AEU coppersmiths were real coppersmiths who just happened to be members of another union and the two could work amicably together, sharing the same jobs. They would each try and wean members away from the other union but that was all part of the game and no hard feelings.

In just one more attempt to reduce demarcation disputes the NEC met with the plumbers' executive in 1939 and decided unanimously that it would be advisable to reach agreement on all disputes without the intervention of a third party. The district committees of both unions were to be told to try and arrive at a solution to such cases on their own. A guideline in deciding who was entitled to do the job, recommended by the two executives, was that the purpose to which the pipe was to be put should be taken into account. Nothing more was heard of this.

A number of proposals for amalgamation were put forward over the years, sometimes by one branch, sometimes by another, each influenced by local experience of working with the other kindred trades which varied at different periods. But the pride in craft and desire to remain independent was usually stronger than the desire for unity or for this solution to the problem of demarcation, especially as the general secretary generally spoke in opposition to amalgamation.

This was the position at the delegate conferences of 1928, 1930 and again in 1936 when motions in favour of amalgamation both with the sheet metal workers and with 'kindred trades' did not even get voted on after being dismissed as 'impossible' by the General Secretary. It was said that the sheet metal workers should first accomplish their own amalgamation and that they should lift their rates and organisation to the level of the coppersmiths.

So problems of demarcation continued to occupy both the time and the energy of Society members at all levels, and the struggle to hang on to or take over as many jobs as possible was the main preoccupation of the Society as a whole to the detriment of other necessary activities. A national conference of shipyard delegates from all over the country spent the whole time in reports and discussion 'who was doing what' in the various yards.

Failures to agree led to endless conferences on local, district and national level, the outcome of which was work shared out to give the least cause for conflict so that, while no one was satisfied, everyone had something which they would not want to risk losing.

The need to strengthen the Society numerically and organisationally was apparent but no practical steps were taken to bring it about. A proposal to appoint a national organiser was turned down by the 1938 delegate conference after the General Secretary had ruled it out as too expensive and unlikely to yield sufficient members to reimburse the Society the £500 a year that an organiser would cost. In fact, he did not think there were so many unorganised coppersmiths.

But as trade improved some organisation did take place. A branch was set up in Doncaster, based on the railway shops and a small branch at Yeovil of 'smiths working at Westland Helicopters.

Coppersmiths also staked out a claim in the new aeroplane industry. At least one member was in it from the very beginning. Tommy Wilkins was said to be hammering away in a tin hut on the banks of the Basingstoke Canal as early as 1897; he was the grandfather of the Farnborough branch, which was set up in 1913. Before the First World War others followed him to try their hand at their new work. They took part in the building of all kinds of flying machines, including airships. Between 1914 and 1918 they helped to produce hundreds of fighter planes, at the same time establishing union organisation.

In 1913 Shorts opened a seaplane factory at Sheerness and the branch secretary urged members to get in there quickly. Members were also employed at Saunders Roe at Cowes, Supermarine at Southampton, A. V. Roe's at Manchester and the British and Colonial Aeroplane Co. of Filton, Bristol, and other aeroplane shops, mostly, at that time, small establishments.

Work fell off with the ending of hostilities but picked up again in the 1930s with the increasing possiblity of war. In addition to Westlands Helicopters, members were working at Blackburn aircraft works at Dumbarton – the first accredited aircraft works in Scotland and the Brough, Yorkshire aircraft works. The Weybridge branch was re-formed with members working at the various aircraft works there. There were reports that attempts were being made to sectionalise work at Hawker's, de Havilland and at Rolls Royce, which was allowed by the NEC providing the Society maintained control. Shops were also opened at Portsmouth and near Edinburgh for servicing Fleet Air Arm planes.

In April 1939 a delegate conference from all branches with members working in aircraft shops was held in London. Discussion ranged over general problems connected with the aircraft shops and what demands there were in the industry for coppersmiths. Later in the year the NEC decided to set up an experimental committee for a period of 12 months to be based at Derby. Its role would be to co-ordinate recruitment activities in aircraft subcontract shops then springing up in the Midlands. They were said to be employing boys and girls but with some ex-members of the Society working there. The NEC promised full support to all organising activity at aircraft works and urged members to give membership application forms to all their workmates working as coppersmiths.

The early days of the Second World War revealed a great shortage of coppersmiths, particularly in the shipyards, and the employers were soon calling for dilution. Already in 1939 when the big increase in shipbuilding taxed the manpower resources of the Society to the utmost, it was decided to admit dilutees – classified as assistants – under strict control of the Society, and a special section was created for them. Later, women were brought into the shops and in 1941 it was agreed they be allowed to join the assistants' section of the Society.

Following pressure for yet more labour an agreement was concluded with the Admiralty in April 1940. This listed the first source of extra labour to be an increase in the number of apprenticies. If this did not prove sufficient, assistants would be allocated under the supervision of a coppersmith. A representative of the shop, together with the management, would allocate the work to be performed by the assistant. Where coppersmiths were available they would be employed before any assistants were taken on and would take the place of assistants, and no coppersmith would be discharged while assistants were engaged on coppersmiths' work. There would also be a temporary relaxation of existing customs but all departures from normal working would be registered and would be terminated as soon as normal conditions returned.

A few months later a similar agreement was concluded with the engineering employers. It was then laid down that a dilutee, working with a coppersmith, should be paid 75 per cent of the craftsman's rate and when working on his own and entirely responsible for the job, he should be paid the full rate. The Society insisted that women assistants be paid on the same basis as men. But agreements were apparently made to be broken – the 'national interest' covered a multitude of evasion, and employers refused to pay women assistants more than the women's rate despite the signed agreement.

Twelve coppersmiths were taken out of Manchester shop and sent around the country while assistants, mainly plumbers, were kept on. When the Society objected the Ministry officials refused to alter their decision, even when their attention was drawn to the written agreement.

Then, as more members of other unions were drafted into coppersmiths' shops, the Society decided to line up with a TUC proposal that unions recognise each other's cards on the payment of 3d a week. In the case of the silversmiths, however, the Society made a special agreement covering both dues payments and union membership. In London, as the result of a personal agreement at the outbreak of war, compositors were taken on as dilutees for the duration.

The only recorded wartime strike involving coppersmiths was that of the apprentices in June 1941 who joined 12,000 Scottish engineering apprentices and came out onto the streets for a pay increase, and, after a few weeks out secured a substantial advance.

Throughout the war, although the coppersmiths were not engaged in any major struggle, officials at both branch and national level were continually taking part in meetings, conferences and tribunals on questions of work, wage awards, manpower and the 101 activities concerned with the prosecution of the war on the home front.

The District Secretary represented his members at Fairfields when the Clyde ship builders repeated their action of the First World War and took two coppersmiths to court for absenteeism. One of them was sent to prison for 30 days and even though the secretary pointed out that the amount of time lost was due to the firm's practice, continued even in war time, of locking out men for half a day if they were more than a quarter of an hour late, the magistrates insisted on sending the man to prison, although reducing the sentence to 20 days. No reprimand was made to the employer for continuing to lock out men who arrived late, however good their reason.

The general activities of the Society also continued. Liverpool reported 100 per cent organisation at Harland and Wolff, for the first time, following dinner-time shop meetings and talks with the men. Branch membership had been pushed up to 300, an all time record. Rosyth branch, which had closed when the dockyard had been put in mothballs, was re-opened. Derby started a sub-branch of men engaged on high grade pipe work at Rolls Royce experimental shop at Hucknall Airport, which later became a branch in its own right. Swindon branch extended its influence with a group of members at Caerphilly – the connection being they were all employed by the Great Western Railway.

An application was made to the shipbuilding employers for an increase in the 3s 4d dirty money being paid on oil tanker repairs. The employers refused to pay more than time and a half for working inside oil tanks and limited to time actually spent working inside the tanks. Work on oil suction pumps and pipes would be at time-and-a-quarter but would not be paid when the tanks had been cleaned. Men working inside tanks on oil burning vessels would be paid time-and-a-quarter, also limited to the time actually worked inside the tanks. Although this was recognised as the dirtiest, heaviest, most dangerous and lowest paid work, the employers refused to pay any other allowances. The Admiralty endorsed the offer so that the officials felt unable to challenge it.

It was not until the end of the war that steps were taken to improve on the war time awards and a number of agreements were concluded for payment to members working in abnormal conditions.

In 1946 Liverpool agreement with the Mersey shipbuilding employers laid down that men working in water ballast tanks or double bottoms, or on work below the engine room and boiler room plates, on masts or funnels 15ft or more above the nearest deck, on uptakes and funnel casings and on the top of boilers, when hot, would receive two hours' extra money for a full day or night, and pro rata. Men using portable pneumatic or electric hammers would receive 8d a day extra, those engaged wholly on electric welding machines 6s to 27s above the rate and on oxy-acetylene welding or burning machines 2s 2d a day. Tinning the inside of pipes, coolers and condensers would be paid at time-and-a-quarter in the shop and time-and-a-half on ships. Work on heavy gauge sheet copper, large pipes and large vessels would get time-and-a-quarter.

Men working in oil-carrying tanks, hatches, oil pump rooms and tunnels on oil tankers would get time and a half, and on wrecks and stranded vessels 2s 6d a day extra. Time-and-a-half would be paid for work on oil fuel pipes.

Men working in spaces where whale oil had been carried would get an allowance of 50 per cent and in the factory and on pipe lines and pumps 25 per cent. Working inside tanks that had carried molasses on the previous voyage would be paid 25 per cent extra, and on any part of an oil tanker that had carried benzine or similar spirit 50 per cent extra. Working inside the smoke boxes of oil fired boilers would be paid $37\frac{1}{2}$ per cent extra and working inside crank cases of main diesel engines carried a 50 per cent extra allowance. Working inside lavatories on board troop ships carried 1s 6d a day extra. But men working inside the actual compartments where explosives were being loaded or unloaded received only an extra 1s 3d per half day.

In an agreement with Cammel Laird men working on submarines when batteries were being charged would receive 1s an hour extra with a maximum of 5s and after the batteries had been charged 6d a day. Working inside tanks carried an allowance of $12\frac{1}{2}$ per cent. Men

Coppersmiths making aluminium tankers, APV, Wandsworth, 1930s

fitting pipes in confined spaces on battleships, cruisers and destroyers would get 1s a day if on the work continuously and 6d a day if for only part of the time.

Even while the war was still in progress the Barrow branch was able to get an agreement with Vicker's on the training of coppersmith apprentices in the yard. In their first year apprentices would work in the workshops with a journeyman coppersmith or senior apprentice, braze small jobs on their own and receive general instruction with various types of brazing torches. Second year: work on submarines, on the dock or general outside work with a journeyman; on general outside work on his own on small jobs. Third year: in the workshop, general training on all types of welding; on the drawing board with a journeyman coppersmith, making templates from drawings and sketches. Fourth year: in the workshops, bending steel pipes of all dimensions along with a journeyman; general training on sheet copper work, brazing large pipes and bending small pipes on his own. Fifth year; general shop work and general outside work. Records were to be kept of the apprentices' progress and abilities and care taken to regulate their training on the lines laid down, as far as it was possible under war time conditions.

Immediately after the war an agreement was made with the railways on apprentice training. Apprenticeship started at the age of 15. They would spend six months on copper and iron pipe repair work; six months on sheet metal work; six months on new copper and iron pipe work; six months on welding and repairing element tubes; 18 months on iron and copper pipe repair work; six months on new copper and iron pipe work; 12 months on sheet metal work; 12 months on copper and iron pipe repair work. A record was to be kept of the actual time an apprenticeship spent in each department and it was considered that by the time he was 21 an apprentice would have had every opportunity of becoming a competent coppersmith.

But would there be work for apprentices after finishing their time in the post war world, or for many of the regular time-served members? This was one of the quesions that was fiercely debated as the war drew to a close. A number of branches reported that work was already being scaled down. They called for an end to dilution and demanded that all assistants and dilutee labour be declared redundant. Sub-contract work should be stopped until the main shops, and particularly the government establishments, had enough work.

This sparked off a general exchange on what should be done about assistants and dilutees in general, with the Society about equally divided. One section could not wait to get back to what they saw as the 'good old days' of before the war, when a coppersmith was a man who had served a five or seven year apprenticeship to the trade. They felt that the assistants had served their purpose in allowing the Society to keep some control over dilution. They now posed a threat. The assistants' section should be disbanded before they started taking the bread out of the mouths of real coppersmiths.

The others argued that disbanding the section would itself provide a threat as the Society would then have no control over the dilutees. A leading spokesman for this viewpoint was Harold Poole, who had been elected London secretary. He pointed out that many upgraded labourers and other dilutees had now had four or five years working with journeyman coppersmiths, they had experience and many had become skilled craftsmen. What would happen if they were turned out on the open market, carrying a chip on their shoulder against the Society that had turned them out? They would man non-union shops in competition with the Society Shops. If the Society would not have them within its ranks, other unions would and use them to get a foothold in the trade. It seems, however, that the policy adopted was 'when in doubt do nothing.'

Internal Changes

It was not until the middle of 1946 that the question again came up for discussion on the NEC. Harold Poole then warned that London alone had lost some 600 dilutees since the end of the war. Some, of course, would have gone back to their original trades. Some were drifting around and many had got jobs as coppersmiths in shops where there was no union organisation. A lot of sub-contract work was being done by these shops. Unless it was decided to widen the scope of the Society and bring in these people they would be a growing menace in the future, but he was afraid the Society had delayed too long.

He urged that all dilutees with experience should be made full members and that all shops employing dilutees and assistants or doing work of a kindred nature, should be organised by the Society.

Harold Poole continued to advocate the organisation of dilutees, particularly after he became General Secretary when H. Stansfield retired in June 1947 after 52 years as a member of the Society and 37 years in its most important office. At the 1950 ADM Poole supported a proposal to set up an auxiliary section that would give control over the semi-skilled, increase the membership and income and provide a pool of labour when needed.

This was turned down as was a proposal later that the assistants' grade be reintroduced in view of the inability of the Society to meet the widespread demand for labour, and the fear that this might lead to the loss of work to other trades.

He never gave up urging that the Society should stop trying to maintain its position as a small body of purely time-served craftsmen. At the October 1951 NEC he again called on the Society to expand as other unions had done by creating a section for people who were not and never would be coppersmiths and so would not be a threat to coppersmiths' jobs. But, although the Scottish district committee had added its voice to the call for dilution in order to allow the Society to keep work going to other trades, he was again defeated by the inflexibility of the rules.

He appealed at the ADM the following year for an ancillary section, pointing out that they were the only craft union without one. This time the question was referred to the NEC, who finally agreed to an ancillary section to include all workers connected with the trade, preparing parts or finishing articles made by trade members. The NEC also urged the enrolment of more apprentices to allow the Society to meet the demand for labour in the future.

At a time when stewards of various unions were forming combine committees and engaging in other forms of joint activity against the employers, the NEC stamped on modest requests from sections inside the Society for closer working. A call by the rail branches for regular rail meetings such as those operating among naval dockyard branches was turned down on the excuse that they could be called together if necessary, something altogether different from the closer working desired. Similarly, a request from Coventry and Cheltenham branches for meetings of branches with shops of the Hawker Siddeley group was ruled out as unnecessary.

Criticism of the way the Society was run had not completely died down during the war. The No. 6 district wanted delegate meetings during the war, as other unions did, complaining that major decisions were being taken without consulting members. There should be a means for members to express their views.

The General Secretary, H. Stansfield, replied that an emergency committee had been set up by the NEC to conduct the affairs of the Society 'during the present exigencies' because of the difficulties of calling together larger bodies like the full NEC or delegate conference. But the coppersmiths were not like the larger unions, they were one big family. He was in constant touch with branch secretaries, NEC members, the general treasurer and the auditors, trustees, shop delegates, etc. Their opinions were often asked on various matters and meetings were held in different parts of the country with representatives of the branches – rather like a daily delegate conference. He claimed that only half the branches had bothered to reply to a call for a delegate conference and the reported attendance of meetings of those which had replied was small.

When the No. 6 district committee refused to withdraw a circular sent out to branches it was disbanded but some time after branches in the district were allowed to set up a new committee.

The next year, the Portsmouth secretary, W. Tooes, complained, as so many others had done, about the committee of management being confined to London members. He also complained that the branches did not have enough contact with the national officers and that members did not get enough information.

Changes in the constitution to meet some of the criticisms were proposed by the NEC after Stansfield's retirement. The period of office of the General Secretary was to be three years, that of the President four years, the full time London and Scottish district secretaries three years and the NEC four years. In all cases retiring members would be eligible to seek re-election.

In future, as with the Scottish district secretary, candidates for the position of London secretary could be nominated by any free member of the Society but election would be by London members only.

District committees would no longer be obliged to meet 'at least quarterly', instead they should meet every six months, or more often if necessary.

But the most important change in the organisation was in the committee of management, which had so often come up for criticism, with members complaining that the London membership was, in effect, running the Society, and the then general secretary resisting any change. In future, the COM would consist of seven full free members of not less than five years continuous membership. But only three of them would reside in the London area; the other four would be elected by the rest of the membership at the national delegate conference from nominations sent in one month beforehand. Their period of office would be two years and they would be eligible for re-election.

But although this damped down criticism, it did not kill it completely. At the 1952 delegate conference the demand that the whole of the COM be elected from all parts of the country surfaced again. The General Secretary opposed it on the grounds that it would cost the Society an extra £400 a year. Even so the proposal was only defeated by 20 votes to 16. It was raised again in 1954 and was lost by 29 votes to 10.

Fermentation vessels for Whitbread's Brewery under construction at APV, Crawley

Criticisms of the undemocratic character of the Scottish district committee were also met with a new basis for elections. Committee members were to be elected annually at a meeting of branch delegates from all over Scotland on the basis of one delegate per 100 members elected at branch quarterly meetings.

In April 1949 it was proposed that a full time officer be elected for the North of England. He would double up as secretary of the Liverpool branch, which had become too big for a voluntary secretary to handle, but he would be responsible for the whole of the North. Nominations would be open to the whole of the Society with election by members of the Liverpool branch only, as with London and Scotland. The period of office was to be three years but could be terminated if the Liverpool branch membership fell below 450 from the then 600.

The Liverpool secretary, F. Bray, a real live wire, was elected. He had been made full time organiser for the North West on a two month trial basis at the end of 1947 and had been re-elected for a second term. During this period he had made a number of new members and re-opened Halifax branch, as well as a new branch in Preston, one at Crewe from members at the railway works, Rolls Royce and Kelvinators and another at Chester, where the fifty members all worked for de Havilland. He appears to have been not too fussy about insisting on only time served men and the 100 he enrolled at the Shell refinery in setting up the Ellesmere Port branch were said to have been pipe fitters rather than proper coppersmiths.

At the same time branches were formed at St Austell in Cornwall, Cardiff, and Kirkaldy where the members were mostly working on back boilers and cylinders. So although the membership did not extend greatly, the spread of organisation made the Society much more like a national union.

Bray sought to build on this, proposing a new branch at Ruabon, near Wrexham, based on a firm making generating plant for the Air Ministry, and another at Blackpool from members working at Hawker Siddley. His aim was to link up with existing branches and form a net-work throughout Lancashire and surrounding areas, which would make recruitment easier. Head office viewed this with caution. Members would be taken from the Liverpool branch for the new branches, perhaps reducing the membership below the level for a full time secretary, so they proposed that they remain in the Liverpool branch. In the end a new branch was formed at Ruabon but not at Blackpool.

The question of demarcation continued during the 1950s. The Barrow branch pinpointed the weakness of the coppersmiths in all demarcation disputes. Even when they were busy they had only 80 to 90 members in Barrow, against 400 to 500 plumbers and even more boilermarkers. So the employer gave in when the boilermakers or plumbers threatened to walk out in defence of their claim for certain jobs, as the employers could not afford to have the whole of the ship stopped. The coppersmiths did not matter. They were small, with no clout, and their work could be done by other trades who would be only too glad to have it. The only answer to the problem was amalgamation but the NEC always shied away from this.

Instead, meetings were held with rival unions. Guidelines were sometimes drawn up but none of them ever solved anything. In June 1950 the NEC met the plumbers' executive to settle the question yet again. The following year a new demarcation dispute broke out with these self-same plumbers, this time centred in Southampton, over who should work on pipes made of two new alloys, Yorkalbro and Yorkcunife – the first 74 per cent copper, 22 per cent aluminium and the rest zinc plus a little manganese; the latter 94 per cent copper, 5 per cent nickel and 1 per cent iron. Both worked like copper and would seem without question to be coppersmiths' work. The Southampton branch claimed them, pointing out that they were not really new, having been in use since 1921 but the cost had precluded their general use. Now they were being used on naval vessels and the plumbers were claiming pipes of these alloys as their work.

Another dimension of the demarcation serial was reported from Barrow where the branch had a dispute with the Heating and Domestic Engineers Union over pipework at Sellafield nuclear power station.

Amalgamation

Amalgamation proposals were voiced by one or two branches almost every year, but not in any strength. In 1950 the Chairman suggested that instead they should have a meeting of all unions covering the pipe trades to try and reach a common policy on work, wages and conditions. On the Secretary's suggestion this was left to the NEC and was quietly buried. In 1952 the coppersmiths had a membership of 5,550 plus 600 apprentices and had just had their 'best year ever', so they saw no need for amalgamation. In 1953 the initiative came from the sheet metal workers with proposals that would be 'for the benefit of all, especially in combatting the unskilled', only to be told that the coppersmiths were not interested in amalgamation. In 1954 the Chairman dismissed the usual amalgamation motion with the old cry that it would mean 'subjugation or submersion' and in announcing the motion lost by 33 votes to 3 declared 'this is the proudest moment of my life.'

Evaporation tube for distilling sea water being formed at Worsamm's marine coppersmiths, London

The following year the Society sent two delegates 'without mandate' to a conference on amalgamation, sponsored by the AEU, and replied to a letter from the plumbers for talks on amalgamation as the best way to solve demarcation problems with the retort that they would discuss demarcation but not amalgamation.

Finally, the financial situation brought a change in attitude. Although the position both of membership and funds was better than it had ever been, rising costs meant further increases in contributions. This would most likely lead to a further increase in arrears, already running at about £3,000 or 10s per member.

The negotiations with the sheet metal works, once they had started, were also no doubt subject to additional pressure as a result of the coppersmiths' participation in the engineering and shipbuilding strike of May 1957 which put the balance of income and expenditure for that year £5,596 3s 6d in the red. To pay for this the National Delegate Meeting had put a £2 'dispute levy' on the membership which was not very well received and had to be spread over two years. The coppersmiths had maintained the practice of the early craft unions of calling for levies to meet contingencies that arose and always some dissatisfaction was expressed.

An invitation had been received from the sheet metal workers in May 1956 for a detailed

Members working on a statue of St Christopher, in beaten copper, made from the flat, erected in the reception hall, Tilbury docks

discussion on amalgamation proposals. The increasing difficulty of keeping a small society in the black and the fact that more and more vital decisions were being taken by the wider trade union movement in which the Society's voice was little above a whisper, were no doubt responsible for this invitation receiving a different response from those of the past. The National Delegate Conference decided that the proposals should be given consideration and that a number of delegates be sent to talk with the sheet metal workers.

It was not until the following year that the Chairman, Stan Pope, gave a report back on the progress of the talks. He told the membership that if they were prepared to continue paying higher contributions they could remain independent and retain their own identity, but the

Society had an obligation to members and they did not want, in eight to ten months' time, to find they did not have the money to meet these obligations.

If they amalgamated on the lines that had been proposed at the joint meetings the coppersmiths would retain their identity in the name of the amalgamated union. It was envisaged that in the early stages there would be little or no interchange of members between one shop and another, as members would generally seek employment in shops best suited to their qualifications and abilities, but it was hoped that eventually there would be common employment.

Branches and branch secretaries would retain their own identity for a considerable period and full time officers and employees would keep their positions for at least eight years. Coppersmiths would also be guaranteed places on the national executive committee of the amalgamated union. Demarcation issues between the coppersmiths and other unions would continue to be handled by officials of the old coppersmiths' society.

The fact that, as the sheet metal workers had lower contributions and higher benefits than the coppersmiths, Society members would be better off in that respect, no doubt helped members to support amalgamation. The General Secretary, Harold Poole, pointed out that despite the difference in the strength of the two societies, the coppersmiths were still able to negotiate with a strong hand, but warned that in ten years' time the financial position might force them to seek shelter under the cover of any union that would take them.

The executive committee decided by ten votes to one to recommend amalgamation and the decision was later endorsed by the national delegate meeting at Morecambe in June 1958. But there was still a lot of discussion before the merger proposals were sewn up. Harold Poole had been largely responsible for pushing the amalgamation through, together with the Chairman, Stan Pope, a lay member still working at the bench, and he stumped the country speaking in favour of amalgamation. A sub-committee of the two executives found few snags in working out a form of merger suitable to both and this was presented to members in a national ballot of all members. The result, 2,582 votes in favour and 728 against, was announced at the final meeting of the coppersmiths' executive at the Great Northern Hotel, Kings Cross, London on 29 June 1959. The coppersmiths brought 6,000 members and £60,000 into the amalgamated union, less than half the per capita funding provided by the sheet metal workers who contributed 43,000 members and £950,000 to the coffers of the joint union. The papers of amalgamation were signed the same day. The amalgamation came into force on 1 July 1959 and the coppersmiths ceased to exist as a separate organisation, becoming part of the National Union of Sheet Metal Workers and Coppersmiths.

1. *McDouall's Chartist Journal and Trades' Advocate*, 18 September 1841.
2. *Northern Star*, 8 February 1841.
3. Goldsmith's Library, University of London.
4. *Northern Star*, 14 August 1841. Place Collection Vol. 53, which gives wages of apprentices as between 7s and 12s a week.
5. *Guiness Times*, Spring 1948.
6. *DCL Gazette*, April 1974.

The main source of information for this chapter, for the earlier years, came from the books and balance sheets of the old London Society of Coppersmiths and for the later years from the branch secretaries' and full-time officials' reports of the National Society of Coppersmiths.

CHAPTER TEN

The Heating and Domestic Engineers

The National Union of Heating and Domestic Engineers dated its history back to the Amalgamated Stove, Grate and Kitchen Range Fitters Protection Society, established on 25 July 1872 in Rotherham.

But in fact, like the other main unions in this history, the Heating and Domestic was a product of a number of amalgamations and take-overs of kindred trades and an equal, or even stronger, element in its make-up was the whitesmiths, whose origins go back much further, to the beginnings of trade unionism in Britain. The stove makers themselves can trace their history back to 1828 if not earlier. Moreover, the two streams were very much intermingled, long before they finally came together in the Heating and Domestic Engineers.

The earliest whitesmiths' society we have been able to discover was the Benevolent Institution of White-smiths, formed in 1807 in a pub off Piccadilly, London – the Coach and Horses in Air Street. The address of its club house when it registered on 7 April 1808 was the Anchor Inn, Chancery Lane. In 1811 it was in the unusual position of having two club houses,[1] the Red Lion, Cross Lane, Long Acre and the Cock, Bow Lane, Cheapside; it was probably already growing too fast to be accommodated in one pub. It later moved back to Chancery Lane, to the Blue Posts which apparently was able to accommodate the then much bigger membership, when its secretary was J. Johnson.

Benevolent Institution

OF

WHITE-SMITHS,

Held at the Houses of

Mrs. SIMMONDS,

THE SIGN OF THE

RED-LION, CROSS-LANE,

Long-Acre,

AND

Mr. BAVERSTOCK,

THE SIGN OF THE

COCK, BOW-LANE,

CHEAPSIDE.

London :

PRINTED BY W. GLINDON, RUPERT-STREET, HAYMARKET.

1811.

The 1825 book of 'rules, orders and regulations'[2] gives as its aims:

> to prevent imposition as much as possible and to procure a fund for the support of each other when out of employ, and to furnish each other with employment, to support the infirm and aged, to decently bury members and their wives and to afford that useful information, by agreeable conversation and useful books, drawings, models and experiments, to make improvements in our trade, and to regulate it.

Although many of the rules were the same as those of the 1798 tin plate workers, the whitesmiths included many novel features. The Society was ruled by a secretary and committee of eleven to fifteen who chose the chairman from among their number. But it was split into divisions, based on areas of residence, of not more than 100 members, the last to be formed to be allowed to go up to 150 before dividing. The divisions met at the same club house on different evenings. Each division was governed by a president and two stewards chosen by nomination from the roll each quarterly night 'by and for the members of the division.'

Whatever the number of divisions, the whole was considered one Society, meeting at the same house, governed by the same rules, using the same books, etc. No division on its own had the power to alter the rules 'or remove the Society without the consent and approbation of the majority as a whole; nor to transact any business but what relates to their own division.' General questions were to be decided at specially-called meetings of the divisions, not by general meetings of the whole Society.

The president of each division, in addition to attending all meetings of his own division, had to visit every meeting of all other divisions, taking part as a member of the committee.

The secretary was common to the whole institution. He was elected by ballot for twelve months and could be removed by a vote of three-quarters of the members assembled in divisions and was allowed to appoint an assistant, if required. His duties included attending all meetings and reporting on the position of the Institution's stock, sending out notices and other communications. He was responsible for the transfer of bonds from one trustee to another and had to produce an annual statement of accounts, copies of which were supplied to members, price ld. All this for a salary of 3d per quarter per member, plus extras for various activities, such as ld for every member he summoned to meetings and 6d a week for paying unemployment benefit on Saturday nights.

Half the committee had to retire each quarter and was replaced by others next on the roll. The whole of the committee had to attend every meeting of all the divisions.

Two 'enquiring stewards' were chosen each quarter by nomination from each division. They had to examine the call book and to see that those out of employ signed their names correctly, together with other particulars and to make enquiries if necessary. One of them had to sign the book every day or be fined. Other members were chosen by ballot as stock-holders, with no two stock-holders holding more than £50.

The duties carried out by the various officers is an indication of the vast amount of work and responsibility required of ordinary working men after long hours of work, in the service of their trade society, receiving little or no remuneration and liable to fines if they ran counter to the rules in any way.

The remuneration included not more than one pot of beer for every officer on all occasions of business and officials were not allowed to 'smoak' during business – surely one of the first anti-smoking rules in the trade union movement.

Contributions were ls 6d a month. The main benefit was unemployment pay of 10s a week for four weeks after which members must work six clear days before becoming entitled to a second benefit. There was a superannuation benefit, the usual death benefit and separate sickness and unemployment funds. Like most trade societies the whitesmiths not only had compassion for members in difficulties, they were also jealous of the good name of their society. The rules laid down that an open subscription would be held for members under severe affliction to save them going on the parish. Others of three years standing suffering from a disease so that they would be unable ever to get their livelihood from the trade could be considered superannuated and allowed 2s 6d a week 'during the existence of his calamity.' It was also laid down that 'every member shall ENDEAVOUR by *active exertion* to promote the welfare and happiness of each other in every way possible and that we do not exact a footing of each other.'

Members became free and entitled to all benefits after twelve months, but new members could become free immediately by paying an extra sum 'that the committee deemed equivalent.'

Each division had the usual box with four separate locks and keys but in addition the whitesmiths had a small wrought iron fireproof box 'with a patent lock and key' to contain all bonds, notes and other valuable property of the Institution, which was kept inside one of the main boxes. The boxes were held by the landlord, or landlady, of the club house, who had to deposit £100 as surety with the Clerk of the Peace.

No one was admitted as a member unless 'well affected to His Majesty and the British Constitution.'

One of the most interesting sections of the rule book is that concerning the library of the Institution. It is, I think, worth quoting in full:

> For the better promoting useful knowledge there shall be a librarian and assistant chosen from each division, the assistant to take the place of the former, and a fresh one chosen every quarterly night.
>
> Duty – they shall attend every Monday, Tuesday, Thursday or Saturday at 8 o'clock and read in their turn, Lectures, with practical experiments on Mechanics, Hydraulics, Pneumatics, Chemistry, etc. that will be conducive to instruction, and devise improvements in trade; they shall keep a catalogue of all drawings, models, books, etc. to be lent to free members on good security for one month: any member keeping any thing longer, shall forfeit sixpence, should they be soiled or injured, the damage to be made good by the member that borrowed them, or he shall be fined double the amount.
>
> And for the encouragement of industry, there shall be annually a premium, or medal, given to him that makes the best drawing, model, or reads the best lecture, which must be delivered in writing and read to the members.
>
> The medal to be voted by ballot of the members who subscribe and to be given on the 23 November; every member shall subscribe twopence on entering the room, for the purchase of books, drawings, models, etc. for philosophical experiments, and elementary schools for teaching drawing, arithmetic, geometry, etc.

The Institution consisted of whitesmiths who had served a legal apprenticeship, who had arrived at the age of maturity, 21, and who were not more than 50 when applying. They were engaged in manufacturing stoves, fenders, jacks, locks, tools, machines, engines, scale-beams, springs, bell-hanging and as house-smiths, who had served not less than seven years to the trade, in the capacity of fireman, viceman or hammerman.

The 1828 rule book mentions five divisions which would indicate that they had over 500 members at that time.

The Society was very active in the early struggles of the London trades. This seems to have been in no small measure due to its energetic secretary, John Johnson who, in 1816, 'deeply impressed' at the distress among smiths, took the initiative in calling together all sections of the craft and kindred trades, including his own whitesmiths and the stove-smiths, to see what could be done to relieve the hardship among fellow tradesmen. He was appointed secretary of the organisation they formed, the United Brethren Benefit Society of Smiths,[3] a benevolent organisation taking in all men working in the trade who were 'sound in wind and limb and well affected to His Majesty and the British Constitution.'

A report in 1812 declared that none of the organised whitesmiths of London earned less than 30s a week and those on high-class work earned a great deal more.[4] Activities continued to improve the conditions of the members. A later Union chairman[5] claimed that there were 4,000 smiths 'in union' when, in 1836 they formed an important element of the joint committee of London mechanics that carried out the big, eight month-long strike costing £5,000 which achieved the 10-hour day – that was 60 hours instead of 63 hours a week – and overtime rates. Some eight years later they took part in further action that brought hours down to $58\frac{1}{2}$ a week.

In 1812 Johnson and his Society took a prominent part in the campaign of the trades throughout the country to retain the apprenticeship regulations. He was particularly interested in working-class education and was one of the artisan leaders serving on the committee of the London Mechanics' Institution.[6] With other trades union leaders connected with that body he helped initiate the trades unions' struggle for the repeal of the Combinations Acts in 1824. The whitesmiths, under his leadership, supported the nation-wide trade union movement of Robert Owen, the Grand National Consolidated Trades Union, in 1836. They contributed both to the fund for the victims of the great lockout of trade unionists in Derby during the struggle for union recognition and to that for the Tolpuddle Martyrs, in the great demonstration for whose release they formed one of the more colourful contingents.[7] The Society also had a representative on the editorial committee of the 1838 trade union newspaper, *The Operative*.[8]

In August 1830 Thomas Matthews of the Derby Smiths' Union met smiths, moulders and fender makers at the George and Dragon, Nottingham[9] to set up a district committee of one of the earliest attempts to form a national organisation of all unions, John Doherty's National Association for the Protection of Labour. Matthews called for unity among the working class, saying 'dissentions in the trade have proved destructive to the working classes and given victory to the avaricious taskmasters.' In 1831 the Manchester Whitesmiths subscribed to the Association and the Derby and Nottingham smiths also supported it. In 1868 the Manchester whitesmiths were represented on the Manchester and Salford Trades Council.

They all seem to have been branches of the United Order of Iron Smiths, Engineers and Mechanics, formed in January 1822 at the Royal Oak Inn, Derby, and later known as the Old Derby Smiths. It was believed to have been a federation or amalgamation, largely of whitesmiths, covering most of the country and was said to have been 'fairly powerful at one time.'[10]

It may have been the same organisation that in July 1835 was known as the Associated Fraternity of Iron Forgers and later referred to as the Old Smiths. Its governing branch was then Manchester and it had 32 branches with 722 members.

The organisation known as the National Associated Smiths or alternatively as the National Associated Friendly Smiths, also with its governing branch in Manchester, could well have been the same organisation with a change of name. By 1840 it had 53 branches with 1,582 members.

It was then part of what was intended as a permanent federation comprised of smiths, millwrights, engineers, moulders and machine builders, mainly located in the Midlands and the North West. The secretary of the smiths, Alexander Hutchinson, was editor of the federation paper, *The Trades Journal*. When 'the Five Trades of Mechanism[12] were urged to develop their federation into a solid amalgamation and form a single union of all the engineering trades, the smiths, as a national body, remained outside, afraid of losing their identity as a small part of a big organisation. But when the amalgamation took place in 1851 to form the Amalgamated Society of Engineers, some branches of Smiths did join and this caused a break-up of the organisation.

The Old Derby Union was thought to have died, as a national organisation, in the 1860s – but it was never completely dissolved. Leamington branch, at least, survived and perhaps others, certainly there were members and at least a memory of organisation to provide a basis for a number of local unions of smiths and fitters, mainly centred on the stove and grate trade, during the revival of trade unionism around the 1870s.

Many of the rules of the 1822 organisation were almost identical in wording with those of the London Benevolent Institution of White-smiths of London of 1808. But an important addition provided that tramps from other societies of smiths would be relieved, providing they had proper credentials or a certificate, when they would be given supper, one pint of beer, one night's lodging and one penny for every mile they had travelled since being relieved. No doubt other smiths' unions reciprocated.

By 1861, when the census reported 9,584 whitesmiths in the country, the organisation was known as the United Order of Smiths, with some fifty branches listed in the National Trade Union directory. Liverpool was then the seat of government of the union and the fortnightly meeting place of the governing body, the Board of Directors. The General Secretary was then Samuel Johnson.

The 1878 rule book of the United Order of Smiths[13] was the result of a rules revision meeting at Bedford, consisting of delegates elected by their lodges. It indicated that the Order was re-formed in 1874, but was originally formed in 1822 under another name. Its registered office was then in Farringdon Road, London. Its general corresponding secretary was Henry Whitehead, its chairman, known as the Grand Master, was R. Clayton and its Vice-Grand Master R. Martin. It operated a system whereby the governing branch of the Order was decided every three years by a majority of all members, the governing branch being allowed to nominate itself for another term of office. The board of directors issued two voting papers to each lodge. These were returned to the board which kept one and sent the other to a town already nominated by delegate conference, which counted the votes and announced the result to all lodges. If any lodge was unable to continue as the governing lodge due to a decrease in membership or other cause, it made known its position to the Society and any other lodge was allowed to offer to take over.

The Society was governed by a board of ten directors elected by branches within a fifteen mile radius of the governing branch. These elected their grand master and vice-grand master and chose a suitable person to be secretary to the board and general corresponding secretary to the Society. He received 15s a week for his services.

The board of directors made an equalisation of funds throughout the Society every twelve months. Those lodges having more than the average funds, according to the number of members, forwarded the balance to the board and they, after deducting monies due to the board, sent the balance to those branches with lower than average funds.

All healthy persons of good moral character between the ages of 19 and 45, capable of earning a living at any of the following trades: engineer, fitter and turner, millwright, smith, whitesmith, gas fitter, brass founder, bell-hanger, grate and range fitter and frame smith was elegible for membership, providing they were receiving the average wage for the district.

Each quarter a door keeper was elected 'to keep out strangers', a book and a money steward, and a marshal-man to fetch any refreshment required, 'but it is better if no beer or spirits are brought in during lodge hours.' It was also laid down that the Society was not responsible for any money owed by members to the landlord.

Any member reading newspapers or books – 'except they are concerned with the Order' – or introducing political or other controversy during lodge hours, was liable to a fine of 6d.

A rule also recorded that the Order repudiated the principle of demanding the payment of footings from members entering strange shops and urged that shops and towns should take steps to have it abolished.

Benefits included unemployment pay of ls 8d a day for 10 weeks and ls 4d a day for eight weeks. Members having an accident or affliction so that they were permanently unable to work would receive a grant of £50 and the secretary was empowered to put on a ls levy to raise the money.

Any member who had been out of work for one week could, with the consent of the lodge officers, go on travel, having 'paid all demands on him.' He was furnished with a travelling card or certificate and received a 'donation' at the different lodges he passed through and in addition was entitled to one to three beds in every lodge house, depending on the size of the town and amount of work, and one for Sunday if required. The lodge secretary was responsible for arranging beds in the lodge house or elsewhere and the lodge had to be satisfied that they were clean and suitable. Non-free members were also eligible providing they were clear on the books. All travellers were informed of the Society pass-word which was changed every three months and issued in the monthly report.

Other rules gave the directors the responsibility of issuing every lodge with printed stationery. Another cautioned lodges that they were not allowed to expend funds on the purchase of regalia – perhaps a hang-over from the days of the 1830s when unions did away with initiation ceremonies following prosecution of the Tolpuddle Martyrs for administering unlawful oaths.

Under 'the rotating system' the governing branch of the Order moved from Farringdon Road to the Sawyers' Arms in Marylebone, from there to the Rockingham Arms, Hosier Lane in the City of London, then in 1878 to the Globe Hotel, Reading and in 1880 to West Derby, Liverpool, where it seems to have remained.

From March 1881 the name of the Society was changed to the Liverpool Order of Whitesmiths and Smiths in General, and its secretary was John Skimming. Members who had been out of work for fourteen days and wanted to go on travel had to make an application to the secretary who called a committee to discuss the case. The Society deprecated strikes but if a dispute did occur and a number of members were thrown out of work, a report of the case had to be forwarded to the secretary who called a committee together to decide if the men were entitled to support. The committee was also called if any lodge or society of Smiths applied to join the Society. No movement for the regulation of wages or hours should, under any circumstances, take place without the sanction of the executive committee.

In July 1889 the name was changed to the Liverpool Whitesmiths' Association,[15] with John Keenan as secretary, meeting at the Oddfellows Hall and with a new rule banning anyone who kept a public or beer house from becoming secretary. One of the secretary's duties was to attend to the vacant book and state therein when and where men were wanted. The money and book stewards were both taken from the roll and remained in office one month, the one collected the money on contribution nights and the other entered it in the books. No member was allowed to hold office for more than twelve months and was not eligible for re-election until after another twelve months.

In December 1890 the Association became part of the Amalgamated Society of Whitesmith[16] which in 1891 added Locksmiths, Bell-hangers, Domestic Engineers, Art Metal Workers and General Iron Fitters to its title, changed yet again in 1894 to General Iron and

Pipe Fitters and finally in 1904 to Amalgamated Society of Whitesmiths, Domestic Engineers and General Pipe Fitters.

In addition to the usual objectives, the Amalgamation added 'to assist other trade societies having their objects the promotion of the interests of workmen.'

The supreme authority of the Society was the triennial conference of delegates, one from branches with under sixty members and two from those with over 100, while branches with less than forty members were grouped together by the NEC. Conferences were not to be held in the same town twice running. As late as 1894 the locality of the seat of government was decided by election every three years. The executive committee was elected by and from the district where the seat of government was located. There was still, too, an annual equalisation of funds. The General Secretary came up for election every three years and the full list of candidates for the position had to be read out at each branch meeting prior to elections. Branches nominating had to be convinced that their nominees had a thorough knowledge of the working of the Amalgamation and were competent to correspond with branches and give information on any subject in connection with Amalgamation business – all very important when many working men were illiterate. A number of minor branch positions were filled from the roll of members and any who refused office were fined.

Any group of over seven members wishing to set up a branch had to apply to the nearest branch secretary, giving their age and how long they had been in the Trade. Members moving to districts where there was no branch had a responsibility to form one.

The EC was specifically given permission, by rule, to put levies on the membership for the purpose of setting up a benevolent fund to help other unions.

The Amalgamation continued to be very craft conscious. The secretary ruled that although a member who 'went over to work as an ordinary smith could continue to keep his position as a member of the Society', they would not take into membership an ordinary smith.

Members on travel must call on a local branch secretary at least once in two days or would lose those days' benefit. If more than five miles from home he was entitled to a 'donation' and a bed, the number of beds available at the club house being recorded in the Quarterly Report. Where it was more than eighteen miles to the next branch a traveller was allowed one day's 'donation' and 2s for a bed, in advance, and where more than 36 miles two days' 'donation' and bed allowance with an extra 'donation' and bed allowance for every additional eighteen miles. Members travelling through towns with no branch had to return their card and remittance to a town specified by the member. Members staying in a town with a branch for more than one day had to sign the vacant book and branch officers had the power to detain any travelling member for a short time if they thought there was a prospect of obtaining employment.

The rule book branded piece-work as 'one of the greatest evils' and any member asking for or accepting piece-work in a shop where it did not exist was fined 20s for the first offence and if he persisted he would be expelled. Where piece-work operated it had to be additional to the proper rate and the balance must be paid through the firm's pay office and not by a piece-master. Fire-iron makers, however, usually worked piece-work, and received 33s for 53 hours where the general minimum was 30s for 54 hours.

The amalgamation membership was only around 85 but by 1892 it had risen to 169, going up to 226 in 1898. A branch was formed in Manchester almost immediately after the amalgamation and in Leeds and Bradford early in 1892. One of the aims of the latter branch was to stop the operation of a team system with a large number of boys employed on repetition work. There had been several attempts to organise a branch in Bradford before this but all had been short lived except for one in 1865 which had lasted about a year. Some 45 men joined in

1892 although it was said there must be hundreds of men eligible in the town, as well as surrounding towns such as Halifax and Huddersfield where there was no organisation. Leeds had 201 members. There was said to be also eight branches in the Midlands.

There were similar societies in other parts of the country. A General Union of Smiths, Bell-hangers and Gas Fitters was formed in Bristol in 1872. Its position in the development of the Amalgamation is vague but a rule concerning wage increases is of interest.

> Any group who want an increase in privileges must apply to the secretary who will put the case before the committee. If agreed the group must choose the best time within the next six months to give the employer three months notice. The Union cannot allow any advance in privileges if the group have had an advance within six months or if other groups are engaged in trying to get an advance. The Union will be prepared to arbitrate with an employer.

The flurry of organisation among whitesmiths generally continued in the final decades of the nineteenth century. The Newcastle-upon-Tyne and District Operative Whitesmiths and Heating Engineers[17] was formed in July 1898 with 69 members. It was open to whitesmiths, hot water and steam heating and ventilating engineers, bell-hangers, locksmiths and blacksmiths employed in whitesmiths' shops. Its objects were to act as a trade defence society, to settle any disputes between the employers and the Society or between the Society and other trades to regulate relations between employers and workmen and to provide burial for members 'and their lawful wives'.

Applicants for membership must have served five years' apprenticeship to the trade, be not less than 21 years of age and of good moral character.

The Society had an organisation of shop and workers' delegates whose duties included keeping the Society's officials fully informed of all proposed or actual alteration of hours, wages or conditions of work likely to be injurious to members. They were also to examine all members' cards periodically and report those in arrears; endeavour to obtain employment for members when vacancies occurred and invite any qualified member coming to work in the shop to join the Society. They were not to use threats or intimidating remarks but if any persistently refused to join the whole matter must be reported to the Society. They also had to 'glean all information possible in cases of dispute between members or any member and a foreman' and lay it before the EC when the case was investigated.

The Society was deregistered in 1904 and seems to have entered into some relationship with the Liverpool-based Amalgamation while retaining its autonomy.

In London the Amalgamated Society of General Smiths, Fitters, Bell-hangers and Whitesmiths[18] was re-formed in 1891, removing 'Amalgamated' from its title. Its clubhouse was the Black Lion Inn, Church Street, Chelsea and its secretary Abraham Whitehouse.

Two branches of the earlier society were still in existence when the new body was formed and soon they had seven branches all in London, including Lambeth, Vauxhall, Kings Cross, Kensington and Chelsea.

A preface to the rulebook declared that the committee had 'endeavoured to consider as closely as possible the welfare of the members, at the same time not losing sight of the employers' interests.' Their aim was to secure good workmanship in all branches with a fair remuneration. They pointed out that

> forming a register of men wanting employment and employers wanting men will be found useful to all concerned. The settlement of a standard rate of wages can also be found to be beneficial, especially to employers making contracts, as it will do away with unfair competition by underpaid and inferior workmen.

It went on to assure employers that

> although the Society is prepared to back up every member in securing his just rights, it will discourage anything in the shape of boasting or unfair dealing towards employers.

The re-formed Society started out with seventy members at the end of 1891 and by 1895 had climbed to 272. It catered for whitesmiths, blacksmiths, stove and range makers, gas, steam, hot and cold water fitters (except when done in lead) and all general iron workers between the ages of 21 and 45 years and receiving the current district rate of wages.

Two books were kept in the branch house, a call book and an application book. Every unemployed member had to sign the application book every day, except Sunday, until he found employment. But any unemployed member could visit any branch house and take a job off that branch's book. If a London firm sent a man to work in the country he had to be paid ls a day, plus lodging allowance, and any man going for less would be fined.

An agreement with the Central Association of Master Builders of London for 1892 fixed wages at 9d an hour and a 50 hour week, starting at 6.30 in summer and 7.30 in winter. An out-of-shop allowance of 6d a day was paid for any distance over six miles, exclusive of travelling expenses, time occupied in travelling and lodging money. Overtime rates were time-and-a-quarter from leaving time until 8pm. Time-and-a-half from 8pm till 10pm and double time after 10pm, after 4pm on Saturdays and all day on Sundays, Christmas Day and Good Friday. No overtime was paid on a weekday until a full day had been made up, except for time lost through bad weather.

The agreement laid down that employers should provide, 'where practical and reasonable', a suitable place at the works for workers to have their meals, with a labourer to assist in preparing this.

The acceptable rate for ironmongers' work was $8\frac{1}{2}$d an hour as they paid all travelling time and allowed extras for certain jobs which builders did not. Members working in jobbing shops also earned more than those working for builders, for the same number of hours − both builders and ironmongers provided tools.

In 1892 the secretary reported that one of the main problems was sweating, especially in big shops where piece-mastering operated, with the work let out to one individual who employed his own men at any price, promising to pay the balance at the end of the job, but dismissing them before the job was finished without honouring his debt.

The secretary also complained of the difficulty of organising with the ASE and the plumbers both claiming this class of work.

The Society was affiliated to both the Building Trades Federation and the London Trades Council. Around 1900 the title was changed to the Society of General Smiths, Fitters, Bell-hangers and Whitesmiths, dropping the word 'General' in 1909.[19]

The whitesmiths considered themselves to be the original stock from which all general engineers developed and the Old Derby Union claimed to be the pioneering union in the engineering trade. They worked in cold metal generally not thicker than $\frac{3}{8}$ inch and could and did both plumbers' and engineers' work. A competent whitesmith could take a piece of metal in the rough and forge, file, dress and finish it, turning out the article ready for sale. They took over pipe fitting, heating and ventilating work, ornamental iron work for lift enclosures and screens for hot water coils. Some stove and grate societies were almost all whitesmiths. This meant inevitably that there were demarcation clashes with plumbers and engineers and the London whitesmiths tried to get a joint committee set up by the Trades Council to deal with these problems but the plumbers refused to take part.

Recruitment for the London whitesmith's societies was from apprentices, learners and a few from journeymen from country towns. Apprenticeship in the 1890s was five to seven years, with some paying a premium of £20 to learn the trade. Learners had no agreements and were usually the sons of journeymen, working either under the supervision of foremen or as mates to smiths and fitters. Opportunities to 'learn by doing' enabled mates to become competent workmen, but those who did not show aptitude were unlikely to advance beyond the status of labourer. In London smiths and fitters usually stuck to their own section of the trade whereas in the country one man did everything.

At the turn of the century the work was hard and heavy, particularly for hot water fitters who mostly worked on wrought iron pipes with few tools. There were no pipe cutters, all wrought iron pipes were filed round and then broken. Thread screwing was all done by solid round dies and all pipes had to be filed so that the dies could get a start. The work lightened a bit when footprints came in, followed by stilsons and split dies.

Mounting boilers meant cutting holes in the boiler and mount with a cramp and ratchet operated drill which replaced the hammer and chisel, then $\frac{5}{8}$ inch holes were tapped by hand. Bending was done by heating the pipe at a portable hearth and took about four heats to get a square bend. If there was no outside work men were put on doors for bakers' ovens with the holes for hinges and catches drilled with cramp and ratchet.

One big whitesmithing firm in Liverpool employed up to sixty smiths in the shop and ten on outside work, largely on shipping – merchant ships, cruise liners, warships and submarines – on heavy cooking equipment – ranges, steam ovens, heavy duty gallies, big fish fryers – as well as hot presses, water condensers, windchutes and winches. They operated before the First World War and throughout the inter-war period, fitting out train kitchens and made all the aluminium cooking equipment for the R101 airship. But in the later period much of the work was done in stainless steel. They made cooking equipment for hotels and institutions and laundry equipment. Another important section of their work was making, fixing and repairing fire grates and domestic back boilers.

The Fitters' Unions

Of the other stream making up the Heating and Domestic Engineers, the stove and grate makers, the earliest organisation we have been able to find was instituted in June 1828. It was known as the Friendly Society of Stove Makers and Smiths and we first hear of it in 1834 when it joined the short-lived Grand National Consolidated Trade Union. In that year, too, a large section of the membership in London took part in a big strike 'on account of the grievous screw-driving of some wholesale dealers in Upper Thames Street.' According to a contemporary account in a trade union paper.[21]

> These taskmasters have had the audacity to propose a reduction of 5s upon a job of 13s 6d. The men instantly refused to work at this low rate, which was bringing them to starvation point, for this job cost them three days' work and besides they have to employ another mechanic to help them in part and pay him out of the sum mentioned. They saw this was merely the commencement of a general encroachment on the trade and if they did not strike, in time all other masters would follow. The Union of the trade has supported the strikers and now they want to caution their fellow workmen against taking work in any of these three workshops which have attempted to undermine their interests.

In 1854 the Society's club house was the Carlisle Arms, Queen's Street, Soho[22] where it still was in 1861. The secretary was then James Challoner. Contributions were ls 6d a month, 6d of it for superannuation.

Each quarterly night the secretary called the roll for men to serve for three months as president and stewards. Any man refusing to stand was fined ls. The trustees, treasurer, secretary and committee of seven were elected annually.

The secretary was to be a person not a member of the Society and remained in office for twelve months, renewable at the pleasure of the Society. His duties were extensive. He had to enter every member's name and residence, post the books, balance the accounts, record bills of expenditure for the month, report on what members were likely to be excluded, post up in the club room a statement of the Society's funds; keep a faithful account of what monies were received, what was expended and on what account; record the minutes of the Society; summon committee meetings, attend all meetings; send letters and notices relative to the Society; summon all members in arrears. He was liable to a fine of 5s if he failed to attend a meeting, was fined ls if half-an-hour late and 5s if one hour late, 'If found screening any member from paying his fines, he shall pay them himself and be fined ls for the offence.'

Out-of-work pay was 10s a week for six weeks, providing there was £30 in the funds and 8s if only £20. A second claim could not be made until the member had worked for three consecutive weeks and only twelve weeks could be claimed in any twelve months. Members leaving work unfinished would be denied all benefits.

Applicants for membership had to be proposed and seconded by two members who knew the applicant's 'character and utilities' and who had to attend in person, having deposited a 2s 6d bond with the Society.

The 1872 ancestor of the H and D, the Amalgamated Stove Grate and Kitchen Range Fitters Protection Society,[23] was said to have immediately set to work to build up again what sections it could find of the Old Derby Union. Most of the fitters' organisations claimed relationship with the old union whose prestige stretched down to the Midlands. The new society helped to give life to moribund societies or formed new ones. Its main success was the Amalgamated Society of Kitchen Range and Stove Grate Smiths and Fitters formed in Nottingham in June as a branch of the Rotherham Society. Together they were responsible for the formation of new branches in Derby, Birmingham and Sheffield. Trade unions were still very fluid at this period. There was not a lot of central control, particularly where governing branches moved around every few years. Branches formed their own associations, changing them when it suited their purpose. Organisation ebbed and flowed. Local organisations were formed during an upsurge of feeling around a strike, a wages application, or some other issue, died down and were resuscitated again in times of need, linking up with others, perhaps, engaged in the same struggle.

The Rotherham fitters' society started with 31 members and at first confined its activities to trade protection, but in 1879 its coverage was extended to include unemployment, accident and funeral benefits. It provided 10s a week for ten weeks, followed by 8s a week for a further ten weeks for members out of work. The funeral benefit was provided by a special contribution of ls 9d a year on top of the basic 6d a week contributions. Dispute benefit was at the discretion of the EC.

While membership in Rotherham climbed only slowly membership of the Society as a whole soared for a time, but that did not last long and by 1880 there were members in only three towns, Rotherham, Nottingham and Derby. In 1886, when membership was down to only 78, the headquarters was moved to Nottingham, which thereafter remained as the governing branch, with R. Anderson as General Secretary. After this membership grew again and by

1890 there were 346 members.

Further confusion to the already complicated scene was provided when a man named Hayden Sanders arrived in Rotherham from Walsall on a 'missionary' visit for the Knights of Labour – an all-purpose industrial and political union of all trades which had its origins and main basis in the United States, and which we saw organising the Lye iron plate workers. Many stove and grate workers were said to have joined and apparently a Knights of Labour local was formed in the town which got the men a 10 per cent rise in wages and a reduction in hours of work from 57 to 54 a week. In 1890 there was a strike in Rotherham, the main seat of the stove and grate industry, and the workers sent for Sanders to help them but this time the Knights of Labour, then rather going into decline, refused support and the stove and grate men left and joined a new National Union of Stove and Grate Workers, formed by Sanders.

The new union, which was to remain outside and in conflict with the amalgamations that went to make up the H and D, was based in Rotherham but soon spread round the country, with branches in the main industrial areas – London, Birmingham, Manchester, Sheffield, Derby and many Northern towns. It took in everyone working in the industry.

Branch officials of the old unions were very bitter over Sanders' conduct, saying that in the early days he asked for and obtained their support in building up his union, promising that he would not take in the smiths and fitters but advise them to join their appropriate craft union. Instead, once he had got established in a factory, he used the numerical strength of his general union to operate a closed shop directed against members of the old craft unions, who were refused employment. He even called strikes against them.

In 1892 the Nottingham-based fitters' society began to recover and expanded its coverage, changing its name to the Amalgamated Society of Kitchen Range, Hot Water and General Fitters. It remained a craft union but did not have indentured apprentices. Applicants for membership were expected to have had five years' experience of the trade. But even this was not strictly adhered to and practical capability, as shown by an ability to earn a living at the trade, was generally regarded as sufficient.

Rules adopted at a special meeting held in Nottingham in March 1886 retained the principle of voting at three-yearly intervals on where the headquarters of the Society would be located, and also the annual equalisation of funds. Half the board of directors were to retire every half-year but were eligible for re-election 'if the lodge think proper.' The rules also made provision for a full-time secretary if an increase in the work of the Society made it advisable. All candidates would come up for election at a delegate conference and if there was no overall winner the two with the highest votes would be put to a ballot of members in the branches.

While it was considered that apprentices came out of their time at 21, they were allowed to work for 4s a week under the rate for the first six months after that date and for 2s under the rate for a further six months.

Should any lodge or society in the trades covered, 'who have books, box, cash or other effects' wish to join the Society they shall, if approved by the board of directors, 'bring and throw the same into the general fund of the Society', and shall stand on the books of the Society the same as they were on their own books and become conformable to the rules of the Society.

Travelling members were given a password and the rules repudiated footings and also prohibited the purchase of regalia by branches, which could be fined 20s for non-compliance. Anderson, the Nottingham secretary, was also secretary of the Amalgamation as a whole, with the clubhouse at the Rose Inn, Mount Street.

A branch of the fitters' amalgamation was formed in Sheffield in January 1890, although in 1861 a stove and grate fitters' union and two unions of whitesmiths, or white metal smiths as they were called, were operating in the city, as well as a branch of the United Order of Smiths and a fender makers' society. The secretary of this new Sheffield branch was C.W. Taylor. It had an initial 39 members but declined to only nine at one time due to the disruptive activities of Sanders' union, which led to 80 per cent of the men working at the trade in the city remaining non-union.

The Sheffield men were mainly on piece-work but prices varied from shop to shop and time to time. The secretary said they would have abolished piece-work if they had been strong enough as the employers reduced prices until only the quickest men could earn a decent living. With the formation of the Union in 1890 they got an increase in prices of 10 per cent without much trouble but the minimum rate was still only 30s for a 54-hour week. They complained of too many lads in the shops and were unable to enforce their new rule of one boy to three men and not more than three boys in any one shop.

The Union opposed moves for an amalgamation of all sections of the stove and grate trade, fearing absorption and that, being small, they would not get justice, quoting fitters in Sanders' union who complained that they were 'sat upon' by the moulders who formed the majority of the union.

The small branch of some twenty smiths and fitters in Derby also fought against amalgamation with the 200-strong local society of stove and grate workers – out of 350 men working at the trade in the town. As in other towns the excessive number of boys in the trade was said to be the greatest evil. In one shop there were more than fifty boys to only 25 men, with the boys kept on repetitive work. Organisation was said to be difficult as work was regular, if poorly paid, and most men had spent all their working lives in one shop.

The United Fitters and Turners and Smiths Society was formed in Birmingham in July 1872,[24] meeting at the Swan with Two Necks in Aston. Originally a branch of the Rotherham stove and grate workers' society, it was reorganised in 1891, its membership having dropped from over 200 to 90 out of some 600 to 700 thought to be working in the trade in Birmingham. All work was piece-work but prices were very low and men had to employ boys in work teams with three or four boys to one man to make a living at all.

A new name, the Amalgamated Society of Kitchen Range, Stove Grate, Gas Stove, Hot Water, Art Metal and Other Smiths and Fitters[25] connected with the above Trades was adopted at a meeting in Birmingham on 30/31 March 1891, with Richard Witham as secretary. It adopted a new rule book similar to that of the Nottingham Society with periodic voting on the location of the seat of government, equalisation of funds, passwords for travelling members, a board of directors, repudiation of footings. The branch also had the power to appoint a wages committee for each branch of the trade to fix the standard rate of wages in each. Any member taking below the rate would be warned and if he persisted he would be excluded from the Society. The Birmingham club house was established at the Coach and Horses, Snow Hill.

Men eligible to join the Society were estimated as 100 kitchen range, stove and grate smiths and fitters with a minimum rate of $7\frac{1}{2}$d an hour; 100 gas stove smiths and fitters with a rate of 7d; 50 hot water smiths and fitters with no established rate but earning between 6d and 8d; 100 jobbing smiths connected with the trade with a rate of 8d. There were also many hundreds of art metal workers whom the Society would willingly accept into membership.

The then evils of the trade were said to be sub-contracting and the usual complaint of too many boys. Many men had three or four boys as underhands who were paid by the piece-master, and always kept on the same job so that when they became older they were unable to earn a decent living. This evil was said to be greatest among the general smiths and fitters, the other, specialised branches, being less willing to take boys under them.

In the 1890s Robert Sewell became secretary and the Society returned to Aston. A branch of the whitesmiths' society was also opened in the city about the same time.

The amalgamated stove and grate union, now with 350 members, approached the Liverpool whitesmiths in 1891, suggesting amalgamation 'as they included similar classes of men.' Negotiations foundered when the whitesmiths insisted on the headquarters remaining in Liverpool while the stove and grate men were equally adamant in support of claims for their own club house, as they were the bigger union.

The stove and grate fitters then approached other unions for an agreement on demarcation questions and a joint committee was set up consisting of four ASE members, four from the Steam Engine Makers and eight stove and grate smiths. They agreed that any member of the three societies could work on each other's jobs providing they did not receive less than the ASE rate.

A National Union

With the adoption, at a three-day rules revision conference in Nottingham in April 1908, of a new, more forward-looking name – The National Union of Operative Heating and Domestic Engineers, Whitesmiths and General Iron Workers[26] – the old stove and grate amalgamation entered the modern world. The old-fashioned annual equalisation of funds, rotating headquarters, passwords, officials taken from the roll and part-time secretaries were all abandoned, although a few old rules, such as that banning regalia, remained for many more years.

Men eligible for membership included kitchen range, stove grate, gas stove, hot water and steam fitters, casement and art metal smiths and fitters, whitesmiths, gas fitters, gate and railing smiths and fitters, brass-workers, toolmakers and general smiths and fitters connected with these trades who had served at least five years' apprenticeship to the trade.

Out-of-work benefit varied on length of membership, from up to £5 in any one year for those with one year's membership, to £9 for those with four years and more. Dispute benefit was 15s a week. Victimised members received their weekly rate of wages until they got a new job. Members suffering disablement so that they were no longer able to work received a lump sum of £50. Superannuated members received 6s a week after twenty years' membership, 8s after 25 years and 10s after thirty years. Breaking with the old tradition of publican treasurers, owners of licensed houses were not eligible to hold office in the society, nor were members who had set up in business, although they could remain members of the society with permission of the branch.

The new union no longer had a club house but a registered office at Queen's Road, Aston, Birmingham. Its first General Secretary was Robert Sewell, previously secretary of the Birmingham branch, who was probably more responsible than anyone for the changes that brought the union into the twentieth century.

This reorganisation laid the basis for a more general amalgamation of the various unions of kindred trades. Later that year, 1908, the Liverpool-based Amalgamated Society of Whitesmiths – which had been formed only a little over 15 years before with the aim of organising all whitesmiths – joined the new National Union, to give a joint total of 738 members and funds amounting to £2,000, £700 of which went to a new superannuation fund. The man who presided over the negotiations, Eli Clarke, had been president of the Birmingham Society, the old United Smiths and Fitters, and was to be president of the National Union for almost the whole of the period until 1931 and then serve as vice-president until his death in 1943.

In September 1912 the Chelsea-based former Society of General Smiths, whose General Secretary was then Charles Fobb, joined, but by then its membership had slumped to around 46. However, it brought the membership up to 1,063 and gave a London base for recruitment as well as contributing £130 to the general fund and £73 to superannuation. The Lambeth branch of the Society was already a member of the National Union.

Then in August 1918 the 97 members of the Newcastle and District Whitesmiths joined, with a contribution of £693 to the funds. By the end of 1913 the Union had 33 branches with 1,771 members. A year later the figures were 35 branches and 1,847 members – nine branches in London, 23 in the rest of England and three in Scotland. The Union, now demonstratably a national union, was on its way.

But the 1914 report showed there was still much to do. Only one branch had more than 100 members, Birmingham with 338 – the London membership being divided into nine branches. At the other end of the scale Mansfield had only eight members, Wolverhampton only 10, Norwich 11, Lincoln 12, Oldham and Sunderland 15 each, Derby 17, Bradford 18 and Huddersfield 19.

In July 1911 the Union signed its first national agreement with the National Association of Master Heating and Domestic Engineers. It covered hours and overtime rates but not the most important item, wages, which were to be still left to local agreements. Overtime rates were to be time-and-a-quarter until 8 pm and time-and-a-half from 8 pm until starting time the following morning. Saturdays from leaving-off time until midnight would be paid at time-and-a-half and all day on Sundays and Christmas Day would be at double time.

For outworking allowances, walking time would be calculated at three miles per hour when the distance to the job exceeded the distance to the shop. Lodging allowance was 1s 6d a day. Travelling time and expenses to be paid at the start and end of a job. Men working more than 20 miles from the shop would be allowed to return at weekends; those working more than 50 miles away could return once a month and if not more than 100 miles away once every eight weeks with travelling expenses and time paid.

The agreement gave the employer the right to employ any working man he wanted, whether or not he was a member of the Union. It also specified one hour's notice of dismissal. But it provided machinery for the settlement of disputes and avoidance of work stoppages. It laid down that apprentices be afforded facilities for acquiring a practical knowledge of the trade and that encouragement be given to them to obtain a theoretical knowledge.

In the early days of the National Union, recognition had to be fought for in all sections and all parts of the country. The 1911 national working agreement had been a partial breakthrough, but the fact that wages were left to local agreement led to a chaotic situation concerning rates throughout the country. The aim of the Union to obtain engineering instead of building industry rates of pay was made more difficult because of this partial lack of national recognition. However, in the 1917 amendment to the agreement the employers association accepted that wages should follow changes in the engineering rate and the first national advance on this basis was paid in August of that year, parallel with an engineering award.

The revised agreement also provided that work on Bank Holidays be paid at time-and-a-half. But an application for an annual paid holiday was turned down. Payments for Bank and local holidays was left to the 'goodwill' of individual employers, and where such payments were made they were usually for 'old hands' only.

In 1919 the provision in the original agreement that allowed a man to ask for overtime was dropped – in the 1911 agreement overtime rates were only paid when the worker was asked to work overtime, if he asked to be allowed to do overtime he worked for flat rates. In 1914 the

Union dropped 'whitesmiths' and 'Iron Workers' from its title, replacing the latter with 'Metal Workers' and bringing to an end the old, highly skilled and respected trade of whitesmith, at least as far as the trade union movement was concerned. This was in line with the development of the industry with the highly-skilled craftsmen able to do any metal work being replaced by specialists.

During the first world war the total membership went up by some 150 per cent to a total of 4,622, continuing to rise until 1920 when it peaked at 7,349 before declining in the slump to 4,432 as members fell into arrears and were excluded. In the brief post-war boom the London skilled rate went up to 2s 3½d in 1920, a figure which was not to be reached again until 1945. In 1922, with trade practically at a standstill as unemployment mounted, rates were cut, slashed three times in 1922 alone and ending up as 1s 7d in 1923.

This period saw the retirement of Robert Sewell, the architect of the National Union, who had held office since 1891, and his replacement by the assistant secretary, Edward Pacey.

The Union only catered for skilled men and the fitters' mates were unorganised, until a separated General Union of Heating and Domestic Engineers' Assistants[27] – generally known as the Mates' Union – was formed in Clerkenwell, London in 1921. It was founded by W.R. Brown, General Secretary of the Union throughout its short life. It organised fitters' assistants and mates, steam and hot water stokers and all those engaged in general trades, including operators of mechanical appliances. It was a successful venture and by the end of the year had 998 members.

The constitution divided the Union into branches but we have been unable to find a reference to any specific branch other than London. It was built on the organisation of a trade benevolent fund, the rules stating that the old benevolent fund was to be divided up among the then existing branches to form the nucleus of branch benevolent funds.

The stated objectives of the Union were to relieve members who were out of employment, to secure a standard rate of wages, to regulate conditions operating between employers and members, to give legal assistance to members, secure legislation for its trade union interests and for the general welfare of members and to provide for the burial of members of 12 months' standing and their wives.

Any desirable person over the age of 21, capable of earning the recognised rate of wages prevailing in the district was eligible for membership. Free members were entitled to unemployment pay of 10s a week for eight weeks and had then to work for another 52 weeks to become eligible to make another claim.

Should a dispute arise on a job the secretary should be immediately informed and should visit the job within 48 hours. If he was unable to get a settlement it should go to the EC. No member should take action without instructions from the EC and members should not be withdrawn from work without proper notice being given. Members ceasing work on EC instructions would receive 2s 6d a day, others affected would get 1s 6d a day for 12 weeks.

The Union was formed at a particularly difficult time, on the eve of the post-war depression. In 1922 £443 was paid in out-of-work benefit when income from all sources came to only £542. With the inevitable depletion of funds a ballot was held which endorsed the EC recommendation that benefits be reduced and contributions lowered. This followed the employers' reduction of the rate by ½d to 1s. In his 1922 report the secretary claimed that despite heavy calls on the funds every legitimate claim had been met in full. However, membership for 1922 was down to 596 and continued to fall, reaching 388 in 1924. Soon after the Heating and Domestic Engineers set up its own auxiliary section and this absorbed members of the Assistants' Union.

A rules revision meeting of the skilled union in Birmingham in 1926 decided to allow the upgrading of fitters' mates; an auxiliary member who had been employed for five consecutive years as an assistant or mate could, on application to his branch supported by two full members, become a full member with the rights and liabilities of a full member.

In addition to the branches of trades set out in the H and D statement in 1914, the following were also eligible for membership – gas muffle and furnace fitters, petrol tank fitters, plumbers, sheet metal workers, brass workers, turners, welders, lead burners, tool makers, aeroplane and motor mechanics, shipbuilders and repairers and constructional ironworkers.

A modification of the old-fashioned method of electing a board of directors from one governing district, appears in the 1926 rulebook with the election of an emergency committee from a 15 mile radius of head office to advise the General Secretary in cases of urgency insufficient to necessitate summoning the EC.

A new position of general organiser was created, elected for three-year terms with possibly an undetermined number of additional provisional organisers. General conferences were to be held every five years, instead of every three years, with one delegate eligible from each branch.

In addition to the usual objectives of the Union concerned with promoting the interest of members, the 1926 rule book included 'to alter the competitive system in such fashion that the worker shall secure his whole share of the fruits of his labour and to alter the present system with a view to taking over the industry.'

After the losses in membership during the post-war depression, the Union began the painful climb-back – to 4,874 in 1925 and 5,067 in 1926, to suffer a set-back to 4,429 after the General Strike. There was another climb in the 1928/29 boom, then came another setback with the 1931 depression. In 1931 membership was 4,641 and by 1935, when recovery was well on its way, membership was still 125 below that total.

In 1931 845 members of the Union were out of work and many more were on short time. In 1932 the unemployed figure had risen to 936, when £5,784 was paid out in 'donations' to members out of work. The year 1933 saw the beginning of recovery, with 612 members unemployed, dropping further to 480 in 1934.

These figures give no indication of the hardship suffered by members. One member, then newly out of his time, reported that when his dole money ran out the means test inspector investigated the income of his whole family – parents, brothers and sisters – and found that the total was 2d (in old currency) more than would entitle him to National Assistance, so he got nothing and was completely dependent on his family. The Labour Exchange officials were continually asking for proof that he was 'genuinely seeking work'. What work was there, he asked when two and a half to three million were unemployed. Another was refused assistance by the means test inspector until he sold the family piano – for which he got £5.

There was little the Union could do with the whole movement in the same position. They tried to stop excessive overtime when men were walking the streets – some country members were said to be working 50 hours a week. They supported moves by the other engineering unions for a shorter working week but the unions no longer had the industrial strength to force concessions out of employers. They also opposed new intakes of fitters into the trade, at least during this period of high unemployment. In 1932 they made a call for 100 per cent union membership, urging that the industry be retained for those organised in it, getting sympathy and support from some employers but the Association was not prepared to comply.

The Union resisted demands from the shipbuilding and repair employers early in the depression for cuts in wage rates and overtime payments, and also demands in 1932 from the engineering section employers for a 2d an hour cut, backed in this by a large majority in a ballot of members, but finally had to give way and in 1932 the London skilled rate dropped to ls 7d.

In the years of the depression the membership figures stood up very well. The five years from 1931 saw 3,308 new members but 2,986 were excluded, mainly for arrears, giving a net increase of 322. There were many ex-members either working in the trade or unemployed, who had been excluded for getting in arrears. They would have liked to rejoin but were unable to afford the double entry fees stipulated in the rules. In July 1933, the EC decided to suspend the rule, with good results in recruitment. The maintenance of membership levels helped the Union recover as the economic situation improved and enabled it to be quick off the mark in attempting to get back something of what had been lost. In November 1934 they were able to get a partial return of wage cuts for the stove, grate and range makers shops, with a 2s 6d a week increase for piece-workers and 1s 6d for time workers.

Demarcation Troubles

Back in 1931 an agreement had been made with the plumbers to set up a confederation to try and bring to an end the interminable conflicts over demarcation. The proposal came from a meeting of the two associations of employers in a joint letter to the two unions.

The industry had a long history of demarcation disputes between the two trades as the plumbers tried to maintain their position when lead pipes were being more and more replaced by other metals and methods. The plumbers resented the intrusion of other metal workers into what had been their preserve in the building industry as the engineering-based heating and ventilating contractors' work increased, carried out by their own men on the site, as well as in the shops. The fact that there had not been a serious national dispute in the industry was probably due to its rapid expansion and its relatively high employment.

In 1902, in the early days of weakness of the Heating and Domestic Engineering Union, the employers of both trades, perhaps leaned on by the plumbers' union, came to an agreement that all lead work would be carried out by plumbers and work in other metals would be regarded as 'neutral' and carried out by either plumbers or fitters. The master plumbers withdrew from that agreement the following year when the plumbers' union refused to accept it, claiming the lot.

In 1906 the master plumbers tried to get all cold and hot water services accepted as plumbers' work but the newly-established National Association of Master Heating and Domestic Engineers would not accept this and was backed by local authorities and architects. An attempt to take the matter to independent arbitration was turned down by the plumbers' union. Then, with the hold-up of a job in Leicester in 1909, the Board of Trade made an independent arbitration award which held the plumbers had not established their claim for exclusive rights to fix and fit all pipes and fittings. Instead, it gave the plumbers all lead and sanitary work, but all other work on hard metal piping in connection with heating, ventilation, laundry, cooking, hot and cold water services to be done by either plumbers or fitters. But the plumbers never accepted the award and later added 'domestic engineers' to their title in an attempt to establish their claim. This constant bickering continued until 1914 when discussion took place on the amalgamation of the two unions, but these broke down in June that year and the war provided more work than either union had members for.

During the latter half of 1914 the Union had to 'repulse aggression' by the plumbers who were carrying out a campaign against fitters doing 'plumbers' work', and claiming any work in which a pipe was used.

It objected to having to use its energies to fight off the plumbers when it should have been engaged in obtaining increased benefits for its members. The secretary told members that only a more complete organisation, together with an unending opposition by the membership, would defeat 'these impudent claims' and allow members to maintain their rights to earn a peaceful living.

In order to establish their position the Union stated their claim for

> the fitting and fixing of all boilers, cylinders, calorifyers, tanks, pipes, fittings or other apparatus in wrought iron and other materials (except lead), either for cold or hot water or any other purpose whatever. This included all work comprised under the terms domestic engineering, water supply, warming, ventilation, cooking, laundry work, fire mains.

It pointed out that the Union claimed for its members the right to execute this work as distinct from claiming a monopoly for it.

At this time the Union was engaged in demarcation disputes in Birmingham, Manchester, Nottingham, Leicester, Newcastle-upon-Tyne, Sunderland and Darlington, with plumbers threatening to walk off the jobs if the Heating and Domestic members were not removed.

The Engineering and Shipbuilding Confederation discussed the issue of demarcation between the two unions in 1920 – although the plumbers refused to acknowledge their right to do so – and confirmed the pre-war Leicester Board of Trade award that the plumbers had not substantiated their case. In 1921 the TUC awarded work on hot and cold water services to the plumbers but strongly advised the fusion of the unions.

The following year on a proposal by the Ministry of Labour a small committee of all concerned was set up to discuss all avenues of agreement – amalgamation, conciliation and arbitration – consisting of representatives of both unions and the two employers' associations, together with the building trades employers and operatives. In February 1925 they reported amalgamation proposals had proved abortive.

The employees had made an attempt to codify the work of the industry into three sections – engineers, plumbers and neutral – but in December 1926 the plumbers' union refused to attend any more demarcation meetings and in 1928 it was decided no further conferences could be held.

It was in this situation that there began the strange saga of employers' intervention in the internal affairs of the unions, which seems to have been considered by all concerned as nothing out of the ordinary. A joint meeting of the employers proposed that some form of confederation be attempted by the unions. This was accepted by both unions who agreed to the creation of a federation to cover a four-year period, in the fourth year of which the two union executives would review the position with a view to ultimate amalgamation.

This federation gave members of each union the right to execute work that had previously been a 'bone of contention'. The Heating and Domestic Union leaders had seen it as 'a strict compact for mutual support' with both sections of workers 'equally employable' on any job and giving the members of both unions the opportunity to get to know each other.

But apparently the plumbers saw things rather differently and John Stephenson, the plumbers' General Secretary, said the move was only a means of getting a trouble-free respite so that amalgamation proposals could be properly considered and developed. Many disputes were taken to the National Reference Committee which had been set up with one representative from each of the four bodies. These claims 'made nonsense of the confederation.' The H and D complained that the plumbers continued to press their individual claims, citing local custom and practice and the H and D, which was not a party to building trade agreements, said they always seemed to get the worst of the deal, with decisions either against them or, at best, being ordered to share what they saw as their work, with the plumbers.

The employers continued to play a leading part in deciding what the unions should do, with apparently no objections from either union. In 1932 a 'Committee of Eight' – two from each party, both employers and unions – was set up to report on the methods and basis of confederation.

In December of that year, a general meeting of the Heating and Domestic Engineers Association recommended that the interim confederation being operated by the two unions should be terminated and that the two unions create a permanent amalgamation. A four-party conference of unions and employers, in May 1933, unanimously accepted that the amalgamation proposals be put to the members. Ballots were taken of the two unions and in December 1934 it was reported that the Heating and Domestic had decisively turned down amalgamation by a majority of 2,509 out of a vote of 3,317 while the plumbers had just as decisively voted in favour with a majority of 8,895 out of a vote of 11,560. This result, said the H and D leadership, was hardly surprising in view of the attitude of the plumbers to the fitters in recent years.

The Heating and Domestic Engineering employers turned on the Union as being responsible for the failure to get agreement after four years of negotiations and threatened that if the Union did not come up with some agreement 'with the other three interests', the Association would advise its members to execute their contracts without reference to the Union.

The Union met this threat with a campaign throughout the country, visiting local employers and their associations, informing them of the position and the Union's case, and meeting with some support, so they finally got a 'stay of execution'.

Then in January 1933 the Association gave three months notice to terminate all working agreements, offering nothing in their place. When, with the three months' notice nearly up, the Association entered into closer relations with the plumbers, the Union thought it was time to take action and 'went to the country' again. A new national agreement was signed late in 1935 and although it did not give the Union all they desired, they 'could have fared worse.'

But that same year, after asking the unions to reconsider the position and adjourning the Four-Party Conference, the Association entered into direct discussion with the plumbers' union and the master plumbers, leading to a Three Party Agreement in 1936, with the Heating and Domestic Union out in the cold. The excuse they gave was that 'harmony established during the confederation should not be lost.'

The plumbers union then claimed that a certain number of their members should be employed on all contracts of members of the Heating and Domestic Engineers' Association, with members of both unions used 'indiscriminately' – plumber-fitters on heating work and hot-water fitters on cold or hot water services 'according to their skill.' The principle established, the plumbers then said it was difficult to fix a ratio of fitters and plumbers and proposed that the rights of the plumbers to domestic supplies work should be recognised, so giving them a standing in Association firms. The Association proposed 10 per cent of workers employed be plumbers for the first three years, rising after that to 15 per cent. In April a joint conference of the three organisations was held and the Three-Party Agreement was duly signed, without any reference to the Heating and Domestic Union, a somewhat strange way of 'maintaining harmony.' In July 1937 the Association informed the Union that it could not, as a body, discuss allocation of work.

The Union could not take this without some protest, and certainly not the men on the job. In September 1937 came the historic Leeds dispute, 'the most serious demarcation dispute in the history of the industry.' H and D members stood firm and the employers eventually signed the first Four Party Agreement, incorporating a section on 'allocation of work'. The master plumbers then referred to the building trade agreements and as the Heating and Domestic employers were not prepared to be bound by building trade decisions over which they had no control, the Three Party Agreement declined.

After the Second World War the two unions discussed closer working and eventually the two executives made a joint recommendation in favour of amalgamation. But in a ballot vote in February 1953 the Heating and Domestic members again decisively rejected it by a majority of 7,195 out of a vote of 9,884, representing 85 per cent of the membership with the plumbers again voting overwhelmingly in favour, although less than 20 per cent of their members took part. In retaliation, the plumbers officially and unilaterally ended the procedure agreement between the two unions and rejected an H and D proposal for a joint recognition of cards as a move to peace. They refused to operate a conciliation clause agreed with the employers, demanding all work on domestic hot water supply, calling strikes against the H and D on jobs in Edinburgh, Newcastle, Middlesborough, Oldham and the Midlands. Len Green, assistant General Secretary, called on his members to resist and the old conflict was back again.

Changing Work Patterns

In 1935 trade was generally picking up over the country and the year saw an increase in membership, particularly on the heating side. The Union put in a claim for a 2d an hour all-round increase and managed to get 1d, restoring the cut that had been made in the depths of the depression, in 1932, and returning to the 1s 8d skilled London rate of ten years earlier. The rate was thereafter pushed up by ha'pennies and pennies until, at the end of 1939, it reached 1s 10d – still well below the 1920 figure.

In 1935 the Union put in a claim for an advance for adult fitters' mates and assistants throughout the country. Attempts had been made since 1919 to get a national agreement for mates but it was not until they were organised in the early 1920s that any agreement was obtained, and then it was limited to London. An auxiliary section of the Union had been set up around 1925/26 into which mates around the country had been recruited – though not without objections from districts which refused to organise any except skilled workers. These auxiliary members were now complaining, justifiably, that nothing was being done for them. The 1935 national claim saw the first breakthrough. At first the employers dismissed it, declaring that the unskilled should be left to the general workers' unions, but the Union was able to persuade them that it would be better, if there were to be negotiations, that they be carried on by one union rather than get another union in from outside the industry.

A 1d increase was obtained, giving a rate of 1s 3d an hour in London and of 1s 2d in the rest of the country. The mates also got an out-working allowance similar to that of the fitters. (They had previously received 1s a day against the fitters' 1s 6d 'because receiving lower wages than a tradesman, they had a lower standard of living.' 'I have never yet met a landlady who charged less for lodgers who were not skilled tradesmen,' commented one mate.) While this agreement gave only partial recognition the Union felt it gave future hopes for a full recognition that the Union spoke on behalf of mates. But it took the war to bring about the desired change and an end to separate agreements with the adoption in 1940 of the first national agreement covering both skilled and unskilled.

Despite the general improvement in the work position, changes in methods of manufacture brought unemployment and short time working in the stove, grate and range shops, particularly among the older members.

But long before that the old stove and grate and casement shops had been taking an ever less

important part in the Union organisation. The advent of bigger buildings around the end of last century brought a great emphasis on the site work of the Union. The big blocks of expensive flats in London and to a lesser extent in other big cities, blocks of offices, stores, hospitals, asylums, prisons and other institutions, factories and other industrial buildings demanding efficient space heating and ventilation followed later by air conditioning systems, sprinklers, hot water and other services with their labyrinth of pipes and ductwork, gave a great fillip to the industry. The old brick-built boilers gave way to the Ideal and Robin Hood types that were installed by H and D members, the heavy radiators to the panel system with coils encased in the walls and underfloor heating. More and more sophisticated systems became standard practice and heating and ventilating-engineering craftsmen became a regular part of the workforce on all construction sites. Oil refineries, chemical works producing drugs, plastics and detergents, power stations brought hundreds of members on to a site, with some staying on as maintenance workers after the jobs were completed. Later members took part in constructing oil rigs – some afterwards forming part of the maintenance crews when the rigs were operating in the North Sea.

Fawley, on Southampton Water, set the pattern for these oil refinery jobs, the dozen or so unions working through the Confederation of Shipbuilding and Engineering Unions which dealt with the management on behalf of them all. This was followed by the Isle of Grain in the

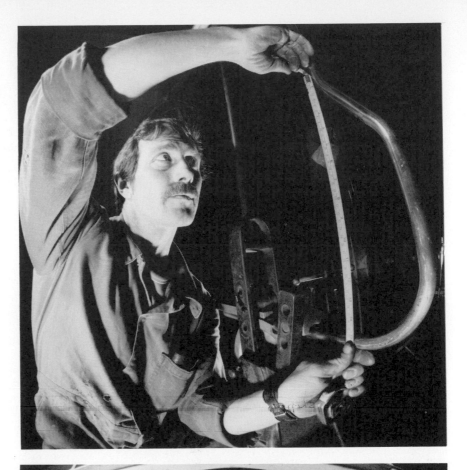

On opposite page: operative checking ductwork and lagging after installation; ductwork, carrying many piped services are a feature of modern construction jobs

Right: shaping a copper pipe for a domestic heating service in North London

Right, bottom: fitting a fan housing for the air-conditioning system in London's tallest building, the National Westminster Bank in the City, it has seven miles of ductwork

Thames Estury where in 1955 700 members of the Union worked on 600 miles of pipes criss-crossing the site, carrying water and steam, crude oil, petrol, kerosene, lubricating oils and diesel fuel. Some 500 members attended the meeting to elect the Union's chief steward on the job.

At the other end of the scale the Union claimed the fitting of boilers, pipes and other equipment for domestic central heating which had become a big industry, though poorly organised. A number of members were also engaged in thermo insulation work on power stations, oil refineries and other big contracting jobs.

Apprentices and Training

In 1936 a new apprentices' agreement was negotiated on pay, conditions of work and standards of training. The employers agreed to pay enhanced rates to apprentices who had attended an approved technical school for two years. They also agreed that, when practical, technical training should take place in the day time without loss of wages, but apprentices were also encouraged to continue with evening classes in the winter.

Apprentice training had featured in the first national working agreement between the Union and the employers' association in 1910. Progress was delayed by the start of the 1914-1918 War but in 1917 a revision of the agreement made further provisions relating to apprentices – on pay, length of service and also against exploiting boy labour with an agreement that no apprentices be sent out on fitters' work.

In February 1918, a deputation to the Ministry of Labour consisting of representatives from both the Union and the employers put the case for a joint industrial council (JIC) for the industry. The Ministry tried to get them to go in with the building trade JIC but this was rejected by both sides of the industry and the Heating and Ventilating JIC was finally launched in May 1919.

Originally its objects included negotiations on wages, conditions of employment, welfare and research into working conditions. However, in 1942 it was decided that these be left to the Union and the employers' association, leaving the JIC to concentrate solely on the education and training of operatives, mainly apprentices, working in co-operation with the education authorities.

The Council comprised elected representatives of the Heating and Ventilating Contractors' Association and the Union, together with representatives from the education and employment ministries, the Institute of Heating and Ventilating Engineers, the Association of Technical Institutions and teachers' organisations. A number of others with special qualifications were co-opted onto the Council. They took a full part in meetings and the work of the council and were allowed to vote on all except financial matters; all decisions were taken on a two-thirds majority and those coming from outside the industry were not allowed to outnumber the Union and employers' representatives. The Council also had direct contact with the City and Guilds of London Institute and the Construction Industry Training Board. The Union and Association provided the chairman in rotation, the other providing the vice-chairman.

The Council played an important part in the life of the Union whose top men sat on its committees and quite a sizeable part of the Union's quarterly journal was taken up with very full reports of its activities.

The first Agreement of Services for Operative Apprentices was adopted in 1921 and the same year the Council began co-operating with the City and Guilds Institute, which included examinations in heating and ventilating in its 1928/29 programme.

Right: apprentice setting up test piece; *below*: apprentice practicing bronze welding; above: HVCA apprentice's medal

Day release classes were recommended by the Council as early as 1923 and area committees were set up in various parts of the country to facilitate this in 1928 when classes were started in London, Birmingham, Newcastle, Manchester, Liverpool and Nottingham. They had become common by 1947 and were later replaced by block release courses. In 1965 the length of apprenticeship was shortened from five years to four, with the proviso that four complete academic years at the technical college should be covered. The courses were modified from time to time to meet the industry's changing technical needs. The Council also concerned itself with the recruitment of suitable apprentices. It also provided a guide for training on site with a log book in which the apprentice records the actual on-site training received.

In the field of post-apprenticeship training, the Council issued a syllabus for short courses on site administration and organisation for young potential charge-hands. One feature of operative apprentice training was the provision of a 'bridge' from the craft to the drawing office apprenticeship which it expected to be much used in the future. The minimum qualification for recognition as a craftsman was decided as a pass in the practical test for a fitter in the appropriate City and Guilds of London Institute examinations. It was decided that trainees should be required to pass the same test, and also applicants for up-grading to fitter. The Council took on the supervising of these tests and the registration authority for certificates of welding competency. In the 1930s the Council began providing scholarships, prizes and a challenge shield to stimulate interest.

During the 1939-1945 War the Council began registration of apprenticeship agreements. By 1970 there were 2,290 indentured apprentices, compared with only 50 in 1924.

The scope of present-day training, in the securing of which the Union has been very active, should be contrasted with that of an apprentice whitesmith in the early years of this century whose activities in the shop consisted of dressing rough castings, a period with the pattern maker, then time on drilling and planing machines, assisting the grinder on buffing and whetstone, acting as striker for the blacksmith and such tasks as preparing killed spirits for soldering, making silver solder sticks from old watchcases and soluble oil for drilling from Hudson's dry soap.

War and Post-War

In 1940 it was decided that the EC remain in office for the duration of the war and that the general conference be deferred 'to a more appropriate time', which does not seem to have occurred until the end of the War. One useful innovation, however, was the six monthly war-time meeting with the employers for a 'periodic review of wages', which included other problems that arose.

In 1941 one of these joint Union/employer meetings agreed that the industry's National Joint Industrial Council should have the power to take any action of a consultative or advisory nature which might appear likely to achieve the advancement of the industry, providing that the measures had not already been the subject of agreement between the two sides. The Council was given the power to act for the industry in all matters affecting the education of apprentices.

It was reported that then only one in eight of the boys employed in the industry was apprenticed and the Union wanted an agreement that apprenticeship be the only means of entering the industry. This was brought up again at a special one-day conference of the Union in Leicester in 1944 as an item of the post-war policy of the Union.

In 1943 a scheme to give one week's holiday with pay was started, in which the worker had a holiday credit card stamped by the employer for every week the worker was in his employment and operated among all firms in the Association.

A similar form of stamped cards was favoured for a non-contributory sick scheme, put into effect in May 1965 with transfers when members moved from one Associated firm to another. Operators claimed from their employer who passed the claim on to an insurance company – benefits were £3 10s for industrial injury and £2 2s for sickness, with a maximum period of 13 weeks, two weeks between claims counting as two separate claims.

Unlike the end of the 1914-1918 War when, after a short boom there was a prolonged slump, the end of the Second World War, which saw the election of a Labour government, brought a prolonged advance. The 1947 Triennial Conference was told that membership had topped 16,000 but the old problem remained, how to consolidate the membership? If all who had joined the Union in the previous seven years had stayed in, the membership would have been 40,000. Lapsing members continued to be the main problem confronting the Union, inevitable, perhaps, in an organisation whose members were constantly changing their work place and, almost as often, their employer.

On the other hand, when long service badges were introduced in the 1950s it became apparent that a particularly large number of members were eligible, revealing many years of service to the Union. No less than 80 members were entitled to the 50-year loyalty badge. Of these, one Sunderland member had been branch secretary for 27 years and another branch chairman for 18 years.

A Bristol member had been branch secretary for 28 years, for 19 of which he was also a member of the EC. On his retirement he was followed in both jobs by his son; two other brothers were members of the committee and an uncle had been branch chairman for 35 years. The Kilburn branch recorded a father and seven sons who were all members of the branch at the same time, with one of the sons branch chairman and another the secretary. Another Union family, in the Downham branch, had a total of 166 years, over four generations, all working at the same firm. The great grandfather joined in 1858 – at the time of the Friendly Society of Stove Makers and Smiths. He retired in 1908 and was followed by his son and grandson; his great grandson joined in 1945 and was still a working member at the time of amalgamation.

The 1959 Triennial Conference decided to make a drive for 100 per cent Union organisation and to improve the bad arrears position. In some places, it was said, only half the workers were in the Union, it was estimated that some 8,000 eligible workers in the industry were not Union members and members were urged not to work with nons.

At the end of the War the NEC called for greater attention to be given to shop stewards, but it was not until 1957 that it was decided – 'with fairly general agreement' – to approach the employers to recognise shop stewards, particularly on big contracts. The EC statement urged greater attention be paid to the appointment of stewards, the protection of those appointed and their recognition by the employers. It was proposed that a shop stewards' hand-book be produced giving stewards instructions on how to carry out their duties. The EC decided that an attempt should be made to get a national stewards' agreement with the employers for general recognition. The Union was not very successful, the employers preferring the position then existing in which stewards were recognised by individual companies and were 'granted reasonable facilities providing they acted constitutionally.' This rather ambiguous position was allowed to remain, with the EC assuring active members who were prepared to act as shop stewards that they would have full Union support 'so long as they carried out their duties in a proper manner.'

It was not until 1966, on the eve of amalgamation, that a national agreement was reached with the employers for a general recognition of stewards. In signing the agreement the employers laid down conditions, which the Union accepted, that stewards must be craftsmen and be in at least their second year of membership of the Union and employment with the firm.

Outside Affiliations

From 1913 to 1918 the Union was affiliated to the General Federation of Trade Unions, an organisation set up by the TUC to help small unions in strikes and lockouts by spreading the financial burden. It was also affiliated early on in its life to the Confederation of Shipbuilding and Engineering Unions, and its predecessor and to the Trades Union Congress. In 1950 it affiliated to the National Council of Labour Colleges and the Workers' Educational Association.

It was one of the few manual unions of any size that was not affiliated to the Labour Party, and did not maintain a political fund. The principle was accepted at a Union policy conference in 1944 and the question of putting the principle into practice was raised from time to time in the post-war years. A decision was taken to hold a ballot on the question in 1949 but for some reason, instead of a ballot, the branches were circularised asking their opinions. There was a very poor response and the General Secretary, L. Green, complained of a lack of political interest in the branches. The 1963 Quinquennial Conference decided by a majority of three to one to seek affiliation but again no ballot appears to have been held and no political fund existed when the amalgamation with the sheet metal workers took place in 1967.

The H and D was also one of a minority of unions that operated the 'black circular' from the 1930s banning Communists from holding office in the Union. The rule stated that no member of the Union 'who is also a member of the Communist Party or fascist organisation' shall retain or hold any position in the Union at any time, either as executive member, full-time or part-time officer or branch official. Members standing for office were obliged to make a declaration that they were not a member of the Communist Party. In a reply in 1939 to the Croydon branch, the Union claimed that as it was affiliated to the TUC it 'must adhere to the declaration of Congress relative to disruptive bodies.' But in fact it was only a small minority of unions that operated it and of those few were still doing so by 1939. But the EC went on to advise the Croydon branch to disaffiliate from their local trades council, apparently because it was 'tainted with communism.' In 1950 a ballot on whether communists be allowed to stand for office reaffirmed the ban and the 1956 Triennial Conference, after turning down a motion that members of the Communist Party be allowed to hold office, went on to extend the ban to shop stewards and temporary acting members of the EC, officials or branch officers. When calling for nominations for national conferences, the EC always reminded branches that those nominated must make the declaration and regularly restated that the rule must be maintained in all ballots for office. The H and D must have been the last union to operate the ban as it was still in regular use at the time of the 1967 amalgamation, after which it was omitted from the new joint rule book – the TUC General Council had agreed to the withdrawal of the circular in 1943.

Amalgamation

Despite the overwhelming majorities by which the members had twice rejected amalgamation with the plumbers the leadership of the Union still nourished hopes of a merger. The plumbers

Left: H&D General Secretary, signs the amalgamation documents while Les Buck, General Secretary, Sheet Metal Workers and Coppersmiths (*centre*) SMW President, G. Kellet (*right*) and H&D Vice-President, W. Bawden, look on, April 1967

EC continued to press for fusion and in 1955 refused to attend a meeting to discuss a wage claim, saying they would only meet to discuss amalgamation. So there was no meeting. No progress had been made with the plumbers whose recent actions in claiming what the H and D considered their work had embittered many, including some who favoured amalgamation. But another big stumbling block to getting agreement was that the plumbers' superannuation and other benefits were much lower than those of the H and D.

The policy of the Union was for federation with kindred trades. Nevertheless it sent delegates to a meeting called by the AEU in 1956 to consider setting up one big union for engineering workers. A meeting with the boilermakers to discuss either closer working or amalgamation was more in line with the NEC ideas and it was decided to continue to send delegates to discuss federation but not amalgamation.

The General Secretary, Len Green, drew the Union's attention to the TUC call for mergers of smaller unions where there were similar interests and demarcation problems. He felt that the Union should not wait for the TUC to tell them what to do, this would considerably weaken the Union's bargaining power. He reported that the sheet metal workers were interested in amalgamation but would perhaps consider federation as a first step. He thought amalgamation would be acceptable providing the Union did not lose its identity; the present title would have to be incorporated in the name of any merged union.

Reporting to the 1963 national conference, he said that neither the boilermakers nor other kindred unions were interested in federation and the sheet metal workers had shown the most interest. During the next few years there would be great changes in heating and ventilating techniques with fewer radiators and more trunking, ductwork and ventilating equipment, made by sheet metal workers, so a linking with their union would enable the Union to control an essential part of the heating and ventilating industry. With proper safeguards, the Union had a bright and prosperous future with the industry expanding at a rapid rate. Talks with the sheet metal workers showed it would be to their mutual advantage to have a close working arrangement.

Talks were held between the two unions, sub-committees were set up which drew up proposals for amalgamation which were eventually accepted by the two sides. The Heating and Domestic national executive recommended acceptance of the amalgamation proposals.

The members accepted the EC's recommendation and by a large majority voted in favour of amalgamation. So, on 1 April 1967 the National Union of Sheet Metal Workers, Coppersmiths, Heating and Domestic Engineers came into existence and the old H and D carried on its life, pursuing the interests of the workers in the trade as part of a larger organisation. The General and Assistant General Secretaries, Len Green and Cyril Bransby, became Assistant General Secretaries of the new amalgamated union. For a time the area committees of the H and D remained in being but were soon absorbed in the old district committees of the sheet metal workers and coppersmiths Some branches of the two organisations merged but others decided to retain their local organisation, particularly in London where the small local branches of the H and D remained in being, part of the No. 7 district, alongside the big London branch of sheet metal workers and coppersmiths. In September 1967 a special joint national conference of delegates from the branches of the two organisations was held which agreed on a joint rule book. Within a few years London H and D members had formed their own shop stewards association which provided an organisation for officially co-ordinating activities in the furtherance of specific Heating and Domestic problems and interest.

1. 1811 Rule Book, R. and E. Frow, Working Class Movement Library, Manchester. The rule book carries a statement from the magistrates at the Middlesex Quarter Sessions that the rules had been 'examined, allowed and confirmed.'
2. 1825 Rule Book, author's collection.
3. Rules, orders and regulations of the United Bretheren Benefit Society of Smiths and Iron workers, held at Mr Phillips's, The George, East Harding Street, Gough Square, Fleet Street. The inaugural meeting was held on 9 January 1816.
4. *Records of the Borough of Nottingham, VIII, 1800-1835*, Nottingham 1952. Prothero, *Artisans and Politics*. E. Thompson, op. cit.
5. *The Times*, 19 May 1859.
6. Prothero, *Artisans and Politics*.
7. *Northern Star*, April 1838.
8. *Operative*, 4 November 1838.
9. *United Trades Co-operative Journal*, 4 September 1830.
10. BLP&ES Webb Collection.
11. Ibid.
12. S and B. Webb *History of Trade Unionism*, London 1894.
13. PRO FS/7/4/168.
14. BLP&ES Webb Collection.
15. Ibid.
16. PRO FS7/12/556.
17. PRO FS24/1149.
18. BLP&ES Webb Collection.
19. Ibid.
20. PRO FS7/4/18.
21. *Pioneer*, 1 March 1834.
22. PRO FS7/4/68.
23. Board of Trade Reg 153, TUC Library.
24. BLP&ES Webb Collection.
25. Ibid.
26. Ibid.
27. TUC Library.

Material on other years was obtained from reports and other publications of the Heating & Domestic Engineers Union and the Heating & Ventilating Contractors Association.

Alderman J.V. Stevens, President of the Birmingham Society, 1880, General Secretary 1894-1919

CHAPTER 11

The Birmingham Society

Advertisements for tin plate workers had been appearing in the Birmingham papers from the last decades of the eighteenth century, if not before,[1] but it was not until the beginning of the nineteenth century that the trade spread in any strength to the town from neighbouring Wolverhampton.

Birmingham had grown with the Industrial Revolution from a cluster of villages, and so had no guild basis to provide a corps of skilled journeymen with a background of organisation. The workers probably graduated from the travelling tinkers who had served the villages.

By then Birmingham was hailed as 'the greatest[2] centre of general hardware manufacture in the world', town of 101 minor metal trades in which the craft of the tin plate worker was establishing a position. Quasi-independent craftsmen with their labourers were providing 'an amazing range of products' from tin and iron plate, copper and brass. Few masters employed more than 20 workers. The norm was the workshop where a small master laboured alongside the one or two men and boys he was able to employ.

There were still a number of artisan outworkers who collected material from an employer and made up the work in a shed in his backyard, working by the piece, helped by members of his family, or perhaps by another journeyman, a labourer or a boy or two he might employ. The better, more profitable end of the market was monopolised by the richer capitalist, leaving the poorer, cheaper class of goods to the mass of small men, working from hand to mouth and often dependent on the main contractor for materials as well as orders.

Birmingham was a matrix of small workshops where the journeyman had a measure of independence in that, if he were not satisfied, he could leave one master for another – at least when trade was good. Or, as very little capital was needed, he could become a small master himself. Most of these small employers would revert to the status of workman – some of them making the transition each way many times – through getting in debt, or in times of bad trade, such as the general depression of 1817 'when poor-houses were full and the pawnbrokers were holding hundreds of pounds worth of tools.'[3] Indeed, the workhouses were dubbed 'the tinmen's rest'.[4] But even in the best of times there was little enough to separate the mass of small masters from the employed journeymen, the former often getting little if any more money, than the journeyman.

For both it was a hard life, slogging away in hot, unventilated shops some 14 hours or more a day, six days a week, with an hour or two of overtime and even longer hours in the summer months. In these circumstances 'St Monday'[5], and the amount of beer drinking that accompanied it, was honoured almost universally by the Birmingham trades.

This attitude of rough independence, of 'devil take the hindmost', and the possibility of 'rising' to become a small master always before the more responsible journeymen, did not provide the best soil for nurturing trade unionism. But the situation was changing as the increasing supply of labour coming into the expanding town, and the cycles of trade depression, heightened competition for jobs.

The earliest tin plate workers' society in Birmingham of which we have found any mention was said to have been formed in 1812 'to protest at low wages.' However, there is a Book of Prices for the manufacture of Tin Goods in the Town of Birmingham, dated 10 July 1810.[6] This bears no imprint of any society of workers or masters but its cover is decorated with four clasped hands and clasped hands are usually used by trades societies rather than employers. This is perhaps confirmed by a hand-written note inside that that the price list had been 'agreed and sanctioned' by a list of eleven named Birmingham manufacturers. If this was indeed produced by a trades society it would mean there was a society much earlier than was thought as it would take some years of organisation before a society was able to produce such a prices book. What we do know is there was a Birmingham Society affiliated to the Union of 1821 to 1825, which was credited with a membership of 30 in 1824.

From time to time down the years there are references to a Birmingham Society which would seem to suggest a continuing organisation. Its members made financial contributions to the London bookbinders' strike in 1838. Walter Thorn, was secretary in 1841 when he attended a meeting in the Grand Turk Hotel, Bell Street, to set up a local committee to support the stone masons on the new Houses of Parliament who were on strike. Thorn was still a leading member of the Society in January 1847, working closely with the Wolverhampton Society, when W. Hall was Birmingham secretary and the club house was the Bull's Head in Deritend.[7] Birmingham members appear on the tramp accounts of the Liverpool Society in the 1840s. Then in 1846 when, according to the *Northern Star* the tinmen 'were very numerous in the town', there was a big strike, taken 'only in defence of their just rights', when the employers tried to cut wages by 20 per cent. This was followed by another, in 1855, in defence of prices.

A reorganised Society was formed on 12 February, 1859,[8] as the result of a meeting held at the Grand Turk, from which time there is documentary evidence of a continuing history. It was stated that

at the earnest request of a few of the tin plate workers in Birmingham it was thought it would be advisable to call a general meeting of as many of the men working in the town as possible together to take into consideration the formation of a New Trade Society.

The meeting resolved that the new society be called the Birmingham Co-operative Tin Plate Workers Society and the decisions were confirmed at a general meeting on 17 May 1859.

The reason it was thought necessary to form a new society is something of a mystery. There is no doubt that a society already existed. Two items in the minute book of the new society confirm this. One is a resolution at the meeting of 2 August 1859 'that Mr Hall pay to the treasurer the £10, the funds of the old society', the other records a decision that five members of the old society be placed on the books of the new society as free members.

Writing more than 30 years later, the then secretary of the Society, E. Fooks, says that by 1855 'the trade was large and important enough' to draw up a uniform list of prices based on those of Wolverhampton, which was accepted by the men. However, 'it became difficult to enforce the prices."⁹ So in 1859 it was decided to form a new society which, it was thought, would be able to defend the list and enforce the prices.

There is no reference to any of this in the minutes of the new society, nor any indication of a struggle to get the new prices paid by the employers, in fact the minutes appear to indicate that the first few years of the new society were very quiet. The only items that might possibly bear some relation to it are a minute of 6 December 1859 'that no member goes to work at Mr Harriott's unless he get the full book price'; and in July 1860 a member was told to ask his employer, Mr Griffiths, if he would pay the book price for pumps that had been made; if not the Society would allow the member sufficient money to take the case to the magistrates. A decision recorded at that same meeting laid down 'that no man contracts himself to another,' but these are all ordinary run of the mill occurrences for a craft union and in no way add up to a campaign to enforce book prices. Nor would the employers be likely to pay quietly the new prices just because a new society had been formed.

The records available do not indicate the number of members who joined the new society, but a later president says that when he joined, in 1862, there were only 20 members.

The first officers were Joseph Smith, secretary, Samuel Reeves, president, and Thompson, treasurer, but at the 2 August meeting a new president, Griffiths, was elected, as well as 12 committeemen and two auditors. Six trustees were installed and when money was deposited in the bank it was done by means of two cheques, each signed by three trustees. Three of the trustees were appointed key bearers, each taking care of one of the keys for the three locks of the Society's box. One of the original trustees of 1859, Robert Musgrove, was still a trustee when he died in 1898.

The Grand Turk was chosen as the club house 'to hold meetings and receive contributions', which were fixed at 6d a week. At the same time it was decided that committeemen be paid a 6d refreshment allowance for attending meetings. More than 20 years later this, 'wet rent' principle, as it was called, was still practised, the stewards receiving 3d drink checks for their services.

The secretary wrote to the tin plate workers' societies in all the main towns in England asking them to acknowledge and co-operate with the new Society and to relieve tramps calling on them with the Society's cards. It was also agreed that any tramp with a card of any other society, who was not free, could be relieved to the extent of 2s, and tramps without cards to receive 1s, if the secretary thought it proper.

The committee ordered 50 tramp cards for members who had been in the Society between six and 12 months, who were to be allowed 10d a day, and 50 for free members, who were to be allowed 1s 8d a day. Another 100 cards were ordered in September 1862 and a further 100 'for the two-year membership' in May 1864. There is nothing in the records, either of particularly high unemployment or of any industrial action pending, that would indicate why such a large number of tramp cards were thought necessary.

Two hundred copies of the Society's rules were also ordered, to be sold to members at 2d each. These would appear to be rules taken over from the old society as there was no indication of a committee meeting to draft new rules, nor would there have been time to do so.

From the start, the new Society was generous in the help it gave to others. Already at the 2 August 1859 meeting it was resolved 'that we give the committee of the gun makers, now on strike, the sum of £1 and the sum of 5s per week for four weeks and if the strike should continue longer they are requested to apply to our committee again.' In November £5 was sent to the London building workers and a further £3 the following January. In August £2 10s was voted to the Coventry ribbon weavers 'providing a vote taken at each manufactory is in favour.'

In 1863, the Society contributed £10 to help alleviate the distress among the tin plate workers in Lancashire due to the 'cotton famine'. The 1867 balance sheet showed that donations were made of £10 to the London tailors, another £10 to the Operative Iron Plate Workers and £2 to the Birmingham Co-operative Basket Makers, considerable sums for a society that started out with only £10 a few years before, and who, the previous year, with only 61 members and funds of £224, was shown by the balance sheet to have made a gift of £25 to the London tin plate workers' strike and £2 to the striking Cradley chain makers. In 1865, the Society took five shares in the Wolverhampton lock makers' co-operative which had been formed during a lockout.

Birmingham also gave support to the *Beehive* newspaper, organ of the London Trades Council and of the First International, as did the London and Wolverhampton societies, giving two donations of £1 in answer to appeals and decided that in addition to the paper taken for members to read in the club house, to order some for sale to members. Many years later, it was to do the same for the Birmingham Labour Party paper, the *Town Cryer*, taking 100 copies a week for sale.

But in 1870 the committee decided that it could not support the emigration movement proposed by London.

The visit of the Italian patriot, Garibaldi, to Birmingham gained the enthusiastic support of the Society, as it seems to have with the whole of the English working-class movement – trade unions, friendly societies and political groups – who turned out in their thousands wherever he went. The Society elected a committee of eight and voted £5 to defray expenses of participating in the demonstration. The stampers and burnishers were allowed to join in with the Society in the procession.

That was in 1864. In 1867 the Society began preparations for participation in the big demonstration for electoral reform. Already in 1861 the Society informed the Reform League that it would do everything in its power in the cause of Reform, in the way of obtaining signatures.

Now it was decided that the Society should have its own banner. On the front was to be painted 'Birmingham and Operative Tin Plate Workers Society' and the trade arms with two supporters in working dress, leather aprons with bibs, paper hats, shirt sleeves turned up, one with a mallet and the other with a pair of compasses in hand and the motto 'United to support but not combined to injure'. On the back, the eye sign over a beehive; the rose, shamrock and thistle in a wreath; two bundles of sticks; joined hands and the motto 'United we stand Divided we fall'. Two men were appointed to 'get up the banner' and four men engaged to carry it at 5s each. It cost £10 plus 3s 6d for a wrapper.

A 'splendid brass band' was hired at a cost of £5. On the day, the committee conducted the banner through the streets. Three hundred circulars were distributed, giving an invitation to a meeting at the Society's club house, the Pump Tavern in the Bull Ring, and drawing attention to the fact that the new banner and the 'splendid brass band' would be there. Again a dinner was provided at the club house at which tin plate workers who were not members of the Society were invited to take part. But a request from the Reform League for a donation was turned down, although members were recommended to join the League privately and the Reform League medal was adopted by members taking part in the demonstration.

Despite this enthusiasm for electoral reform, a request soon afterwards for the Society to join a committee to consider sending a working man to Parliament for Birmingham was 'not entertained'.

In November of that year, a meeting of the Society considered a proposed Act of Parliament relating to combinations and trade societies but found the Act 'too restrictive in its provisions and therefore cannot be supported.'

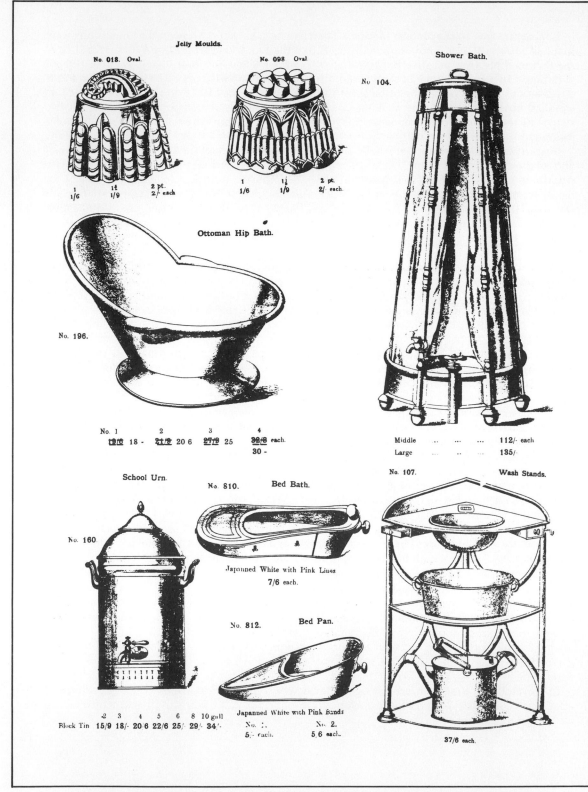

Jelly Moulds.

No. 018. Oval.

No. 098. Oval.

1	1¼	2 pt.
1/6	1/9	2/ each.

1	1½	2 pt.
1/6	1/9	2/ each.

Shower Bath.

No. 104.

Middle	...	...	...	112/- each
Large	...	...	..	135/-

Ottoman Hip Bath.

No. 196.

No. 1	2	3	4	
18 -	20 6	25	30 -	each.

School Urn.

No. 160.

	2	3	4	5	6	8	10 gall
Block Tin	15/9	18/-	20 6	22/6	25/	29/-	34/-

No. 810. **Bed Bath.**

Japanned White with Pink Lines
7/6 each.

No. 812. **Bed Pan.**

Japanned White with Pink Bands

No. 1.	No. 2.
5/- each.	5 6 each.

No. 107. **Wash Stands.**

37/6 each.

Items from the 1912 catalogue of R. Hookman, general sheet metal workers, Birmingham

An expression of international solidarity resulted from a dispute in 1865 at the old-established firm of Griffiths and Browett, with whom the Society clashed on a number of occasions. This time, in an attempt to defeat the strikers, the firm sent representatives to Germany and brought back a number of tin plate workers, not telling them that a strike was in progress. The proposed strike-breakers were secretly taken into the firm's premises during the night. When the pickets arrived outside the factory the following morning the German workers came to a window and one of them who could understand English was told of the position. He conveyed the information to his fellow countrymen who immediately threw all their tools out of the window and then came out and joined the pickets. A number of them remained in Birmingham and joined the Society. Two were later elected auditors of the Society, Julius Stahlmann in 1868 and William Schultz in 1874.

Smith resigned as secretary in 1862 and was followed by a number of stop-gaps, all of whom held the position for only a few months each. First William Westwood, a wheeler, then Thomas Beston and Henry Fell, former presidents who, it would appear, took over in an emergency.

William Evans

Then in 1864 the Society elected as secretary William Evans, who had served as auditor, committeeman and steward and who was to rule the Society until his death on 9 November 1889. He was a strong character and left his imprint deep on the Society.

Evans was born in Gloucester in 1838 and apprenticed to a local firm, but he soon moved to neighbouring Tewkesbury where he was apprenticed to an ironmonger. When he was 19 he moved back to Gloucester where he got a job making ships lamps, leaving after a short time for Birmingham, where he became a founder member of the 1859 Society.

He was said to be a handsome young man and something of a 'gentleman tinman', always wearing a silk top hat and frock coat, even to go to work, as did many of the 'superior' workmen of the time, and for many years later, the custom not dying out entirely until the First World War. On contribution nights he would sit in state, a distinguished figure between the two money stewards, one calling out the contributions and the other taking the cash. The Secretary lent dignity to the occasion, always smoking a cigar 'which seemed to fit the man and the occasion'. He was said to have been respected by the members, as well as by the employers who found him 'a hard nut to crack'. His accounts and books 'were always accurately and well kept.'

One of the first activities of the Society under his leadership was an attempt to establish a trade price list. This was the first of a long line of prices books of the numerous articles of sheet metal in everyday use, compiled by the Society, revised and added to over the years, in constant use by generations of members until the last one was issued in 1915. One item from this early list will be sufficient to indicate the kind of prices these old tin plate workers received for their work:

Job No. 391 Coffee Pots (Best common) Planished throughout, body formed, handles and spouts rivetted and grooved, bodies grooved inside, bottoms paned down, bright tops cut, formed and polished, well cleaned but not scoured, the finished article to be in perfect saleable condition. Price per dozen 3s 3d.

It was during his rule, too, that a superannuation fund was started although the credit for this is said to be due to the then President, J.V. Stevens.

Evans was largely responsible for the original coming together of the Midlands societies in the Amalgamated Tin Plate Workers of Birmingham, Wolverhampton and District. He was convinced of the need for this by the way the employers constantly played off one society against the other during negotiations. He was also one of the delegates of the Birmingham Society who took part in the extension of the organisation into the National Amalgamated by bringing in the London and Edinburgh societies.

In disputes with the employers he declared himself to be always in favour of trying conciliation 'previous to taking more harsh steps.' While this seldom failed when trade was good, during slackness there were always employers trying to take advantage of the situation to cut prices or worsen conditions. He reported in 1877 an attempt by one employer to introduce a system of sweating or division of labour in making mess tins, which was 'an encroachment on our rights and principles, we were compelled to resist, or otherwise sanction a system whereby the foundations of our Union would have been undermined.'

In that same report he dealt with those critics of the trade unions who, ever since their formation, have accused them of all the evils under the sun:

> The slackness of trade which has been general throughout the country, has brought forward an unusual number of persons of all ranks – Noblemen, Members of Parliament, Ministers of Religion, tradesmen and others, in condemnation of Trade Unions; and while each of them attribute the distress to the action of Unions in reducing the hours of labour, and raising wages, they all seem to forget that greater distress had existed at other times when few Unions were in existence, and when men, women and children were worked as many hours and for what remuneration their employers chose to offer them.
>
> There are many features in trades unions which its caluminators studiously avoid mentioning, amongst which may be named, assistance to members out of employ, in sickness, old age and in the provision of a decent interment when their earthly labours cease. I feel convinced if the various amounts distributed in these forms throughout the country were compiled and published it would make them blush, or cease their one-sided accusation.

A further insight into the man is provided by his forthright attack on non-unionists, particularly how they turn up during a dispute to get any handouts that might be forthcoming without paying a penny in contributions.

> Like the placid stream, disturbed by a storm, the dregs or sediments rise to the surface, so, in like manner, we found men turn up who were previously unknown to us and join those who had been withdrawn and need I add, partake of our bounties; but who cared little what system they worked under when there was no dispute on hand, and most of whom ceased their connection with us when our support was withdrawn.

When Evans took over the Society was a trades club of some 35 members. He left it a trade union of nearly 1,000 members, respected in trade union circles in the Midlands and beyond. This was all accomplished – as was usual in the many craft unions of that time – in his spare time, after a working week of perhaps 54 hours, for this he received a salary of £8 a year.

Fooks, who followed Evans as Secretary, claimed that in 1870 the Society numbered only about 200 members 'although there must have been three times that number working in the trade in the town.' The reason was that the Society then only admitted into membership the cream, 'the very select workers and those in the best jobs', leaving the great majority completely unorganised and for the most time unconsidered.

In this they were following the pattern and attitude that prevailed among the members of the Wolverhampton Society at that time. Birmingham had long looked up to Wolverhampton, its elder brother and mentor. There was still a close working relationship between the two societies on questions of pricing and in times of dispute. In 1886 the bath makers of the two towns were called together to discuss anomalies of prices and the demand of one manufacturer for a reduction in prices which he said was necessary to meet the competition of other makers. He was told that different forms of manufacture were responsible for the variation in prices, but that most makers paid book prices.

As late as 1906 the two societies got together to fix overtime rates for both day and piece-works. It was felt that if the employers had to pay extra for overtime working it would stop members doing regular and excessive overtime when men were walking the streets without a job.

But back in 1874, said Fooks, 'the little section of highly skilled and well-organised men' who formed the membership of the Society, succeeded in getting their employers to pay a bonus of 10 per cent on top of the old piece-work prices. Soon after, the employers in the rest of the trade agreed to make the same payment to their tinmen. But in 1879 the employers in the unorganised shops took away the bonus. The Society men, 'being the pick of the trade and well-organised' were able to maintain the prices and the bonus. This state of things, with two different sets of prices for the organised and unorganised shops, continued until 1889. The employers of the trade shops then notified the Society that they could no longer continue in competition with the large number of employers who were paying lower wages. The Society would have to see that the bonus was paid to all the non-union shops or they would not get it themselves.

This 'led to considerable agitation.' After a lot of discussion the Society was thrown open to all skilled men working in the trade. Organising meetings were held all over the town and the Society increased its membership so rapidly that in a year or two it comprised practically the whole trade. The membership topped the 1,000 mark 'and not more than 20 or 30 non-union tinmen were left in town.'[10]

Even so, strikes to maintain or obtain the 10 per cent continued into 1892, some of them lasting many months before the employers gave in. However, towards the end of the year, the 10 per cent was generally conceded throughout the trade in Birmingham.

Having consolidated the organisation the membership figure remained generally constant around the 1,000 mark, losing some members in times of bad trade and high unemployment and recovering them when trade improved.

The whole history of the trade was one of slump and boom, with more slump than boom. The year 1885, the Society leaders reported, 'was one that would stand as the very worst in their experience for lack of employment and bad trade, straining their resources to the utmost.' Contributions were raised from 6d to 7d a week, but this was still totally inadequate with, at one time, 65 members signing the book. Contributions had to be pushed up to 1s a week, but even then, with contributions doubled and the men short of money, 'the Society did not lose a single member.'

A benefit fund was set up for those out-of-work who had used up all their entitlements. In one week £22 was raised by donations and collections in the shops and £15 came from 'a gentleman of independent means who had always helped Birmingham trade unionists in their struggles.' This enabled the Society to give a good Christmas dinner to all members out of work. Although a 3d levy was put on for nine months the funds drained away as the depression dragged on for a couple of years more. Concerts and shop collections helped to provide something for those who had long ago run out of benefit. To help relieve funds the Society modified its old ruling and allowed members to work in non-trade shops until the situation improved. Inevitably, in the end, members were lost. Some employers used the situation to try and cut prices and to introduce women and boys onto sheet metal work, but the men stood firm on this and won the day.

After a brief improvement in 1889 the depression returned and by 1893 and 1894 the situation was proclaimed worse than ever. Then the tide turned and in 1897 and 1898 work was plentiful. The Society took the opportunity of advancing piecework prices by 5 per cent and pushing up day work rates to a minimum of 7d an hour. The employers agreed to grant the advances on condition that the Society organised the 'outside shops', brought up their rates correspondingly, so doing away with unfair competition. Then in 1889 the whole of the trade was very unsettled with hundreds of men having to change their jobs, and a large number who could not find work left the trade.

But the South African war brought prosperity to Birmingham and the Society was able to bring out a new prices book for government work. The end of the war brought a return to trade depression and jobs were scarce. However, even in Birmingham, the heart of the general trade, new lines were taking over. There was something of a boom in cycle lamps and gear cases. The rise of the motor car brought more and more jobs and with a few ups and downs trade continued to expand until the beginning of the First World War. By 1913 membership had topped 2,000.

Writing in 1892, when he was Secretary of the Society, E. Fooks claimed that it was one of the strongest unions in Birmingham with funds amounting to £2,000. Although the minimum day work rate was only 6½d an hour, 8d was more often paid. Piece-workers, who accounted for the majority of the members, were still paid on the 1855 list of prices 'which is a great bulky volume, with numerous additions for new articles, but is still the same in its staple goods.' The main body of members were on general work.

Since 1890, in particular, a great amount of machinery had been introduced into the general trade, particularly for stamping out parts.

> This is seen as a very great advantage to the men, relieving them of the hard labour part of the work, and so allow them to do much more work in less time. The men allow so much off the price for the amount of work done by machinery, but the money allowed is not so much as the amount of work actually done by the machines. The men have never resented the use of machinery, recognising that it would be a real improvement in their position if they could take advantage of it, as they have succeeded in doing.

The percentage of the price to be allowed for the work done by machinery was decided by the shop pricing committee, which also priced new articles. There was no need for the foreman to check over the prices, he said, they were all members of the Union and any complaints could be taken before the committee of the Society.

In the reorganisation of the Society in 1889/90, determined action succeeded in stamping out the piece-mastering system which in the previous twenty years had grown to a considerable extent and had become an evil. It was prohibited by rule which forbade members from either working for or employing other men. Outworking had also been prohibited, members had to work in the shop or factory of their employer – but, in any case, the increase in machinery had largely made outworking impossible.

Machinery had also brought a lot of women into the tin ware shops and 200 were then employed in the industry. There had always been a number of women and girls engaged on soldering and other odd jobs. With machinery taking over the heavy work, women were doing the small, cheap, shoddy goods. He claimed that the men were indifferent to this and never

Left: making oil and fuel tanks in a Coventry motor and general shop in the early 1920s; *bottom*: tinshop, Singer Motor Co., Coventry, 1926

tried to oppose it. In fact they were glad to be relieved of the ill-paying work. This may have been the reaction of many of the men on the shop floor, but it was certainly contrary to the Society's policy, which strictly prohibited members from working with women.

In 1895 the Society engaged in a one-month strike against women working in sheet metal shops and a report declared that female labour was a serious thing and was growing: 'Before long it must engage the serious attention of the Union.' Again, in 1897 the Society called a strike that lasted three months against female labour, declaring that they would rather lose the shop than give up their principles.

Fooks admitted that women were not allowed to join the Society and said that some time before there had been an attempt to get them into a union, without success. 'Another attempt will have to be made before long to get them to form their own union.'

He also said that apprentices were not limited or regulated at that time. Boys who were not bound apprentices were being taken into the shops. They worked for a percentage of the men's prices, until they were 18 when they had to join the Society. Then at 18 to 19 they would go and work in another shop at the full men's rate of prices. 'Some members thought that this arrangement was an advantage in some ways, others considered it an evil which led to a large number of lads being taught the trade.' The Society was then considering what should be done. The question of training had been before the Society a few years before when, in 1886, J.V.Stevens had reported that technical lectures had been held in Birmingham and had been well attended by local 'tinners'. But it was said that although technical education was desirable it came second to putting apprentices to the trade.

Fooks said that there was no system of arbitration in the trade but claimed that general relations with the employers were very good and disputes in a factory were settled with the individual employer. The employers had no formal organisation of their own but would meet when something important occurred.

In 1892 the committee revised prices for government contract work which was accepted by all employers and brought increased wages for the men. They also had a try at abolishing sweating.

Soon afterwards it was reported that special attention had been given to the organisation of the trade which had brought a big increase in numbers and in funds. The Society's rooms were looked upon, both by the employers and the Press, as 'the labour exchange of the trade.' The employers were sending to the Society for men, instead of advertising. Organisational work during 1897, 'a year of unchecked progress and prosperity', brought in shops never previously connected with the Society, and some that the officials had never even heard of had been brought in wholesale, adding between 300 and 400 to the ranks. Prices were brought up to a proper standard and day workers received increases. Advances of 5 per cent to 30 per cent were obtained on trunks, and up to 50 per cent on steamship work. They 'attacked evils in the trade that had existed for years' – once again abolishing piece-mastering.

In 1899 the employers tried to reduce wages, but the Society 'was a tower of strength' with its position improved by the organisation of the non-Society shops and the strengthening of the weak places in the organisation of the trade shops.

In 1900 and 1901 the organising continued with a lot of attention given to consolidating prices and getting uniformity of prices and conditions of work. The method of pricing was also centralised, with all new work submitted to the trade committee for pricing instead of letting each shop price its own work.

Mr Birmingham Society

In 1894 J.V. Stevens was elected secretary of the Society, receiving a salary of £106 13s a year, retaining the position until he retired in 1919.

For these 25 years Alderman John Valentine Stevens JP was 'Mr Birmingham Society'. He was much more than a General Secretary, he was the Union, and what he said went. During his rule he controlled the Union and moulded it in the way he thought it ought to be. He was born in Bristol in 1852 and served his apprenticeship in that city, moving to Birmingham when he came out of his time. He joined the Society in 1874 and six years later was elected President. In 1885 he was elected Secretary of the Amalgamated Society and it was under his energetic secretaryship that it developed into the National Amalgamated Tin Plate Workers.

In addition to his work in the Society he was also active in the wider labour movement. He was president of the Trades Union Congress when it was held in Birmingham in 1897; was a one-time Secretary of the Birmingham Trades Council and three times President of that body, but that was not untypical of the life of a trade union official of his time.

He entered general public life with his election to the Birmingham Schools Board in 1887 and followed this up with election to the City Council in 1889, defeating no less a person than Austen Chamberlain, and held the seat for 18 years. But when he stood for Parliament in 1900 as a Liberal-Labour candidate he was defeated by 2,000 votes after a massive campaign against him by the Tory party during which Joseph Chamberlain advised the working men in the constituency not to send to parliament a man who was doing so much good locally or they might find themselves short of someone to fight their local labour battles.

He was as energetic and dominant in the council as he was in trade union activities, a strong advocate of municipal ownership, particularly of the tramway system, and was largely responsible for the fair wages clause being inserted in council contracts, as well as improving the wages of the council's own employees. For six years he was a governor of King Edward's Grammar School.

He was also the first president of the national Committee for Organised Labour, an organisation claiming membership of 1,500,000 organised workers, formed to obtain old age pensions for the mass of the people.

Like so many trade union officials of the period he was also very active in the friendly society movement. He was a member of the Court of the Ancient Order of Foresters and for many years secretary of the 'Friar Tuck' court and of its High Court Investigating Committee. He could hardly have had a free moment to himself.

He also espoused the cause of free speech after being arrested when speaking at a perfectly orderly and legal open-air meeting in support of a fellow councillor's election campaign. He was incarcerated in the nearest police station on a charge of shouting in the street, based on an old local bye-law intended to restrain the raucous calls of street hawkers. After some rough handling and an hour in the cells he was grudgingly released on bail, which had at first been refused. The next day the charge was dismissed by the magistrates. When the police refused to make an apology he sued them for illegal arrest, which he won, with £40 damages and costs.

There seems no doubt that J.V. Stevens was a strong character and an outstanding personality. In addition to being extremely energetic, astute and able, he appears to have been something of an autocrat, quick tempered and allergic to criticism. In reply to a letter from the London Society criticising organisation of the trade in Birmingham, as it affected prices, Stevens wrote back a snorting letter accusing London of all the crimes in the craft union's calendar, and more, including aiding and abetting 'female and Jewish labour.'

He appears to have been the driving force in the walkout of the Birmingham Society from the Amalgamated and, in the early years, of its refusal to return to the fold – perhaps he preferred to be the big shot in a local union than a district secretary of a national body whose main full-time officer had already been chosen.

In his obituary his fellow trustees paid tribute to 'his extremely able advocacy of the claims of labour' and hailed him as a 'zealous guardian' of working-class interests. He was said to be devoted to the Society and 'a valiant fighter' who strove to obtain but one object in life, an improvement in the lives of members of the Society and the working-class in general. He was 'a warrior in the working-class movement who remained loyal to the end to the class in which he was born.'

But the obituary recorded that all who had at some period been connected with the administration of the Society had heard administered or received from him a 'thrashing', although 'a very kindly spirit underlay this apparent harshness.'

There was no false modesty about the man. In his letter of retirement addressed to the Society he stated his own claim to the members' gratitude:

> During my Secretaryship great progress has been made. Our total membership at the time of my appointment was just over 700 and it is now 3,055. Our total funds at that time stood at £1,751 14s 0½d, our funds now stand at £32,438 19s 11½d. I have been a member for 45 years, and have held office for nearly the whole of that period. The work I am most proud of is the scheme of superannuation brought out and established when I was president in the year 1880, six years after I joined the Society. This scheme has proved a great blessing to many of our aged members in their declining years, and a great help to the Society in retaining members.'

Loath to let him go, the Society paid him a retaining fee for a while and he remained a trustee of the Society until he died in 1924.

One of J.V. Stevens' pet schemes that did not come off was a co-operative business making tin plate wares. When originally proposed, during a period of severe trade depression, as a means of absorbing some of the many unemployed members, the Society decided that such a step would be taken 'only for defence.' However, Stevens was an energetic advocate of the scheme and in June 1887 the Midland Productive Tin Plate Workers Society Ltd was opened in Birmingham with £200 capital invested by the Birmingham Society. The Society later increased its investment to £400 and Stevens persuaded the National Amalgamated to invest £200. Both had representatives on the board of directors and although it was suggested from time to time that they should play a bigger part in the running of the works it was inevitably left to the full-time professional management, which was obviously very incompetent. The reports show that the management was never very satisfactory and the business was often in the red. The 1897 report, like so many others, was one of losses, but the union directors said that in the ten years it had been in operation it had brought thousands of pounds in wages to members of the trade. The co-operative bought the rights to manufacture the Speedwell cycle gear case, and this, according to the management, was to be its salvation. Money was spent on machinery and advertising. But concentrating on this, the management neglected the general work which was its bread and butter.

The Co-op staggered on until March 1918 when it was reported the business was defunct and the machinery was sold – for a lot less than it was worth. J.V. Stevens continued to defend what he called 'the child of his own creation.' Society members working there had reaped a benefit. The failure was no reflection on the capacity of trade unionists to manage co-operative production. The principles of co-operatives remained as sound as when they were founded – to provide for the emancipation of the workers by returning to them the full product of their labour.

The Lamp Makers

During 1891 the Birmingham Carriage Lamp Makers Society joined up with the Society, bringing in 149 members. We know nothing about this society, it may have been the same Birmingham Lamp Makers Society that was formed in 1825[11] or have been brought into being because according to one report the early Birmingham Society did not accept lamp makers of any kind as members of their society. When this ban was lifted we do not know, but there were certainly lamp makers in the Society in 1868 as in that year an employer, Webb, had demanded a reduction of 25 per cent in the price of ships' port and starboard lamps, but the men had stood out and Webb had agreed to go on paying the same as other employers.

By 1900, if not before, the Society had a lamp committee and in 1906 it was reported that considerable progress had been made in organising carriage lamp makers and by far the larger proportion of the men working in that section of the trade were said to be in the Society. The men were determined that something had to be done to improve their position and to guarantee them greater security and rates of wages. 'If the men show that they are in earnest, this Society will help them to raise the standard to that which some fair employers are paying at the present time,' said the trustees' report. The next year they were able to report that the carriage lamp makers had been able to establish a minimum rate of wages and to fix certain piece-work prices. The lamp committee was preparing a list of prices for general carriage work which it was believed would 'ensure to the men a fair reward for their labour, and also be the means of preventing undue and unfair competition among the manufacturers.' The committee was still engaged on the prices book in 1908.

There was a big development of lamp work at that time, first with cycle lamps and then with various lamps for motor cars as well as many of the various other kinds of lamps that had been Birmingham's stock in trade for decades.

By far the biggest employer in the cycle and motor car lamp trade in the country, was Joseph Lucas, who had been making lamps in Birmingham since 1876. He had a long connection with the Society with whom he was on such good terms that it was reported in 1890 that 'on the suggestion of, and with the help of Mr Joseph Lucas, the noted lamp manufacturer, the Society's business was removed from a public house to a private office.' In spite of that, within a few years he was locked in bitter struggle with the Society, determined to do without union members.

In May 1905 Lucas was advertising for non-union labour and putting the new men to work in special shops with youths. The Society men began to get suspicious that this was the beginning of an attempt to fill the shops with non-union labour. The union officials protested to the management. They asked what would happen if they recruited the new men into the Society and were told that the men would have to leave.

It then transpired that Lucas was also recruiting women and putting them on motor car lamps. The Birmingham Society prepared to do battle. They called on the London Society and the National Amalgamated to help, pointing out that the struggle was one of principle.

On 5 May the 65 Society men employed in the various Lucas shops gave in their notices after a general meeting at which they expressed their determination to resist to the utmost. They soon gained the support of the men and youths in the non-society shops.

The Allied Trades arranged a meeting with Lucas but he refused to move, saying that he could deal with the other trades, the brass workers etc but not with the tin plate workers. Stevens said that he was prepared to discuss anything with Mr Lucas provided no cardinal points connected with the rules of the Society were touched. Lucas insisted that he must have women on car lamps, as otherwise he could not compete with foreign competition. But the officials pointed out that he had the market sewn up and that half the lamps in London were of Lucas manufacture. In any case, he was told he had no possible chance of employing women on motor car lamps. This issue would be fought to a finish and the Society had the other trades behind them.

Then, suddenly, Lucas climbed down. With the men's notice due to expire on 13 May, he called their deputation in on the 12th and conceded all the Society's demands. He agreed that the new men could join the Society, but they must not be coerced into doing so. On their part the management would do nothing to hinder the men from joining. The fifteen lads who were in a shop of their own would be drafted into the men's shop on the basis of one to five, where they would be able to learn the trade. And finally, the women would be withdrawn from motor work.

The reason for the Birmingham Secretary's determination not to give in to Lucas was not only the Society's long-standing rejection of female labour but also his resolve that the Society should control the motor industry and this meant that women must be kept out. He emphasised time and time again that women must not be allowed to be employed on motor work.

J.V. Stevens was an astute man with an eye to the main chance – the coralling of as much work as possible for his members. He saw that the old staple goods of the general trade were being taken over by machine-made substitutes as far as the mass of day-to-day products were concerned, and he wanted something to take their place. He saw from the very first that the introduction of the motor car was a possible alternative. 'Mechanical inventions seem to favour this utilitarian trade of ours. We have good reason for believing that the New Motor Car will find considerable employment for good Sheet Metal Workers: we have already five men on this work in receipt of good wages,' he declared in 1897: in all probability the men referred to were working at Daimler. And he campaigned to get that work for the tin plate workers, not only in Birmingham and Coventry, but all over the country, aware that this was going to be a national industry and must be claimed by the tin plate workers nationally.

The Premium Bonus Dispute

In 1903 he called a meeting of all interested societies to thrash out a policy for the new industry, mainly dealing with rates and the problem of boy labour. As these discussions were largely ignored throughout the country, he called another conference in Birmingham in 1907. Stevens expressed concern at working methods in the shops on motor car work. The Midlands strictly enforced day work in their shops but various forms of piece-work were being introduced and he felt that a 'guarded form of piece-work' should be allowed in order to maintain a grip on the industry and forestall attempts by other trades to take work away from members and to stop the extension of the premium bonus system.

In June that year he called another national conference specifically to deal with the Premium Bonus system and its application to the Daimler Motor Company in Coventry. Representatives attended from 22 sheet metal workers' societies, coppersmiths from Liverpool, Manchester, Wigan and Coventry, from two London coppersmiths' societies, from the London braziers and two from the ASE. The first day's meeting, in Birmingham, was confined to sheet

Panel shop, Daimler Motor Co., Coventry, around 1905

metal workers' societies, the second day the conference moved to Coventry and was open to delegates from all societies and concerned itself with means of eliminating the system at Daimlers and stopping its spread throughout the country. Conference carried a resolution condemning the system and prohibiting members of societies attending from operating it, the ban was to take effect from 1 September 1907. They further declared that while pure day-work was preferable to any form of piece-work or bonus system and no form of premium bonus could be countenanced, a form of straight piece-work might be tolerated.

A strong deputation visited Daimlers but the management refused to end the contentious system, saying the men were free to work it or not, as they liked. A number of union members at Daimler panel shop defied the societies' instructions and continued working the Premium Bonus system as they could earn more money. The sixteen who were members of the Birmingham Society were expelled by 278 votes to 21 at 'a large and enthusiastic meeting' at Birmingham. The men expelled from the various societies formed a new organisation, the Coventry Progressive Society of Sheet Metal Workers which built up membership in the works and elsewhere. The Unions then called out all members still working in the shop but the London coppersmiths allowed their members to continue working at the factory and were strongly condemned by the Birmingham Society. It was later reported that work in the panel shop was in full swing manned by members of the Progressive and coppersmiths' societies but only 14 of the full complement of 60 were still working in the erecting shop. Birmingham Society called another meeting of interested societies in February 1908 which ended the strike and blacked the works, closing it to all union members. A blacklist of sheet metal workers still working there was drawn up and circularised to all societies.

The Birmingham Society joined with the National Amalgamated in taking the coppersmiths before a committee of the TUC which found, however, that the coppersmiths' society had not broken faith with the sheet metal workers or taken the place of any members on strike. The sheet metal workers pointed out that the committee had completely ignored the fact that a society, without a single member in Coventry, had sent members into the Daimler works and deliberately undermined conditions established by a kindred trade.

A number of other attempts were made to defeat the Premium Bonus system at Daimler but it was not until 1917 that the system was ended there and the shop was opened to members.

In an apparent attempt to save other shops for the trade Stevens took action on the lines laid down at the 1907 meeting, allowing piece-work as a defensive action. In 1909 he sent round the various societies a copy of a letter he had sent out to motor employers in the Midlands. In it he stated that the committee of the Birmingham Society had decided to let all their members on motor work operate piece-work on the conditions generally observed in the large shops in the trade. These were that any man on piece-work who was unable to earn the regular day work rate would be paid the deficit, but this could be deducted from any excess earned above the day work rate in the following three months. Overtime rates were laid down for men on both day and piece work. The men were to price their own work or come to an arrangement with the firm: but where the work was made in 'competition shops' to supply motor manufacturers, and where the articles being made were the same, trade prices should be arranged.

Over these years an increasing number of motor shops appeared from time to time in the books of the Society. After Daimler in 1897, there was Wolseley in 1907, Humber and Austin in 1908, Deasey, Rover and Motor Radiators in 1911, Rudge and Wolseley panel shop in 1912 – when the company's car production was second only to Ford in Britain. A motor committee was set up by the Coventry branch in 1910 and Birmingham formed a motor tank committee in 1913. The motor industry was then an established part of the work of Society members.

The first recorded strike at the Austin Motor Company, Longbridge, took place in March

1910, sparked off by the firm taking on youths after they had refused a Manchester Society man a job. Stevens took this as a challenge to his resolve that the motor industry should be run by union labour, as far as the sheet metal workers were concerned. He withdrew all the Birmingham Society men and circularised the trade, urging local societies not to send men to Longbridge. Within ten days Austin's agreed to give the man a job and to withdraw the youths, and the first Austin strike was over.

The same kind of trouble arose in 1912 with Serk, who owned the Motor Radiator Company. He ran a chain of radiator depots in various parts of the country, and although the main shop at Coventry and the London shop were staffed by Union men and well paid, most of the works were non-union. In his Birmingham works he employed one or two non-union men and a number of youths. Stevens saw this as an attempt by Serk to do without union labour altogether throughout his whole business, when convenient, and took up the case of the Birmingham shop. He called out the Birmingham Society men working in the Coventry shop and called for united action throughout the whole country. The dispute lasted eight weeks and came to a rather inconclusive end.

The First World War

In 1914, at the beginning of the war, the Birmingham Society experienced for some months the same problems as other local societies, with a large number of members thrown out of work. But a flood of government work soon provided jobs for all, and although there were periods and pockets of unemployment after that, the bigger problem was finding men for the jobs.

A number of new firms sprang up on war work, and while the majority worked with the Union, and observed established procedures and conditions, a few gave trouble. Some tried to employ women on skilled men's work. Others failed to observe the House of Commons resolution on fair wages. These were reported to the Ministry and the officials had an interview with one of the war ministers who turned the case over to the Chief Industrial Commissioner for an investigation, and generally the Society made use of the official machinery when it could be used in the interest of the trade.

In 1915 the Society accepted an invitation to send a representative to join other union members on a visit to the Western Front, as a means of getting greater support for the 'war effort'. A trustee and former president, G.W. Challenor, was nominated and on his return spoke at a number of meetings and his report was printed as a pamphlet by the Society. He said everything must be done to back up 'our class' fighting over there, and nothing done to jeopardise their lives. At the same time he stressed that everything must be done to maintain their rights as citizens and trade unionists and to maintain trade union and social conditions as they left them. Any attempt to reduce their pay as soldiers and the allowances to their dependants had to be resisted; when they returned to the workshops any changes should be for the better.

In 1916 wage increases were obtained in most sections, but not enough to meet the increases in the cost of living. Some employers refused to pay the increase and strike action had to be used to get the award. The Munitions Act was no use to the workers against the employers' attempts to worsen rates, and the men had to rely on the strength of their Union.

The employers also tried to force dilution on the Society, complaining that they could not get labour. The Birmingham Society sent out a call to all other local societies and 400 members turned up at Birmingham and effectively scotched the threat of dilution on that occasion.

The committee was now meeting daily. New articles were being produced all the time and had to be priced 'to obtain uniformity and to place all employers on an equal footing when tendering for work.' It took from June to October to obtain an advance on government and general work, although no advance had been given on government work since the start of the war. An agreement was drawn up, after talks with the Ministry and employers, giving 15 per cent on government work and 12½ per cent on general work, but the employers refused to honour it. This led to a great strike at the end of the year in which every trade union shop in Birmingham, Wolverhampton, Coventry, Redditch and Worcester was closed. The strike ended when the government representatives gave a promise that the agreement would be carried out. All that the members got was the promise – it was never honoured.

The same situation arose in the meter trade and the men had to strike to obtain their just rights. In the face of united and solid action by the Birmingham meter makers, and with financial help from London and elsewhere, the employers conceded their demands and a general advance followed in the meter trade throughout the country.

The attempts of the employers, aided and abetted by the government, 'to feather their own nests by means of cheap labour in the form of dilution' was one of the main causes of labour unrest throughout the War. There was widespread mistrust of all promises and assurances coming from the government and the employers broke very nearly every promise they made, said a Society report at the end of the War. Agreements were drawn up by astute lawyers serving the capitalists. They were full of hidden snags designed to misguide the workers' representatives who failed to notice them at the time, but they were 'fatally revealed' a little later. 'Acts of Parlaiment, said to be in the interest of labour, did not provide what the workers were given to believe they would provide.' The unions received no help from the government. and when they resorted to strike action to get justice they were reviled by the newspapers as unpatriotic.

It was in the light of this experience that the committee considered 'after-the-war problems.' They believed that in all probability there would be large-scale unemployment in the turn over from war work to commercial work while at the same time the men in the forces would be being demobbed. To provide for this and other possible difficulties, it was recommended that contributions be increased to build up a contingency fund. The members 'readily agreed to this.'

During the period of the war the Society increased its membership by nearly 50 per cent, the total number on the books going up from 2,183 in January 1914 to 3,055 by the end of 1918.

Post War Problems

As the Society had foreseen, the end of the war in 1918 brought a vast amount of unemployment, and the situation worsened during the next two or three years, while the cost of living continued to rise, with rents going up 30 per cent.

All kinds of fund-raising activities were undertaken to help provide for the unemployed – collections in the shops brought in over £3,000. A special effort to provide a decent Christmas for those out of work raised £152 in three days.

The employers seized this opportunity to cut wages, reducing the war bonus from 26s to 10s a week. The struggle against this cost the Society over £6,000 in 1921, while out-of-work pay shot up to a record total of £8,500. On top of all this the Society was badly hit by the 'managerial functions' lockout which cost them nearly £3,000 in lockout pay they could ill afford.

To try to obtain the best possible standards for members in this very difficult situation, the

Radiator shop, Rover Motor Co., Coventry, 1919-20; women brought in as dilutee labour during the war were still working there

Society concluded a series of agreements with the employers over a whole range of industries. But the fact that conditions of work and rates of pay were largely maintained in Society shops in the first half of the 1920s was to a very great extent due to the members and their organisation in the shops, said the committee. In particular, the shops were able to maintain their position by keeping out non-union labour and so operating from a position of greater strength. This demanded continual vigilance, particularly on the part of the shop stewards whose key position in industry was becoming recognised in the Society.

Although the numbers out of work continued high, trade gradually improved. Then came the General Strike and the miners' lockout in which many of the Society's members were involved. Collections were taken in the shops and branches for the miners and their families and the Society hailed the strike as a splendid example of working-class solidarity, even though it had failed, although it suggested that it would be wrong to blame anyone for its failure. But, unlike some unions, the Society was not frightened by general strike action as a result; instead it declared that mistakes made on that occasion should be learned in case such action was needed again, pointing out that the government was considering legislation to curb the unions.

The First World War was a watershed; members entered the war tin plate workers, they came out sheet metal workers.

The war had been a forcing house of new ideas and new ways of doing things, particularly in industry. The Society's world had changed much more as the result of five years of war than in the decades before it. The Society had to accommodate itself to this world and to provide the appropriate organisation to deal with the new problems.

General work, that had been the backbone of the Birmingham trade for generations of tinmen, had shrunk considerably. The wide variety of lamps that had been made in

Jobs done by 83-year old Percy Bliss (*left*) of Birmingham, are typical of the trade. He started at Alldays and Onions in 1912 on cycle work; during the First World War, he made ventilator fans for the first tanks to be sent to France. He then made bodies for Alldays and Onions cars until 1926, going on to make fuel tanks for tractors. In the Second World War, he made fans for barrage baloons; he is pictured here at the age of 80, making blowers for heating and ventilator systems.

Birmingham since the early days of the trade were now made by machine and unskilled labour, but although it is about as far from the sea as it is possible to get in Britain, Birmingham continued as a centre for making ships' lamps – navigation lamps, masthead, port and starboard, poop, stern and bow lamps, galley and engineeroom lamps, morse code, globe, telegraph lamps and many others. In the 1930s they made the lamps for the *Queen Mary* and later for the *QE2*. Another job was making the big headlamps for US locomotives. In the later years, when the trade had further declined, about 50 men were employed, many of them on fancy work, in a couple of firms in Birmingham – another firm in Glasgow was also engaged in the trade.

There was a strike of churn makers, but it was one of the last signs of life in a declining dairy industry.

The motor industry took a much more important place in the employment of society members in Birmingham and Coventry. It had a large number of small factories and shops but was dominated by a few big factories employing large numbers of men. The years since the War had seen the development of these mass production, highly mechanised factories with their giant presses. The Society had to consider the position for the maximum number of members in conditions that called for completely different methods of work to those of which members had experience and in factories where the sheet metal workers were a small, if often influential minority.

In 1928 the Society began an organisation campaign in the motor industry, particularly directed toward the big factories. It moved outside the Midlands to tackle the giant Pressed Steel Company of Oxford, which made all-metal bodies for Morris, and to a lesser extent for other manufacturers. It seems to have made a foothold there, if little more. But for some reason it does not appear to have made any attempt to organise the nearby Morris Motors factories, with their sheet metal, radiator, press and soldering shops that might have been thought to be the ideal Society territory, despite a strong anti-union attitude by William Morris. However, it did get some members in a few of the larger shops in the Midlands, reporting that in 'at least one large shop we are making considerable progress.'

In the next few years dozens of new members were made in motor shops such as Austin, Wolseley and, above all, at Fisher and Ludlow, which would seem to suggest that organisation in the industry was very poor. We first encountered Fisher's making army mess tins in the Boer War. By 1930 it was one of the bigger of the new steel pressing firms that were changing the face of the industry. Thanks to a core of active members, including the works' convenor, Alf Cooper, who was to later become General Secretary, a good shop organisation was built up there. But organising the Union in these large factories was extremely difficult and 'ringleaders' were candidates for the sack.

More problems arose when in 1932 Fishers started an 'endless band' method of manufacture with a two-shift system on the basis of a 40-hour week, and then in 1934 proposed a system of measured daywork. This latter was resisted by the men who favoured straight piece-work. (That also applied at Standard of Coventry where the same method of working had been put forward.) After a lot of Union pressure, including a number of mass meetings, the firm agreed to withdraw the system and return to straight piece-work.

The following year, in the worst of the slump, when the Society had had to make cuts in superannuation and funeral benefits, the men at Fisher's refused to work overtime as long as men were walking the streets out of work.

The shop stewards were now playing an increasingly important role in the activities of the Society, and the first of a regular series of shop stewards' meetings, convened by the EC, was held in October 1933, attended by some fifty stewards. Shop organisation in a number of factories was strengthened. A reorganised shop stewards and committee set-up was instituted at Fisher's, with stewards in all shops and a 'chairman of the central committee.' Now, when the stewards in one shop called a meeting of his members the stewards in the other four shops attended so that all stewards knew what had been decided and could act accordingly.

At the Austin the number of stewards was increased to serve the increased number of members working there and they were told to appoint collectors to serve under them. Wolseley was also affected, many new members had been recruited and in 1935 a deputation from the shops visited head office to discuss organisation at the firm.

The following year a mass meeting of some 300 meter makers from all the Birmingham meter shops was held at the Central Hall and discussed the position of the trade. It was decided to set up a permanent meter committee composed of representatives of all the meter shops in the City, who remained members as long as they worked in the shop. The names of the committee members were registered at the Union office, tying it in with the Union machinery. National Union members could be co-opted onto the committee on special occasions but all permanent committee members would be Birmingham Society men. The mood of the meeting was that the meter trade was in decline and they must take drastic measures to save what could be salvaged.

Later, members at Parkinson and Cowan complained of prices in the meter, geyser and lamp shops. More particularly they objected to being asked to work in shops where women were employed on street lamps. A deputation reported that the firm had started to work the Bedeaux system and two members had been clocked on jobs. Members were told that they must not work under the system nor must they go into the lamp shop unless the women were taken off the job.

Similar problems continued in the various sections of the trade. Even at Cadbury's, where some thirty members were employed, a deputation was elected and sent to head office to complain at the method of pricing moulds for chocolate making.

In 1938 the men at Austin Motors walked out when the firm put a rate fixer in the sheet metal shop. The men returned only when the management agreed to remove him and promised that there would be no victimisation; the action led to a tightening up of organisation in the shops.

From the mid-1930s a number of aircraft shops were opened in Birmingham, many by firms connected with the motor industry. The Society decided to get in on the ground floor and began organising as the shops went into operation. The Austin Aero Works was set up in 1938 and a meeting of 700 members was held in the 'mess hall' to discuss organisation. Joseph Lucas also opened two aircraft shops and the steward reported that almost 100 per cent organisation had been achieved, with the main shop paying the district rate of 57s plus 25 per cent plus 18s and the detail fitting shop paying 50s plus 25 per cent plus 18s.

There was a turn-out of 110 stewards at the February 1939 shop stewards' meeting,where the secretary reported that an aircraft committee was being set up on which every shop engaged on aircraft work would be represented. The recruiting drive in the big motor and aircraft shops was reflected in the membership figures, topping the 4,000 mark for the first time in 1936 and going over the 5,000 a couple of years later.

With the introduction of war work on the eve of the Second World War, the Society came to an arrangement with the local district of the Union of Gold, Silver and Allied Trades, covering silversmiths who might go onto work in sheet metal shops.

It was agreed that silversmiths over the age of 50 would be allowed to work in society shops and have a card as a senior member on payment of ls a week, but they would not be entitled to any benefits. The Society would have the right, at the end of the war, to call in any card issued under this agreement. Any silversmith member of the Society would then have to declare whether he wanted to remain in the sheet metal workers or return to the silversmiths. If he wanted to return to his old trade he would have to surrender his card immediately and the silversmiths' district secretary would be responsible for seeing the card was returned. Silversmiths under 50 years of age with at least ten years' membership of their trade would be allowed to join the sheet metal workers and at the same time retain their membership of the silversmiths' society on the payment of 5s a year. They would be recognised as sheet metal workers, pay full contributions and receive full benefits. They could, if they wanted, return to their old society when the war was over, in which case their membership of the sheet metal workers would cease. They would then have to surrender their card and would receive no further benefits after that date.

It was agreed that all sheet metal work done in all shops under the silversmiths' control would have to be done at rates and under conditions not less favourable than those in Society shops and paid at piece-work prices not less than in those shops under the Society's jurisdiction. In shops where neither had control the two societies would jointly organise the shop with any silversmiths joining the silversmiths' union and any sheet metal workers joining the Birmingham Society.

The Society also concluded, in 1940, a wartime agreement with the coppersmiths' society. Following a dispute over rates at Wilmot Breeden, the two societies agreed that no member of either society would start on aircraft work at less than 57s plus 10 per cent plus 25s national awards. They also agreed that a joint committee would look into all membership applications and report on the advisability or otherwise of accepting them into membership of one or other society.

An agreement the Birmingham Society made with the National Union stipulated that except for the Galvanised Hollowware workers, who would remain firmly under the control of the National Union, the Birmingham Society would be the negotiating body for all work in its area of jurisdiction. A further agreement laid down that auxiliary cards issued by the two unions would not be issued to men to work on sheet metal work but only for welders and men working with sheet metal workers and not themselves on sheet metal work.

The Out-of-Town Branches

At the turn of the century, having consolidated its organised position in Birmingham, the EC began to look at some of the towns in the surrounding area. There had long been members in various shops in a number of nearby towns but they were individual members, without any organisation. Now it was becoming apparent that if the Society was to get the trade organised, so that the non-union out-of-town factories did not pose a threat to the organised Birmingham shops by undercutting, there would have to be local branches. The first of these was started in Coventry.

The first report we have of any Society members in Coventry was in 1895 when it was said that some 30 Birmingham Society members were working in the City, mainly on cycle lamps. The Society negotiated an eight-hour day, overtime rates and increases of 1d and 2d an hour for them.

From the Society's books it would seem that the Coventry branch was started in 1899. Its secretary was H.Robinson and it affiliated to the Coventry Trades Council in 1903.

According to reports Birmingham Society members were working in the infant motor industry at least by 1903 and were working at Daimler even before that.

Coventry, which had been a centre of the watch-making and cycle trades, and therefore had a large section of mechanics among its workforce, was ideally placed to take advantage of development of the motor industry. Membership of the Society increased by leaps and bounds. Men came from all over the country to work there, some belonging to other local branches of the National Amalgamated or General Union, others did not belong to any union. The development of aircraft factories and expansion of other engineering plants in the City during the First World War boosted branch membership still further.

By the end of that war the branch had become so large that it was decided to upgrade the branch secretary to a full-time position. Richard Baston was elected in 1919 and held the position until he was elected General Secretary of the Society in 1939. We do not know the number of members in the Coventry branch at that time, but branch contributions amounted to £1,731 compared with a total of £6,009 for the Society as a whole that year, when the total membership of the Society was 2,995.

As was to be expected, membership dropped at the end of the war. The branch ran a 'back to the union' organising campaign which seems to have been very successful in that contributions, which had dropped to £1,740, shot up to £2,074 and remained in the £2,000 range. The branch committee then urged members to take over as much of the panel work as they could 'with the object of obtaining complete control of this section of the motor industry, a position that was ultimately obtained.'

The pattern of work, with high wages one month and dole the next, was probably responsible for the Coventry workers' reputation for militancy and political awareness. In the First World War it had been one of the centres of the engineering shop stewards' movement, and it was to continue this militancy under the leadership of the shop stewards in the Second World War and in the post-war struggles.

There was a lot of grumbling about this way of working but the economic depression stopped anything being done about it in the inter-war years.

As early as 1925 the branch helped to organise a meeting for the miners of the nearby Midlands coalfield then engaged in a struggle with the mine-owners against demands for a cut in wages and increase in hours. Then in 1926, 'a vital year in the history of the trade union movement,' to quote the branch secretary, the branch 'answered the general strike call of the TUC General Council to a man.' They also collected over £660 for the dependants of the local miners. In the city, like everywhere else, the defeat of the General Strike saw attacks on union organisation, and the branch balance sheet records the payment of £113 12s 6d in victimisation benefit.

A few years afterwards came the great slump: 1931 was said to be the worst year members of the branch had experienced, with continued mass unemployment reducing membership and depleting resources. The 1930s saw many old-established shops go out of business: motor shops, in particular, disappeared or were taken over, some of them having employed Society members since before the First World War.

In 1938, with shops going down all around them, the EC held a special meeting which decided that a 10 per cent reduction in piece prices be offered to the Coventry-based Singer Motor Company – which employed a lot of Society members, including officials – as a contribution to the firm's struggle to keep its head above water. This would continue until there was an improvement in business. A deputation from the stewards and the branch committee was told that this was only temporary and after the firm had pulled round the EC expected the 10 per cent to be returned. Meanwhile there could be no loosening of trade union conditions.

However, despite the continuing slump it was not all gloom in the motor industry and some recruitment continued, notably at SS Motors, later to become Jaguar cars, and which was then becoming an organised trade shop.

Relations with members of other sheet metal workers' societies had been a problem for the Coventry branch of the Birmingham Society since its early days. In the period of the First World War and immediately afterwards there were probably more members of outside societies than of the Coventry branch itself, with all the problems of discipline, checking cards for membership, collecting and transferring contributions and the many sources of friction inevitable in this situation.

Although some of these problems were solved with the formation of the National Union and the setting up of the Coventry National Union branch in March 1921, there still remained many areas of friction although the National Union continued to recognise the right of the Society to negotiate area rates and conditions on behalf of members of both unions.

Generally, however, relations in the shops, where members of both unions worked side by side, were good, as realities of day-to-day life on the shop floor did not let either of them forget that the 'enemy' was the employers.

Concern of the Society for the position in Coventry built up, however, when the National Union appointed a full-time district secretary in 1933. The EC expressed its fears that the National Union would appoint its own shop stewards and shop organisation, bringing dual control and undermining the Society's own organisation in the city. The EC's fears were increased when they were told that some National Union members were already acting as stewards, representing members of both unions. Assurance was given that these National Union stewards did not take full part in meetings of Society members, nor attend meetings where domestic affairs of the Society were discussed.

The EC instructed the Coventry branch to see that all shop stewards were Birmingham Society members, a demand which it was impossible to put into practice. The EC was somewhat placated, however, when the National Union assured them that their new full-time officer was only a financial secretary and all general negotiations would continue to be undertaken by the Birmingham Society.

In the 1940s the Coventry branch reported 'an unfriendly attitude' on the part of the National Union district secretary in muscling-in on negotiations and the EC advised that 'a close watch should be kept throughout the district.' The situation cannot have been easy, especially at times of work shortage.

Branches were formed in 1913 at Rugby and Burton-on-Trent. The latter was very small with the members working mainly on refrigerators, but with some on brewery work. There was little change in the branch until the Second World War when a number of new factories engaged in war work opened in the town, the main one a dispersal works of Daimler of Coventry. The branch had difficulty with the management who wanted to pay the lower Burton rates and help was needed from the parent factory to get Coventry rates.

More success was obtained in organising the other dispersal factories and building up the branch. But after the war most of the factories closed and branch membership dropped back, continuing to slide until 1955 when the branch was closed.

The Rugby branch was about four times the size of Burton, the members mainly engaged on general work in the sheet metal department and maintenance section of the big AEI works, later taken over by GEC. During the last war some dispersal factories opened in the town, bringing more work and more members. In the post-war period membership was maintained and the branch was able to record full employment. Membership increased in the mid-1960s with the arrival of new sheet metal factories which were promptly organised.

This unexciting but satisfactory situation continued, except for a drop for a short period when GEC reduced their sheet metal shop. Rugby was the only branch except Coventry to survive until the fusion with the National Union.

A branch was opened in Redditch in 1914, most of the members being employed in the Austin Motor Company. Like the other smaller branches dispersal factories brought new members to Redditch, doubling the membership by 1942. These new shops were said to give 'greater interest to the branch.' But after the war the branch declined and seems to have died in 1955.

There were pockets of 'outside' members in a number of Midland towns. In the small market town of Ludlow in Shropshire members were employed at Hurry Heaters during the war. At Malvern and Defford members worked side-by-side with National Union members at the government radar establishments, RTE, and others worked in various shops in Worcester. All of these Society members were serviced by Birmingham, coming under the South Birmingham branch which lasted from 1949 to 1959 and was otherwise largely consisting of members working at Austin Motors.

In 1945 a branch was opened in Dudley in the Black Country which specialised in hearth furniture. It was hoped that this would pick up post-war with the restarting of house building. The branch closed in 1952 but during its short life it was able to organise a number of new shops and employers were going to the branch for labour.

After a number of requests by delegations of local members, a branch was opened at Loughborough in 1949. One of its first jobs was to find work for a large number of members made redundant by the local coach works. This left the main employers Rolls Royce at Mount Sorrel and Brush Electric. In 1960 the branch reported membership had risen to over 100 but during the next ten years it dwindled and the branch disappeared from the books in 1968.

The Second World War

As with the 1914-1918 war, the most immediate problem the Society had to deal with after the outbreak of the Second World War was that of dilution.

Already by 1940 the Society, together with the National Union, had had to enter into a dilution agreement with the engineering employers. In a message to members, the Society expressed the hope that it would be tackled in most shops 'in the right spirit' by both employers and members. However, members were told to keep a watchful eye on any employers who tried to exploit the situation to their own advantage. When changes in production were inevitable, shop organisations must insist that all changes be registered, as was stipulated in the agreement, so that the Society would be in a position to safeguard the trade in the post-war period. They were also to demand that the union rate be paid whoever did the job – it was reported that when that had been done many employers lost interest in dilution.

The agreement was confined to male dilution and on some occasions the Society withdrew its members when managements put women on sheet metal work. Although the Ministry was informed the officials did not want to know and rarely intervened with the employers who were pressing for a new agreement on female dilution. The two unions emphasised this was not on, although they were prepared to consider extending the general dilution agreement to cover women.

As the war progressed, skilled members on war work, who had been reserved at eighteen, became eligible for call-up. The Society complained that while skilled men were being called up, rivetters remained reserved. The Ministry promptly took the rivetters off the reserved list so that they were the same as sheet metal workers. The Society then put in a further complaint that skilled men were being called up while dilutees remained. This brought a letter from Lord Terrington at the Ministry to the effect that sheet metal workers would not be called up for combat duties until the problem could be sorted out.

Already in 1940 the committee had realised that the Society's rule prohibiting juniors from working in motor and aircraft shops – a decision adopted to stop the boys being used as cheap labour – meant that they would be eligible for the army. The EC was therefore allowed to make changes in the rules to allow juniors between the ages of 20 and 21 to be drafted on to aircraft or vehicle work on the distinct understanding that this would only be used for 'military reasons.'

Early in 1943 redundancy became a problem, although the displaced men were fitted in here and there. But later in the year the secretary reported difficulty in placing redundant members and expressed concern on the effect this might have on their call-up. So far they had been able to retain members under 24 who had received their calling-up papers, by the frequent use of Lord Terrington's letter. When the Ministry withdrew this concession and again started calling up members, the Society compiled a list of dilutees who had registered under 30 years of age 'to assist in the calling up of dilutees' while reserving skilled men. This was later supplemented by a list of members who had joined the Society since the outbreak of the war who should be called up in preference to more established members. Attempts were then made to get skilled men out of the forces and returned to the shops, or else to be transferred from combat duties to technical branches where their skills could be utilised.

Redundancy again arose as a problem in 1944 when 'an abundance of war materials' was received from the United States. There were a number of lay-offs and some unemployment for a time, but eventually all were placed in other jobs.

As the war seemed to be drawing to a close the EC began to give consideration to the post-war policies of the Society.

Members at the Austin plant were told to build up organisation, taking into account the post-war position. They should take in all men working on sheet metal work with the necessary qualifications who were prepared to fight for the full Society rate.

At a special EC meeting in August 1944 on post-war policy to prepare the basis for pricing peace-time work, a questionnaire sent to 94 shops employing 4,870 members showed an average wage of 4s 4½d, inclusive of national bonus, ranging from 2½ per cent on only 2s an hour to 50 per cent earning 5s an hour or more. Together with further information obtained from the shops they were able to formulate a pricing policy for post-war motor and aircraft work to give a member of average ability the possibility of earning 3s 4½d an hour, plus full awards. The gas meter committee was to consider what the meter policy should be and general and other sections would be considered later.

With the end of the war the Society had to contend with rapidly rising unemployment. At the beginning of September 1945 some 200 were signing the books, going up to 350 on the 18th, 500 on the 24th, 750 on 1 October and 1,000 on 9 October. By the end of the year 12½ per cent of the total membership was out of work.

At the same time men continued to be called up and by the end of 1945 there were 1,643 members in the forces out of a total membership of 7,260, an increase of some 1,600 since 1939.

In this situation the Society insisted that the number of dilutees who were still doing sheet metal work under the war-time agreement, should be first on the redundancy lists, followed by the members who had joined during the war whose ability and experience should be taken into account. A large number of the silversmiths who had been brought in under a special agreement between the two unions, had already returned to their own trade and it was expected that the rest would do so within a period of three months.

An approach was made to the Ministry of Labour to deal with the question of ending the registration of dilutees under the Restoration of Pre-War Practices Act of 1942, when the Minister, Ernest Bevin, had promised that the sacrifices of skilled workers would be safeguarded. The Minister replied that it had not been decided when this Act would be put into operation.

Return to Normal

With one thing and another the return to pre-war 'normalcy' proved long and difficult. The Society expressed its dissatisfaction at the speed, or lack of it, with which craftsmen were being demobbed two years after the end of the war, with 700 members still in the forces at the end of 1947.

Having had almost no unemployment or dispute payments to make during the war the Society's funds were fortunately in a position to deal with the cost of unemployment arising from the change-over to a peace-time economy, followed by closures and part-time working arising from shortages of fuel and raw materials which beset much of industry for a number of years after the war.

In this situation the Society took part in the movement for a 40-hour week which many unions backed as a means of reducing unemployment, as well as providing greater leisure for members.

The EC congratulated the Society on the arrangements that had been made with the shop stewards before the end of hostilities which had done much to help stabilise conditions inside the various factories. Building on this, 1947 saw a general improvement in shop organisation. Agreements were made with Fisher and Ludlow, Singer Motors and Serk Radiators which marked a big step forward in the organisation of the trade. A lot of thanks for this again was due to the shop stewards and shop committees which had become an essential part of the organisation of the Society, its official status recognised by monthly meetings of shop stewards from the various factories.

A new attempt was made to organise workers in Pressed Steel at Oxford. A meeting was held with former members at the factory and 80 application forms were received, cards were issued and a further meeting arranged. Attention was given to other factories where pressings had taken the place of the pre-war hand-built motor car bodies. Men working in the all-metal body department at Wolseley Motors were organised. The work on rectification of panels from the press was claimed at Armstrong, as was the operation of wiring machines at Fisher and Ludlow. Organisation at Austin had become strong enough for the whole of the membership at the West Works to stop when two non-Society men were started.

But the work position in the 1950s continued difficult, particularly in the motor industry in which a considerable section of the membership was by then employed. Members opted for short-time working wherever possible to share out what work was available, which resulted in a number of clashes with managements.

Membership at this period fluctuated within the 8,000 band with a high level of lapsings keeping the total from going above 9,000. It was not until 1960 that the registration of 795 skilled members and 460 auxiliaries during the year brought the total to 9,530.

Heat exchangers under construction at Marston's, Wolverhampton; *below*: welding a condenser incorporating six brazed aluminium heat exchangers for an oxygen plant; *on opposite page*: a pre-cooler for a B1-11 aircraft

But the early years of the 1960s saw a continuation of unemployment from closures and short-time working in the aircraft industry.

But 1968 was a different story, enabling the Society to record 'real full employment' and 'the unique but pleasing experience of having more vacancies than unemployed members', with a number of companies offering a variety of pay and productivity deals to attract workers.

This situation did not last long, and by 1972 unemployment was again a major problem. In that year lay-offs in Jaguar involved the Society in the largest single item of expenditure in 20 years, with further lay-offs at Chrysler, Coventry, adding to the difficulties – both the result of disputes in other unions.

Political Action

The Society was rather late in setting up a political fund. It was not until 1944 that a decision was taken 'by a large majority' to affiliate to the Labour Party. In April 1945 a ballot was held on whether the Society should have a political fund with 629 voting in favour and 64 against. It was not until May 1947 that it was decided to apply for affiliation to the Labour Party on a membership of 3,750.

After some funds had been accumulated in the Political Account the Society affiliated to the Birmingham Borough Labour Party and delegates were proposed for five new constituency parties. A political section was started with a Secretary and chairman who attended head office every Saturday to receive members who wanted to take part in its activities. After a few months the officers reported that the section had nominated Society representatives to 11 of the 13 Labour Party constituency management committees in the area. Members of the section held meetings, debates and discussions, took teams of canvassers into marginal wards, and distributed Labour Party literature in the shops. However the activities, though not the fund, seem to have petered out after the Secretary, V. O'Hara, became Secretary of the South Birmingham branch of the Society.

Another political decision taken at this time was to invest £200 in the People's Press Printing Society, the publishers of the *Daily Worker*, which was carried unanimously at a general meeting at the end of 1945 and the EC appointed a delegate to attend membership meetings.

General Secretaries

Stevens was followed as General Secretary in 1919 by Charles Brett, a very different character. He led the Society through the difficult inter-war years and during the General Strike was a member of the Birmingham trades action committee. In 1927 he was made SecretaryTreasurer and built up the Society's finances to a respectable position. He died in harness in 1939 and was followed by the Coventry branch secretary, Richard Baston, an able negotiator who put his Coventry experience to good use. He also died in harness in 1951 to be followed by Harry Townsend who had been filling the new position of Assistant General Secretary. He continued in office until 1958 when he was replaced by the President, Alf Cooper. His period of office registered many changes including the end of its life as an independent Society and amalgamation with the National Union.

Alf Cooper had a rough and tough childhood in the back-to-back streets of Birmingham's slumland before the First World War and an early life rich in personal experience of unemployment, and he never forgot it. He told of going barefoot; fighting other boys for a crust and dripping; his bathroom the canal with a sack for a towel, their bed coverings the family's supply of coats; clothes supplied by charities and recognisable as such to all; a continual war against bugs that would swarm from·one terraced house to another; clashes with the police; how his honeymoon was two years on the dole, helped out by food parcels from collections made by the local newspaper.

He had a great deal of experience of the trade, particularly in the motor industry from 1920 at Wolseley onwards. He had worked in most motor shops, helped by a facility for getting elected shop steward which was like putting in for the sack. His record was getting elected steward at 2 o'clock and getting the sack at five past, and on another occasion had three jobs in one morning. As an active rank-and-filer, in 1928 he was sent by the Society into the big Pressed Steel Company works at Oxford to try and organise it as the rates and conditions were undermining the motor shops in Coventry. It was difficult to get men to stay there so the Society paid them 10s a week to encourage them to stay. They did get a shop of 30 to 40 members at one time with a shop organisation but they were swamped with unskilled men driven into the works by unemployment. The management would place five or six unskilled on the same bench as a skilled man and told them to watch what he did and copy him. But as soon as trade picked up the Birmingham members drifted back home. He said they might have got somewhere if only the National Union leadership had been interested in organisation and had collaborated. The factory was never organised until the Transport and General took it on in the 1950s; they were successful as they first organised the fork lift truck drivers who moved steel plates, pressings and other material from one shop to another, and if they stopped the whole works stopped. They had a few men doing skilled work at Morris Motors, Oxford, but never managed to get an organised shop, only individuals, generally those passing through. He was best known in the Society for his work at Fisher and Ludlow, a big works with 120 wheeling machines lined up. When he started there they had only 250 members and poor organisation, when he left it was a closed shop 1,300 strong.

During the war he worked in a number of aircraft shops and was elected to a succession of positions inside the Society, an EC member in 1940, then trustee, vice-President and then President. In 1950 he organised the resistance to seasonal work which had been the lot of pre-war motor workers, and established the right to short-time working to share the work and keep men off the dole, cutting their piece-work earnings throughout the whole membership by 1s an hour for four weeks. He fought for restricted night-work shifts demanded by the men: first for a short Friday night and then, when the 40-hour week was won, for the 40 hours to be worked in four shifts, almost completely isolated in the Confederation of Shipbuilding and Engineering Unions, on the issue.

He played an important part in the 1956 BMC strikes against redundancy, organising the pickets at the Austin works, clashing with the police, organising the mass pickets to lie down in the gateways to stop lorries and negotiating with the police to remove the horses, keeping marbles in his pocket just in case. He organised coach and car loads of Birmingham members to man the gates in the weaker factories, Nuffield's and Morris Motors, in one of the early 'flying pickets.' He was very proud that his own Fisher and Ludlow men were out solid.

He was a great believer in piece-work both as a means of getting the best possible wages and, more particularly, because of the strength it gave to the shop organisation to allow members to control their own working lives. Earnings ceilings would be lowered or raised to suit circumstances, adjusted to share work and stop redundancies, to control the speed of the line, to maintain prices. He mourned the passing of the piece-work system and with it, as he saw it, the end of real workers' control.

In his period as General Secretary membership of the Birmingham and Midlands Society went up by some 20 per cent and its funds trebled. Of all his contributions his greatest was probably his part in bringing about amalgamation with the National Union which was 'very desirable.' But he admitted that the drive for amalgamation had always come from the Coventry branch where the two unions worked very closely together at all levels with joint committees. Birmingham never had such a relationship and therefore never such a strong feeling for amalgamation.

Although he was never an indentured apprentice, Alf Cooper had great pride of craft and was particularly happy working on copper. When planishing a job on a polished anvil with a six-pound hammer he would generally be singing 'Soldiers of the Queen' to get the right rhythm for the hammer strokes. When he finished a job in copper he would lovingly polish it and look at it 'for hours' saying 'Ain't I good?'

Amalgamation

From time to time after it had broken away from the National Amalgamated in 1908 the Birmingham Society received invitations to rejoin the main body.

One such invitation was received in 1914. Birmingham replied with a draft scheme of 'solid amalgamation.' Representatives of the Amalgamated had a number of meetings with the Society and then put forward their own proposals which were rejected by Birmingham as not going far enough – there were no rules proposed to govern such an amalgamation, no provisions for district committees and no central fund.

Another invitation was received at the end of the war when discussions were taking place on the constitution of the new National Union. The Birmingham Society could not accept a number of the proposals put forward by the Amalgamated, particularly on the formation of district committees and the right of societies to withdraw and take their share of the funds. But the main objection was over superannuation. J.V. Stevens, who could be said to have an emotional interest in the Birmingham superannuation fund, his special 'brainchild', emphatically declared that under no circumstances would Birmingham be prepared to pool their superannuation funds, neither could the Society's trustees agree to merge the funds, which they considered as sacred. He finally stated that if the Amalgamation delegates were particularly desirous of forming a national union they would be able to do so among themselves without waiting for Birmingham to join. And, summing up, the Society's President, G.W. Challenor, pointed out that as they could not agree with the Amalgamated delegates on the points put forward it was useless for them to retire and discuss the situation. Their instructions were definite and they would report back to their members. They then walked out, which was the end of that attempt.

After the formation of the National Union, which left Birmingham the only major society outside, it continued to receive further invitations from time to time. In January 1923 the Society received a deputation from the National Union to whom it put questions on superannuation, the duplication of branches in some towns and a number of financial matters. But the replies were not considered satisfactory and nothing came of it. The National Union made another approach in 1935 but the Society replied that they saw no point in further meetings.

Soon after the election of Richard Baston as secretary, a letter was received from Charles Hickin, General Secretary of the National Union, for talks to bring a fusion of the two organisations, and a meeting was held in Birmingham on 20 October 1939.

Hickin urged that the war situation demanded the closest unity and fullest co-operation of the joint forces of the two unions. Other unions were trying to encroach on the craft and the National Union was not going to allow the fact that they were working with the engineers and the coppersmiths to be used to bring dilution. It was in the best interest of the trade that there should be complete understanding and that they have a clear-cut policy with the objective of one union for the sheet metal industry. He called for the setting up of a committee to consider thoroughly the whole question of amalgamation.

Baston said that full consideration would be given by the EC but it was too early to say with what result. He then went on to raise more day-to-day matters, saying he favoured discussions on dilution and military service and the question of detail fitting on aircraft which he considered sheet metal work. Joint efforts were needed and Birmingham would be pleased to co-operate in attending deputations and in talks with the Ministry.

In November, the EC considered the meeting on amalgamation and a suggestion that the proposed joint committee be set up, but Baston urged that it be left until after a further joint meeting. It was later decided to set up a sub-committee of the Society to discuss thoroughly how it would be affected by amalgamation.

A joint sub-committee met early in 1941 and agreed on proposals of the Birmingham Society that after amalgamation there would be one Midlands district comprised of Birmingham, Wolverhampton, Coventry, Rugby, Burton, Redditch, Worcester, Stourbridge and other towns in the area. The district office would be situated in Birmingham with sub-district offices in Wolverhampton, Coventry and Lye. There would be no alteration in the constitution of the district for five years unless the majority of members desired. After receiving endorsement by the National Union, the Birmingham Society then raised the disparity in the funds of the two organisations. The general fund of the Birmingham Society equalled approximately £8 6s per member against only £5 16s 2d for the National Union and the Birmingham superannuation fund equalled £3 13s 10 per member compared with £1 0s 8d for the National Union. No way could be found for dealing with this and it was suggested that it would be better to leave further consideration until more normal times. In view of the advisability of maintaining relations with the National Union it was decided that Birmingham would go further into the matter and report to a joint body.

From time to time the Society sent representatives to conferences to discuss a more general amalgamation of the unions in the engineering industry mostly called by the AEU but most members realised that before there could be any wider amalgamation they must forge a national united union for all sheet metal workers.

In 1944 a letter was sent to the National Union stating that the Society did not want to break off negotiations but it was thought it would be better to remain separate for the duration of the war while continuing the working relationship. Immediately after the war negotiations could be reopened.

In October 1945 the secretary did write to the National Union suggesting a joint EC meeting to discuss amalgamation. Meetings were called of the branches – Coventry, Burton-on-Trent, Dudley, Rugby and Redditch – to discuss the whole question of amalgamation, which was accepted in principle. It was proposed that the Society should have representatives on the NEC as soon as amalgamation was agreed; the Midlands district should continue to have a seat on the EC of the Confederation of Shipbuilding and Engineering Unions; certain other autonomy claims were made for Midlands branches and the current motor and aircraft rates should be preserved. The proposal was put to the members at a general meeting and the report was approved at meetings of Birmingham and branches by 837 votes to three, with the proposal to have a ballot of the membership agreed by 813 to 44. When the ballot was held in 1946 the proposal was rejected by a mere 74 votes, 1,704 against 1,629, over 50 per cent of the membership having voted when allowance was made for members in the forces.

The result was obviously a great surprise. In his message to members the General Secretary said that this was a 'vital question' and it was essential that the relations between the two societies should be as close as possible. 'Their interests, obviously, are our interests, and our interests must be bound up in the general sheet metal industry.' The EC would be keeping the situation under review and no stone would be left unturned 'to obtaining a close working arrangement with our friends of the National Union.'

He appealed to members working with National Union members to realise how essential it was that unity should prevail between members of the two organisations within the shops. Although at that time it was impossible to take any further steps he asked members to do nothing that would tend to lead to disunity. The EC was quite determined 'that this matter should be ever before them', and no effort would be spared to cement the friendship between the two organisations. This was by far the strongest appeal for unity between the two unions since the break in 1908.

Arrangements were immediately made for a closer working arrangement and although the Society feared that it would not be possible to raise the question again for about two years, the secretary promised to get in touch whenever a move could be made.

The following year he reported that 'it would appear that the arrangements between the two societies were working very smoothly and were undoubtedly serving a useful purpose.'

The Society later asked the National Union for a proper working agreement to cover the old bones of contention, the allocation of jobs, methods of collecting contributions and shop organisation. This improved relations for a time although friction continued. Talks continued between the leadership of the two unions and in 1964 it seemed that it would be possible to go forward to another ballot but in 1964 a ballot of members unexpectedly voted by 3,530 to 3,240 against continuing with talks on amalgamation. However, after a discreet interval talks were renewed against a background of deteriorating employment prospects. In 1970 sub-committees of the two executives got down to detailed discussion, the main concerns being the forms of organisation in the Midlands after merger with the integration of branches and shop organisation; and the situation concerning benefits, particularly concerning the superannuation fund which had long been a main area of controversy in amalgamation discussions. In 1972 the EC accepted the proposals agreed by the sub-committee and recommended acceptance in a ballot of members. This was held in March 1973 with 3,729 voting for and 1,586 against, and the Birmingham Society took its place in the organisation of the National Union. Alf Cooper, the Society's General Secretary, became an Assistant General Secretary of the amalgamated union, based in Birmingham, with the officials of the Society taking over the new Midlands district of the Union.

1. W.H.B. Court, *Rise of Midland Industry*, London 1938, declares Birmingham had been making tinplate since 1740. According to Joseph Parker, *State of Trade in Birmingham*, Birmingham 1826, there were then 33 master brazier and tin plate workers in Birmingham, but he gave no indication of how many journeymen they employed. E.P. Thompson, *The Making of the English Working Class*, said that at the beginning of the nineteenth century the wide range of metal products made Birmingham 'the metropolis of the small master.' In 1791 Young, in his *Tour in England and Wales*, thought artisans wage rates in Birmingham were high, ranging from 10s to 25s a week, with the latter rate predominating 'to make the City's wages the highest in Europe.' W. Cobbett, *Rural Rides*, London 1830, records that in the surrounding area of the Black Country 'the truck or tommy system generally prevailed,' forcing the workers to buy from stores set up by their employers, instead of being able to get their necessities in the cheapest market.
2. J. Rule, *The Experience of Labour in the Eighteenth Century*, London 1981.
3. Ibid.
4. A. Briggs, op. cit.
5. The custom of taking Monday off from work which was widely observed in Birmingham and the industrial Midlands. H. Pollitt, in his autobiography, *Serving my Time*, London 1940, tells how, in the Merseyside shipyards before the First World War, every Monday morning the leading boilermaker would gather all the tradesmen around him and told an apprentice to throw a hammer into the air: 'if it stays up we remain at work, if it comes down we leave.' Rule suggests that excessive hours of work during the rest of the week, necessitated by the low piecework prices, was responsible for the custom.
6. Birmingham Public Library.
7. Letter from Wolverhampton Society secretary. W. Brodie, to G. Swainston, secretary of the London Co-operative Tin Plate Workers' Society, 29 January 1847.
8. MS minute book 1859.
9. BLP&ES, Webb Collection.
10. Ibid.
11. The Society consisted of 'Journeymen Brass Lamp Makers, gas lamp Makers and Carriage Lantern Makers.' Place Coll. Add 27803 Vol. XV. Other sources were the Society's MS minute books, reports and other publications, correspondence and interview with retired members and officials.

CHAPTER TWELVE

The War and After

The war saw the further expansion and development of the Union, strengthening its position in industry and in the wider labour movement, continuing generally along the lines established during the latter years of the inter-war period.

At the beginning of the war the General Secretary, Hickin, laid down the policy for the Union: to fight dilution, the policy pursued during the First World War. A circular setting this out was sent to all branches. It emphasised that men must be drawn from non-essential work and drafted on to aircraft work while taking care not to deplete the other firms so that they would be unable to keep going. A list must be drawn up of men on gas meters and other 'non-essential' work who would be prepared to place themselves at the disposal of the secretary to be sent where most necessary in the fight against dilution. But no dilution would be allowed while men were on the books.

As the war progressed the clamour for dilution, and particularly for women to work on sheet metal jobs intensified, with the employers backed by the Ministry. In June 1940, at a meeting with the employers 'aimed at expediting production', the National Union and Birmingham Society were put under pressure to relax existing customs and agreed that where skilled sheet metal workers were not available, dilutees would be allowed for the duration of the war, providing they were registered and paid the Union rate. But the employers were told, 'in no uncertain terms,' that the Union would not agree to women on sheet metal work and the employers had to accept in order to get the general dilution agreement, although stating that the question might have to be reviewed later.

The Union took a number of steps to deal with the situation. The NEC was given powers to operate a dilutee section. Members were urged to work overtime to get the work out. Men in non-essential jobs were urged to transfer to shops doing war work or to press for war work to be placed in shops engaged on non-essential work. While Union members had accepted 'in principle' they used every means of getting round it in practice, keeping their big guns for repulsing the main enemy, women in the sheet metal shops, a danger the Union had fought since its formation. The members were firmly of the opinion that the employers wanted 'dilution for dilution's sake', to get women established on sheet metal work so that they could be retained as cheap labour after the war. The Union made every endeavour to meet all demands for skilled labour made on them. In the middle of 1940 the employers said they must have 660 sheet metal workers immediately and a further 6,500 three months later. Soon after they demanded 350 fully skilled sheet metal workers immediately for aircraft repair. They were using 'men with very little skill supervised by others with very little training.' The Union pointed out that the employers had hardly made use of the male dilutees since the previous year's agreement and that a lot of skilled men were wasted in the forces. The members, recognising that there might come a time when resistance was no longer possible, gave the NEC powers to 'control' women labour, using all possible means, including insisting on payment of the men's rate for the same job, which they felt would be the most effective way of cooling the employers' ardour for female labour.

In order to provide some protection to apprentices, the Union issued an Apprentice Certificate in 1942 as the employers had not provided any document to take the place of the old indentures. This new card enabled apprentices to establish their skilled status if required to do so. It was endorsed each year by the local district secretary and finally signed by the General Secretary when the apprentice had finished his time.

A host of problems surrounded the Schedule of Reserved Occupations which stopped the call-up of skilled sheet metal workers engaged on the manufacture of aircraft, vehicles and ship building and repair and other 'protected work' at 18 years of age and 35 for non-protected work. But fights with the military developed from time to time as they tried to ride roughshod over the provisions of the Schedule. So 'eternal vigilance' became the watchword for the whole question of call-up and the problem of meeting manpower demands.

Among other wartime regulations was the Essential Work Order which laid down that no worker could be dismissed 'except for serious misconduct' and that no worker could leave his job without the written permission of the National Service Officer. The National Arbitration Order banned strikes and lockouts. Despite this latter order members continued to take strike action when they felt it was necessary. Coventry members were out three days over the victimisation of a steward; 200 members struck over a foreman at Hawker's, Kingston, 300 at Handley Page over piece-work prices; Lagonda and Turner and Savage of London had short strikes over prices; members at Northern Aircraft, Ashton-under-Lyne, came out when the firm introduced a clock-timing system; members at Metropolitan gas meter shops at Nottingham and London came out in support of the Cheltenham shop which struck in protest at a dilutee being put on skilled men's work. They returned but refused to make parts to be used by blackleg labour. During this strike the Union had to accept that gas meter work was of national importance and therefore subject to the agreement on the Relaxation of Existing Customs.

This pattern of disputes continued in various parts of the country, usually of short duration, concerned with conditions, piece-work prices, or demarcation. A few led to the courts. One steward was prosecuted when the shop came out over a member refusing to observe the shop 'limit'. The branch briefed D.N. Pritt, KC, who got the man acquitted. Occasionally the Union was able to use the Ministry against the employers as when 172 members at Cornercroft, Coventry, took the law into their own hands after the firm had refused to let them knock off officially at 4 o'clock on Christmas Day. They were all sacked but won in an appeal. The firm refused to reinstate them until the Union brought in the Ministry of Labour.

In March 1942 agreement was reached between the unions and the engineering employers on the setting up of joint works production committees throughout federated establishments. Their object was to establish consultative and advisory committees for the exchange of views between management and workers on the improvement of production and increase of efficiency for the war effort. The workers' side of the committees was elected by ballot in the shops, with a maximum number of ten representing all sections of workers in the factory. Each side elected its own secretary and meetings were held monthly with emergency meetings if necessary. They discussed maximum utilisation of machinery, upkeep of fixtures, jigs, tools and gauges, improvement in methods of production, efficient use of hours of work, elimination of waste, efficient use of materials, proper regard for safety precautions. These were generally welcomed by the left as a contribution to the war effort and as a foot in the door for the post-war take-over of capitalist enterprises. Many of the old craft unionists, however, were deeply suspicious of the whole idea and were not much interested. This was reflected in the mixed results.

A report by the General Secretary in the national Journal for January 1941 pointed out that with the fall of the Chamberlain government the attack on wages had ceased. Nothing was heard of it throughout the summer when the threat of invasion seemed great and the workers were urged to put out every ounce of effort possible to increase production in the war effort. But when the immediate danger lessened in September, the attack on wages was resumed, first cautiously, then more and more openly with the *Times, Telegraph, Financial Times* and other papers representing the employers' interests coming out with demands for a wages policy.

A number of branches complained of Air Ministry investigators touring aircraft firms and interfering with prices agreed by the Union and management. Finally a union application for a wage increase was turned down by the director of the engineering employers, Sir Alex Ramsay, in a statement that the country could not afford it and a request to the government to consider a national policy of pegging wages. The unions replied with a wage application covering three million workers. The claim went to national arbitration which awarded an increase of 3s 6d a week.

Throughout 1942 the Union was preoccupied with the problem of getting realistic wage increases for members in a wartime situation. In March, a national meter conference was held and made a call for a 'substantial increase' on repair prices. Six months later the meter stewards put in for a general increase of 10s a week, were offered 7s 10d which they refused and then put in a simultaneous application by all stewards for a rate of 2s 6d an hour, which was backed by the NEC. Shipping members did the same, arguing that their jobs were skilled, heavy and dangerous but were the worst paid. The aircraft stewards joined in with a demand for prices that would enable an efficient panel beater to earn 5s an hour and a flat worker 4s 6d. The employers were told that if they did not meet the Union the men would stop work. Increases were received in shipbuilding after members had taken a day off for a mass meeting in London's East End in support of their claim, giving the employers seven days to arrange piece-work. This was followed by increases for gas meter, rail, hollowware, engineering, the Royal Ordnance factories and ICI.

With new factories on aircraft and other munitions work springing up in the outlying towns, the London district turned its attention to organising them and bringing them into the Union. The secretary visited Basingstoke and made 40 members at Thorneycroft's. New branches were set up in Reading and Rochester. The problem arose of how to integrate them into the organisation of what had been a one-branch district. It was decided to group them for representation on the district committee. More immediate was the problem of getting members in the shops brought into the activities of the branch in a period when maximum overtime was being worked on a regular basis and the whole area was subject to a continual threat of air raids. A proposal was made that shop representatives attend general branch meetings and report back to the shops, but this was modified and it was finally agreed to endeavour to get greater shop steward involvement.

A Shop Stewards' Co-ordinating Committee was set up similar to the Central Shop Stewards' Committee that had operated at the end of the 1914-1918 war, with representatives from each sectional stewards' association. The 'doodle-bug' raids a year later brought problems of getting meetings of even shop stewards' associations. The aircraft stewards' answer was the production of a bulletin to keep the shops informed. So, in October 1944, the *Sheet Metal Workers' Aircraft Shop Stewards' Bulletin* was first published with the Association secretary, Fred Rawson, as editor. However, it soon ran into official opposition. The district secretary, Blackburn, himself a former aircraft steward, branded it as 'dangerous' and 'not factual'. He objected to an 'official' paper being produced without supervision by the district office. After long discussions he agreed that publication could continue providing copy was submitted first to the district committee and a district committee member appointed to the

Left: stainless steel shell of the nose cases for BAC's Skylark rockets for use in the Eurospace weather-monitoring project under construction at Hudson badger works, Leeds; *below*: making cowlings for Rolls Royce jet engines, used on Vickers Viscount aircraft, at BAC, Weybridge

editorial board. With the end of the war it became the organ of the London Shop Stewards' Co-ordinating Committee with a representative from each stewards' association on the editorial board. The first issue of the new paper, renamed *Fusion*, came out in September 1946 with Henry Baines as the first of a string of editors. It was acknowledged that it served a useful purpose in the London organisation of the Union and its circulation extended far beyond the confines of the London district, providing news of the various associations and London district branches and a forum for members during a very active period of change in the Union until it was wound up in 1969.

The unofficial rank-and-file aircraft (later Engineering) Shop Stewards' National Council continued to play an active part in promoting organisation of factories, particularly in the aircraft industry. Together with its monthly paper the *New Propellor*, later *The Metal Worker*, it was particularly useful in helping to build a militant organisation in the dispersal factories in areas remote from the general industrial scene. A number of sheet metal shops and stewards were active in the organisation to the chagrin of the officials who generally distrusted any organisation they could not control. In June 1941 the NEC denounced a printed circular, 'published by what is called the shop stewards' council', inviting sheet metal workers to attend a meeting in Manchester. This was said to be 'alien to the rules and constitution of the Union' and was viewed 'with grave concern' by the NEC, which 'could not countenance the abrogation of the rules by unauthorised bodies.' There is no record of any disciplinary action being taken against any shop or steward.

The Union's own Aircraft Shop Stewards' Association only covered the London district, although it did have communication with shops in other districts, but within its own area it was very active, was recognised as part of the Union machinery and was generally encouraged and consulted. The Union organisation in most of the aircraft shops at this period was the envy of many trades and gave shop-floor leadership out of all proportion to its membership.

But a call by London for shop stewards' associations for the various sections of the trade to be set up in other parts of the country with a national co-ordinating committee to link them together was rejected by the NEC 'as it would be forming a union with the Union.'

With the beginning of the war the sub-contract aircraft shops that had started up in the late 1930s multiplied like mushrooms after rain, many of them staffed with militant individuals from the motor shops who saw to it they were Union shops. Together with the well-established main shops, greatly expanded and fully organised, they made the SM Aircraft Shop Stewards' Association a force to be reckoned with.

The Aircraft Stewards demanded better support from officials for auxiliary workers. It was only with great reluctance that the Union agreed that in shops where all the members were in the auxiliary section an auxiliary could serve as shop steward. There was no doubt that the auxiliary members were in the union on sufferance, as temporaries. The auxiliary section had been set up in July 1940 only because it was the only way the Union could control dilutees and stop them being organised in other unions. The officials and the 'traditionalist' members expected the section to be disbanded after the war when the dilutee question would have gone away.

A proposal from Wolverhampton at the 1943 National Conference that welders in the auxiliary section with five years' experience could be 'brought into full membership' was defeated by 63 votes to 67 after the General Secretary, Brotherton, had warned that if this motion went through welders could be elected to office and have to negotiate on behalf of sheet metal workers. And a motion from London that auxiliary workers who proved their ability to operate as sheet metal workers could be transferred to the skilled section with the approval of the branch secretary was also lost, by 280 votes to 461.

In 1947, when it was generally accepted that the auxiliary section had come to stay, it was laid down that auxiliary members were entitled to attend all shop and general meetings, to vote in elections for all shop officials and committee members and receive all ballot papers. But no auxiliary member could be a shop official when full members were available. The NEC accepted that there would have to be upgrading of members who had come in under the relaxation agreement and the 1947 conference accepted a Liverpool amendment that after five years on skilled work they should become eligible for membership of the skilled section.

London tried to get agreement for the organisation of all engaged on sheet metal work not catered for by the skilled section, stressing the need to move with the times and that firms were breaking down jobs and the skilled men were losing them. But after the General Secretary said it would bring the Union into conflict with other unions and would be 'taking away the craft nature of the union' it was defeated by 50 votes to 84. London made another attempt in 1949 and it was again defeated by those who feared it would result in an industrial union and would bring women into the Union, although the movers had stressed there was a rule preventing that. On the basis of a questionnaire sent to branches the NEC felt the rules were adequate 'to cover those workers eligible' and it would be 'impractical' to open the Union ranks to sections of workers being catered for by other unions. The General Secretary said that if the majority of members were not skilled the position of the Union would be weakened and the value of the craft must deteriorate further. To try and take the Union into a wider field would mean competing with other unions and at best only bring in 1,000 auxiliaries. But the critics were not satisfied, complaining that the Union was just drifting while jigs and sectionalisation were taking work away from members and allowing other unions to encroach on sheet metal work. Sheet metal was becoming universally used in industry but Union members were not getting it. They were being restricted to prototype and experimental work and the job was then given to other labour. Hawker's were opening a factory in Blackpool with no skilled workers, which was bound to affect the main Kingston factory. The NEC view again prevailed.

As the war progressed the Union began making preparations for a return to peace-time activities. Already in early 1945 it was agreed to set up a motor stewards' association to try and obviate the chaos that followed the 1914-18 war. The Union had started off the war with some 24,000 members and many of those of only recent origin. By the end of 1945 it had over 40,000 with 6,000 in the forces. It was thought that it would be difficult to find jobs for such a number in peace-time conditions; in fact the change-over went fairly smoothly, the main difficulty being to get members to take jobs where they were needed, and for some time the officers were faced with a shortage of labour.

The employers also made their preparations. They demanded a wage cut citing what they called 'large earnings' by members on piece-work in aircraft shops but the demand fell flat. The Union had already put in a claim which included two weeks' paid holiday plus six statutory paid days off, a 3s an hour minimum and the right to hold trade union meetings on the factory premises. A general demand for a shorter working week brought a cut to 44 hours in 1946 without too much difficulty.

One of the urgent problems before the National Union was that of reorganisation of the Union structure to meet the changes brought about by the war, with the scattering of members resulting from the dispersal of industry. In London this meant pressure for more peripheral branches and in 1946 branches were finally set up in Farnborough, Hayes and Luton, although it was said that the latter 'would need a lot of nursing'. Stop watches 'and other odious practices' were being operated at Vauxhall's, the main factory in the town. A branch was also opened in Slough a year later.

Construction of HS125 business jet aircraft at British Aerospace, Chester

Retiring Officials

The war saw many changes in the leadership of the National Union. In 1941 Charles Hickin, then 70 years of age, retired as General Secretary, a position he had held since 1922 when he was elected to succeed J.C. Gordon, who had retired because of ill-health. He joined the Wolverhampton Society in 1891 as soon as he had finished his time in a local general shop, the diversity of whose products gave him a wide experience of the craft which was to serve him and the Union well in the succeeding years. In his early days he was active in the Independent Labour Party and later in the Social Democratic Federation, then, in 1910 he was elected to the Wolverhampton Town Council on a Labour ticket. He was elected president of the Wolverhampton Society in 1903 after five years as a member of the EC. During this period he was active in organising sheet metal workers in other Midlands towns, establishing branches in Stourbridge, Hadley, Nottingham, Stafford and a special welders' branch. In 1908 he was elected president of the National Amalgamated while retaining his presidency of the Wolverhampton Society and became full-time assistant general secretary of the Amalgamated in 1915. By this time the National Amalgamated had become an approved society under the National Insurance Act which necessitated the General Secretary devoting much of his time to administrative work. This meant that much of the organisation work was left to Hickin who helped with the formation of branches in Norwich, Ipswich, Peterborough, Lincoln, Huntingdon, Rochester, Cheltenham, Yeovil and other areas, concentrating in particular on areas where new aircraft shops had been opened. With the formation of the National Union he became Assistant General Secretary.

Hickin was succeeded by the Assistant General Secretary, Archibald Kidd, who in 1906 became assistant general secretary of the General Union, succeeding Wiltshire as General Secretary in 1913. Kidd, said to be 'of a studious disposition', joined the Liverpool Society as soon as he was eligible. After only one year he became a member of the EC and from then until his retirement he was never out of office – a period of 49 years. On the formation of the National Union he became secretary of the No. 2 district covering Lancashire and the

Harry Brotherton at the 1953 national conference with Les Buck in the chair

North-East, taking over as Assistant General Secretary on 1 January 1923. A keen advocate of federation, he served on the NEC of the old Federation of Engineering and Shipbuilding Trades, first as representative of the General Union and then of the National Union and was responsible for the drafting of the resolution that brought the Confederation of Shipbuilding and Engineering Unions into being. He was a committed Labour Party member and keenly interested in independent working-class education, active in the Labour College movement from its early days. He retired in 1943 on reaching the age of 70.

Harry Brotherton, as the then Assistant General Secretary, was the next in line of succession. He joined the London Society in 1911 after serving his apprenticeship in the meter trade. He soon became active in the Union, playing a leading role during the First World War and the post-war period in the London shop stewards' movement, helping to form stewards' associations in both the aircraft and motor industries. He was the first secretary of the Motor Stewards' Association and a leading member of the Central Committee of Shop Stewards' Associations. He was a major influence in the National Union from soon after its formation, becoming full-time London assistant district secretary in 1926 and district secretary three years later. He retired in 1961 when 70 years of age after 18 years at the helm of the Union and 32 years in important full-time positions in the National Union, a period of major changes in the trade during which time he used his undoubted authority to block changes in the Union. Brotherton also played an important part in the wider trade union movement, having the distinction of being elected unopposed as president of the Confederation of Shipbuilding and Engineering Unions – often called the little TUC – for ten consecutive years. Even after that period of office he had great difficulty in persuading the Confederation to accept his resignation although the post had always previously been an annual one and reverted to this system after Brotherton's retirement.

His successor as General Secretary of the Union was Ted Roberts, a member of the Leeds Society from before the First World War, who before taking national office was secretary of the Yorkshire district. He died after only one year in the top position, after being overshadowed by

Brotherton for some 20 previous years; he was popular and generally recognised as an able man.

Brotherton's retirement brought the end of an era. The new people who came along were from a very different school, brought up in a new age of trade unionism. Les Buck, who took over in 1961, came from the motor industry, and had been London district secretary. His period of national office was beset with many problems arising from both amalgamation and from fundamental changes in industry. With his election to the TUC General Council he helped to increase the stature of the Union and draw it into wider participation in the decisions of the general trade union movement. Throughout his general secretaryship he played a leading part in the decisions and activities of the Confederation of Shipbuilding and Engineering Unions. He resigned as general secretary in 1977 when appointed director with responsibility for personnel on the board of the newly-nationalised British Aerospace, with the full approval of the NEC of the Union. He was the nominee of the Confed. which had been asked by the Secretary State for Industry in the Labour government to put forward a representative of the unions. Union officials said that during his term of office the industry experienced its most fruitful period since the war, both from the point of view of the workers in the industry and the country as a whole.

His successor, George Guy, also a former London district secretary, followed in the footsteps of Brotherton in that he had served his apprenticeship in meters, going on to aircraft during the war and then on to the motor industry. But although his path through the trade and the Union was similar, the intervening 40 years had brought a very different world and a revolution in the trade, needing a completely different outlook which Guy provided. George Guy was a forceful character and a persuasive and authoritative speaker who gave strong leadership during one of the most difficult periods in the Union's long history. He became London District Secretary in 1961, was elected to the NEC in 1964 and became National president in 1972, Assistant General Secretary in 1974 and General Secretary in 1977. He paid great attention to education and training and was a governor of Ruskin College, Oxford, as well as being a member of the Engineering Training Board. He presided over the formulation and implementation of policy to deal with the revolutionary change in the organisation and the work of members following the impact of high technology. His vision of new technology as a challenge and opportunity for the Union's members to obtain great benefits was the basis of his puruit of amalgamation.

Merger talks

Even after the outbreak of war, amalgamation talks with the Birmingham Society continued although it was the National Union that made all the running. The National Union was not put off by the stated wide divergence between the two unions on the attitude to dilution, the main preoccupation of the National Union throughout the war. It was said that the policy of the Birmingham Society was to accept dilution, train the dilutees on sheet metal work and get them into the Union while insisting they get the rate for the job. There were also complaints from the National Union Midlands district that the Birmingham Society refused to recognise National Union stewards.

During the talks Birmingham rejected proposals that the whole of the National Union funds be put into the Amalgamation with the Birmingham Society contributing on a pro rata basis. This, they said, would weaken the organisation and it was up to the National Union to increase its funds to the Birmingham level. The Birmingham Society valued its 6045 members at £12 3s 6d each against £7 2s 10d each for the 28,000 National Union members. The National Union replied that the weekly financial improvement it was enjoying would bring up the member valuation without a levy or any other measures. It also noted Birmingham's concern over superannuation funds and hoped that the Society would not let all the work that had been done go to waste.

After the meeting Brotherton reported that the National Union had done as much as could be expected after Birmingham had put forward 'impossible proposals' at a gas meter conference and when they had not been accepted told their members that the National Union had let them down. He claimed that the door of amalgamation was always open but the next move must come from Birmingham.

Meanwhile the Amalgamated Engineering Union was urging the National Union to take part in amalgamation talks, but was told that the Union must first complete amalgamation with kindred trades.

As the end of the war approached a general feeling prevailed that at last real moves would be taken for one union for all sheet metal workers. The possibility of reopening talks with the Birmingham Society was being hopefully canvassed. The Zinc and Copper Roofers had already made advances for a merger. But when Brotherton took advantage of discussions with the coppersmiths over recognition of each other's cards to make overtures on amalgamation he found that Stansfield, the coppersmiths' secretary, 'was not helpful.'

Amalgamation with the Birmingham Society meant to the National Union much more than an addition of 7,210 members to the fighting strength of the Union – a little over half the organised sheet metal workers in the Midlands, one of the main centres of the trade – important though this was. It meant the healing of a split, the coming together in unity and the strength that could only come from a single united body. And in 1946 it seemed that this split of over 30 years was about to be healed. Brotherton reported that the year 'showed real progress in our endeavours for one union for sheet metal workers.'

The recommendations for amalgamation put forward by the joint sub-committee, approved by the ECs of both unions, were accepted unanimously by delegates to a special conference of the National Union. The National Union members were told that the Birmingham Society branches had also voted in favour and it went to a ballot of the whole Birmingham membership with a recommendation for acceptance – the members turned it down by a mere 75 votes. The whole sad business had to be started all over again.

So, with something of an anti-climax, the first post-war amalgamation on which such high hopes had been built was with the London Society of Zinc and Copper Roofers and General Sheet Metal Workers with less than 100 members. This had started up as a breakaway organisation made up of members of the old Zinc and Copper Roofers' Society who would not accept the terms of benefits at the time of amalgamation with the old London Society 30 years before, and had broken away and restarted their old society. They were all skilled men working at one firm, Braby's, then the main London roofing firm; one of the best known jobs they carried out was the building of the Dome of Discovery, one of the main features of the 1951 Festival of Britain on the South Bank of the River Thames. They retained their shop organisation and their individual financial valuation was reportedly greater than either the National Union or the Birmingham Society.

Instead of amalgamation, the National Union and the Birmingham Society drew up an agreement on relations between the two societies covering shop stewards, membership transfers, negotiations and collection of contributions.

During this time amalgamations had been started with another 'kindred body', the Sheet Iron and Light Platers' Society, whose 1,000 or so members were engaged in shipbuilding and repair, concentrated in Scotland and the North East coast with branches in Glasgow,

Greenock, Newcastle and North Shields. It had been formed in Glasgow in 1900 as the Sheet Iron Workers, Light Platers and Ships' Range Makers and there had been bitter demarcation battles between its members and those of the old General Union before the 1914-1918 war and carried on in the inter-war years. Now discussions went along remarkably smoothly with agreement on branches, benefits, funds and officials settled without difficulty. The only hold-up occurred when the Sheet Iron Workers' General Secretary, H. Mulholland, retired and was replaced by John Fender and the Head Office transferred from Glasgow to Newcastle. The Sheet Iron Workers' EC was unanimously in favour and a ballot of members gave more than the statutory consent of two-thirds of the membership and the two joined forces on 2 October 1950. The amalgamation necessitated a reorganisation of the Union structure with the creation of a new district in the North East covering Newcastle, Sunderland, Hartlepool and Stockton branches of the National Union, and the Newcastle and North Shields branches of the Sheet Iron Workers carved out of the old Lancashire and Northern district, with Fender as district secretary. The Scottish branches of the Sheet Iron workers became branches of the National Union Scottish district.

On 1 July 1959 a real new step forward was taken on the road to one union for all the sheet metal trades when the two old craft unions of sheet metal workers and coppersmiths came together in a new united union.

The National Union had made a number of overtures to the coppersmiths but it was not until Stansfield retired and Harold Poole became General Secretary that there was any response. Poole, who had long seen that splendid isolation was no longer a viable proposition, was aided by the harsh facts of rising prices in persuading his EC to take a more positive attitude. Poole had promised his old craft-orientated members that their Society would not be submerged and that 'coppersmiths' would remain in the title, which was accepted by the National Union. The fact that all the National Union benefits were higher than those of the coppersmiths – except for 'auxiliary burial' – for lower contributions, and that the coppersmiths would operate under National Union rules also probably had some influence. While coppersmiths' branches and those of the metal workers would continue, it was hoped that time would bring them into their own local amalgamations with interchange of members both in the branches and in places of work. It would seem that the coppersmiths did very well, with their officials guaranteed in office for eight years but the terms were agreed to unanimously and not considered a dear price to pay for unity. The coppersmiths amalgamated on a membership of 5,590 and brought in funds to the value of £57,708.

Most of the branches integrated but a few maintained separate coppersmiths and sheet metal workers' branches in the same town, in Portsmouth, for example, which had a strong coppersmiths' branch in the dockyard, and the Derby railway coppersmiths who insisted on their own organisation; the final decision was left to members. In 1975 the naval dockyards introduced new coppersmiths' apprenticeship schedules orientated toward sheet metal work instead of toward plumbers' work, which would enable future journeymen to undertake work in either craft.

In Coventry there was joint organisation down to shop level. At Bristol Siddeley the two shops – the metal workers with some 250 members and the coppersmiths with over 100 – had formed joint committees to deal with questions common to both, including demarcation on jobs with the objective of safeguarding jobs rather than individual trades. All future bound apprentices were to be sheet metal workers/coppersmiths with a curriculum covering both trades. They spent six months at training school covering both trades, then general sheet metal work for eight months and general coppersmithing work, including brazing, soldering, cleaning and testing for 10 months. Welding – gas, spot, argon arc – took four months. They then had three months in the jig and tool drawing office and planning office three months, followed by six months on plant sheet metal work and six months on test plant maintenance. After two months on rocket development they finished off six months in the coppersmiths' department and six months in the sheet metal department. At 21, it was calculated, apprentices should be able to work on either trade. At other places members worked out relationships to suit themselves. In London, AEC, Napier's and Lyons all soon had joint organisation and other shops followed.

On the initiative of the Northern Ireland district, overtures were made to the Irish Sheet Metal Workers Union, the only affiliate to the National Amalgamated which did not join the National Union in 1921 but preserved its independence. In 1948 mutual recognition of cards was arranged and the secretary and president of the Irish union attended the Union's national conference. But the hope that this would lead to amalgamation was not realised.

The question of amalgamation continued throughout this post war period. Firstly there was the aim of one union for sheet metal workers and after the coppersmiths had been brought in this really meant the Birmingham Society. This was always in the background of National Union activities as relations between the Birmingham Society and the National Union in the Midlands continued with their downs and ups.

But the high and mounting cost of running a union meant that many other unions were looking to amalgamations to help them keep out of debt. The engineers and to a lesser extent the boilermakers and plumbers made tentative enquiries, but were told the Union wanted to first get in the kindred trades. The General Secretary declared that the Union was not concerned with amalgamation with kindred trades purely for the sake of increased numbers but for the increased strength that comes from this type of organisation, the strength of skilled unions with identical interests. The Midlands branches pressed for amalgamation with the vehicle builders which for some reason never made much of an impact, probably because it was the bigger union and members were in the mood for taking over, not being taken over. The members in the shipping industry wanted fusion with the boilermakers or plumbers, both were also bigger unions. There was a need for the craft unions to unite to survive and to solve demarcation problems, said the Liverpool branch.

After a certain amount of 'sounding out of unions that might be prepared to amalgamate', a meeting was held in York between Les Buck, Alf Roberts, General Secretary of the National Union of Vehicle Builders, Frank Briggs of the Metal Mechanics and Len Green of the Heating and Domestic Engineers' Union for a preliminary discussion on amalgamation. Soon, however, the NUVB and the Metal Mechanics dropped out and discussion continued with the H and D.

The NEC reported to the 1964 conference on those preliminary discussions and received endorsement to continue executive sub-committee negotiations. The General Secretary spoke of the growth of air-conditioning and ventilating in recent years that had seen an increasing number of National Union members engaged on this work. The erection of ducting and pipefitting had proved a fruitful field for organisation by the H and D. A combination of the two unions should prove of mutual assistance in the work of organising this continually expanding industry with the chemical and other industries providing additional areas of organisation. He pointed out that the full title of the Heating and Domestic included 'general metal workers' and they partly derived from the old whitesmith who worked in tin-plated iron. The important position the amalgamated union would occupy in the heating and ventilating industry would not be able to be ignored. It would give a membership of 75,000 and a better base from which to deal with other amalgamations. In October the National Union members balloted on the amalgamation proposals endorsing it with a vote of 19,758 to 5,172 – the Heating and

Front and rear views of five 7 ft diameter ducts for blasting air at temperatures between −20 and 180°C on Concorde at Filton, Bristol, to test for metal fatigue. Sheet metal maintenance workers made and fitted the ducts and SM production workers took part in the construction of Concorde

Domestic had also voted in favour by 9,516 votes to 3,012. A special conference was called to hammer out a new rule book for the amalgamated union which went through without much controversy.

The Heating and Domestic had 138 branches in eight areas and the National Union then had 122 in nine districts. A two-year period for consolidation and clearing the decks was allowed before making any other advance, although talks still continued with the Birmingham Society.

Political Fund

One unforeseen result of the amalgamation with the Heating and Domestic Engineers was that the Union was without a political fund for the first time for some 50 years. This came about because the H and D did not have a fund and the law required that a ballot should be held to determine whether the combined Union wanted one. The Union leadership apparently thought that the ballot was a mere formality and the result a foregone conclusion, and so no real work was done to prepare the membership. The only lead from Head Office seems to have been an article by the general secretary on an inside page of the Journal, which was then in magazine format and not designed to act as a campaigning sheet. As it was, the Journal was delayed and did not come out until after the ballot had been held. As a result of general apathy, antagonism on the part of some H and D members together, it was thought, with some opposition to the policies of the then Labour government, only one in five of the membership bothered to vote, giving 6,003 in favour and 9,508 against.

Two years later, after a resolution had been carried at national conference calling for a new ballot and re-affiliation to the Labour Party, voting took place again. But again nothing in the nature of a real campaign was organised, the main call coming from an article on the front page of the then newspaper-style Journal. But there was still a very low vote and the proposal was again defeated, although only by a small majority, a mere 650, with 8,495 voting in favour and 9,145 against.

Then came amalgamation with the Birmingham and Midlands Society and as they already had a political fund another ballot had to be held. This was in 1973 and the situation was entirely different. First there was the adhesion of the Birmingham members who could be expected to vote to retain their own fund. But, more important, there was a new political situation. Apathy, which had brought defeat in the two previous ballots, had been banished with opposition to the government-ordered four-day week and the General Election some weeks before, which had turned out the Heath Government. The leadership had also learned its lesson. The whole of the front page of the Journal had been given over to the campaign and circulars were sent out to all branches. This time 28,755 members returned voting papers with 16,718 voting in favour, but there was still a sizeable minority of 9,787 against. So, after seven years, the Union was able to return to affiliated membership of the Labour Party. Re-affiliation allowed branches to affiliate to local Labour parties, take part in their activities, be represented on the local party management committees and to nominate members to panels of local government candidates.

But reaffiliation was not enough. There still remained the problem of getting members to pay the political levy. It was pointed out that of 28,000 members of the Union in 1941 only 8,000 were paying into the political fund. And the position had not changed very much since. In the mid-1950s it was reported that 5,482 members had 'deliberately contracted out.'

The campaign for a political fund and reaffiliation to the Labour Party was in line with the

London district banner dating from the 1950s (*left*), and the Northern Ireland banner of the 1960s

greater political involvement of the post-war Union, particularly from the 1960s. This emergence as a 'political union' was a development of the political activities of the 30s when the dominant London district was being influenced by the left-wing leadership of the aircraft and motor workers, spreading in the war years to other districts, and the translation of these people into officials.

In its later years the Union was labelled as a militant, left-wing union. It supported left wing candidates in elections to the Labour Party NEC, and joined in Party campaigns. It supported demonstrations for higher old age pensions and members participated with Union support in the various marches for jobs. Earlier it opposed German rearmament, took a continuing active part in the peace movement and the campaign against nuclear weapons; opposed the US war in Vietnam; denounced apartheid and supported black trade unions in South Africa; opposed the Chilean junta and expressed solidarity with the Chilean workers. It was active in opposition to Britain's membership of the Common Market, vigorously opposed any form of wage freeze and generally sided with the 'left' at TUC and Labour Party conferences. In later years the union Journal carried regular advertisements for the *Morning Star*. Its action on these and similar causes took the form of resolutions from branches, districts and the national executive to the Government or appropriate authorities, and all national conferences gave time to political resolutions; it sent delegates to conferences; used the Journal to publicise these activities. The London district banner was usually to be seen in demonstrations in support of these and other movements, later supported by the Southend branch banner, though often followed only by the faithful few. But demonstrations in other districts increased after the NEC in 1979 provided each district with a standard banner.

The London district banner was always out on TUC demonstrations, such as the big marches against the Tory Government's anti-trade union legislation. Before all districts were issued with a banner, it was treated rather like a national banner, leading a contingent of national officials on demonstrations. The Union also took a more leading role in the general trade union movement with Brotherton's ten-year spell as president of the Confederation of Engineering and Shipbuilding Unions followed at intervals and for the statutory one-year period by Poole of the Coppersmiths, Green of the Heating and Domestic and Buck of the SMW and all General Secretaries were regularly elected to the Confederation executive. In 1970 Buck first stood for election to the TUC General Council, and received the respectable vote of 2.5 million. He was elected in 1972, holding the seat until he resigned as General Secretary of the Union in 1977 – the first time a sheet metal worker had been a member of the TUC leadership since the Birmingham Secretary, J.V. Stevens, was President in 1898. He was followed by G. Guy after he had succeeded as General Secretary of the Union. Guy held the position until 1983 when he was unseated in a drive by right wing union leaders against the left in which Guy, as a member of the Communist Party, was a main target. In Ireland, A. Barr, the district secretary, was elected president of the Irish Confederation of Trade Unions.

The National Union was very active in opposition to the 1972 Tory Government's anti-trade union legislation attempt, and had the dubious honour of being the first union prosecuted in the National Industrial Relations Court. As the result of a strike over a pay claim at Kaymet Engineering, a small firm at Peckham, three National Union stewards and one from the Metal Mechanics were ordered to appear before the NIRC to answer a charge of inducing employees to break their contract. The full force of the law was invoked to haul them before the Court at an hour's notice. The district officials were mobilised to represent them and the authority's resolution to make an example of the men dissolved and the two sides were told to get together again. The employer made another offer which was accepted. The following year saw the more famous case when the Court jailed five dockers and trade unionists all over the country –

including National Union members – walked off their jobs and took to the streets so that the Heath government had to discover a long-forgotten official, the Public Solicitor, to get the five men out, which effectively stopped the Court's anti-trade union activities.

Organisation

Post-war attacks on the 'one big branch attitude' in London, saw new moves to break-up the 11,457-strong London branch, partly to make the London branch more democratic by making it easier to attend branch meetings, and partly as a means of recruitment and building up organisation. H. Brown had been elected as a third full-time London officer with a responsibility of organising the outlying branches. The promised Farnborough branch was set up soon after the war and with 130 members soon had a union shop at Dennis Bros, the fire-engine makers of Guildford and members at Basingstoke, including some working in artificial limb shops. Weybridge, with 464 members, was making 'steady progress' in organising Vickers Armstrong, long a weak spot in Union organisation. The branch asked for help in organising the many unorganised shops in Surrey, but the branch membership was much below the number entitling them to a full time official, and potential was not something the Union recognised. Hayes had over 500 members and Reading was pressing for organising drives in Oxford and the Harwell area. A branch with 84 members was set up in Brighton at the end of 1948. (In fact there was a branch in the town in 1824 with 15 members; in 1847 a Society had its club house at the Hammers in North Street and its secretary, Artridge, was in communication with the Wolverhampton Society.) All this was only in the London district, but London was of great importance as it still accounted for about one-third of the total Union membership.

Things were also happening elsewhere. Branches were formed at Plymouth, Cardiff, Scarborough, Bournemouth and Jarrow, followed by more in the area around London, including Basildon, Crawley and Dagenham.

The disorganisation of industry through fuel and material shortages at a time of exceptionally bad weather brought some unemployment, a lot of short time working and staggered working hours without overtime rates. But that apart, most of this period from the end of the war through the 1950s was a time of full employment with the Union on occasion finding it difficult to provide the labour required, except for the early 1950s when there was unemployment and short time working. The membership totals remained remarkably stable, first around 38,000, then 40,000 gradually building up to 42,750 in the latter half of that decade. These were genuine increases, not due to amalgamations, showing a consolidation and spreading of the organisation. This was despite the fact that 11,248 had been removed from the register in 1948 for arrears, 7,866 of them skilled section members and 3,382 others.

In 1957 the big dispute in the engineering and shipbuilding industries pushed dispute benefit payments up by £90,000 and brought a setback in what had been a steady improvement in finances. At the beginning of the 1960s the early stages of inflation began to undermine financial stability, with total expenditure exceeding income by £24,240 in 1960 and by £23,000 in 1961. The Union was forced to put up contributions but pointed out that in 1921 contributions were ls 2d a week, in 1928 ls 8d, in 1938 2s, in 1952 2s 6d, in 1962 with the proposed increase, they would be up 50 per cent on 1928 during which time wages had gone up from an average £4 a week to £16.

Back to Basics

The controversy that had been carried on for decades between those who wanted a strong all-embracing organisation and those, mostly older members who felt that the strength of the union was best upheld through limiting the membership strictly to time-served men was continued after the war. The proposal for full time organisers that had been the demand of the 'get them all in' school of thought voiced from time to time since the formation of the National Union was first made in the post-war years by J. Parker and G. Guy, both of whom were to become London district secretaries. They asked that an organiser be appointed for the London district on a temporary basis, to be made permanent if justified. The appointment of organisers was also urged at the 1953 conference, when the call was made for five organisers covering the whole country. The work of the organisers would be to get into the Union the large number of skilled sheet metal workers still unorganised. The proposers called on the Union to change its approach and go out after members, not just wait for them to approach the Union. Like their predecessors, these motions were defeated after the General Secretary, Brotherton, had expressed doubts about there being a large number of skilled men still unorganised. He also claimed that the system of organisers was dying out and declared that a system of full-time district and branch secretaries was preferable, although it had been pointed out that this was no substitute for organisers whose work would be directed to recruitment. Brotherton expressed horror that people 'might be taken in wholesale' urging that there must be 'some discrimination about who could be admitted.' An attempt to get the unskilled workers engaged on a wide range of sheet metal work into the Union and for upgrading those who became qualified was overwhelmingly defeated. Brotherton complained that too many were being upgraded already by branch secretaries all over the country although trade was bad and skilled men were out of work.

In 1966 W. Warman, Midlands district secretary and NEC member, called for greater urgency in recruitment of members. He charged that the old craft outlook, still held by many members, must bear the responsibility for so many lost opportunities of enrolling members. The Union could not afford to be selective, as it had in the past. It must change with the changing times. With the spread of industry to areas new to the Union there must be a spread of Union organisation to cover the whole country.

Although appeals and demands for a militant attitude to recruitment continued, tradition and self-satisfaction went too deep and was too widespread, while the sprinkling of full time officials was too involved in looking after the existing membership for there to be any real change in Union outlook on recruitment. Such decisions that were made on recruitment were therefore not followed up. It was not reasoning but the economic facts of industrial life, and particularly inflation, that forced the Union to accept auxiliaries and other semi-skilled workers into membership, with up-grading into the skilled section of those who had been engaged on skilled sheet metal work for a period of years.

The old controversy – a problem of the First World War – on whether to accept welders as skilled members flared up again in the 1950s. An attempt to get welders accepted as skilled members with right of election to branch committees, though on a limited scale, was defeated at the 1953 national conference. This was said to be the main reason the Birmingham Society turned down amalgamation with the National Union later that year.

This attitude was reaffirmed at the 1956 conference when the NEC moved a change in rule which would endorse the segregation of skilled welders, confining them to their own section, 'kept separate and apart.' They would be allowed to attend branch meetings but could only take part in debates and vote on questions that directly affected their section. This was defended on the grounds that if they were given the same rights as skilled sheet metal workers they might get elected as shop stewards, or even full-time officials and have to negotiate for sheet metal workers An unsucessful amendment from Scotland and London would have removed the restriction on their rights of discussion and voting. It was argued that with the changing methods of work, welders were part of the trade and were essential for maintaining the earnings of sheet metal workers. Their skill was recognised in so far as the shops now had welder apprentices. The Boilermakers and others were recruiting welders who were joining because they did not suffer the same restrictions as they did in the National Union. Nevertheless, the NEC's motion was accepted.

Life on the shop floor brought changes in the attitude to welders and the adhesion of the Birmingham Society, which accepted welders into the skilled section, forced a change of attitude on the part of the NU leadership. The next move was to integrate the welders into general sheet metal work. In places such as the Derby Engines Division of Rolls Royce, the welders were classed as skilled and served an apprenticeship which covered some sheet metal work, while sheet metal apprentices received some welding tuition. This gave a flexibility that enabled a man in one section to do the work of another when one or the other department was short of work.

The Post-War Years

The post-war years saw a big upsurge in organisation, when perhaps the Union was stronger then it had ever been. There was a feeling of confidence and authority, at least among the active sections of the membership who ran the Union. This was perhaps the result of the special place the trade unions occupied in the factories and in the country during the war, which was carried on into this new period. The employers had had to talk to them, even to consult them, in relation to many aspects of 'the war effort.' This was followed by the landslide victory for Labour in the general election, putting 'our people' into power. Even the period of immediate post-war fuel and material shortages could not dim this feeling. This time it was the unions that were on the offensive – although they were prepared to modify their demands in the interest of the country – a major difference from 1918. Many shops and workers were organised for the first time and shop organisation in general was stronger than ever before.

The Union was built on shop organisation, with shop secretary, chairman and committee, a shop fund and regular meetings together with a discipline that was backed by the branch and district committee concerned. The organisation was rooted in the experiences of the past, going back some 150 years to the early tin plate workers' bodies. William Lovett, the Chartist cabinet maker, has told how when the London craftsmen had something to discuss they would call the shop together by striking their hammer on some available metal. Shop meetings were still being called in the post war years on the decision of the shop committee to discuss business considered urgent. It was regarded as an important trade union right and was stoutly defended when any suggestion was made to ban the practice. Its operation depended on the strength and awareness of the organisation in the shop. It was often a preliminary to strike action but in many cases such meetings enabled a settlement to be made on an immediate question that might otherwise have festered and developed into a strike.

Members in the London shops began to extend and rebuild their shop stewards' organisation which had long been the basis of their strength in some sections. With the return

Wheeling a panel for a Rolls Royce at Mulliner Park Ward, London

of gas meter makers to their pre-war jobs the Meter Stewards' Association got a new lease of life, taking in even the gas companies' shops that had been a source of weakness in the past. Now there was hardly a gas meter shop anywhere in the country that did not make Union membership a condition of employment. In 1951, in an attempt to organise the most effective opposition to this threat to their trade, the London Association tried to get similar associations formed in other meter centres. In January 1952 they reported one established in Manchester and expressed the hope of having others operating in every large town by the end of the year, but no more were reported.

Although the aircraft industry had shed many workers on the cessation of hostilities, it was now an up-and-coming industry with sizeable shops already established in many parts of the country, and others coming into existence. Although depleted in strength with the loss of most of the sub-contract shops, the Aircraft Stewards' Association was still a power in the London district.

The motor industry, too, was almost daily growing in importance as firms returned to their old products, taking up where they left off in 1939, while preparing new post-war models. utilising the experiences of new methods and materials developed in wartime. But the post-war motor stewards' association was very different from that of between the wars. The old luxury, hand-made coach-built section that dominated the pre-war motor trade in London district had been decimated. The merged Mulliner and Park Ward firms had become the body department of Rolls Royce: Van den Plas had been taken over by Austin's and Thrupp and Mabberley by Rootes. It was a period of mergers and rationalisation. Bus and coach firms like Park Royal Vehicles and Weyman's of Weybridge accounted for a large number of the members in the motor section. But some small independent panel shops had opened, doing work for small sports car firms like Allard and Lotus. One weakness of the Association was that the big mass-production companies – Briggs, Ford and Vauxhall, where the bulk of the membership was on experimental work – were not affiliated. Only the BLSP (Rootes) shop, where 40 per cent of a total of some 200 members were directly engaged on line production, was a member of the Association.

There were also a number of bus and coach stops in the provinces: Eastern Coach Works in Lowestoft, Rowe of Leeds and Paxtons of Scarborough.

But the heart of the motor industry remained in the Midlands where five firms employed some 3,000 members between them – Standard, Rootes and Jaguar in Coventry with about 250 members each and Austin and Fisher Ludlow in Birmingham with 1,200 or more each in the mid-1950s, plus a number in the large panel and component shops.

On the edge of the motor sections was the car radiator trade. This included established national firms like Serk and Delaney Galley with branches in various parts of the country; Willenhall Radiators in the Black Country; Marston's in Leeds and others, including some trade shops in London employing 40 to 50 members each, two or three others employing around 30, some two-thirds of them in the Union. These were engaged on both new work and repairs, while a host of smaller firm's with one or two Union members but largely unorganised were mainly concerned with repairs, many of them repairing petrol tanks, wings, panels and lamps, picked up from the garages who were customers for radiator repairs. It was not a well-paid section of the trade, ranging from medium to poor. The bigger car repair shops employed some members and panel beaters, generally freelance, visited the smaller firms, like those under the railway arches.

Varied Work of Members

In November 1946 a meeting of stewards from 23 London shops formed a General Shop Stewards' Association. These were different from the old general shops whose basis was the domestic tin ware trade. The post-war general trade consisted of mainly small shops making a wide variety of articles, most of them with their own specialised line, lighting or other electrical speciality, customs built cabinets with almost any job in sheet metal to fill in; and a strange and varied collection of jobs came their way. In one London shop jobs given out included special fluorescent lighting fitments for the British Museum reading room, infra-red lamps for a pig farm and three dozen tinplate spittoons 2 feet 6 inches high and 12 inches in diameter for tea tasters. A Coventry shop whose basic jobs were one-off items for experimental or racing cars, received an order for 30 sheet iron battle helmets for the Royal Shakespeare Theatre at nearby Stratford-on-Avon.

One Lowestoft shop generally had a few dodgem cars or swans from the tunnel of love from the local seaside funfair lying around the shop to be repaired. The main work of some shops in London and Coventry was fair ground equipment. Dodgem cars were hand-made throughout, shaped with the wheel and hammer; the bodies made from 16 and 18 guage steel offcuts welded together where necessary; they were built to withstand the bumps and bashes that may have got rid of someone's frustrations. Model railways to carry children were made from 18 gauge mild steel sheet and the engine's 'steam dome' was of hand-beaten copper. Helter-skelter towers had 14 gauge light alloy panels and 18 gauge domes.

There was a great lot of skill around in some of those shops, developing jobs from a rough sketch, and often working with worn-out tools. There was a lot of organising work to be done in some of these places, wages were low more often than not, and the conditions Dickensian. They were not all like that, of course; many, such as those on the catering side, which were affiliated with the General Steward's Association, had conditions as good as could be found anywhere.

One shop where members were called upon to carry out very diverse jobs was Trinity House based in east London. This was essentially a medieval guild, dating from the time of Henry VIII which was responsible for 'beacons, marks and signs from the sea'. It was then responsible for the upkeep of 55 manned lighthouses, 36 light vessels and 600 buoys, some 200 of them carrying lights. In the workshops they could be working on copper flue pipes that had to follow the shape of a lighthouse, copper pipe work with a number of intricate bends, shaped steam pipes, lead pipes, water and gas pipes, the repair or renewal of many different types of oil lamps, making copper or tin oil cans, petrol tanks, oil trays, ventilators or any of a dozen other jobs. They could be sent out on a job at any time, which could be on lighthouses, light vessels or buoys, where they might be called on to make their own drawings of a job and estimate the length of time it would take. They might be working on the top of a lighthouse, repairing the roof 'holding on with one hand with the wind blowing to make it more difficult,' or inside an oil tank lining it with lead. As one tinman observed, 'Because of the weather you could go out for a week and remain a month.'

An Artificial Limb Shop Stewards Association was formed in 1957 serving a developing industry. The main firm in this industry was J.E. Hanger, of Roehampton in West London. It was originally an American firm which in 1914 opened a London branch that later became independent and operated under the Ministry of Pensions. From an original staff of two it had been built up to 150 by the end of the 1914-1918 war, and the old wooden legs had given way to metal. By 1944 duralumin was being used and production was around 13,000 limbs a year, all different, custom built for the individual. In 1940 the works was organised, and from that time on the unions operated a closed shop policy. Rates of pay, however, remained low for what was a highly skilled, hand-made job. The industry expanded and Union officials gave it a lot of attention, a number of old members well known in other sections of the trade went to work there and helped to strengthen the organisation. In 1959 a strike brought improved earnings on a payments-by-results basis. More firms came on the scene – Vessa's opened shops in Alton and Roehampton, Blatchford's opened one in Clapham, Vokes had a shop in Guildford, Kelly's, part of the Vokes group, started up in Dundee and Steepers opened a shop in London, making only arms.

But basic rates remained low compared with other sections of the trade until 1979 when the Union took their case to the Central Committee of Arbitration which awarded increases that almost doubled the wages of craftsmen in some of the small branch shops and gave everyone a substantial increase. Perhaps more important was the fact that the award embraced the small branch shops in hospitals all over the country. These branches of the major makers consisted of a handful of craftsmen adapting the individual limbs in each of the various fitting centres. They had been mainly unorganised but were now enrolled in the Union, bringing the total membership to over 1,000. They each had their own shop representatives and were brought into the machinery of the shop stewards' association through the shop organisation of the parent firms. As the provincial shops were already enrolled, this meant that the stewards' association then covered the industry over the whole country.

In April 1959 a meeting of stewards from shops on fine limit work set up a Precision Sheet

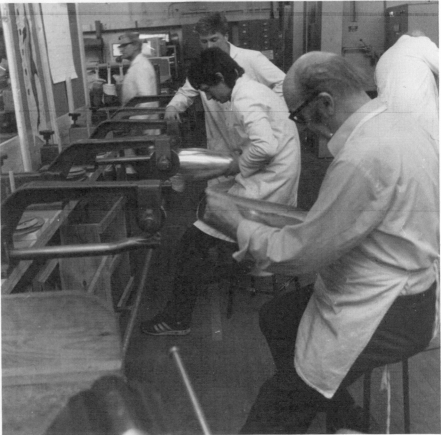

Making artificial limbs at
Hangars, Roehampton

Metal Workers' Association, with some 35 shops affiliating. This section of the trade was tied up with the rapidly developing electronics and allied industries. Most of the shops were engaged on development work, working to thousandths of an inch, using verniers and height gauges. Representatives came to meetings from shops in many parts of the district and there was some contact with shops elsewhere in the country.

A stewards' association was formed in the late 1960s by representatives of a number of shops in the metal signs industry. There were many shops in this section of the trade, most of them small with little or no Union organisation, giving great potential for recruitment. There was some initial enthusiasm, with stewards from shops as far away as Margate on the Kent coast attending its meetings. But it did not last, repeating a pattern of some ten years earlier when the district secretary, H. Brown, tried to get an organisation of sign-making shops going, and although two of the main shops, Pearce and Franco-British, were interested it did not get off the ground.

At the same time he tried to bring the car radiator shops together in their own organisation, but without success. The ventilation section had a new lease of life after the war with the building boom, the development of large buildings with heating, ventilating and other services carried in ductwork made on an individual basis. However, as these services became the norm standardisation was introduced which allowed much of the ductwork to be machine made and the bottom dropped out of another line that had produced craftsmen highly skilled in pattern development and fabrication over many years, leaving only a few small shops with a pool of skilled men for specialised one-off jobs.

The small but effective Shipping Stewards' Association continued to serve a separate body of members who worked in the half-dozen shops that carried out ship repairs in the Port of London, a section that had always been a body apart from the mass of the London membership.

Immediately on the entry of the Coppersmiths' Society into the Union in 1960 a coppersmiths' section was started, giving way later to a Coppersmiths and Stainless Steel Shop Stewards Association. Most of the affiliated shops were engaged on brewery, dairy, catering and chemical industry work.

These associations provided a forum where representatives of shops engaged on the same type of work could regularly get together and discuss problems common to all, exchange information on rates and conditions, the position of work, organisation and prevailing trends, the question of sub-contracts, hammering out a common policy for their section of the trade. They provided help in disputes, strengthened organisation in the shops and gave the weak shops and inexperienced members some confidence, as well as helping to organise the non-union shops in conjunction with the district officials.

Railway workers in different parts of the country also felt the need for closer relations. In

Finishing a body scanner in stainless steel and aluminium at J.B. Morton, Burton-on-Trent

1947 there were some 500 members working in rail shops: Crewe had 55, Darlington 25, Derby carriage and wagon works 109, Derby locomotive 34, Eastleigh carriage works 60, Horwich 32, London passenger transport board 14, London (Stratford) 25, Newcastle 17, Swindon 75, Wolverton 30, York 13, Glasgow 16 and Edinburgh two, men and apprentices. Their request for some kind of co-ordinating body was refused; even a plea for a national meeting of railway shops was rejected and they were told that if they wanted information from another shop they could forward their enquiry to head office, via their branch and it would be passed on.

However, despite some opposition, one-day national sectional conferences were held for representatives of members in both the railway and aircraft sectors of the trade during Buck's period as national President, 1953/6. Other sectional national meetings were held in the 1960s after he became General Secretary, with more meetings for representatives from the railway shops and others for members working at government establishments.

Right to Work

The organised workers, particularly those in the car industry – where the Union had much more influence than could be expected from its size alone – brought a new idea into the post-war world, 'the right to work'.

The first strike to hit the headlines based on this demand was the Duple strike of 1950 which Les Buck, sheet metal shop secretary at the time, described as 'something of a trail-blazer'. Duples in North London, was one of the old style motor coach makers which did not recognise trade unions although the unions had established a works council. It was the kind of family firm where a strike was unheard of. It operated a piece-master system and the manager was inclined to sack a man on the spot for anything he thought a flagrant case of *lèse-majesté*. In 1950 an engineer was brought in and a new method of working adopted with a batch system of working instead of the old make to order. Changes were made without any consultation or consideration of how the workers' earnings were effected. The shop stewards objected and all the stewards, members of the works committee and others who had spoken up were sacked, whereupon the sheet metal shop went on strike. After three weeks out all the strikers returned, taking the sacked men with them. That was in June. Soon after the management had another go, informing all the unions of impending large-scale redundancy. After rather superficial negotiations the management unilaterally broke off talks with the union officials and on 19 October the men were all out.

A strike committee was set up with Les Buck elected chairman and the strike was run with the efficiency supposedly displayed in a military exercise. Headquarters were set up in a room within sight of the factory gate, which was immediately picketed. The committee was in daily session with its first job the setting up of a machine to run the various activities. Members of the committee were given individual responsibilities and gathered a team around them to run their section. One was in charge of pickets, arranging rotas, seeing those on duty were provided with oilskins and food, receiving a lot of help and sympathy from local traders. This group also arranged the picketing of the Earls Court Motor Show. The team looking after finances also did a very good job. About 100 men, with a number of cars and motor cycles spoke at many trade union branch meetings, visited some 1,200 factories and asking for support, one group bluffing their way into an aircraft factory and holding a meeting in working time. Altogether they raised £12,000 in two months.

Others looked after the mail, sending receipts, replying to all letters containing contributions, and seeing that the books were audited weekly. A 'social security' group provided benefits to strikers' dependants in cases of hardship. A press and publicity group wrote to national and local papers and put out a quarter of a million statements, leaflets and other publicity materials. A transport group with 30 cars and 20 motor cycles provided dispatch riders, transported speakers as well as carrying banners and placards for meetings. Another booked halls and made other arrangements for meetings. Black work was trailed from the factory gate half way across the country to its destination, and workers were urged not to touch the work. Progress was reported to the strike committee which was reported to the membership at twice-weekly mass meetings.

In the face of this sustained solidarity, so different to the pre-war general lack of fight in the largely unorganised motor factories, the management held talks with the union officials without any return to work. Meetings with the management, TUC and Ministry of Labour eventually came up with a formula for returning to work which included giving notice to all those sacked. This was rejected out of hand by a mass meeting and the case went to a national tribunal at the request of the firm, which was represented by a KC against Harry Brown of the National Union and W. Roberts of the vehicle builders. Talks went on until the management conceded the strikers' terms and redundancy notices were withdrawn, when the men returned on 18 December.[1]

The strike registered an important step in the fight against mass sackings and for the right to work. It also had an effect inside the Union, no doubt contributing to the election soon afterwards of Les Buck as national President, the first time a member had been elected straight from the shop floor. From there he went on to become London district secretary and eventually General Secretary.

The right to a job demand was carried forward by the 'redundancy strike' at the big mass production Standard factory at Coventry in 1956, in which 250 sheet metal workers participating out of a total of some 5,000 of all trades on strike. This was one of the strikes that helped force the hand of employers and show the employers that the motor workers were not going back to the old days of 'hire and fire' said Bill Warman, who was chairman then of the strong Standard works committee at the time. In 1956 the management gave notice of changes at their Canley factory, including a lot of redundancies: the stewards fought back and the redundancies were withdrawn. Then the management stated they would be closing the factory to retool, making 2,000 redundant. The stewards put forward proposals for retooling without sacking men. As they were discussing this with the management, staff were putting up notices of closure and giving the workers notice. The stewards walked out of the meeting, called mass meetings in the shops and struck. Pickets were out but not a single worker tried to go in. The Unions took the dispute through procedure to York and the officials recommended a return to work. Rather than defy the unions the strikers returned and many were made redundant. The only gain was that the officials were made to see such action was going to lose members and the following BMC dispute was declared official.

Later, the British Motor Corporation sacked 6,000 workers. But the various BMC factories were not the same as those same plants before the war. The vast Morris factories, once the bastion of the hire and fire philosophy, were now organised, although mainly by the Transport and General Workers and the engineering union, with very few sheet metal workers. The Austin works in Birmingham had been fully organised during the war. Instead of 2,000 union members out of a workforce of 18,000, 1956 saw strongly organised plants with some 600 shop stewards and 25,000 members, including some 1,600 sheet metal workers, 500/600 members of the National Union and 900/1,000 of the Birmingham and Midlands Society.

In the immediate post-war period, when the motor firms could sell all the cars they could make, the firm recognised and consulted with the shop stewards. Then things got more difficult and the motor manufacturers reverted to type, shaking off the influence of wartime co-operation. The first redundancies came in 1951 and were met with strike action. But the men were divided after the first few days. They had not got used to the idea of there being a 'right to work', accepting in their minds the old seasonal sackings with the, fatalistic attitude 'this was the motor industry'. They returned with very little that could be claimed as gains.

BMC then announced more redundancies with 3,000 of all the sackings at Austin's. The stewards called a strike but the first day saw only 2,000 outside the gates. Then it began to build up with mass pickets on all the gates and flying pickets sent to bolster up pickets at the weaker plants such as Morris at Oxford, Nuffield, and the smaller links of the chain like MG at Abingdon. After two weeks a compromise was worked out and at Austin all marched back, dropping workers at the various departments as they passed them. It was agreed that men would be stood off but they would receive redundancy payments and an undertaking given to take them all back when trade picked up. Although the unions did not win all their demands the idea of the right to work was implanted in workers' minds and has remained. It was reinforced by the redundancy payments, an acknowledgement of that right, which originated in the 1956 strike and was later taken over as a state-run system.

Another battle in the right to work took place in 1961 at British Light Steel Pressings, West London, where some 200 members of the Union played a leading part in the 14-week long strike against redundancy. This ended in defeat with the men returning on more or less the employer's terms and a number of the more militant members were not taken back.

In 1971 the fight for the right to work was carried a stage further with the Upper Clyde Shipbuilders' 'work-in' which forced the Tory government to change its policy and saved shipbuilding on the Upper Clyde for a period while gaining support from the mass of trade unionists throughout Britain and many countries overseas. About 120 Union members were involved (a reduction from a shop of 250, all coppersmiths) and the NEC provided financial assistance while calling on all shops to make regular collections.

The 'York Memo'

After the war the Union again took up the struggle against the long line of procedure that the employers insisted must be followed 'for the avoidance of disputes'. This had its roots in the settlement forced on the defeated workers after the 30-week engineering lockout of 1897/8 which was later revised under the Carlisle agreement of 1907. The employers further strengthened their demands on procedure to be followed in 1914 – the first 'York Memo' which laid down a procedure of works, local and national conferences – up to York throughout which the employers' position would be maintained as the status quo until a settlement was reached. In a further revised agreement enforced by aggressive employers after the workers were again defeated in the 1922 lockout. They insisted on the sanctity of their right to manage their businesses as they saw fit, including the right to hire and fire at will. The sheet metal workers continued to resist this for some years after it had been generally accepted, but finally had to give way.

In the post-war struggle the unions forced the employers to make some concessions in 1955 but this did not meet the workers' objections and they continued to press for an equitable agreement. Unable to get any satisfaction after two-and-a-half years of talks, the unions withdrew from the agreement in December 1971 after due notice had been given. Continued pressure finally got rid of the hated 'York Memo' and the status quo clause, forced on the unions when they were weak. A new procedure on disputes was agreed in 1976 limited to a local conference consisting of the management, the employers' federation, the workers and the unions. If this could not arrive at a satisfactory settlement both sides would be free to take what action they thought fit.

The End of Meters

Changes were on the way for what had long been a bulwark of organised membership. Meter makers as a body tended to remain static, so forming a good basis for organisation. At G. Glover's, Chelsea, in 1951, of the 50 members in the shop no less than 25 had served their apprenticeship there. Of the rest, half-a-dozen had worked in the shop for 25 years or more and there had not been any change in the complement of the shop for four years. Joe Morphew had been shop secretary for 20 years, in pre-war days, only leaving to become assistant London district secretary. Other shops had a similar record.

When long service badges were first issued in 1952 meter makers had by far the largest number of any section of the trade in the London district. The 22 members at T. Glovers who received badges on that occasion had more than 1,000 years membership of the Union between them. There were 21 recipients from Smith's, 12 from Parkinson's, 11 from Willy's, with proportionately similar numbers from the smaller shops.

Over 7,000 years of craftsmanship and skill in all sections of the trade were represented when 140 of the 182 members of the Wolverhampton branch eligible for long service badges attended a special presentation meeting. Neighbouring Lye branch members received 92 silver badges. Manchester 99, including one who had 71 years membership, Glasgow 56, Liverpool 50, Birmingham 35, Bury 20, Bristol 19, Leeds 21, Hull 18. The London branch found it impossible to present badges personally to the 311 members eligible; 170 were sent out directly to members, the big shops sent delegations to the general meeting to collect badges for their shopmates and make presentations in the shops, the rest were presented at general meetings of the branch. At the same time some of the branches were celebrating 150 years of continuous life. The meter shops were well represented on many of these.

Meter maker members had not long settled down to their old trade after the wartime disruption followed by a spell of four-day working, when the shadow of a threat to eliminate the tin plate meter that had provided reasonably well-paid jobs for a section of members for generations, began to loom. It came in the form of the die-cast meter, most of whose earlier faults had been overcome and, assembled by cheap labour, was a serious threat.

Even with this threat of the guillotine hanging over their heads, the normal business of protecting living standards had to continue and the meter stewards put in a claim for a wage increase. The meter section had their own peculiar wage pattern. With a large number of individual prices for various jobs – some of which, on repairs, cost as little as 1d – working out wage increases was difficult in this piece-working trade. Since the First World War this had been done by percentages plussed on the amounts men booked in at the end of the week. By 1931 this plussage stood at $33\frac{1}{3}$ per cent but during the slump the employers reduced this to 25 per cent. In 1945 it was pushed up to $27\frac{1}{2}$ per cent – figures which coincidentally were the amounts of engineering piece-workers' earnings above day-work rates. As the employers linked the two to suit their own ends when in 1951 engineering rates went up to 45 per cent and the meter makers put in a similar claim. This was turned down by the employers and at a mass meeting meter makers denounced the NEC handling of their case.

Soon the meter makers had real problems with, in 1951, the introduction of the die-cast meter into Smith's. Parkinson's answer to this was a line-assembled tin plate meter, offering

Union labour and the old rates to get Union support. But with it went the closure of one of the oldest London shops, Cowan's, the first of what was to be a long series of closures that would decimate the meter industry in London.

A national meter makers' conference was held in May 1950. It was reported that the Northwest Gas Board had already ordered 25,000 of the new meter which was no longer a phantom but there in cast iron. The members were told that the old methods and practices were on their way out and meter makers had better see if they could put something in their place, they should get together with the employers. Glasgow reported that one local manufacturer had already started line production of the tin-plate meter but was not cutting prices to the customer, although getting more output. It was reported that the same was happening in London and the London Meter Stewards Association had decided there would be no more alteration of methods unless the savings were passed on to the customer.

Already in 1953 the NEC was writing off the meter section and were prepared to give away high frequency soldering as not skilled work. But the rank and file wanted to keep all work previously done by Union members and at national conference successfully moved the reference back to the NEC report on soldering machines. A lot of haggling on 'who does what' continued; members at Smiths managed to secure the full operation of the soldering machine and reported that almost all were able to earn top rate. But all this was an attempt to provide jobs for older members remaining in the trade. While members might hang on, getting into another shop when their own closed, at first, the meter section was on its way out. In 12 months it lost 100 members, then one-fifth of working meter makers.

In 1959 Willys shop closed, the fifth in two years, the others being Alder and Mackay, J. Braddock, Sutherland and South Suburban. The remaining firms combined to produce three power groups. They had ended the price ring the year before and now were engaged in a price war to get what orders were available, closing the small shops and concentrating work in the big establishments. In 1960 G.Glover was taken over and the shop closed; the men, many of whom had spent all their working lives in the shop – as had others elsewhere – were left looking for jobs. Dougal's and Sawyer and Purves went the way of the rest, as did Parkinsons at Cottage Lane, which had been employing Union members for 100 years or more. Finally T. Braddock was taken over by Wilsons, then owned by the asset strippers, Slater Walker. The men were issued with a notice to quit and production switched to the Coventry shop. The whole sad business reads like a roll call at a meter stewards' meeting. Soon there was nothing left. The London Meter Stewards' Association closed down in October 1972 and from then the whole of the London gas meter trade consisted of seven men at Smith's producing steel meters on a line system, with a handful of others engaged on repairs at other places.

Heating and Domestic Stewards

In 1975, when most of the other London stewards' associations were in decline, the district committee, prompted by the district secretary, R. Marsh, started an association for the heating and ventilating industry, and it proved to be as lively as any in the past. At that time there were some 6,000 to 7,000 members in the industry in London and its environs, but as industry generally declined, and capital investment plummeted, the heating and ventilating industry was particularly badly hit and membership in London dropped to around 4,500.

Organising on the sites was a necessary but always difficult task, and one that was never-ending. Members once made were not made for life. When their contribution to one contracting job finished they moved to another – at least when there was work around – and if

Working on ductwork of the air-conditioning system of the Barbican Arts Centre, City of London

there was no work in their own area they would travel to other parts of the country. If the job was not organised, which was the case five times out of six on a new site, they lapsed, perhaps becoming Union members again if some keen member came on the site and started agitating for Union organisation, there was a drive for membership or a visit from a full-time official brought organisation. The continual changing around of stewards was not conducive to a strong, permanent stewards' association. However, the organisation was adapted to suit the circumstances. The Southend branch, with whom the idea originated, provided a permanent base with the branch secretary, Martin Gould, acting as Association chairman until he became a full-time officer specialising in heating affairs. Other secretaries of the old Heating and Ventilation branches also gave stability. But even with the basic fluidity of organisation, it was surprising how often the old faces popped up at the Association meetings. It seemed that in many cases it was 'once a steward always a steward.' Experienced men, who had been stewards before, got known and when a steward was wanted he got nominated, perhaps by the full-time officer who was organising the site, if the member himself was not responsible for the organisation. But there was not a great deal of competition; there were always more kicks than ha'pence and on many jobs it was as good as asking for the sack.

One of the activities of the Association, consequently, was fighting the black list which most employers kept and surreptitiously referred to when a man applied for a job. The heating branches were responsible for regular motions on national conference agendas demanding action on black lists and there were a few strikes on the issue. In 1974 at the Shell oil refinery job at Stanford-le-Hope, Essex, the men were out for 13 weeks, with some 150 National Union members involved out of a total of about 800 to 900 members of all unions. There was another in 1979 at Mobil Oil's new refinery at Coryton with 30 Heating and Ventilating members out of 120 of all trades. This lasted 30 weeks. But there was not a great deal of success in either case and the problem remained.

Another of the Association's activities was to get 'civilised' conditions in the 'shut-down jobs'. When the big plants like Ford's closed down for two or three weeks for their summer holidays, contractors were employed refitting the works, ducting, pipe fitting, fans, extractors, sprinklers repaired or replaced and similar jobs. The men were Union members, the regular workers at the plant would insist on that, but until the Association got on the job they were worked all hours, often with no proper overtime rates and sometimes not getting the Union rate, conditions were poor and in many cases there was no concern for health and safety. Association members gave a lead and help in changing that. The contractors had the two or three weeks to get the job finished and could not afford trouble, so they generally accepted the conditions demanded.

The Association also helped with the organisation of sites, getting the stronger site organisations to help the weaker, gave support to new stewards, provided a forum to help formulate policy and demands, provided links with the Union machinery, and exchanged information on the situation on the various sites.

The Association became particularly active in the later years in backing up wage claims, with meetings of stewards to decide on action, bringing out leaflets and getting them distributed on the sites, holding meetings of members and building up an informed membership. Sites were requested to pass resolutions in support of claims which went to Head Office and employers made aware of them. Calls were made for deputation from the sites and branches to lobby the negotiations with banners and placards publicising their demands, supplemented with loud-hailers, backing up the Union negotiators, providing them with that extra bit of muscle needed to get an agreement.

As the result of London motions at National Conference at the beginning of the 1980s similar associations were formed in Birmingham to cover the Midlands and Manchester, covering Lancashire and Cheshire, and later one for Scotland. Conference resolutions were also responsible for the organisation of annual National Industrial Councils for the heating industry in 1982 with some 40 mainly rank and file delegates appointed by the district committees, together with some full-time officers. The Council set up a national campaign committee to back up the 1983 wage claim with a view to it being a regular part of the organisation, putting out national leaflets and similar activities.

At one time this section of the Union had become largely a body of pipe fitters and with the miles of pipe work on all refineries, gas installations and many other construction jobs, this provided a great amount of work. But in 1980 the National Union officer responsible for the section, S. Nugent, reported moves to expand into new fields or those that the Union had allowed to go by default. He told the national conference of work poached by other unions and that the Union had not claimed although it came into the category of heating and ventilating work. Thermo and acoustic insulation – generally known as lagging – which had been the work of the Union since before the First World War, had been almost completely lost to general unions but was now being won back, particularly on the big oil depot sites in South Wales, where one job alone was providing work for 500 members. Domestic heating was an industry employing some 20,000 workers and although these were scattered over a large number of small firms, many of them were cowboy employers and cowboy workers, it too wanted to establish its own separate identity and own agreements, giving the Union a foothold.

New technology was bringing new problems and challenges to members, but also giving them chances to get in on types of work previously neglected. Fire protection was an expanding industry which was changing its character. The old sprinkler system was no longer suitable for buildings containing intricate and expensive computers, delicate machinery and valuable records, and it was rapidly being taken over by new technology. Inert and in some cases active gases were already being used with their own transporting systems requiring special sensors and their own instrumentation. The Union and the industry were concerned with providing training and suitable apprenticeships to deal with these new developments.

Heating members on maintenance kept the presses rolling in Fleet Street, and had their own branch of the London district; some 800 others staffed the steel mills throughout the country. Members worked on making rigs and maintained the flow of North Sea gas, worked on the off-shore rigs, on the on-shore termini and on the pipe-lines and distributing systems. They helped build nuclear power stations and worked on the Thames flood barrage.

Union organisation was very patchy. Although almost all heavy construction jobs were 'closed shops'. The same was by no means the case on the heating and ventilating jobs where there was much non-unionism and domestic heating provided work for very few members.

While the amount of work on erecting ductwork for the ever-growing number of services multiplied during the post-war period, the number of workers making ducting dropped catastrophically. There was a boom in the sheet metal shops making ducting in the 1950s but

Working off-shore: preparing a 4″ pipe at a welding station on a pipe-laying barge at the North Sea Leman Bank field, Bacton, 1967, during the laying of a 30″/4″ gas pipe line.

Preparing a section of complex 42″ pipe for installation at an oil refinery in Pembrokeshire

the miles of ducting used meant that the custom-built trunking soon gave way to factory made, which the Union did not organise, and by the end of the 1970s there were very few ventilating shops left.

The ventilation shop stewards association was not the only one to disappear, the economic slump, cuts in public spending with the consequent reduction in capital construction, technical changes and the drift of industry from London combined to bring a reduction in London membership and the decline of the shop stewards movement as a whole.

New materials were taking the place of metal, weakening the position of the Union. Plastic of various kinds was being used more and more in ventilating work, and replacing metal utensils and pipes in the brewing and chemical industries. Glass fibre was in widespread use in the coachbuilding trade; carbon fibres were introduced in the aerospace industry where milling from the solid block of metal had in many cases taken over as a way of producing shaped panels previously formed on the wheel by panel beaters and increasingly new machines were taking the skill out of sheet metalwork.

The policy of the NEC was to claim as much of the work as possible on the grounds that it had previously been done by sheet metal workers or other members of the Union. Some of the jobs were allowed to go by default, members rejecting it as unskilled and allowing it to go to other labour. The advent of these new materials or new processes meant a fight to retain work with 'winning some and losing some' usually resulting in a nett loss of jobs. Even the victories

Prototype work at Abbey Panels, Coventry, for new British Leyland models, 1980s

were not won for all time but had to be continually defended. But the effect on the Union was not so catastrophic as some had forecast, and demands for the traditional skills of sheet metal workers continued. When British Leyland set up the production line for its new Metro model in 1980, the most robotised car assembly line in the country, the management found that they could not do without the skills of the sheet metal workers. Indeed, after they had engaged what they considered the necessary labour to start production they found they needed another 120 skilled metal workers in addition to the 1,100 already employed at the Longbridge works. When advertising did not attract the necessary labour they applied to the Union's district office in Birmingham to provide the necessary skilled men – the first time Longbridge had done so in some 70 years of car production.

Women members

Fundamental changes were taking place everywhere. The Union's long opposition to women working on sheet metal work came to a decided halt in 1975 when such discrimination became illegal under the Equality of Opportunity Act. There had been women in the Union before this, brought in through the amalgamation with the coppersmiths who had a few women members, though not as many as the General Secretary, Poole, wished. He claimed that the Union would not have lost work on $\frac{3}{8}$ inch copper pipes if they had recruited the women who did a better job on this work than men. A special women's auxiliary section had been formed but little or no attempt was made to recruit others.

There had even been a few women on skilled sheet metal work over the years. We have a copy of an indenture of one, Ada Turner of Birmingham, who in 1890 was apprenticed to a local master tin plate worker for four years to learn the art of tin tea pot making. But she was not taken into the Union.

The first time-served woman sheet metal worker to become a member of the skilled section of the Union was able to join because of the law. She was Lyn Ridgeway who completed her apprenticeship at Vicker's shipyard, Barrow in 1981 and became a member of the skilled section of the Union. The same issue of the Journal that recorded Lyn Ridgeway's breakthrough reported that 18-year-old Tracy Englis had started as an apprentice at a general sheet metal shop in Poole, Dorset and had joined the Bournemouth branch.

The new law necessitated changes in the rule book, with immediate temporary modifications until complete new rules could be drafted and passed by conference. The women's section was disbanded, the women members transferred to the respective general sections and what was called a 'tidying-up resolution' passed, so that the rule book carried the correction 'references in the rule to the male gender includes female for the terms of membership of the Union.'

Health and Safety

The trade-union scene became more diverse and complicated throughout the period following the Second World War. Officials, both lay and full-time were constantly having to deal with problems never even imagined by their predecessors. They had to provide expert advice and guidance on a whole range of issues, often having to pit their skills against technical experts and lawyers when representing members at hearings and tribunals. As so often happens in the trade-union movement, the job made the man in many cases. One of the areas where this was often the case was that of health and safety. The Labour government's 1946 Industrial Injuries Act and the publicity surrounding the introduction of the National Health Service brought greater activity in the area of health and safety at work. The old first aid box in the foreman's office with its iodine bottle, odd assorted bandages and a few old burn dressings was no longer enough.

The National Union joined in the trade union pressure for legislation to complement and assist the unions in their activities to improve industrial safety and to minimise the risk to health from materials and processes used in workplaces. This concern became much more widespread from the 1960s.

In addition to bringing pressure to bear on the authorities through the TUC, the Union also alerted and educated members on the many hazards connected with various jobs. These included the dangers of cancer from working with asbestos, which applied particularly to heating members; respiratory diseases and other hazards connected with welding; the dangers of cadmium poisoning to coppersmiths and other members doing silver soldering; the dangers of lung cancer from working with glass fibre, particularly among members on coach building; the dangers of lead poisoning for metal finishers. The Union campaigned on the question of industrial deafness with resolutions at the Trades Union Congress and representation to the TUC and government ministries. On the one hand the Union pressed to get members included under the legislation that listed workers covered by industrial deafness provisions and on the other for legislation to reduce noise in the workshops. The first compensation award for industrial deafness came in 1971. In 1982 the Union obtained £192,853 in claims made on behalf of 153 members. In 1983 no less that 382 claims were for industrial deafness, the highest classified group out of a total of 988 claims. The 1982 lists of awards included £73,000 for six claims for asbestosis and £43,784 for four claims for cadmium poisoning.

This aspect of the Union's work was greatly expanded with the enactment of the Health and Safety at Work Act in 1974, the result of widespread trade union agitation. Day and weekend schools on the provisions of the Act and the attitude of the Union toward it were held for officials, district and branch officers, stewards and safety representatives. Shops were urged to set up shop floor health and safety committees and to back proposals for safety representatives on a shop and factory level, and on the sites. In Coventry the Union organisation in the shops joined with other trades in setting up a Coventry Health and Safety Movement which held lectures, gave assistance to shop stewards, organised conferences, checked up on the position in the various workplaces and generally exchanged experiences and gave advice on all matters connected with health and safety.

Education and Training

Considering that their members were very craft conscious, the old tin plate workers' and early sheet metal workers' unions had little time for training and education. For some 50 years, the Union's education facilities had been provided by the National Council of Labour Colleges – and its predecessor, the Plebs League – with its emphasis on 'independent working-class education' and its basis in Marxian economics. The old General Union of Sheet Metal Workers had been something of a pioneer in its own small way in its support for this 'education for emancipation' and succeeding generations of tinmen had had their class consciousness raised by NCLC politico-economic courses and learned their public speaking and report-writing from its classes. But there was nothing dealing specifically with the Union's own organisation and problems. Membership participation, too, was purely voluntary and very much a hit and miss affair, depending on the individual member's own initiative, perhaps in response to articles, reports or advertisements in the Journal or persuasion from an enthusiast in the shop. It has been estimated that less than 0.5 per cent of the Union members participated. Even so, the NCLC generated great loyalty among members involved – perhaps this delayed the introduction of a more considered education policy.

The change came from outside with proposals in 1946 by two of the main backers of the NCLC, the miners and the railwaymen, for a rationalisation of working-class and particularly trade union education then being carried out separately by the NCLC and the TUC. In 1962 the two merged, something in the nature of a shot-gun marriage, to avoid overlapping and competition for the same students, it was said, and to provide education suited for post-war needs and possibilities, directed mainly at improving trade union work and administration. This was to be financed initially by a levy of 4d per head of the affiliated membership. The old NLCL, in effect, disappeared.

The changed attitude to education was part of a whole process of change taking place in the post-war trade union movement, reflecting their new position in society. The part the unions had played in the war, their greater numerical strength and the advent of a Labour government in power all helped to give the unions a new and enhanced status, and ensured they would be consulted by government and non-governmental organisations, as well as more and more by industry. At the same time the old stalwarts in the leadership of the trade unions, who were brought up in the old traditional ways of doing things and were resistant to change, were being replaced by a new generation. These new, younger men had a different attitude to education. They did not have the distrust of 'theory' and were persuaded that it was not sufficient for officials to learn by doing. Learning from experience was still a necessary part of a union official's development but should be supplemented by whatever else was available. The struggle continued but in a new form.

Along with others, the National Union leadership was changing, particularly with the retirement of Brotherton as General Secretary, the last of the old traditional craft union leaders, one whose involvement dated back to before the First World War.

It took the Union some years to decide what they were going to do about education now that it was to be Union business and could no longer be a decision to be taken by the individual member with the Union's contribution limited to the payments of affiliation fees and electing a representative to attend NCLC annual meetings.

In 1960, proposals for a very modest programme of education with two weekend schools in each district every year and the provision of places for two young members to study at Ruskin College, Oxford, was defeated at national conference. In 1970 it was reported that most education was still of a shop floor character, learning by experience, supplemented by TUC correspondence courses and TUC training classes. The Union had started running an annual summer school at Ruskin College, its first step toward education based on the Union. A report the following year on a sub-committee investigation of the problem proposed that the NEC and each district and branch should appoint an education officer. F. Barnes, Assistant General Secretary and the first national education officer, said union education was not to be an academic exercise but would be for the specific purpose of better equipping members to carry out the work of the Union and the general trade union movement. Education facilities should be as broad as the Union could afford and should be integrated into the work of the Union. In 1974 the NEC had worked out its programme and invested £5,000 in education, mainly directed toward the training of officers. The Union had always believed that the best officials came from the bench; men who knew the trade, who had been a steward or branch secretary, active in many ways and had become a full-time official because of support received from members he had served. What was lacking was a final polish, and the education was designed to give that polish. There was to be a course for new officers before taking over, followed by continuing courses for officials, manuals and courses for part-time officers and district schools for shop stewards and activists, largely given by officials of the Union. Groups of active shop stewards were taken through a range of courses over one or two years to develop leadership within the districts and a special shop stewards' handbook was produced. This development in the Union's education took a number of years and varied in different parts of the country, depending on the commitment of the local officials. Together with it went TUC day, weekend or week-long schools on such subjects as negotiations, work study and job evaluation methods, general administration, the Health and Safety at Work Act and the increasing amount of other legislation, agreements and other matter with which the modern trade union official had to be familiar.

In later years there were classes or courses on new technology, as it affected the Union and the skilled craftsman. With the increasing attacks on the unions some officials included political education as a regular feature. Education, such as there was, had been one of the responsibilities of the Assistant General Secretary – as had the editorship of the Journal – and after this position had been eliminated with the creation of a number of national officers. One of these, Tom Nelson, was given the now important task of developing education as part of his duties. At the same time, the editorship of the Journal was given to a professional journalist, with Union connections.

As Union education developed, so did the attitude to apprentices and their training. Until the 1914-1918 war, and in some places between the wars, apprentices were kept in their place, essential for providing the future membership of the Union but a nuisance in themselves except for such errands as fetching a ha'penny mug of beer from the barrel kept in the yard or the breakfast steaks and chops that each morning frizzled on the firepots of some London meter shops before the First World War. But apprentices were not allowed to take part in Union activities. In fact, it was only after persistent pressure by some apprentices on the eve of the formation of the National Union that they were given permision to join the Union in the latter years of their apprenticeship, and that right was granted with a great deal of reluctance. Even after the rule book gave apprentices over the age of 18 the right to vote up to and including national ballots, they were still not allowed to attend shop meetings in many places and in others, while they were allowed to attend they could not speak or vote. This was contrary to the rules, a hangover from the past. Although this attitude was eventually discarded, it was not until 1959 that the first London meeting for apprentices was held. It was hailed as a success; 150 apprentices turned up to hear talks on their various problems from the General Secretary, Brotherton, and the London district secretary, H.Brown, who was responsible for the innovation. A second meeting was held six months later and it, too, was lively, although only 50 apprentices attended. It was to have been a regular feature but after that it was more sporadic and was later dropped. A call by London and Glasgow branches for a regular national apprentices meeting was opposed by the NEC and was defeated at national conference, as was a 1970 motion that districts should, by rule, call quarterly meetings of junior members.

Early minute books tell of little or no discussion on the form or content of apprentice training; any negotiations that took place dealt only with conditions. There was much discussion and many disputes over the number of apprentices allowed, but that was due to concern that they would be used as cheap labour, rather than for the effect it would have on their training. After the Second World War concern switched to a growing shortage of apprentices, and calls were made for recruitment drives. In the later years it was said that in Birmingham, firms like Lucas had up to 200 sheet metal workers but only four or five apprentices. The General Secretary condemned the employers for refusing to invest in apprentices because they could not see them providing a profit This continued to be a problem and increased with the development of the depression.

Aluminium core for a nuclear reactor under construction at APV, Crawley

Despite the undoubted deficiences in the training of apprentices in a large number of shops, there was always some interest in the articles and drawings on pattern development which had been a regular feature of the Journal from its early days. Apprentices were also generally encouraged to attend evening classes at technical schools and to sit for their City and Guilds examinations, at least in the better organised shops. Some branches were even responsible for getting technical classes started, sometimes providing the instructors and giving prizes for the best work. They also kept up pressure for day release and later block release schemes to take the place of evening classes. In general the big firms accepted this, but in many places it took a long hard struggle to convince the numerous small employers to release their apprentices – and to pay them for studying. It was not until the late 1950s that the Union nationally provided incentives by operating a regular grant payment to apprentices passing their City and Guilds examinations.

Traditionally training in many, perhaps most shops, had consisted of the apprentices watching the journeymen do the job and then being allowed to do the more simple tasks gradually passing on to more skilled operations. But after the Second World War a number of firms began more systematic apprentice training. They included some government establishments, aircraft companies, together with some other more enlightened firms. One such was APV of Crawley, makers of high-class equipment for the brewing, dairy, food and chemical industries, in stainless steel, aluminium, nickel and titanium. They opened their own special training school at the works and operated a training programme agreed upon with the Union stewards and presided over by a Union member. Apprentices spent their first two years mainly in the school, their work there supplemented by day release courses at the local technical school on theory. Their third and fourth years were spent on getting practical experience on the great variety of jobs on the shop floor under the supervision of journeymen.

In the post-war world great changes were taking place in work and in training. The passing on of skills at the bench over a seven or five year apprenticeship was giving way to a position where much of the craft skills was being learned away from the bench, supplemented by experience in the factory during four years of apprenticeship. In the engineering and metal trades there was a movement to transferrable skills, enabling a man to move from one job to another. In 1959 a training agreement was signed between the engineering employers and the Confederation of Shipbuilding and Engineering Unions.Then in 1964 the government had stepped in after pressure from the employers who complained of lack of adequate training throughout the industry. Parliament brought in the Industrial Training Act with powers to levy all employers of 40 workers or more and distribute the proceeds among firms that carried out training to Industrial Training Board standards and to enforce the quality and quantity of training generally. Initially the Union decided to proceed with some caution but to make sure that the interests of the trade and craft were safeguarded. In later years it became associated with the boards in which members had a direct interest. It favoured their continuance and urged the government not to scrap the levy system.

The courses were designed particularly for small firms that did not have the facilities or resources to do their own training. The sheet and metal plate work syllabus covered 50 weeks: six weeks bench fitting; four weeks hard and soft soldering and tinning; six weeks oxy-acetylene welding; six weeks development, two weeks each on brazing, rivetting and copper pipe work, followed by 22 weeks on general sheet metal work exercises.

In 1978 the engineering employers called for a new form of training apprentices based on modules instead of time served. This new training had been accepted in 1966 as a system of craft and technician apprenticeship. The employers proposed that an agreed number of apprentices be taken into the industry each year, of which the employers would take a certain

Lyn Ridgeway, the first time-served woman member of the Union's skilled section, who completed her apprenticeship at Vicker's shipyard, Barrow, in 1981

number and the training board take up the shortfall for employment in the industry when trade picked up. School subjects should be linked to training in industry, and the aim was to show how mathematics, science, technology and craft practice were allied to industry and how learning was used in the workplace. Pupils achieving CSE grades two or three would be accepted as achieving the equivalent of the first six months of an apprenticeship. Two modules should be achieved by the age of 18 when the apprentice would receive the craftsman's rate and examination of achievement would be at the training centres. The aim should be for greater flexibility among craftsmen which would be achieved by learning other modules to become a 'multi-skilled craftsman', with extra payments for each module.

The General Secretary, Guy, called for the widest discussion on the proposals at all levels in the Union on whether this could be accepted or, indeed, if it could be refused. He said changes would not mean the end of the craftsman, but they would be taking a different way forward by improving the standard of skills within their range and move to higher technical achievement. There had always been a minority of craftsmen who had gone on to become draughtsmen and technicians, but now all skilled craftsmen with the ability and interest could tread that road. There was some questioning of the effect of this on the Union, how would it be decided, what union apprentices joined and what would be Union attitude to members of other unions doing 'their' work under the flexibility agreement.

In 1983 the Confederation reached an agreement with the employers to change over to the new method of training, enabling industry to make effective use of available manpower and accelerate the acquisions of new skills to meet the changing needs of technology. Training standards would be that of the Engineering ITB certificate of craftsmanship and the length of training sufficient to achieve two modules of approximately 12 months each. The General Secretary recommended the agreement and the New Training Initiative as making good sense, providing highly skilled craftsmen trained to the needs of the new technology. The needs of the future would probably be for fewer but better trained craftsmen, capable of great skills and providing great opportunities for advance to technicians' status. He urged members to consider retraining for the complete technological changes that lay ahead. He was sure that craft groupings of the future would be smaller and less orientated to a single skill, with a much clearer connection with technicians. The change in training methods was not just a matter of new technology and new courses in colleges, but heralded in a complete new structure in industry and trade unions in the years ahead.

Financial Problems

The financial position, the constant struggle to balance the books, played a significant part in the decision to join up with a larger union. This was particularly the case in the late 1970s and early 1980s when mass unemployment struck the Union and all other trades, cutting down income when prices continued to rise. Right up until 1977 the Union carried a heavy burden of friendly society benefits that were an anachronism in the post-war world – unemployment, disablement, funeral, sickness and superannuation. Although collectively their cost was a heavy burden on the Union, individually the amounts paid out were derisory, yet members fought to retain them. In 1970, when the NEC proposed putting an end to sickness benefits conference delegates were told that in addition to the £60,000 paid out in sick benefit that year, the cost of administering the benefit amounted to a further £20,000. Even so the delegates turned down the proposal. At the 1976 conference the NEC only managed to get their motion to end sick benefit carried by 806 votes to 634 and that to end unemployment benefit by 837 votes to 531, even though they sugared the pill with an increase in dispute pay. Supporters of the abolition of the benefits saw this as an end to the old friendly society conception of the Union, and a clearing of the decks for a struggle against the employers for full employment and to get a proper occupational sick pay.

An even greater problem was superannuation, which was a great and increasing drain on funds. In 1970 it was agreed that no new members would be accepted into the superannuation scheme. Payment would continue to those already in receipt of the benefit and others, then paying, would be allowed to continue if they wished. Otherwise they, and all other members would be eligible for a grant on retirement. Even so, superannuation would continue to drain away funds and in a review in 1976 it was reported that 36 per cent of all contributions went to old members. In 1980 it was decided that while the 3,687 retired members actually drawing superannuation would have this guaranteed until their death, the 5,032 working members who had decided to go on paying in would have to transfer to retirement grants.

The General Secretary reported that the superannuation was being subsidised to the extent of £191,000 a year. The law now stipulated that pension funds should be properly funded. To do this without making changes or increasing benefits would cost £1,131,000 and the Union did not have that kind of money. Even with the proposed changes £450,000 would have to be transferred to the fund over the next three years and a further £72,000 paid in each year for the next six years. The fund would then have to be supported in accordance with actuarial valuation from 1983.

Even with these expensive benefits hived off costs continued to mount with the deterioration in the economy and rising inflation. The Union, rather reluctantly, had to continue to ask for more money. But when these demandswere accepted contributions were always chasing inflationary costs, never catching up. The loss of members that always followed increases in contributions intimidated the NEC into putting in for lower contributions than were really needed. Even so there was generally opposition to increases asked, although it was pointed out that contributions as related to wages were only about a quarter of what they were pre-war. Although in his reports the General Secretary did emphasise that the Union was by no means 'broke' he did point out the deteriorating financial position and the difficulties this would lead to if continued. There is no doubt that it did contribute to the feeling of inevitability of amalgamation.

Amalgamation

Despite the unexpected setback in the 1946 ballot, amalgamation with the Birmingham Society remained a major aim of the National Union and although there were clashes between members of the two societies, talks were kept going.

Meanwhile the two societies had to live together and at the beginning of 1951 the Birmingham Society accepted a working agreement although modifying the National Union proposals. But the good relations that had been built up deteriorated and by the end of the 1950s it was said that there was no harmony in the Midlands, rather that the situation was more one of war between the two societies. This was partly the result of personality clashes, with some strong opposition among leading personnel of the local National Union organisation as well as on the other side, and partly because of fears of job losses as motor work, particularly, contracted.

The establishment of new leadership in the Midlands district brought weekly communications between the two societies with lists of vacancies, members wanting jobs and positive action on problems such as collection of contributions in the shops. The joint struggle against massive redundancies in the motor shops had already laid the foundation for closer working. But amalgamation prospects suffered another setback when in 1964 the Birmingham Society members voted in a ballot against engaging in merger negotiations. Nevertheless the National Union continued to see merger with Birmingham as a priority and indicated to various suitors that this must be settled before there could be any wider amalgamation.

After 1970, with the deteriorating economic position, both of the unions and of the trade generally, talks between sub-committees of the two unions dealt with differences in superannuation payments and other benefits and integration of the two organisations on a district and national level. In 1972 proposals of the joint subcommittees were agreed by the two ECs which recommended acceptance. In March 1973 both unions voted for amalgamation by overwhelming majorities, bringing to completion attempts to heal the breach which had extended over 65 years.

Although the amalgamation was welcomed by those who had pressed for it for so long, and its effect on morale was considerable, it had come almost too late for the Union to take full advantage of the new unity. The separate organisation of the Birmingham Society had a detrimental effect on the development of union organisation in the trade, both on the National Union and on the Birmingham Society itself. The split restricted the organisation of sheet metal workers and weakened organisation in one of the most important areas of the trade. The rivalries, the duplication of organisation, the time spent on merger talks, the difficulty of mounting recruitment drives, had interfered with the organisation of the trade for years. It had also delayed the amalgamation with kindred trades making it possible for those in the coppersmiths, plumbers and others who opposed proposals or attempts at amalgamation to demand that the sheet metal workers first put their own house in order. It also delayed wider amalgamation with such unions as the boilermakers, as the National Union itself felt it must complete the unity of the kindred trades and particularly of the sheet metal craft.

During the long years of talks with the Birmingham Society other unions had been probing the possibilities of the National Union amalgamating with them. The engineers, boilermakers and electricians had all been interested. Amalgamation with them, however, would be a very different matter to those that had gone before. Up to then, it had largely been a matter of 'kindred trades' coming together; and perhaps more important, the other unions had been joining the National Union. Amalgamation with any of these three unions would mean the National Union going in with them as the junior partner and that was not so welcome. Many members feared that this would be a take-over to a greater or lesser degree, their Union would be absorbed and they would lose their skilled craft status. Although there had been an agreement with the Birmingham Society that there would be no more amalgamations for at least two years following their merger, and despite the lack of enthusiasm by many sections of the membership, the probing and the talks went on.

In 1956 there had been talks with the plumbers on a more or less equal basis. But whether they would lead to anything was dependent on the outcome of negotiations they were already having with the electricians, with whom they eventually amalgamated. The EEPTU took up where the plumbers left off, offering similar terms to those accepted by the plumbers and offered the use of their computer as an incentive. There was some support for this link-up, particularly from heating members. However, the EEPTU was itself having merger talks with the General and Municipal Workers' Union and the National Union would not agree to any merger that might land them up in a general union. The ban on Communists holding office was also a stumbling block, but the EEPTU said that if that were be the only outstanding question it could be considered.

Preliminary talks were also held that year with the Boilermakers, whose conference had instructed its officials to pursue amalgamation with the National Union and whose president, McGarvey, said nothing should be allowed to stand in the way of achieving this.

The problems raised in amalgamation with the Amalgamated Union of Engineering Workers were more difficult, with the National Union covering as wide a spread of industries as the engineering union itself. The talks with the AUEW president, Scanlon, provided no solution on how the National Union could fit in the federated structure as a separate section and it was finally suggested that National Union members might have to join engineering branches.

The following years saw a continued struggle inside the Union for joining one or other of the 'contestants' in the struggle for members, power and solvency. The line-up was mainly based on the section of the trade in which branch members were employed but there was also an underlying political element.

At the 1972 national conference there was a tussle between those supporting the AUEW, including the NEC and those who favoured the Boilermakers, based on the 'shipping branches', with the Northeast coast branch representatives led by the district secretary, A. Tarn, among the most vocal. Proposals were put forward by the Transport and General Workers' Union but received no support and no further moves were made by the electricians.

The NEC motion seeking authority to continue discussion with the AUEW for a separate section was defeated by 564 to 949. The motion favoured by the General Secretary, Les Buck, for amalgamation with the boilermakers, offering an equal partnership in a new metal workers' union with the boilermakers retaining the presidency and the National Union the secretaryship was carried by 822 votes to 725. But a vote to 'stay as they were' obtained a minority of nearly one-third of the votes, 513 against 957.

In 1978, after a period of consolidation following the amalgamation with the Birmingham Society, delegates to national confederence overwhelmingly supported a Birmingham motion that further amalgamation was inevitable. The position of the Union was that income was down, membership in decline and expenditure rising. In this situation the Union could still negotiate from a point of comparative strength but dare not delay further in case the situation deteriorated. New techniques and materials were eroding demarcation lines and eliminating members' jobs. The National Union was unable to compete with the big unions and had to

New technology: coppersmith operating a computerised pipe-bending machine at Vosper Thorneycroft's Shipyard, Southampton, 1984

give way to them in negotiations – this was particularly the case with the decline of piece-work. The NEC was instructed to discuss the possibilities of amalgamation with interested organisations and to prepare a report with its own recommendations.

After meetings with the Transport and General Workers' Union, the electricians, boilermakers and the four sections of the AUEW, a special conference was held in September 1979 which overwhelmingly accepted terms negotiated with the AUEW engineering section and instructed the NEC to finalise the details of the transfer of engagements. The report said that the terms agreed maintained the identity and craft associations of the Union, which would have its own sheet metal, coppersmith, pipe and heating section which would remain separate until members agreed otherwise. It would retain its own branches and districts, its own section balloting procedure and 'certain of its rules'. Officers would be guaranteed eight years' employment, there would be five years to rationalise contributions, the Union's solicitor would be retained and the Journal retained for five years. It would have two members on the National Executive Committee and 23 on the joint national committee, as well as representation on other committees. The agreement was supported by the General Secretary, G. Guy, and the NEC. The General Secretary reported that membership of the AUEW would improve service to members, give the organisation a stronger base, allow the membership to put in their contribution before AUEW policy was made and provide a step forward to the long-held aim of one union for engineers. He reported that although the recruiting campaign had added 1,258 members since 1975 this was due to increases in apprentices and auxiliary members, the skilled membership, the core of a craft union, had decreased by 828, while costs continued to rise. At the end of 1978 arrears totalled £150,495. The Union was not broke, and it could continue on its own, but contributions would continue to increase. Even if the Union became a section of the AUEW the recruiting campaign could not be stopped, for if membership shrank, the survival of the section would be threatened.

It was reported that in carrying out the decision of the 1978 national conference, the NEC had held talks with the Metal Mechanics and Pattern Makers who expressed interest but were not planning to amalgamate; the Associated Metal Workers' Union had a conference decision not to discuss amalgamation. The Boilermakers were directing their energies toward an amalgamation with the General and Municipal Workers. The Transport and General Workers made a good offer but it was thought members would not want to join with a predominantly general union. The NEC felt that the National Union could not play any effective part in the EEPTU structure and unless radical changes were made the Union would sink its identity. The only affinity between the two unions was between the Union's heating members and the plumbers. The NEC therefore went ahead with working out an agreement with the AUEW engineering section.

However, before any agreement could be made, a dispute arose within the AUEW between the engineering and technical sections which resulted in court action. At the same time the leadership of the engineering section moved further and further to the right both politically and industrially. This was strongly condemned at the conference the following year, in particularly the attitude of the AUEW president Duffy during the British Leyland wage claim and his refusal to back the sacked BL shop stewards' convenor, Robinson. However, although the General Secretary, George Guy, fully agreed with the criticisms he said it was organisations that mattered not individuals and asked for and got agreement to continue with the ongoing talks. He later reported in the Journal that as soon as the legal position had been resolved the certification officer would be asked to approve the Union's terms for transfer of engagements to the AUEW.

With the legal dispute concerning the AUEW still unresolved and deteriorating relations with the engineering section, the 1982 national conference decided by an overwhelming majority to set aside the decision of the 1979 special amalgamation conference which instructed the NEC to go ahead and finalise the transfer of engagements with the AUEW. Conference decided instead to open simultaneous discussions with two unions they had previously turned down, the AUEW technical section and the Transport and General Workers. The result would be put to a special conference within 12 months. The General Secretary said they had no alternative but to give up attempts for an agreement with the engineering section of the AUEW as their leadership apparently felt themselves all-powerful and not bound by rules. Agreements made by them were not worth the paper they were written on.

The agreement negotiated with the Amalgamated Union of Engineering Workers (Technical and Supervisory Section) – AUEW (TASS) – would mean that after amalgamation National Union members would become members of a craft sector of AUEW (TASS) – one of the four sections of the AUEW – but the identity of the National Union would be preserved in the new rules with a separate identity guaranteed to the craft sector. There would be rules covering both sectors and others that applied only to the craft or technical sections. Some of these rules would need the agreement of both sections before they could be changed, including rules relating to structure. The National Union's existing branches and districts would continue and the EC would become the National Craft Committee. There would be an annual conference of delegates from both sections to deal with matters affecting the whole union, after which the conference would break up into the separate sections to consider their own questions. There would also be district conferences. All officials would continue to be elected as in the National Union but members of the craft section would also be eligible for the posts of General and Deputy General Secretary and could participate in the appointment process. Conduct of business, method of admission and of collecting contributions would not change. The representative council, the supreme policy-making authority of the amalgamated union would have members from both sections proportionate to their membership.

The Transport and General Workers proposed that the National Union should form a new skilled trades group within the present Transport and General structure. It would recruit all skilled men of whatever trade or category within the engineering and construction industries. The branches would continue to operate unchanged, district committees would also continue to function and representation would be provided on the regional committees. The national committee of the skilled trade group would have representation on the General Executive Council and would have delegates to the national biennial conference. Arrangements would be made for co-ordination with the existing engineering, automotive and power groups of the Transport and General Workers' Union. Branch secretaries and other lay officers would continue and full time officers would become officials of the skilled group with two electoral periods of office guaranteed. Vacancies in the trade group officials would be filled by members of the group for the next eight years. It was envisaged that in the future, probably in eight years, there could be a merger of the new skilled group with the automotive and power engineering groups.

The Union was sharply divided on the issue. The amalgamation sub-committee of the NEC divided three to two in favour of recommending transfer of engagements to TASS, but the NEC reversed this also by a majority of one. At the special one-day conference speeches were about equally divided and the vote on the amendment, to accept the terms negotiated with the AUEW (TASS) and proceed to a national ballot of the membership, instead of the Transport and General Workers' Union as recommended by the NEC, was carried by 575 votes to 517. There was no amendment by those wanting to remain independent and their number was not known.

The main support for the linkup with the Transport and General came from the important Midlands district, strongly advocated by the district secretary, T. Henderson, and a number of former members of the old Birmingham Society. It had its basis in the fact that the strength of the district membership lay in the Midlands' motor industry in which the main union was the T&G automotive section, essentially the old National Union of Vehicle Builders, which the Midlands district saw as its natural affinity. Solid support for this amalgamation also came from the North East district whose district and branch representatives strongly opposed going in with AUEW TASS, largely on the grounds that its members were the representatives of the management in the workshops.

The very left wing political complexion of TASS was undoubtedly an attraction for the London district and other sections of the Union led by the left. It also had the support of the many who saw it as a step toward the long-held goal of one union for engineering workers as well as those who feared absorption into the broad masses of a general union and felt it to be the best form of amalgamation offered that might preserve the identity of the Union.

A big campaign was mounted, led by the General Secretary, to get the maximum vote, with meetings, leaflets and two special issues of the Journal.

A total of 57,376 ballot papers were distributed and 24,485 were returned by 24 October 1983, the final date for the return of papers – 43 per cent of all those eligible to vote. A total of

George Guy, last General Secretary of the Union, greets Ken Gill, General Secretary, AUEW-TASS, on the amalgamation of the two unions

Tom Nelson, formerly Coventry branch secretary, first Secretary of the craft sector of AUEW-TASS, working at the bench in Coventry

19,102 voted in favour of the transfer of the Union's engagements to AUEW (TASS) and 5,279 against, with 104 spoilt papers.

The future in store for the Union was still not very clear. The last General Secretary, of the independent Union, George Guy, who retired in May 1984 after the final national meeting of the Union, declared that this would be a step toward the long-cherished dream of one union for engineering workers. But the links between TASS and the rest of the AUEW was by then even more tenuous than before as the other three sections were in the process of solid amalgamation. There was some hope expressed by both the National Union and TASS leadership that the craft sections would be augmented by the adhesion of other unions, such as the Pattern Makers and the Metal Mechanics. TASS already had one small craft affiliate, the old gold and silversmiths, as the precious metals section.

That, however, was perhaps something for the future. From May 1984 the new craft section was to be led by Tom Nelson, senior national officer of the old National Union, who had been nominated for the position by 54 branches from all over the country and elected unopposed as General Secretary.

So, on 20 December 1983, after some 200 years of life, the National Union of Sheet Metal Workers, Coppersmiths, Heating and Domestic Engineers, itself a product of some 100 mergers of separate kindred societies over the years, ceased to exist as a separate Union and became the craft section of the Amalgamated Union of Engineering Workers (Technical and Supervisory Section).

1.   A report of the strike, *How Duples Won*, published a pamphlet by the strike committee, sold 75,000 copies and was used as a guide to running a strike in a number of disputes.

The material for most of this chapter came from the books of the National Union, journals, the national press, leaflets and pamphlets, from interviews, discussions and correspondence with various active and retired members of the Union and from personal experience as an active member of the Union over many years.

Index

Index

Aberdeen, 29, 54, 58, 128-30, 133, 153-4, 159, 162-3, 225, 289, 291, 297

Accrington, 58, 100, 183, 198-9, 208

AEU, 243, 264, 272, 307, 316, 347, 394

Admiralty, 226, 228, 232, 242, 253, 286, 292, 302, 310

Aircraft, 145, 148-50, 242, 266-73, 308-9, 372, 387-9, 404

Aircraft Committee, Birmingham, 372

Aircraft Manufacturing Co., 149, 242

Aircraft shop stewards, London, 150, 270-3, 387, 389

Aircraft Shop Stewards' National Council, 266, 271-2, 389

Aircraft Workers, National Council of, 272

Air Ministry, 315, 387

Airships, 268, 308, 328

Allied Trades Movement, 190, 218, 219

Alloa, 298, 305

Altringham, 48, 58, 213

Amalgamated Tin Plate Workers of Birmingham, Wolverhampton and District, 162, 203, 222, 356, 361

Apprentices, 21-3, 25, 28, 32, 36, 39-40, 63-7, 82, 119-20, 137-9, 155-7, 159, 163, 169, 171, 181, 183-4, 193, 200-1, 206, 258, 273-6, 280, 283-5, 296, 306-7, 309, 311, 322, 342-4, 359, 386, 393, 421-3

Apprentices, Statute of, 63-7

Apprentices, strikes of, 306-7, 309

Apprenticeship Certificate, 386

APV Crawley, 423

Arbroath, 58, 153

Argyle Motors, 293

Armstrong Siddeley Motors, 263, 267, 378

Armstrong Whitworth Aircraft, 271, 378

Armourers Company, 18, 30, 31

Arrol Johnson Motors, 293, 305

Artificial Limb Stewards Association, 256, 406

Artisans' General Committee, 64-5, 67, 73

ASE, 100, 216, 287, 292, 295, 323, 332

Ashford, 228

Ashton-under-Lyne, 48, 53, 58, 172-3, 180-1, 183, 198, 203-4, 208, 240, 248-50, 386

AUEW, 427-9, 431

AUEW-TASS, 429-32

Austin Motors, 245, 261-2, 366-7, 371-3, 375-6, 378, 381, 405, 410-11; Aircraft, 372

Auxiliaries, 150, 180, 219, 229, 240-1, 262, 273, 309, 312, 334-5, 339, 385, 389-90, 418

Ayr, 58, 153, 158

Back boilers, 293, 298

Banners, 75-6, 86-7, 111, 113, 141, 157, 176, 196-7, 215, 251, 279, 353, 400

Barkers, 147, 259-61

Barnsley, 53, 185

Barr, A., 400

Barrhead, 155, 158

Barrow, 58, 204, 209-12, 218-20, 229-30, 289, 297, 302-3, 305, 311, 315, 418

Basildon, 401

Basingstoke, 387, 401

Baston, R., 373, 380, 383

Bath, 53-4, 70, 77, 194

Bedford, 143, 220, 268

Beehive, 110-11, 136, 164, 353

Belfast, 54, 58, 77, 100, 171-2, 204, 287, 297-8

Bell Inn, 95, 100, 106, 108, 111, 113

Benevolent Institution of Whitesmiths, 319-21

Berwick, 58

Bilston, 54, 77, 94, 103, 167-8, 170-1, 222, 224

Birkenhead, 212

Birmingham, 24, 30, 40, 48-51, 53-4, 58, 72-3, 77, 85-6, 91-4, 97, 100, 103-5, 113, 118-9, 126, 136, 138, 140, 142, 146, 156, 167-72,

174, 177, 206, 222, 224, 226-7, 229, 231-4, 244-5, 256, 261-2, 264, 273, 280, 292, 294-6, 305, 329-3, 337, 344, 350-85, 393-4, 396, 398, 402, 405, 410, 412, 415, 418, 426-7
Birmingham gas meter committee, 377
Birmingham Journal, 40, 72, 81, 94
Blackburn, 53, 56, 58, 95, 172-4, 183, 198-9, 203-6, 208, 213, 215-6, 268
Blackburn, H., 148-9, 272-3, 387
Blackburn Aeroplane Co., 267-8, 273, 308
Black Circular, 20, 386
Black Country, 94, 103, 168, 188, 244, 357, 405
Black Jack, 109, 111, 279
Board of Trade, 275, 336-7
Boilermakers, 122, 177, 189, 211, 247, 258, 292, 347, 396, 403, 426-9
Bolton, 48, 53, 56, 58, 92, 95, 100, 140, 172, 177, 183, 197-200, 206, 212-5, 219
Bonny Bridge, 155
Boulton and Paul, 268, 270
Bournemouth, 401, 418
Boy labour, 67, 119, 130, 142-4, 148, 169, 171, 226, 240, 270-1, 280, 289, 293, 303, 331-2, 363
Boyle, J., 271, 273
Bradford, 53-4, 58, 86, 90, 100, 140, 172, 174, 182-5, 188, 203-4, 229, 287, 293, 295, 325, 333
Bransby, C., 348
Brassfounders, Braziers and Coppersmiths Armour Association, 279
Brassfounders, Braziers and Coppersmiths, Society of, 50, 72, 74-5, 83-4, 87, 89, 273, 278, 364
Brassworkers, 173, 177, 262, 270, 286, 289, 293, 307
Braziers, 17-22, 25, 28-30, 40, 48, 50, 52-3, 56, 63-4, 66, 70, 73, 83-4, 87-8, 90, 92, 94, 138-9, 201, 280, 364
Brett, C., 380
Brierly Hill, 169-70
Brighton, 53-4, 58, 77, 291, 401
Briggs Bodies, 261-2, 405
Bristol, 29-30, 53-4, 58, 68, 70, 77, 82, 86, 91-2, 94, 96, 100, 133, 138, 167-8, 171-2, 180, 184, 193-4, 227-8, 231, 240, 250, 256, 272-3, 280, 286, 308, 326, 345, 361, 412
Bristol Aeroplane Co., 267, 269

British Aerospace, 393
Bristol Channel ports, 286
British Leyland, 418
British Light Steel Pressings, 262, 405, 411
Broadhurst, MP, H., 226
Brotherton, H., 242, 275, 289, 392-4, 400, 402, 420, 422
Brown, H., 401, 408, 410, 422
Brown and Melhuish, 150, 242, 246, 268
Brough, 269, 308
Buck, L., 393, 396, 400, 409-10, 427
Burnley, 183, 204
Burns, MP, J., 226
Burton-on-Trent, 285, 287, 289, 307, 375, 382-3
Bury, 53, 58, 92, 100, 118, 144, 183, 198, 203-4, 207-8, 212, 215, 412
Buxton, MP, S., 119, 226

Canister makers, 128-31, 133, 140, 219, 226
Cardiff, 94, 227-8, 286, 315, 401
Cardington, 268
Carey, P., 272-3
Carlisle, Richard, 22, 52, 85
Car radiator stewards, 408
Carriage Lamp Makers Society, Birmingham, 49, 363
Census (1831), 53-4, 58; (1861), 285, 323
Central Organisation of London Trades, 95
Challoner, G., 332-3, 367, 382
Charter, The, 92, 94
Chartism, 92, 93, 95, 100, 138, 278
Chatham, 284, 286, 292
Chelsea, 94, 326, 333
Chelmsford, 143, 228
Cheltenham, 53-4, 58, 77, 181, 194, 228, 267, 271-3, 302, 304-5, 313, 386, 391
Chester, 29, 48, 53-4, 58, 314
Chesterfield, 208
Chrysler, 379
City and Guilds, 275, 342, 344, 423
Clyde, 158, 294, 297-8, 306-7, 309, 411
Colchester, 54, 194
Communist Party, 250, 271-2, 302, 346, 400
Combinations Acts, 35-6, 41, 65-73, 75, 79, 82, 85, 166, 322
Combinations of Workmen Bill, 174-5
Conciliation and Arbitration Bill, 175

Confederation of Shipbuilding and Engineering Unions, 340, 346, 381, 383, 392, 423

Conspiracy and Protection of Property Act, 118-9

Co-operative production, 87, 138, 362

Cooper, A., 371, 380-1, 384

Coppersmiths, 17-8, 21, 25, 28-30, 40, 48, 50, 52-3, 56, 64, 66, 72-3, 87-8, 90, 93-4, 111, 113, 122, 138, 173, 201-2, 207, 209-10, 214, 230, 244, 278-318, 364, 366, 372, 394-5, 426

Coppersmiths and Stainless Steel Shop Stewards Association, 408

Corbett, J., 191, 193, 228

Cork, 54, 78, 82, 204, 298

Corn Laws, 85

Cotton Famine, 113, 173, 198, 353

Councils of Action (1920), 219; (1926), 248, 264

Coventry, 53, 71, 147, 230-1, 245, 250, 262-6, 271, 275, 287, 293, 295, 297-8, 302, 304, 307, 313, 364, 366, 368, 371, 373-5, 380, 382-3, 386, 395, 405, 410, 413

Coventry Sheet Metal Joint Shop Stewards' Committee, 231, 266

Coventry Sheet Metal Workers' Committee, 231

Crawley, 401, 423

Crewe, 191, 193, 227-8, 231, 314, 409

Criminal Law Amendment Act, 118, 157, 162, 175

Crossley Motors, 213, 267, 305; Aircraft, 220

Croydon, 249, 268, 346

Crucefix, H.J., 150

Daley, R., 273

Dagenham, 261, 401

Daily Citizen, 215, 235

Daily Herald, 181, 215, 235, 244, 250

Daily Worker, 380

Dairy equipment workers, 120, 123-4, 126, 190, 245, 307, 370

Daimler Motors, 147, 230-1, 248, 293, 298, 364, 366, 373, 375

Darleston, 168

Darracq, 148, 235, 246

Darlington, 209, 212-3, 293, 300, 337, 409

Deanes, J., 121, 161

De Havilland, 240, 267-71, 273-4, 308, 314

Demarcation, 29, 168, 177, 189, 201, 211, 258, 273, 286, 295-6, 298, 307-8, 315, 336-9, 396

Derby, 53-4, 58, 70-1, 77, 86, 88, 189-90, 204, 212-4, 218-20, 230, 232, 275, 286, 289, 295, 298, 304, 307, 309-10, 329-31, 333, 395, 403, 409

Devonport, 94, 284, 286, 302

Dewsbury, 184, 204

Dilution, 150, 220, 246, 270, 294-5, 309, 312, 367, 376, 385

Dockyards, Naval, 286, 292, 302, 313

Doherty, J., 71, 87-8, 322

Doncaster, 53-4, 58, 77, 172, 212, 228, 303, 308

Dorchester, 29, 90

Dorchester Committee, 90, 91, 93

Dorchester 'Victims', 90

Downham, 228, 345

Dublin, 48, 54, 58, 77, 100, 172, 177, 182, 219, 293

Dudley, 58, 103, 168-71, 375, 383

Dunfermline, 27, 29

Dunscombe, T.S., 95, 97

Duples, 409-10

Durham, 58

East London Society, 118, 122-3, 127, 131, 224-5, 227

Eastern Coachworks, 405

Eastleigh, 191, 193, 228, 291, 294, 409

Edinburgh, 29, 53-4, 58, 77, 86-7, 113, 115, 118, 133-4, 153, 156, 160-3, 181, 188, 198, 200, 213, 225, 233, 239, 245, 249, 289, 297, 307-8, 339, 356, 409

Education and training, 120, 159, 171, 177, 184, 194, 216, 273-6, 306, 311, 342-4, 360, 395, 420-4

EEPTU, 427, 429

Electricians, 427-8

Ellesmere Port, 314

Employers' Liability Bill, 215

Employers' organisations, 237-8, 243-5, 251, 277, 301, 306, 333, 336-8, 342, 387, 423-4

Engineers, 209, 216, 271-2, 276-7, 291, 297, 322, 429

Engineering Industry Training Board, 424

Equal Opportunities Act, 418

Essential Work Order, 386

Evans, W., 222, 355-6

Exeter, 53, 133, 144, 227

Factory Act, 170
Fair prices, 119, 180, 184, 188, 225-6
Fairey, 150, 245, 269-70, 272-3
Falkirk, 159
Falmouth, 302
Farnborough, 148, 150, 229, 245, 294-5, 304, 308, 390, 401
Federation of Coppersmiths, 287, 289
Federation of Engineering and Shipbuilding Trades, 189, 211, 234, 238-9, 243, 301-2
Fleetwood, 298
Fender, J., 395
Fisher and Ludlow, 371, 377-8, 381, 405
Flying pickets, 381, 411
Fooks, E., 351, 356-8
Ford, 215, 261-2, 298, 366, 405, 415
Founders Company, 18-24, 31-2, 50, 278
Fraserburg, 128
Friendly Society of Iron Plate Workers, 49, 126, 166
Friendly Society of Tin Plate Workers, 21, 41-4, 320
Fusion, 389
Fyld, 298

Galvanised hollowware workers, 168, 171-2, 188, 235, 244, 372
Garibaldi demonstrations, 111, 133, 136, 175, 353
Gas meters, 87, 90, 105, 109-11, 113, 115-8, 120, 131, 140-1, 143-5, 156, 161-2, 178, 180-1, 184-5, 188, 190, 199-200, 213, 227, 229, 245, 249, 253, 259, 262, 275-7, 368, 371, 387, 412-3; meter firms, Alder and MacKay, 161, 413; Braddock, J., 413; Braddock, T., 413; Cowan's, 115, 118, 143-4, 161, 199, 413; Crossley, 90, 116; Donaldson's, 161; Dougal's, 413; Edge's, 116; Glover, G., 115, 143, 249, 412; Glover, T., 115, 243, 412; Grant's, 161; Laidlaw's, 161; Metropolitan, 386; Milne's, 119, 161, 188; Parkinson's, 115, 141, 145, 371, 411-3; South Suburban, 413; Smith's, 412-3; Sutherland's, 413; Wilson's, 413; Willey's, 227, 413; Wright's, 119, 143-4
Gas meter repairs, 115, 182

Gast, J., 67, 72, 83
Gateshead, 53, 94
Gear cases, cycle, 166, 190
General Aircraft, 245-6
General Federation of Trade Unions, 171, 346
General and Municipal Workers' Union, 427-9
General sheet metal work, 117-8, 120-1, 123, 141, 144, 146, 165, 194, 213-4, 226, 245, 253-4, 256
General stewards' association, 48, 51, 405-6
General Strike, 1842, 94
General Strike, 1926, 247-50, 258, 261, 263-4, 303-5, 369, 374
General Union, 59, 175, 180-3, 185, 189-90, 194, 202-21, 225-6, 227, 229, 231, 237, 292, 335, 420
Gerrard, H., 272
Glasgow, 28-9, 31, 48, 53-4, 56-8, 70, 77, 81-2, 86, 88, 91-2, 103-4, 113, 118, 140, 152-7, 159-60, 162-3, 172, 188-9, 225, 231-2, 243-4, 251, 278, 280, 286-7, 289, 297, 300, 302, 304-6, 394-5, 409, 412, 422
Glossop, 58
Gloster Aeroplane Co., 181, 267, 269, 271-2, 302, 305
Gloucester, 29, 53-4, 78, 194, 228, 256, 355
Gorbals, 31, 54
Gordon, J.C., 119, 123, 127, 130, 132-3, 140, 143, 150, 184, 191, 193-4, 227-9, 238, 391
Gorgon, The, 71
Gould, M., 414
Govan, 31, 54
Government work, 119, 170, 225, 358-9, 368
Grand National Consolidated Trade Union, 89, 91-2, 96, 273, 278, 322, 328
Green, L., 339, 346-8, 396, 400
Greenock, 53, 153-5, 159, 289, 302, 304-6, 395
Greenwich, 53
Grimsby, 30, 128, 189, 204, 208, 210, 291, 297
Guildford, 401
Guy, L.G., 393, 400, 402, 424, 428-9, 431

Hadley, 229, 231, 391
Halesowen, 133, 227
Halifax, 53, 183-4, 188, 204, 206, 208, 213, 220, 287, 293, 298, 314, 326
Hammermen, 227-9; Aberdeen, 29; Dunfermline, 27, 29; Edinburgh, 29; Glasgow,

28-9, 31, 51, 86

Handley Page, 150, 242, 267, 269-70, 272-3, 386

Hanley, 193

Hangers, 406

Hawker's, 269-72, 308, 313, 315, 386, 390

'Hands off Russia' Movement, 181, 219

Hartlepool, 208, 395

Harwell, 401

Hayes, 390, 401

Health and safety, 419-21

Heating and Domestic Engineers' Union, 302, 307, 315, 319-49, 396, 398

H and D Assistants' Union, 334

Heating and Domestic Engineers' Stewards Association, 348, 413-5

Heating and Ventilating JIC, 342, 344

Hebburn, 212

Henderson, T., 430

Henson, Gravener, 71

Heywood, 57, 172

Hereford, 29

Hicken, C., 191, 245, 268, 277, 382, 385, 391

Hillman Motors, 262

Holburn, MP,. G., 162

Hooper's, 147, 245, 260-1

Horwich, 200, 212, 409

Hospital and Laboratory Equipment Stewards, 256

Howden, 228

Huddersfield, 53, 90, 92, 184, 188, 204, 206, 208, 229, 326, 333

Hull, 54, 77, 96, 118, 189, 204, 208, 210-1, 218, 258, 267-8, 272, 286, 297, 412

Humane Society of Tin Plate Workers, Liverpool, 46

Humber Cars, 262-3, 293, 366

Hunger Marchers, 250-1

Huntingdon, 143, 228, 302, 391

Independent Labour Party, 162, 184, 215, 391

Industrial Relations Court, 400

Industrial Training Act, 423

International Working Men's Association, 113, 353

Invergordon, 294, 298

Inverness, 58, 153

Ipswich, 228, 391

Irish Confederation of Trade Unions, 400

Irish Sheet Metal Workers' Union, 396

Iron braziers, 166

Ironmongers' Company, 18, 27

Iron plate workers, 49-50, 53, 72, 126-8, 166, 172, 231

Isle of Wight, 268, 286, 294, 303, 306, 308

Jaguar, 374, 379, 405

Jarrow, 294, 401

Jewish tin plate workers, 126, 131-6, 142, 194, 362

Johnson, J., 85, 319, 322

Johnstone, 155

Joiners, 122, 177

Joint Production Committees, 386

Jones, Tom, 109-11

Journal, The, 210, 216, 248-51, 271, 295, 297-8, 306, 386, 398, 418, 420, 423, 429-30

Journeymen's clubs, 25, 31-3, 35-6, 38-9

Jowett Cars, 185

Keighley, 204

Kendal, 53, 183

Kidbrook, 248

Kidd, A., 209-10, 216, 391-2

Kilmarnock, 53, 155, 159, 291, 298

Kirkaldy, 163, 293, 315

Knights of Labour, 167, 169, 330

Labour College Movement, 181, 216, 346, 392, 420

Labour Electoral Association, 194, 199

Labour Government, 302, 398, 403

Labour Party, 188, 234-6, 250, 304, 353, 379-80, 392, 398, 400

Labour Representation Committee, 178, 180, 188, 199, 234

Lagonda, 386

Lamp Makers' Society, 49, 363

Lamps, 33, 49, 50-1, 85, 87, 97, 105, 119, 145-6, 156, 184-5, 193, 195, 213, 226, 259, 363-4, 369-70

Lancaster, 48, 53, 58-9, 70, 203-4, 206

Lane, F., 263

Largs, 155

Leamington, 58, 323

Leeds, 53-4, 58, 70, 78, 86, 90, 100, 184-8,

203-4, 206, 272-3, 286-7, 293, 304, 325-6, 338, 392, 405, 412
Leicester, 88, 144, 229, 293, 306, 337, 344
Leyland, 214, 218, 240
Limerick, 204
Lincoln, 29, 228, 333, 391
Liverpool, 39-41, 46, 48, 53-4, 56-9, 65, 68, 70, 72, 76-7, 84, 92, 99, 100, 104-5, 118, 138, 159, 167-8, 172-82, 185, 189, 193-5, 198, 203-4, 210-3, 226, 251, 280, 286-7, 289, 294, 303-5, 310, 314-5, 324, 332, 344, 364, 391, 396, 412
Liverpool United Society of Coppersmiths, 289
Llanelly, 194, 228
London Amalgamated Tin Plate Workers, 115, 117-9, 121-3, 131, 206, 224-5, 356, 363
London Amicable Society of Workers in Copper, 48, 278
London Central Stewards' Committee, 219, 239, 242, 252, 270, 387, 392
London Co-operative Tin Plate Workers, 97, 105, 109, 113, 115, 117-8, 193
London Gas Meter Makers' Stewards' Association, 109-11, 113, 115-8, 128-9, 144-5, 225, 241, 248, 371, 404, 413
London Operative Tin Plate Workers, 57, 82, 89-92, 95-7, 104-10, 113, 115, 122, 129
London Society of Tin and Iron Plate Workers, 123, 126, 132, 134-5, 137, 139, 213, 231, 268
London Tin Plate Workers' Pension Society, 52, 107-8
London Trades Council, 67, 110-1, 118, 136
London sheet metal workers' unemployment committee, 251
London Working Men's Association, 92-3, 111
Long service, 345, 412
Lotus, 405
Loughborough, 228, 375
Lovett, W., 91, 93, 403
Lowestoft, 128, 130, 220, 228, 405
Lucas, J., 363-4, 372, 422
Luddism, 75, 375
Luton, 143, 262, 390
Lye, 167-71, 194, 227, 330, 382, 413
Lytham, 293, 298

Macclesfield, 53

Machinery, 75-6, 93, 129, 142, 169, 254, 264, 358, 370
Maidstone, 54, 77, 194
Malvern, 195, 375
'Managerial functions' lockout, 238, 243-4, 301
Manchester, 30, 39, 41, 46, 48, 50, 53-4, 56-9, 70-1, 73, 77, 86-8, 90, 94, 96, 99-100, 103-4, 106, 140, 144, 156, 159, 167-8, 172-3, 181-3, 195-204, 206-7, 210-1, 213-6, 218, 220, 231, 244, 247, 267, 272, 277, 280, 286-7, 289, 293, 295-6, 302, 304-5, 307-9, 322, 325, 330, 337, 344, 364, 404, 412, 415
Mansfield, 333
Marsh, R., 413
Marstons, 405
Martin, MP, M., 235
Marx, Karl, 113, 216
Marylebone, 94
Mason, F., 210, 219
Master and Servant Act, 119
Mass production, 261, 371
Means Test, 251, 371
Mechanics Institutes, 85, 89, 322
Mechanics of the Metropolis, 64
Mechanics Protective Association, 174
Metal mechanics, 396, 400, 429, 431
Metal Propellors, 367-8
Metal Trades Federation, 180
Metal Worker, 389
Merthyr, 53, 86
Metropolitan Trades Committee, 94-5
Middlesborough, 204, 209, 212, 339
Midlands, 88, 94-5, 103-5, 142, 144, 147, 171, 209, 214, 222, 226, 254, 264, 293, 309, 326, 329, 339, 364, 370, 384, 393-4, 396, 402, 405, 415, 430
Ministry of Labour, 238, 337, 342, 377, 386, 410
Minority Movement, National, 250, 266, 302
Moody, J., 231, 264
Morgan, 195
Morris Motors, 261-2, 366-7, 370, 380-1, 410-1
Motors, 141-2, 146-8, 179, 194, 213-4, 229-30, 240, 242, 245, 253, 259-62, 267, 370, 404, 430
Motor Stewards' Association, 242, 245-6, 392, 404-5
Munitions Act, 294, 367

Munitions, Ministry of, 220, 235-6, 238
Munitions of War Bill, 220
Musical instrument makers, 140

Nantwich, 48, 58
Napier, 147-8, 291, 396
National Amalgamated Tin Plate Workers, 118, 123, 127, 130, 133, 137, 150, 159, 163, 171, 180-2, 184-5, 191, 193-4, 203, 206-7, 210-1, 213, 215, 221-37, 296, 356, 361, 363, 366, 373, 381-2, 391
National Arbitration Order, 386
National Association for the Protection of Labour, 87-8, 96-7, 107-8, 322
National Association of United Trades for the Employment of Labour, 96, 100
National Association of United Trades for the Protection of Labour, 95, 107-9, 174-5, 185
National Council of Aircraft Workers, 272
National Council of Labour, 250
National Craft Committee, 429
National Political Union, 86
National Society of Coppersmiths and Braziers, 287
National Union of Municipal and General Workers, 427, 429
National Union of the Working Classes, 86-7
Nelson, T., 421, 431
Newcastle-upon-Tyne, 30, 53, 70, 86, 90, 113, 204, 206, 208-9, 211-3, 219, 294-5, 326, 333, 337, 339, 344, 395, 409
Newport, 228, 286
New Propellor, 271, 273, 389
Newton Heath, 212
New Training Initiative, 424
Nine Hours League, 173, 183, 199
Northampton, 54, 78, 93
North-east Coast, 53, 204, 208-10, 212, 298, 394-5, 427, 430
Northern Ireland, 396
Northern Star, 95, 278, 351
North Sea, 340, 416
North Shields, 113, 209, 294, 297, 302, 393
Norwich, 29-30, 53-4, 71, 77, 96, 227-8, 268, 294, 333, 391
Nottingham, 53-4, 58, 70-1, 86, 100, 144, 172, 204, 206, 208, 229, 329-30, 337, 344, 386, 391

Nugent, S., 415

Oil refineries, 414-5
Operative, The, 92, 322
Oldham, 53, 58, 100, 174, 180, 198, 203-4, 206, 213, 227, 247, 333, 339
Organ Pipe Makers, 139
Osborne Judgement, 234, 250
Oswestry, 172
Owen, Robert and Owenism, 85, 89, 91, 96, 278, 322
Oxford, 24, 54, 79, 88, 191, 261-2, 305, 370, 378, 380, 401, 411

Pacey, E., 334
Paisley, 153-5, 289, 305-6
Parker, J., 402
Panhard, 148
Park Royal Vehicles, 405
Park Ward, 148, 260-1, 404
Pattern makers, 166, 429, 431
Paris, sheet metal workers in, 100, 111
Pattison, R.B., 150, 271
Pembroke, 294
Pendleton, 213
Peterborough, 58, 143, 289, 295, 302, 391
Petition to magistrates, 35, 41, 52, 61-2
Perth, 54, 78, 163
Philanthropic Hercules, 67
Pickets, 118-9, 130, 188, 304, 381, 410
Pioneer, The, 90
Place, F., 66, 71-3, 86, 91
Plumbers, 122, 157, 177, 211, 286, 289, 298, 307, 315-6, 336-9, 346-7, 396, 426-7
Plymouth, 53, 70, 401
Poor Man's Guardian, 90
Political fund, 194, 234, 250, 304, 346, 379, 398
Poole, H., 312, 318, 395, 400, 418
Pope, S., 317-8
Port Glasgow, 155
Portland, 291
Portsmouth, 53, 229, 284-6, 291-2, 298, 304, 308, 313, 395
Precision work shop stewards, 406, 408
Premium Bonus, 143, 147-9, 190, 214, 218, 220, 229, 231, 272, 298, 304, 308, 313, 395
Pressed Steel Co., 147, 213-4, 230, 261-2, 289, 298, 305, 314, 370, 378, 380, 405

Preston, 30, 48, 53-4, 57-8, 77, 82, 95, 172-3, 177, 198, 203-4, 212, 220, 298, 314

Prices · lists, 33, 35, 48, 50-1, 61-3, 81, 97, 104-6, 117, 119, 126-7, 134, 146, 148, 150, 152, 164, 167, 170, 172-3, 181, 191, 194, 197, 226, 254, 279, 351-2, 355, 358

Procedure for Settling Disputes, 242-3, 247, 253

Progressive Sheet Metal Workers, 230-1, 366

Queen Caroline, 73-5, 279

Quinton, C., 285

Rae., W., 127

Railway shopmen, 189-91, 193, 200-1, 212, 228, 256, 258, 284-5, 289, 291, 305

'Rats', 48, 77, 79, 82, 196

Reading, 29, 54, 77, 143, 147, 324, 387, 401

Redditch, 368, 375, 382-3

Reform movements, electoral, 85-7, 92, 111, 113, 116, 157, 353

Relaxation of Existing Customs, 386

Restoration of Pre-war Practices Act, 377

'Right to work' movements, 141, 409-11

Roberts, E., 392

Rochdale, 58, 96, 172, 174, 183, 196, 198, 203-4, 271

Rochester, 140, 229, 267-8, 387, 391

Roe, A.V., 215, 220, 267, 308

Rolls-Royce, 147, 190, 213-4, 230, 245, 259, 261-2, 274-5, 289, 298, 307-8, 310, 314, 375, 403, 405

Rootes, 262, 405

Rotherham, 293, 298, 303-4, 329-31

Rosyth, 271, 294, 297, 310

Rover, 293, 366

Rugby, 372, 375, 382-3

Ruskin College, 216, 393, 421

St Austell, 315

St Helens, 173, 204

Salford, 94, 197

Salisbury, 29, 280

Saunders Roe, 268, 308

Scarborough, 401, 405

Schedule of Reserved Occupations, 220, 386

Scientific instrument makers, 140

Schofield, T., 271, 273

Scottish TUC, 162

Serk Radiators, 367, 377, 405

Sewell, R., 332, 334

Sheerness, 286, 304, 308, 329

Sheet Iron and Light Plate Workers' Union, 177, 179, 209-12, 244, 394

Sheffield, 40, 53-4, 73, 77, 86, 95-6, 108, 157, 174, 207-9, 218, 229, 329-31

Shrewsbury, 172

Shields, 204

Silversmiths, 140, 207, 270, 373, 377, 430

Singer, 263, 374, 377

Shipbuilding and repair, 121-2, 141, 177, 189, 210, 238-9, 258-9, 289, 291, 305, 310-1, 387, 408

Ship repair stewards, 408

Shipbuilding Securities, 305

Shipwrights, 292

Shop delegates, 46

Shop stewards, 179, 190, 194, 202, 218, 220, 237, 241-2, 270, 295, 297-8, 369, 371-4, 377, 392

Shop Stewards' Co-ordinating Committee, 387, 389

Shorter hours, 31, 88, 157, 160-1, 172-3, 179, 183, 189, 197, 216, 218, 297, 377, 390

Short's, 140, 267-8, 275, 308

Sign makers' stewards, 408

Slough, 143, 390

Social Democratic Federation, 199, 391

Sopwith, 145, 148-9, 267

South African war, 226, 358, 371

Southampton, 53-4, 77, 229, 258, 272-3, 280, 285-6, 291-2, 294, 297, 308, 311, 315

Southend, 400, 414

Southport, 214, 220, 245

South Shields, 113

Spanish war, 250, 266

Stafford, 204, 229, 391

Standard Motors, 293, 371, 405, 410

Stansfield, H., 287, 295-8, 301, 303, 312-3, 394

Stevens, J.V., 142, 146, 194, 227, 229, 232-3, 356, 360-4, 367, 380, 382, 400

Stills, whisky, 289, 298, 305-6

Stockport, 48, 53, 72, 172, 199-200, 273

Stockton, 204, 209, 395

Stourbridge, 172, 227, 361-3, 382, 391

Stovemakers, 319, 321, 323, 327-31, 336, 339

Strikes and lockouts, 1756, Liverpool tin plate workers (TPW) and coppersmiths, 40; 1822, Wolverhampton TPW, 55; 1842, Wolverhampton TPW, 58; 1844, 1846, Birmingham TPW, 58; 1812, St Pancras TPW, 69-70; 1819, Wolverhampton TPW, 70; 1810, London TPW and braziers, 70; 1821, Wolverhampton TPW, 79-80; 1824, London TPW, 80-1; 1824, Glasgow TPW, 80-1; 1824, Cork TPW, 82; 1824, Preston TPW, 82; 1826, Liverpool braziers, 84-5; 1828, London TPW, 85; 1850, Wolverhampton TPW, 97-100; 1842, Wolverhampton TPW, 104; 1846, Birmingham TPW, 104-5; 1855, Birmingham TPW, 105; 1886, London TPW, 117-8; 1893, London TPW, 119; Jewish TPW, 133; 1843, Birmingham braziers, 138; 1912, London tin case makers, 140; 1897, London TPW, 146; 1904, London TPW, 148; 1864, Glasgow TPW, 155; 1896, Clyde sheet metal workers (SMW), 158; 1900, Glasgow case makers, 159; 1907, Glasgow SMW, 159; 1919, Glasgow SMW, 160; 1874, Edinburgh meter makers, 161; 1886, Aberdeen TPW, 163; 1867-8, 1881, Birmingham iron plate workers (IPW), 166; 1889, Birmingham IPW, 167; 1892-3, Midlands IPW, 168; 1870, Wigan TPW, 182; 1868, Accrington SMW, 183; 1911, Bradford SMW, 184; Bradford tin case makers, 184; 1898, Oldham SMW, 198; 1871, Blackburn TPW, 198; 1912, Manchester SMW, 215; 1897, general engineers, 216; 1918, Manchester SMW, 220; 1877, Wolverhampton SMW, 222; 1888, Wolverhampton SMW, 224; 1922, national engineering lockout, 243; 1926, General Strike, 247-9; 1930, London meter makers, 259; 1933, London motor workers, 262; 1935, Cheltenham and London aircraft workers, 271; 1939, Stockport aircraft workers, 273; 1852, London coppersmiths, 281; 1866, London coppersmiths, 282; 1866, London coppersmiths, 285; 1897, London coppersmiths, 286; 1917, Eastleigh railway coppersmiths, 294; 1937, apprentices, 306-7; 1957, general engineering and shipbuilding, 316; 1836, whitesmiths, 322; 1828, stovemakers, 328; 1895, 1897, Birmingham SMW, 360; 1910, Birmingham SMW, Austin, 366-7; 1957, national engineering and shipbuilding, 401; 1950, Duples, 409-10; 1956, Standard, 410; 1960, BMC, 410; 1974, 1979, oil refineries, 415

Sub-contract shops, 246, 266, 273, 289, 404
Sunday Worker, 250
Sunderland, 53, 73, 204-6, 305, 333, 337, 345, 395
Superannuation, 42, 52, 107, 115, 137, 176, 183, 188, 190, 197, 199, 209, 233-4, 321, 329, 333, 347, 425-6
Swansea, 53, 86, 228, 286
Swindon, 191, 228, 256, 258, 281, 289, 304, 307, 310, 409

Taff Vale Judgement, 180, 234
Talbot cars, 147, 262
Tarn, A., 427
Taunton, 53
Thames Flood Barrage, 416
Thorne, W., 91-4, 351
Thrupp and Mabberley, 147, 150, 260, 405
Time and motion studies, 106, 150, 270, 371
Tin case makers, 130, 140, 159, 184, 200
Tin Plate Workers' Company, London, 20-3, 25-30, 32-3, 35, 40-1, 59, 61, 64, 83, 109, 121
Tin roller makers, 180
Tolpuddle, 46, 89-90, 278, 322, 324
Townshend, H., 380
Trade Card Scheme, 285, 295
Trades councils, 67, 110-1, 118, 136, 157, 162, 166, 174-5, 180-1, 183-4, 188-9, 191, 195, 199-200, 215, 261, 322, 327, 346, 361, 373
Trades Dispute Bill 1905, 162, 164, 188
Trades Dispute Act, 1913, 234
Trade Union Bill, 1871, 164, 175
Trades Unions Reform Act, 1927, 249
Trades Newspaper, 83-4
TUC, 100, 118-9, 170-1, 175, 180, 183, 215, 219, 222, 230, 234, 247-9, 251, 286-7, 291, 303, 309, 337, 346, 361, 366, 374, 393, 400, 410, 419, 421
Training Board, Engineering, 293, 424
Tramping system, 32, 38, 40, 42, 46, 48, 54-9, 79-80, 161, 165, 177, 180-3, 185, 189-90,

193-6, 212-3, 285, 323-5, 330, 351-2
Transport and General Workers' Union, 380, 410, 427-30
Triple Alliance, 242, 248
Truck Act, 170
Turner and Savage, 386
Tyne and Wear, 113, 211-2, 291, 297

Unemployed Workers' Movement, National, 250
Unemployment, 55, 85, 87, 106, 108-9, 141, 154-5, 159, 162, 165, 168, 170, 179-80, 183, 194, 205-6, 219, 226, 239, 250-1, 270, 302, 305, 335, 350, 357-8, 371, 374
Union, The, 48, 51, 54-5, 76-83, 172, 189, 193, 351
United Artisans' Committee, 64
United Coppersmiths of Glasgow, 287
United Machine Workers' Association, 87
United Tin Plate Workers for Scotland, 152-4
United Trades Association, 87
United Trades Co-operative Journal, 88
Uttoxeter, 204

Van den Plas, 148, 214, 405
Vauxhall, 147, 262, 390, 405
Vehicle builders, 396, 410, 430
Ventilating trade, 142, 179, 199, 255-6, 259, 347-8
Ventilating Stewards, 417
Vickers, 211, 218, 267-8, 270, 273, 289, 311, 401, 418
Vulcan Motors, 214, 220, 245

Wakefield, 53, 188
Wales, 26, 53-4, 103, 209, 262
Wallsend, 292
Walsall, 167-8, 330
Warman, W., 266, 402, 410, 420
War Munitions Volunteers, 220, 235
War Office, 119, 170, 213, 251
Warrington, 48, 53, 58, 183, 208, 213, 218
Webb, Simion, 169, 171-2, 244
Welders, 180, 119, 229, 295, 389, 391, 395, 402-3
Westland Helicopters, 308
West London branch, 107, 252

West of Scotland Sheet Metal Workers' Society, 160
Weybridge, 210, 229, 273, 306, 308, 401, 405
Weyman's, 405
Weymouth, 286, 291, 295
Whitesmiths, 29, 54, 64, 85, 87-8, 90, 92-4, 177, 289, 319, 328, 330, 332-4, 344, 396
Whitley Councils, 302
Wigan, 48, 53, 58, 172, 177, 181-3, 198-9, 203-4, 206, 364
Wilberforce, MP, W., 68, 70
Willenhall Radiators, 405
Wiltshire, J., 54, 207-9, 212, 391
Windovers, 147, 260
Wire Workers, 140
Wolseley Motors, 260, 366, 371, 378, 380
Wolverhampton, 41, 44-6, 53-5, 58, 70, 77, 79, 92, 97, 99-100, 103-5, 118-9, 126, 133, 142, 144, 156, 163-8, 170-1, 174, 177, 181, 195-6, 198, 206, 222, 224, 227, 229, 231, 233, 235, 243-5, 251, 273, 294-5,, 297, 305, 333, 350, 353, 356-7, 368, 383, 389, 391, 401, 413
Wolverhampton Tin Plate Workers' Friendly Society, 44, 46
Wolverton, 193, 228, 409
Women workers, 119, 130, 142-4, 150, 159, 161, 169, 171, 219, 222, 233, 358, 360, 362-4, 376, 385-6, 418-9
Women's Trade Union League, 171
Woolwich, 53, 81, 121, 143, 248, 285
Worcester, 53-4, 77, 88, 118, 195, 222, 368, 375, 382
Working Men's Association, 93
Workshop Act, 287
Wrexham, 172

Yarmouth, 96, 189, 220, 228
Yeomanry, 24-5
Yeovil, 88, 229, 308, 391
York, 29-30, 48, 53-4, 58, 78, 92, 94, 212, 256, 277, 396, 409-11
York Brassfounders' and Coppersmiths' Company, 29

Zinc workers, 66, 111, 113, 118, 136-7, 151, 160, 174, 177, 184, 207, 256, 294